COUNSELING THE
ADOLESCENT

Individual, Family, and School Interventions
FIFTH EDITION

Edited by Jon Carlson and Judith Lewis

Governors State University

LOVE PUBLISHING COMPANY®
Denver • London • Sydney

To Kirstin, Chris, Keith, Christine, Matthew,
Karen, Benjamin, and Kali

Some chapters in this book are adapted from selected issues of
Counseling and Human Development, Family Counseling and Therapy,
and *Focus on Exceptional Children*, Copyright by Love Publishing Company,
Reprinted by permission.

Published by Love Publishing Company
Denver, Colorado 80222

Fifth Edition

Library of Congress Catalog Card Number 2006920936

Copyright 2007, 2002, 1998, 1993, 1988 by Love Publishing Company
Printed in the U.S.A.
ISBN 0-89108-320-0

Table of Contents

PART TWO:
Individual Issues and Interventions   59
by Jon Carlson and Judith A. Lewis

13 School Violence and Disruption: Rhetoric, Reality, and Reasonable Balance 287

by Peter E. Leone, Matthew J. Mayer, Kimber Melmgren, and Sheri M. Meisel

14 Promoting a Safe School Environment Through a Schoolwide Wellness Program 321

by Patricia A. Gallagher and Linda S. Satter

15 Intervention Procedures for Traumatic Crises in Schools 343

by Beverley H. Johns and John P. Keenan

16 School Crisis Intervention: Building Effective Crisis Management Teams 361

by Alan Basham, Valerie E. Appleton, and Cass Dykeman

PART FOUR:
Family-Based Interventions 429

Preface

Adolescents face a variety of challenges as they transition from childhood to adulthood, and those challenges continue to evolve and develop as society advances. While some of the issues remain constant throughout the decades—such as suicidal tendencies, depression, and relationships with peers and parents—other issues are beginning to emerge as more pressing topics in this day and age, such as bullying and school violence.

The physical, intellectual, and emotional changes that adolescents experience, along with the trends of modern society, shape this period of rapid growth, for better or for worse. It is our job as counselors and educators—indeed, our passion—to help adolescents through this turbulent and vulnerable time, helping them make smart choices and deal with the issues with which they are confronted. Although there are no simple answers to the complex problems of adolescence in modern society, some fresh perspectives can enhance our understanding and give direction to our efforts. This book, in its fifth edition, gives voice to those perspectives, addresses the special needs of adolescents, and provides suggestions for action.

The first part of this book deals with the cultural, ethical, and collaboration contexts in which adolescent counseling takes place, addressing some of the barriers that may hinder progress. The second part of the book, entitled "Individual Issues and Interventions," focuses on important concerns in the individual realm, such as resilience, depression, and school violence. The following section on school-based interventions directs its attention to the schools, discussing preparation and practice, strategies, balance, crisis intervention, and group work. The final section of the book, called "Family-Based Interventions," describes the changes in contemporary family life that may have strong effects on adolescents and how to deal effectively with those influences.

Each contributing author blends theory and practice to focus on a specific issue in adolescents' lives. Every topic is described in detail, examined, and discussed in terms of interventions and strategies. The goal for everyone involved—the authors and you, as a reader and future counselor—is to learn more about adolescents, the issues they face today, and workable ways for us to help guide them to success as they make this crucial life transition.

Adolescent Counseling in Cultural, Ethical, and Collaboration Context

The first three chapters in this text set the stage for new, innovative approaches for the counseling of adolescents. Culture, ethics, and collaboration, along with environment, play critical roles in understanding the best practices for counseling adolescents. The impact of cultural forces on adolescent counseling needs to be understood and become part of the helping skills used with young people today.

Collaboration of institutions can be of considerable help in working with children and youth. Agencies, families, communities, schools, and service clubs can make positive contributions if they work together. It requires good leadership and support of policies that work.

Judith A. Lewis begins this text by addressing the cultural context of adolescence development and how this impacts both the modality and content of counseling sessions. Culturally sensitive counselors must adjust the approaches they use to the needs and ethnic backgrounds of their clients. Interventions focused on individuals, schools, and families need to include cultural context as an essential part of the agenda.

Three major issues are addressed by Peggy Kaczmarek from an ethical and legal standpoint: competence, confidentiality and privileged communication, and informed consent. She examines an ethical decision-making model for working with children and adolescents and applies it to a case vignette. This results in a highly stimulating chapter with recommended actions to help counselors stay current with ethical and legal issues.

In chapter 3, Steven Adelsheim explores the barriers that affect young people's development and learning and the ways in which we can attend to the issues. Collaboration is the key, and Adelsheim discusses why professionals should and how they can develop collaborative practices, offering as an encouraging example the efforts of the state of New Mexico in this field. Adelsheim also offers implications for future policy, practice, and intervention.

CHAPTER 1

Working With Adolescents: The Cultural Context

Judith A. Lewis

Counselors who work successfully with adolescents usually find that they need to use multifaceted approaches that combine interventions at a number of levels. The counselor's focus at any one time may be on the individual, the family, the school, or the community. Regardless of the level of the specific intervention, however, the effective counselor is always aware that the system being addressed exists within a broader cultural context.

The Cultural Context of Adolescent Development

As adolescents make the transition from childhood to adulthood, they are faced with an astonishing array of challenges. In the few years that divide the onset of puberty and the attainment of full adult status, each individual must adjust both to a new body and to a new place in the world. Counselors and human development specialists have long recognized that adolescence brings with it the need to accomplish a number of important developmental tasks (Havighurst, 1972). What mental health professionals are beginning to see more clearly now is that the nature and meaning of these tasks are powerfully affected by cultural factors. As Lee (1995) reported:

> The process of human psychosocial development must be considered within the context of cultural diversity as it relates to the dynamics of race/ethnicity. Specifically, culture needs to be understood in terms of the developmental dynamics of those young people from racial/ethnic groups who trace their cultural origins to places outside of a Western European, European-American conceptual framework. (pp. 6–7)

What criteria should be used to decide whether a developmental task has been completed successfully? What are the earmarks of a well-adjusted adolescent and an effective adult? The answers that would be provided by the dominant culture do not necessarily represent universal values.

Dominant Versus Traditional Values

As noted by Koss-Chioino and Vargas (1992), "What is 'normative' is culturally determined" (p. 12). Consider, for instance, the commonly held view that the important tasks of adolescence include separating from the family of origin and gaining an independent self-identity. Placing a premium on the adolescent's attainment of individualism and independence reflects a value that is central to the dominant culture in the United States but that is not shared by all ethnic groups. Sue and Sue (1990) pointed out that most cultural groups "place greater value on families, historical lineage (reverence of ancestors), interdependence among family members, and submergence of self for the good of the family" (p. 123). Inclan and Hernandez (1992) also emphasized that the concepts of separation, individuation, and clear boundaries are not universally accepted across cultures. They cautioned that helpers who overemphasize the goal of personal autonomy may inadvertently be imposing definitions of normality that are at odds with a client's culture. This issue, while important throughout the life span, is especially crucial when the client is an adolescent.

During adolescence, young people raised in nondominant cultures often feel forced to reconcile conflicting pressures. They may try to conform to dominant values at school while adhering to the traditional norms of their culture at home. Discussing issues concerning Asian American youth, Yagi and Oh (1995) pointed out:

> As acculturation occurs, cultural conflict may become a reality for many Asian American youth. Socialized in a highly collectivistic culture where individual identity is often indistinguishable from family identity, many young people experience anxiety, confusion, and stress when exposed to the value of individuality characteristic to the predominant American culture. . . . Significantly, many of the psychosocial issues that confront school counseling professionals in working with Asian American students focus on the stress of meeting parental obligations while striving for individuality. (p. 64)

According to Koss-Chioino and Vargas (1992), conflicts around the issue of autonomy are also prevalent among Hispanic youth. Modern and traditional values in this area vary widely. As these authors stated, "When Hispanic parents do not lead children into autonomous behaviors that prepare them for separation from the family at the cessation of high school, and when they groom their female (and often male) children to remain at home until they marry, therapists who insist upon a certain degree of adolescent autonomy provoke misunderstandings and confusion in their clients" (p. 8).

Thomason (1995) observed that Native American students also face potential conflicts in the school milieu.

> In addition to the normal identity crises that all young people face, Native American children and teenagers often experience pressure to ignore their traditional

values and assimilate into American culture. A student's family may emphasize the importance of traditional values, whereas at school teachers and peers consciously and/or unconsciously reinforce adherence to the values of mainstream society. (pp. 110–111)

Clearly, the kinds of conflicts described by these authors do not affect all adolescents of color. Counselors can never assume that an individual student's ethnicity determines the unique values that he or she holds. Rather than stereotyping the members of any population, counselors need to recognize the heterogeneity within ethnic groups and to be aware that many of the generalizations that have found their way into the literature are based on inadequate research (Zapata, 1995). With this caveat in mind, culturally competent counselors explore with each client the nature and salience of the cultural factors that affect him or her. Only in this way can they avoid the kind of harm that can be caused by a counselor who is not awake to cultural norms.

Ina (1994) reported a distressing story that epitomizes the problems that can occur if a counselor is not awake to cultural norms. A Japanese American student was referred to her for counseling because he had been in a deep depression since his estrangement from his family. His former therapist, after constructing a genogram, had diagnosed his family relationships as dysfunctional, citing that (a) the men in the family seemed authoritarian and emotionally unavailable, (b) the boundaries between subsystems within the family seemed diffuse, and (c) the family's communication patterns involved the habit of sending messages to one another indirectly through a third party. The therapist had encouraged the student to air his concerns by confronting his father in public. It was the confrontation that had brought about his exclusion from the family.

Ina saw what the former therapist had missed. This family's interactions were not pathological; rather, they were based on the family's traditional values. The son's new behaviors, encouraged by his former therapist, had been so much in opposition to these values that his humiliated father would not speak to him. Under Ina's guidance, the student successfully reintegrated into the family by asking his eldest sister to act as an intermediary (the kind of communication that the previous therapist had viewed as dysfunctional). The culturally sensitive perspective that Ina brought to the situation allowed the family to avoid what could have been a permanent schism.

The Context of Oppression

Just as the conventional wisdom views developmental tasks from within a mainstream cultural perspective, it also works under another assumption that may be erroneous. This inaccurate assumption is that adolescents can address their developmental tasks within an environment that is essentially friendly. A related premise is that if a young person develops normally, he or she will be able to find a comfortable niche in society. Unfortunately, the existence of racism and other forms of oppression makes these assumptions unrealistic for a large number of young people. Discussing problems faced by African American children, Greene (1992) wrote:

> The image of childhood as a protected developmental period is clearly not the case for a majority of African American children, particularly those who are economically impoverished. These children grow up under conditions that sharply contrast with those of many white children, the life-styles they view in the media, and the formally espoused values of the dominant culture. Survival becomes an ongoing struggle. (p. 67)

Greene asserted that the optimal development of African American children and adolescents is threatened by an antagonistic environment that embodies "the dominant culture's insidious devaluation of persons of color" (p. 66).

Factors related to economic class place additional hazards in the paths of developing youth. Schools that serve children and adolescents in poor neighborhoods work with only a fraction of the resources available to their suburban counterparts. Reacting to the common terminology of the lack of a "level playing field," Kozol (1991) explained:

> Unlike a tainted sports event . . . a childhood cannot be played again. We are children only once; and, after those few years are gone, there is no second chance to make amends. In this respect, the consequences of unequal education have a terrible finality. Those who are denied cannot be "made whole" by a later act of government. Those who get the unfair edge cannot be later stripped of what they've won. Skills, once attained—no matter how unfairly—take on a compelling aura . . . the winners in this race *feel* meritorious. (p. 180)

People who have that "unfair edge" of privilege tend not to notice their advantage and to attribute success to their personal competence. The reverse is also true. People who are victims of oppression often internalize the negative views that are communicated so powerfully by the dominant culture. Lewis and Arnold (in press) noted:

> The most insidious effect of oppression is the internalization of the distortions and lies of the oppressor by the victims of oppression. . . . Internalized oppression is the acceptance, most often unconscious, of the myths, misinformation, and stereotypes the dominant culture constructs about one's own group. Victims take on the values and norms of the dominant group and cast aspersions on the experiences and traditional values of their own group. In order to take on the values of the dominant culture, one must repudiate one's self and live with contradictions in how one experiences self-in-the-world. . . . The process is often conflictual because it involves what would seem to be mutually-exclusive emotional responses of acceptance and rejection of one's oppressor.

The contradictions inherent in this experience are especially confusing for adolescents, who are in the process seeking their place in the world. Greene (1992) contended that African American children, as they learn to be bicultural in a hostile environment, "must learn to imitate the dominant culture whether they accept its values or not" (pp. 65–66). Sage (1991) stated that "close identification with the non-Indian world increases the American Indians' sense of invisibility, which decreases their sense of identity and self esteem" and that, "conversely, not identifying with the dominant culture (non-Indian world) leads to isolation, passivity, increased stress, anxiety, and depression" (p. 26). This conflict was also addressed by Herring (1991), who, in a discussion of the attempts of Native American youth to live as both Native Americans and Americans, wrote, "This dualistic life places much stress and strain on these young people" (p. 42). Members of all oppressed groups have to deal with both the harsh realities of external persecution and the destructive force of internalized oppression. Whether intervening at the individual, family, or school level, counselors working with young people need to use approaches that acknowledge these obstacles to development. At the same time, their approaches need to reflect an appreciation the positive resources in the client's life. As Greene (1992) pointed out, despite the barriers created by racism and poverty, "African American children have succeeded against the odds for generations" (p. 68), at least in part because of the supportive emotional environments created by family and community.

Interventions Focused on Individuals

Cultural factors and issues of oppression have implications for both the modality and the content of counseling in sessions with adolescents.

Counseling Modalities

As they work with young people of varied ethnic backgrounds, culturally sensitive counselors learn to adjust the modalities they use to the needs and preferences of their client populations. Thomason (1995), for example, presented suggestions for working with Native American students in the school milieu. He recommended that when working with individual clients the counselor be available for informal conversations that focus on problem solving and avoid intrusive questioning. He suggested, however, that group and family counseling are more valuable approaches than individual counseling for this population. Group work, he asserted, "relieves individual students of some of the pressure to talk and self-disclose and allows them to learn from the experiences of the other students" (p. 116). Family counseling is helpful both because of the family's strong influence and because "the family can provide the student with strength and support, which may not be readily available to the student in the school environment" (p. 113). Thomason also advocated the use of tribal network therapy.

> In this approach, as many as 40 people—who are related to the client by blood, friendship, need, or proximity—are called together to provide support for the client. The goal is to build the coping skills of the client within the context of the group, both to resolve the current problem and improve the client's ability to handle future

problems. This approach makes clear that problems exist in groups, rather than just in individuals, and the group is a powerful agent of change. (pp. 113–114)

Similarly, Jackson (1995) focused on group work as an appropriate vehicle for addressing the needs of Arab students, pointing out that as long as group members are all of the same sex, "group counseling would be an activity that reflects the Arab value of collectivism" (p. 49). Ho (1992) recommended group modalities for Asian clients as well:

Asian children are taught at an early age that there is pervasive awareness of mutual interdependence, and an Asian child who values interdependence and cooperation can gain significantly from the power and strength of collective group feedback. The group atmosphere can be less threatening than individual treatment. (p. 188)

Of course, while guidelines for working with specific adolescent groups are useful for practicing counselors, they can never replace careful assessment of the needs of one's own clients and setting.

Counseling Content

The content of effective counseling reflects the counselor's ability to notice the impact of environmental factors on the client. This competence is especially important when working with clients who are members of oppressed groups. As stated by Carlson, Sperry, and Lewis (1997), "The process of oppression is insidious because targeted people must face a lethal combination of overt bigotry, covert discrimination, and a socialization process that encourages internalization of negative self-views" (p. 130). To be effective, the counseling process has to address these issues directly.

In some cases, the client may be well aware that oppression is part of the problem but fearful that the counselor will avoid discussing it. Boyd-Franklin (1993) pointed out that African American clients who are concerned about racism often avoid bringing up the topic, believing that counselors "will try to talk them out of what they are feeling because they do not understand the need for African-American individuals and families to vent their rage about situations in which there is an undercurrent of racism" (p. 56). Yet, as noted by Franklin (1993), "If the impact of racism is ignored, it's unlikely that therapy will go anywhere" (p. 36). Sometimes, clients need time to explore oppression-related issues before they are ready to talk about planning for personal actions. The counselor must ensure that this process is not only allowed but encouraged.

Often, the impact of racism and other forms of oppression is not readily available in the client's consciousness. In such cases, the counseling process can help the client to understand the relevance of oppression to a particular situation. "Clients who recognize the role of oppression in their lives are most likely to be able to move from the morass of self-blame to the solid ground of self-management" (Carlson,

Sperry, & Lewis, 1997, p. 132). Without this understanding, they might remain mired in the self-condemnation that accompanies internalized oppression.

Interventions Focused on Families

As school-based family counseling becomes more prevalent, increasing numbers of counselors are working with adolescents and their families. As is the case with individual counseling, differences between norms of the dominant U.S. culture and those of other cultures soon become apparent. As already discussed, different cultural groups value individuation and family unity to varying degrees, but other cultural variations are just as important. In fact, the most basic concepts and definitions of *family* vary across cultures. Sue and Sue (1990) noted, "Middle-class white Americans consider the family unit to be nuclear (husband/wife and children related by blood), while most minorities define the family unit as an extended one" (p. 120). Most cultures characterize family life in terms of extended kinship systems that include supportive members who are not necessarily related by blood.

Extended Families

Extended family networks are common among Native Americans (Ho, 1987; Thomason, 1995), African Americans (Boyd-Franklin, 1989), Hispanics (Inclan & Hernandez, 1992), and Asians (Sue & Sue, 1990). Counselors working with diverse populations of young people need to ask their clients how they define their families rather than making unsupported assumptions based on a lack of cultural knowledge. Falicov (1994) related the story of a Puerto Rican child who was hospitalized with a serious illness. His godmother, an elderly great-aunt, spent hours at the hospital, praying and overseeing his treatment. The health care providers were upset about what they interpreted as her interference and wondered why the child's parents had allowed this person to usurp their role. These health professionals were unaware that some cultures define "family" in a way that encompasses kinship bonds, shared parenting, and multigenerational involvement.

Another story highlighting the importance of understanding family structure, which hits closer to home for counselors, was related by Sue and Sue (1990). A school counselor, working with an adolescent Latina in crisis, arranged a family conference. The counselor was surprised that, in light of the father's difficulty in taking time away from his place of employment, the student's mother was hesitant to arrange an appointment on her own. When the participation of both parents had finally been negotiated, the counselor was astonished once more. A brother-in-law, who was the student's godfather, accompanied the parents. As described in Sue and Sue (1990):

> The counselor reported being upset at the presence of the brother-in-law when it became obvious he planned to sit in on the session. At that point, she explained that

a third party present would only make the session more complex and the outcome counterproductive. She wanted to see only the family. The counselor reported that the session went poorly with minimal cooperation from the parents. (p. 119)

The helping professional here, too, showed a lack of awareness concerning the variability of family structures. The result of this misunderstanding was that the family's culturally appropriate behavior was pathologized by the counselor because it did not fit her own limited definition of family life. The counselor's ability to use the resources that could have been helpful to the student was clearly compromised.

Cultural Conflicts Within Families

The work of Szapocznik and his colleagues (Szapocznik & Kurtines, 1993; Szapocznik, Scopetta, Ceballos, & Santisteban, 1994), which began in the 1970s and continues to the present day, has focused on the idea that the individual is embedded in the family, which, in turn, is embedded within a complex cultural milieu. The original focus was on Hispanic adolescents, particularly Cuban immigrants, and their families. The researchers found that the conduct problems of many of the adolescents they studied were associated with family dynamics played out in a cultural context. They learned that they could not view these families strictly in terms of their cultures of origin, instead, they had to recognize that the adolescents and their families lived in a multicultural context, with young people acculturating to the mainstream values of the United States more quickly than their parents, who tended to remain loyal to traditional Hispanic values. In their words:

> The impact of a culturally diverse environment on these families resulted in the emergence of conflict-laden intergenerational acculturational differences in which parents and youths developed different cultural alliances (Hispanic and American, respectively). These intergenerationally related cultural differences were added to the usual intergenerational conflicts that occur in families with adolescents to produce a much compounded and exacerbated intergenerational *and* intercultural conflict. As a consequence, parents became unable to properly manage youngsters who made strong claims for autonomy and who no longer accepted their parents' traditional Cuban ways. (Szapocznik & Kurtines, 1993, p. 403)

It is still true today that families are exposed to a complex array of influences. Many of the older family members value the traditional culture of origin, but "this cultural melange also includes the hybrid culture in which the children are immersed both in school and with acculturating peers" (Szapocznik, Scopetta, Ceballos, & Santisteban, 1994, p. 23).

In response to this issue, Szapocznik and his colleagues designed a structured therapeutic approach called Bicultural Effectiveness Training (Szapocznik & Kurtines, 1993). One of the strategies used is to place the intergenerational/intercultural conflict in the role of the identified patient. The therapists then help family members to reframe their views of the conflict. As family members begin to recognize the cultural determinants of each person's world view, they establish a readiness to build new alliances across generations and cultures.

School Interventions

In any setting, to meet the needs of a diverse group of adolescents, counselors must pay attention to the context of the adolescents' lives. Within the school setting, a contextual approach involves building a comprehensive framework that addresses students' needs for direct services while, at the same time, ensures that their learning environment facilitates healthy development. Table 1.1 provides an illustration of how such a framework can be used to address cultural issues in the school milieu.

As the table indicates, this model distinguishes between direct and indirect services. Direct services provide opportunities for students to develop the knowledge, skills, and attitudes that can help them live effectively, while indirect services address the settings that affect their well-being. In other words, direct services target the students and indirect services target the environment. The model also distinguishes between schoolwide services and focused services. Schoolwide services are provided to meet the needs of the total school population and are therefore focused on development and prevention. Focused services, in contrast, are aimed at students who might need more active assistance. The model encompasses four distinct facets:

1. *Direct, schoolwide services:* These are educational programs that provide direct services to students and that are made available to the school population as a

Table 1.1　Addressing Cultural Issues: A Multifaceted Model

	SCHOOLWIDE SERVICES	FOCUSED SERVICES
DIRECT SERVICES	Multicultural education	Multicultural counseling
	Developmental programs in cultural context	
INDIRECT SERVICES	Address racism and other oppressions in school and community	Advocate on behalf of students who are victimized by racism and other oppressions

Note: Adapted from *Community Counseling: Empowerment Strategies for a Diverse Society,* by J. A. Lewis, M. D. Lewis, J. A. Daniels, & M. J. D'Andrea. Pacific Grove, CA, Brooks/Cole, 1998.

whole. When these services target cultural issues, they include both (a) educational efforts to deal with multicultural issues and (b) attention to cultural context in all schoolwide developmental programs.

2. *Direct, focused services:* These are outreach and counseling programs designed for students who need or desire additional assistance. When these services target cultural issues, they feature multicultural counseling with individuals, groups, and families.

3. *Indirect, schoolwide services:* These are efforts to make the school and community environments more responsive to the needs of the entire population of students. When these services target cultural issues, they address issues of oppression.

4. *Indirect, focused services:* These are programs that intervene in the environments of individuals or groups with special needs on behalf of these individuals and groups. When these services target cultural issues, they emphasize client advocacy efforts.

Direct, Schoolwide Services

Omizo and D'Andrea (1995) and D'Andrea and Daniels (1995) described a set of multicultural guidance activities that they have used with youngsters of various ages. The purpose of the activities is threefold: to help students better understand how people from different backgrounds might be similar to or different from themselves, to foster the development of social skills, and to encourage multicultural sensitivity. Based on structured games, the activities include Multicultural People Bingo, Cultural Warm Fuzzies, Rainbow Poster, Creating a Country, Multicultural Art, and others. The authors emphasized the fact that although these activities were developed and have been carried out by counselors, the counselors have worked closely with teachers in the hope that multicultural education would become infused into the curricula. Of course, a vast array of options are available for age-appropriate multicultural education. Counselors and teachers, working together, can easily design and implement the specific learning strategies that suit their own students.

Culturally relevant programming also includes activities that are not necessarily *about* multiculturalism but that bring cultural awareness into play. Consider, for instance, Zapata's (1995) suggestions for student leadership development. In the kinds of programs Zapata recommended, counselors can identify Hispanic students with potential for leadership involvement and recruit them for participation in leadership training. The program is about leadership, but the context emphasizes diversity.

Direct, Focused Services

Earlier sections of this chapter focused on the kinds of counseling strategies that hold the most promise for working with various client populations. As suggested earlier, the content of counseling should include attention to issues related to oppression. An important awareness for counselors is that although direct counseling will always be a part of their repertoire, it can only be one part. It is clear that if counselors are to be effective, they need to address environmental issues as well.

Indirect, Schoolwide Services

Hilliard (1995) wrote:

> The problem of privilege and oppression or inequity in education is sometimes cast as a problem of stereotyping, intergroup ignorance, or miscommunication. Stereotyping, ignorance, or miscommunication may, in fact, be problematic. However, these "problems" are merely manifestations or components of a total system that is much more complex and pervasive. Consequently, the educator who restricts his or her attention and activity to the elimination of stereotyping, intergroup ignorance, and miscommunication contributes to the appearance of problem solving when, in fact, little of importance may actually be accomplished. Stereotyping, intergroup ignorance, and miscommunication become euphemisms for the deeper problems of privilege, oppression, or inequity, which are much more difficult to address. (p. 149)

Hilliard's conceptualization suggests that the use of euphemisms reduces the scope of the problems discussed herein and makes them easier to address. He suggested that the frightening term *oppression,* could be renamed *race relations* or even *intergroup relations.* But, he noted, this reframing helps people turn their backs on the real issues.

> It is much easier to engage a school district in implementing a program to improve "interpersonal communications" than to focus on problems associated with privilege and oppression. Well-meaning educators and public policymakers succumb to the seduction of euphemisms since they reduce internal and external pressures, soothe sensitivities, and provide the illusion of progress toward important goals. (Hilliard, 1995, p. 150)

It takes hard work and dedication to provide effective direct services to adolescents: to improve "interpersonal communications." However, to address a hostile learning environment takes not only hard work and dedication but also tremendous personal courage. In any school system, counselors are among the first to know when students are victimized by hostile and punitive environments. That knowledge is what gives counselors their courage.

Indirect, Focused Services

As counselors examine the learning environment that affects all children in a school, they generally become aware of individuals and groups who need stronger advocacy on their behalf. As noted by Lewis and Arnold (in press), counselors know that

> poor children, children of color, and children for whom English is a second language are often neglected, labeled, and left to wither in the lowest tracks in our schools. Just as counselors in agency settings alert the community to the oppression

of its members, so can school counselors voice opposition to oppressive and punitive practices affecting children and youth. Just as agency counselors participate in alliances with community organizations seeking change, so can school counselors affiliate with groups working toward the creation of schools that are distinguished by warm and welcoming climates for learning.

Atkinson, Morten, and Sue (1993) suggested that, in a society characterized by oppression, client advocacy may be the service of choice.

> As an advocate, the counselor speaks on behalf of the client, often confronting the institutional sources of oppression that are contributing to the client's problems. . . . In this role, the counselor represents a client or group of clients who have brought a particular form of discrimination to the counselor's attention. Being an empathic counselor who suggests alternative ways of coping with a particular problem is not enough. (p. 301)

Summary

As counselors examine the cultural context of adolescent development, they become aware that the society's conventional view of developmental tasks may be culture-bound. For example, the mainstream, European culture in the United States dictates that adolescence is the time for young people to separate from their families and become independent. Yet, most cultures emphasize family interdependence and frown on autonomy. Recognizing the context within which adolescents live also increases awareness of racism and other forms of oppression that place barriers in front of their development.

This knowledge affects the work counselors do as they focus on individuals, on families, and on schools. Cultural competence makes counselors consider the diverse world views of their clients when they make choices about counseling modalities or emphases. It makes them ask their clients how they define their own families and whether all of the family members would answer that question in the same way. It makes counselors aware that, in their school-based interventions, they need to focus not just on providing direct services to the students but also on making the school as a whole a supportive environment for learning.

References

Atkinson, D. R., Morten, G., & Sue, D. W. (Eds.). (1993). *Counseling American minorities: A cross-cultural perspective* (4th ed.). Madison, WI: Brown & Benchmark.

Boyd-Franklin, N. (1989). *Black families in therapy: A multisystems approach.* New York: Guilford.

Boyd-Franklin, N. (1993, July/August). Pulling out the arrows. *Family Networker,* pp. 33–39.

Carlson, J., Sperry, L., & Lewis, J. A. (1997). *Family therapy: Ensuring treatment efficacy.* Pacific Grove, CA: Brooks/Cole.

D'Andrea, M., & Daniels, J. (1995). Helping students learn to get along: Assessing the effectiveness of a multicultural developmental guidance project. *Elementary School Guidance & Counseling, 30,* 143–154.

Falicov, C. (1994, August). *Cultural change on a global scale: Crossing cultural borders.* Paper presented at the 1994 Annual Convention, American Association of Marriage and Family Therapy, Chicago.

Franklin, A. J. (1993, July/August). The invisibility syndrome. *Family Networker,* pp. 33–39.

Greene, B. A. (1992). Racial socialization as a tool in psychotherapy with African American children. In L. A. Vargas & J. D. Koss-Chioino (Eds.), *Working with culture: Psychotherapeutic interventions with ethnic minority children and adolescents* (pp. 63–81). San Francisco: Jossey-Bass.

Havighurst, R. J. (1972). *Developmental tasks and education.* New York: McKay.

Herring, R. D. (1991). Counseling Native American youth. In C. C. Lee & B. L. Richardson (Eds.), *Multicultural issues in counseling: New approaches to diversity* (pp. 37–47). Alexandria, VA: American Counseling Association.

Hilliard, A. G. (1995). *The maroon within us.* Baltimore: Black Classic Press.

Ho, M. K. (1987). *Family therapy with ethnic minorities.* Newbury Park, CA: Sage Publications.

Ho, M. K. (1992). Differential application of treatment modalities with Asian American

youth. In L. A. Vargas & J. D. Koss-Chioino (Eds.), *Working with culture: Psychotherapeutic interventions with ethnic minority children and adolescents* (pp. 182–203). San Francisco: Jossey-Bass.

Ina, S. (1994, April). *Culturally sensitive family therapy.* Paper presented at the national conference of the American Counseling Association, Minneapolis, MN.

Inclan, J., & Hernandez, M. (1992). Cross-cultural perspectives and codependence: The case of poor Hispanics. *American Journal of Orthopsychiatry, 62,* 245–255.

Jackson, M. (1995). Counseling youth of Arab ancestry. In C. C. Lee (Ed.), *Counseling for diversity: A guide for school counselors and related professionals* (pp. 41–60). Boston: Allyn & Bacon.

Koss-Chioino, J. D., & Vargas, L. A. (1992). Through the cultural looking glass: A model for understanding culturally responsive psychotherapies. In L. A. Vargas & J. D. Koss-Chioino (Eds.), *Working with culture: Psychotherapeutic interventions with ethnic minority children and adolescents* (pp. 1–22). San Francisco: Jossey-Bass.

Kozol, J. (1991). *Savage inequalities: Children in America's schools.* New York: Harper Perennial.

Lee C. C. (1995). School counseling and cultural diversity: A framework for effective practice. In C. C. Lee (Ed.), *Counseling for diversity: A guide for school counselors and related professionals* (pp. 3–17). Boston: Allyn & Bacon.

Lewis, J. A., & Arnold, M. S. (in press). From multiculturalism to social action. In C. C. Lee & G. Walz (Eds.), *Social action: A mandate for counselors.* Greensboro, NC: ERIC/CASS and American Counseling Association.

Lewis, J. A., Lewis, M. D., Daniels, J. A., & D'Andrea, M. J. (1998), *Community counseling: Empowerment strategies for a diverse society.* Pacific Grove, CA: Brooks/Cole.

Omizo, M. M., & D'Andrea, M. J. (1995). Multicultural classroom guidance. In C. C. Lee (Ed.), *Counseling for diversity: A guide for school counselors and related professionals* (pp. 143–158). Boston: Allyn & Bacon.

Sage, G. P. (1991). Counseling American Indian adults. In C. C. Lee & B. L. Richardson (Eds.), *Multicultural issues in counseling: New approaches to diversity* (pp. 23–35). Alexandria, VA: American Counseling Association.

Sue, D. W., & Sue, D. (1990). *Counseling the culturally different: Theory and practice* (2nd ed.). New York: Wiley.

Szapocznik, J., & Kurtines, W. M. (1993). Family psychology and cultural diversity: Opportunities for theory, research, and applications. *American Psychologist, 48,* 400–407.

Szapocznik, J., Scopetta, M. A., Ceballos, A., & Santisteban, D. (1994). Understanding, supporting and empowering families: From microanalysis to macrointervention. *Family Psychologist, 10*(2), 23–27.

Thomason, T. C. (1995). Counseling Native American students. In C. C. Lee (Ed.), *Counseling for diversity: A guide for school counselors and related professionals* (pp. 109–126). Boston: Allyn & Bacon.

Yagi, D. T., & Oh, M. Y. (1995). Counseling Asian American students. In C. C. Lee (Ed.), *Counseling for diversity: A guide for school counselors and related professionals* (pp. 61–84). Boston: Allyn & Bacon.

Zapata, J. T. (1995). Counseling Hispanic children and youth. In C. C. Lee (Ed.), *Counseling for diversity: A guide for school counselors and related professionals* (pp. 85–108). Boston: Allyn & Bacon.

The Ethical and Legal Context of Adolescent Counseling

Peggy Kaczmarek

Before discussing specific ethical and legal issues related to working with child and adolescent clients, a case vignette is presented to demonstrate some of the issues. Readers are encouraged to consider this vignette in reference to the information presented in the chapter and then to work through the ethical decision-making model provided to determine how they would handle the case if they were the treating professional. Readers are encouraged to compare their approach with the one I suggest and to discuss with colleagues about areas of agreement and disagreement. The vignette has not been constructed from an actual case.

Ethics Vignette

A 13-year-old girl named Sarah is seen on a walk-in basis at a nonprofit counseling agency. Sarah's parents have been divorced for 5 months and, although she lives primarily with her mother, she reports that she spends time with both parents on a regular basis. Sarah is an only child, and she is sad as a result of the continued tension between her parents. The divorce has not stopped the bitterness or her parents' inability to agree on decisions related to her.

Sarah's parents often ask questions about the other parent and how they spend time with her. They also ask her if the other parent is dating. Sarah reports that she has trouble falling asleep and sleeping at night because she thinks about her changed family. She is having trouble concentrating at school, and her grades have been going down. This is causing some tension with her mother.

This chapter is dedicated to its author, the late Peggy Kaczmarek, a dedicated counselor who spent many years making significant contributions to her field and touching people's lives through her work. She is greatly missed.

Sarah has lost 5 pounds and has little appetite. She is highly pessimistic about the future. She reports that she has thought about suicide but does not have a plan and says she would not do that because it would make her parents and her boyfriend too sad. Sarah's boyfriend attends the same school. Her mother likes the boyfriend and approves of their seeing each other. Her father believes she is too young to have a boyfriend and wants his daughter to break up with him.

Sarah is seeking a counseling relationship that does not involve her parents. She wants some place to go where she can sort out her feelings about her changing family circumstances without worrying about hurting anyone's feelings. Sarah mentions specifically the importance to her of having a confidential therapy relationship. She reports that if the counselor involves her parents, she will not participate in therapy. Sarah also reports that her father does not support counseling; he believes that individuals should be able to handle their own problems, and if the counselor tries to involve him, he probably will forbid her to continue.

This chapter explores the differences associated with working with children and adolescents and with adults. The ethical codes will be reviewed for references to clients of minor age. Ethical and legal discussions focus on issues of competence, confidentiality, privileged communication, and informed consent. A sample professional disclosure statement for children and adolescents is provided. An ethical decision-making model is described and applied to the case vignette. Last, I provide recommendations for staying current in regard to ethical and legal issues related to children and adolescents.

Differences in Working With Minor Clients

Children and adolescents have been described in the literature as a specialized population (Corey, Corey, & Callanan, 1993), a multicultural subgroup based on age. Children are not miniature adults, and adolescents are neither children nor adults. Some of the clinically significant differences associated with working with minor clients are as follows:

■ The developmental stage of the child or adolescent can have significant implications related to minors' capacity to understand and consent to therapy, as well as limiting their autonomy in decision making. Depending on the age and cognitive maturity of the child or adolescent, parents or guardians may legally hold the decision-making capacity. Age is an important factor in deciding how much autonomy to provide minors, with children under the age of 11 more governed by their parents, adolescents age 15 and older more like adults related to decision making, and more gray areas associated with adolescents 11–14 (Sobocinski, 1990).

■ Frequently the child or adolescent does not independently seek services, but a parent or another significant adult decides that the child or adolescent would benefit from therapy and, therefore, a third party intrudes into the therapy relationship. This context raises the ethical issues of voluntariness and the right to refuse treatment.

- Conflicts of interest may be prominent for professionals who work with minors, as the parents may have identified goals that conflict with those identified by the child (Sondheimer & Martucci, 1992) or the adolescent. Whenever a professional works with a minor client, the professional and the parents are engaging in a dual relationship because the best interests of the minor may diverge from those of the parents (Koocher and Keith-Spiegel, 1990).

- Confidentiality is a frequently occurring ethical dilemma that is more complex with minors because of the greater need to consult with collateral contacts—parents, teachers, step-parents, physicians, and so on. The clinician will have to identify a stance on what kind of confidentiality the child/adolescent client will have in relation to the parent or significant adult seeking services. Younger children have less serious concerns than pre-adolescents and adolescents about confidentiality.

- The clinician has to have an identified approach as to how parents will be consulted in regard to treatment, which should incorporate the wishes of the child/adolescent client.

- The parents might identify the child or adolescent as the problem when the issue might be more of a lack of parenting skills or a family systems issue that the parent has difficulty accepting. The therapist may lose the chance to work with the family if the parents are confronted before a relationship is established.

- Parents may consciously and unconsciously sabotage therapy. They may not want someone else to succeed where they have failed, or they may become jealous of the relationship that develops between the client and the therapist. On the other hand, parents can be a good source of background information and an ally in therapy. Axline (1969) stated that the therapy proceeds more quickly when the parents are involved.

- Parents may decide when to terminate therapy irrespective of the needs of the child/adolescent or the therapist's recommendation.

- Managed care guidelines are established along the line of adult contacts and may have to be adapted for work with children. Some managed care organizations permit the therapist to divide one unit into two 30-minute sessions without penalty, and others will not.

- The therapist dealing with children or adolescents may have to assume more of a role of child advocate (Koocher & Keith-Spiegel, 1990), just as social workers are trained to provide. This may involve school personnel or community agencies so the child or adolescent can receive needed services.

- Child therapists may have to guard against being paternalistic or parental with minor clients. Child therapists have to create a role that is different from that of a parent or a teacher and that is more of a facilitator.

- Counseling with minor clients means providing services that may be of shorter duration than adult sessions and may be more activity-oriented, depending on the client's developmental level (Vernon, 1999). Clearly, work with minor clients raises numerous issues that do not have standard answers.

Professional Codes of Ethics

Although ethical codes of conduct establish general guidelines for working with clients, these codes are based primarily on the premise that the professional relationship will be between counselors and adult clients. Therefore, the professional must generalize or adapt the guidelines to children and adolescents with little guidance or training about how to proceed (Koocher & Keith-Spiegel, 1990; Corey, Corey, & Callanan, 1993). Ethical and legal issues courses typically do not address issues related to minor clients in any depth. No seminal resources or ethical/legal casebooks are available to assist the clinician in adapting ethical codes in their work with children and adolescents. Current textbooks on child counseling, such as *Counseling Children* (Thompson & Rudolph, 2000) provide limited attention to ethical and legal issues and current journal literature is limited in this area (Lawrence & Robinson-Kurpius, 2000). Although the school counseling literature provides some guidance, resources for clinicians who work in nonschool settings are sparse.

Legal Considerations With Minors

Historically, children were viewed as the property of their parents, and the law has been reluctant to interfere with parental rights. Children and adolescents are legally defined as minors. *Black's Law Dictionary* (Garner, 1999) defines a minor as "a person who has not reached full legal age." Children and youth are viewed as incapable of making certain decisions legally, and the law defers to the parents or legal guardians to know what presumably is in the best interest of the child. Several classic court cases, however, have resulted in the expansion of rights for minors, such as in re Gault, which extended Miranda rights to minors (cited in Koocher & Keith-Spiegel, 1990).

In legal cases involving minors, the courts may appoint a *guardian ad litem* to protect the interests of minors. Many states allow minors to receive treatment for substance abuse, birth control, and medical treatment of venereal disease without involvement or notification of the parents (Kitchner & Robinson, 2000). The rationale is that treatment is in the best interest of the adolescent and that this may not occur if parents need to be notified.

The ability of a minor to obtain an abortion without parental involvement also differs by state. In Great Britain, the Children's Act of 1989 formally recognized that children are individuals and not the property of parents (Honig & Bentovim, 1996). This act provides for different levels of minors' autonomy based on age, developmental stage, and capacity to understand. These rights of minor children still need to be balanced with the legal responsibility of parents for their minor children.

Each state has mental health statutes that govern work with clients. Clinicians have to know the statutes in the state in which they practice. The differences in the law across states can be significant. For example, in most states parental permission is required to treat minor clients, but in New Mexico any child, with no age limit imposed, is entitled to verbal therapy with or without the permission of the parents (Chapter 32A, New Mexico Children's Code). Though accepting a minor client for services without parental permission may be legally possible, it might not be in the best interest of the client to exclude parental involvement.

References to Minors in Professional Ethical Codes

The ethical codes of four major professional counseling organizations are reviewed here to determine the guidance they provide in working with minor clients. Specific sections of the code are referenced and discussed.

American Psychological Association

The Ethical Principles of Psychologists and Code of Conduct (APA, 1992) includes adaptations based on age in the following sections:

- *Principle D: Respect for People's Rights and Dignity* discusses the need for professionals to be sensitive to cultural differences based on age along with additional factors.

- *2.04: Use of Assessment in General and with Special Populations* directs psychologists to be watchful for situations in which interventions or assessments may have to be adapted based on the client's age and additional factors.

- In *4.02: Informed Consent,* minor clients are discussed more directly in that permission for interventions must be obtained from an adult if the client is not legally able to give consent. The code makes it clear, however, that the clinician is expected to present information to minors in language they can understand so their consent can also be obtained.

- *4.03: Couple and Family Relationships* discusses the complexities of working with multiple parties so boundaries are established and all parties are clear on who the client is.

- In *5.01: Confidentiality,* professionals are required to discuss the limitations of confidentiality with clients, and "to the extent feasible, minors, or their legal representative."

- In *6.11: Informed Consent to Research,* researchers must provide information about the project in terms that are understandable to minors and to obtain their consent in addition to their legal representative.

American Counseling Association

The *Code of Ethics and Standards of Practice* (American Counseling Association, 1995) has both direct and indirect references to minors:

■ *Section A: The Counseling Relationship, A.1: Client Welfare* suggests that: it may be helpful to involve family members as a positive addition to therapy.

■ *A.3: Client Rights* emphasizes the need for the client to have freedom to chose to enter therapy or decline and *"Inability to give Consent:* When counseling minors or persons unable to give voluntary informed consent, counselors act in these clients' best interest."

■ *A.8: Multiple Clients* suggests that if a counselor is working with parents and children, the counselor must clarify who the client is and the boundaries that will be established with other individuals who are involved.

■ *B.3: Minor or Incompetent clients:* "When counseling clients who are minors or individuals who are unable to give voluntary, informed consent, parents or guardians may be included in the counseling process as appropriate. Counselors act in the best interest of clients or take measures to safeguard confidentiality."

■ *B.2: Groups and Families* suggests that in family counseling, the counselor works to protect the confidentiality of all members and does not reveal information from an individual member without his or her permission.

American School Counselor Association

Even though many of the professionals who work with children and adolescents are not in school settings, they may find some guidance from the American School Counselor Association's (1998) Ethical Standards for School Counselors, which speaks more directly than other professional codes to the issue of working with minor clients. It is divided into subheadings that address the responsibilities of the counselor to multiple groups: students, parents, colleagues and professional associates, school and community, self, and the profession. Even though the code addresses the various roles the counselor may perform, it highlights the importance of confidentiality in the counseling relationship and the need to provide students with a written disclosure document that identifies the limitations associated with confidentiality and the need to have the client sign the document after discussion.

In the section outlining responsibilities to parents, the code recognizes that parents have legal rights and responsibilities related to their children, and the counselor is encouraged to establish a collaborative relationship with parents when appropriate. Although the code recognizes the importance of a confidential relationship with the client, it suggests that parents have to be informed.

American Association for Marriage and Family Therapy

The American Association for Marriage and Family Therapy's (AAMFT, 1991) Code of Ethics is unique because it addresses the complexities of working with multiple clients in families. Related to confidentiality, the code stresses that "therapists respect and guard confidences of each individual client." It also states that related to release of information, when more than one member of a family receives counseling services, all legally competent members must sign a release for information to be provided.

A review of the preceding ethical codes illustrates the difficulty of balancing responsibilities to parents and children and identifying clear boundaries when working with more than one family member.

Ethical/Legal Issues Related to Work With Child and Adolescent Clients

Three major issues will be addressed from an ethical and legal standpoint: competence, confidentiality and privileged communication, and informed consent.

Competence

A basic ethical issue related to work with children and adolescents is the need to have the professional competence to work with this group and to demonstrate knowledge of the significant age-related developmental differences that will influence therapy. Children, adolescents, and adults are distinct populations. Counselors who work with children should have specialized training in: theory and techniques of counseling applied to children, play therapy techniques, child psychopathology, assessment techniques for children, and supervised practica working with child clients and administering assessments to this population (Kaczmarek & Wagner, 1994). Kaczmarek and Riva (1996) suggested the following specialized training for working with adolescent clients: knowledge of adolescent development, career counseling, theory and technique of adolescent counseling as applied to individual and group counseling, assessment with adolescents, and supervised experience working with adolescents at different developmental levels. In addition, it seems important that clinicians take a course that focuses on ethical and professional issues unique to children and adolescents.

Confidentiality

Confidentiality and privileged communication are related but are different terms. *Confidentiality* is the ethical obligation of the professional to protect information provided in counseling from disclosure (Koocher & Keith-Spiegel, 1990). *Privileged communication* is a legal right established by state statutes stating that information that clients provide to specified professionals may not be revealed in a court setting without the client's consent (Arthur & Swanson, 1993). The law establishes which professions will be granted privilege. The privilege belongs to the client, and in the case of minor clients, it is held by the parent.

Confidentiality is the foundation on which the therapeutic relationship is built, and this is equally true for children and adolescents. Most preadolescents and adolescents are familiar with the concept of confidentiality and they expect it (Gustafson & McNamara, 1987), but they often hold expectations of "absolute" confidentiality. Schulte and Cochrane (1992) described confidentiality as a "therapeutic promise" made by the therapist. Nemiroff and Annunziata (1990) defined confidentiality as a "one-way secret" to 4- to 7-year-olds. Their book explains the importance of confidentiality to parents and children.

Gustafson and McNamara (1987) discussed the use of the following criteria to decide the extent of confidentiality to grant to minor clients: age, cognitive maturity, identified problem, wishes of the client, and wishes of the parents. The age of the child is important, although age can be an unreliable indicator of maturity. Therefore, age should be combined with an informal assessment of cognitive maturity. The wishes of the child/adolescent are important, and often as children get older, they desire more privacy from parents. Parents' wishes is a factor that has to be considered, as is the quality of the relationship between the parent and the child/adolescent. Decisions regarding confidentiality and autonomy should be based on the competence of the child or adolescent to make rational choices (Sobocinski, 1990).

When Collins and Knowles (1995) surveyed 13- to 18-year-olds related to their beliefs about confidentiality, 56% said confidentiality was *essential* in the therapy relationship and 46% said it was *important*. There was no difference between the responses of 13-year-olds and 18-year-olds. It also was interesting that the respondents did not realize that parents or other adults might have a right to information about what goes on in counseling and that counselors have legal obligations. Elementary counselors were more likely to breach confidentiality than were secondary counselors (Isaacs & Stone, 1999).

Prior to beginning treatment the therapist should discuss with the parents and the child or adolescent a confidentiality agreement that includes a discussion of the pros and cons of confidentiality with minor children (Welch, 1999; Lawrence & Robinson-Kurpius, 2000). Parents need to understand the importance of confidentiality in the therapeutic relationship and be agreeable to granting it. The therapist is trying to balance two systems—the rights of parents to knowledge about their children and adolescents and the advantages of their involvement for the client versus the right of the minor client to confidentiality and autonomy, which may promote more self-disclosure, provided they are not a danger to themselves or to others. Parental access to information may become more important as various state courts have begun to enact laws that hold parents responsible for the illegal actions of minors.

The therapist has to decide how to access background information. The therapist might have a consultation session with the parents first so they can talk freely. Or, in the case of adolescents, it might be better to meet with both the parents and the adolescent jointly so the client does not feel the clinician has aligned with the parents. Younger children may require more parental involvement so parents can promote environmental changes that may have a positive impact. Adolescents may prefer less parental involvement.

The counselor should identify in advance how parental phone calls will be handled so as not to lose trust with the adolescent. Parents may choose to try to contact the therapist either to provide information about the adolescent or to ask questions. I inform parents that if they contact me between sessions, I will let the adolescent know.

Confidentiality is not an absolute for clients of any age (Huey & Remley, 1996). The limits of confidentiality must be clearly explained verbally and in writing, and all parties—parents and child or adolescent client—must sign a confidentiality agreement. The discussion must be clearly understandable to the developmental level of the child or adolescent. Positions the counselor can negotiate in establishing boundaries of confidentiality related to the parent/child/adolescent are the following (adapted from Hendrix, 1991 as cited in Lawrence & Robinson-Kurpius, 2000):

1. With parental approval, the minor client is given confidentiality and only general information is shared with parents.

2. No confidentiality is provided for the minor client.

3. The client is provided limited confidentiality; the therapist decides what information should be shared with the parents.

4. Limited confidentiality is provided, with the client and the therapist deciding in advance what information will be shared with the parents, and the therapist is open to the client's perspective not to disclose certain information.

All of the preceding declarations of confidentiality have associated problems. If the therapist promises confidentiality, he or she may not be able to honor this commitment, and legally, depending on the age of the minor, the parents may be able to access information about him or her. If no confidentiality will be provided, the therapist may discourage children, especially adolescents, from seeking therapy or disclosing in therapy, especially if they wish to discuss some issues about which they would prefer that their parents not have knowledge.

Lawrence and Robinson-Kurpius (2000) suggested that it is important to have an agreement between the child, parents, and therapist about what approach to confidentiality will be used, and to work to empower the minor client to make disclosures to parents as appropriate. Haley (1987) described the therapist as the "gatekeeper of information," with the responsibility of deciding when secrets are to be shared and when they need to be kept, a function that can serve to strengthen the therapeutic alliance between the client and the therapist. If parents are too removed from the therapeutic arrangement, however, they may terminate therapy (Taylor & Adelman, 1989).

The most critical issue is that all parties be clear about the approach to confidentiality. The therapist has to check the client's level of understanding to be sure he or she fully understands.

Work with child clients often involves the need to make more collateral contacts for information about how the child is doing in different systems. If the teacher, social worker, probation officer, or physician is going to be contacted, the child or adolescent should be asked for his or her permission. Younger children often have no objections, but mid-school and high-school students might object. The wishes of the child or adolescent client should be considered when making collateral contacts.

Informed Consent

Informed consent has both ethical and legal implications. Clients have a right to information that is presented in an understandable way so they can make an informed decision about whether they want to participate in therapy (Welch, 1999). Nagy (2000) identified the following aspects of informed consent:

1. The client must be presented with information about therapy that is understandable. In the case of child and adolescent clients, the therapist must explain the therapy process in terms that are appropriate given the client's cognitive developmental level. For example, parents can be asked to read to their children *A Child's First Book About Play Therapy* (Nemiroff and Annunziata, 1990), written for children between 4 and 7 years of age. The book can be used to provide general information to children and parents about the process of therapy and confidentiality.

2. The client must be able to provide consent to treatment. In many states, parents must provide consent for minor clients. The law tends to view chronological age as the marker for establishing consent (Powell, 1984). Under the age of 11, consent is seen as primarily belonging to the parents; for age 15 and older, consent on the basis of maturity can be argued for the minor; however, between 11 and 14 years of age, the therapist will have to make some fine discriminations (Sobocinski, 1990). Autonomy must be based on an assessment of the competence of the adolescent to make rational decisions. Several states permit minors to access counseling services without parental permission. New Mexico is one such state and there is no age limit.

3. The client must voluntarily agree to receive services. When parents consent to treatment for their children or adolescents, the minors must give their assent to treatment (Reid, 1999). Even though parents have the right to make decisions concerning their children, the cooperation of the child or adolescent is important if therapy is to be effective.

Powell (1984) discussed the necessity, at times, of being paternalistic, or overriding the autonomy of minors, when it promotes the well-being of the minor to receive treatment or if clients are determined to endanger themselves or others. By observing the clients and parents together, the therapist can determine if the minors are being coerced into entering therapy, and this will have to be addressed.

When discussing therapy with children and adolescents, the therapist should give them general information about why parents are seeking services for them and to get their agreement to enter counseling. If they are reluctant, they should feel free

PROFESSIONAL DISCLOSURE STATEMENTS FOR MINOR CLIENTS

Welcome. I am pleased to have the chance to get to know you better. I am a licensed psychologist, and I specialize in work with children and adolescents. I am not a medical doctor, nor do I provide medication. As a psychologist, I have been trained to help individuals deal with problems by talking about them and engaging in activities. I am often consulted when children or adolescents are having difficulty at school, when they are having trouble getting along with family members or with friends, or when they have strong emotions, such as anger or sadness, that may be related to negative events or changes that have occurred in the family.

In counseling, it is important that you and I work together. I will help you talk about your feelings and learn how they may affect your behavior. You will develop a better understanding of your strengths, and you may develop new skills that will help with problem solving. I have available a play and activity room, and you may choose to have our sessions there.

Confidentiality

Confidentiality, the duty to keep private what you share with me in counseling, is an important part of our working relationship. I will try my best to protect your privacy. You need to be aware, however, that in a few situations I am legally and ethically bound to break confidentiality.

1. If you tell me that you are being abused.
2. If you appear in my judgment to be in danger of hurting yourself or someone else.
3. If you request that I release information to someone else.

You, your parents, and I will negotiate a confidentiality agreement that will identify the role your parents will have in the therapeutic process, what kind of information will be provided to them, and what type of contact they will have with me. I will try to honor your request, but you need to be aware that, legally, your parents may be able to access information about your counseling sessions.

I will always try to discuss with you in advance any information that may be released. In this state, the age of consent is _____. If you meet this age limit, legally you are able to decide who will be able to obtain information about therapy and you will have to sign the release of information forms.

Responsibilities of Child and Adolescent Clients

Child and adolescent clients are responsible for:

1. Attending scheduled counseling sessions.
2. Actively participating in deciding what to work on.
3. Trying to complete agreed upon assignments.
4. Calling the therapist between sessions if in distress.

Rights of Child and Adolescent Clients and Parents [some of these have been adapted from Huey, 1986; Jacob & Hartshorne, 1991; Koocher & Keith-Spiegel, 1990; Ross, 1980; and Simmonds, 1976, as adapted and cited in Prout, DeMartino, & Prout, 1997].

Child and adolescent clients have the right to:

1. Be treated with respect and dignity.
2. Have confidentiality and its limits explained.
3. Develop a confidentiality agreement with the parents related to therapy.
4. Participate in decision making to the fullest extent possible.
5. Have the process of therapy and the techniques used clearly explained.
6. Contribute to the development of treatment goals.
7. Provide an opinion about what role parents, step-parents, legal guardians, or other significant adults are preferred to have in therapy.
8. Be able to ask questions and to receive answers that are understandable.
9. Have assessment results explained in clear language.
10. Provide the therapist with feedback about the counseling relationship.
11. Not be labeled as the identified client when the problem may be a family issue.
12. Receive treatment.
13. Refuse treatment as long as it is not legally mandated or school-mandated.
14. Decide who will receive information about therapy.

Parents have the right to:

1. Seek services for their children and adolescents.
2. Access information that pertains to their child or adolescent.
3. Control release of information for minor children.

Please sign that you have read the brochure and that you are in agreement with entering therapy.

_____   _____

Signature of client   **Date of Birth   Date**

_____   _____

Signature of parent   **Date**

to discuss their reservations openly. Children and adolescents need to become involved in the therapy process. To make an informed choice, written information should be provided at an appropriate level of understanding for minor clients. A brochure designed for children age 8 to 14 for example, should be concise but comprehensive. The language used should be at the client's level of understanding. Counselors should provide the client information about their credentials and training, approach to therapy, client rights and responsibilities, parental rights, and limits of confidentiality.

Finally, it is important to document in the client record that the information was discussed and understood and questions were answered (Krener & Mancina, 1994).

Ethical Decision-Making Model

An ethical decision-making model provides a systematic way to problem solve. This is especially important in cases related to children and adolescents, as the professional codes must be adapted to the context of working with minors. The following is an example of an ethical/legal decision-making model for working with children and adolescents, adapted from Tymchuk (1981) and Haas and Malouf's (1989) work (as adapted and cited in Koocher & Keith-Spiegel, 1998).

1. *Recognize that certain ethical/legal issues are related to child and adolescent clients.* Just as clients are evaluated for suicidal and homicidal ideation during the initial session, all cases should be reviewed for current or potential ethical or legal dilemmas. Zuckerman (1997) discussed developing an ethical and legal consciousness that would keep the clinician proactive. For example, in work with children, parents could possibly divorce and attempt to involve the therapist in a custody battle. By anticipating ethical and legal issues, the clinician has time to research and reflect on the issues.

2. *Identify the specific ethical and legal issues and consult the relevant sections of the current professional code and the state mental health statutes for guidance. Once the relevant sections of the code and the statutes have been identified, adapt the information to a child or adolescent context.* All practicing therapists should have a current copy of their professional ethical code, a copy of their state mental health statutes, including a children's code if applicable, and a current copy of the rules and regulations developed by their professional licensing board. In addition, clinicians might develop a personal library of ethical and legal resources, such as books and articles, on topics related to children and adolescents, to be better able to make adaptations for this population (Koocher and Keith-Spiegel, 1998). For example, clinicians who work with adolescents should have resources that address suicide assessment in this population and a copy of suicide assessment criteria and a "no harm contract." An effective system of paperwork and forms will help to demonstrate that the clinician has thought through many of the ethical and legal issues associated with work with minor clients (Zuckerman, 1997).

3. *Reflect on personal beliefs and values that may influence your judgment.* It is impossible to perform value-free therapy (Corey, Corey, and Callanan, 1998). Ethical and legal issues may create strong emotional reactions in clinicians. One way to assess the impact of personal values on decision making is to have clinicians complete the Ethics Position Questionnaire (Forsyth, 1980). The questionnaire has 20 items, with 10 reflecting level of idealism and 10 reflecting level of realism. The final score provides clinicians with feedback about which one of four ethical ideologies they may favor when making ethical-decisions: situationalism, absolutism, subjectivism, and exceptionalism.

The influence of values is demonstrated in research reporting that various professionals can apply the same ethical code and arrive at different decisions (Haas, Malouf, & Mayerson, 1986). Personal variables such as gender, ethnicity, age, years of experience, and theoretical orientation also may impact decision making (Koocher & Keith-Speigel, 1998).

4. *Identify the rights and responsibilities of the child, adolescent, parents, or significant others involved.* It is important to analyze the case from the perspective of the child, the adolescent, the parents, or significant others, such as step-parents. When working with minor clients, verification of who is the custodial parent is essential. Zuckerman (1997) discussed the importance of documenting written consent from both parents to provide therapy to children when parents share a joint custody arrangement.

5. *Identify all possible courses of action, being overinclusive rather than underinclusive, and then rank order them.*

6. *Identify consequences associated with each identified action and its impact on all of those involved.*

7. *Formulate an action plan, and then consult at least two professional colleagues who have extensive experience in working with children and adolescents. Consult an attorney if legal issues are involved.* The clinician should struggle with the dilemma first and formulate a tentative course of action before consulting with colleagues. Clinicians should ask colleagues for their opinions and then provide them an opportunity to respond to the tentative plan the clinician has developed. The colleagues should be experienced in working with children and adolescents. The clinician also may choose to consult with state and national ethics committees or with an attorney experienced in mental health law. Clinicians are encouraged to document their consultations.

8. *Analyze all of the information and then make a decision.* Recognize that all courses of action may be problematic.

9. *Act on the decision.* Even though professionals may be aware of the appropriate course of action to take, they may choose not to follow through (Bernard & Jara, 1986).

10. *Document the decision, the decision-making process, the references consulted, and the rationale for the choice.*

Ethical Decision-Making Model Applied to Vignette

I now will apply the preceding ethical/legal decision-making model to the case vignette at the beginning of the chapter and share my "thinking aloud" processes. The legal issues will be addressed from the perspective of New Mexico law.

1. *Recognize that ethical/legal issues are related to minor clients.* The professional's ethical/legal sensitivity radar should send out an alarm in response to this scenario. Clinicians should be asking themselves if they can honor the minor's request to provide confidential services without involving the divorced parents. The clinician should be asking what lies behind the adolescent's request for absolute secrecy. The clinician also should be recognizing that the parents seem to disagree and be hostile in regard to issues surrounding the adolescent. The clinician must keep in mind, however, that this is only one perception of the family situation. If both parents were interviewed, other perspectives might emerge.

2. *Identify specific ethical and legal issues and then consult the relevant sections of the ethical code and the state legal statutes, recognizing that the clinician may have to adapt the guidelines of the code to work with minor clients.* As with many clinical scenarios, multiple ethical and legal issues are involved, beginning with best interest of the client, confidentiality, informed consent, and right to treatment. Initially legal issues include right to treatment, informed consent, and privileged communication.

For the sake of illustration, the ethical code of the American Psychological Association (1992) will be consulted for guidance:

■ Principle E: Concern for Other's Welfare applies as there is a 13-year-old who describes symptoms that would benefit from treatment. She has the maturity to recognize that she is in need of help and is requesting services.

■ 4.02: Informed Consent to Therapy requires that the person seeking services has the mental capacity to provide consent to treatment. To make this determination, the clinician has to be able to make an informal assessment of cognitive functioning.

■ 4.02(b) suggests that when the client is not able to legally consent to treatment, consent is sought from those who have that legal standing, such as parents.

■ 5.01: Confidentiality discusses that the limits of confidentiality have to be explained to the client. Because the parents are not involved in initiating therapy, it is not possible to discuss a confidentiality agreement with all parties in advance of services being provided. This could set in motion an angry reaction from parents if they later find out about therapy being provided, and they may demand to know information related to counseling.

The client is 13 years old, and there is a legal question related to whether an adolescent may seek mental health services without the consent of her parents. The clinician may have to make an argument for a mature minor, if the clinician decides to accept the client in therapy. In New Mexico, children are legally permitted to receive counseling services without parental consent. This does not mean it is in the best interests of the minor client to exclude the parents. In New Mexico, even though children can seek services, they do not achieve greater autonomy until they reach the age of 14—therefore this client would have to be informed that the parents could very well access information related to the services provided.

The parents are divorced, and it sounds like a joint custody arrangement, but the clinician does not know the final disposition of custody. The adolescent is troubled by the situation with her parents, and leaving them out of the counseling process may create additional conflict if they find out. Another consideration is the administrative policy from the organization that employs the clinician, as to whether the organization would support treating the minor client without parental permission.

3. *Reflect on personal beliefs and values that may influence judgment.* In this particular case, I need to explore my ethnic values, which may tend to emphasize the rights of the individual rather than looking at issues related to the family. I also would have to consider the culture of the client and the parents and contrast it with my own. Because I am a parent, I may have strong feelings about excluding parents from decision making related to their children, especially since, by client report, they seem to be the source of some of the adolescent's distress.

I have completed the Ethics Position Questionnaire, and my score has placed me in the situationalist category. I tend to be influenced by the individual circumstances of a given case, which could mean that individual circumstances may lead me to interpret the code differently in various contexts.

As a female, I also am concerned about relationship issues, and I am in the process of developing a relationship with the female adolescent. I firmly believe that treatment is better than no treatment for this client at this moment in time. I recognize that the parents, especially the father, may be highly upset with me if they find out that I accepted their daughter into counseling. I also may believe that if I involve the parents at this point, the entire case is likely to become more highly charged and complex and the adolescent probably will lose autonomy in terms of pursuing therapy.

4. *Identify the rights and responsibilities of the child, adolescent, parents, or significant others.* The clinician is caught between the rights of the adolescent and the rights of the parents. The adolescent has a right to receive treatment, and she is describing symptoms that would benefit from therapy. Nevertheless, she seems to want to set conditions for treatment that may not be in her best interest. She does have a right to autonomy in decision making, especially if she is acting in her own best interests and if she is sufficiently mature cognitively. If the client is accepted into therapy, she has a right to a confidential counseling relationship. But the clinician cannot guarantee confidentiality because the parents have been totally excluded at the adolescent's request. If the client were accepted and subsequently were to become suicidal, the therapist would have to contact the parents.

The parents in this scenario have the right to be involved in decisions that affect their child. It sounds as if their involvement potentially could lead to a change in the home environment that would have a positive impact on the client. Several times I have been pleasantly surprised when I met parents after I had listened to an adolescent describe them. Parents have a right to know of their daughter's distress and to be kept apprised of her progress in therapy.

5. *Identify all possible courses of action and then rank order the possibilities in terms of their level of acceptability.*

The following four proposed action plans are listed in order of their acceptability in my opinion.

■ Encourage the client to involve her parents in the decision, and allow the client some time to think it over. If she is still opposed, accept the client for therapy, as she appears to be a mature minor. The client is requesting services and is experiencing several symptoms of depression, which may become more severe if untreated. Spend time discussing with her the limits to confidentiality, given her minor status. She has a level of cognitive maturity that can be used to argue for autonomy in decision making.

   The parents are creating stress for her, and you may be able to work with her to reduce her symptoms enough so that she will be willing to try to include the parents later. The client has to recognize that the parents, by not being included from the beginning may be able to access her counseling records. Before the therapeutic relationship begins, the client has to fully understand the limits to confidentiality and when the therapist is bound to break confidentiality.

■ Inform the client that you will have to contact at least one parent before you can work with her, and suggest that it can be the parent of the adolescent's choice. Work with the client to find the best way to inform the parent, and see if you can get the parent to consent to therapy and to confidentiality for the adolescent.

■ Inform the client that if she wants to see you in therapy, you will have to schedule a meeting with her and her parents, so you can all discuss the distress that is being generated. Let her know that, because she apparently is in a joint custody arrangement, both parents have to be contacted, although you could meet with them separately. Work with the client to help make these meetings successful. Try to get the parents to work toward the client's best interest.

■ Suggest to the adolescent that you contact her school to see if it has a divorce adjustment group that may help the client deal with her current situation. Suggest that the client's church might have some resources available that the parents would see as acceptable.

6. *Identify consequences associated with each proposed action and its impact on all involved parties.*

■ The first option is to try to change the restrictions the adolescent placed on the therapy arrangement but agreeing to see her even if she did not change her mind. It is hoped that therapy would be able to reduce current symptoms and make her more amenable to including her parents in the future. If the parents are included later, they may be highly resentful about being excluded initially and might terminate therapy or try to access their daughter's records, which could have a negative impact on the therapeutic relationship.

Your practice is in a small town and someone may see the client leaving the center and ask one of the parents about this. The client could become angry with a parent and say that her therapist stated that parents should not place children in the middle between feuding parents. The client might become suicidal, in which case the therapist would have to notify the parents and also to inform them that she had been seeing the client in therapy. The client may be harboring a secret that may require taking action on the part of the client. Because the home environment may continue to be distressed, therapy might not be as effective as if the parents were involved.

■ Accept the client if she will permit you to obtain permission from one parent, whom she can choose. If the client chooses the mother, you may be able to negotiate a confidentiality agreement for the client and may promote a better relationship between the two. You may, however, alienate the client from the other parent, who may become hostile if he finds out that he has been left out of the process. He also may be able to access records if it is a joint-custody arrangement. The excluded parent might place the adolescent in an even more distressed environment. The client may find the terms unacceptable and decide not to enter therapy.

■ The client may find the terms of contacting both parents for permission unacceptable and decide not to enter therapy at this time. Or she may agree to invite the parents for a meeting with you and the parents may decide that therapy is not needed and the adolescent will have lost autonomy of decision-making. The client's symptoms could worsen without intervention. The parents may decide against therapy, but they may have more empathy for their daughter's current situation and make some changes.

■ The client might be willing for you to investigate school programs to see if group counseling is available, without using her name. The clinician must check to see if parental permission is required for participating in school counseling. The client might be able to present this concept more easily to her parents than the individual counseling option. She might be amenable to talking with someone from her church to try to persuade her parents to permit her to enter counseling. Or the church or another agency in town might have a divorce adjustment group, but parental permission likely would be sought for participation.

7. *Formulate an action plan, and then consult with at least two colleagues who have extensive experience working with children and adolescents. Consult with an attorney for legal advice.* I had decided to tentatively choose the first course of action described above, which was to lobby the adolescent to involve her parents, but if not successful, to accept her as a client. Having formulated a decision, I proceeded to consult with two psychologists in private practice and an attorney. The first child and adolescent psychologist was concerned that the adolescent did not want any parental involvement or even notification. The psychologist thought this was significant and should be explored more fully. She also was concerned that the adolescent might be keeping something from the therapist, waiting to receive some assurance of confidentiality, at which time she might reveal something that would necessitate the par-

ents' involvement, such as abuse or potential suicide. The psychologist also postulated that the adolescent was presenting one perspective on the family and information from other individuals might be useful, as well as providing a different perspective.

Further, if the therapist agreed to see the client, the client would have to be informed about the limits of confidentiality and the parents legally might be able to access her records. The psychologist recommended countering the adolescent's objections so the parents could be contacted.

The second child and adolescent psychologist in private practice responded that it might be possible to see the adolescent, but that agency rules and administration should be consulted for guidelines. She was aware that New Mexico law would not prohibit her from accepting the adolescent client. But she was bothered by the restrictions and the control that the adolescent was trying to exert over the therapeutic relationship. This psychologist did not want to agree to such a handicapped relationship, and she believed that her autonomy as a therapist was being compromised, possibly manipulated. For example, a referral for medications might be needed in the future, and this was an option that might not be available without parental involvement.

I also consulted an attorney who was experienced in mental health law. He reported that it made a difference that the adolescent was seeking therapy on her own. In New Mexico, the Children's Code states that children are entitled to verbal therapy and parental consent is not required. He cautioned, however, that if one parent in a joint custody situation would seek to initiate services for a minor client, the therapist would have to contact the other parent for consent as well, as joint custody implies joint decision making on important issues.

As the reader will note, three different professionals were consulted—and each had a slightly different perspective. This is why multiple consultations are important. The treating professional, however, must make the ultimate decision and accept the responsibility for the action and any consequences.

8. *Analyze all of the information and then make a decision.* Following consultations with colleagues and the administrator of the agency, I am beginning to rethink my decision to accept the client in counseling without parental involvement. Legally, I can see the client without parental permission, but I am not able to promise confidentiality in reference to the parents. I recognize the client's reluctance to involve hostile parents, but because they are contributing to the current problem, it would seem to be in the best interest of the client to involve the parents from the outset. I believe it would be highly conflictual if therapy were initiated and the parents were to find out later.

I practice in a small town, and the chance that a friend of the family might see the client at the agency is relatively high. The client might have to lie to the parents about her activities, and this would not be in the client's best interest. I would want to know the client's objections to contacting the parents, and I would try to work with her to overcome them. I could role-play with the client about how to approach her parents, and I would offer to support her through this process. I would offer to meet separately with each parent if this would be seen as a more acceptable option. But it may be more difficult to refuse her after talking with her than to make a decision in the abstract.

If the client were unwilling to involve her parents, as a secondary approach I would encourage her to join a group at school or at church so she could receive support. I also would encourage her to talk to her parents or another relative about how she was feeling.

Creating and Maintaining a Personal Ethical and Legal Stance in Clinical Practice

One way to generate ideas about how to stay current in the field is to ask yourself how you would respond if you were asked by a client, a colleague, a prospective employer, or an attorney to demonstrate that you are an ethical professional who practices within the scope of your state's laws. The following are some recommended actions which will help to ensure that you are staying current in ethical/legal issues in your state.

1. Join at least one national professional organization and seek membership in divisions that bring together professionals who have an interest in children and adolescents. Divisions provide an opportunity for closer networking with professionals who have similar interests.

2. Have a copy of the current ethical code of your professional organization in your desk and know the year of its publication. I observed an attorney embarrass a clinician who could not provide the date of publication of the current ethical code. More important than having a copy of the code, be sure to review it periodically. As an instructor, I assign students to read the code, and we discuss it in class. Ethical codes are dynamic, not static, and they are continually in a process of revision. The practicing clinician must take responsibility for staying current. Read the professional journals and newsletters that you receive from professional organizations, as they will discuss the revision process and upcoming changes in the ethical code.

3. Have a current copy of the state mental health statutes and any laws that specifically apply to minors. Have a copy of state statutes related to confidentiality, informed consent, and release of information related to the treatment of minor clients. The American Psychological Association is in the process of publishing a series entitled *Law and Mental Health Professionals* for each of the 50 states.

4. Research and identify an ethical decision-making model that you will apply to ethical dilemmas. The decision-making model provides a systematic way to analyze the situation. Cottone and Claus (2000) have compiled a literature review of several decision-making models.

5. Develop a personal library with resources addressing ethical and legal issues that occur with high frequency in your practice. Start an ethical file of journal articles and relevant materials. Include references that discuss the current ethical code and legal issues in your state. Inquire about obtaining continuing-education texts for home-study courses on relevant topics.

6. Join a state professional organization. They often sponsor workshops addressing legal changes within the state, and they have an ethics committee that also can provide consultation. Their newsletter will provide current relevant state information.

7. Have a copy of the current rules and regulations from your state licensing board. This resource will keep you informed about state laws.

8. Identify at least two professionals who are experienced in working with children and adolescents whom you can call upon for consultation when needed, and identify a professional whom you can consult on legal issues.

9. Attend at least one continuing-education workshop annually on ethical or legal issues. Several liability insurance companies provide a discount for such continuing-education activities.

10. Attend the national conference from your professional affiliation, and include at least one workshop on ethical issues.

11. Check professional organization websites for updates about ethical issues. Some suggestions are the following:
    www.apa.org./ethics/Code.html
    www.counseling.org/resources/codeofethics.htm
    www.schoolcounselor.org/ethics/standards.htm

References

American Association for Marriage and Family Therapy. (1991). *Code of ethics.* Washington, DC: AAMFT.

American Counseling Association. (1995). *Code of ethics and standards of practice.* Washington, DC: ACA.

American Psychological Association (APA). (1995). *Ethical principles of psychologists and code of conduct.* Washington, DC: APA.

American School Counselor Association (1998). *Ethical standards for school counselors.* Alexandria, VA: ASCA.

Arthur, G. & Swanson, C. (1993). *Confidentiality and privileged communication.* Washington, DC: American Counseling Association.

Axline, V. (1969) *Play therapy.* New York: Ballantine Books.

Bernard, J. L. & Jara, C. S. (1986). The failure of clinical psychology graduate students to apply understood ethical principles. In D. N. Bersoff (Ed.). *Ethical conflicts in psychology* (pp 67–71). Washington, DC: American Psychological Association.

Collins, N., & Knowles, A. (1995). Adolescents' attitudes towards confidentiality between the school counsellor and the adolescent client. *Australian Psychologist, 30,* 179–182.

Cottone, R. & Claus, R. (2000). Ethical decision-making models: A review of the literature. *Journal of Counseling & Development, 78,* 275–283.

Corey, G., Corey, M. S. & Callanan, P. (1993). *Issues and ethics in the helping professions.* (4th ed.) Pacific Grove, CA: Brooks/Cole.

Corey, G., Corey, M. S., & Callanan, P. (1998). *Issues and ethics in the helping Profession* (5th ed.). Pacific Grove, CA: Brooks/Cole.

Forsyth, D. (1980). A taxonomy of ethical ideologies. *Journal of Personality & Social Psychology, 39,* 175–184.

Froese, A. (1991). Minors' right to psychiatric treatment. *Canadian Journal of Psychiatry, 36,* 452–455.

Garner, B. (Ed) (1999). *Black's law dictionary* (7th ed.). St. Paul, MN: West Group.

Gustafson, K. E., & McNamara, R. J. (1987). Confidentiality with minor clients: Issues and guidelines for therapists (pp. 193–197). In Bersoff. (Ed). *Ethical conflicts in psychology.* Washington, DC: American Psychological Association.

Haas. L., Malouf, J., & Mayerson, N. (1986). Ethical dilemmas in psychological practice: Results of a national survey. In D. N. Bersoff (Ed.), *Ethical conflicts in psychology* (pp. 90–98). Washington, DC: American Psychological Association.

Haley, J. (1987). *Problem-solving therapy.* (2nd ed.) San Francisco: Jossey-Bass.

Herlihy, B. & Corey, G. (1996) *ACA ethical standards casebook.* Alexandria, VA: American Counseling Association.

Honig, P., & Bentovim, M. (1996). Treating children with eating disorders—ethical and legal issues. *Clinical Child Psychology & Psychiatry, 1,* 287–294.

Huey, W. C., & Remley, T. P. (Eds.) (1986). *Ethical and legal issues in school counseling.* Alexandria, VA: American School Counseling Association.

Isaacs, M. L., & Stone, C. (1999). School counselors and confidentiality: Factors affecting professional choices. *Professional School Counseling, 2,* 258–266.

Kaczmarek, P. & Riva, M. (1996). Facilitating adolescent optimal development: Training considerations for counseling psychologists. *Counseling Psychologist, 24,* 400–432.

Kaczmarek, P., & Wagner, W. (1994). Future training requirements for counseling psychologists: Competence with children. *Counseling Psychologist, 22,* 426–443.

Kitchener, K. & Anderson, S. (2000). Ethical issues in counseling psychology: Old themes—new problems. In S. D. Brown and R. W. Lent (Eds.). *Handbook of counseling Psychology* (pp. 50–82). New York: John Wiley.

Koocher, G., & Keith-Spiegel, P. (1990). *Children, ethics, and the law.* Lincoln, NE: University of Nebraska.

Koocher, G., & Keith-Spiegel, P. (1998). *Ethics in psychology.* New York: Oxford Press.

Krener, P. K., & Mancian, R. A. (1994). Informed consent or informed coercion? Decision-making in pediatric psychopharmacology. *Journal of Child & Adolescent Psychopharmacology, 3,* 183–200.

Lawrence, G. & Robinson/Kurpius, S. (2000). Legal and ethical issues involved when counseling minors in nonschool settings. *Journal of Counseling & Development, 78,* 130–136.

Milne, J. (1995). Analysis of the law of confidentiality with special reference to the counselling of minors. *Australian Psychologist, 30,* 169–174.

Nagy, T. (2000). *Ethics in plain English.* Washington, DC: American Psychological Association.

Nemiroff, M. & Annunziata, J. (1990). *A child's first book about play therapy.* Washington, DC: American Psychological Association.

Powell, C. (1984). Ethical principles and issues of competence in counseling adolescents. *Counseling Psychologist, 12,* 57–68.

Prout, S. M., DeMartino, R. A., & Prout, H. T. (1999). Ethical and legal issues in psychological interventions with children and adolescents (pp. 26–48). In H. T. Prout & D. T. Brown (Eds.), Counseling and psychotherapy with children and adolescents. (3rd Ed.). New York, NY: Wiley & Sons.

Reid, W. H. (1999). *A clinician's guide to legal issues in psychotherapy.* Phoenix: Zeig, Tucker, & Co.

Schulte, J., & Cochrane, D. (1995). *Ethics in school counseling.* New York: Teachers College Press.

Sobocinski, M. (1990). Ethical principles in the counseling of gay and lesbian adolescents: Issues of autonomy, competence, and confidentiality. *Professional Psychology: Research & Practice, 21,* 240–247.

Sondheimer, A., & Martucci, C. (1992). An approach to teaching ethics in child and adolescent psychiatry. *Journal of American Academy of Child & Adolescent Psychiatry, 31,* 415–422.

Taylor, L. & Adelman, H. S. (1989), Reframing the confidentiality dilemma to work in children's best interest. In D. N. Bersoff (Ed.), *Ethical conflict in psychology* (pp. 198–201). Washington, DC: American Psychological Association.

Thompson, C., & Rudolph, L. (2000). *Counseling children* (5th ed.). Belmont, CA: Wadsworth/Thompson Learning.

Vernon, A. (1999). *Counseling children and adolescents.* (2d ed.). Denver: Love Publishing.

Welch, B. (1999). The hazards of working with children and adolescents. *Insight.* Amityville, NY: American Professional Agency.

Zuckerman, E. (1997). *The paper office.* New York: Guilford Press.

Addressing Barriers to Development and Learning: School, Family, Community, and Agency Partnerships in New Mexico

Steven Adelsheim

*E*very day, too many youngsters encounter external and internal barriers that interfere with healthy development and positive learning. This unfortunate reality ultimately makes it difficult for them to become productive members of society. Among those living in poverty, major inequities of opportunity interfere with school readiness, and this contributes to the large proportion of learning and behavior problems in urban and rural schools, especially those serving economically impoverished families. For all youngsters, a host of interfering factors arise from physical, mental health, and psychosocial concerns such as neighborhood and domestic violence, physical and sexual abuse, exposure to disease, relationship difficulties, school adjustment and attendance problems, encounters with the juvenile justice system, substance abuse, youth pregnancy, dropping out of school, homelessness, and so forth.

This chapter underscores the nature and scope of barriers to young people's development and learning, stresses the importance of collaboration for efforts to address such barriers, and offers a few implications for future policy and practice. With respect to collaboration, the emphasis is on highlighting the value of adopting a unifying concept around which prospective partners can rally and illustrates how one state, New Mexico, is doing this.

Barriers to Learning

From the perspective of schooling, barriers to development and learning encompass any factor that interferes with satisfactory performance at school, including factors that make it difficult for teachers to teach effectively. The problems are exacerbated as youngsters face the frustrations of confronting barriers to development and learning and the debilitating effects of performing poorly at school (Adelman & Taylor, 1993; Allensworth, Wyche, Lawson, & Nicholson, 1997; Carnegie Council on Adolescent Development, 1989; Comer, 1988; Dryfoos, 1990, 1998; Knitzer, Steinberg, & Fleisch, 1990; Schorr, 1997).

The number of youngsters affected is large and growing. How many are affected? Estimates vary. With specific respect to mental health concerns, between 12 percent and 22 percent of all children are described as suffering from a diagnosable mental, emotional, or behavioral disorder, with relatively few receiving mental health services (Costello, 1989; Hoagwood, 1995). Of the approximately 20 percent of children with mental health problems, however, 50 to 80 percent do not receive mental health care; 70 to 80 percent of children from disadvantaged families do not receive critical mental health services (Richardson et al., 1996).

If one adds the many others experiencing significant psychosocial problems, the numbers grow dramatically. Harold Hodgkinson (1989, p. 24), director of the Center for Demographic Policy, estimates that 40 percent of young people are "in very bad educational shape" and "at risk of failing to fulfill their physical and mental promise." The problems these students bring to the school setting often stem from restricted opportunities associated with poverty, difficult and diverse family circumstances, lack of English language skills, violent neighborhoods, and inadequate health care (Dryfoos, 1990, 1998; Knitzer et al., 1990; Schorr, 1997). The reality for many large urban and poor rural schools is that over 50% of their students manifest learning, behavior, and emotional problems.

One view of this issue is provided by a 1997 survey of 28,000 New Mexico public school students, grades 7 through 12, by the state's Office of Epidemiology in the Department of Health (New Mexico Department of Health, 1999). The survey focused on substance use, self-esteem, depressive symptoms, and school behavior. The number of students abusing substances other than alcohol showed an increase from a previous study done in 1993. Of particular note: Marijuana use increased to approximately 25 percent of boys and 22 percent of girls, and other drugs of abuse, particularly inhalants and crack cocaine, continued to increase.

Those who reported any substance use were much more likely to have had problem behaviors at school, such as having stolen things, ditched school, put down others, or hit others on purpose. Students who reported higher rates of depressive symptoms, such as feeling sad, discouraged or hopeless, also reported more problem behaviors at school. Those reporting high rates of substance use, too, had higher scores on a measure of depressive symptoms (e.g., they too indicated feeling sad, discouraged, and hopeless), raising the suspicion that the students reporting more substance use also were the students reporting depressive symptoms. It was not clear whether the depression these students identified was a result of their substance use or their substance use secondary to self-medication for depression. National data indicate that 20 to 40 percent of adolescents with substance abuse problems also may have co-morbid depressive disorders (Stowell & Estroff, 1992; Riggs et al., 1995; Weinberg et al., 1998).

Similar problems were seen in a "snapshot" study of incarcerated youth done by the New Mexico Children, Youth, and Families Department (1996). Among a sample of approximately 550 incarcerated youth in New Mexico detention facilities in 1995, high proportions reported histories of school failure (67 percent), substance abuse (63 percent), mental health problems (52 percent), special education involvement (36 percent), and abuse and neglect (34 percent). Among students served by the six school-based health center sites operated through the University of New Mexico in 1997–98, an average of 37 percent of students had a mental health diagnosis or problem. These numbers are particularly large at the middle schools, where more than half of the students seen had primary mental health or substance abuse issues.

The most frequent diagnoses were depression and dysthymic disorders, general counseling needs, family disruptions, and academic problems leading to potential adjustment disorders. Many face high rates of poverty, lack of support at home, and multiple stresses that make it hard for them to be successful in a school environment. For many, the problems were so severe as to raise concerns about post-traumatic stress disorder.

Clearly, young people are facing many barriers to their successful development and learning. It is critical to deal with these barriers in ways that enable more youth to achieve successfully in school and become productive members of society. As is widely acknowledged, however, the tendency has been to address these matters in a marginalized and highly fragmented manner in policy and practice (Adelman & Taylor, 1997, 1998, 1999). Many of these youth, in fact, often do not end up with the educational supports to which they may be entitled, such as Section 504 of the Rehabilitation Act or the Individual with Disabilities in Education Act (IDEA). Frequently, at least in New Mexico, many of these students are suspended or expelled, or drop out, leaving them on the streets, where they end up in trouble and in the juvenile justice system. In the 1999 Kids Count poll, New Mexico led the nation with the most students in the nation out of school and not working (Annie E. Casey Foundation, 1999).

The Need for Collaboration for Early Identification

Many students throughout New Mexico are suspended or expelled from school or drop out without first receiving an adequate assessment of their individual barriers to successful learning. Clearly, New Mexico's data show that a major part of their school behavioral problems are tied to a failure to identify children early who may have mental health or substance abuse issues. Providing such an assessment identifies children at risk for problem behaviors or violence, as well as children with potential disabilities.

Unfortunately, the majority of the current school and community processes that are supposed to lead to early identification and intervention for children and teens in

New Mexico lack a strong mental health component. Early Periodic Screening, Diagnosis, and Treatment screens, a part of the federal Medicaid program, do not include a mental health component and often are administered by providers with no mental health training. Under Medicaid Managed Care, fewer students are being identified, as community services for children have not been expanded, and inpatient and residential services are decreasing. New Mexico's State Children's Health Insurance Plan (SCHIP) provided for funds for school mental health assessment, but this plan was rejected by the Health Care Finance Administration (HCFA) and is in legal limbo.

As a result of this lack of mental health assessments from medical providers, as well as the responsibilities schools face with the Individuals with Disabilities in Education Act (IDEA) and Section 504 to identify children with disabilities, schools must bear the burden for most of these assessments. Unfortunately, schools do not currently have the systems or resources in place to provide these critical assessments. This may be related to the fact that New Mexico was the last state in the United States to accept funding from IDEA. Even those early educational processes that do include mental health assessments and supports (Child Find and Head Start) often fail to help preschoolers make the transition into the general school system, and individual progress is lost.

Furthermore, parents frequently are left out of the assessment and evaluation process and are not aware of their rights to have their child assessed. The New Mexico State Department of Education General Screening Process most often consists of simple vision and hearing tests and does not address children's mental health needs. Student Support Processes, which also are mandated by the State Department of Education, are functioning below par in some schools and are nonexistent in others. The quality of school-based assessments is too dependent upon an individual school's commitment and the expertise and availability of trained personnel. Many special education or 504 evaluations that do take place have minimal mental health and substance abuse components, and often psychological staffings on children provide only cursory mental health evaluations.

As stated, most of the students who are involved in school violence show early warning signs of mental health or substance abuse issues prior to these incidents. The ratio of school counselors, social workers, and other school personnel to students, however, is so poor that schools are not able to take on the sole responsibility of evaluating the vast numbers of these children. Even when children's behavioral issues become serious enough that administrators consider suspension or expulsion, children and teens rarely have a mental health or substance abuse evaluation. The lack of assessment at this critical juncture leaves many students on the street without school or treatment. This results in high costs both in terms of increased violence in our communities and general fund expenditures for juvenile justice intervention. The need for improving collaboration among schools, families, and communities in meeting these overwhelming demands cannot be overstated.

Collaboration to Deal With Problems

In recent years, an increasing number of collaborative arrangements within, between, and among agencies, schools, families, and communities have emerged to address the needs of young people and their families, and a growing body of literature helps to clarify the policy and conceptual bases and available data related to these endeavors (see, for example, Adelman, 1995; Adelman & Taylor, 1997; Adler & Gardner, 1994; Allensworth, Wyche, Lawson, & Nicholson, 1997; Carnegie Council on Adolescent Development, 1988; Center for Mental Health in Schools, 1997; 1999; Dryfoos, 1994, 1998; Lawson & Briar-Lawson, 1997; Melaville & Blank, 1998; Schorr, 1988, 1997; Tyack, 1992). The nature and scope of collaborative activity varies from community to community and site to site and may be initiated by one or more agencies, schools, family-oriented organizations, or a wide variety of community entities.

Terms used to designate their activity include school-linked services, integrated services, school-community partnerships, family resource centers, one-stop shopping, wraparound services, seamless service delivery, systems of care, comprehensive school health programs, co-location of services, and community schools. The arrangements encompass concerns for promoting well-being, preventing problems, and addressing existing problems through early intervention and remediation/treatment of chronic and severe problems. Prevention programs and interventions may be offered to everyone, to those in specified cohorts, or to those identified as at-risk. For the most part, however, high poverty communities don't come close to having enough resources to meet their needs, which makes collaborative use of existing resources an essential strategy in maximizing use of what is available.

Analyses of trends indicate that a basic intent of policies for collaboration is to move from *fragmentation* to *cohesive intervention* and from a *narrow focus on specific problems and specialist-oriented services* to *strategies that encompass comprehensive approaches.* Partnerships offer hope for reducing fragmentation and minimizing wasteful use of limited resources and also seem fundamental for enhancing efficacy by weaving limited resources together into increasingly comprehensive, multifaceted, and integrated approaches.

Moving toward comprehensive approaches requires more than a desire to collaborate. It involves overcoming marginalization and fragmentation by elevating the priority level assigned to the policies that address the problems that young people experience and creating stronger linkages between policy and practice. For this to happen, the many forces currently advocating for specialized concerns have to develop partnerships around a concept that unifies responses to a wide range of psychosocial and health factors that are interfering with young people's learning and performance. Adoption of such an inclusive unifying concept is pivotal in convincing policy makers to move to a position that recognizes the essential nature of comprehensive, multifaceted, and integrated approaches. The concept of addressing barriers to development and learning represents such a unifying concept.

One State's Efforts to Address Barriers to Learning

New Mexico's children currently face some of the highest rates of poverty, substance abuse, suicide, and school dropout of any children in the United States. New Mexico has the largest number of children in poverty, the third highest teen pregnancy rate, the fourth highest dropout rate, and the fifth highest teen suicide rate in the United States (Kids Count, 1999). No wonder New Mexico is consistently rated one of the two or three worst states in which to raise a child (Children's Rights Council, 1999).

Unfortunately, as indicated in *The Status of Children's Mental Health in New Mexico* (New Mexico Department of Health, 1998), the majority of those with problems are not receiving appropriate support or intervention. In part, this lamentable state of affairs is a result of the limited availability of school- and community-based programs and services, and in part from the difficulty public systems have in working together to address these matters. New Mexico has been taking active steps to alleviate many of these difficulties.

One trend across the country for improving the situation involves expanding school-based and linked programs and services by enhancing the policy focus at the state level. In New Mexico, the strategy for accomplishing this builds on current windows of opportunity that have opened because of policy initiatives encouraging collaborative infrastructures to enhance how schools address physical and mental health. As a result, school health has become a high priority within New Mexico. In establishing relevant collaborative arrangements throughout the state, the concept of addressing barriers to development and learning has had a unifying and energizing influence.

Using Windows of Opportunity to Enhance Collaboration

In recent years, various opportunities have emerged for funding and working with schools to address a variety of barriers to development, learning, and teaching. State agencies in New Mexico have been aggressive in taking advantage of the open windows. Of particular note is the way the state has used federal initiatives designed to encourage states to build a collaborative infrastructure to enhance (a) coordinated school health (Marx & Wooley, with Northrup, 1998), and (b) mental health in schools (Adelman, Taylor, Weist, Adelsheim, et al., 1999).

As new initiatives were introduced, establishing collaboratives to enhance the focus on school health clearly would require strategies that accounted for the reality that schools are not in the health business. Their primary mission is to educate. Therefore, any effort to establish high-priority collaborations with education agencies and schools must operate within a framework that reflects their mission. In this respect, schools were found to value the idea of working with others to address the barriers that get in the way of their students benefiting from instruction.

Therefore, many of the efforts to expand physical and mental health in schools were pursued by framing them as facets of a comprehensive component for addressing barriers to learning. From this perspective, it was much easier to connect school health initiatives with federal educational initiatives such as the Safe and Drug Free Schools program and with special education. It also was easier to encourage building collaboratives that combined the efforts of agencies, schools, families, and communities and to incorporate a strong school health emphasis in the plan for the state's Children's Health Insurance Program (SCHIP).

Translating Policy Into Collaborative Practices

The work of New Mexico's Office of School Health illustrates the progress being made. The Office, with its 18 staff members, is in the Health Systems Bureau of the Public Health Division of the New Mexico Department of Health. Its role is to promote school health programs and services for all children, whether in school, home-schooled, suspended, or expelled. Programs and services promoted by the Office of School Health range throughout the whole continuum of care, from prevention to early intervention to treatment services. Programs supported by the Office include prevention efforts such as the A+ Awards program, which supports schools in developing successful school/ community partnerships in one of the eight school health component areas promoted by the Center for Disease Control's model of coordinated school health (Marx and Wooley, with Northrup, 1998).

Other programs include development and expansion of School Based Health Centers (SBHCs) throughout the state, with a particular focus on the mental health and substance abuse services that these centers provide. Furthermore, the Office of School Health has grown dramatically in the last few years, with expansion of the New Mexico School Mental Health Initiative (Adelsheim, 1999). Funded by a federal Maternal and Child Health grant, this collaboration of state agencies, schools, families, and community partners has made great strides in expanding both programs and support for addressing the mental health needs of students so they may be successful in school.

As one of the key agencies working to develop an effective infrastructure for a health focus in schools, the School Mental Health Initiative has played a catalytic role in enhancing connections among divisions within the Health Department (e.g., collaborations among the Office of School Health, the Behavioral Health Division, and the Division of Health Improvement, which monitors the effectiveness of interventions). It also has had to deal with the challenge of how to enhance collaboration among the various state agencies responsible for health, education, juvenile justice, child protective services, and the Human Services Department. (This last agency has been actively involved in school health issues because it administers both Medicaid-managed care and the Medicaid in the Schools Program, and because under welfare reform, it requires children to stay in school for a family to receive financial benefits.)

The task of establishing interagency partnerships and other collaborative working relationships has been facilitated by emphasizing the reality that addressing barriers to development and learning is an overlapping concern for all public agencies that deal with youth and their families (Coalition for Cohesive Policy in Addressing Barriers to Development and Learning, 1998, 1999).

Developing State-Level Interdepartmental Relationships

Adopting the unifying concept of "addressing barriers to learning," the staff of the School Mental Health Initiative reached out to organizational representatives and other key stakeholders to create the Interdepartmental School Behavioral Health Partnership. This state level, interdepartmental collaborative has coordinated and expanded critical school mental health programs for New Mexico's children.

Members include representatives from the Divisions of Public Health, Behavioral Health, and Health Improvement in the Health Department; Data and Analysis and Special Education Divisions in the Department of Education; staff from the Children, Youth and Families Department; and the Medical Assistance Division of the Human Services Department. Together, these agencies have combined to provide more than $1 million in staff and program support for school mental health programs in a true state-level partnership.

Developing State-Level School Mental Health Infrastructure

Initially, the staff of the School Mental Health Initiative consisted of the child psychiatrist director (funded through three different state agencies and the federal grant), a master's-level social worker as program director, and an administrative assistant. To be responsive to the needs of schools for training in school mental health directed to teachers, it became important to obtain state support to add a position for a teacher with strong background in working with the social/ behavioral needs of students in a classroom. For this reason, the *Behavioral Educational Consultant* position was created, and a former special education teacher with a strong background in teacher training was hired. Later, as the four existing staff worked to meet the demand for their technical assistance, support, and training services, the four School Mental Health Advocate positions were created.

Each regional School Mental Health Advocate, a master's-level trained therapist with school mental health experience, was assigned to one of the four state Public Health district offices to work closely with local schools, parents, health professionals, and mental health providers. These critical community partners have provided essential technical assistance, training, and support to schools, families, and communities to expand regional and local capacity to provide collaborative prevention, early intervention and treatment support for students. These School Mental Health Advocates worked with more than 37 communities statewide and provided more than 120 trainings to more than 4,000 people in school mental health during 1999. They also have played a critical role in bringing community partners together to address the barriers to learning unique to each school and community.

Collaborative Workgroups

The first step in implementing the initiative at the community level was to establish statewide workgroups. An *Advocacy Workgroup* was created to promote legislation and expand policy support for school mental health. A *Training Workgroup* focused on expanding the capacity of school teachers and other school health professionals to recognize children at risk for problems so they can be properly directed to help. Workgroups also enhanced university linkages for preservice and inservice training of school and community providers.

The initial emphasis of the *Families, Schools, and Communities Linkages Workgroup* was on ways to improve understanding and use of Section 504 of the 1973 Rehabilitation Act, which provides general education classroom modifications for children with behavioral and physical disabilities. These workgroups played a critical role in expanding initial linkages between state government and community partners in determining local priorities and providing direction for future initiatives.

School/Community Collaborative Pilot Sites

An additional step has involved interagency and community partnerships to develop four demonstration sites across the state for use as models of school/community school mental health collaboration. Funded by the Interdepartmental School Behavioral Health Partnership, these pilot programs were designed to expand mental health and psychosocial interventions to the schools by expanding linkages to the community and provide additional resource support for these school/community partnerships. Projects at these sites include the restructuring of student support teams in schools, the development of parent and peer mentorship models in middle schools, and improving access to case management and other mental health services on school grounds.

Other nonfunded sites throughout the state receive regular technical assistance and training for developing school/community mental health collaboration to expand their capacities to provide school-linked services and programs. In fact, 10 sites that were not initially funded received mini-grants for education and training opportunities that led to many of them obtaining other funds for their collaboratives.

Expanded School-Based Mental Health Services

School-Based Health Centers (SBHCs) are important components of school health interventions in New Mexico. The Office of School Health, with additional financial support from the Interdepartmental School Behavioral Health Partnership, currently provides funding for 17 school-based health centers statewide, which serve more than 40 schools. In New Mexico, at least one-third of children who come to school-based health centers have a primary mental health or substance abuse issue, which becomes apparent after several visits. While most states with school-based health centers have a large number of mental health providers, New Mexico initially had mental health providers in only one-third of its school-based health centers.

One of the goals over the past several years has been to expand the capability of these sites to provide mental health and substance abuse support by linking them more effectively with community children's mental health and substance abuse providers. In 1999, the Office of School Health restructured its request-for-proposals process to reflect this by expanding the level of funding available to school-based health centers that provide coordinated primary care, mental health, and substance abuse services on site. Also in 1999, funding was created for stand-alone school-based mental health centers. In addition, the Office of School Health is in the process of developing state standards for provision of mental health and substance abuse services, including the provision of psychotropic medication in school-based health centers.

New Mexico moved to Medicaid-managed care in the middle of 1997. Since that time, community-based services have not yet been expanded to a great degree under Medicaid-managed care and New Mexico's public mental health systems continue to have difficulty identifying and bringing children into treatment services. As New Mexico moved to Medicaid managed care, the School Mental Health Initiative worked to develop relationships with community Medicaid providers to link them with schools through the behavioral health systems of Medicaid-managed care.

A pilot project in school-based Medicaid managed care behavioral health services in the Albuquerque Public Schools now provides for full-time clinical social work services for Medicaid-eligible children in all 12 schools in one high school cluster. Through this pilot, social workers from community provider agencies work in conjunction with school health professionals employed by the school district and are able to see students regardless of their assigned Medicaid provider.

As a result of statewide efforts to expand this model, the Medical Assistance Division of the Human Services Department, in a joint effort with the Health Department and the Medicaid-managed care providers, is awaiting final approval for a grant from the Center for Health Care Strategies to expand the relationship between Medicaid-managed care and school-based health centers. In addition, the School Mental Health Initiative is collaborating with other state and school partners on a *Medicaid in the Schools* Guidebook. This document will give schools additional technical information on how to utilize their Medicaid in the Schools dollars more effectively to support school mental health and other programs.

School Behavioral Health Assessments

As stated, the School Mental Health Initiative has worked to expand the statewide effort to provide school behavioral health assessments for students. The Initiative took the lead in developing the School Behavioral Health Assessment component of the state SCHIP plan. This meant convening a group of more than 30 representatives of state and local agencies, parent organizations, school health providers, and others to come to consensus about how to develop a system of school-based behavioral health assessment. As stated earlier, New Mexico's entire Phase II SCHIP plan was rejected by HCFA and is still under negotiation. If it is finally approved, the plan will provide for more than $9 million per year for school behavioral health assessment and school health interventions. The SCHIP Assessment component, which would take place in childcare, daycare, or schools whenever possible, focuses on identifying early risk factors in children and serves as a gateway to other SCHIP services and to Medicaid-managed care services, school interventions, and community resources and services.

As a result of the hold-up on the SCHIP plan, other efforts have been made to bring mental health assessments to schools. A legislative memorial was approved in 1999, and followed by legislation in the 2000 legislative session that, if approved, would target mental health assessments for students in kindergarten through grade 3. The goal would be early identification of high-risk youth, supportive intervention for the child and family, and a plan to get the child back on track and successful in the classroom. This legislation is accompanied by funds for teacher training in school mental health and funds for assessments tools, as well as service dollars.

Training for Teachers and Other School Professionals

An additional component of collaboration includes statewide and local community training with a specific focus on strategies for enhancing the capacity of schools to identify students with mental health issues early and linking to appropriate intervention. This effort includes a partnership with the Department of Education's Special Education Division as well as New Mexico State University and is designed to expand awareness and training for teachers on how to identify children's mental health issues in the classroom and link them to intervention.

This train-the-trainers model, known as *Supporting Teachers Supporting Students*, is based on a model developed by the Training Workgroup of the School Mental Health Initiative. In this model, teachers, administrators, and school health professionals from local school districts are trained in adult education techniques and then an array of school mental health topics. The trainees then practice their own presentation skills with others being trained before going back to their home districts and providing two workshops for colleagues in their home schools.

In the first training pilot in the spring of 1999, 30 teachers from five New Mexico school districts attended the training and then provided workshops for 600 colleagues at their home schools. This group's presentations were well-rated, with requests for more training in specific school mental health areas. Currently, 55 school personnel from nine school districts are participating in this training process. It is hoped that additional funds will be obtained to expand this training in the coming year and give it a truly regional focus. This effort represents true collaboration among state, university, and school agencies.

In addition, the School Mental Health Initiative collaborates with the Office of School Health in the yearly *Head to Toe: A Conference on School Health.* This conference is now in its fourth year with attendance of more than 400 and brings together school personnel, parents, students, and providers from throughout New Mexico to collaborate on school health issues. Also, in collaboration with the Department of Education's Special Education Division, Section 504 training has been implemented for teachers and administrators throughout the state. Other workshops have focused on topics ranging from adolescent substance abuse to grant-writing (so school/community collaborative partners can learn how to pursue additional funds for needed interventions).

Collaboration Among Parent and Youth Organizations, Higher Education, and Professional Guilds

Collaboration with parents and parent advocates has been one of the critical priorities of the School Mental Health Initiative. With parent organizations, the initial thrust has been one of joint advocacy for increased support to address children's mental health concerns such as expanded awareness of mental health symptoms and improving access to services. The School Mental Health Initiative is currently collaborating with Parents for Behaviorally Different Children, New Mexico's parent advocacy organization for children with neurobiological disorders, to develop a *Guide for Parents on School Mental Health Issues,* which includes diagnostic and resource information, as well as updates on parent rights under Section 504 and IDEA.

The School Mental Health Initiative provides for reimbursement for parent transportation and time to attend meetings and asks for parents to co-present to legislative committees. Acknowledgement of parents as the true experts in understanding the needs of their children and the community has been one of the cornerstones of the School Mental Health Initiative's collaborative model.

With youth organizations, one emphasis has been on ensuring students a greater voice in policy and legislation, particularly regarding efforts to provide alternatives to suspension and expulsion. An additional youth-related effort is development of the Peer Navigator's Program, a peer mentorship model and training guide, created by School Mental Health Initiative staff with community and youth involvement. This prevention program and workbook for school personnel provide a leadership model for high-risk youth to develop self-esteem and find success in school through positive peer role-modeling. Now implemented in seven school districts within New Mexico, schools are finding strategies to reach out to some of their at-risk students to keep them involved in their schools in productive ways.

With institutions of higher education, the focus has been on expanding preservice and inservice training for school personnel and for community mental health providers who work within schools. The Initiative is working with a statewide school health collaborative on higher education to bring models of school mental health to teachers, administrators, school nurses, and counselor training. Some of the School Mental Health Initiative social work staff provides linkages for state social work training programs to develop internships for their social work students at local schools. Furthermore, the School Mental Health Initiative staff is linking with the state Legislative Education Study Committee and the State Board of Education to develop a plan for prioritizing school mental health issues in classroom education and state curricula.

With the state Pupil's Services Alliance, the emphasis has been on linking with school nurses, school social workers, school psychologists, school counselors, and child psychiatrists to bring a collaborative effort to expand attention to the mental health needs of our students. These efforts include multidisciplinary training on school mental health issues, as well as advocacy to expand the ratios of school health professionals and community providers on site in schools.

Building Awareness of Children's Mental Health Needs

The School Mental Health Initiative also has undertaken major efforts to expand statewide awareness of the mental health needs of children. In the summer of 1999, the School Mental Health Initiative, along with the Interdepartmental School Behavioral Health Partnership, brought together parents, religious leaders, school personnel, legislators, providers and youth from throughout the state to discuss the need to expand support for children's mental health. With consultation from a national media firm with expertise in children's mental health campaigns, the New Mexico Children's Mental Health Awareness Project was born. The target audience of this effort is parents and families, school personnel, and policy makers. The two priorities of the project are (a) to promote issues of awareness of children's mental health problems in the state, and (b) to improve access to programs and services.

The first activity of the group is to bring the art exhibit Childhood Revealed to New Mexico. This exhibit was coordinated by staff from the New York University Child Study Center and highlights artwork of children with mental illness from across the United States. Plans are under way to bring this exhibit to three sites in New Mexico. The Awareness Project intends to build a series of lectures, media events, and materials around this exhibit, which will highlight these critical issues. Schools and universities from around the state are joining the project to develop curricula and classroom projects to help New Mexico youth derive the maximum understanding from this exhibit. This exhibit certainly will galvanize community collaboratives from around the state to discuss the impact of childhood mental illness while also addressing the stigma issues that complicate communication around this issue.

Moving Ahead

Indications of the initial impact of the various collaborative efforts with respect to enhancing statewide attention to youth problems is reflected in establishment of the first state Summit on Children's Mental Health (done in conjunction with the Governor's Mental Health Planning Council) and passage by the legislature of a special Memorial in support of expanded school mental health. In the fall of 1998, the School Mental Health Initiative took the lead in developing the first New Mexico Summit on Children's Mental Health. Attended by more than 200 people its first year, this summit brought together statewide advocates for youth, parents, and providers, to share information about children's mental health in New Mexico. The next summit is scheduled for May of 2000.

The Mental Health in the Schools Memorial formally called for maximizing intra- and interagency collaboration and training to enhance school mental health programs. State agencies involved were the Departments of Health; Public Education; Children, Youth, and Families; Human Services; Corrections; the Administrative Office of the Courts; the Children's Subcommittee of the Governor's Mental Health Planning Council; the Developmental Disabilities Planning Council; and the IDEA Council. In addition, the text called for inclusion of consumers, advocates, and providers working in the mental health field and schools. The Memorial recommendations were made following four regional meetings on school mental health around the state. More than 240 New Mexicans spent one-half day discussing these issues in small groups and making recommendations. Some of the final recommendations, such as the SCHIP plan and other legislation, became policy, but are still awaiting final state approval.

With awareness of the expanding numbers to be served and the growing emphasis on wraparound services, New Mexico's legislature and state government is increasingly coming to understand that effective collaboration is essential to addressing barriers to development and learning. In keeping with this understanding, the state is making school- and community-level collaboration a priority and is building an infrastructure that can effectively turn policy into practice.

Implications for Future Policy and Practice

New Mexico's efforts to enhance collaboration for addressing barriers to development and learning represent moves in the right direction. Nevertheless, the problems of fragmentation and marginalization related to efforts for addressing barriers to learning are generally well-entrenched and difficult to change. These problems frequently stem from categorical policy making and funding, along with the specialized, self-protective focus and relative autonomy of units within agencies and among agencies. It is well documented that, although agencies often are dealing with "the same client" (Hodgkinson, 1989), they tend to do so with little in the way of a "big picture" framework, little or no coordination, and sparse attention to moving toward integrated efforts.

Cohesive Policy, Comprehensive Intervention

Ultimately, addressing barriers to learning and enhancing healthy development must be viewed from a social policy perspective. It is becoming increasingly clear that a major policy shift is needed to move (a) *from* fragmented *to* cohesive interventions, and (b) *from* narrowly focused, problem specific, and specialist-oriented services *to* comprehensive programmatic approaches. This shift encompasses an expanded focus on addressing barriers and enhancing the cohesiveness of existing policy. It also should include efforts to fill critical gaps in current initiatives designed to reform and restructure education and link to those efforts to restructure community health and human services.

From a societal perspective, the goal is to foster development of a comprehensive, multifaceted, and integrated continuum of community and school programs for local catchment areas. The framework for the continuum emerges from analyses of social, economic, political, and cultural factors associated with the problems of youth and from reviews of promising practices. It is built on holistic and developmental perspectives that are translated into an extensive continuum of programs focused on fostering the well-being of individuals, families, and the contexts in which they live, work, and play.

This continuum ranges from primary prevention and early-age intervention, through approaches for treating problems soon after onset, to treatment for severe and chronic problems. Included are programs designed to promote and maintain safety at home and at school, programs to promote and maintain physical and mental health, preschool programs, early school-adjustment programs, programs to improve and augment ongoing social and academic supports, programs to intervene prior to referral for intensive treatments, and programs providing intensive treatments. Implied is the importance of using the least restrictive and nonintrusive forms of intervention required to address these problems in a culturally appropriate manner. This scope of activity underscores the need to develop formal mechanisms for essential and longlasting interprogram connections (collaboration in the form of information sharing, cooperation, coordination, integration) on a daily basis and over time (Center for Mental Health in Schools, 1999).

One tool to foster greater cohesion in educational and health policy and practice is Adelman and Taylor's concept of an *enabling component* as a policy-oriented notion around which to unify efforts to address barriers to learning (see Adelman, 1996a, 1996b; Adelman & Taylor, 1994, 1997). The concept is intended to underscore two major concerns:

1. Current reforms are based on an inadequate two-component model for restructuring school and community resources, with the result that efforts to address barriers to development and learning are marginalized.

2. It is essential to move to a three-component model if student achievement is to increase significantly.

(As delineated in the publications cited above, a three-component model calls for elevating efforts to address barriers to the level of one of three fundamental and essential facets of education reform and school and community agency restructuring. All three components are seen as essential, complementary, and overlapping.)

By calling for reforms that fully integrate a focus on addressing barriers to learning, the concept of an enabling component responds to a wide range of factors interfering with development and learning. By providing a framework for restructuring school-owned enabling activity and blending school and community resources, the concept provides a helpful unifying focus upon which to formulate new policy and foster collaboration.

Adequate Underwriting for Essential Capacity-Building

A policy shift and programmatic focus are necessary but insufficient. For significant systemic change to occur, policy and program commitments must be demonstrated through allocation and redeployment of resources (e.g., finances, personnel, time, space, equipment) that can adequately operationalize policy and promising practices. In particular, there must be sufficient resources to develop an effective structural foundation for systemic changes. Existing infrastructure mechanisms must be modified in ways that guarantee that new policy directions are translated into appropriate daily practices. Well designed infrastructure mechanisms ensure local ownership, a critical mass of committed stakeholders, effective capacity building (including staff development), processes that can overcome barriers to stakeholders working together effectively, and strategies that can mobilize and maintain proactive effort so changes are implemented and renewed over time.

Institutionalizing comprehensive approaches requires redesigning mechanisms for governance, capacity building, planning-implementation, coordination, daily leadership, communication, information management, and the like. In reforming mechanisms, new collaborative arrangements must be established and authority (power) must be redistributed. All this obviously requires adequate support (time, space, materials, equipment) — not just initially but over time — to those who operate the mechanisms. And appropriate incentives and safeguards must be provided for those undertaking the risks involved in making major changes.

Concluding Comments

As Melaville and Blank (1998) note:

> One of the most important, cross-cutting social policy perspectives to emerge in recent years is an awareness that no single institution can create all the conditions that young people need to flourish.

Here it is evident that agencies, schools, families, and communities must work closely with each other to meet their mutual goals. For example, schools find that they can provide more support for students, families, and staff when they are an integral and positive part of the community. Reciprocally, agencies can make services more accessible to youth and families by linking with schools, and they can connect better with and have an impact on hard-to-reach clients.

The interest in working together is bolstered by concern about widespread fragmentation of interventions. The hope is that by integrating available resources, as New Mexico is attempting, a significant impact can be made on at-risk factors. In particular, appropriate and effective collaboration and teaming are seen as key facets in addressing barriers to development, learning, and family self-sufficiency.

Though informal linkages are relatively simple to make, establishing major long-term connections is complicated. These require vision, cohesive policy, and basic system reform. The difficulties are seen readily in any attempts to evolve comprehensive approaches. Enhancing the effectiveness of intervention in addressing barriers to development and learning requires collaboration among agencies, schools, families, and communities that

- is cohesive;
- provides the resources necessary for transforming the nature and scope of intervention efforts so comprehensive, multifaceted, and integrated approaches can be developed;
- creates necessary infrastructure and provides for effective capacity-building to ensure appropriate implementation of these comprehensive approaches;
- provides the resources necessary for implementing widespread scale-up.

Inadequate policy support related to any of these matters decreases the likelihood of enhancing intervention effectiveness on a large scale. Thus, the task ahead is one of ensuring that policy makers appreciate this fact and act appropriately.

References

Adelman, H. S. (1995). Clinical psychology: Beyond psychopathology and clinical interventions, *Clinical Psychology: Science & Practice, 2,* 28–44.

Adelman, H. S. (1996a). *Restructuring support services: Toward a comprehensive approach.* Kent, OH: American School Health Association.

Adelman, H. S. (1996b). Restructuring education support services and integrating community resources: Beyond the full service school model. *School Psychology Review, 25,* 431–445.

Adelman, H. S., & Taylor, L. (1994). *On understanding intervention in psychology and education.* Westport, CT: Praeger.

Adelman, H. S., & Taylor, L. (1997). Addressing barriers to learning: Beyond school-linked services and full service schools. *American Journal of Orthopsychiatry, 67,* 408–421.

Adelman, H. S., & Taylor, L. (1998). Reframing mental health in schools and expanding school reform. *Educational Psychologist, 33,* 135–152.

Adelman, H. S., & Taylor, L. (1999). Mental health in schools and system restructuring, *Clinical Psychology Review, 19,* 137–163.

Adelman, H. S., Taylor, L., Weist, M. D., Adelsheim, S., Freeman, B., Kapp, L., Lahti, M., & Mawn, D. (1999). Mental health in schools: A federal initiative. *Children Services: Social Policy, Research, & Practice, 2,* 99–119.

Adelsheim, S. (1999). School mental health in New Mexico, *Adolescent Psychiatry 24.* New Jersey: Analytic Press, 101–107.

Adler, L., & Gardner, S. (Eds.). (1994). *The politics of linking schools and social services.* Washington, DC: Falmer Press.

Allensworth, D., Wyche, J., Lawson, E., & Nicholson, L. (Eds.). (1997). *Schools and health: Our nation's investment.* Washington, DC: National Academy Press.

Annie E. Casey Foundation. (1999), *Kids count data book.* New York: Annie E. Casey Foundation.

Carnegie Council on Adolescent Development. (1988). *Review of school-based health services.* New York: Carnegie Foundation.

Carnegie Council on Adolescent Development's Task Force on Education of Young Adolescents. (1989). *Turning points: Preparing American youth for the 21st century.* Washington, DC: Author.

Center for Mental Health in Schools. (1997). *Addressing barriers to learning: Closing gaps in school-community policy and practice.* Los Angeles: Author.

Comer, J. (1988). Educating poor minority children. *Scientific American, 259,* 42–48.

Costello, E.J. (1989). Developments in child psychiatric epidemiology. *Journal of the American Academy of Child & Adolescent Psychiatry, 28,* 836–841.

Dryfoos, J. G. (1990). *Adolescents at risk: Prevalence and prevention.* London: Oxford University Press.

Dryfoos, J. G. (1994). *Full-service schools: A revolution in health and social services for children, youth, and families.* San Francisco: Jossey-Bass.

Dryfoos, J. (1998). *Safe passage: Making it through adolescence in a risky society.* New York: Oxford University Press.

Hoagwood, K. (1995). Issues in designing and implementing studies of non-mental health care sectors. *Journal of Clinical Child Psychology, 23,* 114–120.

Hodgkinson, H. L. (1989). *The same client: The demographics of education and service delivery systems.* Washington, DC: Institute for Educational Leadership./ Center for Demographic Policy.

Knitzer, J., Steinberg, Z., & Fleisch, B. (1990). *At the schoolhouse door: An examination of programs and policies for children with behavioral and emotional problems.* New York: Bank Street College of Education.

Lawson, H., & Briar-Lawson, K. (1997). *Connecting the dots: Progress toward the integration of school reform, school-linked services, parent involvement and community schools.* Oxford, OH: Danforth Foundation and Institute for Educational Renewal, Miami University.

Marx, E., & Wooley, S. F., with Northrop, D. (Eds.). (1998). *Health is academic: A guide to coordinate school health programs.* New York: Teachers College Press.

Melaville, A., & Blank, M. J. (1998). *Learning together: The developing field of school-community initiatives.* Flint, MI: Mott Foundation.

New Mexico Children, Youth, and Families Department. (1996), *Restoring justice: Snapshot: juveniles in custody,* New Mexico.

New Mexico Department of Health. (1999). *1997 New Mexico school survey final report,* Santa Fe: Dept. of Health.

New Mexico Department of Health. (1998). *The status of children's mental health in New Mexico.* Santa Fe: Dept. of Health.

Richardson, L. A., Keller, A. M., Shelby-Harrington, M. L., & Parrish, R. (1996). Identification and treatment of children's mental health problems by primary care providers: A critical review of research. *Archives of Psychiatric Nursing, 10*(5), 293–303.

Riggs, P. D., Baker, S., Mikulich, S. K., Young, S. E., & Crowley, T. H. (1995). Depression in substance-dependent delinquents. *Journal of the American Academy of Child & Adolescent Psychiatry, 34,* 764–771.

Stowell, R. J. A., & Estroff, T. W. (1992). Psychiatric disorders in substance abusing adolescent inpatients: A pilot study. *Journal of the American Academy of Child & Adolescent Psychiatry, 31,* 1036–1040.

Schorr, L. B. (1988). *Within our reach: Breaking the cycle of disadvantage.* New York: Doubleday.

Schorr, L. B. (1997). *Common purpose: Strengthening families and neighborhoods to rebuild America.* New York: Anchor Press.

Tyack, D. B. (1992). Health and social services in public schools: Historical perspectives. *Future of Children, 2,* 19–31.

Weinberg, N., Rahdert, E., Colliver, J. D. & Glantz, M.D. (1998). Adolescent substance abuse: A review of the past 10 years. *Journal of the American Academy of Child & Adolescent Psychiatry, 37,* 252–261.

Individual Issues and Interventions

Jon Carlson and Judith A. Lewis

The essays that make up this section examine concerns that affect adolescents on an individual level. Each author combines knowledge of adolescent development with an awareness of the behaviors that tend to place young people in jeopardy.

In chapter 4, M. Lewis Putman describes the problems experienced by adolescents with special emphasis on those with learning disabilities, as they seem to be more at-risk than their non-disabled peers. The dramatic physical, emotional, psychological, and social changes of adolescence pose unique challenges for individuals with learning disabilities.

Rosemary Lambie, Susan Leone, and Christopher Martin discuss how important resilience can be in working with at-risk children and youth. The authors offer many ideas as to how resilience can be increased.

In chapter 6, John Maag and Steven Forness provide an overview of child and adolescent depression. They describe the treatment studies that have been completed with depressed children and adolescents, as well as some of the common psychopharmacological interventions that are used. In addition, they discuss the prevalence of depression in populations with disabilities and the treatments that are available.

Next, Dave Capuzzi addresses another problem of great urgency: adolescent suicide. He provides an overview of possible causes for adolescent suicide, identifying common misconceptions and describing developmental, family, and environmental factors that may relate to the recent increase in adolescent suicide rates. He suggests a number of strategies for recognizing and preventing potential suicides and provides guidelines for managing crises that could not be prevented.

Barry Weinhold shows how bullying and school violence can lead to tragedy such as that experienced at Columbine High School. Dr. Weinhold describes effective long-range prevention methods that address many of the hidden elements present in a culture of violence.

In chapter 9, Radha Horton-Parker builds on Weinhold's ideas and presents a firm foundation for pro-social behavior that is essential for curbing violence during the adolescent years. This chapter presents information that the counselor can use to assist parents in developing practices that will lead to pro-social outcomes in young children and last throughout their lives.

Finally, the authors in this section share a vision of counseling that encompasses *prevention* as well as intervention. Each chapter provides a set of practical suggestions for services to address a particular issue. The guidelines presented have a number of common characteristics, including the following:

- a recognition that complex problems require multifaceted strategies for resolution and that no single method will always be appropriate;

- an awareness that interventions should fit the developmental level and special needs of the individual at risk and that careful assessment should be the basis for the approach to be used;

- a focus on the roles of family, peer group, and other systems in the development and resolution of problems;

- an appreciation of the need to use honest, straightforward, two-way communication in dealing with adolescents;

- a combination of broad, preventive measures and specific, targeted interventions to address each issue.

Adolescence is, for many, a difficult transitional stage. Because of the complexity of the issues involved, counseling clients who are at this stage in their development is demanding. The chapters in this section do not oversimplify this challenge, but they do provide some practical, positive strategies for coping with it.

Crisis Intervention With Adolescents With Learning Disabilities

M. Lewis Putnam

Here are just a few of the challenges we face:

- Every 31 seconds an adolescent becomes pregnant.
- Every 2 minutes an adolescent gives birth.
- Every 78 seconds an adolescent attempts suicide.
- Every 90 minutes an adolescent commits suicide.
- One million adolescents drop out of high school (*Children and Teens Today Newsletter,* 1987; Mann, 1986).

This chapter provides a discussion of several social issues that all adolescents must deal with daily. This information is critical to special education teachers because students with learning disabilities (LD) are not immune to involvement in these and other social issues.

Depression and suicide, alcohol and other drug use, teenage sexuality and school dropout, along with many other pressing social issues, place adolescents at risk for social, emotional, and psychological problems. Adolescents often are involved with more than one of these social issues. They attend schools where they are expected to be attentive, complete assignments, learn in a classroom setting, earn credits toward high school graduation, and eventually enter the world of work or attend an institution of higher education. Many adolescents succeed despite their involvement in these social issues, but increasing numbers need social, emotional, and educational interventions aimed at increasing their coping skills or at reducing their involvement. Adolescents with LD are at even greater risk for involvement with these social issues than their nonhandicapped peers. Thus, special education teachers should understand the incidence, possible causes, identification, and appropriate interventions.

Problems of Adolescence

Adolescence is a developmental stage characterized by experimentation, confusion, risk-taking behaviors, and a sense of immortality and invulnerability. Teachers often hear student comments such as, "I got so blasted Saturday night that I don't remember anything," or "It's not cool to use a condom!"

Public School Responsibility

Public schools increasingly are expected to address social issues that previously were the responsibility of the family, religious organizations, and social agencies. Educators often feel overwhelmed and underprepared to deal with adolescents at-risk for depression and suicide, alcohol and other drug use, sexual activities, school dropout, and other complex social issues facing today's adolescents.

Adolescents At Risk

Many professionals use the term *at risk* to describe a certain category of students. Never precise, the meaning of this term varies considerably in research and in classroom practice. McWhirter et al. (1993) defined "at risk" as "a set of presumed cause/effect dynamics that place the [adolescent] in danger of negative future events" (p. 6) such as not graduating from high school (Slavin, Karweit, & Madden, 1989). Those authors contended that "at risk" also might be viewed as a relative term, like a series of steps along a continuum rather than as a distinct category. The continuum in Figure 4.1 ranges from adolescents who are minimally at risk to those who are involved more actively in risk-taking behaviors.

Minimal risk. Adolescents who come from high socioeconomic settings, attend good schools, and have loving, caring relationships with their friends and families are assumed to be at minimal risk for involvement with these social issues. These adolescents, however, cannot be considered as "no risk," because no adolescent can escape altogether the influences of events such as death, divorce, and so on. The extent to which these and other events lead the adolescent to risk-taking behaviors depends upon factors such as age, developmental level, personality, available resources (social and mental health support), coping skills, and so on.

Remote risk. An adolescent reaches the point on the continuum at which risk-taking behaviors, though still remote, seem more possible because of negative demographic markers involving family, school, and so forth. A combination of these markers moves the adolescent along the at-risk continuum. For example, an adolescent who is from an "impoverished, dysfunctional, ethnic minority family and who attends a poor school in a marginal neighborhood" (McWhirter et al., 1993, p. 8) is further along the continuum than an adolescent with fewer markers. Most adolescents in this group do survive these difficulties and function well. Therefore, although these markers are important, they are only partially predictive of at-risk status for an adolescent.

MINIMAL RISK
> favorable demographics
> positive family, school, and social interaction
> limited psychosocial and environmental stressors

REMOTE RISK
> negative demographics
> less positive family, school, and social interaction
> some stressors

HIGH RISK
> negative family, school, and social interaction
> numerous stressors
> development of personal at-risk markers
> negative attitudes and emotions
> skill deficiencies

IMMINENT RISK
> development of gateway or threshold behaviors and activities

AT-RISK CATEGORY
> at risk for more intensive maladaptive behavior
> adolescent's activity solidly places him or her in the at-risk category
> at risk for other categories

Source: Based on Orr & Brack (unpublished data)McWhirter, J. J., McWhirter, B. T., McWhirter, A. M., & McWhirter, E. H. (1993). *At-risk youth: A comprehensive response.* Pacific Grove, CA: Brooks/Cole. Reprinted with permission.

Figure 4.1   The At-Risk Continuum

High risk. The next set of circumstances that moves a adolescent along the continuum is the demographic markers combined with an adolescent's negative attitudes or emotions. Adolescents at this point often experience depression, anxiety, and exhibit aggressive and risk-taking behaviors. These markers often signal that an adolescent is not coping with various stressors (e.g., poor grades, few friends) and certain demographic markers.

Imminent risk. As the adolescent moves along the continuum, at-risk status becomes even greater. At this point the adolescent may begin to use alcohol or other drugs occasionally to reduce some of the stressors or may appear to be depressed at times. These behaviors, referred to as *threshold behaviors*, often progress to increasingly more frequent and severe risk-taking behaviors. For example, cigarette use is considered a threshold to alcohol use, which can be a threshold to marijuana use, which in turn can be a threshold to crack cocaine use.

At-risk. The final step in the continuum is reached when the adolescent participates in behaviors that define the at-risk categories. According to McWhirter et al.

(1993), these adolescents no longer are at risk because they may have already attempted suicide, become involved in the abuse of alcohol and other drugs, become sexually active, or dropped out of school.

Teenage Depression and Suicide

Suicide is a growing problem among adolescents. The number of 15- to 24-year-olds who have committed suicide has risen 200% (Tomlinson-Keasey & Keasey, 1988) and now ranks as one of the top three causes of death for individuals under 24 years of age (Guetzloe, 1989).

How Many Adolescents Attempt Suicide

Suicide *ideation* (thoughts about suicide) and *parasuicide* (attempted suicide) both show a significant increase with age, particularly during adolescence (Rutter, 1986). As many as 7,000 adolescents commit suicide each year, and 400,000 to 1 million attempt to do so (Capuzzi & Golden, 1988; Robertson & Mathews, 1989). According to the results of a Gallup poll, 33% of 1,152 adolescents 15 to 19 years old have thought about suicide, 15% have seriously considered killing themselves, and 6% actually have made attempts (Peterson, 1991). In the United States, 20% of male suicides and 14% of female suicides involve adolescents (Hendlin, 1982; Robertson & Matthews, 1989). Females attempt suicide three times as often as males, but males complete suicide three times as often as females. This difference results from the more violent means, such as guns, that males use. The rate of completion by teenage girls, however, is increasing rapidly (Steele, 1983). These estimates are low because suicides often are reported inaccurately. Because of family embarrassment or religious beliefs or because of school and community discomfort, many suicides are reported as accidental or undetermined deaths (McWhirter et al., 1993).

Knowledge of the incidence of suicide by adolescents with LD is even less clear, as only a few studies directly compare depression and suicide by adolescents with mild disabilities and those without disabilities. The limited number of studies, however, suggests a discouraging picture. Adolescents with mild disabilities seem to have higher anxiety levels, more frequent and more serious bouts of depression, and higher rates of suicide than adolescents without disabilities (Dollinger, Horn, & Boarini, 1988; Hayes & Sloat, 1988; Maag & Behrens, 1989; Ritter, 1989).

Societal Myths Related to Suicide

Our society presents a negative view of suicide and of individuals who attempt suicide. As a result, many myths are associated with suicide. Accurate knowledge is one of the keys to understanding the causes and characteristics of adolescents who are at risk for taking their own lives. The most common myths are shown in Table 4.1.

Table 4.1   Societal Myths Related to Suicide

MYTH	FACT
People who talk about suicide do not attempt suicide.	8 out of 10 people who attempt to kill themselves do leave clues to their intent. Simply talking about suicide, however, does not mean a person will not attempt. Every verbal threat or reference to dying must be taken seriously. To discount a person's threat or reference is a direct rejection of his or her cry for help.
Suicide happens without warning.	Suicide often seems to be a sudden, unprovoked act only because we missed the warning signs. Sometimes, however, the clues are much more indirect unless we know what to look for. Statements such as "You won't have to worry about me much longer," or behavior such as withdrawing from friends or giving away many of their possessions can be signs that a person is preparing to die. The point is that expressed statements about dying must be taken seriously. We must learn the warning signs that the suicidal person provides.
Suicidal persons are fully intent on dying.	Most suicidal persons are ambivalent about dying. Many, especially teens and younger children, never believe they will die but that they will be rescued. Ninety percent of teenage suicide attempts are made in the home between early afternoon and midnight when parents are likely to find them. The fact that clues and warning signs most often precede the attempt also points to the ambivalence. It must be remembered, however, that the ambivalence does not reduce the risk involved.
People who attempt suicide are mentally ill.	The overwhelming despair a suicidal person feels can be caused by a sudden emotional upset, a long physical illness, the sudden loss of a loved one, or the feeling that he or she truly is a burden to others. A frequent theme of suicidal children is that they feel they are the cause of their parent's unhappiness. Suicide in most cases is not the act of psychotic persons, but persons who feel that the pain in their lives will not die, so they must. Only 12% of those who commit suicide are mentally ill. The attitude that suicide is the act of a deranged mind is exactly what keeps many potentially suicidal persons from being more open about their feelings. They fear that if they reveal their suicidal feelings, others will attempt to commit them to a psychiatric hospital. This reaction is, by far, the least helpful and is most often unnecessary.
Children are not capable of knowing how to kill themselves.	Television has given adolescents the knowledge necessary to kill themselves. They are aware of what acts are potentially lethal.
Children who attempt suicide have parents who are callous, insensitive, ignorant, and incapable of loving a child.	Most parents are sometimes the last to see the pain in their child because they love the child so much that they don't want to recognize that their child is in pain. Most parents, however, once approached, will do whatever is necessary to help their child.
People who attempt suicide are merely looking for attention.	People who threaten to attempt suicide are reaching out for help, not "merely" attention.

Source: Steele, W. (1983). *Preventing teenage suicide.* Novato, CA: Ann Arbor Publishers. Reprinted with permission.

When an Adolescent May Be Suicidal

For many, adolescence is filled with stressful events and adjustments. We must be able to distinguish between the typical turmoil that occurs during adolescence from turmoil that is life-threatening. Too many adolescents at risk for suicide have been viewed mistakenly and sometimes tragically as simply going through a stage (Metha & Dunham, 1988).

The exact cause of suicide remains a mystery. Professionals generally agree that suicidal behavior results from a complex interaction of numerous factors with no single cause (Hawton, 1986; Pfeffer, 1986). Thus, no one type of adolescent is more suicidal than another. It could be any student from the homecoming queen to the most reserved and quiet student in class.

The single most predictive factor for adolescent suicide is a previous attempt (Shaffer, 1974). Any problem that contributes to feelings of depression, worthlessness, helplessness, or hopelessness has the potential to trigger suicidal behavior in a vulnerable adolescent. Table 4.2 summarizes the most common warning signs that an adolescent may be thinking about committing suicide.

Certain psychological, social, and school characteristics can help distinguish between adolescents who are able to cope with their turmoil and those who are at risk for taking their own lives.

Psychological characteristics. These characteristics include suicidal threats or statements, extreme changes in behavior, and "getting the house in order" (e.g., giving away prized possessions) (Guetzloe, 1987). Frederick (1985) contended that suicidal individuals often suffer from the "three H's: haplessness, helplessness, and hopelessness" (p. 15). For example, suicidal adolescents may have had a series of misfortunes over which they had little or no control, such as their parents' divorce and a subsequent move (haplessness). The adolescent may not have the coping skills, such as seeking help or advice from a friend or professional, to deal with these events (helplessness). As a result, the adolescent may feel hopeless, and suicide may seem to be the only answer ("I don't know what else to do!").

Another key psychological characteristic, depression, is highly correlated with suicidal behavior. Estimates of the prevalence of depression among the general school-aged population have ranged from 1.8% to 13.9% (Pfeffer, Zuckerman, Plutchik, & Miznuchi, 1984), with higher rates reported among older adolescents. We must become aware of the signs of depression among adolescents so we can provide appropriate interventions or refer the adolescent to the school counselor or to a local social or mental health agency.

According to the *Diagnostic and Statistical Manual of the American Psychiatric Association, Third Edition, Revised (DSMIII-R)* (APA, 1987), a consideration of major depression requires at least five of the following nine behaviors and must include either a depressed mood or loss of interest or pleasure. These behaviors must have been evident nearly every day for at least 2 weeks and represent a change from the adolescent's previous behaviors:

1. Depressed or irritable mood

Table 4.2   Suicide Warning Signs

BEHAVIORAL CLUES

- Sudden changes in behavior
- Drinking, taking drugs
- Decline in school performance
- Inability to concentrate
- Withdrawing from others
- Studying all the time to the exclusion of outside activities and friends
- Fighting physically with family members
- Running away
- Giving away possessions

VERBAL CLUES

Direct:
"I feel like killing myself."
"Sometimes she makes me so mad, I feel like hanging (shooting, etc.) myself."
Indirect:
"Everyone would be better off without me."
"If this happens again …"
"I just can't take anymore. …"
Any denial that problems exist when problems are obvious to others. Sudden interest in suicide, questions about it, ongoing discussion about it, etc.

SITUATIONAL CLUES

- Loss of relationships, friends, etc.
- Loss of status or sudden traumatic event (not making grades or team, or exclusion from peers)
- Divorce of parents
- Violence within the family
- Parental overemphasis on achievement
- First year of college
- Period of time immediately following a long bout of depression
- Physical problems along with changes in behavior or performance

---

Source: Steele, W. (1983). *Preventing teenage suicide*. Novato, CA: Ann Arbor Publishers. Reprinted with permission.

---

2. Loss of enjoyment or interest in normally pleasurable activities

3. Change in weight, appetite, or eating habits

4. Problems with sleeping

5. Psychomotor agitation or slowness

6. Loss of energy; feeling of fatigue

7. Feelings of worthlessness, inadequacy, self-reproach, self-depreciation, loss of self-esteem

8. Diminished ability to attend, think, or concentrate

9. Recurrent thoughts of death or suicide

Social Characteristics. One of the major social characteristics of teenage suicide is the cluster suicides that follow or imitate another suicide. Teenagers who are part of a cluster may attempt suicide out of an impulsive reaction to someone else's suicide. When one adolescent commits suicide, the act somehow becomes "normalized" for others, and those who previously had experienced the "three H's' may begin to see suicide as a viable option. The incidence of cluster suicides suggests that one adolescent's suicide is a powerful event that influences others to take their own lives (Sturner, 1986).

A second social characteristic is related to the adolescent's home situation. Suicidal youths are more likely than non-suicidal youths to have lost a parent. Specifically, 50% to 72% of adolescent suicide attempters or completers have lost a parent through death, divorce, or abandonment (Tomlinson-Keasey & Keasey, 1988; Tomlinson-Keasey, Warren, & Elliott, 1986).

Violence in the home is another social characteristic. Some researchers have reported that nearly 60% of suicidal adolescents have experienced some degree of sexual or physical abuse at home (Kosky, 1983). In addition, a family history of suicide is prevalent in adolescents who attempt or complete suicide. According to one study, nearly 38% of adolescent suicide attempters had a close relative who had committed suicide (Metha & Dunham, 1988).

School Achievement Characteristics. Suicide also is related to the adolescent's school achievement. In one study of 12-to 15-year-olds hospitalized for self-destructive behavior and threats of suicide, 20% were not enrolled in school, 45% reported that they did not attend school regularly, and 50% were performing below their expected grade level (Gispert, Wheeler, Marsh, Davis, 1985). As we are all too aware, poor school achievement often initiates a spiral of self-doubt, failure, and negative thoughts, which may lead to depression or suicide attempts.

Identification

In addition to being aware of these psychological, social, and school achievement characteristics, two useful methods are available to determine an adolescent's suicide ideation. Teachers who feel uncomfortable about using these procedures should refer the adolescent to another professional, such as the school counselor.

Interviews. Interviews, which can disclose the severity and lethality of suicide ideation, probably are the most effective and informative way to determine the adolescent's suicide risk (McWhirter, 1993). These are conducted with adolescents who appear to be depressed or suicidal and with their parents, teachers, and friends. Information to be solicited during the interview includes the following:

(a) History of the presenting problem (depression, anxiety, etc.)

(b) The family structure and relationships (divorce, physical or sexual abuse, alcoholism, etc.)

(c) The developmental, medical, and academic history of the adolescent

(d) The status of interpersonal relationships

(e) Previous suicide attempts

(f) Verbal warning signs

(g) Behavioral warning signs

(h) Any stressor events that may trigger a suicide attempt (McWhirter et al., 1993, p. 195)

If suicide ideation is suspected, the degree of risk of the adolescent acting upon those thoughts must be determined. Because suicide ideation by itself is not a great risk, the severity of the threat or suspicion depends on the specificity and the lethality of the method of choice.

Therefore, we need to be knowledgeable about the risk factors of a suicidal threat as listed by Steele (1983):

1. *Suicidal plan.* The more specific a person is about the way he or she will die, the greater is the likelihood of an attempt.

2. *Availability of method.* The risk is higher whenever the method is readily available. (Example: a person who says he or she has thought of carbon monoxide poisoning but does not have a car is less at risk than the person who has a car available.)

3. *Location.* If a person has determined the place and it is accessible, the risk of suicide is high, especially if the location is inaccessible to others.

4. *Time.* If the time is specified, the risk is higher. Teens most often attempt suicide in their own homes between mid-afternoon and midnight.

5. *Ingestion of alcohol or drugs.* Whenever anyone is drinking or taking other drugs and talking suicide, the risk is very high because drugs reduce self-control and significantly increase impulsivity.

6. *Accessibility for rescue.* If a person plans to commit suicide at a time or place when or where no one is expected or able to get to, the risk is high.

7. *Lack of support.* If the person has no friends, parents who are not concerned, or if the suicidal person refuses to give information necessary to reach friends or those who could help, the risk is high. A recent loss coupled with talk of suicide portends high risk. A loss that may seem insignificant to us can be painful for that person, especially if followed by other losses. Loss may be in the form of a friend or a pet, for example. Not getting an "A," not winning an election, not being accepted into peer groups, or being rejected from a peer group can be significant losses.

8. *Previous attempts.* Those who have attempted suicide in the past are always at high-risk for suicide.

9. *Illness.* Chronic physical illness or long-standing emotional problems raise the risk for suicide.

Self-Report Inventories. The second method that can be used to determine the level of depression in adolescents is the self-report inventory. Two useful inventories are the *Beck Depression Inventory* (BDI) (Beck et al., 1961) and the *Scale of Suicide Ideation* (SSI) (Beck, Kovacs & Weissman, 1979). The BDI indicates whether an adolescent is severely depressed and at-risk for suicide. The SSI focuses more on attitudes about living and dying, the characteristics and specificity of suicidal ideation, and background factors such as previous suicide attempts.

By using interviews and self-report inventories and by being aware of the warning signs and myths associated with depression and suicide, we are better able to identify adolescents who may be depressed or experience suicide ideation. Before accurate identification is possible however, we must be aware of two primary difficulties:

1. Adolescents tend not to actively volunteer information about their emotions, turmoil, and so forth (Garrison, Lewinsohn, Marsteller, Langhinrichsen & Lann, 1991).

2. Adolescents are reluctant to say that they are thinking of taking their own life or that they may be thinking of death (Reynolds, 1985).

Prevention, Intervention, and Postvention

Suicide *prevention* tends to focus on the factors that lead to suicidal ideation or parasuicide, while *intervention* is directed to treatment after an unsuccessful suicide attempt. *Postvention* consists of activities for surviving family members, friends, the school, and the community after a parasuicide or successful suicide.

Prevention. Most school-based suicide prevention programs deal primarily with detecting signs of depression and suicide ideation. In addition, prevention efforts attempt to help students to be successful in school, to grow emotionally, and to achieve up to their academic potential. School-based prevention efforts include modifying the student's school situation (e.g., changes in schedule), providing a tutor, or reducing the student's credit load. In addition, students with LD may need a change in their individualized education programs (IEPS), such as reduced time in either the special or general education classroom, and specific instruction in social skills or problem solving.

Intervention. Intervention efforts usually are initiated after an adolescent is determined to be depressed or has exhibited suicidal behaviors or attempted suicide. The focus here should not be on why adolescents view suicide as an option to their current situation but, rather on solving problems, in the home, school, or community, so suicide is no longer considered an option. The major stressors (e.g., grades, friends) that triggered the suicidal behavior or thoughts should be identified, and steps taken to reduce the pressures through school-based counseling or support groups. Again, a change in IEP may be necessary for students with LD, to address specific stressors.

At times an adolescent may have to be referred to services outside of the school system, such as a counseling center or a mental health agency. Regardless of whether interventions are in or outside of the school, the immediate task is to provide relief from feelings of the "three H's", to explore alternatives to suicidal behavior, and to instill feelings of being in control of their life (Frederick, 1985). With appropriate interventions, depressed and suicidal adolescents usually show considerable improvement (Peck, 1985), but warning signs can recur. More than 40% of adolescents who commit suicide are thought to have made previous attempts (Shaffer, 1974), and 3%–10% do so within 15 years (Otto, 1972). Therefore, school-based prevention and intervention efforts must be combined with long-term intervention and follow-up efforts, because an adolescent with suicidal tendencies may be at risk for several years after the initial threat or attempt (Guetzloe, 1988).

When teachers find themselves in a situation of interacting with a depressed or suicidal adolescent, the following set of guidelines proposed by McGee and Guetzloe (1988) may be helpful.

1. Never take suicide threats or gestures casually.

2. Don't be afraid to bring up the subject of suicide.

3. Question the student closely and carefully about a possible suicide plan.

4. Do not debate the morality of suicide.

5. Identify the major stresses or events that precipitated the suicidal behavior.

6. Do not convey the message that suicidal thoughts are ridiculous or that make the student suffer guilt.

7. Encourage the student to use other support systems such as parents, friends, church leaders, school personnel, or a counseling center.

8. If the suicidal behavior was precipitated by the loss of a romantic relationship, don't downplay it. The adolescent may view such a loss as the end of any hope for a loving relationship.

9. Don't leave the suicidal student alone.

10. Dispose of anything in the immediate environment that could be used as a weapon.

11. Mention school or community events that will be coming up later in the day, the next day, or the next week that might elicit their interest.

12. Be aware of the student's responses to your statements.

13. Be sure that the student has the telephone number of a crisis center, the suicide hotline, or a member of the school staff.

14. Do not promise to keep a student's suicidal behavior a secret.

15. Try to get a commitment from the student that he or she will not hurt himself or herself and that if he or she feels any kind of suicidal impulse, he or she will call a teacher, a counselor, or a hotline worker.

16. Always make a referral to a school guidance counselor or other appropriate professional.

These guidelines are not to be used in lieu of notifying parents or guardians or seeking other professional help.

Postvention. Despite prevention and intervention efforts, all adolescent suicides cannot be prevented. When a suicide does occur, the school should provide postvention activities. These efforts deal with issues such as cluster suicides and the grief and shock of family members, friends, and other students.

Adolescents will talk about the suicide whether we do or do not provide them with the opportunity. They need a chance to remember that having suicidal thoughts is not unusual and thinking about suicide does not mean they are destined to attempt suicide. If they talk about the suicide without adult leadership, however, their conclusions may be incorrect or negative. The leadership that the school can provide can help adolescents who might have suicidal ideations. Berkan (1986, pp. 29–30) suggested the following postvention activities:

- The building principal should brief all teachers and staff on the situation.
- The building principal should request assistance from the district's psychologists, social workers, and counselors to spend several days in the school and/or district talking to small groups of students about their feelings and reactions to the suicide.
- All first-hour or homeroom classes should be informed about the facts of the situation and given an opportunity to have a short discussion of their feelings and be told about the small group sessions.
- The immediate peer group of the student who has committed suicide should be identified and called in at once for special sessions with the support staff.
- All students need to be told as to whom to ask for help if they or a friend are thinking of suicide.
- Support groups should be scheduled for those who need them during school time.
- Do not dismiss school; students need to follow a normal schedule as much as possible.
- Do not encourage a general student body attendance at the funeral if it is held during school hours; excuse only those students who have a parental request to attend.
- Do not dedicate a room, garden, etc., to the student's memory.
- If the students or staff want to do something, in memory of the student, suggest helping to plan a suicide prevention effort in the school or community.
- Emphasize that suicide is not a good choice to solve problems, that help is available, and that people care.
- Emphasize that no one is to blame, not friends, parents, or teachers; the student chose to die by suicide and no one forced it on the student.

Alcohol and Other Drug Use

Alcohol and other drug use among adolescents is widespread and has remained stable at high levels since 1975. Marijuana remains the most commonly used drug, followed by stimulants, inhalants, hallucinogens, sedatives, and tranquilizers (Johnston, O'Malley, & Bachman, 1986). The average age at which alcohol consumption begins is 12 years, 5 months, and 23% of young people between ages of 12 and 18 have a serious drinking problem (Horton, 1985). Regardless of the substance used and the age at consumption, even occasional use can have disastrous results. The leading cause of death in adolescents is accidental death, related to the consumption of alcohol in at least 40% of cases (American Academy of Pediatrics, 1988).

Incidence

Although the substance of choice among adolescents is alcohol, estimates of alcohol consumption and other drug use vary greatly depending upon definitions. Results of two nationwide studies indicated that anywhere from 60% to 66% of high school seniors nationwide reported alcohol consumption during the month prior to the study, 4.2% - 5% of seniors reported that they drank every day, and 37.5% reported at least one incident of heavy drinking (five or more drinks in a row). In addition, about 2%-6% admitted to using stimulants, 9% used inhalants, and 5% had used cocaine. Furthermore, 16%-33% reported having experimented with marijuana (Newcomb & Bentler, 1989).

Limited data are available on the prevalence of alcohol and other drug use by adolescents with mild disabilities. Existing data are mixed, stemming primarily from clinical studies and geographically limited samples, as well as from studies with questionable technical adequacy. Devlin and Elliott (1992) found that 51% of a sample of students classified as behavior disordered (BD) showed patterns of high drug use. Only 14% of a matched nondisabled control group showed similar rates of usage. Only 28% of the BD students reported no drug use, compared with 74% of the control students. Others (see Dean, Fox, & Jensen, 1985; DiNitto & Krishef, 1984; Issacs, Buckley, & Martin, 1979; Krishef, 1986) have contended that the incidence of alcohol and other drug use in adolescents with disabilities may be greater that it is among the general population. Still others (Elmquist, Morgan, & Bolds, 1989; Leone, Greensburg, Trickett, & Spero, 1989) see no reason to believe that adolescents with disabilities have higher levels of substance use than nondisabled students.

These and other reported incidence rates probably underestimate the prevalence and incidence of drug use by adolescents. Most research studies do not include school dropouts, who are at even higher risk for alcohol and drug abuse.

Why Do Adolescents Use Alcohol and Other Drugs?

The reasons for alcohol and other drug use among adolescents are difficult to determine. Typical reasons for use of alcohol and other drugs often are linked to social influences (e.g., peer use of drugs), whereas reasons for abuse often are tied to internal processes (e.g., use of alcohol and other drugs as medication against depression, anger, frustration) (Long & Scherl, 1984).

Research suggests that some environmental, behavioral, psychological, and social risk factors are so consistently associated with alcohol and other drug use that they can be considered true causal factors (Newcomb & Bentler, 1989). This information can be used to determine the likelihood of alcohol and other drug use by students and then used to provide appropriate interventions. The more risk factors with which an adolescent is associated, the greater is the probability of alcohol and other drug use.

The most reliable predictor of future alcohol and other drug use is prior use (McWhirter et al., 1993). Adolescents who use alcohol and other drugs before age 15 have more problems of abuse in later life (Kellam & Simon, 1980). Risk factors for alcohol and drug abuse that have been identified by numerous researchers include the following (American Academy of Pediatrics, 1988; Capuzzi & LeCoq, 1983; Horan & Strauss, 1987; MacDonald & Blume, 1986; Webb, Baer, McLaughlin, McKelvey, & Caid, 1989):

Early and persistent behavior problems
Low commitment to school
Peer rejection in the elementary grades
School failure
Antisocial and deviant behavior
Tolerance for deviance
Sensation-seeking
Peer and parental approval and use of alcohol and other drugs
Poor relationship with parents
Family history of alcoholism or other drug use or abuse
Peer use of alcohol and other drugs
Depression
Low self-esteem
Poor parent-child communications

Use Versus Abuse

Many adolescents experiment with alcohol and other drugs but perform well in school and go on to lead productive lives. Their use does not necessarily equate to abuse. With this in mind, we must keep the entire issue of alcohol and other drug use versus abuse in perspective. Because there is such a fine line between use and abuse, some informal identification procedures may be helpful. We must consider the context, frequency, type, and purpose for which alcohol or other drugs are used.

Informally, one of the best ways to determine an adolescent's use of alcohol and other drugs is through our own knowledge of the issue and the relationship we have established with students. The more we know about the students, the better the chances are that we may pick up on signs of alcohol and other drug use, as listed in Table 4.3.

In addition to these warning signs, teachers should be knowledgeable about the most common drugs adolescents use, their street names, and their effects. Also, to be

Table 4.3   Signs of Alcohol and Drug Abuse

CHANGES IN PERFORMANCE:

- Distinct downward turn in grades—not just from Cs to Fs, but from As to Bs and Cs
- Assignments not completed
- Loss of interest in school; extracurricular activities
- Poor classroom behavior such as inattentiveness, sleeping in class, hostility
- Missing school for unknown reasons
- In trouble with school, work, or the police
- Memory loss

CHANGES IN BEHAVIOR:

- Decrease in energy and endurance
- Changes in friends (secrecy about new friends with different lifestyles)
- Secrecy about activities (lies or avoids talking about activities)
- Borrows lots of money, or has too much cash
- Mood swings, excessive anger, irritability
- Preferred style of music changes (pop rock to heavy metal)
- Starts pulling away from the family, old friends, and school
- Chronic lying, stealing, or dishonesty
- Hostile or argumentative attitude; extremely negative, unmotivated, defensive
- Refusal or hostility when asked to talk about possible alcohol or other drug use
- Slurred speech

CHANGES IN APPEARANCE/PHYSICAL CHANGES:

- Weight loss or gain
- Uncoordinated
- Poor physical appearance or unusually neat; striking change in personal habits
- New interest in the drug culture (drug-related posters, clothes, magazines)
- Smells of alcohol, tobacco, marijuana
- Frequent use of eyedrops and breath mints
- Bloodshot eyes
- Persistent cough or cold symptoms (e.g., runny nose)
- Always thirsty, increased or decreased appetite, rapid speech
- AOD paraphernalia (empty alcohol containers, cigarettes, pipes, rolling papers, baggies, paper packets, roach clips, razor blades, straws, glass or plastic vials, pill bottles, tablets and capsules, colored stoppers, syringes, spoons, matches or lighters, needles, medicine droppers, toy balloons, tin foil, cleaning rags, spray cans, glue containers, household products)

Source: Elmquist, D. L. (1991). School-based alcohol and other drug prevention programs. *Intervention in school and clinic, 27,* 10–19. Reprinted with permission.

able to distinguish between the occasional user from the adolescent whose use has moved to abuse, teachers should be familiar with the patterns of progressive alcohol and drug use, shown in Table 4.4.

A more formal means of determining an adolescent's alcohol and other drug use is the *adolescent drinking index* (ADI) (Harrell & Wirtz, 1989). The ADI is a 24-item scale that measures the severity of drinking problems of adolescents. Severity is measured by determining the number of different areas (e.g., school, grades) in which the adolescent has had alcohol-related difficulties and the extent or intensity of the problem in those areas.

Prevention and Intervention

Prevention programs are the most common form of intervention for alcohol and other drug use, for students who have not yet experimented with the substances. At the same time, treatment for threshold drug use is instituted for students who are already users.

Many school-based prevention programs are provided through extracurricular clubs and activities that are open to all students and require no special training or selection process. These programs alone cannot be expected to have a significant effect on alcohol and other drug use and related problems. They should be *part* of a comprehensive school-based alcohol and other drug use program. The following are a few examples of clubs and activities that schools may offer to their students.

Students Against Driving Drunk (SADD). SADD meets regularly as a school club to promote the nonuse of alcohol and other drugs by peers and their parents, particularly when driving. A major component of this program is a contract for life, in which the adolescents and parents agree in writing to call for help or transportation if they are in a situation where they have been drinking and need to go home. SADD sponsors activities such as putting up posters in stores, restaurants, and bars; giving presentations in the community; arranging for speakers at school-wide assemblies; and giving presentations to students in middle and elementary schools to encourage early commitment to preventing alcohol and other drug use.

Just Say No Clubs. These clubs advocate the nonuse of alcohol and other drugs among its members and classmates. Members receive current and accurate information regarding alcohol and other drug use, as well as training in how to say no to peers, how to have fun without using alcohol and other drugs, and how to support each others' nonuse. Meeting during and after school, they often sponsor alcohol- and drug-free activities for the club and the entire school.

Lock-Ins. The lock-in is an overnight alcohol- and drug-free activity sponsored by parents, students, or other clubs. Participating students engage in activities such as volleyball, basketball, swimming, and watching videos on a weekend evening. Students obtain parental permission and are not allowed to arrive or leave between certain hours, usually 9:00 P.M. until 7:00 A.M. the following morning. Lock-ins often have a special theme, and the school or local groups or agencies donate money, food, and prizes. The students are locked in to help prevent alcohol and other drug use.

Table 4.4   Patterns of Progressive Drug Abuse

EXPERIMENTATION

Behavior	*Frequency of Use*	*Emotional State*
Little effect	1 to 5 times	Excitement/daring
Denial of negative consequences	(total)	Mild euphoria
		Possible discomfort
		Mild guilt

SOCIAL/SITUATIONAL

Behavior	*Frequency of Use*	*Emotional State*
Decreased academic performance	2 to 4 times	Excitement
Loss of interest in hobbies	per week	Being "in" with the crowd
Loss of interest in special activities		Feels better with drug than
Begins to seek out drug-using friends		without it
Changes in clothing habits		Less guilt—"Drugs are OK,
Some uncharacteristic behavior		I can handle them."

HABITUAL

Behavior	*Frequency of Use*	*Emotional State*
Most friends use drugs	Daily use	"Need" for euphoric state
Beginning of family problems		Highs are very high, and
due to drug use		lows are very
Major loss of interest in		uncomfortable
school and other activities		More guilt and depression
Impulsiveness		
Erratic mood swings		
Uses drug alone		

OBSESSIVE/DEPENDENT

Behavior	*Frequency of Use*	*Emotional State*
Skips school regularly	Multiple times	Needs drug to feel "normal"
Weight loss or gain	per day	Severe discomfort if drug is
Messy, unclean appearance	depending	not available
Loss of ability to concentrate	on drug	Disorganized thoughts
Severe paranoid or depressed	Erratic behavior	
thoughts		May become psychotic or
Dangerous aggression, suicidal		suicidal
thoughts		
Stealing to obtain drugs		

Source: Kerr, M. M., Nelson, C. M., & Lambert, D. L. (1987). *Helping adolescents with learning and behavior problems.* Columbus, OH: Merrill. Reprinted with permission.

Sufficient supervision and administrative support are essential for success of these events.

Adventure-Based Programs. These programs are designed to fill the adolescent's need for adventure and risk-seeking behaviors. They provide stimulating and exciting activities as alternatives to alcohol and other drug use. Students build self-confidence and self-esteem and learn group problem solving and teamwork as they develop new skills and find new strengths. Canoeing, camping, mountain climbing, sailing, and hiking are some of the many possible activities.

Mini-Courses and Wellness Days. Schools offer these programs to promote individual well-being and fun without alcohol and other drug use. For one day or all week students participate in presentations by community volunteers and professionals with themes such as wellness, hobbies, noncompetitive games, alcohol and other drug-use issues, and skills in resisting peer pressure and saying no.

School Climate Teams. Schools sponsor positive school activities that build school spirit and community pride. The goal is to prevent alcohol and other drug use by making the school a better place to be—more caring, nurturing, and personal. Activities include a special day for encouraging friendship, decorating lockers for birthdays, and special events that give students a sense of belonging and bonding within the school.

To ensure that these clubs and activities are effective (Contrucci, 1991), schools should take care of the following:

- Activities should be comfortable and safe for all participants.
- A variety of individual, small-group, and whole-group activities should be offered to add diversity and interest to the program.
- Activities should be flexible to meet individual school, and community needs.
- Participation must be voluntary.
- Realistic expectations should be set for each activity.
- Advisors and school staff must receive basic training. (p. 47)

Many educational materials are available to teachers. These can be incorporated in daily instruction or utilized as part of the activities of these clubs and activities.

Teenage Sexual Activity

During the developmental stage of adolescence, sexuality takes on new dimensions. Feelings become more intense, relationships become more complex, and the consequences of sexual activities are altered radically. These changes affect not only the behavior of adolescents but also the behavior of their families, peers, and educators. Despite public opposition from a variety of sources, the need for adequate school-based sex education programs is pressing (Romaneck & Kuehl, 1992). Issues related to adolescents' sexual activities are broad and complex, including sex education, the use of contraceptives, date/acquaintance rape, sexually transmitted diseases (STDs), sexual orientation and sexual harassment.

Extent of Adolescent Activity

Although the age of first sexual intercourse varies by gender and ethnicity, the majority of adolescents are sexually active by age 18 (Hofferth, Kahn, & Baldwin, 1987; Orr, Wilbrant, Brack, Rauch, & Ingersoll, 1989). In a Time/CNN telephone survey of 500 teenagers, Gibbs (1993) found that 19% of 13- to 15-year-olds and 55% of 16- to 17-year-olds have had sexual intercourse. Further, 61% of teenage girls reported that they have had multiple sexual partners, up from 38% in 1971. In addition, 61% of the same population reported using birth control every time they had sex; 26% reported sometimes, and 13% reported never using birth control.

Why Do Adolescents Become Sexually Active?

The reasons adolescents become sexually active are varied. Economic status, educational goals and attainment, perceived life options, parental involvement, and familial role models are among the most influential factors associated with adolescent sexual activity. Additional factors include the adolescent's values of independence and achievement, level of self-esteem, and peer influence (Muccigrosso, Scavarda, Simpson-Brown, & Thalacker, 1991).

Family factors are highly associated with adolescents' decisions about being sexually active. Adolescents with working mothers and from single-parent families may be more likely to be sexually active (Fick, 1984). Beyond the effects of income and educational status females whose older sisters are role models and those from large families seem to be more sexually active. The extent of sexual activity by adolescents also is related directly to the quality of parent-child communication in the home. The more involved that parents are in the lives of their adolescent, the less likely their children are to be active sexually (Foster, 1986; Paget, 1988).

Sexual activities commence at a younger age in male and female adolescents who live in poverty, teenage males and females who are low achievers educationally, and females whose mothers and older sisters are low educational achievers (Foster, 1986). According to Gibbs (1993), "In the inner cities the scarcity of jobs and hope for the future invites kids to seek pleasure with little thought of the fallout" (p. 63).

Sex Education Programs

The consequences of an adolescent's sexual behavior are so potentially serious for themselves, their families, and society that learning and practicing responsible sexual behavior is imperative. The overall goal of sex education is to teach adolescents sexual responsibility and to promote the "positive perception of an individual's sexuality" (Kempton, 1988, p. 24). Adolescents learn sexual responsibility as they grow up in a family, by watching and copying the way responsible adults behave. Adolescents need to know that good relationships can suffer from acting upon one's sexual feelings. Unless adolescents understand the meaning of sexual responsibility, they are unprepared to engage in any sexual activity.

Sexual responsibility can be summarized as the following:

■ both partners discussing birth control and agreeing to use it every time to prevent an accidental pregnancy

■ both partners being honest about their sexual health and agreeing to use condoms to prevent sexually transmitted diseases (STDs)

■ knowing that sex involves commitment and mutual consent

■ understanding the positive and negative consequences that sex can have in their lives (Stang, 1989, p. 3).

Although sex education is still highly controversial, one study indicated that 85% of parents favor sex education in the schools and believe it fosters a healthy attitude toward sex (Harris, 1987). Much of the debate over teaching sex education in the public schools focuses on the morality of and our own attitudes toward human sexuality. As a result, it is a difficult issue on which to build consensus among teachers, administrators, and parents. The issue is complicated further by the flaunting of sexuality in the media, the lack of appropriate role models who practice responsible sexual behavior, and societal attitudes regarding sexuality.

In describing the needs for sex education for adolescents with disabilities, Shapiro (1981) stated:

Exceptional children experience the same physical and emotional changes that [nondisabled] children do, as well as the same anxiety which often accompanies adolescence. Thus, they must cope with all the emotional conflicts of their [non-disabled] teenage counterparts in addition to those produced by their handicaps. (pp. 25–26)

Price (1987) concurred that

[adolescents with handicaps] are influenced by the same pressures affecting the sexual decision making of every adolescent and teen, such as peer pressure, movies, and television. The differences lie in the [disabled] person's lack of appropriate information about physical and emotional changes of adolescence, sexuality, and birth control (p. 154)

Conger (1988) recommended three general approaches to sex education: (a) family-life planning, (b) increasing the accessibility of contraceptives to adolescents, and (c) enhancing the life options of adolescents.

Family-Life Planning. All students need current, relevant, accurate, and appropriate family-life education from the early school through high school years. Unfortunately, many students receive little information about sexuality from their parents. Only 30% of 13- to 15-year-olds and 27% of 16- to 17-year-olds reported that they learned the most about sex from their parents; 26% of the 13- to 15-year-olds and 37% of the 16- to 17-year-olds reported learning about sex from their friends, Gibbs (1993). This is discouraging because we all have heard the type of information about sex that students hear from their friends (for example, "If you have sexual intercourse while standing up, the girl can not become pregnant").

Although sex education in the context of family-life planning is important, it is not sufficient to resolve the problem of adolescent sexual activity. Sex education improves knowledge, but little conclusive proof exists that behavior is influenced by knowledge alone. Therefore, educational programs that work on improving relationships, boosting self-esteem, and teaching decision-making skills must be combined with life-planning programs (McWhirter et al., 1993).

Increased Accessibility to Contraceptives. A second approach to sex education is the availability of contraceptive options to sexually active adolescents. Decisions about birth control are complicated. Age at onset of sexual activity, family income, belief in the risks associated with unprotected sexual activity, and the availability of confidential contraceptive services are crucial variables in adolescents' use of contraceptives (Muccigrosso et al., 1991).

Contraceptives cannot be forced on adolescents, but they should be available. Access can be provided best through community- and school-based clinics that offer comprehensive, easily accessible, and high-quality health services. School-based clinics are particularly useful so sexuality can be dealt with in the context of overall health care by a school nurse who is aware of adolescents' special sexuality concerns and needs. The various methods of contraceptives available to adolescents are varied, controversial, and confusing. Therefore, adolescents should ask themselves some serious questions about their choice of contraceptives, such as the following:

■ Would an accidental pregnancy be a big problem for me and my partner?

■ How safe is this method for me?

■ How easy is this method to use? Will I use it the right way every time, even if it sometimes is a hassle?

■ How much will this method cost to use? Can I afford it?

■ How does my partner feel about birth control? Can we work together to use this method?

■ Will I feel embarrassed about using this method? Will my partner feel embarrassed? Will I use it even if I feel embarrassed?

■ How do I feel about touching my body?

■ How often do I have sex? Do I want a method that is always in my body? Or can I pick a method to use only when I have sex?

■ Do I have more than one sexual partner?

■ Do I have religious or moral feelings about using birth control? Does this method fit with my religious beliefs?

At this point, the few clinics that provide comprehensive health services, including dispensing contraceptives, have shown promising results. In one school district the overall annual rate of first-time pregnancies was reduced from 80 per 1,000 to 29 per 1,000; repeat pregnancies were reduced to 1.4%, compared to 33% nationally (Kirby, 1984; Schorr, 1988).

Using contraceptives every time an adolescent has sexual intercourse can help protect against pregnancy and STDs, however, the most commonly-used form of contraceptive, the use of condoms, is still not 100% foolproof. Condoms can break, partners can be careless, and mistakes can happen. The only surefire method of contraception is abstinence. Adolescents should take the attitude that being abstinent does not mean they are not grown up but, rather, they are being sexually responsible.

Until the majority of adolescents elect abstinence, those who are sexually active should be urged to practice safe sex. Safe sex means more than using contraceptives. It also requires knowing your partner and your partners sexual history. A person is having sex not only with the partner but also with whomever the partner has ever had sex with (Adams & Gullotta, 1989).

Enhanced Life Options. A third approach to sex education attempts to improve adolescents' life options. McWhirter et al. (1993) contended that "when young people feel good about themselves and have a clear vision of a successful and self-sufficient future, they will be motivated to avoid pregnancy" (p. 147). In addition, Edeleman (1987) proposed that "the best contraceptive is a real future" (p. 58). A future requires opportunities to build academic and work-related skills, job opportunities, assistance with life-planning, and access to comprehensive-health services. Adolescents who are working toward personal and economic self-sufficiency tend to be more sexually responsible (McWhirter et al., 1993).

Sexually Transmitted Diseases. To many adolescents, STDs (formerly called venereal diseases) are not a concern. Thus, the risks for adolescents' contracting an STD are extremely high. Any sex education program offered in the public schools must include information on STDs, including the human immunodeficiency virus (HIV) that causes the acquired immune deficiency syndrome (AIDS). Short of abstinence, there is no surefire way to prevent contracting STDS.

The rates of STDs are escalating in adolescents. More than 2.5 million adolescents contract an STD annually (Office of Population Affairs, 1988). Nearly one-fourth of adolescents contract some STD each year (Gibbs, 1993). Adolescents must understand how STDs are contracted and their symptoms, as shown in Table 4.5.

The incidence of STDs in adolescents has increased because of the following:

1. More adolescents are sexually active.

2. Adolescents tend to have more sexual partners.

3. Many adolescents who are asymptomatic do not know that they have an STD and spread the disease unknowingly (Gale, 1989).

AIDS is an STD caused by the human immunodeficiency virus (HIV). Over time, HIV damages the body's immune system, resulting in life-threatening infections and cancers. These illnesses are called *opportunistic diseases* and do not develop in healthy people.

Table 4.5   The Most Common Sexually Transmitted Diseases

STD	CAUSE	SYMPTOMS*	TRANSMISSION
HIV	virus	general illness swollen glands pneumonia skin cancer (Kaposi's sarcoma)	sexual contact (via blood, semen) blood transfusion dirty needles mother to fetus
Chlamydia	bacteria	itching or burning in genital or urinary areas	sexual contact mother to fetus
Giardia diarrhea	bacteria	diarrhea abdominal pain	sexual contact blood feces
Gonorrhea	bacteria	discharge from penis or vagina	sexual contact
Herpes Type I Type II	virus	painful sores around mouth and/or vagina burning or pain during urination	sexual contact
Syphilis	bacteria	pimple-like sores on genitals	direct sexual contact with sore mother to fetus
Vaginal infections	bacteria fungi yeasts	bad-smelling vaginal discharge pain during intercourse	sexual contact some infections spread on objects (towels, douche equipment)
Genital warts	virus	warty growths in genital area	sexual contact mother to infant

*may not experience all of these or may be asymptomatic

Source: Scott, M. (1988). *Family living and sex education* (p. 126). New York: Globe. Reprinted with permission.

Without doubt, AIDS is the most dangerous of the STDs that adolescents risk through their sexual activity. Because at this time AIDS is always fatal, adolescents who engage in high-risk behavior—principally, unprotected sexual intercourse or intravenous (IV) drug use are vulnerable to contracting HIV. The number of adolescents infected with HIV is unknown, but it is believed to be much higher than the prevalence of AIDS in adolescents and is doubling each year (Brooks-Gunn, Boyer, & Hein, 1988).

Approximately 1% of those diagnosed with AIDS are adolescents (Centers for Disease Control, 1989); however, individuals 20 to 29 years of age constitute 21% of those with AIDS (Hein, 1989). Given the 7- to 10-year latency period between HIV infection and the diagnosis of AIDS (National Academy of Sciences, 1989), 20% of the individuals diagnosed in the 20-29 year-old range were infected during adolescence (Centers for Disease Control, 1989). The source of infection varies substantially by gender: 38% of males are infected by homosexual activity and 37% by hemophilia; females are more likely (45%) to be infected through heterosexual activity (Centers for Disease Control, 1989).

Until researchers find a cure for AIDS or a vaccine for HIV, the only weapon against the epidemic is education. Many adolescents receive contradictory and confusing information, not only from peers but also from parents and teachers. Adolescents' lives and the lives of all their sexual partners depend on their having accurate information about AIDS. This is not an overstatement or a scare tactic. Adolescents no longer can afford to think about the pleasures of sex without knowing the risks of contracting the HIV virus.

A number of studies have found significant deficiencies in adolescents' AIDS-related knowledge and beliefs (Hingson, Strunin, Berlin, & Heeren, 1988; Strunin & Hingson, 1987). Many beliefs related to AIDS put adolescents at risk for exposure to the HIV virus. For example, 12% of a national sample believed that birth control pills provide some protection against HIV infection, and 23% believed that one can tell whether a person has AIDS by looking at them (Anderson et al., 1990). In addition, Tatum (1988) contended that adolescents often associate HIV/AIDS with gays and bisexuals ("the gay disease") , which frequently leads to homophobia (fear and mistrust of gays and lesbians).

Much of this misinformation is the result of hastily conceived programs, curricula, and educational materials that provide inaccurate information on HIV and AIDS. To ensure that the information shared with students is accurate, it must be obtained from reliable sources. The local public health department, Red Cross chapter, local and national AIDS agencies, and the public library can provide or recommend up-to-date, accurate information and educational materials.

Information provided to adolescents about HIV/AIDS should take into account the following information:

1. The risk of becoming infected with HIV can be virtually eliminated by not engaging in sexual activities and by not using illegal IV drugs.

2. Sexual transmission of HIV is not a threat to uninfected individuals who engage in monogamous sexual relations.

3. HIV can be transmitted through sexual contact with an infected person, by using needles that an infected person has used, and from an infected mother to her infant before or during birth.

4. Although no transmission from deep, open-mouth ("French") kissing has been documented, it theoretically could transmit HIV from an infected to an uninfected person through direct exposure of mucous membranes to infected blood or saliva.

5. Adolescents who engage in sexual intercourse with individuals who are at risk or whose infection status is unknown should use a latex condom and a water-based lubricant to reduce the likelihood of becoming infected.

6. Behavior that prevents exposure to the HIV virus also may prevent unintended pregnancies and exposure to STDs (*Morbidity and Mortality Weekly Report,* 1988).

Regardless of the amount of information provided to adolescents about HIV/AIDS, many continue to engage in sexual activities. These adolescents can take several precautions to greatly reduce their risk for contracting HIV (American College Health Association, 1990; Gale, 1989):

1. Make careful choices about sexual activity in (a) choosing whether to be sexually intimate, (b) choosing a partner, (c) choosing how to be sexually intimate, and (d) choosing when to be sexually intimate.

2. Communicate assertively with your sexual partner and negotiate for safer sexual practices.

3. Develop skills to express your feelings and concerns.

4. Remove alcohol and other drug use from the context of sexual activities.

5. Use latex condoms and water-based lubricants for sexual intercourse.

6. Do not share IV needles.

Date/Acquaintance Rape

Dating violence is "a pattern of abusive and coercive behaviors or actions whereby one dating partner seeks to control the other," and sexual abuse is "any sexual activity forced upon a person without his or her consent" (Tomaszewski, 1991, p. 5). All adolescents, males and females, should recognize that forcing anyone into unwanted sexual activity is rape. Forced sex is illegal, even if the person is a friend, a relative, or a date.

Rape is the most frequently committed violent crime in the United States today, and violence in dating couples does exist in adolescent relationships. Coles and Stokes (1985) reported that 14% of adolescent females in their study said they had been raped. When asked to identify the rapist, they indicated the following:

Identity of Rapist	Percentage
friend	30
stranger	29
boyfriend	16
relative	13
neighbor	9
gang rape	4

These abusive behaviors rarely stop without some form of intervention. Violence in an early intimate relationship is as an indicator of violence in future adolescent and adult relationships (Tomaszewski, 1991). Clearly, education about date/acquaintance rape is a necessary step toward prevention and early intervention.

The goals of educational programs are "to provide adolescents with information about the dynamics of violence, teach interpersonal relationship skills that could reduce the likelihood that one partner will be abusive or abused, and provide resources to either change the abusive behavior or help an abused teenager leave the relationship" (Tomaszewski, 1991, p.4). Education should focus on sexual responsibility and "sex as a loving act" (Gale, 1989, p. 120). Sex requires two consenting persons and requires that each person set his or her own limits and be accepting of their partner's limits. All adolescents should be advised to give a clear and firm message in setting their limits and not to let themselves get talked or bullied into a situation they do not want (Gale, 1989). When a partner says "no," it means NO.

Teachers cannot prevent their students from being in situations where they are forced to participate in sexual activity without their consent. Nevertheless, teachers can offer some suggestions for lessening this risk:

1. If you feel uncomfortable about going somewhere or being alone with someone, don't go.

2. Be cautious of someone who invades your personal space by doing things such as standing or sitting too close, staring at your breasts or crotch, or touching you more than you want; tell him or her clearly to stop it.

3. Be careful of someone who is domineering and selfish, who tries to get what he or she wants at your expense.

4. Be especially alert at parties involving alcohol and drugs; they lower resistance and self-control.

5. Don't accept a ride home or go somewhere alone with someone you just met.

6. Always have a back-up to get a ride home or a way out of a potential risky situation.

7. For girls—be aware that boys may misinterpret a girl's manner of dress or behavior, and be prepared to set your limits.

8. If you get in a situation in which you are being coerced, pressured, threatened, or forced, respond quickly and firmly, flee or try to flee, fight back and yell (Gale, 1989, pp. 122-124).

Sexual Orientation

Among the many controversial topics in school-based sex education programs, none has raised so many red flags as that of sexual orientation, "the emotional and physical attraction a person feels for the [opposite] and/or same sex" (Humm, 1992, p. 14). Orientation to the opposite sex is heterosexuality; to the same sex, homosexuality;

and to both sexes, bisexuality. Many female homosexuals prefer to be called lesbians, whereas many male homosexuals prefer to be called gay. Being gay is not a disease, a mental illness, or a choice. The American Psychiatric Association removed homosexuality from its list of mental disorders in 1973.

Estimates of the prevalence of homosexuality in the general population range from about 2% to 10%–12%. In multiple studies of gay men, the mean age of acknowledging sexual orientation has been identified retrospectively around the age of 13–14. Although these men usually did not consider themselves as gay until young adulthood, the feelings were there much earlier.

Because homosexuality is a sensitive subject for most adolescents, as well as their parents and teachers, we tend to avoid discussing it. Nevertheless, we may find ourselves in a situation in which a student asks us about sexual orientation. At one time or another, many adolescents wonder whether they are gay. For most, these are just mild concerns that cease as they grow older. For others, however, feelings about being gay can be confusing and emotional. As a result, they may "spend their time trying to look and act like other [adolescents] and being afraid to do anything that might make them different" (Gale, 1989, p. 111). Often they fight their feelings and, because of this insecurity, many adolescents tend to confuse masculinity/femininity with sexual orientation. The male who does not match the subjective definition of "masculine" or the female who does not match that of "femininity" are suspected of being gay.

For fear of arousing anyone's suspicions, adolescents often hesitant to discuss their feelings and think they are the only ones with the same feelings. Gay and lesbian adolescents are more likely than their heterosexual peers to drop out of school, become runaways, and abuse alcohol and other drugs. The suicide rate for gay and lesbian adolescents is two to six times higher than that of heterosexual adolescents (Pender, 1990).

In addition to the many emotions that gay and lesbian adolescents experience, they also must cope with parental, peer, and societal negative reactions to being gay. A significant amount of ridicule, discrimination, stigmatization, anger, and physical attacks (known as "gay-bashing) is directed at gays and lesbians simply because of their sexual orientation.

Although many sex education programs include the topic of sexual orientation, the information is limited and often presented in a negative, nonaccepting fashion. Many state mandated HIV/AIDS education programs, however, have opened up discussions about sexual orientation. School districts are beginning to take the initiative in educating adolescents about sexual orientation and are beginning to provide more of a healthy and safe environment for students who consider themselves to be gay. As examples: schools in Los Angeles operate a counseling and support program called "Project 10" for gay and lesbian youth; in San Francisco each school is required to designate a "gay-sensitive" staff member to whom students can turn if they have concerns; and schools in Fairfax, Virginia, integrate homosexuality into the family living/sex education curricula (Humm, 1992).

Sexual Harassment

One of the most persistent problems related to the issue of sexual harassment has been the "absence of a widely agreed upon definition, one that is broad enough to comprehend the variety of experiences to which the term refers, and yet specific enough to be of practical use" (Fitzgerald, 1992, p. 9). Because of the confusion over a definition, many students hesitate to discuss incidents with other students or school administrators. Students often feel helpless and without witnesses. Further, the burden of proof falls largely on the adolescent. The other side of the coin is that many teachers hesitant to interact with their students (put their arms around students in a friendly manner) for fear of being falsely accused themselves.

According to the American Association of Colleges (1978), behaviors that may be considered sexual harassment include the following:

- Verbal harassment or abuse
- Subtle pressure for sexual activity
- Sexist remarks about someone's clothing, body, or sexual activities
- Unnecessary touching, patting, or pinching
- Leering or ogling at someone's body or body parts
- Demanding sexual favors accompanied by implied or overt threats concerning one's grades, etc.

A coed expressed the following emotions after being sexually harassed by one of her teachers: "I still slink down one hall, cowering, frightened because of a teacher whose classroom is there. . . . Whenever I see him, my heart jumps a beat, I begin to sweat and I try to avoid eye contact as he stares at me" ("The Pain of Harassment," 1993). This student's feelings were the result of numerous sexual harassment incidents such as the teacher passing her in the hall and blowing her a kiss or patting her on the back or the buttocks in class; calling her "sweetheart," "honey," and "cutie"; and walking by her desk and discreetly slipping his hand inside the waistband of her jeans. Ultimately, the student informed the school's administration about the harassment. After a year of investigations and interviews, the teacher was suspended without pay with a warning that further incidents would not be tolerated.

In terms of education, adolescents need to become aware of behaviors that are considered inappropriate and what to do if they believe they are being sexually harassed. In addition, administrators must establish a school atmosphere that encourages students to report these behaviors.

Teaching Sex Education

Because sex education is such a sensitive topic, a student's question or behavior at times may be beyond what a teacher feels comfortable or knowledgeable about discussing. A model developed by Jack Annon (discussed in Muccigrosso et al., 1991), the PLISSIT model, is designed to determine the parameters and when a referral to a professional in or outside of the school is indicated. The model outlines four levels of intervention: permission, limited information, specific suggestions, and intensive therapy.

Permission (P). Some potential problems can be eliminated simply by giving permission to adolescents to experience their sexual development. Adolescents need to know they are normal in their sexuality, through statements such as, "All girls have periods. It's normal and part of being a girl. It means you're growing up, and that's exciting!" (Maksym, 1990, p. 109). This may be helpful in relieving anxiety over sexual thoughts, fantasies, and arousal (Kempton, 1988) for boys and girls alike.

Limited information (LI). This level of information provides more details but only enough to answer specific questions. Information presented through a sex education program must be keep simple: "Some bleeding comes from the vagina each month; it comes from the uterus inside the girl's body" (Maksym, 1990, p. 110). This type of information dispels myths and concerns about sexuality.

Specific suggestions (SS). Often questions can be answered by giving specific and concrete suggestions: For example, you might say to an adolescent, "Having a period is a private thing. You can talk about it just with your mother or your teacher or your best friend. Not to people on the bus, or people you don't know" (Maksym, 1990, p. 110).

Intensive therapy (IT). Teachers should not provide intensive therapy unless they have been trained in both the physical and the psychological aspects of human sexuality. This is the level at which teachers usually suggest that the individual student obtain professional counseling.

A lot of information about human sexuality can be provided to students through informal and unplanned interactions. When discussing these topics, teachers should not overemphasize technical detail, or misrepresenting facts, or omit essential options. The goal is to provide accurate, complete, and relevant information so adolescents can make informed, responsible decisions. Throughout these interactions, the following personal characteristics are essential for effective instruction in human sexuality (Romaneck & Kuehl, 1992, p. 24):

1. *Credibility.* The ability to win the confidence and respect of students.

2. *Knowledge.* Awareness of the subject matter and confidence in one's ability to present the material in an open and straightforward manner.

3. *Trust.* Engendering in students the feeling that they can communicate freely and openly with the teacher.

4. *Acceptance.* The ability to accept individual differences.

5. *Approachability.* Communicating to students that they can express highly sensitive or private feelings to the teacher.

6. *Flexibility.* The capability of dealing with student input in a nonrigid fashion.

7. *Authenticity.* The ability to maintain an honest and sincere posture toward students.

Numerous commercial curricula are available for more formal sex education programs. Regardless of the program used, Thomas et al. (1985), have suggested that the following components be part of a sex education curriculum:

Unit 1
Introduction to human growth
and development
Communication and decision making

Unit 2
Growing up male
—anatomy and physiology
—sexual orientation
—pressures
—laws

Unit 3
Growing up female
—anatomy and physiology
—sexual orientation
—pressures
—laws

Unit 4
Teen pregnancy
—health and psychosocial risks

Unit 5
Personal hygiene for males
and females

Unit 6
Birth control
—benefits
—risks
—alternatives
—access and laws

Unit 7
Sexually transmitted diseases
—prevalence

—prevention
—detection
—treatment
—health risks
—laws

Unit 8
Factors influencing reproductive
health
—smoking
—alcohol and other drug use
—nutrition and medical care

Unit 9
Labor and pregnancy

Unit 10
Positive parenting and pregnancy
alternatives

Unit 11
Date rape and stranger rape
—prevalence
—prevention
—laws
Sexual harassment
—prevalence
—prevention
—laws

Unit 12
Conclusion
—course review
—development of personal
   reproductive life plan

In addition, Muccigrosso et al. (1991), have suggested some effective techniques for teaching sexuality to adolescents, as follows:

1. Draw out what the students already know or think they know.

2. Establish ground rules to make it safe to talk about sexuality, such as
   ■ no put-downs;

- don't share information outside of the class;
- everyone can pass (e.g., refuse to discuss a topic);
- no private stories;
- show respect for one another;
- all questions are good questions.

3. Agree on commonly understood vocabulary.

4. Use visual aids such as models, videos, and slides.

5. Create opportunities for role plays.

6. Incorporate group discussions and cooperative learning.

7. Be as concrete as possible; demonstrate and illustrate.

8. When possible, have coeducational groups.

9. Team-teach—male and female whenever possible.

10. Start with topics that are comfortable to you and the students.

School Dropout

Dropping out of school has a significant impact on a student's life as well as economic and social repercussions for the society at large. Unemployment rates are high among high school dropouts. In one study, 60% of dropouts in Miami and 46% in Philadelphia reported being unemployed and not enrolled in vocational or academic programs. In addition, high school dropouts who are employed tend to earn less than high school graduates (Dropouts' Perspective on Leaving School, 1988). The result is a loss of earnings, taxes, and social security, as well as a lack of qualified workers.

Most dropouts later regret their decision to leave school (Peng & Takai, 1983). This dissatisfaction only intensifies the low self-esteem typical of dropouts (Ekstrom, Goertz, Pollack, & Rock, 1986). Teachers, therefore, must provide appropriate opportunities for all students to learn, to be successful, and to graduate from high school as a means of reducing the ever-rising dropout-rates.

Numbers of Dropouts

One problem with the current research on dropouts is the lack of a standardized definition and inconsistent accounting procedures across school district and research studies (MacMillan, Balow, Widaman, Borthwick-Duffy, & Hendrick, 1990). The Office of Educational Research and Improvement (1987) defined a *dropout* as a student who leaves school before his or her program of study is complete, before graduation, without transferring to another school.

Another definition of school dropouts, by Voss, Wendling, and Elliott (1966) differentiated three types of dropouts:

1. Involuntary dropouts who have to leave school because of unavoidable circumstances such as a family emergency

2. Students . . . who leave because they lack certain skills

3. Capable students who voluntarily drop out for other reasons

A conservative estimate of the dropout rate nationwide is 15%–25.9% of all high school students (Mann, 1985; State Education Performance, 1990). The incidence of students with mild disabilities who drop out of school may significantly exceed that of the nondisabled; approximately one in four students with mild disabilities drop out of school (Cohen & deBettencourt, 1991).

Studies that report dropout rates separately for different categories of handicapping conditions generally indicate that two groups have a higher propensity than others to leave school before graduation. The estimated dropout rate of students with severe emotional disturbances is approximately 50% (Kaufman, 1987), and for adolescents with learning disabilities, between 25% and 50% (deBettencourt, Zigmond, & Thornton, 1989). In a comparative study Zigmond and Thornton (1985), reported that half of the students with learning disabilities who began 9th grade left school before graduation. This rate was significantly higher than that for nondisabled adolescents in the same urban school.

Kinds of Students Who Drop Out of School

Numerous characteristics of students at risk for dropping out of school have been identified. Ekstrom and her colleagues (1986) focused on a sample of high school sophomores over a 2-year period and found that those who stayed in school ("stayers") differed from those who left ("leavers") across a wide variety of dimensions. Students in low socioeconomic and racial/ethnic minority groups were disproportionately represented among the leavers and were more likely to be older and male.

Specifically, these researchers found that the leavers tended to come from homes with fewer study aids and fewer opportunities for nonschool-related learning. Further, the leavers were less likely to have both birth parents living in the home, more likely to have employed mothers (who had less education and lower educational expectations for their children), and to have less parental monitoring of their in- and out-of-school activities.

The leavers also were less likely to be involved in extracurricular activities and had lower grades and test scores than the stayers. Too, the leavers did less homework— an average of 2.2 hours a week compared to the 3.4 hours reported by the stayers. The leavers also had more discipline problems in school than the stayers, were absent and late more often, cut more classes, got suspended from school more often, and had more trouble with the police.

Differences between leavers and stayers also were found in the social domain. Many of the leavers reported feelings of alienation from school. Few leavers reported being satisfied with their academic work and being popular with other students. They tended to choose friends who also were alienated from school and who had low educational expectations. Finally, the leavers were likely to have worked more hours during their high school years than the stayers. Their jobs were more enjoyable and important to them than school. Additional characteristics of dropouts and related school factors are summarized in Table 4.6.

Table 4.6   Characteristics of Drop-Out Students

Demographic Factors	School Factors
Ethnic group	Weak leadership from the principal
Gender	High level of disempowerment experi-
Community type	enced by staff
Social and Family Factors	Small amount of time teachers
Socioeconomic status	engage in instruction
Single-parent family	Low percentage of teaching time
Educational or motivational support	spent in interactive learning
at home	Tracking
Personality Factors	Misuse of standardized tests
Low self-concept	Fiscal arrangements that encourage
Externalized locus of control	early dismissal of dropouts
Low needs for self-development	
Early Transition into Adulthood	Overcrowding
Pregnancy	Underachieving student body
Marriage	High failure rates
Having a job	
Deviant Behavior in Society	Low degree of order and discipline
Institutionalized or incarceration	Low attendance rate
Delinquency	
Drug use	
In-School Factors	School reform
Low academic achievement and low grades	
Low IQ; reading problems	
Being held back; being over age	
Low educational and occupational	
aspirations	
Behavior problems; poor attendance	

Source: Wolman, C., Bruininks, R., & Thurlow, M. L. (1989). Dropouts and dropout programs: Implications for special education. *Remedial and Special Education, 10,* 6–20. Reprinted with permission.

Although the profile of adolescents who drop out of school helps to identify potential dropouts, the data do not tell us why these students decide to leave. Some say that factors identified by Ekstrom and her colleagues (e.g., truancy, poverty, low expectations) actually cause students to drop out of school (SMERC, 1986). Over the past 30 years dropouts have consistently reported (Dropouts' Perspective on Leaving School, 1988) their main reasons for leaving school before graduation are as follows:

A dislike for school
The opinion that "school is boring" and not relevant
Low academic achievement and poor grades
A desire to work full-time and a need for money
Lack of belonging and a sense that nobody cared

Prevention

Literally thousands of school programs have been designed to reduce the number of students who drop out of school. Successful programs share several common features: small size, inclusion by choice, flexibility, view of school as a community, and involvement of the community outside the school (Cuban, 1989).

Nationwide, school districts are adopting a variety of programs to reduce high school dropout rates. The underlying premise of many of these programs is to provide opportunities for student success (ways to get students through school and to accumulate credits toward high school graduation) and to improve their self-image. Many interventions emphasize support systems designed to help students overcome obstacles such as low motivation and large class size. The programs also tend to stress flexibility with regard to course requirements and grading systems, school climate, support from teachers and administrators, teacher-student contact strategies, instructional approaches, and vocational and school-community educational programs (Cohen & deBettencourt, 1991).

Some common dropout prevention programs are as follows:

- Remedial and basic skills classes
- Reading programs
- Tutoring programs
- Motivational development activities
- On-the-job training
- School-supervised work experience
- Counseling activities
- Parental involvement
- Self-awareness classes
- School-age parenting classes
- Evening or weekend classes

Generally, educators say the needs of students at risk for dropping out of school are complex and defy easy solutions (Rodenstein, 1990). Moreover, the reasons frequently are multiple (e.g., a young girl is pregnant, low-achieving, and poor) and vary from student to student.

Crisis Intervention Efforts

A number of professionals (Caplin, 1964; McWhirter et al., 1993) separate prevention into three levels: (a) *primary prevention*, efforts to reduce the incidence of involvement; (b) *secondary prevention*, efforts to work with adolescents who are involved already; and (c) *tertiary prevention*, efforts directed toward rehabilitation of the adolescent.

Primary Prevention

Primary prevention has been defined as "a process which promotes health by empowering people with the resources necessary to confront complex, stressful life conditions and by enabling individuals to lead personally satisfying, enriching lives, (Berkan, 1986, p. 4). This approach encompasses a variety of activities that help adolescents develop a positive self-image and better coping skills. Most primary prevention programs promote behavioral changes of adolescents to reduce their risk-taking behaviors. Shaw and Goodyear (1984) noted that primary prevention must

— be group-oriented and individually focused,

— be a before-the-fact effort targeted to groups or individuals not yet involved in the social issue,

— rest on a solid knowledge base that suggests the program holds potential for preventing involvement. (p. 625)

Primary prevention approaches are of four main types: information, affective, alternative, and social competence (Elmquist, 1991).

Information. Prevention efforts are considered generic when they are thought to be appropriate for all students, not just those presumed to be at-risk. Often, these efforts are information-based with the assumption that more balanced, factual knowledge about the consequences of at-risk behaviors, such as alcohol and drug use, sexual behaviors, and so on, will create more negative attitudes toward and reduce the likelihood of the adolescent's involvement.

Educators must provide accurate and timely information about these social issues. Hansen et al. (1988) found that information about relatively immediate consequences had greater effect than information about long-term consequences. In addition, adolescents are more likely to be suspicious of information presented in an obviously one-sided and biased manner than information presented in a balanced and neutral manner (Botvin & Willis, 1987).

The information approach includes scare tactics. We all have seen the television commercials that dramatically demonstrate the effects of drugs on the brain by cracking an egg into a sputtering skillet. However, scare tactics neither provide information nor prevent drug use (Horan & Straus, 1987; Newcomb & Bentler, 1989).

Fortunately, we are beginning to move away from the information approach. According to Goodstadt (1986), information-based efforts, especially alcohol and other drug-use education programs, have failed for four reasons: (a) changes in attitude do not automatically lead to changes in behavior; (b) alcohol and other use drug or sex education courses often are taught as though all students involved are nonusers or nonparticipants; (c) education programs do not make necessary links between the classroom and reality; and (d) most education programs have not been evaluated in terms of learning outcomes. Finally, Eiser, Eiser, and Bocker (1988) questioned teachers and found them dissatisfied with information-based interventions, preferring approaches based on teaching students how to make appropriate decisions.

Affective. Affective educational programs promote self-understanding and responsible decision making. They address value clarification, problem solving, self-awareness and self-esteem, and coping skills (Barnea, 1989; Jaker, 1985). An adolescent faces many decisions that require these skills (Should I have sex? Should I try marijuana? Should I have another beer?). This prevention/intervention approach is based on the assumption that by improving their psychological traits, clarifying values, and developing responsible patterns of assertiveness, refusal and decision making skills, and skills in resisting peer pressure, the adolescent will decide not to become involved in alcohol and drug use, sexual activities, and so on (Elmquist, 1991). For example, instead of focusing on actual alcohol and drug use, affective education programs attempt to eliminate the underlying reasons for their use (Bell & Battjes, 1987). Several professionals (e.g., Moskowitz, 1989; Tobler, 1986), however, claim that affective education is ineffective in influencing values, self-esteem, or behaviors.

Alternatives. The alternative prevention approach is based on the premise that an individual exhibits risk-taking behaviors because of a need to be involved in rewarding, exciting, and thrilling activities (Barnea, 1989). Adolescents often drink alcohol because they want to belong and have fun with friends. To be effective, alternative intervention programs have to offer healthy, legal alternative activities, such as the alcohol and other drug use activities and clubs described earlier, as a means of meeting these needs (Bell & Battjes, 1987).

Alternative programs have proven effective in decreasing alcohol and other drug use and in improving self-esteem, coping skills, relationships with family and friends, school attendance, school behavior, leadership skills, and academic performance (Contrucci, 1991). Participants enjoy a sense of belonging to a group that engages in meaningful, worthwhile activities where they have some responsibility and control. Using the dynamics of positive peer pressure, peer support, peer influences, and peer interaction, these programs bring together a group of unique and diverse students with the common interest of wanting to help others.

Social Competence. The social competence approach is based on the assumption that alcohol and other drug use, sexual activities, and so on often are a result of poor personal and social competence (Elmquist, 1991). An adolescent with appropriate social skills can resist and counter these pressures (Botvin, 1983).

A major component of this approach is active student participation through peer helper programs. Specially selected, responsible students are trained in specific skills and are given the opportunity to have a positive influence on their fellow students (see Contrucci, 1991, for selection and training procedures).

Secondary Prevention

Secondary prevention involves identifying adolescents who show beginning signs of depression or involvement in undesirable behaviors for whom prompt diagnosis and effective treatment might ward off more serious involvement. Simply, it is the action taken following recognition of the problem, such as the steps discussed earlier related to teenage depression and suicide.

Tertiary Prevention

Tertiary prevention consists of treating adolescents who are seriously involved in alcohol and drug abuse, sexual activities, and so on. This treatment is similar to the concept of rehabilitation—to help those who already are affected to lead as normal a life as possible (for more information see Adams & Gullota, 1989; Thompson & Rudolph, 1992).

Comprehensive Efforts

Schools should adopt a comprehensive prevention approach because no *one* approach reaches every adolescent. A comprehensive approach differs from what many schools and educators currently provide, such as the problem-of-the-week approach (Jessor, 1991) wherein efforts are mobilized to fight teenage pregnancy one week, drunk driving the next, alcohol and drug use the next, and so on.

A comprehensive approach is based on the assumption that many adolescents are involved not only in alcohol and other drug use but also in risky sexual activities. For example, the three behaviors that place individuals at highest risk for HIV infection typically are initiated during adolescence. These are (a) unprotected sexual intercourse, (b) intravenous drug use, and (c) the use of drugs and alcohol before or during sexual behavior (Rotheran-Borus & Koopman, 1991). Professionals have identified common components of comprehensive dropout prevention programs (Guetzloe, 1988; Rogers, 1991):

1. Initiated early and dealt with antecedents, not results of failure

2. Gave one-on-one attention to students

3. Supplied, fostered, and encouraged the development of basic skills and socialization skills

4. Located in school and involved parents, students, and educators

5. Had an obvious connection with the real world

6. Had exciting leaders who related well to adolescents

7. Were broad-based, communitywide efforts

8. Involved multiple agencies

Dryfoos (1991) provided examples of successful communitywide prevention programs that incorporated different kinds of programs and services (e.g., schools, public and private community agencies, parent groups, media, police, courts, clergy, businesses, universities, and students). For example, a number of efforts combined community education, media, and school interventions. In the alcohol and other drug abuse area, a communitywide health promotion campaign used local media and community education in conjunction with alcohol and other drug use prevention curricula in the local schools. A successful program in pregnancy prevention concentrated on community education through the media and a speaker's bureau; training of parents, clergy, and other community leaders; and development and implementation of comprehensive sex and family life education unit in the schools. In another example a school dropout program was implemented successfully by an all-out community effort that involved the schools with local businesses, local government agencies, and universities in planning, teacher training, and training and job placement of adolescents.

Summary and Conclusion

As we explore adolescents' involvement in social issues and as we consider prevention and intervention activities, we must keep in mind the enormous changes adolescents go through. The dramatic physical, emotional, psychological, and social changes of adolescence occur rapidly, at a rate unsurpassed at any later point in life. To this great change within adolescents we must add the changes in social expectations, changes in the structure and content of formal education, the effects of difficult conditions in our society, and the effects of having a mild disability. Only then can educators imagine how tough the transition into adulthood can be for many adolescents. As educators, we must ask how we can establish more supportive environments for adolescents' transition to adulthood in a society that place many obstacles in their paths. Hepworth and Shernoff (1989) contend that "to be effective, education must motivate people to recognize personal risk and to take action to change behaviors that put them at risk" (p. 48).

References

Adams, G. R., & Gullota, T. (1989). *Adolescent life experiences.* (2d ed.) Pacific Grove, CA: Brooks/Cole.

American Academy of Pediatrics. (1988). *Substance abuse: A guide for health Professionals.* Elk Grove Village, IL: Author.

American Association of Colleges (1978). *Sexual harassment: A hidden issue.* Washington, DC: Author.

American College Health Association (1990). *HIV infection and AIDS.* Baltimore, MD: Author.

American Psychological Association. (1987). *Diagnostic and statistical manual of mental disorders* (3d ed. rev.) Washington, DC: Author.

Anderson, J. E., Kann, L., Haltzman, D., Arday, S., Truman, B., & Kolbe, L. (1990). HIV/AIDS knowledge and sexual behavior among high school students. *Family Planning Perspectives, 22,* 252–255.

Barnea, Z. (1989). A critical an comparative review of the prevention of drug and alcohol abuse in Israeli *Journal of Drug Education, 19,* 59–81.

Beck, A. T., Ward, C. H., Mendelson, M., Mock, J., & Erbaugh, J. (1961). An inventory for measuring depression. *Archives of General Psychiatry, 4,* 53–63.

Beck, A. T., Kovacs, M., & Weissman, A. (1979). Assessment of suicidal ideation: The scale of suicidal ideation. *Journal of Clinical and Consulting Psychology, 47,* 343–352.

Bell, C. S., & Battjes, R. J. (1987). Overview of drug abuse prevention research. In C. S. Bell & R. J. Battjes (Eds.), *Prevention research: Determining drug abuse among children and adolescents* (National Institute on Drug Abuse research Monograph

No. 63, DHHS Publication No. ADM-85-1334). Washington, DC: U. S. Government Printing Office.

Berkan, W. A. (1986). *Suicide prevention: A resource and planning guide.* Madison: Wisconsin Department of Public Instruction.

Botvin, G. J. (1983). *Life skills training (Teacher's Manual).* New York: Smithfield.

Botvin, G. J., & Willis, T. A. (1987). Personal and social skills training: Cognitive-behavioral approaches to substance abuse prevention. In C. S. Bell & R. J. Battjes (Eds.), *Prevention research: Determining drug abuse among children and adolescents* (National Institute on Drug Abuse research Monograph No. 63, DHHS Publication No. ADM-85-1334). Washington, DC: U.S. Government Printing Office.

Brooks-Gunn, J., Boyer, C. B., & Hein, K. (1988). Preventing HIV infection and AIDS in children and adolescents: Behavioral research and intervention strategies. *American Psychologist, 43,* 958–964.

Caplin, G. (1964). *Principles of preventive psychiatry.* New York: Basic Books.

Capuzzi, D., & Golden, L. (1988). Adolescent suicide: An introduction to issues and interventions. In D. Capuzzi & L. Golden (eds.), *Preventing adolescent suicide* (pp. 3–28). Muncie, IN: Accelerated Development.

Capuzzi, D., & Le Coq, L. L. (1983). Social and personal determinants of adolescent use and abuse of alcohol and marijuana. *Personnel and Guidance Journal, 61,* 199–205.

Centers for Disease Control. (1989, December). AIDS cases reported through

November 1989. *HIV/AIDS surveillance.* Atlanta, GA: Author.

Children and Teens Today Newsletter (1987, February), p. 3.

Cohen, S. G., & deBettencourt, L. V. (1991). Dropout: Intervening with the reluctant learner. *Intervention in school and clinic, 26,* 263–271.

Coles, R. , & Stokes, G. (1985). *Sex and the American teenager.* NY: Rolling Stone Press.

Conger, J. J. (1988). Hostages to fortune: Youth, values, and the public interest. *American Psychologist,* 43, 291–300.

Contrucci, V. J. (1991). *Alcohol and other drug abuse programs: A resource and planning guide.* Madison: Wisconsin Department of Public Instruction.

Cuban, L. (1989). At-risk students: What teachers and principals can do. *Educational Leadership, 45,* 29–33.

Dean, J. C., Fox, A. M., & Jensen, W. (1985). Alcohol and drug use by disabled and nondisabled persons: A comparative study. *The International Journal of the Addictions, 20,* 629–641.

deBettencourt, L. U., Zigmond, N., & Thornton, H. (1989). Follow-up of rural learning disabled graduates and dropouts. *Exceptional Children, 56,* 40–49.

Devlin, S. D., & Eliott, R. N. (1992). Drug use patterns of adolescents with behavioral disorders, *17,* 264–272.

DiNitto, D. M., & Krishef, K. (1984). Drinking patterns of mentally retarded persons. *Alcohol, Health, and Research World, 8,* 40–42.

Dollinger, S. J., Horn, J. L., & Boarini, D. (1988). Disturbed sleep and worries among learning disabled adolescents. *American Journal of Orthopsychiatry, 58,* 428–434.

Dropouts' Perspective on Leaving School (1988). *CAPS Capsule,* 2–3.

Dryfoos, J. G. (1991). *Adolescents at risk: Prevalence and prevention.* New York: Oxford University Press.

Edeleman, M. W. (1987). *Families in peril: An agenda for social change.* Cambridge, MA: Harvard University Press.

Eiser, C., Eiser, J. R., & Bocker, M. (1988). Teachers, evaluation of a "life-skills" approach to drug education. *Educational Research, 30,* 202–210.

Ekstrom, R. B., Goertz, M. E., Pollack, J. M., & Rock, D. A. (1986). Who drops out of high school and why? Findings from a national study. *Teacher's College Record, 87,* 356–373.

Elmquist, D. L. (1991). School-based alcohol and other drug prevention programs: Guidelines for the special educator. *Intervention in school and clinic, 27,* 10–19.

Elmquist, D. L., Morgan, D. P., & Bolds, P. (1989). *Substance abuse among adolescents with disabilities.* Unpublished manuscript, Utah State University, Department of Special Education, Logan.

Fick, L. (1984). *Adolescent childbearing decisions: Implications for preventing.* St. Louis, MO: The Danforth Foundation.

Fitzgerald, L. F. (1992). *Sexual harassment in higher education: Concepts and issues.* Washington, DC: National Education Association.

Foster, S. (1986). *Preventing teenage pregnancy.* Washington, DC: Council of State Policy and Planning Agencies.

Frederick, C. I. (1985). An introduction and overview of youth suicide. In M. L. Peck, N. L. Farberow, & R. E. Litman (Eds.), *Youth suicide* (pp. 1–33). New York: Springer-Verlag.

Gale, J. (1989). *A parent's guide to teenage sexuality.* Henry Holt: New York.

Garrison, C. Z., Lewinsohn, P. M., Marsteller, F., Langhinrichsen, J., & Lann, I. (1991). The assessment of suicidal behavior in adolescents. *Suicide and Life-Threatening Behavior, 21,* 217–230.

Gibbs, N. (1993, May 24). How should we teach our children about sex? *Time,* 60–66.

Gispert, M., Wheeler, K., Marsh, L., & Davis M. S. (1985). Suicide adolescents: Factors in evaluation. *Adolescence, 20,* 753-761.

Goodstadt, M. S. (1986). School-based drug education in North America: What is wrong? What can be done? *Journal of School Health, 56,* 278–281.

Guetzloe, E. C. (1987). *Suicide and depression, the adolescent epidemic: Education's responsibility.* Orlando, FL: Advantage Consultants.

Guetzloe, E. C. (1988). Suicide and depression: Special education's responsibility. *Teaching Exceptional Children*, 20, 25–28.

Hansen, W. B., Graham, J. W., Wolkenstein, B. H., Lundy, B. Z., Pearson, J., Flay, B. R., & Anderson-Johnson, C. (1988). Differential impact of three alcohol prevention curricula on hypothesized mediating variables. *Journal of Drug Education, 18*, 143–153.

Harrell, A. V., & Wirtz, P. W. (1989). *Adolescent drinking-index.* Odessa, FL: Psychological Assessment Resources, Inc.

Harris, L. (1987). *Inside America.* New York: Vintage.

Hawton, K. (1986). *Suicide and attempted suicide among children and adolescents.* Beverly Hills, CA: Sage.

Hayes, M. L., & Sloat, R. S. (1988). Suicide and the gifted adolescent. *Journal for the Education of the Gifted, 13*, 229–244.

Hein, K. (1989). AIDS in adolescence: Exploring the challenge. *Journal of Adolescent Health Care, 10*, 105–355.

Hendlin, H. (1982). *Suicide in America.* New York: W. W. Horton.

Hepworth, J., & Shernoff, M. (1989). Strategies for AIDS education and prevention. In E. Macklin (ed.), *AIDS and Families*, p. 35–48. New York: Harrington Press.

Hingson, R. W., Strunin, L., Berlin, B. M., Heeren, T. (1988). Beliefs about AIDS, use of alcohol and drugs, and unprotected sex among Massachusetts adolescents. *American Journal of Public Health, 78*, 460–461.

Hofferth, S. L., Kahn, J. R., & Baldwin, W. (1987). Premarital sexual activity among U.S. teenage women over the past three decades. *Family Planning Perspectives, 19*, 46–53.

Horan, J. J., & Straus, L. K. (1987). Substance abuse. In M. Hersen & V. B. Van-Hasselt (eds.), *Behavior therapy with children and adolescents: A clinical approach* (pp. 440–464). New York: Wiley.

Horton, L. (1985). *Adolescent drug abuse.* Bloomington, IN: Phi Delta Kappa Educational Foundation.

Humm, A. J. (1992). Homosexuality: The new frontier in sexuality education. *Family Life Educator, 10*, 13–18.

Issacs, M., Buckley, G., & Martin, D. (1979). Patterns of drinking among the deaf. The *American Journal of Alcohol and Drug Abuse, 6*, 463–476.

Jaker, G. F. (1985, August). *Lessons learned: A review of the research in drug education.* Anoka: Minnesota Prevention Resource Center.

Jessor, R. (1991). Risk behavior in adolescence: A psychosocial framework for understanding and action. *Journal of Adolescent Health, 12*, 597–605.

Johnston, J., O'Malley, P. M., & Bachman, J. G. (1986). *Drug use among American high school students, college students, and other young adults.* Washington, DC: U.S. Government Printing Office.

Kellam, S. G., & Simon, M. C. (1980). Mental health in first grade and teenage drug, alcohol and cigarette use. *Journal of Drug and Alcohol Dependency, 5*, 273–304.

Kempton, W. (1988). *A teacher's guide: Sex education for persons with disabilities.* Santa Monica, CA: Stanfield.

Kirby, D. (1984). *Sexuality education: An evaluation of programs and their effect.* Santa Cruz, CA: Network.

Kosky, P. (1983). Childhood suicidal behavior. *Journal of Child Psychology and Psychiatry, 24*, 457–467.

Krishef, C. H. (1986). Do the mentally retarded drink? A study of their alcohol usage. *Journal of Alcohol and Drug Education, 31*, 64–70.

Leone, P. E., Greensburg, J. M., Trickett, E. J., & Spero, E. (1989). A study of the use of cigarettes, alcohol, and marijuana by students identified as seriously emotionally disturbed. *Counterpoint, 9*, 6–7.

Long, J. V. F., & Scherl, D. J. (1984). Developmental antecedents of compulsive drug use: A report on the literature. *Journal of Psychoactive Drugs, 16*, 169–182.

Maag, J. W., & Behrens, J. T. (1989). Epidemiologic data on seriously emotionally disturbed and learning disabled adolescents reporting extreme depressive symptomatology. *Behavioral Disorders, 15,* 21–27.

MacDonald, D. I., & Blume, S. B. (1986). Children of alcoholics. *American Journal of Disorders of Children, 140,* 750-754.

MacMillan, D. L., Balow, I. H., Widaman, K. F., Borthwick-Duffy, S., & Hendrick, I. G. (1990). Methodological problems in estimating dropout rates and the implications for studying dropouts from special education. *Exceptionality, 1,* 29–39.

Maksym, D. (1990). *Shared feelings: A parent guide to sexuality education for children, adolescents and adults who have a mental handicap.* North York, Ontario: The G. Allan Roeher Institute.

Mann, D. (1985). Action on dropouts. *Educational Leadership, 43,* 16–17.

Mann, D. (1986). Can we help dropouts: Thinking about the undoable. *Teachers College Record, 87,* 307–323.

McGee, K., & Guetzloe, E. (1988). Suicidal emotionally handicapped students: Tips for the classroom teacher. *The Pointer, 32,* 7–10.

McWhirter, J. J. (1993). Will he live? A suicide assessment interview. In L. Golden & M. Norwood (eds.), *Case studies in child counseling* (pp. 89–98). New York: MacMillan.

McWhirter, J. J., McWhirter, B. T., McWhirter, A. M., & McWhirter, E. H. (1993). *At-risk youth: A comprehensive response.* Pacific Grove, CA: Brooks/ Cole.

Metha, A., & Dunham, H. (1988). Behavioral indicators. In D. Capuzzi & L. Golden (eds.), *Preventing adolescent suicide* (pp. 49–86). Muncie, IN: Accelerated Development.

Morbidity and Mortality Weekly Report. (1988, January 29). *Guidelines for effective school health education to prevent the spread of AIDS.* Atlanta, GA: Centers for Disease Control.

Moskowitz, J. M. (1989). The primary prevention of alcohol problems: A critical review of the research literature. *Journal of Studies on Alcohol, 50,* 54–88.

Muccigrosso, L., Scavarda, M., Simpson-Brown, R., & Thalacker, B. E. (1991). *Double Jeopardy: Pregnant and parenting youth in special education.* Reston, VA: Council for Exceptional children.

National Academy of Sciences. (1989). *Confronting AIDS: Directions for public health, health care, and research.* Washington, DC: Author.

Newcomb, M. D., & Bentler, P. M. (1989). Substance use and abuse among children and teenagers. *American Psychologist, 44,* 242–248.

Office of Educational Research and Improvement. (1987). *Dealing with dropouts: The urban superintendents' call to action.* Washington, DC: U.S. Government Printing Office.

Office of Population Affairs. (1988, November). *Family life information exchange.* U.S. Department of Health and Human Services, Public Health, Resource Memo. Washington, DC:

Orr, D. P., Wilbrant, M. L., Brack, C. J., Rauch, S. P., & Ingersoll, G. M. (1989). Reported sexual behaviors and self-esteem among young adolescents. *American Journal of Diseases of Children, 143,* 86–90.

Otto, U. (1972). Suicidal acts by children and adolescents. *Acta Psychiatry Scandinavia, 233,* 7–123.

Paget, K. (1988). Adolescent pregnancy: Implications for prevention strategies in educational settings. *School Psychology Review, 17,* 570–579.

The pain of harassment, *Seattle Times,* Nov. 2, 1993, p. E-8.

Peck, M. L. (1985). Crisis intervention treatment with chronically and acutely suicidal adolescents. In M. Peck, N. Farberow & R. Litman (eds.), *Youth suicide* (pp. 1–33). New York: Springer-Verlag.

Pender, L. (1990). Growing up gay. *Cincinnati Magazine* (February). 26–29.

Peng, S. S., & Takai, R. T. (1983). *High school dropouts: Descriptive information from high school and beyond.* Washington,

DC: National Center for Educational Statistics (ERIC No. ED 236-366).

Pfeffer, C. R. (1986). *The suicidal child.* New York Guilford Press.

Pfeffer, C. R., Zuckerman, S., Plutchik, R., Mizruchi, M. S. (1984). Suicidal behavior in normal school children: A comparison with child psychiatric patients. *Journal of American Academy of Child Psychiatry, 23,* 416–423.

Price, M. (1987, December). Physically, mentally disabled teens require special contraceptive care. *Contraceptive Technology Update,* 154–156.

Reynolds, (1985). Depression in childhood and adolescence: Diagnosis, assessment, intervention strategies, and research. In T. R. Kratochwill (ed.), *Advances in school psychology* (Vol. 4, pp. 133–189). Hillsdale, NJ: Lawrence Erlbaum.

Ritter, D. R. (1989). Social competence and problem behavior of adolescent girls with learning disabilities. *Journal of Learning Disabilities, 22,* 460–461.

Robertson, D., & Mathews, B. (1989). Preventing adolescent suicide with group counseling. *Journal for Specialists in Group Work, 14,* 34–39.

Rodenstein, J. M. (1990). *Children at-risk: A resource and planning guide.* Madison: Wisconsin Department of Public Instruction.

Rogers, D. E. (1991). Adolescents at risk conference: Summation. *Journal of Adolescent Health, 12,* 644–647.

Romaneck, G. M., & Kuehl, R. (1992). Sex education for students with high-incidence special needs. *Teaching Exceptional Children, 25,* 22–24.

Rotheran-Borus, M. J., & Koopman, C. (1991). HIV and adolescents. *The Journal of Primary Prevention, 12,* 65–82.

Rutter, M. (1986). Depressive feelings, cognitions, and disorders: A research postscript. In M. Rutter, C. E. Izard, & P. B. Read (eds.), *Depression in young people* (pp. 491-519). New York, NY: Guilford Press.

Schorr, L. B. (1988). *Within our reach: Breaking the cycle of disadvantage.* New York: Doubleday.

Shaffer, D. (1974). Suicide in childhood and early adolescence. *Journal of Childhood Psychology and Psychiatry, 15,* 275–291.

Shapiro, C. (1981). *Adolescent pregnancy prevention: School-community cooperation.* Springfield, IL: Charles C. Smith.

Slavin. R. E., Karweit, N. L., & Madden, N. A. (1989). *Effective programs for students at risk.* Boston: Allyn & Bacon.

SMERC. (1986 January). *Information for professional excellence: Dropouts.* Redwood City, CA: San Mateo County Office of Education.

State Education Performance, 1982 and 1989. (1990, May 9). *Education Week.*

Steele, W. (1983). *Preventing teenage suicide.* Novato, CA: Ann Arbor Publishers.

Strunin, L., & Hingson, R. (1987). Acquired immunodeficiency syndrome and adolescents: Knowledge, beliefs, attitudes, and behavior. *Pediatrics, 79,* 825–828.

Sturner, W. Q. (1986). Adolescent suicide fatalities. *Rhode Island Medical Journal, 69,* 471–474.

Tatum, M. L. (1988). The AIDS challenge: Controversial issues in the classroom. *Family Life Educator, 7,* 15–19.

Thomas, L. L., Long, S. E., Whitten, K., Hamilton, B., Fraser, J., & Askins, R. V. (1985). High school students' long-term retention of sex education information. *Journal of School Health, 55,* 274–278.

Tobler, N. (1986). Meta-analysis of 143 adolescent drug prevention programs: Quantitative outcome results of program participants compared to a control or comparison group. *Journal of Drug Issues, 16,* 537–567.

Tomaszewski, E. P. (1991). Adolescent dating violence. *Family Life Educator, 10,* 4–8.

Tomlinson-Keasey, C., & Keasey, C. B. (1988). "Signatures" of suicide. In D. Capuzzi & L. Golden (eds.), *Preventing adolescent suicide* (pp. 213–245). Muncie, IN: Accelerated Development.

Tomlinson-Keasey, C., Warren, L. W., & Elliott, J. E. (1986). Suicide among gifted women: A perspective study. *Journal of Abnormal Psychology, 95,* 123–129.

Voss, H. L., Wendling, A., & Elliott, D. S. (1966). Some types of high-school drop-outs. *Journal of Educational Research, 59*, 363–368.

Webb, J. A., Baer, P. E., McLaughlin, R. J., McKelvey, R. S., & Caid, C. D. (1989). Risk factors and their relation to initiation of alcohol use among early adolescents. *Journal of American Academy of Child and Adolescent Psychiatry, 30*, 563–568.

Zigmond, N., & Thornton, H. (1985). Follow-up of postsecondary age learning disabled graduates and drop-outs. *Learning Disabilities Research, 1*, 50–55.

Fostering Resilience in Children and Youth

Rosemary A. Lambie, Susan D. Leone, and Christopher K. Martin

Resilience in children and youth at-risk has become a topic of interest within the field of education during the last few decades. Studying resilience in children who otherwise would be expected to fail provides us with clues for helping children who are living under similar circumstances. What is resilience? Simply put, resilience is about *beating the odds* (Haggerty, Sherrod, Garmezy, & Rutter, 1994; Wang & Haertel, 1995). Of students considered at-risk, 19% were found to be resilient (Peng, Wang, & Walberg, 1992). As caring professionals, our challenge is to increase the number of children who fall in the resilient category. Resilience is a valuable topic because it focuses on the positive factors that can accompany challenging life circumstances (Cowan, Cowan, & Schulz, 1996; Kaplan, Turner, Norman, & Stillson, 1996).

At-Risk Children and Youth

Professionals from varied fields have written and hypothesized about at-risk children and youth for some time (Haggerty et al., 1994; Rutter, 1994). An early definition from education is that at-risk students are those who are likely to fail either in school or in life (Frymier, 1992; Frymier & Gansneder, 1989). Risk is related to negative experiences faced, their severity and frequency, as well as other circumstances in the child's life. Professionals generally share the opinion that risk also relates to internal aspects such as biophysical factors innate to the individual (Masten, 1994).

In about 1991, professionals in the field seem to have discontinued the quest to define the term *at risk* and began to focus more on resiliency. Perhaps this is a result of the definitive study by Frymier (1992), funded by Phi Delta Kappa, providing answers sought about the terminology, etiology, and characteristics of the at-risk population.

Earlier, Slavin and Madden (1989) indicated that "a practical criterion for identifying students at risk is eligibility for Chapter 1, special education, or other remedial services under today's standards" (p. 4). Frymier and Gansneder (1989) found that between 25% and 35% of the students in their study were seriously at risk for failure. This was defined by 45 factors that previous research had linked to being at risk.

Cuban (1989) offered a new and different explanation for students considered at risk. He departed from the previous notion that these students are the cause of their own poor performance, or that their families neither prepared them for school nor provided proper support. His alternative view was that the school failed to meet the needs of the child by disregarding or devaluing the family and culture. Cuban contended that teachers from the middle class often reflected those values and criticized children with behavior and values that varied from the dominant culture. Cuban also indicated that diverse abilities and interests were not accommodated, nor were adaptations made to meet individual needs.

Slavin and Madden (1989) agreed with Cuban's view. They identified the following risk factors: low achievement, retention in grade, behavior problems, poor attendance, low socioeconomic status, and attending school with a large number of poor students.

Liontos (1991) said the term *at-risk* had become a cliche "used both as a description and a prediction" (p. 5). She viewed the term as one that describes personal, educational, and societal ills, in particular as they relate to families who are poor.

The concept of risk is familiar in medical fields as well. According to Jens and Gordon (1991), the concept of risk had recently entered the field of education and was misunderstood by many. The term implies possible negative outcome as well as the possibility of avoiding a negative outcome. "Resiliency" is the term used when the negative outcome is avoided or ameliorated.

In this chapter we provide counselors with information about, and means of working with, at-risk students, their families, and communities. We focus on the nonacademic factors related to social, personal, and environmental influences—not academics. We recognize that all children who face serious life challenges may be or might become at risk for failure. For the purposes of determining eligibility for specific programs and allocating funds, the government sets certain socioeconomic parameters to define children who are at-risk or have special needs. In actuality, children who are identified as at-risk can be found in any classroom and in every socioeconomic and ethnic group.

Lambie (in press) found that, over time, the literature on at-risk students has reflected greater emphasis on the positive. Practitioners including counselors, educators, other mental health professionals and their professors, and sociologists are focusing on possibilities and abilities; shared meaning, values, power, and experience, as well as the importance of developing of an internal locus of control within students and their families. Guidance and counseling professionals are in a unique position to be of help, having a history of working with clients' strengths and abilities. Counselors, however, have typically focused on identification of at-risk youth but have not focused specifically on increasing the characteristics of resiliency in its wholeness (Rak & Patterson, 1996).

This emphasis on the positive might be seen as a simplistic means of dealing with tightening budgets, shifting interests on the part of society, or a denial of overwhelming pain in the face of perceived hopelessness. Nevertheless, *if you train your eye to look in the right direction, you will see much beauty.* Many who work with children and youth considered at risk have overcome many family-life and personal challenges. Nietzsche wrote, "That which does not kill me makes me stronger."

Perhaps all of us who succeed are resilient and have something to offer in our stories of resiliency (Henderson & Milstein, 1996). Many counselors have painful stories that others would never imagine—stories like those told by the students who are working to beat the odds and being taught by a professional who has beaten the odds in spite of adversity. So where we choose to train our eyes and the example that this gives to others become important in our efforts to increase resilience. Proust said, "The real voyage of discovery consists not in seeking new landscapes but in having new eyes." The eye to the positive is a voyage of discovering how our vulnerable children can rise from the ashes like the Phoenix of mythology.

Models of Resilience

Professionals who have beaten the odds and risen from the ashes can make excellent models, especially when they speak from experience, offer compassion, and have chosen *a path with heart* (Shepard, 1995). This article is about them and for them and others who wish to learn from their experiences. It is about our communities joining to be part of the whole, serving not as islands but as part of the main. In being allowed the opportunity to give, we are vital links in the chain, and we know we are valuable. George Bernard Shaw said:

> This is the true joy in life, the being used for a purpose recognized by yourself as a mighty one; . . . being a force of Nature instead of a feverish little clod of ailments and grievances complaining that the world will not devote itself to making you happy.

Research demonstrates that resilient individuals beat the odds because they recover from or adapt to stress and problems found in life (McMillan & Reed, 1994; Rhodes & Brown, 1991). Professionals benefit from knowing what helps to build resiliency in children so those program attributes can be reinforced, thereby increasing resiliency.

Today, school personnel speak about a school population in which the dropout rate reaches 30% to 50%, and in which more and more students are impoverished, are classified for special education, come from various ethnic and cultural backgrounds, and have academic difficulties in our schools (Barr & Parrett, 1995). At the same time, our economy is becoming less tolerant of individuals without skills and the ability to learn and adapt. If the schools do not address the at-risk population effectively, the consequences for at-risk children and our society are clear. With the growing numbers of at-risk children and youth in America (Barr & Parrett, 1995), we must find ways of helping our schools and communities increase the numbers of resilient, at-risk students. Increasing resiliency among at-risk children is a *community* responsibility, rather than the school's responsibility alone (Waddock, 1995).

Many professionals from varied fields have written on resiliency in children (Garmezy & Rutter, 1983; Haggerty et al., 1994; Henderson & Milstein, 1996; Hetherington & Blechman, 1996; Joseph, 1994; Rhodes & Brown, 1991; Wang & Gordon, 1994; Weissbourd, 1996). We first describe factors related to resilient at-risk students in terms of personal, family, and school factors. Then we discuss characteristics of successful school programs for the at-risk population. The remainder of the chapter is devoted to increasing resiliency by promoting the wise use of resources from many contexts, including school, family, social supports, and the community at large. Counselors are encouraged to serve as *web weavers*, helping coordinate the evolution of a caring community (Noddings, 1995).

Factors Related to Resilient At-Risk Students

In this section we describe three factors related to resilience: personal, family, and school domains. Understanding these factors will enable counselors to influence and develop programs and interventions within schools and communities.

Personal Factors

Teachers have described resilient children as social, optimistic, energetic, cooperative, inquisitive, attentive, helpful, punctual, and on-task (Sagor, 1996). They laugh at their own mistakes (Young-Eisendrath, 1996). The resilient child has a personality, manifested in early childhood, that elicits a positive response from others. These children are affectionate, good-natured, cuddly, and easy to get along with (McMillan & Reed, 1994), and they actively seek out relationships (Wolin & Wolin, 1996). As they grow older, they play alone comfortably, and as they seek challenging experiences, they appear to be self-reliant and have little fear. They use art, play, and humor as creative outlets that help them escape painful circumstances (Wolin & Wolin, 1996).

They also request and receive help from adults when required (Werner, 1984). Positive reciprocity emerges at an early age. Resilient youth reach out to others assuming they will receive help. Thus, their positive attitude results in responsiveness from others. Resilient children view the world as affirming in spite of challenging circumstances. The positive attitude relates to respect for others, being prepared for school, volunteering, and being at ease with school (McMillan & Reed, 1994).

In addition, resilient at-risk children have an internal locus of control and are highly motivated to succeed (Henderson & Milstein, 1996). They feel personally responsible for their success, which they view as their own (McMillan & Reed, 1994; Wolin & Wolin 1996). They do not blame others or their environment (external locus of control) for their failures or other situations. They have clearly defined goals that they articulate in a mature manner, and they recognize the importance of goal setting as a method by which they can improve their circumstances. Thus, mastery of new experiences is important for all at-risk students. Counselors can help teachers see the importance of providing self-fulfilling activities for students that reinforce their development of an internal locus of control.

Resilience is seen in the potential individuals have for creative development (Young-Eisendrath, 1996). Resilient students often seek refuge from their troubled environments in extracurricular activities. These activities may keep them away from potentially detrimental activities such as drug abuse. Resilient youth welcome alternative positive experiences such as sports and academic clubs (McMillan & Reed, 1994). Working successfully in groups with peers and emerging as a leader within one's peer group can be rewarding to the at-risk child or youth. The recognition associated with extracurricular activities can motivate students to participate. Counselors who recognize this can collaborate with teachers and parents to encourage belief in the student's ability to succeed.

Choosing to volunteer is another personal factor related to resilient children and youth (Henderson & Milstein, 1996). A few possible volunteer experiences are tutoring, helping in the home, and visiting nursing homes. Having a purpose that aids others is associated with resiliency (Keith, 1997). Young-Eisendrath (1996) wrote of the desire, as well as ability, to "feel and understand the needs of other" and "the ability to compromise and to delay meeting one's own desires in order to meet the needs of others" (pp. 71-72). Equally valuable in extracurricular activities and volunteering alike is the exposure to a positive adult who leads or facilitates the activities and serves as a role model for resilient behavior.

The personal characteristics of resilient children and youth lend themselves to success in the face of adversity. They have achieved a wisdom that allows them to engage life's meaning as well as their personal limitations (Young-Eisendrath, 1996). Resilient children in dysfunctional and abusive homes have the capacity to develop insights about their circumstances and don't blame themselves for their family's troubles. They seek safety for themselves by creating physical and emotional distance from unpredictable parents and find productive activities to fill their time (Wolin & Wolin, 1996). Some at-risk children from families having a parent who has a psychological disorder are able to maintain a sense of separateness from their parents, making peace with them and assuming a resilient life (Rak & Patterson, 1996).

Though peers may struggle in school as well as daily life, the resilient child emerges from a stressful environment able to cope successfully. Resilient children are the kind of people whom other people want to be around. They survive and thrive despite the odds against them. A resilient child is our modern day *phoenix*. This child rises with much to teach us about life, and, if we listen and observe, we will more ably serve all children and youth and their families.

Family Factors

Family demographic factors are not predictive of resiliency. Children in intact families have no higher incidence of resiliency than single-parent families do. What influences resiliency is a strong parent-child relationship and support (Hetherington & Blechman, 1996). Parental commitment gives the family a sense of coherence. Out of this family experience, resilient children learn to feel that life makes sense and that they can exercise control of their lives. This sense of meaning is basic to their motivation.

Receiving family support is another important family factor that can promote resiliency in children (Liontos, 1991). Parents of resilient children have higher educational expectations for their children, which in turn influence the children's achievement orientation; and resilient children have more of the necessary tools and materials for learning at home and are more frequently taken to community educational activities than are those who are nonresilient (Henderson & Milstein, 1996). Under-education of parents relates to nonresiliency. Peng et al. (1992) found that less than 11% of children were resilient in families in which the parents had not earned a high school diploma. Of students whose parents had at least a high-school diploma, 23% were considered resilient. This statistic alone points to the need for parenting training in low-income and high dropout areas.

A hallmark of resilient children is that, at early ages, they seek out and access adults whom they can trust (Hetherington & Blechman, 1996; McMillan & Reed, 1994; Rak & Patterson, 1996). Trust is established in the early years. It forms the building blocks for later adjustment at school, translating to reciprocal relationships with teachers and other role models. It is difficult to "exaggerate the importance of anchors in their lives—children and adults outside their families who are caring and attentive over time" (Weissbourd, 1996, p. 63).

Parents, though important, are not essential to building trust. Other adults may provide this necessary ingredient. These adults often become as close as family. Many resilient adults recount stories of a special neighbor or a teacher who took an interest in them (Wolin and Wolin, 1993). This connection made the children feel confident in their ability to build other strong relationships. Counselors are, by training and responsibility, in a position to provide this important relationship.

A personal recollection from a resilient adult follows:

> I remember when it seemed as if everything in our family life was a struggle. My father was ill and had to retire in his 40s. My mother was overwhelmed with the responsibilities of her nursing job, my father's heart attacks and strokes, and raising us kids. When I was in sixth grade, my father went into the hospital, and the day he got out, my mother went in.

A friend of my mother's, Elena, stepped in and filled some empty spaces in my life. Elena continued to be an important person in my life throughout life. I can still hear some of the things she would say, and they serve as guides to me today. She was fun to be with and had lots of advice about dating.

When my grandmother died, Elena was right there with me at eighth-grade graduation while my mother was at the funeral across the country. Elena was also right beside me a few months later when my dad died. She was a teacher of mine in grade school and for life. She taught me a lot about people and how to lighten up. I don't think I would have made it without her presence in my life.

School Factors

Children who are resilient find support outside of the home. This often takes the form of support in school. Resilient children usually get along well with their peers and have at least one close confidante from their school. They have an informal network of people whom they can access in crisis, as well as for help in academic and other areas (McMillan & Reed, 1994).

Resilient children usually are involved in extracurricular activities and find them to be supportive, providing a sense of belonging and increased self-esteem (Werner, 1984). Service learning has become a major thrust in education, and taking advantage of the opportunities it presents will help build resiliency (Henderson & Milstein, 1996; Keith, 1997).

Resilient students often mention that teachers, counselors, and other school staff have provided personal interest in and support for them (Geary, 1988; Coburn & Nelson, 1989) that influenced them to succeed. Resilient students find the interpersonal relationship aspect as well as the competence of these adults to be important (Geary, 1988). The resilient student wants school professionals to demonstrate caring, respect them for who they are, be able to get along with ease, listen without being intrusive, take them seriously, be available and understanding, provide encouragement, and share humor. In terms of competence, resilient students want the teacher to foster group goals, listen beneath the surface before disciplining, be fair in grading and instruction, encourage success, and know them academically (McMillan & Reed, 1994).

Characteristics of Successful School Programs

Richard Sagor (1996) identified five attributes that schools can integrate within the curriculum to encourage resiliency: competence, belonging, usefulness, potency, and optimism. Sagor asserted that educators must incorporate these attributes in educational experiences. This is neither difficult nor time-consuming. Sagor pointed out that good teaching and resiliency-building are the same. Educators continue to do what already works—what already helps instill resiliency within students.

Ten attributes of successful programs have been identified for at-risk students (McMillan & Reed, 1993; Westfall & Pisapia, 1994). These categories, expanded upon in the following pages, relate to characteristics and problems of at-risk students.

Early Intervention

As has been learned from experiences such as Head Start (Berrueta-Clement et al., cited in Trachtman, 1991) and special education (Fewell, 1995), early educational experiences in quality preschool programs can serve to decrease school failure stemming from poverty. Early monitoring of progress and providing assistance can help at-risk students avoid the all too frequent school failure and high dropout rates associated with challenging life circumstances. Early education has been related to better intellectual performance, reduction in the dropout rate, and reduction of placement in special education (Trachtman, 1991). Early educational intervention can also unlink negative family patterns and habits from low school success rates and increase early exposure to resiliency-building factors.

School Climate

A welcoming and pleasant school atmosphere will help students enjoy coming to school and increase the likelihood of their success. Noddings (1995) wrote that personal manifestations of care are "more important in children's lives than any particular curriculum or pattern of pedagogy" (p. 676). Cooperative learning (Johnson & Johnson, 1994), a sense of belonging (Edwards, 1995), and a positive environment (Mullis & Fincher, 1996) can be encouraged through alternative and enrichment activities, total school programs, more direct contact with teachers, counselors, and administrators, and use of positive reinforcement. Lewis, Schaps, and Watson (1995) wrote of developing the child's ethical and social aspects through a caring community. They said formation of trust and mutually satisfying relationships are important features of schools. School counselors can assume responsibility by their involvement in and coordination of total school programs that enhance community and unity.

School Personnel

The teacher plays a significant role in creating a positive school climate and in motivating students (Hetherington & Blechman, 1996). To be successful, school professionals must be positive and believe that they and their students can be successful. They are advised to be flexible, approaching each student as an individual with different needs, providing activities that lead to the development of an internal locus of control and a positive self-image, and offering students visible touchstones of their success. School professionals do well to keep themselves focused on the positive and the possible rather than on deficits. Thus, we must include students in creating a classroom community through classroom meetings, problem solving, and democratic procedures (Lewis, Schaps, & Watson, 1995). Counselors are pivotal in helping school personnel emphasize the positive, through staff development, as models, and by promoting wellness and resiliency in all facets of school life.

Small Class and School Size

Class and school size affect how much individual attention a teacher, counselor, or administrator can provide, how flexible the counselor or teacher can be in meeting individual needs, and how quickly a counselor or teacher will be able to notice and address problems as they develop. Small classes make it easier to provide a positive school climate and to interact personally and in a timely manner with parents, resulting in fewer behavior problems and higher achievement (Achilles, 1996, 1997; Finn, 1998).

Beyond class size, Sergiovanni (1995) focused on size of high school, reiterating Goodlad's findings in *A Place Called School*, and the value of smaller schools. Wynne and Walberg (1995) seconded this value on smaller schools, especially intimacy in education that can be developed more easily in smaller schools. According to Weissbourd (1996), many larger high schools are "creating more personal environments—environments in which children spend the bulk of their day with the same group of teachers and students—by clustering teachers and students, for example, or by creating schools within schools or houses within schools" (p. 63).

Parent Involvement

When parents work with their children to prepare them for preschool, the children experience fewer difficulties when they do enter school. Counselors can impact growing families when they work with parents of students who have preschool siblings. Later, parents should be invited to be participants in their child's education both at home and in the school building (Slavin, Madden, Dolan, & Wasik, 1996). Empowering parents as co-planners in their child's education is an effective way to increase their participation and to encourage them to reinforce academic activities at home (Lambie, in press). Special education, with its emphasis on parental involvement, is a model that general education can borrow for at-risk families (Pell & Cohen, 1995).

Counselors can advocate for meaningful family involvement in the schools by helping teachers and administrators recognize its importance and overall positive impact on adjustment, achievement, and self-esteem of students (Christianson, 1997). Henry (1996) challenges us to communicate with parents in ways that encourage collaboration, value diverse perspectives, and utilize problem solving to benefit the child.

Self-Esteem Building and Support

Increasing self-esteem is critical with at risk-students (Joseph, 1994). The first step in increasing self esteem may be finding an area in which a student can be successful and recognizing the student for the success. This can *hook* the student on success.

Volunteer projects and service learning can provide students with opportunities to feel good about themselves and their ability to contribute to their world (Keith, 1997; Lewis, Schaps, & Watson, 1995; Yoder, Retish, & Wade, 1996). Including students in decision making also helps to develop a sense of ownership and influence in the school community, building self-esteem in the process. Groups led by counselors can focus on increasing self-esteem/self-efficacy of students (Sonnenblick, 1997).

Guidance and Mental Health Counseling

Schools should provide opportunities for individual and group counseling support for individual students as well as their families, both at school and in the home (Edwards & Foster, 1995; Rak & Patterson, 1996). Confidentiality must be maintained, and meetings have to be held discreetly so students and families remain comfortable with the process. Counselors who remain creative, flexible, and nonjudgmental can work successfully with this population. Brief, solution-focused approaches should recognize cultural diversity. Consultation services (Kaplan, Turner, Norman, & Stillson, 1996) are invaluable with at-risk families and students.

Social and Life Skills/Vocational Education

Prerequisites for school success are having and using social skills (Sugai & Lewis, 1996). Good social and life-skills training as well as vocational programs make education relevant to students and increase their feeling that education is worthwhile (McMillan & Reed, 1993). Counselors can use the group context effectively to help students who come to school with insufficiently developed social skills to develop appropriate human interaction skills.

Although some (e.g., Barr & Parrett, 1995) question that vocational and career education programs succeed with at-risk students, others (McMillan & Reed, 1993; Westfall & Pisapia, 1994) indicate that students involved in vocational education tend to complete school. They also related that vocational classes tend to provide many of the positive attributes described previously, including smaller classes and positive classroom climate. Counselors are in a unique position to point out these advantages to the family and students who are at-risk for school failure. They can also be instrumental in countering the stigma that vocational education has in some communities. Comprehensive career guidance programs, coordinated by the counselor, should include community and family involvement and emphasize social and life-skills.

Extracurricular Activities

Many positive benefits are associated with extracurricular activities, including a sense of belonging and community, as well as greater opportunity to pursue interests and learn new things, both of which can increase self-esteem (Geary, 1988;

McMillan & Reed, 1994; Werner, 1984). After-school activities provide students with a safe, supervised atmosphere. Evidence cited in a review of at-risk students, by McMillan & Reed (1993), also suggests that extracurricular activities decrease the likelihood that a student will drop out of school.

We have to do more than offer these activities, though, because at-risk youth often do not feel connected to the school community. Counselors and other school personnel should invite, encourage, and facilitate youth participation. All school personnel must recognize the importance of positive leisure activities in developing resiliency. Extracurricular involvement must be seen as an integral part of the education experience that fosters resiliency and wellness.

Easing Grade Level Transitions

Students tend to drop out of school when they are making the transition between grades and school levels, such as between middle and high school. Schools can provide activities and services that prepare students for and support them through the transition. The counselor's role in this is paramount. Assistance with transitions and orientation of students, a traditional counselor role, fosters resiliency in students. Looping teachers with classes across grades is another way of dealing with transition problems (Lewis, Schaps, & Watson, 1995). Noddings (1995) encouraged this practice as a means of strengthening relationships. Small groups providing support for students who are retained a grade level are effective in countering the sense of loss and failure that students may experience when they are retained.

Together, these 10 characteristics of school programs serve as a guide for educators to increase resiliency in students who are at-risk for failure. School programs alone, however, will not foster resiliency to the extent desired. The environment beyond the school must be actively engaged as well (Waddock, 1995).

Resourcing and Creating Community

A child's behavior is influenced by many factors, only one of which is environment. Other factors include biological constitution, disposition, and developmental level. This last area—resourcing and creating community—is the major topic of this chapter. It focuses on the role of environment in fostering resilient behaviors.

Systems theory holds that behavior is affected by many interrelated systems. Thus, change in one subsystem (for example, the community) will reverberate throughout other interrelated systems including the classroom and schools. With Wang and Haertel's (1995) contention that resilience "provides a conceptual base for an intervention that calls for responsive classroom, school, and community environments" (p. 159), the importance of community joining with schools to build resilience in youth is clear. The counselors' coordination function facilitates this joining and places them in the role of *weaver of webs* and collaborative consultant (Keys, Bemak, Carpenter, & King-Sears, 1998).

One of the most successful means of encouraging resiliency is to create a school community that is positive and fosters a sense of belonging (Wang, Haertel, & Walberg, 1994). The African proverb says, "It takes a village to raise a child." In postmodern America the heart of that village is the school. A school has the opportunity to become the hub of a community that links and provides services through collaboration with external resources (businesses, volunteers, retirees, YMCAs and YWCAs, Boys/Girls Clubs, synagogues, mosques, and churches, as well as social-service agencies) that support and enhance everyone's efforts to rear healthy and whole children (Fowler & Corley, 1996). Resourcing and Creating Community provides for exploration of opportunities that schools offer to strengthen the proverbial village, through linking families and students to professional service providers and, perhaps more important, by creating a supportive and nurturing community by which students and families are connected in a caring manner (Lewis, Schaps, & Watson, 1995; Noddings, 1995; Wynne & Walberg, 1995).

Rationale for Creating Community

There is no better time than now for transforming communities to build resiliency in children and youth. Our society is on the edge of possibility. Our families are changing demographically, and technology has revolutionized the worlds of home and work. Yet the rise of poverty, crime, sexual promiscuity, drugs, and depression have made it difficult for families and schools to support and care for the nation's youth the way they once did. Zill and Nord (1994) and Waddock (1993) concluded that families today are less able to provide nurturing, supportive, safe, and secure environments where children can develop and learn. Communities must take stock and rearrange our resources to help children grow up to become responsible and actively productive members of this society (Dryfoos, 1994). With the intention of building both better learners, school personnel have an opportunity to lead the way as family and child advocates.

With a vision of social transformation, counselors and other educators can become partners not only in the development of a child but also in the preservation and development of the entire community (Booth & Dunn, 1996; Dryfoos, 1994). To achieve this, Haas (1993) suggested that schools must move away from the factory model of production with raw materials and move into a new era where schools adopt the metaphor of *family resource schools*—in which schools, as extensions of a child's family, provide the scaffolding for the child's growth that was once provided solely by relatives and neighbors. This will require a shift of attitudes about the roles of the school and of school personnel that must expand and evolve to meet the needs of the at-risk population. School counselors have been challenged to become advocates for school and community partnerships and to coordinate networks of resources for children and youth who are considered at-risk (Hart & Jacobi, 1992). Schools must go beyond the traditional "three Rs" and include the teaching and nurturing that parents have traditionally been expected to provide. Counselors and other school personnel must also reach out to parents through parent education, training, and support groups.

Although schools cannot be all things to all people, they must become more things to more people than they have in the past. Schools are in the unique position to help increase resiliency in children and youth by becoming part of a cohesive community that meets the needs of families of at-risk students. This is critical, not only for individual students and their families but also for the continued health and viability of our society. As an outgrowth of the National Commission on Children, Nickolas Hobbs (1975) wrote *The Futures of Children.* He stated, "Our failure to act today will only defer to the next generation the rising social, moral and financial costs of our neglect. Investing in our children is no longer a luxury, but a national imperative." This point is as appropriate today as it was in 1975, and the evidence of Hobbs' grave warning surrounds our cities and our people.

The presence of a support network is one of the most important factors in family adjustment during life-cycle changes and stresses. Schools can encourage support and should act as liaisons, linking at-risk students with public and private institutions, businesses, churches, retirees, and volunteers interested in and capable of providing services (Beck, 1994). The heart of service is in the relationship that is formed through interpersonal contact (Noddings, 1995). Schools can and should diagnose needs, collaborate and network, and share information as well as resources. They must also keep in mind that it is relationship that builds resiliency (Noddings, 1995). Mentoring, lunch buddies, Big Brothers/Big Sisters, tutoring by retirees, e-mail pen pals that link students with professors, and similar experiences will provide opportunities for the relationship building that fosters resilience (Rak & Patterson, 1996).

Schools must become part of the fabric that *gives back* to the community. Native American cultures emphasize giving back (Attnaeve, 1982), and those who give to others are held in highest regard. Service learning provides an opportunity for the school to connect with the community (Keith, 1997; Kleinbard, 1997). A class of adolescent students in a program for troubled youth might provide tutoring to kindergarten children who need to hear stories from supportive people. These same adolescents may be visited by senior citizens from the nearby community for retirees who share the experience of gardening. In this way all involved will benefit and realize the vital part they play in community life. In community we are inexorably linked with one another in ways that are critical, yet we forget the importance of sharing, community, and relationship—the human connection that gives meaning to our lives (Noddings, 1995). A gentler nation is aware of its potential and is in touch with its soul, connected across generations.

James Coleman (1987) concluded that the success students experience in parochial schools could be attributed to the crossing of generations encountered by religious organizations. "They are among the few in which the social capital of an adult community is available to children and youth." (p. 37). Therefore, community involvement is important for the success of children in school and as adults. Schools have to take a proactive stance to include citizens of all ages in meaningful relationships with children and youth, and members of the community must view themselves as central to the school's mission (Waddock, 1995).

At times, families need access to professional resources from the community. The goal of resourcing or referral is not to encourage family dependency on outside resources. Nor should families be expected to solve all their problems alone or be responsible for meeting all the needs of its members. Services are provided with the goal of reminding each family of its own resources so that, working together, they can draw out, through mutual clear and honest communication, the strengths, knowledge, and wisdom that are already there. The underlying belief here is reflected by the poet Gibran (1923) in the section from *The Prophet* titled "Teaching":

> No man can reveal to you aught but that which already lies half asleep in the dawning of your knowledge . . .
> If he is indeed wise he does not bid you enter the house of his wisdom, but rather leads you to the threshold of your own mind. . .
> For the vision of one man lends not its wings to another man. . . (pp. 56-57)

Counselors who assist families through referral to community resources from this frame of reference will develop important linkages and will foster resiliency-building in the process.

Frames of Reference

The counselor's understanding of the concepts of family resources and deficits will affect plans for, as well as interactions with, at-risk members. The individual and family may not be able to interpret the professional's attitude; however, when they deal with professionals who respect and view them as resourceful and consult with them as equal partners, trust is more likely to develop. To focus on the resources of an individual and family, the professional must assume that each has a wealth of assets that can be tapped (Dunst, Trivette, & Deal, 1994a). This does not mean that professionals ignore the family's deficits. Both resources and deficits can be acknowledged at the same time. The goal is to view the family's wholeness and strength.

Counselors must deal with and think about their frames of reference—how they view people in general, as well as how they view specific individuals. Discounting those who are at-risk and assuming that their lives are tenuous will lead to further losses and, in a subtle manner, may support self-fulfilling prophecies of those at-risk for failure in school or life (Rak & Patterson, 1996). If professionals' expectations for families who have children at risk are negative, they may miss the family resources as well as the possibilities the resources present for wholeness. Our society has had a jaundiced view of at-risk individuals and has focused for decades upon seeing deficits in those who have special needs—thereby failing to attend to the possibilities and resources.

The conceptualization of families as resourceful is an essential view with which to engage family members (Cameron & Vanderwoerd, 1997). When professionals view the family as resourceful and as a positive resource, they recognize that the need for additional resources is secondary and temporary. They also recognize that at certain times in the family's life cycle, the family may face an overload when attempting to meet demands. An appropriate analogy was presented by Imber-Black (1986): "The family has not suddenly become bankrupt in terms of its own resources, although its assets may be temporarily frozen or creating no interest" (p. 149).

A resource model of family functioning assumes that families continually create their own norms as they interact with history, culture, ethnicity, social class, politics, interpersonal relationships, individual quirks, and more. Counselors and other school professionals can frame their views of the family with this in mind and recognize the impact of context. Seeing context as significant, the professional is better able to make sense of family observations instead of seeing the family as abnormal. This focuses on the assets of the family while recognizing, but deemphasizing its deficits.

Sharing Information With Families

We provide the following information important to resourcing, focusing on areas in which school professionals serve as agents that link traditional and nontraditional families with supportive resources, thereby precluding their students from falling through the cracks (Greenawalt, 1994).

Helping individuals and family members not to be overly dependent upon outside resources is certainly good, but being independent does not mean having to meet all needs alone or within one's own family. The focus here is on sharing information that allows family members to learn more about family life and healthy communication and to know how to link with beneficial resources. Interdependence is the outgrowth of connection with others and builds the fabric of the community, which is relationship. This is a critical factor in producing resiliency.

Although sharing information with most families of at-risk students will present no difficulty, some will resist input from school professionals (Campbell, 1993). Some family members will consider it to be bordering on an invasion of privacy or indicative of perceived failure or inadequacy of the parent. Other parents may conjure up a racial, religious, or gender bias.

For example, in one family the suggestion that a child join a little League Team may be considered a positive intervention that fits the child's developmental level and offers a social outlet. In another family the same suggestion may be seen as squelching the child's natural creativity by requiring the child to take part in an organized sport rather than allowing exploration of unique physical and social needs. The professional who is aware of the uniqueness of families might recommend to the second family that members take time to play as a family and to explore each individual's creativity through interaction. Suzuki, a form of teaching a musical instrument that involves teaching the parent as well, or the family learning a foreign language together would fit such a family.

Resourcing

Not all at-risk families are dysfunctional; however, most would benefit from having resources available at times of increased stress. Assistance in resourcing can allow families to take advantage of their family and social networks, as well as free or low-cost social services. A support system is one of the most important factors in family adjustment to life-cycle changes and stresses. This support includes school-community resourcing, family resourcing, social systems resourcing, and external resourcing.

School-Community Resourcing

Characteristics of effective school and community programs are as follows, along with some suggestions for establishing effective services.

Schools as a Source of Support. Aside from the informal support that families receive from friends, relatives, and each other, school personnel are often the main source of support for families who need assistance (Burke & Cigno, 1996). Frequently, the schools are the first to recognize a problem and to contact the parent when a problem arises. Just a few of the challenges that students face and bring with them when they enter school are poverty, drug abuse, learning problems, health problems, child neglect and abuse, teen pregnancy, homelessness, and even single-parent families and two-parent families where both parents work. Thus, schools have become a place where basic education alone is not enough.

Unfortunately, a student's problems too often are left to the teacher or building principal and eventually are shuffled on from elementary to middle school or junior high and on to high school where a once preventable problem grows to crisis magnitude. Counselors have the necessary skills and training to ensure that families know about and benefit from the myriad services available in most communities.

Support Based on Need. The kinds of support services provided should depend on the family's desires and needs, the community resources available, and the specific challenges encountered. In today's complex society, families cannot meet all of their needs. Sooner or later, they will need and benefit from different kinds and levels of support. Although one might expect that two-parent, nonminority homes experience low stress and are able to cope, communicate, and parent effectively, this is not always the case (Allen, Brown, & Finlay, 1992). Whereas middle-income families are less likely to need financial help to pay for child care or health services, they can benefit from peer support or parenting classes as well as a number of other services matched to their needs.

Supportive School Programs. Among the human services located in or facilitated by the school, according to Dryfoos (1994), are school health teams, school-based dental health and general health clinics, mental health services, psychosocial counseling programs for substance abuse, teen pregnancy, and school failure, training in social skills and in parenting, assistance in occupational selection, mentoring programs, recreation and cultural enrichment classes, after-school centers for academic tutoring, and job training with links with businesses, universities, and nonprofit organizations. Programs show up in all shapes and sizes, reflecting the needs of the communities that they serve.

Programs involving senior citizens can be orchestrated or encouraged by counselors. Surrogate grandparents from the community paired with students can serve as tutors, special friends, group co-leaders, or lunch buddies. Nearby senior citizen residences are one source of referrals for a grandparent program.

Counselors can coordinate mentor programs (Christiansen, 1997). These programs could pair older students with younger ones, similar to the Big Brothers/Big Sisters programs, or pair professors from a neighboring teacher-training institution with students. Other sources for mentors include local businesses, service organizations, sororities/fraternities, and college students. Counselors can train mentors to use active listening skills, to listen for problems that might require professional intervention and referral, and to recognize new avenues for building resilience in children and youth throughout the community. In this role they serve as ambassadors within the community and beyond.

A worthwhile investment for schools is a family resource library in a room dedicated to family involvement. By defining a space for family members to gather and support their children's educational program and personal development, schools speak to the value of family involvement. A parent guidance advisory committee involves parents in meaningful ways with schools and provides another means of doing this. Involvement of and input from parents regarding the school environment, what programs and activities to include, and the school's mission and goals can facilitate the community building necessary for enhancing resiliency in students.

Counselors, school psychologists, and school social workers can organize and facilitate time-limited or ongoing support groups for parents. The nature of the groups will vary by community and other variables related to the children and families. Techniques such as enactment (mentioned later in this document) are powerful means of eliciting change in these groups.

Sibling group counseling is meaningful for siblings of children who are at-risk or have special needs. *Sibshops* (Meyer & Vadasy, 1994) is an excellent resource model for counselors to use when arranging and implementing sibling groups. Family retreats led by counselors with training in working with families allow family members the opportunity to get away from home to learn from other families as well as the professionals that facilitate the retreat. Family play group counseling led by counselors provides an avenue for increasing resiliency-building in families and healing wounds in a supportive and nonjudgmental environment. Teaching conflict resolution (Johnson, 1997) in group contexts is useful for families who need to develop their skills in dealing with intense feelings. Conflict resolution that is taught in schools and practiced in families and community settings will reinforce the skills and enhance resiliency-building beyond the school environment.

Counselors can generate many more ideas that encourage school-community resourcing. A planning committee that involves the counselor with representatives from students, family members, administration, and teachers can assume responsibility for generating, as well as orchestrating, practical means of providing school-community resources through needs assessment, program planning, and evaluation.

Prior to the opening of Saltonstall Elementary School, linkages with city officials, college faculty, and teachers were already in place. One feature that developed is the *Friday Club.* Every Friday community partners teach elementary students how to do a variety of things. For example, one club built, painted, wallpapered, and decorated doll houses. In another, students learned to play soccer. Meanwhile, teachers spent the 2 hours planning lessons (Fowler & Corley, 1996).

Sonnenblick (1997) described a middle-school program for girls identified as at-risk for dropping out and for membership in youth gangs. The program consisted of weekly club meetings and mentor relationships with school staff and some parents. It offered service activities and recreational events designed to promote personal growth and release from pressure to act "street-smart," impress boys, and deal with excessive family responsibility.

The Monticello, Arkansas, schools work with HIPPY (Home Instruction Program for Preschool Youngsters) to help parents develop social and interpersonal skills to reduce feelings of isolation (Greenawalt, 1994; Harvard Family Research Project, 1995). For example, parents of children entering kindergarten shared their feelings of inadequacy with the school counselor.

Schools in Indianapolis, Indiana, indicated that they wanted more contact with parents and more parent participation in the schools. Working with Parents In Touch (PIT), schools have set aside 20 minutes a day for parent-teacher conferences, created activity calendars to inform and make suggestions to parents, set up homework contracts, homework hotlines, call-in services, parent workshops, and even medical and dental services. Many parents have received other assistance through the various services the school system provides (Harvard Family Research Project, 1995).

Before schools can effectively begin to create programs and links to help students and their families, schools and school districts must decide what they want to achieve and provide. The possibilities abound, and counselors can assist in the planning process by serving along with other school personnel, parents, and community representatives on an advisory committee that assesses school/community needs and resources, establishes goals, and implements programs to promote community pride and improve school morale and climate.

According to the Harvard Family Research Project's *Raising Our Future* (1995), after 25 years of scientific research, Ramsey and Ramsey (1992, p. 5) determined that effective programs embody seven characteristics:

1. They start sooner and continue longer.
2. They increase the frequency of interactions with participants.
3. They give students direct learning experiences.
4. They provide for comprehensive services to students.

5. They take learning style into consideration for at-risk students.

6. They support students who are making a transition into elementary school.

7. They enhance cultural beliefs, traditions, and practices.

Weissbourd (1996) presented 11 principles for schools to use when working with vulnerable children. Counselors can support and help implement these principles in the school and community.

1. Emphasize academics that focus on results and academic achievements.

2. Respond to students' emotional/social challenges and material needs.

3. Develop a safe, orderly school environment.

4. Imbue students with high expectations across all areas of school functioning.

5. Collaborate with parents and children in a respectful manner, and when a problem develops, systemically view the roles of the student, family, community, and school.

6. Identify underlying causes of problems so negative interactions become cycles of success.

7. Share authority with parents and engender a sense of belonging; reaching out to all parents by creating experiences in which they can be involved meaningfully.

8. Engage the noncustodial parent and significant other adults in the child's life.

9. For administrators: Cull out the benefits of experienced teachers' wisdom, and find them the "time, support, and resources they need to work with struggling students" (p. 181), and foster teachers' professional development.

10. For administrators: Support counselors and nurses, and encourage all school staff members to support one another.

11. Form "effective partnerships with community services, businesses, and other community resources. These partnerships are designed to achieve specific goals that further children's academic achievements" (p. 181).

In school-community resourcing we have emphasized school personnel building resilience in students by utilizing strengths within the school. Today's circumstances demand that counselors adopt a systemic view and reach out to families and communities to build resilience in children.

Family Resourcing

Family resourcing encourages counselors to identify family strengths and builds on Weissbourd's principles of collaboration, highlighting the interdependence of systems. We initially define family resources, then provide information about four family resource areas that can be tapped during interactions with the family members. School personnel can catalogue resources and problems for later use. *Cataloging* means tracking family patterns on a family-by-family basis. This allows for a greater use of family resources. Strategies for counselors to encourage the wise use of family resources are as follows.

Definition of Family Resources. Several types of family resources have been identified in the literature (Attneave & Verhulst, 1986; Dunst, Trivette, & Deal, 1994b; Hansen & Coopersmith, 1984; Hansen & Falicov, 1983; Karpel, 1986a). Karpel (1986b) defined family resources as "those individual and systemic characteristics among family members that promote coping and survival, limit destructive patterns, and enrich daily life" (p. 176).

Karpel's (1986b) first element of family resource is the *ability to access coping and survival techniques.* Families face a variety of predictable as well as unexpected stressors throughout the family life cycle. Families vary widely in their resources for promoting coping and survival (Pell & Cohen, 1995). Some families cope well with the challenges, while others struggle. Those who struggle with coping daily may benefit from family resourcing. Assistance can be a means of promoting resiliency in all family members.

Another element of family resources identified by Karpel (1986a) is the *ability of the family to limit destructive patterns.* This relates both to external stressors and to internal patterns such as attacking, demeaning, neglecting, or diminishing another. Limiting destructive patterns helps to prevent stressors from piling up (McCubbin & Patterson, 1982) within the family. Some families seem to resist destructive patterns, which Karpel (1986a) paralleled with immunological resistance. Examples of resistance are a wife's resisting her husband's invitation for a co-alcoholic marriage, parents exercising a clear hierarchy over an acting-out teenager, and a child's resistance to being triangulated into the parents' conflicts.

A third element of family resource relates to the *ability to enrich and enjoy daily life* (Karpel, 1986a). This element goes beyond dealing with problems and centers on life's more rewarding aspects—caring and sharing, satisfaction, and pleasure. The ability to bounce back—one characteristic of resiliency—is enhanced by the family's ability to enjoy simple aspects of daily life.

Karpel (1986a) expanded upon this three-element definition and described *personal resources* as well as *relational resources* in families. Examples of personal resources include self-respect, protectiveness, hope, tolerance, and affection. Relational resources include respect, reciprocity, reliability, repair, flexibility, family pride, and loops of interaction.

Personal and relational resources within families are affected by three characteristics: capacity, rules, and active efforts. For example, the relational resource of reciprocity, or give-and-take, in a family relates to how the family balances and holds fair play. Counselors can assess each family member's capacity for reciprocity and consider this in conjunction with the family rules (e.g., Dad is the disciplinarian). Finally, active efforts by family members to initiate and collaborate on reciprocity can be considered. Counselors, school social workers, and psychologists are the professionals most likely to look closely at these factors. Observations can be added to the catalog of family process, noting strengths and challenges faced by family members.

Areas of Family Resource. Imber-Black (1986) described four family resource areas that direct professionals' attention to the family's strengths as opposed to their deficits. The first area has to do with *religious, cultural, and racial identity.* McGoldrick, Giordano, and Pearce (1996) have addressed the issue of ethnicity and family therapy, and Carter (1995) has focused on the importance of racial identity.

Avoiding stereotypical thinking about people from other backgrounds is beneficial to healthy family-professional interactions. Counselors should be aware of their own values and any prejudices they may have. Looking for strengths in others' ethnic background is helpful, and being aware of differences is critical to avoid misinterpreting behavior. For example, Mexican-American families typically are cooperative rather than competitive. A counselor who tries to use a competitive strategy to motivate a Mexican-American child may get lackluster results that counselors might misunderstand. This child could easily be seen as unmotivated, whereas in truth the child might be easily motivated by a cooperative learning task. The cooperative task would serve as a resiliency-building strategy as well.

Counselors should observe family interactions with an eye toward recognizing and cataloging family identity, if any. Families also identify with religious groups, and these allegiances serve as a family resource. Some church groups have considerable resources that might be tapped in helping families. This linkage is important as schools reach out to community resources and form partnerships for mentoring and other resiliency-building programs.

A second area (Imber-Black, 1986) relates to the family's *inner language,* which identifies it as a family both to family members and to others. The professional should look for myths, metaphors, jokes, humor, and words or phrases with special meaning to the family members, note any examples, and use them at appropriate times. For example, a family may refer to itself as having "dogged determination." When the family is going through a particularly rough time, the counselor could provide support and encouragement in terms of the family members' own view of themselves by complimenting them on "hanging in there with dogged determination," a resiliency characteristic to be reinforced.

A third area of resource categorized by Imber-Black relates to *individual and family commitments, loyalties, or a sense of connections.* Counselors should be aware of and publicly recognize commitments and loyalties. Examples are a grandmother who takes over the custody and rearing of her unmarried teenage daughter's child, and a family that goes to all ends to be sure the wheelchair-bound child does not miss out on family outings. Counselors should validate family convictions about including everyone in the family fun, thus reinforcing several aspects of resiliency.

The fourth area (Imber-Black, 1986) relates to the *capacity of the family to interact with the outside world* in such a way that preserves and enhances its integrity as a family. The outside world is defined as everything beyond the family. Families have rules for dealing with the external world, beyond family, in the same way that rules develop for family relationships. Counselors should build upon family resources in dealing positively with people outside the family. School professionals are members of that outside world, and it is valuable to know how the family has interacted in the past with school professionals. If prior experiences with the schools have been negative, the current school professionals should attempt to engage the family members, which may mean overcoming negative expectations on both sides.

For example, former school professionals may have seen parents as recalcitrant. If the counselor views the family as having been protective rather than antagonistic, he or she will be better able to focus on the family's positive resources and functional survival skills for making it through an antagonistic situation.

Strategies. School professionals can assess, monitor, and reinforce all four areas of family resources. Again, when collaborating with any family, it is good to look for resources versus deficits (Malatchi, 1997). Everyone who has contact with the family of an at-risk student can contribute to cataloging. A file on each student is valuable, to which information on family resources can be added. The file can be divided into the resource areas described here or according to any other system that meets the needs of the counselor or other professional.

There is good reason to include family members in the process of recognizing their resources. Team meetings might include an agenda item on family resources. When family members attend meetings, professionals can observe the family's use of inner language, as well as how they interact with the outside world.

It is important not only to note but also to reinforce family resources. When counselors are in meetings with family members or in one-to-one interactions, they should take every opportunity to validate family resources related to resiliency. For example, a counselor might tell a mother, "I can see your son Timmy takes after the rest of your family when it comes to being gentle. I wish you had seen him with the new student from Iran."

It is also important to validate and encourage healthy family functioning that enhances resiliency. When spouses take a vacation together and tell the schools they will be out of town, school professionals should verbally reinforce their taking care of their marriage and encourage them not to worry about the child at school ("We can handle whatever might come up here").

The sibling subsystem also should be validated as a source of support and a valuable family resource. Too often, people think the siblings are in a rivalry. Counselors need to help frame existing or potential sibling relationships positively (Meyer & Vadasy, 1994; Powell & Gallagher, 1993; Seligman, 1991). Kahn (1986) has an excellent chapter about the sibling system with bonds of intensity, loyalty, and endurance. Knowing whether the family is either disengaged or enmeshed can also be helpful when making comments that might encourage balance and sibling support. When the family is disengaged, the school professional can facilitate alignment between siblings, fostering the resiliency-producing relationship bonds. For example: "I've noticed that you and your brother act quite differently, but it seems as though the two of you have had a similar experience in your family."

Dysfunctional family interaction patterns or roles, such as scapegoating (Satir, 1988), can be changed. For example, the professional might say, "It looks as if Sandy is the 'fall guy' in this family. I wonder if she might be bringing a fresh perspective instead?" Another dysfunctional role that can be transformed is that of *parentified* child, frequently the oldest daughter in families that are extremely stressed. Counselors can suggest the family allow the daughter an opportunity for extracurricular activities, thereby fostering resiliency. School professionals should not unwittingly reinforce *parentifying* (Nichols, 1996). For instance, comments about what a "great little mother" a child is are inappropriate.

Another resource of potential strength lies in the extended family. Family members may overlook the real possibilities the extended family has to offer. We can learn from African American families in which extended family members often pitch in, not only to care for but also to participate in, rearing the children in their families (Hines & Boyd-Franklin, 1996). The counselor can ask whether a grandparent, aunt, uncle, or other relative might be able to help with various functions. A simple suggestion that an unmarried aunt or uncle babysit once a week so that the parents could have time together might never have occurred to the family. Extended family members can serve as important role models for coping with stress and for increasing resiliency in children and youth.

Family retreats, family play-group counseling, and parent education groups can be implemented using flexible scheduling, with babysitting provided for infants and toddlers. When focusing on family as resource, the school professional can be creative and energizing. Many possibilities exist. It is up to the creative professional to make these possibilities real and to bring them to the school's attention.

Social Systems Resourcing

Cameron and Vanderwoerd (1997) defined social networks as "the actual, reccurring linkages between a focal person and significant others in her or his environment" (p. 27). Social support is from "instrumental, educational, social, and psychological assistance actually received by the focal person" (p. 27).

Extensive research shows that social support helps some individuals and families to cope better with a stressful event and improve health (Hobfoll & Stephens, 1990), life expectancy (Kennedy, Kiecolt-Glaser, & Glaser, 1990), and success on exams and other academic tasks (Goldsmith & Albrecht, 1993). Paradoxically, other evidence suggests that some forms of support may be detrimental (Kaplan & Toshima, 1990; Swann & Brown, 1990; Goldsmith, 1992). Advocating for continued social support, Burleson, Albrecht, and Sarason (1994) indicated that supportive communication can contribute in positive or negative ways to recovery from illness, coping with loss, managing chronic health problems, dealing with daily disruptions, performing tasks, and feeling good about themselves and their quality of life (p. xiii).

Families should be encouraged to pursue supportive relationships that reduce their stress and increase their well-being. Schools can help to facilitate social support by connecting people with others who face similar challenges or to people in their community who could serve as positive role models. The counselor, for example, could encourage designation of a room for families to meet with other families who share the same needs and with families who have already overcome similar obstacles. The room should be inviting, with careful attention to selecting the leaders that will facilitate the meetings. Counselors, social workers, and psychologists should all be particularly aware of the impact that social support networks have on individuals and families. Group co-leadership by a helping professional and a "veteran" successful parent can facilitate interaction and minimize the resistance of individuals who are defensive or mistrust professionals.

Researchers interested in at-risk families have written about social network interventions and the value of social support (Berger, 1984; Coopersmith, 1983; Dunst, Trivette, & Deal, 1994a; Dunst, Trivette, & Cross, 1986; Friedrich & Friedrich, 1981; Intagliata & Doyle, 1984; Kazak, 1987; Kazak & Marvin, 1984; Rueveni, 1979). Just as the resources of the immediate and extended family are valuable, so, too, are the resources of the family's social network.

Families that face a high level of stress will look to their social network for resources that enable them to reduce and better cope with that stress. Unfortunately, the social network may unwittingly add to the stress by providing contradictory and competing suggestions. One person may suggest a favorite intervention, and another might offer a diametrically opposing idea. This can be confusing. Thus social network interventions can be invaluable in getting all interested parties to understand and support realistic strategies.

Background. Systems theorists propose that social networks, with their attendant support, directly and indirectly influence attitudes, expectations, behavior, and knowledge of family members and other members of the network. Bronfenbrenner (1979) described ecological units or social networks topologically. He saw them as a nesting of concentric structures, one embedded within the other. The child and family are at the center. Broader ecological systems move out in concentric circles, to include relatives, friends, neighbors, and other acquaintances. Beyond that are larger social units (discussed under External Resourcing), encompassing the neighborhood mosques, churches, and synagogues, as well as social organizations, the workplace, play areas, and school.

Waddock (1993) also described ecological units or social networks topologically. She saw them as webs of influence outward from the center, where the child and school are center. Broader ecological systems move outward and include social workers, then the larger community where services are provided, then state policies, until at the outer edge of the web lies the nation and federal government. Counselors can serve as *web weavers* to develop linkages that promote resiliency-building for families and students between and among these systems.

Social systems theorists contend that these ecological units do not function in isolation but, rather, interact within and between levels. Thus, changes in one unit or subsystem will reverberate and impact upon other units or subsystems. When professionals understand this dynamic, reciprocal, systemic relationship, they will be more likely to plan appropriate interventions that promote resiliency by considering input from the school, the family, and the community, and its impact on students considered at-risk.

Definition of Social Support Systems. Social support networks are links among individuals and groups. These links relate to size, satisfaction, density, connectedness, and frequency of contacts. As Dunst, Trivette, and Cross (1986) indicated, "Social support is a multidimensional construct that includes physical and instrumental assistance, attitude transmission, resource and information sharing, and emotional and psychological support" (p. 403). They added that a consensus of social systems theorists view social support networks as serving the function of nurturing and sustaining links that support others daily as well as in times of need and crises.

Turner (1981) named social support as a component of psychological well-being. Although he did not study at-risk families, he did study four diverse populations, one of which was adults with hearing losses. He also traced research about social support and concluded that social support is most important in stressful circumstances. In his study, Turner adopted Cobb's (1976) view of social support, in which Turner related social support as providing information that result in people believing they are cared for and loved, esteemed and valued, and belong to a "network of communication and mutual obligation in which others can be counted on should the need arise" (pp. 358-359).

Findings and Strategies for Social Systems Resourcing. Social networks, with their attendant support, directly and indirectly influence the attitudes, expectations, behavior, and knowledge of family members and other members of the network alike. In this web of influence, counselors have the distinct opportunity, through the "collective anchoring of the individual life" (Haas, 1993, p. 215), to develop students by providing the tools that allow them to forge a tranquil, thriving, and equitable society.

The Harvard Family Research Project (1995) stated, "The heart of family support programs is the web of relationships connecting staff with families, parents with children, and parents with other parents" (p. 11). This study found that schools had to overcome some formidable obstacles including the negative images held toward schools, reaching families that are poor and isolated, and overcoming transportation and child-care barriers that make parents reluctant to leave their neighborhoods. Thus, counselors and other professionals must be willing to go into the communities to meet parents in their homes or, possibly, at a neutral establishment such as a library, mosque, church, synagogue, community center, park, or even a fast-food restaurant to strengthen relationships and to provide the necessary assistance.

As the Harvard Family Research Project (1995) found, outreach programs are complex and difficult. Professionals must be adept at disarming resistant and often dysfunctional attitudes and also able to convince the family of its need for assistance. A frame of reference that stresses the family's resources and ability to overcome challenges will facilitate this task. Many valuable concepts in family systems approaches can help counselors effectively share information with parents of at-risk and special-needs students, thereby promoting resiliency and reducing harmful stress.

A variety of findings presented in the literature on social network systems indicate the value of considering social systems as essential assets in reducing stress on family members. Dunst et al. (1986) examined effects of social support on parents of children with mental retardation and physical impairment, as well as developmentally at-risk children. These researchers were concerned with the impact of social support on "personal well-being, parental attitudes toward their child, family integrity, parental perceptions of child functioning, parent-child play opportunities and child behavior and development" (p. 403). Their findings supported the positive impact of social support systems on families having children with disabilities.

Kazak and Marvin (1984) studied stress and characteristics of social support networks of families with and without a child with a disability. They found that mothers are particularly subject to personal stress. Unlike previous research findings, they did not find a significant difference in the stress levels of marital dyads. They suggested that professionals view the differences between families (and their networks) as appropriate accommodations to raising a child with a disability. Specifically, they found both the overinvolvement of the mother and child and the peripheral role of the father in parenting to be appropriate and to be respected by professionals, "unless there is ample evidence that the marital relationship is impaired" (p. 75).

Kazak (1987) examined mothers and fathers of children with disabilities or chronic illnesses and compared them with matched parents of children without disabilities. She considered personal stress, marital satisfaction, and size and density of the social network. She found that only the mothers of the children with disabilities experienced higher levels of stress. Again, her findings indicated no differences in marital satisfaction. Finally, Kazak found that mothers of children with disabilities had higher-density social networks than comparison mothers.

Intagliata and Doyle (1984) examined social support for parents of children with developmental disabilities by training them in interpersonal problem-solving skills. From this pilot study, they concluded that enhanced problem-solving skills of these parents was relevant and could be a helpful intervention.

Friedrich and Friedrich (1981) compared parents of children with a disability with a control group of parents of children without disabilities. One of many measures included social support. They concluded that "an appropriate avenue of intervention might increase the availability of social support for these parents to help them cope with this additional stress" (p. 553).

Minuchin and Fishman (1981) described the technique of *enactment*. In enactment, people act out the problem as contrasted with simply talking about the problem in the family. For example, if a student is disobedient to the parents during a social systems networking session, the counselor might ask the parents what they plan to do. This allows the counselor to see the problem as it evolves naturally. It may also present an opportunity for the counselor to intervene while serving as a model for the whole social systems network.

Berger (1984) recommended the use of enactments in network interventions. He suggested creating a context in which those in attendance act differently toward one another. This helps when attempting to look at the family and social network as valuable resources: "Network interventions, then, are especially powerful contexts for the use of enactments that alter network members' definition of the handicapping condition or of what needs to be done about that condition" (p. 134).

Social support has a positive impact upon families with at-risk children. School professionals must consider this when relating to families (Rak & Patterson, 1996). Counselors, social workers, and psychologists in the schools should be particularly aware of the influence of social systems on building resilience.

External Resourcing

External resource networking helps families form supportive links with resources outside their family, school, or social network. This might include tapping into volunteer groups, social service agencies, support groups and counseling services.

A host of potentially valuable resources are available in every community and state, as well at the national level, which most professionals know about only generally. Every school should have a resource file that all professionals can consult in their efforts to provide resource information to families. As professionals learn about additional resources, they can add to the file. School professionals might even find resources beneficial for themselves or their families.

Each file should contain evaluation information, including feedback from family members who have used the resources. They can be asked to respond to a brief questionnaire covering their impressions and reactions to different resources. Space should be allotted for general comments from family members who have used the resource. If any school professionals have used a resource or know someone who has, they can add their comments to the evaluation. Neither parents nor professionals should be required to sign the questionnaire, nor should they quote or identify by name anyone receiving confidential services.

These files should be checked and purged at least once a year. Telephone numbers and contact people change regularly, as do opportunities for group as well as individual support. It is frustrating to hear of a resource that is no longer available. When this happens, parents may decide not to follow any other leads.

To generate a file, a group of professionals can get together and divide the workload and pool their findings. A search of resources in the community begins by contacting the local school board for brochures or information on agencies and services available to families. Then the community mental health center should be contacted for information on its services, as well as other resources with which the personnel are familiar. Community parks and recreation associations can also be contacted. Another source of services consists of local churches. The local United Way may also be a source of agencies that provide services and support, as well as a clearinghouse for agencies needing volunteer assistance.

Beyond the local community, professionals can contact state agencies such as the Department of Education for information on state-level services and opportunities for networking with families of at-risk and special-needs children. The division responsible for special education in the state should be contacted, along with the Department of Mental Health. The division on volunteerism within the state government may also be of service.

National agencies should be investigated. These are beneficial contacts for a variety of types of disabilities. Also, many organizations can be found through a national directory. Examples include the Association for Retarded Citizens (ARC), Learning Disabilities Association (LDA), and Bereaved Parents/Compassionate Friends. The textbook by Lambie (in press), on which this publication is based, contains a lengthy resource list in an appendix, which will be helpful in finding national resources.

References

Achilles, C. M. (1997). Small classes, big possibilities. *School Administrator, October,* pp. 6–15.

Achilles, C. M. (1996). Students achieve more in smaller classes. *Educational Leadership, 53,* 76–77.

Allen, M., Brown, P., & Finley, B. (1992). *Helping children by strengthening families: A look at family support programs.* Washington, DC: Children's Defense Fund.

Attneave, C. (1982). American Indians and Alaska Native families: Emigrants in their own homeland. In M. McGoldrick, J. K. Pearce, & J. Giordano (Eds.), *Ethnicity and family therapy* (pp. 55–82). New York: Guilford.

Attneave, C. L., & Verhulst, J. (1986). Teaching mental health professionals to see family strengths: Core network interventions in a hospital setting. In M. Karpel (Ed.), *Family resources* (pp. 259–271). New York: Guilford.

Barr, R. D., & Parrett, W. H. (1995). *Hope at last for at-risk youth.* Boston: Allyn & Bacon.

Beck, V. (1994). "Opportunity plus": A school and community based tutorial program for elementary students. *Elementary School Guidance and Counseling, 29,* 156–159.

Berger, M. (1984). Social network interventions for families that have a handicapped child. In J. Hansen & E.I. Coopersmith (Eds.), *Families with handicapped members* (pp. 127–136). Rockville, MD: Aspen.

Booth, A., & Dunn, J. F. (Eds.). (1996). *Family-school links: How do they affect educational outcomes?* Mahwah, NJ: Lawrence Erlbaum.

Bronfenbrenner, U. (1979). *The ecology of human development.* Cambridge, MA: Harvard University.

Burke, P., & Cigno, K. (1996), *Support for families: Helping children with learning disabilities.* Brookfield, VT: Ashgate.

Burleson, B. R., Albrecht, T. L., & Sarason, I. G. (Eds.). (1994). *Communication of social support: Messages, interactions, relationships, and community.* Thousand Oaks, CA: Sage.

Cameron, G., & Vanderwoerd, J. (1997). *Protecting children and supporting families: Promising programs and organizational realities.* Hawthorne, NY: Aldine de Gruyter.

Campbell, C. (1993). Strategies for reducing parent resistance to consultation in the schools. *Elementary School Guidance and Counseling, 28,* 83–91.

Carter, R. T. (1995). *The influence of race and racial identity in psychotherapy: Toward a racially inclusive model.* New York: John Wiley & Sons, Inc.

Christiansen, J. (1997). Helping teachers meet the needs of students at risk for failure. *Elementary School Guidance & Counseling, 31*(3), 204–210.

Cobb, S. (1976). Social support as a moderator of life stress. *Psychosomatic Medicine, 38,* 301–314.

Coburn, J., & Nelson, S. (1989). *Teachers do make a difference: What Indian graduates say about their school experience.* (ERIC Document Reproduction Service No. ED 306 071)

Coleman, J. A. (1987). Families and schools. *Educational Researcher, 16*(6), 32–38.

Coopersmith, E. I. (1983). The family and public service systems: An assessment method. In J. Hansen & E. Keene, (Eds.), *Diagnosis and assessment in family therapy* (pp. 83–100). Rockville, MD: Aspen.

Cowan, P. A., Cowan, C. P. & Schulz, M. S. (1996). Thinking about risk and resilience in families. In E. M. Hetherington & E. A. Blechman, (Eds.), *Stress, coping, and resiliency in children and families* (pp. 1–38). Mahwah, NJ: Lawrence Erlbaum.

Cuban, L. (1989). The "at-risk" label and the problem of urban school reform. *Phi Delta Kappan, 70,* 780–784.

Dryfoos, J. G. (1994). *Full-service schools: A revolution in health and social services for children, youth, and families.* San Francisco: Jossey-Bass.

Dunst, C. J., Trivette, C. M., & Deal, A. G. (1994a). Resource-based family-centered intervention practices. In C. J. Dunst, C. M. Trivette, & A. G. Deal (Eds.), *Supporting and strengthening families: Volume 1, Methods, strategies and practices* (pp. 140–151). Cambridge, MA: Brookline Books.

Dunst, C. J., Trivette, C. M., & Deal, A. G. (1994b). *Supporting and strengthening families: Volume 1. Methods, strategies and practices.* Cambridge, MA: Brookline Books.

Dunst, C. J., Trivette, C. M., & Cross, A. H. (1986). Mediating influences of social support: Personal, family, and child outcomes. *American Journal of Mental Deficiency, 90,* 403–417.

Edwards, D. L. (1995). The school counselor's role in helping teachers and students belong. *Elementary School Guidance & Counseling, 29*(3), 191–197.

Edwards, D. L., & Foster, M. A. (1995). Uniting the family and school systems: A process of empowering the school counselor. *School Counselor, 42*(4), 277–282.

Fewell, R. R. (1995). Early education for disabled and at-risk children. In M. C. Wang, M. C. Reynolds, & H. J. Walberg (Eds.), *Handbook of special and remedial education: Research and practice* (2d ed., pp. 37–60). New York: Elsevier Science.

Finn, J. D. (1998). *Class size and students at risk: What is known? What is next.* Washington, DC: U.S. Department of Education. (On-line www.ed.gov/offices/oeri/at-risk)

Fowler, R. C., & Corley, K. K. (1996). Linking families, building community. *Educational Leadership, 53*(7), 24–26.

Friedrich, W. N., & Friedrich, W. L. (1981). Psychosocial assets of parents of handicapped and nonhandicapped children. *American Journal of Mental Deficiency, 85,* 551–553.

Frymier, J. (1992). *Growing up is risky business, and schools are not to blame.* Bloomington, IN: Phi Delta Kappa.

Frymier, J., & Gansneder, B. (1989). The Phi Delta Kappa study of students at-risk. *Phi Delta Kappan, 71*(2), 142–146.

Garmezy, N., & Rutter, M. (Eds.). (1983). *Stress, coping, and development in children.* New York: McGraw-Hill.

Geary, P. A. (1988). *"Defying the odds?": Academic success among at-risk minority teenagers in an urban high school.* (ERIC Document Reproduction Service No. ED 296 055)

Gibran, K. (1923). *The prophet.* New York: Alfred E. Knopf.

Goldsmith, D. (1992). Managing conflicting goals in supportive interaction: An integrative theoretical framework. *Communication Research, 19,* 264–286.

Goldsmith, D., & Albrecht, T. L. (1993). The impact of supportive communication networks on test anxiety and performance. *Communication Education, 42,* 142–158.

Greenawalt II, C. E. (1994). Educational outreach programs. In C. E. Greenawalt (Ed.), *Educational innovation: An agenda to frame the future* (pp. 413–433). Lanham, MD: University Press of America.

Haas, T. (1993). School in communities: New ways to work together. In G. A. Smith (Ed.), *Public schools that work: Creating community* (pp. 215–245). New York: Rutledge.

Haggerty, R. J., Sherrod, L. R., Garmezy, N., & Rutter, M. (1994). *Stress, risk, and resilience in children and adolescents: Processes, mechanisms, and interventions.* Cambridge, UK: Cambridge University.

Hansen, J. C., & Coopersmith, E. I. (Eds.). (1984). *Families with handicapped members.* Rockville, MD: Aspen.

Hansen, J. C., & Falicov, C. J. (Eds.). (1983). *Cultural perspectives in family therapy.* Rockville, MD: Aspen.

Hart, P. J., & Jacobi, M. (1992). *From gatekeepers to advocate: Transforming the role of the school counselor.* New York: College Entrance Examination Board.

Harvard Family Research Project. (1995). *Raising our future: Families, schools, and communities joining together.* Cambridge, MA: Author.

Henderson, N., & Milstein, M. M. (1996). *Residence in schools: Making it happen for students and educators.* Thousand Oaks, CA: Corwin.

Henry, M. (1996). *Parent-school collaboration: Feminist organizational structure and school leadership.* Albany, NY: State University of New York.

Hetherington, E. M., & Blechman, E. A. (Eds.). (1996). *Stress, coping, and resiliency in children and families.* Mahwah, NJ: Lawrence Erlbaum.

Hines, P. M., & Boyd-Franklin, N. (1996). African American families. In M. McGoldrick, J. Giordano, & J. K. Pearce (Eds.), *Ethnicity and family therapy* (2d ed., pp. 66–84). New York: Guilford.

Hobbs, N. (1975). *The futures of children.* San Francisco: Jossey-Bass.

Hobfoll, S. E., & Stephens, M. A. P. (1990). Social support during extreme stress: Consequences and intervention. In B. R. Sarason, I. G. Sarason, & G. R. Pierce (Eds.), *Social support: An interactional view* (pp. 497–481). New York: John Wiley.

Imber-Black, E. (1986). Toward a resource model in systemic family therapy. In M. Karpel (Ed.), *Family resources: The hidden partner in family therapy* (pp. 148–174). New York: Guilford.

Intagliata, J., & Doyle, N. (1984). Enhancing social support for parents of developmentally disabled children: Training in interpersonal problem solving skills. *Mental Retardation, 22*(1), 4–11.

Jens, K. G., & Gordon, B. N. (1991). Understanding risk: Implications for tracking high-risk infants and making early service decisions. *International Journal of Disability, 38,* 211–224.

Johnson, D. (1997). *Reaching out: Interpersonal effectiveness and self-actualization (6th ed.).* Needham Heights, MA: Allyn & Bacon.

Johnson, D., & Johnson, R. (1994). *Learning together and alone: Cooperative, competitive, and individualistic learning.* Needham Heights: MA: Allyn & Bacon.

Joseph, J. M. (1994). *The resilient child: Preparing today's youth for tomorrow's world.* New York: Insight Books/Plenum.

Kahn, M. D. (1986). The sibling system: Bonds of intensity, loyalty, and endurance. In M. Karpel (Ed.), *Family resources: The hidden partner in family therapy* (pp. 235–258). New York: Guilford.

Kaplan, C. P., Turner, S., Norman, E., & Stillson, K. (1996). Promoting resilience strategies: A modified consultation model. *Social Work in Education, 18*(3), 158–168.

Kaplan, R. M., & Toshima, M. T. (1990). The functional effects of social relationships on chronic illness and disability. In B. R. Sarason, I. G. Sarason, & G. R. Pierce (Eds.), *Social support: An interactional view* (pp. 427–453). New York: John Wiley.

Karpel, M. (Ed.). (1986a). *Family resources: The hidden partner in family therapy.* New York: Guilford.

Karpel, M. (1986b). Testing, promoting, and preserving family resources: Beyond pathology and power. In M. Karpel (Ed.), *Family resources: The hidden partner in family therapy* (pp. 174–234). New York: Guilford.

Kazak, A. E. (1987). Families with disabled children: Stress and social networks in three samples. *Journal of Abnormal Child Psychology, 15,* 137–146.

Kazak, A. E., & Marvin, R. S. (1984). Differences, difficulties and adaptation: Stress and social networks in families with a handicapped child. *Family Relations, 33,* 66–77.

Keith, N. Z. (1997). Doing service projects in urban settings. In A. S. Waterman (Ed.), *Service-learning: Applications from the research.* Mahwah, NJ: Lawrence Erlbaum.

Kennedy, S., Kiecolt-Glaser, J. K., & Glaser, R. (1990). Social support, stress and the immune system. In B. R. Sarason, I. G. Sarason, & G. R. Pierce (Eds.), *Social support: An interactional view* (pp. 253–266). New York: John Wiley.

Keys, S. G., Bemak, F., Carpenter, S. L., & King-Sears, M. (1998). Collaborative consultant: A new role for counselors serving at-risk youths. *Journal of Counseling & Development, 76,* 123–133.

Kleinbard, P. (1997). Youth participation: Integrating youth into communities. In J. Schine, (Ed.), *Youth participation: Integrating youth into communities* (pp. 1–18). Chicago: University of Chicago.

Lambie, R. (In press). *Family systems within educational contexts: Understanding at-risk and special-needs students.* Denver: Love.

Lewis, C. C., Schaps, R., & Watson, M. (1995). Beyond the pendulum: Creating challenging and caring schools. *Phi Delta Kappan, 76,* 547–554.

Liontos, L. B. (1991). *Involving the families of at-risk youth in the educational process.* (ERIC Document Reproduction Service No. ED 328 946)

Malatchi, A. (1997). Family partnerships, belonging, and diversity. In L. Power-deFur and F. Orelove (Eds.), *Inclusive education: Practical implementation of the least restrictive environment* (pp. 91–115). Gaithersburg, MD: Aspen.

Masten, A. S. (1994). Resilience in individual development: Successful adaptation despite risk and adversity. In M. C. Wang & E. W. Gordon, *Educational resilience in inner-city America* (pp. 3–25). Mahwah, NJ: Lawrence Erlbaum.

McCubbin, H. I., & Patterson, J. (1982). Family adaptation to crises. In H. McCubbin, A. Cauble, & J. Patterson (Eds.), *Family stress, coping and social support.* Springfield, IL: Charles C Thomas.

McGoldrick, M., Giordano, J., & Pearce, J. (Eds.). (1996). *Ethnicity and family therapy.* New York: Guilford.

McMillan, J., & Reed, D. (1993). *Defying the odds: A study of resilient at-risk students.* Richmond, VA: Virginia Commonwealth University, Metropolitan Educational Research Consortium.

McMillan, J., & Reed, D. (1994). At-risk students and resiliency: Factors contributing to academic success. *Clearing House, 67*(3), 137–140.

Meyer, D. J., & Vadasy, P. F. (1994). *Sibshops: Workshops for siblings of children with special needs.* Baltimore, MD: Paul H. Brookes.

Minuchin, S., & Fishman, H. (1981). *Family therapy techniques.* Cambridge, MA: Harvard University.

Mullis, F., & Fincher, S. F. (1996). Using rituals to define the school community. *Elementary School Guidance & Counseling, 30,* 243–251.

Nichols, W. C. (1996). *Treating people in families: An integrative framework.* New York: Guilford.

Noddings, N. (1995). Teaching themes of care. *Phi Delta Kappan, 76*(9), 675–679.

Pell, E. C., & Cohen, E. P. (1995). Parents and advocacy systems: A family systems approach. In M. C. Wang, M. C. Reynolds, & H. J. Walberg (Eds.), *Handbook of special and remedial education: Research and Practice* (2d ed., pp. 371–392). New York: Elsevier Science.

Peng, S. S., Wang, M. C., & Walberg, H. J. (1992, April). *Resilient students in urban settings*. Paper presented at annual meeting of American Educational Research Association, San Francisco, CA.

Powell, T. H., & Gallagher, P. A. (1993). *Brothers and sisters: A special part of exceptional families* (2d ed.). Baltimore: Paul H. Brookes.

Rak, C. F., & Patterson, L. W. (1996). Promoting resilience in at-risk children. *Journal of Counseling & Development, 74*(4), 368–373.

Rhodes, W. A., & Brown, W. K. (1991). *Why some children succeed despite the odds*. New York: Praeger.

Rueveni, U. (1979). *Networking families in crisis: Intervention strategies with families and social networks*. New York: Human Sciences.

Rutter, M. (1994). Stress research: Accomplishments and tasks ahead. In R. J. Haggerty, L. R. Sherrod, N. Garmezy, & M. Rutter (Eds.), *Stress, risk, and resilience in children and adolescents: Processes, mechanisms, and interventions* (pp. 354–385). Cambridge, UK: Cambridge University.

Sagor, R. (1996). Building resiliency in students. *Educational Leadership, 54*(1), 38–43.

Satir, V. (1988). *The new peoplemaking*. Mountain View, CA: Science and Behavior Books.

Seligman, M. (1991). Siblings of disabled brothers and sisters. *The family with a handicapped child* (2d ed., pp. 181–201). Boston: Allyn and Bacon.

Sergiovanni, T. J. (1995). Small schools, great expectation. *Educational Leadership, 53*(3), 48–52.

Shepard, H. A. (1995). On the realization of human potential: A path with a heart. In D. Kolb, J. Osland, & I. Rubin (Eds.), *The organizational behavior reader* (6th ed., pp. 168–178). Englewood Cliffs, NJ: Prentice Hall.

Slavin, R. E., & Madden, N. (1989). What works for students at risk: A research synthesis. *Educational Leadership, 46*(5), 4–13.

Slavin, R. E., Madden, N. A., Dolan, L. J., & Wasik, B. A. (1996). *Every child, every school: Success for all*. Thousand Oaks, CA: Corwin.

Sonnenblick, M. D. (1997). The GALSS club: Promoting belonging among at-risk adolescent girls. *School Counselor, 44,* 243–245.

Sugai, G., & Lewis, T. J. (1996). Preferred and promising practices for social skills instruction. *Focus on Exceptional Children, 29*(4), 1–16.

Swann, W. B., Jr., & Brown, J. D. (1990). From self to health: Self verification and identity disruption. In B. R. Sarason, I. G. Sarason, & G. R. Pierce (Eds.), *Social support: An interactional view* (pp. 150–172). New York: John Wiley.

Trachtman, R. (1991). Early childhood education and child care: Issues of at-risk children and families. *Urban Education, 26*(1), 25–42.

Turner, R. (1981). Social support as a contingency in psychological well-being. *Journal of Health & Social Behavior, 22,* 357–367.

Waddock, S.A. (1993). The spider's web: Influences on school performance. *Business Horizons, 36*(5), 39–48.

Waddock, S. A. (1995). *Not by schools alone: Sharing responsibility for America's education reform*. Westport, CT: Praeger.

Wang, M. C., & Gordon, E. W. (Eds.). (1994). *Educational resilience in inner-city America: Challenges and prospects*. Hillsdale, NJ: Lawrence Erlbaum.

Wang, M. C., & Haertel, G. D. (1995). Educational resilience. In M. C. Wang, M. C. Reynolds, & H. J. Walberg (Eds.), *Handbook of special and remedial education: Research and practice* (2d ed., pp. 159–200). Hillsdale, NJ: Lawrence Erlbaum.

Wang, M. C., Haertel, G. D., & Walberg, H. J. (1994). Educational resilience in inner cities. In M. C. Wang & E. W. Gordon

(Eds.), *Educational resilience in inner-city America: Challenges and prospects* (pp. 45–72). Hillsdale, NJ: Lawrence Erlbaum.

Weissbourd, R. (1996). *The vulnerable child: What really hurts America's children and what we can do about it.* Reading, MA: Addison-Wesley.

Werner, E. E. (1984). Resilient children. *Young Children, 40*(1), 68–72.

Westfall, A., & Pisapia, J. (1994). Students who defy the odds: A study of resilient at-risk students. *Research Brief #18.* Richmond, VA: Virginia Commonwealth University, Metropolitan Education Research Consortium.

Wolin, S. , & Wolin, S. J. (1996). Beating the odds: Some kids who have been dealt a losing hand end up winning the game. What can we learn from them? *Learning, 25,*(1), 66–68.

Wolin, S. J., & Wolin, S. (1993). *The resilient self: How survivors of troubled families rise above adversity.* New York: Villard.

Wynne, E. A., & Walberg, H. J. (1995). The virtues of intimacy in education. *Educational Leadership, 53*(3), 53–54.

Yoder, D. I., Retish, E., & Wade, R. (1996). Service learning: Meeting student and community needs. *Teaching Exceptional Children, 28*(4), 14–18.

Young-Eisendrath, P. (1996). *The gifts of suffering: Finding insight, compassion, and renewal.* Reading, MA: Addison-Wesley.

Zill, N., & Nord, C. W. (1994). *Running in place: How American families are faring in a changing economy and an individualistic society.* Washington, DC: Child Trends.

Depression in Children and Adolescents

John W. Maag and Steven R. Forness

Depression in children and adolescents is a mood (affective) disorder whose magnitude and clinical importance has only recently permeated the concern of educators. Once considered exclusively the domain of psychiatrists, depression can and should be considered by school personnel in identification, assessment, and treatment (Reynolds, 1984). Unfortunately, professionals in special education have been slow to recognize that depression affects a wide range of school-related functioning (Maag & Rutherford, 1987, 1988). A survey by 47 nationally recognized experts in education of the behaviorally disordered, for instance, did not even mention depression as an important research issue in the field (Epstein & Cullinan, 1984). Youngsters with behavioral disorders are not the only handicapped group at risk for developing depression. Depression has been identified in children and adolescents with mild mental retardation, learning disabilities, and speech and language disorders (e.g., Cantwell & Baker, 1982; Reynolds & Miller, 1985; Stevenson & Romney, 1984).

Depression may be overlooked as a potentially important area of concern in special education, in part, because of its colloquial presence and associated ambiguity (Kendall, Hollon, Beck, Hammen, & Ingram, 1987). At one end of the spectrum, depression is a commonly used term to denote "feeling a little bummed out." At the other end of the spectrum, depression refers to a clinical syndrome or disorder. Kazdin (1990) provides the following distinction:

> As a *symptom*, depression refers to sad affect and as such is a common experience of everyday life. As a *syndrome* or *disorder*, depression refers to a group of symptoms that go together. Sadness may be part of a larger set of problems that include the loss of interest in activities, feelings of worthlessness, sleep disturbances, changes in appetite and others. (p. 121)

These distinctions are more than a matter of semantics—different definitions and uses of the label "depression" have important implications (Kendall et al., 1987). The syndrome of depression can be present, in secondary ways, in other disorders. For example, a schizophrenic individual may manifest depressive symptomatology without meeting diagnostic criteria for major mood disorder (American Psychiatric Association, 1987).

In this chapter we are providing only a brief overview of the current status of knowledge in the area of child and adolescent depression. For in-depth reviews, see Dolgan (1990), Kazdin (1990), and Reynolds (1985). We describe diagnostic criteria and identification procedures as well as assessment methodology and intervention strategies. The focus is on depression in handicapped populations in school settings and the implications for special educators.

Current Perspectives

For many years, controversy has surrounded the nature of depression in children and adolescents (Kaslow & Rehm, 1991). For example, conventional psychoanalytic doctrine postulates that depression cannot exist until the onset of adolescence and the development of the superego (Rie, 1966; Rochlin, 1959). A popular view during the 1970s reflected the belief that depression in children was "masked" and must be inferred from underlying behaviors such as hyperactivity, aggression, irritability, delinquency, and poor school performance, to name a few (e.g., Cytryn & McKnew, 1974; Malmquist, 1977). Lefkowitz and Burton (1978) suggested that depression represents a transitory developmental phenomenon which abates spontaneously without intervention; and Seifer, Nurcombe, Scioli, and Grapentine (1989) currently suggest that depression is but one symptom usually found in a pattern of other symptoms that seem to cluster together in children.

The current consensus among researchers and clinicians, however, is that depression in children and adolescents parallels that found in adults. Consequently, the diagnostic criteria for diagnosis of depression in adults also is appropriate and applicable to children and adolescents (Carlson & Cantwell, 1980; Chambers et al., 1985; Chiles, Miller, & Cox, 1980; Kashani, Barbero, & Bolander, 1981; Mitchell, McCauley, Burke, & Moss, 1988).

Diagnostic Criteria

The primary diagnostic system that researchers and clinicians currently use is the *Diagnostic and Statistical Manual for Mental Disorders—Revised* (DSM-III-R) (American Psychiatric Association, 1987). The DSM-III-R criteria for all mood disorders in adulthood, including depression, are applied to children as well. Although depression is a clinical condition that can be diagnosed in children, adolescents, and adults, its specific symptoms, associated features, and clinical course can vary as a

---

DSM-III-R Criteria for Major Depressive Disorder

At least five of the following symptoms must be present during the same 2-week period; at least one of the symptoms is either (1) depressed mood, or (2) loss of interest or pleasure.

■ Depressed mood most of the day, nearly every day (either by subjective account; e.g., feels "down" or "low" or is observed by others to look sad or depressed)

■ Loss of interest or pleasure in all or almost all activities nearly every day (either by subjective account or is observed by others to be apathetic)

■ Significant weight loss or weight gain (when not dieting or binge-eating) (e.g., more than 5% of body weight in a month) or decrease or increase in appetite nearly every day (in children consider failure to make expected weight gains)

■ Insomnia or hypersomnia nearly every day

■ Psychomotor agitation or retardation nearly every day (observable by others, not merely subjective feelings of restlessness or being slowed down) (in children under 6, hypoactivity)

■ Fatigue or loss of energy nearly every day

■ Feelings of worthlessness or excessive or inappropriate guilt (either may be delusional) nearly every day (not merely self-reproach or guilt about being sick)

■ Diminished ability to think or concentrate, or indecisiveness nearly every day (either by subjective account or observed by others)

■ Thoughts that he or she would be better off dead or suicidal ideation, nearly every day; or suicide attempt

---

function of development (Kazdin, 1990). DSM-III-R provides a standardized nomenclature, but this system does not help to identify developmental differences. Cicchetti and Schneider-Rosen (1986) have suggested that depression becomes a problem when it interferes with social, cognitive, or emotional competencies necessary for the successful resolution of developmental tasks. A developmental perspective complements DSM-III-R criteria by providing a broader framework for understanding the nature of depression in children and adolescents (Carlson & Garber, 1986).

Depressive symptoms may be included in other types of disorders. Separation anxiety disorder, adjustment disorder with depressed mood, and uncomplicated bereavement are conditions associated with depressive symptoms such as sadness and loss of interest in usual activities. Severity, duration, and precipitants of the symptoms are major determinants of the type of depressive disorders diagnosed (Kazdin, 1990). A scheme depicting a continuum of mood disorders and selected differential problems is presented in Table 6.1.

Table 6.1 Classification Scheme for Mood Disturbances

PATHOLOGY	UNIPOLAR	BIPOLAR

Severe	Major depression:
	  Single episode*
	  Recurrent**
		Bipolar disorder:
		  Manic
		  Depressed
		  Mixed

Moderate	Dysthymia***	Cyclothymia***
Mild	Atypical depression	Atypical bipolar disorder

	Adjustment disorder:
	  Depressed mood
	  Withdrawal
		Adjustment disorder
		  with anxious mood

Differential	Schizophrenia Schizoaffective disorder Separation anxiety	Paranoia Schizoaffective disorder
Nonpathological	Demoralization Bereavement	(no equivalent)

*** Estimates are that more than 50% of individuals having a first single episode will eventually have recurrent episodes.
*** Major depression, recurrent, may predispose to development of bipolar disorder
*** Dysthymia and cyclothymia may predispose to development of a major mood disorder.

Distinctions should be made between depression and dysthymia. The latter is seen as relatively less severe but recurring over a longer period, often punctuated by periods of normal mood that may last for days or even weeks. Another important distinction is between unipolar and bipolar depressive disorders. Unipolar depressive disorders consist of continuous or intermittent periods of dysphoric mood or anhedonia (inability to have fun), whereas bipolar disorders involve alternating episodes of depression and inappropriate euphoria, excessive energy, grandiosity, impulsivity, and poor judgment (Rizzo & Zabel, 1988). Common conditions of both differential pathological and nonpathological origin are noted in Table 6.1 as well; the former are those of similar severity but different pathological nature, and the latter are within the range of normal emotional responses.

Little is known about manic conditions in children, as they are believed to be rare and difficult to diagnosis in this age group (Kovacs, 1989). Criteria for major depressive disorder and dysthymia generally are necessary in the diagnosis of bipolar disorder and cyclothymia, respectively, along with specific criteria for alternating manic features. It is interesting to speculate whether the episodic nature of a bipolar disorder could render an afflicted child ineligible for special education in that he or she would fail to meet consistently the criterion of a "pervasive mood of sadness or depression" even though bipolar disorder is possibly more debilitating than depression per se (Forness, 1988).

Subtypes of Childhood and Adolescent Depression

The classification scheme illustrated in Table 1 represents a continuum of mood disorders, from the DSM-III-R, that may be present in children and adolescents. Childhood depression can further be classified into several distinct subtypes, each positing a slightly different etiological base and, therefore, having implications for identification, assessment, and treatment (Maag & Rutherford, 1988). Different subtypes of depression are presented in Table 6.2.

Several important distinctions exist between each subtype. *Anaclitic depression*, also termed the "deprivation syndrome" (Spitz & Wolf, 1946), develops in an infant after loss of a caregiver and no provision of a substitute. *Reactive depression* differs from anaclitic depression in that loss of the caregiver does not invariably lead to anaclitic depression; poor parent-child relationships have the most impact on development of reactive depression (Abrahams & Whitlock, 1969). *Acute depression* develops in response to some traumatic event, such as the loss of a loved one, and the prognosis for recovery is good (Cytryn & McKnew, 1972). *Chronic depression*, in contrast, is more extreme and has no immediate precipitating events but is punctuated by repeated separations from the caregiver during early infancy. Finally, *endogenous depression* is thought to be genetic or biochemical in nature, and possibly related to learning disabilities in some children (Brumback & Stanton, 1983).

Table 6.2   Subtypes of Childhood and Adolescent Depression

SUBTYPE	CHARACTERISTICS
Anaclitic Depression	Loss of caregiver with no provision for a substitute; period of misery followed by loss of interest in environment.
Reactive Depression	Trauma or loss frequently accompanied by feelings of guilt for past failures; poor parent-child relationship is important factor.
Acute Depression	Onset occurs after some traumatic event; prognosis for recovery is good if relationship with caregiver is healthy.
Chronic Depression	Repeated separations from caregiver beginning in infancy; presence of depression in mother; no immediate precipitating event; periodic recurring emotional-depriving experiences; suicidal ideation early in childhood.
Endogenous Depression	Genetically or biochemically determined; no identifiable stressors; believed to exist, to some degree, throughout life of child; may reach psychotic or suicidal proportions.

Identification and Assessment

Upon examining prevalence figures of depression in children and adolescents, the importance for educators to identify this disorder becomes alarmingly apparent. The extent to which children and adolescents experience depressive symptomatology has been studied in school-based and clinical populations. Prevalence estimates usually are determined either through DSM-III diagnostic criteria or rating scales in which a score is translated into levels ranging from nondepressed to severely depressed (Reynolds, 1985). Because DSM-III focuses on clinical syndromes or symptom-clusters, prevalence estimates using this approach tend to be more conservative than those obtained for rating scales that provide only global indicators of symptom-severity. In fact, children obtaining rating scale scores in the severe range occasionally fail to meet DSM-III diagnostic criteria for depressive disorders (Kazdin, Colbus, & Rodgers, 1986).

Prevalence Estimates

Using DSM-III criteria, about 2% of school-based children (Kashani et al., 1983; Kashani & Simonds, 1979) and 10% to 20% of clinic-based children (Puig-Antich & Gittelman, 1982) have been diagnosed as depressed. When depression is identified using extreme scores on self report scales, between 2% and 17% of students attending general education school classes manifested moderate to severe levels of depressive symptomatology (Friedrich, Jacobs, & Reams, 1982; Kaplan, Hong, & Weinhold, 1984; Lefkowitz & Tesiny, 1985; Reynolds, 1983; Smucker, Craighead, Craighead, & Green, 1986; Teri, 1982a). Special education populations tend to have a much higher prevalence: Between 14% and 54% of learning disabled (LD) and seriously emotionally disturbed (SED) students manifested severe depressive symptomatology (Maag & Behrens, 1989a; Mattison et al., 1986; Stevenson & Romney, 1984).

A summary of selected prevalence studies is presented in Table 6.3. Only fairly recent studies employing large samples are included because they tend to be more accurate; however, considerable variability is evident, often depending on choice of diagnostic criteria and instrumentation.

Another reason prevalence estimates tend to be somewhat inchoate stems in part from the failure of researchers to consider variables such as gender and age. Gender differences in prevalence of depression usually do not surface until adolescence, when more females than males experience severe symptomatology (Angold, Weissman, John, Wickramaratne, Drusoff, 1991; Kashani et al., 1983; Lefkowitz & Tesiny, 1985; Lobovits & Handal, 1985; Mezzich & Mezzich, 1979; Reinherz et al., 1989; Reynolds, 1985). Similar results have been obtained with LD and SED adolescents; females are three times more likely to report severe depressive symptomatology than their male counterparts (Maag & Behrens, 1989b).

In regard to age, except for very young children (aged 1–6), who have low rates of depression (Kashani, Cantwell, Shekim, & Reid, 1982; Kashani, Ray, & Carlson, 1984), age differences in both handicapped and nonhandicapped populations tend

Table 6.3   Selected Prevalence Findings in Childhood and Adolescent Depression

STUDY	SAMPLE TYPE	PERCENT DEPRESSED
School-Based General Education Samples		
Lefkowitz & Tesiny (1985)	3,020 3rd-, 4th-, & 5th-grade children, mean age 9.8	5.2%
Reynolds (1983)	2,874 adolescents, ages 13–18	7%
School-Based Special Education Samples		
Maag & Behrens (1989a)	465 LD and SED adolescents ages 12–18 attending resource programs	21%
Mattison et al. (1986)	109 students ages 6–18 referred for SED placement	18% (ages 6–12) 51% (ages 13–18)
Stevenson & Romney (1984)	103 LD students ages 8–13 attending resource programs	14%
Clinic-Based Samples		
Cantwell & Baker (1982)	600 children and adolescents ages 2–16 presented to a community clinic for speech and language evaluation	4%
Carlson & Cantwell (1980)	102 children and adolescents ages 7–17 presented for psychiatric evaluation to an outpatient department	58%
Colbert, Newman, Ney, & Young (1982)	282 children and adolescents ages 6–14 admitted to a child and family practice unit	54%

to be mediated by gender (e.g., Fleming & Offord, 1990; Maag & Behrens, 1989a; Rutter, 1986). Adolescents in general, however, seem to experience higher rates of depression than children do (Forness, 1988; Kazdin, 1990).

Educators' Perspectives on Depression

Given the unsettling prevalence of depression in schoolbased populations, educators clearly should play a strategic role in early identification. Youngsters spend more time in school than in most other structured settings outside the home, and their most consistent and extensive contact is with educators (Grob, Klein, & Eisen, 1983). Consequently, school personnel may be the first professionals to notice developing problems (Powers, 1979). To facilitate the identification process, school personnel must be knowledgeable of depression and sensitive to students who might exhibit it. Although school personnel possess some general knowledge of depression, they cleave to several misconceptions.

Maag, Rutherford, and Parks (1988) had a sample of regular education teachers, special education teachers, and school counselors complete a questionnaire assessing their ability to identify characteristics of depression. Their answers were coded into similar response categories and compared to information about depression drawn from empirical research. School counselors possessed the greatest knowledge of depression, whereas general and special educators identified only global characteristics. Of particular note, special educators tended to identify characteristics related to externalizing problems (e.g., disobedience, aggression) more frequently than internalizing problems (e.g., sadness, loneliness, crying). Externalizing behaviors tend to correlate more highly to depression scores for males, and internalizing problems and negative view of self correlate more highly with depression scores for females (Smucker et al., 1986). More males than females typically receive special education services, so the belief in masked depression should not be resurrected.

In a similar study, Clarizio and Payette (1990) surveyed school psychologists. Although the school psychologists in the study possessed considerable knowledge of depression, their responses diverged relative to the literature in two important areas. *First*, a substantial number of school psychologists believed that childhood depression was substantively different from adult depression. They almost unanimously agreed that masked depression exists, even though this conceptualization has been discounted for several years (Kaslow & Rehm, 1991). *Second*, projective techniques (e.g., TAT, sentence completion) were one of the most frequently named methods for assessing depression. This finding contradicts evidence that projective tests are not sensitive enough to identify specific psychiatric conditions in childhood, including depression (Gittelman, 1980).

More alarmingly, some evidence suggests that educators may respond more negatively to depressed students than to their nondepressed peers. Peterson, Wonderlich, Reaven, and Mullins (1987) had teachers rate their feelings in response to four films in which a child was portrayed as either depressed or nondepressed and as having experienced either high or low life stress. The children who were both depressed and stressed received the most negative reactions from educators; the children who were either depressed or stressed were viewed less negatively; and the children who were neither depressed nor stressed received the most positive reactions. Depression clearly influenced educators' responses in ways that could serve to maintain a child's depression. Educators who communicate less positive and more negative behavior to a depressed child may enhance feelings of low self-esteem, dysphoria, inadequacy, and helplessness.

Because the risk of suicide also is greatly heightened with depression (Myers et al., 1991), educators have a particular need to be sensitive to this disorder. Guetzloe (1989) discusses issues of suicidality in school settings.

Early Identification

Early identification of depressed children and adolescents in school settings is desirable, but Reynolds (1986a) recognized several factors that make this goal problematic:

1. Prevalence figures may be somewhat misleading as depressive symptomatology tends to be overendorsed on the first administration of a self-report measure of depression. A second administration of the same measure shortly thereafter may not show depressive symptomatology. What happens is that a specific event or stressor may trigger a depressive episode, which may account for many cases of depression identified in prevalence surveys.

2. School personnel often have difficulty identifying specific symptom clusters associated with depression. To complicate matters, secondary teachers have limited contact with students.

3. Depressed students rarely refer themselves for help.

4. Some parents deny that their child may be suffering from a mood disorder.

On the basis of findings from prevalence studies of depression in children and adolescents and the lack of self-referral, teacher referral, or parent referral, Reynolds (1986a) developed a three-stage screening program to identify depressed children and adolescents in school settings: (a) conducting large-group screening with self-report depression measures; (b) 3 to 6 weeks later retesting children who, on the basis of the large-group screening in Stage 1, meet cutoff score criteria for depression; and (c) conducting individual clinical interviews with children who manifest clinical levels of depression at both Stage 1 and Stage 2 evaluations.

Classroom teachers can conduct group assessment of students, utilizing a self-report depression measure appropriate for children or adolescents. Self-report is particularly important in assessing depression because primary symptoms such as sadness, feelings of worthlessness, and loss of interest in activities reflect subjective feelings and self-perceptions (Kazdin, 1990). Common self-report measures for children and adolescents are given in Table 6.4.

Reynolds (1986a) has suggested that teachers avoid telling students they are being tested for depression because this information may induce lower levels of mood awareness. Instead, students can be informed that the school is interested in how they are feeling about themselves. This information can be restated to students involved in a second screening. The second screening serves to weed out students who experienced a transient depressed mood during the initial screening or exaggerated their depressive symptomatology. During the last stage, individual clinical interviews are conducted with students who met depression criteria at both previous

Table 6.4   Commonly Used Measures for Childhood and Adolescent Depression

MEASURE	RESPONSE FORMAT	DESCRIPTION
Self-Report (Child)		
Children's Depression Inventory (Kovacs, 1985)	27 items, each rated on a 0–2 point scale	Derived from Beck Depression Inventory (Beck, Ward, Mendelson, Mock, & Erbaugh, 1961). Items reflect affective, cognitive, and behavioral symptoms.
Reynolds Child Depression Scale (Reynolds, 1986b)	30 items, each rated on a 1–5 point scale	Items selected to measure depression in school characteristics (e.g., suicide) are replaced by less severe behavior (e.g., hurting oneself).
Self-Report (Adolescent)		
Beck Depression Inventory (modified for adolescents) (Chiles et al., 1980)	33 items, each on a scale varying from 0 to 2, 3, or 4 points	Changes in language, not content of Beck Depression Inventory (Beck et al., 1961).
Reynolds Adolescent Depression Scale (Reynolds, 1986c)	30 items, each rated on a 4-point scale	Items derived from symptoms included in major, minor, and unipolar depression.
Clinical Interviews (Child)		
Bellevue Index of Depression (Petti, 1978)	40 items, each rated on a 4-point scale of severity and 3-point scale for duration	Administered separately to child, parents, and others; helpful to combine scores from different sources.
Children's Depression Rating Scale (Poznanski, Cook, & Carroll, 1979)	16 items scored after interview; symptoms rated on a 6-point scale for severity	Derived from Hamilton Depression Rating Scale (Hamilton, 1967) for adults. Administered also to parents and others to combine different sources.
Schedule for Affective Disorders for School-Age Children (Chambers et al., 1985)	Multiple items for mood disorders; depressive symptoms rated for degree of severity for scales varying in point values	Patterned after adult Schedule for Affective-Disorders (Endicott & Spitzer, 1978) based on Research Diagnostic Criteria (Spitzer, Endicott, & Robins, 1978). Parent and child are interviewed.
Clinical Interviews (Adolescent)		
Hamilton Depression Rating Scale (Hamilton, 1967)	17-item semi-structured interview with probes	Measures severity of depression and probes for psychotic symptoms; translates well for use with adolescents.
Research Diagnostic Criteria (Spitzer et al., 1978)	11 depression subtypes (e.g., simple, recurrent, unipolar, agitated)	Provides greater specificity than DSM classification; primarily used in research.

Note: For an in-depth review of the characteristics of individual assessment techniques, see Kazdin (1988).

stages. Common interview schedules also are presented in Table 6.4. Obtaining measures other than self-reports is important as some students consistently overestimate or underestimate depressive symptomatology or misinterpret items or response format.

To screen initially for only a single disorder may be neither desirable nor efficient sometimes, especially given limited resources in some school psychology or consulting services budgets. As an alternative to screening only for depression, Walker and Severson (1990) have developed a multi-stage procedure to screen for both internalizing and externalizing disorders. In this process, teachers are asked to nominate and rank order pupils who demonstrate characteristics of these broad-band disorders in their classroom (Stage 1) but then also rate only the top three pupils in each category on brief measures of adaptive and maladaptive behavior as well as on critical events or symptoms (Stage 2). A school psychologist then conducts brief observations of classroom attention and playground social interaction on two different occasions (Stage 3) for any pupils who exceed critical cutoff scores in the first two stages. Although this procedure is not specific to depression, it may identify children with a potential diagnosis of this disorder, which then can be verified using the techniques described above.

Depression-Related Characteristics

Depression influences a wide range of behavioral, cognitive, and affective functioning (Maag & Rutherford, 1987). Many depression-related characteristics vary as a function of developmental level (Kazdin, 1987). For example, infants have not acquired the ability to verbalize and have not experienced the world and therefore express depression through eating and sleeping disorders (Evans, Reinhart, & Succop, 1980). Because preschoolers are motor-oriented, much of their mood is expressed through behavior such as night terrors, enuresis, and encopresis. Older school-age children may become more outwardly aggressive, anxious, and antisocial (Kazdin, French, & Unis, 1983). Depression becomes more overt in adolescents as their better-developed conscience exacerbates feelings of guilt and low self-esteem (Teri, 1982b).

A number of salient characteristics correlate with, if not contribute directly to, depression. Although the range of domains is quite large, several key characteristics occur quite frequently with depression. For example, low self-esteem is likely to be part of the symptom picture of depression. Hopelessness, or negative expectations toward the future, correlates with depression, suicidal ideation and behavior, and low self-esteem (DiGangi, Behrens, & Maag, 1989; Kazdin, Rodgers, & Colbus, 1986).

In addition to cognitive disturbances, social skill deficits often are associated with depression (Helsel & Matson, 1984). Environmental events that induce stress can contribute to the development and maintenance of depression as well (Compas, 1987). These depression-related characteristics often reflect specific theoretical models of depression including social skill deficits, cognitive theory, learned helplessness theory, self-control deficits, and deficits in problem solving.

Descriptions of the relevant models are presented in Table 6.5. A number of measures focus on key areas related to depressive symptoms based on these theoretical models. Table 6.6 lists common measures that are used to assess areas central to current conceptual views of depression and convey areas reflecting specific theoretical models.

Categorizing Problems Associated With Depression

Based on current theoretical models, depression may result from social skill deficits, self-control deficits, learned helplessness attributions, or cognitive distortions or deficits. Interpersonal problem-solving skills contribute to both cognitive

Table 6.5 Theoretical Models Accounting for Depression

MODEL	DESCRIPTION
Social Skill Deficits	Depression results from a lack of social skills necessary to obtain reinforcement from the environment (Lewinsohn, 1974) Low rates of response-contingent positive reinforcement results in reduced activity levels. Punishing and aversive consequences (unpleasant outcomes) may result from person-environment interactions and lead to symptoms of depression.
Self-Control Model	Maladaptive or deficient self-regulatory processes in coping with stress cause depression (Rehm, 1977). Self-regulatory processes include self-monitoring, self-evaluation, and self-reinforcement. Individuals with self-regulatory deficits focus on negative events, set overly stringent criteria for evaluating their performance, and administer little reinforcement to themselves.
Learned Helplessness	Depression results from individuals' experiences and expectations that their responses do not influence events in their lives. Perfidious attributional style filters experiences in such a way as to produce deficits in affect, motivation, and self-esteem associated with depression (Abramson, Seligman, & Teasdale, 1978).
Cognitive Triad of Depression	Depressed individuals have a systematically negative bias in their thinking, which leads them to have a negative view of themselves, the world, and the future (Beck, 1967). Negative cognitions are considered to affect the individual's judgment about the world and interpersonal interactions, and to account for affective, motivational, and behavioral symptoms of depression.
Interpersonal Problem-Solving Deficits	Inability to generate alternative solutions to social problems, engage in means-end thinking, and make decisions exacerbate effects of negative events (Nezu, Nezu, & Perri, 1989). Depression emerges in response to problems of daily living.

Table 6.6   Common Measures for Assessing Depression-Related Characteristics

MEASURE	DESCRIPTION
Social Skills	
Matson Evaluation of Social Skills with Children (Matson, Rotatori, & Helsel, 1983)	Items pertain to social skills, assertiveness, jealousy, and impulsiveness as related to interpersonal interaction. Self-report and teacher-report forms rated on 5-point scale.
Walker-McConnell Scale of Social Competence and School Adjustment (Walker & McConnell, 1988)	Teacher-rated scale consisting of 43 descriptions of peer-related interpersonal social skills and adaptive behavior required for success within classroom instructional settings.
Cognition	
Children's Attributional Style Questionnaire (Seligman & Peterson, 1986)	Self-report measure consisting of 48 forced-choice items that permit assessment of three attributional dimensions considered important in a learned helplessness model of depression: internal-external characteristics, stable-unstable characteristics, and good-bad outcomes.
Children's Negative Cognitive Error Questionnaire (Leitenberg, Yost, & Carroll-Wilson, 1986)	Self-report measure consisting of 24 items presenting hypothetical situations or events followed by a statement about the event that reflects cognitive errors (catastrophizing, overgeneralizing, personalizing, and selective abstraction). Children rate degree of similarity to their own thoughts. This measure is based on Beck's cognitive therapy of depression.
Problem Solving	
Problem Solving Measure for Conflict (Lochman & Lampron, 1986)	Six means-end stories with each stem describing a problematic situation and a conclusion in which the problem was no longer occurring. Children provide the middle. Scores are based on children's responses on three content areas: verbal assertion, direct action, and physical aggression. This measure is based on Shure and Spivack's (1972) means-ends problem-solving test.
Simulated Problem Situations (Gesten et al., 1982)	Measures of children's natural problem-solving behavior when confronted with a simulated problem situation. Interactions between confederates and target children are observed. Scoring is based on number of alternative solutions generated, number of solution variants offered, number of irrelevant solutions generated, total number of solutions generated excluding irrelevant solutions, and effectiveness of solutions.
Stressful Events	
Life Events Checklist (Johnson & McCutcheon, 1980)	Self-report measure consisting of 46 items that list stressful events. Children indicate whether the event occurred in the past year, whether it was bad or good, and degree of impact on their lives.
Life Events Record (Coddington, 1972)	Stressful events varying as a function of age whose occurrence is rated according to life change units. Parents complete the form for young children; older children complete the scale themselves.

---

*Although many problem-solving measures have been reported in the literature, none are ideally suited for either research or practice (Butler & Meichenbaum, 1981).

(continued)

Table 6.6 (continued)

MEASURE	DESCRIPTION
Activities and Reinforcers	
Pleasure Scale for Children (Kazdin, 1989)	Children report on a 3-point scale the extent to which 39 items would make them happy. The instrument measures degree of anhedonia.
Adolescent Activities (Carey, Kelley, Buss, & Scott, 1986)	Adolescents rate the frequency of occurrence of 100 activities for degree of pleasantness and unpleasantness experienced during the last 2 weeks. The measure is based on Lewinsohn's work.
Children's Reinforcement Schedules (Cautela, Cautela, & Esonis, 1983)	Children identify events that can be used as reinforcers. Helpful as a method to assess pleasure children report in response to a variety of events.
Adolescent Reinforcement Survey Schedule (Cautela, 1981)	Parallels Children's Reinforcement Schedules.

and behavioral conceptualizations (Braswell & Kendall, 1988; Nezu, Nezu, & Perri, 1989). Systematically approaching and evaluating problem situations represents a general orientation common to most intervention approaches. In addition, environmental factors, such as inappropriate or absent reinforcement contingencies, inhibit expression of healthy and positive functioning or promote depression and related characteristics.

Figure 6.1 illustrates a four-category conceptualization of problems associated with depression. According to this model, depression can be conceptualized as resulting from social skill deficits, self-control deficits, cognitive distortions or deficits, and learned helplessness attributions. The presence of interpersonal problem-solving skills and environmental factors allows the categorization of depression for the basis of developing appropriate interventions. For example, poor social skills may result from erroneous problem solving or environmental factors. A child who is encouraged by his or her peers to participate in a game and is capable of performing the requisite behaviors but is unable to strategically select them probably indicates erroneous problem solving. Conversely, if the child lacks the behavioral requisites to participate in the game, social skill deficits may be targeted for intervention. Similarly, cognitive disturbances and misattributions may result from the child's inability to evaluate situations appropriately or perform the requisite behaviors.

Treatment of Childhood and Adolescent Depression

The model depicting problems associated with depression presented in Figure 6.1 can be used to develop intervention programs for depressed youth. When developing a

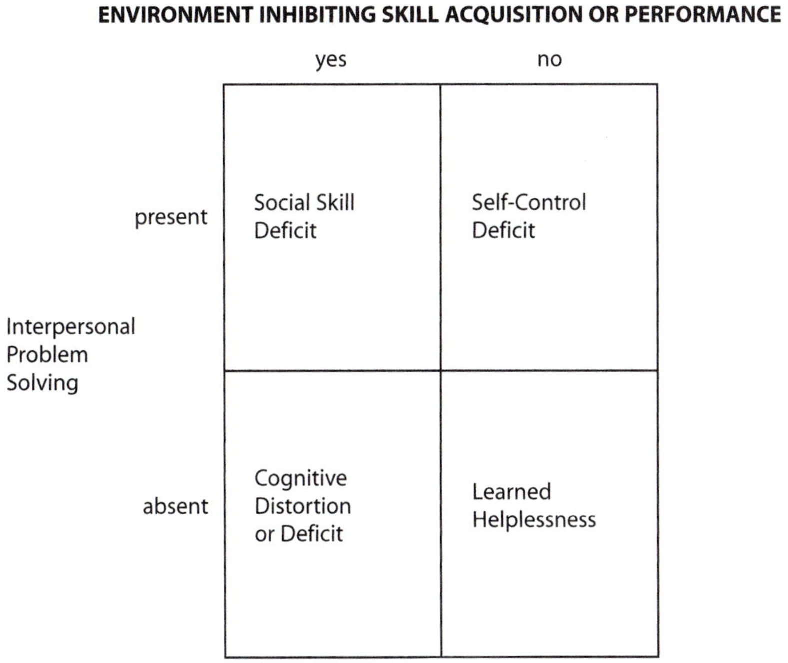

ENVIRONMENT INHIBITING SKILL ACQUISITION OR PERFORMANCE

	yes	no
present	Social Skill Deficit	Self-Control Deficit
absent	Cognitive Distortion or Deficit	Learned Helplessness

Interpersonal Problem Solving

Figure 6.1   Model for Determining the Nature of Depression Deficits

treatment program, the first consideration is whether depressive symptomatology represents a primary condition, (e.g., mood disorder) or is a byproduct of other behavior problems (Kaslow & Rehm, 1991). For example, youngsters who are hyperactive, aggressive, school phobic, or socially incompetent may experience depressive symptomatology and related dysfunctional cognitions as a result of these problems (Maag, Behrens, & DiGangi, 1991). If conventional treatments for these behavior problems are ineffective for ameliorating the primary problem and related depressive symptomatology, specific treatment strategies for depression should be employed.

Table 6.7 presents a summary of treatment approaches relative to theoretical models of depression. Intervention strategies generally reflect either behavioral or cognitive-behavioral orientations. Although techniques based on these models seem promising, only a few studies have investigated their efficacy with children and adolescents (see Maag, 1988a; Stark, 1990). In addition, Kazdin (1990) raises the issue of *comorbidity* (the individual meets criteria for more than one disorder). Several researchers have found that depression coexists with attention deficit disorders, conduct disorders, anxiety disorders, autism, and mental retardation (e.g, Anderson,

Table 6.7   Treatment Strategies Following Theoretical Models of Depression

MODEL	DESCRIPTION
Social Skill Strategies	Main strategies include shaping procedures that use adult reinforcement, modeling or combined modeling and reinforcement procedures, and direct training procedures to make use of the child's cognitive and verbal skills. Specific training techniques include instructions, modeling, role playing, rehearsal, feedback, and self-management techniques. Verbal-cognitive approaches emphasize teaching specific social skills and general problem-solving techniques.
Self-Control Strategies	Self-management strategies including self-monitoring, self-evaluation, self-reinforcement, and self-instruction would be appropriate for remediating self-control deficits. Intervention should take into account children's cognitive developmental capacities and require the practitioner to play an active role in effecting the desired change by utilizing action-oriented techniques and concrete tasks.
Helplessness Strategies	Strategies follow an attribution retraining conceptualization in which children are taught to take responsibility for their failure and to attribute success or failure to effort. Adaptive coping responses are substituted for attributions of helplessness.
Cognitive Strategies	Treatment focuses on determining the meaning of the child's nonverbal and verbal communication. Any distorted cognitions the child expresses must be challenged. Bestowing acceptance and affection are important, as is assigning tasks that ensure success experiences. Techniques are designed to help the child identify, reality-test, and modify distorted conceptualizations and dysfunctional attitudes and beliefs.

Williams, McGhee, & Silva, 1987; Bernstein, 1991; Bernstein & Garfinkel, 1986; Bird et al., 1988; Fendrich, Weissman, & Warner, 1991; Forness & Kavale, in press; McClellan, Rupert, Reichler, & Sylvester, 1990; Strauss, Last, Hersen, & Kazdin, 1988).

Ironically, the phenomenon of comorbidity has led some researchers to suggest that it may be more meaningful to conceptualize depression in terms of the broader classification of internalizing symptoms rather than the more specific symptomatology of depression, which is more difficult to distinguish (Wolfe et al., 1987). This finding is particularly germane to special educators, as problems of an internalizing nature tend to be frequent in children with learning problems (Thompson, 1986).

Determining Choice of Strategies

Given the range of deficits associated with depression, and their implications for treatment, it is important to determine which factor(s) seem most responsible for the development and maintenance of this disorder (Kaslow & Rehm, 1991). Attempting to assess youngsters' relative skills in each area is a tedious and exacting process. Nevertheless, to enhance treatment efficacy, intervention techniques should be matched to identified, specific problems (Maag, 1989).

In this regard, Kaslow and Rehm (1991) suggest sequencing potential intervention strategies and then making decisions on which ones to use in which order, depending on the results of assessment information. For example, if depression is secondary to a conduct or oppositional disorder, social skills training may be essential for the child to obtain an adequate level of response-contingent positive reinforcement in the environment. If the student's social skills are adequate, however, a more appropriate initial technique would be to modify the child's activity level.

Kaslow and Rehm (1991) also stressed the importance of eliciting overt behavior change prior to targeting cognitive factors, because overt behavior is easier to assess than self-reports of children's cognitions. In addition, obtaining an accurate sampling of the child's self-reported cognitions is easier once behavior has been modified. Figure 6.2 presents a modified version of the flowchart developed by Kaslow and Rehm (1991) for determining choice of intervention strategies. This figure is based on the need to accurately identify and define the problem using assessment measures previously described. Targets for intervention reflect three general areas: behavior, cognitive, and cognitive-behavioral. As with any aspect of depression in children and adolescents, care must be taken to modify intervention strategies based on the child's developmental level and level of cognitive, affective, and behavioral functioning (Cole & Kaslow, 1988).

Developing a Conceptual Model for Intervention

Although the treatment literature for childhood and adolescent depression is relatively sparse compared to other areas such as conduct disorders or attention deficit disorders, several new studies have investigated a variety of training techniques. Table 6.8 provides a summary of recent treatment studies for childhood and adolescent depression. One of the difficulties encountered when treating depression is organizing and integrating the various techniques into a structured training format (Maag, 1988a). Attempting to implement all available techniques would be cumbersome and time-consuming. Yet, many depressed youths exhibit a variety of deficits, and employing a single intervention technique may not be sufficient.

A comprehensive training format would provide a structured system for employing various techniques systematically. One conceptual format is offered in the stress inoculation training (SIT) paradigm. SIT is a multi-component intervention format that combines elements of didactic teaching, Socratic discussion, cognitive restructuring, problem solving, relaxation training, behavioral and imaginal rehearsal, self-monitoring, self-instruction, self-reinforcement, and environmental manipulation (Meichenbaum, 1985). SIT should not be viewed as a loose compendium of unrelated methods, but, rather, a set of interconnected techniques that can be combined in a systematic way.

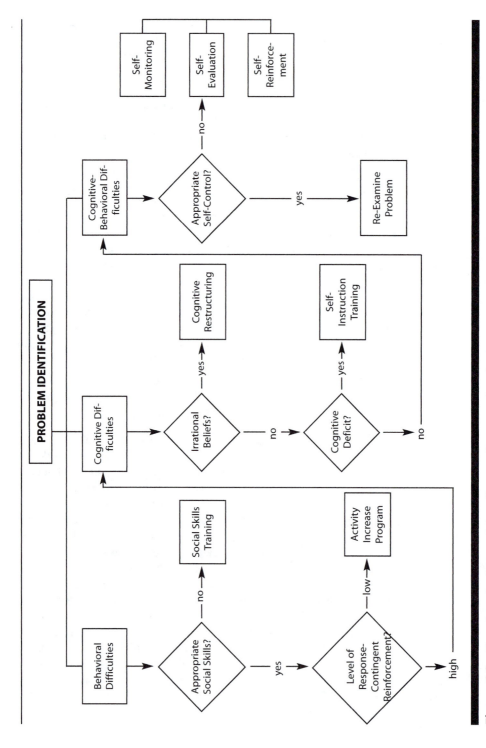

Figure 6.2 Flowchart for Determining Choice of Intervention Strategy

Table 6.8   Treatment Studies With Depressed Children and Adolescents

TREATMENT	STUDY	SAMPLE	FINDINGS
Social Skills Training	Calpin & Cincirpini (1978)	Two depressed inpatients (10-year-old girl, 11-year-old boy)	Improvement for both children on specific social skills (e.g., eye contact)
	Calpin & Kornblith (1977)	Four inpatient boys with aggressive behavior	Improvement of all boys on specific social skills (e.g., requests for new behaviors)
	Fine, Forth, Gilbert, & Haley (1991)	Five groups of 30 adolescent outpatients	Improvement to "nonclinical" levels on depression scales, but to a lesser degree than subjects receiving group therapy
	Frame, Matson, Sonis, Fialkov, & Kazdin (1982)	Borderline mentally retarded 10-year-old depressed male inpatient	Improvement on all target behaviors (e.g., inappropriate body position, lack of eye contact, poor speech quality)
	Petti, Bornstein, Delamater, & Conners (1980)	Chronically depressed 10½-year-old inpatient girl	Improvement on all target behaviors (e.g., eye contact, smiles, duration of speech)
	Matson et al. (1980)	Four depressed emotionally disturbed boys	Increased positive social responses on role-play scenarios for target behaviors (e.g., giving compliments)
	Schloss, Schloss, & Harris (1984)	Three depressed inpatient males	Improvement on five target behaviors (e.g., greets adult, maintains conversation, says goodbye)
Cognitive-Behavioral Interventions	Butler, Miezitis, Friedman, & Cole (1980)	56 fifth- and sixth-grade students	Decreases in depression for role-play and cognitive restructuring conditions; most improvement for role-play
	Maag (1988b)	56 adolescent inpatients	Decreases in depression and negative self-statement for subjects receiving stress inoculation training
	Reynolds & Coats (1986)	30 moderately depressed high school students	Decreases in depression and anxiety for subjects receiving either cognitive restructuring or relaxation training
	Stark, Kaslow, & Reynolds (1987)	29 fourth-, fifth-, and sixth-grade students	Decreases in depression for subjects receiving either self-control or problem-solving training

SIT is implemented in three phases: (a) *conceptualization;* (b) *skills acquisition and rehearsal;* and (c) *application and follow-through.* In Phase I, youngsters are educated about the causes, consequences, and alternative methods of handling depression. Phase II involves training youngsters in relevant skills for coping with depression. In Phase III, youngsters practice applying coping skills *in vitro* and *in vivo* during exposure to regulated doses of stressors that arouse but do not overwhelm their coping skills. SIT has been used to treat depression (Maag, 1988b) and for aggression and anger management (Feindler & Fremouw, 1983; Maag, Parks, & Rutherford, 1988) (see Maag, 1988a for an in-depth description of using stress inoculation training for treating depressed youths).

Pharmacological Treatment

Pharmacotherapy is an essential adjunct to behavioral and cognitive-behavioral interventions, particularly in cases with vegetive symptomatology and family history of mood disorders (Cantwell & Carlson, 1983; Gadow, 1986; Klein, Gittelman, Quitkin, & Rifkin, 1980). Five classes of psychotropics are used in depression; these are depicted in Table 6.9 in terms of their uses, side effects, and related considerations (see Gadow, 1986; Greist & Greist, 1979; Kazdin, 1990; and Petti, 1983 for reviews of pharmacological interventions). Imipramine seems to be the drug of choice for children and adolescents alike (Esman, 1981; Kashani, Shekim, & Reid, 1984; Petti & Law, 1982; Preskorn, Weller, & Weller, 1982; Puig-Antich, 1982); but other drugs, such as lithium and tegretol, are widely used for adolescents who have variant forms of mood disorders (Campbell, Schulman, & Rapoport, 1978; Kishimoto, Ogura, Hazama, & Inoue, 1983).

Although pharmacotherapy is prescribed by psychiatrists, school personnel should be aware of the types of drugs used and their potentially serious side effects. A classroom observation study documenting single-subject classroom effects of imipramine and lithium suggests important considerations for teachers (Forness, Akiyama, & Campana, 1984). Educators need to become much more involved in evaluating effects of such medication on classroom-based measures of treatment outcome (Forness & Kavale, 1988).

Integrating Treatment

Even as treatment of childhood and adolescent depression seems promising, factors external to the child should be considered. Because of parents' influence over their children, Kazdin (1990) suggests that family-based interventions should be incorporated into treatment programs. In this regard, teachers can play a pivotal role by cultivating positive relationships with parents. Positive parent-teacher relationships promote parental feedback to practitioners, enhance treatment outcomes, and extend positive effects of school programming into the home (Heward, Dardig, & Rossett, 1979).

In addition, parents can become trainers of their children by structuring activities and managing behavioral contingencies that promote participation in activities and social interaction (Kazdin, 1990). Parents have effectively implemented reinforcement and punishment techniques and taught prosocial behaviors to their children with externalizing behaviors (e.g., Kazdin, 1985; Patterson, 1982). Parent programs have resulted in decreases in maternal depression and increases in family cohesion (e.g., Eyberg & Robinson, 1982; Forehand, Wells, & Griest, 1980; Karoly & Rosenthal, 1977; Patterson & Fleischman, 1979).

School-based intervention adds several other dimensions as well. Many special educators already conduct social skills training and utilize other cognitive-behavioral techniques for working with aggressive and socially incompetent youngsters (Maag, 1990). Treating depression represents a natural extension of these responsibilities. Furthermore, peers can be recruited for the intervention process as they represent a resource for promoting entrapment (McConnell, 1987) of behaviors that may combat depression. Special educators, therefore, can play a vital role in the early identification, assessment, and treatment of depression.

Summary and Conclusion

Depression represents one of the most significant mental health problems facing children and adolescents. An emerging body of research addresses the nature and characteristics of this disorder in school-aged populations, but educators just recently have begun to address this problem. Part of the difficulty has been educators' lack of knowledge of this disorder and its impact on youngsters' functioning.

Early identification is considered essential, and schools should play an important role in this process. Assessment should focus not only on depressive symptomatology but also on related characteristics, such as social skills. Perhaps most important in treating depression from a school standpoint is that many special educators currently employ many of the intervention strategies that are effective for ameliorating depression for a variety of other conditions such as conduct and attentional disorders. Treatment can be enhanced by sequencing intervention techniques systematically and employing a structured training format.

No one intervention approach will be optimally effective with each youngster. Youngsters who have similar depressive symptomatology may vary greatly with respect to etiological factors, related characteristics, and environmental circumstances. For this reason, depression must be viewed from a holistic framework. This model should guide the development and implementation of treatment decisions. In sum, decisions regarding depression should be made on the basis of empirically based knowledge and the youngster's specific characteristics.

Table 6.9 Common Psychopharmacologic Medication Used With Depressed Children or Adolescents

TYPE (TRADE NAME)	INDICATION	DOSAGE*	THERAPEUTIC EFFECTS	SIDE EFFECTS	OTHER CONSIDERATIONS
Tricyclics: Imipramine (Tofranil)	Unipolar in children	10–175 mg	Improvement in vegetative symptoms at first, followed by improvement in mood some 3 or 4 weeks later	Dry mouth, drowsiness (especially Elavil), blurred vision, constipation, cardiac arrythmias (EKG monitoring is essential and overdose in suicidal patients becomes a concern)	After offset of l month, discontinue gradually over 3 or more months (withdrawal symptoms mimic depression). Has been used to treat separation anxiety, hyperactivity, enuresis.
	Unipolar in adolescents	75–225 mg			
Amytriptyline (Elavil)	Unipolar in adolescents (little research with children)	45–110 mg			
Lithium Carbonate (Lithonate)	Bipolar in adolescents and occasionally in multiple episodes of unipolar	450–1800 mg	Improvement in symptoms in 4–10 days, with most of effect within first 2 weeks; "smooths" rather than eliminates symptoms, but early treatment may suppress recurrences	Nausea, drowsiness, thirst, frequent urination, hand tremor, possible cardiac or kidney problems	Small dose added to tricyclic medication during withdrawal as long-term prophylaxis against recurrence. Has been used to treat aggression.

(continued)

TYPE (TRADE NAME)	INDICATION	DOSAGE*	THERAPEUTIC EFFECTS	SIDE EFFECTS	OTHER CONSIDERATIONS
Monoamine Oxidase Inhibitors (Nardil)	Atypical depression in adolescents	30–60 mg	Gradual improvement over 1- to 3-week period	Nausea, dizziness, fainting, sleep disturbance and possible fatal reactions upon ingestion of certain cheese or yeast products	Used primarily in intractable conditions refractory to other drugs.
Carbamazepine (Tegretol)	Bipolar in adolescents, especially rapid-cycling	30–60 mg	Relatively more rapid onset of improvement	Nausea, drowsiness, weight loss, ataxia in instances, and possible toxic reactions with lithium	Primarily a seizure medication but has been used in lithium-resistant depression.
Fluoxetine Hydrochloride (Prozac)	Unipolar depression in adolescents	20–80 mg	Gradual improvement over 5–6 weeks (long-term effects have not been systematically studied)	Anxiety, nervousness, insomnia, weight loss, hypomania or mania, and seizures	Prozac has not been systematically studied for its potential for abuse, tolerance, or physical dependence

*These are doses in what have generally been considered as optimum levels and, in most cases, are determined on a mg/kg ratio based on body weight. Dosage levels vary widely, so these ranges should be considered with caution.

References

Abrahams, M. J., & Whitlock, F. A. (1969). Childhood experience and depression. *British Journal of Psychiatry, 115,* 883–888.

Abramson, L. Y., Seligman, M. E. P., & Teasdale, J. D. (1978). Learned helplessness in humans: Critique and reformulation. *Journal of Abnormal Psychology, 87,* 49–74.

American Psychiatric Association. (1987). *Diagnostic and statistical manual of mental disorders—Revised* (3rd ed.). Washington, DC: American Psychiatric Association.

Anderson, J. C., Williams, S., McGhee, R., & Silva, P. A. (1987). The prevalence of DSM-III disorders in pre-adolescent children: Prevalence in a large sample from the general population. *Archives of General Psychiatry, 44,* 69–76.

Angold, A., Weissman, M. M., John, K., Wickramaratne, P., & Drusoff, B. (1991). The effects of age and sex on depression ratings in children and adolescents. *Journal of the American Academy of Child and Adolescent Psychiatry, 30,* 67–74.

Beck, A. T. (1967). *Cognitive therapy and the emotional disorders.* New York: International Universities Press.

Beck, A. T., Ward, C. H., Mendelson, M., Mock, J., & Erbaugh, J. (1961). An inventory for measuring depression. *Archives of General Psychiatry, 4,* 53–63.

Bernstein, G. A. (1991). Comorbidity and severity of anxiety and depressive disorders in a clinic sample. *Journal of the American Academy of Child and Adolescent Psychiatry, 30,* 43–50.

Bernstein, G. A., & Garfinkel, D. B. (1986). School phobia: The overlap of affective and anxiety disorders. *Journal of the American Academy of Child Psychiatry, 25,* 235–241.

Bird, H. R., Canino, G., Rubio-Stipec, M., Gould, M. S., Ribera, J., Sesman, M., Woodbury, M., Huertas-Goldman, S., Pagan, A., Sanchez-Lacay, A., & Moscoso, M. (1988). Estimates of the prevalence of childhood maladjustment in a community survey of Puerto Rico: The use of combined measures. *Archives of General Psychiatry, 45,* 1120–1126.

Braswell, L., & Kendall, P. C. (1998). Cognitive-behavioral methods with children. In K. S. Dobson (Ed.), *Handbook of cognitive-behavioral therapies* (pp. 167–213). New York: Guilford.

Brumback, R. A., & Stanton, R. D. (1983). Learning disability and childhood depression. *American Journal of Orthopsychiatry, 53,* 269–281.

Butler, L., & Meichenbaum, D. (1981). The assessment of interpersonal problem-solving skills. In P. C. Kendall & S. D. Hollon (Eds.), *Assessment strategies for cognitive-behavioral interventions* (pp. 197–225). New York: Academic Press.

Butler, L., Miezitis, S., Friedman, R., & Cole, E. (1980). The effect of two school-based intervention programs on depressive symptoms in preadolescents. *American Education Research Journal, 17,* 111–119.

Calpin, J. P., & Cincirpini, P. M. (1978, May). A *multiple baseline analysis of social skills training in children.* Paper presented at Midwestern Association for Behavior Analysis, Chicago.

Calpin, J. P., & Kornblith, S. J. (1977). *Training of aggressive children in conflict resolution skills.* Paper presented at meeting of Association for the Advancement of Behavior Therapy, Chicago.

Campbell, M., Schulman, D., & Rapoport, J. L. (1978). The current status of lithium therapy in child and adolescent psychiatry. *Journal of Child Psychiatry, 17,* 717–720.

Cantwell, D. P., & Baker, L. (1982). Depression in children with speech, language, and learning disorders. *Journal of Children in Contemporary Society, 15,* 51–59.

Cantwell, D. P., & Carlson, G. A. (Eds.). (1983). *Affective disorders in childhood and adolescence: An update.* New York: Spectrum.

Carey, M. P., Kelley, M. L., Buss, R. R., & Scott, W. O. N. (1986). Relationship of activity of depression in adolescents: Development of the Adolescent Activities Checklist. *Journal of Consulting & Clinical Psychology, 54,* 320–322.

Carlson, G. A., & Cantwell, D. P. (1980). Unmasking depression in children and adolescents. *American Journal of Psychiatry, 137,* 445–449.

Carlson, G. A., & Garber, J. (1986). Developmental issues in the classification of depression in children. In M. Rutter, C. E. Izard, & P. B. Read (Eds.), *Depression in young people: Developmental and clinical perspectives* (pp. 399–435). New York: Guilford.

Cautela, J. R. (1981). *Behavior analysis forms for clinical intervention* (Vol. 2). Champaign, IL: Research Press.

Cautela, J. R., Cautela, J., & Esonis, S. (1983). *Forms for behavior analysis with children.* Champaign, IL: Research Press.

Chambers, W. J., Puig-Antich, J., Hirsch, M., Paez, P., Ambrosini, P. J., Tabrizi, M. A., & Davies, M. (1985). The assessment of affective disorders in children and adolescents by semistructured interview: Test-retest reliability. *Archives of General Psychiatry, 43,* 696–702.

Chiles, J. A., Miller, M. L., & Cox, G. B. (1980). Depression in an adolescent delinquent population. *Archives of General Psychiatry, 37,* 1179–1184.

Cicchetti, D., & Schneider-Rosen, K. (1986). An organizational approach to childhood depression. In M. Rutter, C. E. Izard, & P. B. Read (Eds.), *Depression in young people: Developmental and clinical perspectives* (pp. 71–134). New York: Guilford.

Clarizio, H. F., & Payette, K. (1990). A survey of school psychologists' perspectives and practices with childhood depression. *Psychology in the Schools, 27,* 57–63.

Coddington, R. D. (1972). The significance of life events as etiological factors in the diseases of children: A study of normal population. *Journal of Psychosomatic Research, 16,* 205–213.

Colbert, P., Newman, B., Ney, P., & Young, J. (1982). Learning disabilities as a symptom of depression in children. *Journal of Learning Disabilities, 15,* 333–336.

Cole, P. M., & Kaslow, N. J. (1988). Interactional and cognitive strategies for affect regulation: A developmental perspective on childhood depression. In L. B. Alloy (Ed.), *Cognitive processes in depression* (pp. 310–343). New York: Guilford.

Compas, B. E. (1987). Stress and life events during childhood and adolescence. *Clinical Psychology Review, 7,* 275–302.

Cytryn, L., & McKnew, D. H. (1972). Proposed classification of childhood depression. *American Journal of Psychiatry, 129,* 149–155.

Cytryn, L., & McKnew, D. H. (1974). Factors influencing the changing clinical expression of the depressive process in children. *American Journal of Psychiatry, 131,* 879–881.

DiGangi, S. A., Behrens, J. T., & Maag, J. W. (1989). Dimensions of depression: Factors associated with hopelessness and suicidal intent among special populations. In R. B. Rutherford, Jr., & S. A. DiGangi (Eds.), *Severe behavior disorders of children and youth* (Vol. 12, pp. 47–53). Reston, VA: Council for Children with Behavioral Disorders.

Dolgan, J. I. (1990). Depression in children. *Pediatric Annals, 19,* 45–50.

Endicott, J., & Spitzer, R. L. (1978). A diagnostic interview: The Schedule for Affective Disorders and Schizophrenia. *Archives of General Psychiatry, 35,* 837–944.

Epstein, M. H., & Cullinan, D. (1984). Research issues in behavior disorders: A national survey. *Behavioral Disorders, 10,* 56–59.

Esman, A. H. (1981). Appropriate use of psychotropics in adolescents. *Hospital, 12,* 49–60.

Evans, S., Reinhart, J., & Succop, R. (1980). Failure to thrive: A study of 45 children and their families. In S. Harrison & J. McDermott (Eds.), *New directions in childhood psychopathology.* New York: International Universities Press.

Eyberg, S. M., & Robinson, E. A. (1982). Parent-child interaction training: Effects of family functioning. *Journal of Clinical Child Psychology, 11,* 130–137.

Feindler, E. L., & Fremouw, W. (1983). Stress inoculation training for adolescent anger problems. In D. Meichenbaum & M. Jaremko (Eds.), *Stress reduction and prevention* (pp. 451–485). New York: Plenum.

Fendrich, M., Weissman, M. M., & Warner, V. (1991). Longitudinal assessment of major depression and anxiety disorders in children. *Journal of the American Academy of Child and Adolescent Psychiatry, 30,* 38–42.

Fine, S., Forth, A., Gilbert, M., & Haley, G. (1991). Group therapy for adolescent depressive disorder: A comparison of social skills and therapeutic support. *Journal of the American Academy of Child and Adolescent Psychiatry, 30,* 79–85.

Fleming, J. E., & Offord, D. R. (1990). Epidemiology of childhood depressive disorders: A critical review. *Journal of the American Academy of Child and Adolescent Psychiatry, 29,* 571–580.

Forehand, R., Wells, K. C., & Griest, D. L. (1980). AD examination of the social validity of a parent training program. *Behavior Therapy, 11,* 488–502.

Forness, S. R. (1988). School characteristics of children and adolescents with depression. In R. B. Rutherford, Jr., C. M. Nelson, & S. R. Forness (Eds.), *Bases of severe behavioral disorders in children and youth* (pp. 177–203). San Diego: College-Hill Press.

Forness, S. R., Akiyama, K., & Campana, K. (1984, November). *Problems in antidepressant medication and classroom performance.* Paper presented at Annual Conference on Severe Behavioral Disorders of Children and Youth, Tempe, AZ.

Forness, S. R., & Kavale, K. A. (1988). Psychopharmacologic treatment: A note on classroom effects. *Journal of Learning Disabilities, 21,* 144–147.

Forness, S. R., & Kavale, K. A. (in press). School identification and response to conduct disorders. In A. Duchnowski & R. Friedman *(Eds.), Conduct disorders: Research, practice, and issues.* Tampa: Florida Mental Health Research Institute.

Frame, C., Matson, J. L., Sonis, W. A., Fialkov, M. J., & Kazdin, A. E. (1982). Behavioral treatment of depression in a prepubertal child. *Journal of Behavior Therapy & Experimental Psychiatry, 13,* 239–243.

Friedrich, W., Jacobs, J., & Reams, R. (1982). Depression and suicidal ideation in early adolescents. *Journal of Youth and Adolescence, 11,* 403–407.

Gadow, K. D. (1986). *Children on medication: Volume 2. Epilepsy, emotional disturbance, and adolescent disorders.* San Diego: College-Hill Press.

Gesten, E. L., Rains, M. H., Rapkin, B. D., Weissberg, R. P., Flores de Apodaca, R., Cowen, E. L., & Bowen, R. (1982). Training children in social problem-solving competencies: A first and second took. *American Journal of Community Psychology, 10,* 95–115.

Gittelman, R. (1980). The role of psychological tests for differential diagnosis in child psychiatry. *Journal of the American Academy of Child Psychiatry, 19,* 413–438.

Greist, J. H., & Greist, T. H. (1979). *Antidepressant treatment: The essentials.* Baltimore: Williams and Wilkins.

Grob, M. C., Klein, A. A., & Eisen, S. V. (1983). The role of the high school professional in identifying and managing adolescent suicidal behavior. *Journal of Youth & Adolescence, 12,* 163–173.

Guetzloe, E. C. (1989). *Youth suicide: What the educator should know.* Reston, VA: Council for Exceptional Children.

Hamilton, M. (1967). Development of a rating scale for primary depressive illness. *British Journal of Social & Clinical Psychology, 6,* 278–296.

Helsel, W. J., & Matson, J. L. (1984). Assessment of depression in children: The internal structure of the Child

Depression Inventory (CDI). *Behaviour Research and Therapy, 22,* 289–298.

Heward, W. L., Dardig, J. C., & Rossett, A. (1979). *Working with parents of handicapped children.* Columbus, OH: Charles E. Merrill.

Johnson, J. H., & McCutcheon, S. M. (1980). Assessing life stress in older children and adolescents: Preliminary findings with the Life Events Checklist. In I. G. Sarason & C. D. Spielberger (Eds.), *Stress and anxiety* (Vol. 7, pp. 111–125). Washington, DC: Hemisphere.

Kaplan, S. L., Hong, G. K., & Weinhold, C. (1984). Epidemiology of depressive symptomatology in adolescents. *Journal of the American Academy of Child Psychiatry, 23,* 91–98.

Karoly, P., & Rosenthal, M. (1977). Training parents in behavior modification: Effects on perceptions of family interaction and deviant child behavior. *Behavior Therapy, 8,* 406–410.

Kashani, J. H., Barbero, G. J., & Bolander, F. D. (1981). Depression in hospitalized pediatric patients. *Journal of the American Academy of Child Psychiatry, 20,* 123–134.

Kashani, J. H., Cantwell, D. P., Shekim, W. O., & Reid, J. C. (1982). Major depressive disorder in children admitted to an inpatient community mental health center. *American Journal of Psychiatry, 139,* 671–672.

Kashani, J. H., McGee, R. O., Clarkson, S. E., Anderson, J. C., Walton, L. A., Williams, S., Silva, P. A., Robins, A. J., Cytryn, L., & McKnew, D. H. (1983). Depression in a sample of 9-year old children. *Archives of General Psychiatry, 40,* 1217–1223.

Kashani, J. H., Ray, J. S., & Carlson, G. A. (1984). Depression and depression-like states in preschool-age children in a child development unit. *American Journal of Psychiatry, 141,* 1397–1402.

Kashani, J. H., Shekim, W, O., & Reid, J. C. (1984). Amitriptyline in children with major depressive disorder: A double-blind crossover pilot study. *Journal of Child Psychiatry, 23,* 248–251.

Kashani, J. H., & Simonds, J. F. (1979). The incidence of depression in children. *American Journal of Psychiatry, 136,* 1203–1205.

Kaslow, N. J., & Rehm, L. P. (1991). Childhood depression. In R. J. Morris & T. R. Kratochwill (Eds.), *The practice of child therapy* (2nd ed., pp. 27–51). New York: Pergamon.

Kazdin, A. E. (1985). *Treatment of antisocial behavior in children and adolescents.* Homewood, IL: Dorsey.

Kazdin, A. E. (1987). Assessment of childhood depression: Current issues and strategies. *Behavioral Assessment, 9,* 291–319.

Kazdin, A. E. (1988). Childhood depression. In E. J. Mash & L. G. Terdal (Eds.), *Behavioral assessment of childhood disorders* (2nd ed., pp. 157–195). New York: Guilford.

Kazdin, A. E. (1989). Evaluation of the pleasure scale in the assessment of anhedonia in children. *Journal of the American Academy of Child and Adolescent Psychiatry, 28,* 364–372.

Kazdin, A. E. (1990). Childhood depression. *Journal of Child Psychology & Psychiatry, 31,* 121–160.

Kazdin, A. E., Colbus, D., & Rodgers, A. (1986). Assessment of depressive disorder among psychiatrically disturbed children. *Journal of Abnormal Child Psychology, 14,* 499–515.

Kazdin, A. E., French, A., & Unis, A. (1983). Child, mother, and father evaluations of depression in psychiatric inpatient children. *Journal of Abnormal Child Psychology, 11,* 167–180.

Kazdin, A. E., Rodgers, A., & Colbus, D. (1986). The Hopelessness Scale for Children: Psychometric characteristics and concurrent validity. *Journal of Consulting & Clinical Psychology, 54,* 241–245.

Kendall, P. C., Hollon, S. D., Beck, A. T., Hammen, C. L., & Ingram, R. E. (1987). Issues and recommendations regarding use of the Beck Depression Inventory. *Cognitive Therapy & Research, 11,* 289–299.

Kishimoto, A., Ogura, C., Hazama, H., & Inoue, H. (1983). Long-term prophylactic effects of carbamazopine in affective disorder. *British Journal of Psychiatry, 143,* 327–331.

Klein, D. F., Gittelman, R., Quitkin, F., & Rifkin, A. (1980). *Diagnosis and drug treatment of psychiatric disorders in adults and children* (2nd ed.). Baltimore: Williams and Wilkins.

Kovacs, M. (1985). The Children's Depression Inventory. *Psychopharmacology Bulletin, 21,* 995–998.

Kovacs, M. (1989). Affective disorder in children and adolescents. *American Psychologist, 44,* 209–215.

Lefkowitz, M. M., & Burton, N. (1978). Childhood depression: A critique of the concept. *Psychological Bulletin, 85,* 716–726.

Lefkowitz, M. M., & Tesiny, E. P. (1985). Depression in children: Prevalence and correlates. *Journal of Consulting & Clinical Psychology, 53,* 647–656.

Leitenberg, H., Yost, L. W., & Carroll-Wilson, M. (1986). Negative cognitive errors in children: Questionnaire development, normative data, and comparisons between children with and without self-reported symptoms of depression, low self-esteem, and evaluation anxiety. *Journal of Consulting & Clinical Psychology, 54,* 528–536.

Lewinsohn, P. N. (1974). Clinical and theoretical aspects of depression. In K. S. Calhoun, H. E. Adams, & K. M. Mitchell (Eds.), *Innovative treatment methods of psychopathology* (pp. 63–120). New York: Wiley.

Lobovits, D. A., & Handal, P. J. (1985). Childhood depression: Prevalence using DSM-III criteria and validity of parent and child depression scales. *Journal of Pediatric Psychology, 10,* 45–54.

Lochman, J. W., & Lampron, L. B. (1986). Situational Social problem-solving skills and self-esteem of aggressive and nonaggressive boys. *Journal of Abnormal Child Psychology, 13,* 527–538.

Maag, J. W. (1988a). Treatment of childhood and adolescent depression: Review and recommendations. In R. B. Rutherford, Jr., & J. W. Maag (Eds.), *Severe behavior disorders of children and youth* (Vol. 11, pp. 49–63). Reston, VA: Council for Children with Behavioral Disorders.

Maag, J. W. (1988b). *Treatment of adolescent depression with stress inoculation training.* Unpublished doctoral dissertation, Arizona State University, Tempe.

Maag, J. W. (1989). Assessment in social skills training: Methodological and conceptual issues for research and practice. *Remedial & Special Education, 10*(4), 6–17.

Maag, J. W. (1990). Social skills training in schools. *Special Services in the Schools, 6,* 1–19.

Maag, J. W., & Behrens, J. T. (1989a). Depression and cognitive self-statements of learning disabled and seriously emotionally disturbed adolescents. *Journal of Special Education, 23,* 17–27.

Maag, J. W., & Behrens, J. T. (1989b). Epidemiologic data on seriously emotionally disturbed and learning disabled adolescents reporting extreme depressive symptomatology. *Behavioral Disorders, 15,* 21–27.

Maag, J. W., Behrens, S. T., & DiGangi, S. A. (1991). Dysfunctional cognitions associated with adolescent depression: Findings across special populations. Manuscript submitted for publication.

Maag, J. W., Parks, B. T., & Rutherford, R. B., Jr. (1988). Generalization and behavior covariation of aggression in children receiving stress inoculation therapy. *Child & Family Behavior Therapy, 10,* 29–47.

Maag, J. W., & Rutherford, R. B., Jr. (1987). Behavioral and learning characteristics of childhood and adolescent depression: Implications for special educators. In S. Braaten, R. B. Rutherford, Jr., & J. W. Maag (Eds.), *Programming for adolescents with behavioral disorders* (Vol. 3, pp. 55–70). Reston, VA: Council for Children with Behavioral Disorders.

Maag, J. W., & Rutherford, R. B., Jr. (1988). Review and synthesis of three components for identifying depressed students.

In R. B. Rutherford, Jr., C. M. Nelson, & S. R. Forness (Eds.), *Bases of severe behavioral disorders in children and youth* (pp. 205–230). San Diego, CA: College-Hill Press.

Maag, J. W., Rutherford, R. B., Jr., & Parks, B. T. (1988). Secondary school professionals; ability to identify depression in adolescents. *Adolescence, 23,* 73–82.

Malmquist, C. P. (1977). Childhood depression: A clinical and behavioral perspective. In J. G. Schulterbrandt & A. Raskin (Eds.), *Depression in children: Diagnosis, treatment and conceptual models* (pp. 33–59). New York: Raven.

Matson, J. L., Esveldt-Dawson, K., Andraski, F., Ollendick, T. H., Petti, T. A., & Hersen, M. (1980). Observation and generalization effects of social skills training with emotionally disturbed children. *Behavior Therapy, 11,* 522–531.

Matson, J. L., Rotatori, A. F., & Helsel, W. J. (1983). Development of a rating scale to measure social skills in children: The Matson Evaluation of Social Skills with Youngsters (MESSY). *Behaviour Research and Therapy, 21,* 335–340.

Mattison, R. E., Humphrey, F. J., Kales, S. N., Handford, H. A., Finkenbinder, R. L., & Hernit, R. C. (1986). Psychiatric background and diagnoses of children evaluated for special class placement. *Journal of the American Academy of Child Psychiatry, 25,* 514–520.

McClellan, J. M., Rupert, M. P. M., Reichler, R. J., & Sylvester, C. E. (1990). Attention deficit disorder in children at risk for anxiety and depression. *Journal of the American Academy of Child and Adolescent Psychiatry, 29,* 534–539.

McConnell, S. R. (1987). Entrapment effects and the generalization and maintenance of social skills training for elementary school students with behavioral disorders. *Behavioral Disorders, 12,* 252–263.

Meichenbaum, D. (1985). *Stress inoculation training.* New York: Pergamon.

Mezzich, A. C., & Mezzich, J. E. (1979).

Symptomatology of depression in adolescence. *Journal of Personality Assessment, 43,* 267–275.

Mitchell, J., McCauley, E., Burke, P. M., & Moss, S. J. (1988). Phenomenology of depression in children and adolescents. *Journal of the American Academy of Child and Adolescent Psychiatry, 27,* 12–20.

Myers, K., McCauley, E., Calderon, R., Mitchell, J., Burke, P., & Schloredt, K. (1991). Risks for suicidality in major depressive disorders. *Journal of the American Academy of Child and Adolescent Psychiatry, 30,* 86–94.

Nezu, A. M., Nezu, C. M., & Perri, M. G. (1989). *Problem-solving therapy for depression: Theory, research and clinical guidelines.* New York: Wiley.

Patterson, G. R. (1982). *Coercive family process.* Eugene, OR: Castalia.

Patterson, G. R., & Fleischman, M. J. (1979). Maintenance of treatment effects: Some considerations concerning family systems and follow-up data. *Behavior Therapy, 10,* 168–185.

Peterson, L., Wonderlich, S. A., Reaven, N. M., & Mullins, L. L. (1987). Adult educators' response to depression and stress in children. *Journal of Social & Clinical Psychology, 5,* 51–58.

Petti, T. A. (1978). Depression in hospitalized child psychiatry patients: Approaches to measuring depression. *Journal of the American Academy of Child Psychiatry, 22,* 11–21.

Petti, T. A. (1983). Imipramine in the treatment of depressed children. In D. P. Cantwell & G. A. Carlson (Eds.), *Affective disorders in childhood and adolescence: An update* (pp. 375–415). New York: Spectrum.

Petti, T. A., Bornstein, M., Delamater, A., & Conners, C. K. (1980). Evaluation and multimodal treatment of a depressed prepubertal girl. *Journal of the American Academy of Child Psychiatry, 19,* 690–702.

Petti, T. A., & Law, W. (1982). Imipramine treatment of depressed children: A double-blind pilot study. *Journal of Clinical Psychopharmacology, 2,* 107–110.

Powers, D. (1979). The teacher and the adolescent suicide threat. *Journal of School Health, 49,* 561–563.

Poznanski, E. O., Cook, S. C., & Carroll, B. J. (1979). A depression rating scale for children. *Pediatrics, 64,* 442–450.

Preskorn, S. H., Weller, E. B., & Weller, R. A. (1982). Depression in children: Relationship between plasma imipramine levels and response. *Journal of Clinical Psychiatry, 43,* 450–453.

Puig-Antich, J. (1982). Major depression and conduct disorder in prepuberty. *Journal of Child Psychiatry, 21,* 118–128.

Puig-Antich, J., & Gittelman, R. (1982). Depression in childhood and adolescence. In E. S. Paykel (Ed.), *Handbook of affective disorders* (pp. 379–392). New York: Guilford.

Rehm, L. P. (1977). A self-control model of depression. *Behavior Therapy, 8,* 787–804.

Reinherz, H. Z., Stewart-Berghauer, G., Pakiz, B., Frost, A. K., Moeykens, B. A., & Holmes, W. M. (1989). The relationship of early risk and current mediators to depressive symptomatology in adolescence. *Journal of the American Academy of Child and Adolescent Psychiatry, 28,* 942–947.

Reynolds, W. M. (1983, March). *Depression in adolescents: Measurement, epidemiology, and correlates.* Paper presented at annual meeting of National Association of School Psychologists, Detroit.

Reynolds, W. M. (1984). Depression in children and adolescents: Phenomenology, evaluation and treatment. *School Psychology Review, 13,* 171–182.

Reynolds, W. M. (1985). Depression in childhood and adolescence: Diagnosis, assessment, intervention strategies and research. In T. R. Kratochwill (Ed.), *Advances in school psychology* (Vol. 4, pp. 133–189). Hillsdale, NJ: Lawrence Erlbaum.

Reynolds, W. M. (1986a). A model for the screening and identification of depressed children and adolescents in school settings. *Professional School Psychology, 1,* 117–129.

Reynolds, W. M. (1986b). *Reynolds child depression scale.* Odessa, FL: Psychological Assessment Resources.

Reynolds, W. M. (1986c). *Reynolds adolescent depression scale.* Odessa, FL: Psychological Assessment Resources.

Reynolds, W. M., & Coats, K. I. (1986). A comparison of cognitive-behavioral therapy and relaxation training for the treatment of depression in adolescents. *Journal of Consulting & Clinical Psychology, 54,* 653–660.

Reynolds, W. M. & Miller, K. L. (1985). Depression and learned helplessness in mentally retarded and nonmentally retarded adolescents: An initial investigation. *Applied Research in Mental Retardation, 6,* 295–306.

Rie, H. E. (1966). Depression in childhood: A survey of some pertinent contributions. *Journal of the Academy of Child Psychiatry, 5,* 635–685.

Rizzo, J. V., & Zabel, R. H. (1988). *Educating children and adolescents with behavioral disorders: An integrative approach.* Boston: Allyn & Bacon.

Rochlin, G. (1959). The loss complex. *Journal of the American Psychoanalytic Association, 7,* 299–316.

Rutter, M. R. (1986). The developmental psychopathology of depression: Issues and perspectives. In M. R. Rutter, C. E. Izard, & P. B. Read (Eds.), *Depression in young people: Developmental and clinical perspectives* (pp. 3–30). New York: Guilford.

Schloss, P. J., Schloss, C. N., & Harris, L. (1984). A multiple baseline analysis of an interpersonal skills training program for depressed youth. *Behavioral Disorders, 9,* 182–188.

Seifer, R., Nurcombe, B., Scioli, A., & Grapentine, W. L. (1989). Is major depressive disorder in childhood a distinct diagnostic entity? *Journal of the American Academy of Child and Adolescent Psychiatry, 28,* 935–941.

Seligman, M. E. P., & Peterson, C. (1986). A learned helplessness perspective on childhood depression: Theory and research. In

M. Rutter, C. E. Izard, & P. B. Read (Eds.), *Depression in young people: Developmental and clinical perspectives* (pp. 223–249). New York: Guilford.

Shure, M. B., & Spivack, G. (1972). Means-ends thinking, adjustment and social class among elementary school-age children. *Journal of Consulting & Clinical Psychology, 38,* 348–353.

Smucker, M. R., Craighead, W. E., Craighead, L. W., & Green, B. J. (1986). Normative and reliability data for the Children's Depression Inventory. *Journal of Abnormal Child Psychology, 14,* 25–39.

Spitz, R. A., & Wolf, K. M. (1946). Anaclitic depression: An inquiry into the genesis of psychiatric conditions in early childhood. *Psychoanalytic Study of the Child, 2,* 313–341.

Spitzer, R. L., Endicott, J., & Robins, E. (1978). Research diagnostic criteria: Rationale and reliability. *Archives of General Psychiatry, 35,* 773–782.

Stark, K. D. (1990). *Childhood depression: School-based intervention.* New York: Guilford.

Stark, K. D., Kaslow, N. J., & Reynolds, W. M. (1987). A comparison of the relative efficacy of self-control therapy and a behavioral problem-solving therapy for depression in children. *Journal of Abnormal Child Psychology, 15,* 91–113.

Stevenson, D. T., & Romney, D. M. (1984). Depression in learning disabled children. *Journal of Learning Disabilities, 17,* 579–582.

Strauss, C. C., Last, C. G., Hersen, M., & Kazdin, A. E. (1988). Association between anxiety and depression in children and adolescents. *Journal of Abnormal Child Psychology, 16,* 57–68.

Teri, L. (1982a). The use of the Beck Depression Inventory with adolescents. *Journal of Abnormal Child Psychology, 10,* 277–282.

Teri, L. (1982b). Depression in adolescence: Its relationship to assertion and various aspects of self-image. *Journal of Clinical Child Psychology, 11,* 101–106.

Thompson, R. J. (1986). Behavior problems in children with developmental and learning disabilities. *International Academy of Research in Learning Disabilities Monograph Series, 3,* 1–125.

Walker, H. M., & McConnell, S. R. (1988). *Walker-McConnell Scale of Social Competence and School Adjustment.* Austin, TX: Pro-Ed.

Walker, H. M., & Severson, H. H. (1990). *Systematic screening for behavior disorders,* Longmont, CO: Sopris West.

Wolfe, V. V., Finch, A. J., Jr., Saylor, CA. F., Blount, R. L., Pallymeyer, T. P., & Carek, D. J. (1987). Negative affectivity in children: A multitrait-multimethod investigation. *Journal of Consulting & Clinical Psychology, 55,* 245–250.

Adolescent S Prevention and Interve..

Dave Capuzzi

dolescent suicide has become a critical problem in the United States. Recent yearly estimates (Haffen & Frandsen, 1986) report as many as 400,000 attempts and 7,000 completions among the adolescent population in this country. The extent of the adolescent suicide problem is difficult to identify with an exact number because many suicides are confused as accidents or reported as accidents because of family embarrassment, religious beliefs, community discomfort, or denial of the adolescent suicide problem. During the last five years adolescent suicide has moved from being cited as the third leading cause of death among the 11- to 24-year age group to the second leading cause. Only accidents—quite often automobile accidents—rank higher.

Understanding the Problem

Myths About Adolescent Suicide

One of the first steps in developing an understanding of adolescent suicide is to identify the commonly believed myths regarding teenagers who attempt or complete the act of suicide. Some of the most typically cited misconceptions are discussed briefly in the following paragraphs.

- *Adolescents who talk about suicide never do it.* This is probably one of the most widely held misconceptions. In reality almost all suicidal adolescents have made an attempt (verbally or nonverbally—and usually verbally) to let someone else know that life seems too much to handle. A suicide attempt is a cry for help to identify options other than death that will decrease the pain of living. Verbal reats should always be taken seriously and never assumed to be only for the purpose of attracting attention or manipulating others.

■ *Suicide happens without warning.* Most suicidal adolescents leave numerous hints and warnings about their suicidal ideations and intentions. Clues can be verbal or in the form of suicidal gestures such as taking just a few sleeping pills or becoming accident-prone. Quite often the social support network of the suicide-prone adolescent is small. As stress escalates and options other than suicide seem few, suicidal adolescents may withdraw from an already small circle of friends, making it more difficult for others to notice warning signs.

■ *Adolescents from affluent families attempt or complete suicide more often than adolescents from poor families.* This, too, is a myth. Suicide is evenly divided among socioeconomic groups.

■ *Once an adolescent is suicidal, he or she is suicidal forever.* Most adolescents are suicidal for a limited time. In my experience, the 24- to 72-hour period around the peak of the "crisis" is the most dangerous. If counselors and other mental health practitioners can monitor this crisis period and then get the adolescent into regularly scheduled, long-term counseling/therapy, there is a strong possibility that another suicidal crisis will never occur. The more effort that is made to help an adolescent identify stressors and develop problem-solving skills during this post-suicidal crisis period and the more time that passes, the better is the prognosis.

■ *If an adolescent attempts suicide and survives, he or she will never make an additional attempt.* There is a difference between the adolescent who experiences a suicidal crisis but does not attempt it, as in the situation above, and the adolescent who actually tries to bring an end to life. An adolescent who carries through with an attempt has identified a plan, had access to the means, and maintained a high enough energy level to follow through. He or she knows that a second or third attempt would be in the realm of possibility. If counseling/therapy has not taken place or has not been successful during the period following the attempt, additional attempts may be made. Most likely, each follow-up attempt will become more lethal.

■ *Adolescents who commit suicide always leave notes.* Only a small percentage of adolescents who complete the act of suicide leave notes. This myth is common and is one of the reasons why many suicides are classified and reported as accidents by friends, family members, physicians, and investigating officers when suicide actually has taken place.

■ *Most adolescent suicides happen late at night.* This myth is not true for the simple reason that most suicidal adolescents actually want help. Mid to late morning and mid to late afternoon are the time periods when most attempts are made, since a family member or friend is more likely to be around to intervene than would be the case late at night.

■ *The word suicide should never be used when talking to adolescents, because using the word gives some adolescents the idea.* This is simply not true. One cannot put the idea of suicide into the mind of an adolescent who is not suicidal. If an adolescent is suicidal and the word "suicide" is voiced, it can invite him or her to verbalize feelings of despair and help establish rapport and trust. If a suicidal adolescent thinks someone knows that he or she is suicidal and realizes the person is afraid to broach the subject, it can bring the adolescent closer to the point of making an attempt by contributing to feelings of despair and helplessness.

■ *Every adolescent who attempts suicide is depressed.* Depression is a common component of the profile of a suicidal adolescent, but depression is not always a component. Many adolescents simply want to escape their present set of circumstances and do not have the problem-solving skills to cope more effectively, reduce stress, and work toward a more promising future.

■ *Suicide is hereditary.* Suicide, like physical and sexual abuse, tends to run in families, which has given rise to this myth. Although suicide is not genetically inherited, members of families do share the same emotional climate since parents model coping and stress management skills as well as a level of high or low self-esteem. The suicide of one family member tends to increase the risk among other family members that suicide will be viewed as an appropriate way to solve a problem or set of problems.

Causes of Adolescent Suicide

The causes of suicide among teenagers in the United States have been discussed by a number of experts (Haffen & Frandsen, 1986; Davis, 1983; Husain & Vandiver, 1984; Fairchild, 1986). The parameters commonly identified for consideration are (a) the adolescent struggle to develop and integrate a unique identity, (b) familial factors, and (c) environmental factors.

The Adolescent Experience

Early adolescence is second only to infancy in terms of physical growth and emotional development. It is a time during which many of the assumptions of childhood must be left behind as the demands and expectations of others increase with each stage of physical and sexual maturity bringing the adolescent closer to the world of "adults." Even though adolescents may look like young adults quite early, they cannot approach relationships and analyze life circumstances until they have had time to assess a number of areas. Rather than discussing the developmental tasks of adolescence in the traditional sense, the areas of adolescent development that seem to be factors in the development of suicidal tendencies in adolescents will be overviewed.

Self-Esteem. In general, adolescents who become suicidal experience feelings of low self-esteem. These feelings have been present since early childhood, and such a young person may have been other-directed, rather than inner-directed, for a number of years prior to adolescence. Parents of adolescents such as these typically comment that their child seemed to lose control and judgment in the presence of peers, and that quite often they dreaded the arrival of their child's friends for an afternoon visit or a weekend stay.

Poor Communication. Besides low self-esteem, many suicidal adolescents have developed a pattern of poor communication with parents, other adults and, quite often, friends. These adolescents never have been at ease with the prospect of sharing their feelings about parents, siblings, teachers, and friends. As time passes, it becomes easier and more acceptable simply to keep their feelings inside and experience frustration and discomfort than to attempt to deal with those feelings as they arise. Teachers, parents, and neighbors seldom have many verbal cues that relationships, circumstances, or expectations have been upsetting to these children.

Achievement Orientation. In addition to low self-esteem and poor communication skills, suicide-prone adolescents may be quite achievement-oriented. Although it would be a mistake to assume that *all* achievement-oriented adolescents may become suicidal, experience with counseling the suicidal adolescent points to the realization that high achievement is one way to compensate for feelings of low self-worth. Achievement can be focused on any of a number of modalities—high grades, participation in athletic activities, developing a reputation as the "class clown," the best-dressed, most popular. All of these are ways to achieve prominence among peers.

Poor Problem-Solving Skills. Poor problem-solving ability is also characteristic of many adolescents who become suicidal. This trait is usually observable prior to adolescence, epitomized by a lack of resourcefulness in generating options for solving a problem, coping with a difficult relationship, or planning for the future.

Narrow Commitments. Lack of resourcefulness is particularly troublesome in conjunction with another trait that often is part of the developmental pattern of the suicidal adolescent—total commitment to a relationship or to a goal for the future. Suicidal adolescents often develop a tunnel-visioned perspective. A relationship may become so important that other friendships are dropped. A goal may begin to dominate every decision, allocation of time, and thoughts about the future. Commitment, total and unwavering, often becomes the theme for patterning daily, weekly, and monthly activities and priorities. When an important relationship ends or a goal becomes unachievable, self-esteem is lowered, feelings are kept secret and left unexpressed, achievement is roadblocked, and problem-solving skills are frozen in past and current maladaptive patterns, resulting in escalation of stress and anxiety.

High Stress. Most suicidal adolescents have a history of high stress. As they move from childhood to adolescence and the demands of the peer group and the expectations of adults become even greater, they become even less resourceful in their ability to manage stress. During periods of high stress, they may spend more and more time considering the option of suicide and planning for the time, place, and means.

In addition to the above traits that contribute to an adolescent's inclination to consider, attempt, or complete the act of suicide, two other traits should be noted. In my experience, many (though not all) suicidal adolescents have a relatively small network of social support. Friendships that provide opportunities for self-disclosure may be lacking or few in number since the act of sharing feelings or thoughts is usually quite difficult. Finally, I believe that many suicidal adolescents have been bothered by feelings of guilt and not quite "measuring-up" for most of their lives. Adolescents who have low self-esteem and are other-directed usually are never quite satisfied with anything they do, say, or achieve and are likely to feel guilty about their perceived lack of "achievement."

Family Factors

A number of authors (Bigrar, Gauthier, Bouchard, & Jasse, 1966; Jacobziner, 1965; McAnarney, 1979; Otto, 1972; Truckman & Connon, 1962) have discussed family disorganization as a characteristic of the families of suicidal adolescents. Divorce, death, unemployment, drug abuse, physical and sexual abuse, and mental illness are all factors contributing to disorganization. McAnarney (1979) stated that, "In societies where family ties are close, suicidal rates are low and conversely, where families are not close, suicidal rates are high." A number of family factors have become apparent to me as contributing causes of the adolescent suicide crisis in the United States.

Poor Communication. In many families of adolescents who have attempted or completed suicide, family members seem to be lacking in communication. Families report that they have great difficulty communicating clearly and consistently with one another (whether between parents or between parent and child). Even when the family eats breakfast or dinner together, quite often the meal is eaten in silence or with family members' attention directed to a television program. Very often, parents have not modeled a positive, articulate communication style for their children to imitate and develop skills. Parents may have little knowledge of the tribulation their adolescent children experience, and adolescents may have difficulty talking with peers and siblings, while talking with parents may seem unthinkable.

Loss. Loss is something that requires a grieving and adjustment process before daily frustrations and responsibilities can be coped with as before. Losses involving dissolution of the nuclear family because of divorce, death of a family member or close friend, termination of employment, changes in health status, or moves to a new community require the energy to develop changed perspectives and the problem-solving skills to make new beginnings or change life styles. Frequently, suicidal adolescents are from families that have experienced one or more major losses in the preceding one or two years.

Dual-Career Families. More and more American families are finding that two incomes are necessary to support a family. When both parents work, two adults may be bringing the stresses of employment back into the family system. In addition, time to accomplish household tasks, shop for groceries, schedule medical and dental appointments, and complete necessary errands is reduced. Parents may be too tired to spend as much time with their adolescent children as they would like or unable to give undivided attention to an adolescent at a time when he or she needs to talk.

Unless all family members are good at managing both time and stress, saying "no" to unnecessary work-related or other responsibilities, helping one another and meeting each other's needs at the time the needs arise, the family climate may be one of tension and lack of receptiveness. Adolescents may not think they can turn to family members for comfort and assistance.

Single Parenting. The role of the single parent has long been characterized by escalated responsibility, lowered income, high stress, and lack of time. A single parent may be so busy attempting to make a home for his or her children that little time is allotted to the basics of a parent-child relationship. Many troubled adolescents come from single-parent homes.

Blended Families. When two adults who have custody of the children from a previous marriage decide to form a new family, the dynamics of the family constellation can become quite complex. Some adolescents have great difficulty adjusting to a "substitute" parent, a new set of guidelines for behavior and discipline, additional siblings, less personal space, or a different home in a new neighborhood or community. Parents should be encouraged to seek family counseling when adolescent children show signs of depression and poor adjustment to the new family group.

Mid-life Transition. Parents of adolescent children are usually between the ages of 35 and 50. As parents see their children mature to the point of looking like young adults, they may begin the process of assessing themselves as personalities and as partners. They may evaluate their careers and financial progress and begin thinking about employment changes. Issues between partners may surface or resurface if they were not dealt with earlier. Just at the time when children need more time and attention than ever, parents may be too focused on their own status and too concerned about "time running out" to notice and respond to the needs of their adolescent children.

Abuse. Families in which physical or sexual abuse is occurring or in which substance abuse is problematic may be at high-risk for adolescent suicide. Parents who are abusive of each other, themselves, or their children are typically low in self-esteem, stressed, poor communicators and problem-solvers, and financially distressed. Children of these parents have not been taught to feel good about themselves and to problem-solve effectively. During adolescence, escaping the pain of this type of family atmosphere or the self-deprecating viewpoint they have probably developed may become the most predominant motivation for suicide.

Environmental Factors

Adolescents may be concerned and upset about a number of trends in today's society.

Pressure to Achieve. The pressure to achieve academically and vocationally in our culture is often felt keenly by today's adolescents. When families and teachers pressure teenagers to achieve, some may choose to commit suicide rather than to fail and disappoint others.

Mobility. Groups with the greatest amount of mobility are those living in central or rapidly changing portions of a city, immigrants, and families working for large companies that transfer them to different cities every few years (McAnarney, 1979). In addition, adolescents are more mobile than ever before because of improved public transportation and access to private vehicles. Families and their adolescent children often experience alienation, isolation, and loneliness when circumstances result in their changing communities or moving constantly from one neighborhood to another.

Uncertainty About the Future. Many adolescents feel that school and work will only become more competitive and difficult. Many believe that they must prepare for a much lower standard of living than that of their parents because of the escalating costs of housing, utilities, automobiles, and so on in relation to the slower rise in salaries. Some are afraid that no matter how much effort they exert, they already are destined for failure and, perhaps, should not even make a try at life.

Graduation From High School. Although high school students often complain about the expectations of teachers, principals, and school boards and talk frequently about the anticipated joys of finishing school, many teenagers are threatened by the approach of high school graduation. For many, graduation symbolizes the transition to young manhood or womanhood and the initiation of a life more independent of other family members. Even though adolescents tell friends, family members, and other adults that they can hardly wait to finish secondary school and that they have everything under control for later, they may be quite apprehensive. The transition to the next stage of development can be a period of extremely high stress.

Nuclear Threat. Most of today's young people are totally aware of the reality that no nation or component of the world community can be independent or safe from the actions, and the consequences of those actions, of another country. The recent nuclear accident in Chernobyl and resultant radioactive fallout reinforces the fact that no one will be safe during a nuclear war no matter where nuclear detonation takes place. Some adolescents cite these observations as reasons for "opting out."

Drug Abuse. The United States is experiencing an epidemic of drug use and abuse. Opportunities to experiment with marijuana, alcohol, and other drugs are presented to fifth and sixth graders in most school districts. Pressure from peers, a mistaken sense of autonomy and feeling of well-being, and lack of funding to provide school-based prevention, intervention, and after-care programs often result in heavy use and abuse of drugs during the early high school years. Since problem-solving ability, self-esteem, and communication skills—which already may be inadequate—are never enhanced through drug use, suicide-prone adolescents usually become even higher risks as drug experimentation and dependency increase.

Approaches to Prevention

The Role of Families and Friends

In addition to understanding the myths connected with adolescent suicide, as well as the impacts of adolescence as a developmental stage and of certain familial and social factors, family members and friends should familiarize themselves with the signs and symptoms of impending suicide. The four following areas should be assessed by anyone concerned about the welfare of an adolescent child or teenage friend: changes in behavior, verbal cues, themes or preoccupations in thinking, and personality traits.

Noticing Changes in Behavior

In general, any behavior that is decided change for a particular adolescent should be noted. Warning signs include: sudden drops in grades for a good student; difficulty with concentration; loss of interest in friends, hobbies, or goals; changes in patterns of sleeping and eating; experimentation with marijuana, alcohol, and other drugs; lack of cooperation at school or at home; running away; and sexual promiscuity.

Depression is also a symptom of an impending suicidal crisis. When depression, combined with other behavior changes, occurs repeatedly, for periods lasting longer than a week, it is a cause for concern. Family members and friends should realize that when an adolescent who has been struggling with periodic depressive episodes suddenly improves, the possibility of a suicide attempt or completion may be imminent. It is not logical for an adolescent who has seemed troubled for some time to change overnight. Quite often an abrupt change in emotional tenor results after the individual has made the decision about when and how to make a suicide attempt.

Listening for Verbal Cues

Changes in behavior, such as the ones described above, also may be accompanied by a number of verbal warnings. Always listen for statements such as the following:

■ I can't go on.
■ I'm going to kill myself.
■ I wish I were dead.
■ I'm not the person I used to be.
■ The only way out is to die.
■ You won't be seeing me around any more.
■ You're going to regret how you've treated me.
■ Life is too much to put up with.
■ Life has no meaning any more.
■ I'm getting out.
■ I'm tired.
■ If (such and such) happens, I'll kill myself.
■ If (such and such) doesn't happen, I'll kill myself.
■ I'm going home.
■ Here, take this (cassette, jewelry, etc.); I won't be needing it any more.

Although the "language" of adolescents varies from year to year and from one part of the country to another, the above statements convey the meaning that adolescents communicate as their stress and discomfort make suicide seem like an acceptable problem-solving option. Statements similar to the ones listed above invite additional disclosure and description of the person's circumstances and feelings.

Listening for Themes or Preoccupations in Thinking

Themes or preoccupations also seem to dominate the thinking pattern of young persons who are contemplating suicide. Although suicidal adolescents often have difficulty sharing feelings and thoughts, self-disclosure should be encouraged for the following themes:

- Wanting to escape from a situation that seems intolerable (e.g., physical abuse, difficulty at school, drugs, lack of friends)
- Wanting to join a friend or family member who has died
- Wanting to gain the attention of others
- Wanting to manipulate others
- Wanting to be punished
- Wanting to avoid being punished
- Wanting to control when death will occur
- Wanting to end a seemingly unresolvable conflict
- Wanting to become a martyr for a cause
- Wanting to punish the survivors
- Wanting revenge

Noticing Personality Traits

Traits that often characterize suicidal adolescents were discussed earlier. Low self-esteem, poor communication skills, high achievement orientation, poor problem-solving skills, total commitment to a relationship or a goal, high stress, small social support networks, and feelings of guilt should all be noted, especially if they are observed in conjunction with behavior changes, verbal cues, and preoccupations that could serve as motivations for a suicide attempt.

The Role of School Counselors

Suicide prevention measures can and should be taken at the elementary level and continue through middle and high school years. Traits such as low self-esteem, weak problem-solving ability, high stress, and poor communication skills are noticeable in first and second graders. At this level, counseling programs can be initiated for the purpose of enhancing self-esteem or improving communication skills. These services can be continued or begun at middle and high school levels as well. Because these traits are so often part of the profile of suicidal adolescents, early intervention and prevention would seem essential.

Further, counselors who work with students in grades five through twelve can provide information about the signs and symptoms of an impending suicidal crisis through classroom presentations on the topic. These presentations should be direct (the word "suicide" should be used) and should focus upon encouraging students who are concerned about themselves or their friends to ask for assistance. Students should be made aware that when they are concerned about a friend, someone in the school, as well as the friend's parent or parents, should be alerted. The reason for involvement outside of the family is that parents, when told that their child is in difficulty and may be suicidal, often react in the same way as parents who are told that a child is using or abusing drugs—with denial or anger.

Faculty/staff and administration must participate in inservice education on the topic of preventing adolescent suicide prior to presenting programs to students. Not only must school personnel understand the dynamics of the suicidal adolescent, but they also must be sensitive to the necessity of being able to provide or refer a person to counseling services quickly so that attempted suicides can be averted.

Approaching Crisis Management

When called upon to assist an adolescent who is suspected of being in a suicidal crisis, the counselor can take a number of steps to ascertain the severity of the crisis and the lethality or risk that must be monitored.

1. *Be a good listener.* Understanding and respect must be conveyed for everything that is being shared by the young person. Whatever the circumstances, concerns, and feelings are, they are, for this client, reality. Counselors must begin with reality as perceived by the client even if the counselor would not interpret the circumstances in the same way.

2. *Be nonjudgmental.* If an adolescent is suicidal, he or she may have great difficulty communicating the thoughts and feelings that have led to the current feelings of desperation and hopelessness. Rapport cannot be built through comments such as, "You can't be thinking such thoughts," "It's against the teachings of your religion" or, "It would be such an embarrassment to your family."

3. *Be supportive.* When talking with an adolescent who may be at risk, it is important to be reassuring. This does not mean that the counselor should convey messages such as, "Things aren't really that bad" (for the client, things *are* bad) or "The situation will take care of itself" (circumstances usually do not become better without effort on the part of both client and counselor). Being supportive *does* mean that the counselor communicates understanding, reinforces the client for seeking assistance, and outlines some counseling options for the near future. (If the client is experiencing a high level of stress and suicidal preoccupation, counseling will not be effective until the crisis subsides.)

4. *Ask questions to assess lethality.* The following questions will help determine the degree of risk:

■ *What has happened to make life so difficult?* The more circumstances the client describes, the higher is the risk.

■ *Are you thinking of suicide?* Use the word suicide. Doing so will not put the idea of suicide into the thoughts of an adolescent who is not suicidal. Being direct will let the client know that the counselor has listened, is concerned, and is interested in helping.

■ *Do you have a suicide plan?* The more specific the client is about the method, the time, the place, and who will or will not be nearby, the higher is the risk. If the client describes using pills, a gun, a knife, or other specific means, ask if he or she has that item in a pocket or purse, and require that the suicide "weapon" be left with you. (Firearms and highly lethal items, however, should be handled by the police.) Most clients will cooperate since they are most likely at low point, "other-directed," and responsive to taking directions from a trusted adult.

■ *How much do you want to live?* The more difficulty the client has in giving reasons for continuing with life, the higher is the risk.

■ *How much do you want to die?* The more the client discusses ending life, the higher is the risk.

■ *When you think about suicide, how often do these periods of suicidal preoccupation occur, how intense are they, and how long do the periods last?* The more frequent the episodes, the more dysfunctional is the client's behavior during periods of intense preoccupation, and the longer the preoccupation, the more lethal is the situation for the client. Frequent episodes of suicidal preoccupation that are lasting longer and longer mean that the periods of preoccupation with suicidal thoughts are moving closer together and consuming more and more of the client's time.

■ *Have you ever attempted suicide in the past?* If the answer is yes, the client is more lethal. In that case, ask: *How long ago was that attempt?* The more recent the attempt, the greater is the current risk.

■ *Has a family member, neighbor, or friend ever attempted or completed suicide?* If the answer is yes, the client is more lethal because he or she may have learned or come to believe that suicide is an acceptable form of decision making.

■ *On a scale of 1 to 10, with 1 being low and 10 being high, what is the number that depicts the probability that you will attempt suicide?* The higher the number, the higher is the lethality.

■ *Is there anyone to stop you?* This question is extremely important for two reasons. First, if the client has a difficult time identifying a friend, family member, or respected adult who would be worth living for, the risk is higher than if as few as one or two people are named. Second, it is important to obtain specific information about the people identified in response to this question. Names, addresses, phone numbers, and the nature of the current or past relationship may be needed to organize a suicide watch.

5. *Remember the meaning of crisis management.* The word *crisis* means that the situation is not normal or usual because the adolescent you are concerned about is self-destructive. The word *management* means that, for a short time (24 to 72 hours), the client must be directed and monitored. Definite steps must be taken to safeguard the client's well-being, and these steps must be explicated in an assertive, direct manner while conveying concern and empathy. If a young person were in an accident that resulted in life-threatening physical injury and loss of consciousness, paramedics and hospital emergency room physicians and nurses would take decisive action without the permission of the patient to save the patient's life. Managing a suicidal crisis is no different.

6. *Make a decision relative to needed interventions.* If, as a result of the counselor's assessment, the risk factor or lethality is judged to be high, the counselor should develop a management plan to follow until the crisis subsides and long-term counseling can be initiated. If the client is in proximity to a hospital with a psychiatric unit, hospital personnel can undertake additional assessment to determine if hospitalization for a 2- or 3-day period is advisable. Often, if a client has not been eating and sleeping or does not have family or friends to provide a suicide watch, a brief hospital stay will facilitate subsiding of the crisis to the point at which counseling can be initiated.

If hospital services are not available in the community and the counselor believes the risk is high, a suicide watch should be organized by contacting the individuals that the client has identified in response to the question: "Is there anyone to stop you?" After receiving instructions from the counselor, family members and friends should take turns staying with the client until the crisis has subsided and counseling has begun. Under no circumstances should an adolescent in crisis leave the counselor's office until arrangements have been made to monitor the client at all times. Contacting friends and family does break confidentiality, but it does not violate ethical codes of professional groups such as the American Association for Counseling and Development and the American Psychological Association. These steps must be taken to potentially save the client's life.

At times a written contract can be developed with the client, to be used along with a suicide watch (or in place of a suicide watch if the risk is low). The contract should specify activities, time with friends, and the like to which the client will commit, along with phone numbers of individuals to contact if preoccupation with suicide begins again.

A high-risk adolescent never should be left unmonitored, and the counselor should not assume that the client will have the initiative and energy to arrange and arrive for needed counseling when the crisis has subsided enough for counseling to be beneficial. This means that the counselor must be willing to cancel appointments and other scheduled activities to assist if no one else is available to be of support to the client.

7. *Be flexible enough to work with colleagues or crisis center staff.* Responding to a suicidal adolescent and assessing lethality requires patience, energy, and decision making. If another colleague has received training in crisis management, that colleague could help to make an assessment and decide upon the most appropriate crisis management plan. Or it may be necessary to call upon a local crisis center to provide assistance. This is especially true if a suicidal adolescent is on the telephone and someone needs to go to the caller's location to remove firearms, provide transportation to a hospital, or other intervention. The crisis center staff can help determine whether to involve the police and whether emergency medical assistance may be needed prior to arrival at a hospital emergency room.

After a suicidal crisis has subsided, the services of an agency counselor or private practitioner may be necessary to provide follow-up counseling on a consistent and rather long-term basis. Never assume responsibilities that you do not have the expertise to carry through with or the time to provide.

Providing Follow-Up or Postvention Services

As many as six to 10 people are affected, on a long-term basis, for each adolescent suicide attempt or completion. Therefore, planning and offering either individual or group ("survivor group") counseling experiences for family members and friends of the suicide victim or attempter is necessary. On a short-term basis, hundreds of people, if not entire communities, may be in need of assistance ranging from information about the dynamics of suicide to individual or group counseling.

In a school setting, providing information about suicide and offering counseling assistance as a follow-up to an actual suicide are appropriate measures. If an adolescent who has attempted suicide is returning to the same classrooms in the same school, however, suicide prevention programs should not be provided for the first time until a few months have passed, so that the returning student will not be focused upon. But individual or group counseling still can be provided for those who seem to need to talk about their feelings related to the suicide attempt of one of their peers.

Members of both school and community groups must realize that the end of a period of suicidal crisis or the return of an adolescent who has made an unsuccessful attempt does not signify the end of responsibility of school and community groups to provide counseling assistance. The only hope for improved mental health of the adolescent is long-term counseling focused upon overcoming low self-esteem and other traits so that life and its options can be viewed differently.

An adolescent who attempts suicide is reaching out for the help that can be provided only in the context of the helping relationship. School and community groups must plan, network, and fund services to cope with the increasing problem of adolescent suicide in the same way that provisions are made for interventions related to physical and sexual abuse and drug abuse. Family members and friends must affirm the self-worth of all adolescents by being sensitive to their developing individuality, as well as the stresses of the complex, changing society of which they are a part. Only then will the promise of a new tomorrow become the reality of today.

References

Bigrar, J., Gauthier, Y., Bouchard, C., & Jasse, Y. (1966). On the depressive illness in childhood: Suicidal attempts in adolescent girls. A preliminary study. *Canadian Psychiatric Association Journal, 11* (Supplement), 275–282.

Davis, P. A. (1983). *Suicidal adolescents.* Springfield, IL: Charles C Thomas.

Fairchild, T. N. (1986). Suicide intervention. In T. N. Fairchild (Ed.), *Crisis intervention strategies for school-based helpers* (pp. 321–369). Springfield, IL: Charles C Thomas.

Haffen, B. Q., & Frandsen, K. J. (1986). *Youth suicide: Depression and loneliness.* Provo, UT: Behavioral Health Associates.

Husain, S. A., & Vandiver, T. (1984). *Suicide in children and adolescents.* New York: SP Medical and Scientific Books.

Jacobziner, H. (1965). Attempted suicides in adolescents by poisoning. *Journal of the American Medical Association, 191*(1), 101–105.

McAnarney, E. R. (1979). Adolescent and young adult suicide in the United States—A reflection of societal unrest? *Adolescence, 14*(56), 765–774.

Otto, U. (1972). Suicidal acts by children and adolescents: A follow-up study. *Acta Psychiatrica Scandinavica, 233* (Supplement), 5–123.

Truckman, J., & Connon, H. E. (1962). Attempted suicides in adolescents. *American Journal of Psychiatry, 119*(3), 228–232.

Uncovering the Hidden Causes of Bullying and School Violence

Barry K. Weinhold

ecause the bulk of the iceberg that the Titanic hit on April 14, 1912, was invisible to the ship's captain, this great ship sank to the bottom of the ocean. On April 20, 1999, our great nation also hit a largely invisible iceberg at Columbine High School. Since then, the public eye has been focused on the tip of this metaphoric iceberg, known as the "culture of violence." In trying to find ways to avoid further school violence, the larger culture of violence remains hidden from our collective view. Unless this nation changes its course, it surely is headed for more collisions with this invisible iceberg that can cause the deaths of many more innocent people.

Ever since the Columbine tragedy, people have been asking, "How could this have happened?" and "What can we do to prevent it from happening again?" Much of the public commentary about the causes of the Columbine massacre has been directed at assigning blame and finding quick-fix solutions. What might be more useful is uncovering the hidden causes of this tragedy and developing long-range primary prevention strategies to deal with these hidden causes. The goals of this chapter are to (a) examine the hidden elements of the culture of violence that were present in the Columbine tragedy, (b) expose the pervasive nature of bullying and school violence, (c) show how school violence is only a small part of a larger pattern of violence that is fed by the culture of violence, and (d) describe effective long-range prevention methods that address the hidden elements of the culture of violence.

What Is the Culture of Violence?

The most visible forms of the culture of violence that make up the tip of the iceberg of violence are

- youth violence,
- domestic violence,
- road rage,
- gang violence,
- hate crimes,
- community crime and violence,
- global conflict and war.

Ample evidence documents the increasingly negative effects of the culture of violence. For example, juvenile crime is up 47 percent nationally, and almost 3 million violent crimes occur annually at or near schools. The number of violent crimes committed by youth is expected to double by the year 2010 (Perry, 1996a). Similar increases have occurred in reported cases of child abuse and domestic violence (Portner, 1997). According to Sebastian (1996), half of all married women will experience some form of violence from their partners during their marriage and more than one-third are beaten repeatedly.

Feeding this rapidly growing culture of violence is the prevalence of violence on television and in movies and interactive videos. The World Wrestling Federation (WWF), which sponsors professional wrestling matches, particularly glorifies violence by portraying bullies as heroes. Teachers report the influence of WWF wrestling on their students, describing a marked increase in the number of children imitating aggressive WWF gestures and behaviors at school. Many of these teachers also report that parents are becoming more threatening and intimidating toward the teachers when they come to school to complain about something they think is unfair.

Public opinion surveys show that violence in the schools is the number-one education-related concern of Americans (Adler & Springen, 1999). Many schools have adopted get tough policies to deal with violence in the schools. These include initiating zero-tolerance policies, installing metal detectors, hiring more police to patrol the halls, and placing video cameras in school buildings for increased surveillance.

The Hidden Elements in the Culture of Violence

The culture of violence has at least six hidden elements that point toward the occurrence of more Columbine-type shootings:

1. A dominator value system that supports violence

2. An over-focus on negative behaviors

3. The pervasiveness of bullying behavior

4. Collective denial of the effects of bullying behavior

5. The role of post-tramatic stress disorder (PTSD) in the perpetration of violence

6. The effects of parental neglect and emotional abandonment on children

In this chapter I will address each one of these relatively hidden elements of the culture of violence and describe effective primary prevention methods for dealing with these underlying causes of violence.

A Dominator Value System That Supports Violence

What supports this pervasive culture of violence is a system of dominator values (Weinhold & Weinhold, 2000). These values are behind the increase in aggressive and bullying behaviors. Those who live by these dominator values do the following:

- Use power plays involving violence, threats of violence, intimidation, and exploitation to get their way and to bully others
- Have little regard for the rights, needs, or even the lives of others, particularly if they see these others as a threat
- Exploit the needs and rights of others when they perceive them as having less power, status or influence, including women, children, and minorities
- Are on the defensive and never admit mistakes
- Blame others for causing their problems
- Believe that "might makes right"

As evidence of the widespread influence of the dominator system, a study reported that one in three women worldwide has been beaten, raped, or somehow mistreated by men (Heise, Ellsberg, & Gottemoeller, 1999). Dominator values are so tightly woven into the fabric of our culture that they are virtually invisible. For example, most Americans agreed with the United States' bombing of Iraq and Kosovo, even though they knew that thousands of innocent civilians were being killed.

Dominator values are actively promoted by the sports and entertainment industries. For example, hardly anyone even questions the gratuitous violence in wrestling matches sponsored by the World Wrestling Federation or World Championship Wrestling. These matches have some of the highest ratings on cable television. Regular television channels are no better, with daytime shows exemplifying dominator values, such as the Jerry Springer and Jenny Jones programs, commanding huge ratings. Movies such as *The Terminator* glorify violence and pack the theaters. Violent video games such as *Doom* had considerable influence on Eric Harris and Dylan Klebold, the Columbine killers. Violence is a profitable business. Unless these values are changed or supplanted by kinder and more humane values, the culture of violence will continue to grow and flourish in the United States, further undermining all of our democratic institutions.

As a counter balance to the dominator value system is another value system that some call the "humanistic or democratic value system" (Eisler, 1987). Those who espouse these values are people who do the following:

■ Strive to resolve their conflicts with others in peaceful, nonviolent ways so everyone gets their needs met

■ Use the "rule of law" and seek common ground to settle racial, cultural, religious, and political disputes

■ Understand cultural relativity and are able to show tolerance and respect toward people of different cultures

■ Seek equalitarian relationships based on mutual respect, trust, and caring

■ Admit mistakes and strive to learn from them

■ Take responsibility for their actions

These are the values of democracy that we strive to teach our children, but dominator values are undermining the very foundation of our democracy. The dominator value system lurks behind all domestic violence, child abuse, elder abuse, workplace violence, school violence, road rage, hate crimes, and wars.

Over-Focus on Negative Behaviors

Much of people's behavior is motivated by a desire to meet the basic needs for recognition, attention and approval. Over the past 6 years, I visited more than 100 schools, and asked students and faculty members the following question: "Is it easier for you to get noticed or get attention in this school by doing something positive or something negative?" Almost 100 percent of them have replied "negative" (Weinhold, 1999a). This consistent feedback from children and faculty members indicates that children and adults adapt and learn to use negative behaviors to meet their need for recognition because their positive behaviors usually go unnoticed. This is not just a school problem. If someone were to ask the same question of kids in families or workers in companies or in organizations such as the military, they likely would get the same answer.

This focus on negativity is hidden below the tip of our social iceberg and supports the visible culture of violence that we see in the media. For example, have you ever noticed how characters on television sitcoms get the most audience laughter when they make a mistake? This culture of negativity in schools, families, the workplace, and the highway creates an overall climate that breeds violence.

A basic law of psychology says: "What you pay attention to is what you are going to get more of." If we focus too much of our attention on negative behaviors and not enough on positive behaviors, negative behavior will increase. An overwhelmingly negative school climate is damaging to the self-esteem of kids. For example, when kids in kindergarten were asked if they like themselves, 95 percent or more said "yes." By fourth grade, the percentage of these kids who reported liking themselves was down to 60 percent. By eighth grade, the percentage was down to 40 percent, and by twelfth grade, it was down to 5 percent (Weinhold, 1999a).

Columbine High School was no exception. At this upper middle-class suburban high school, every student who was the least bit insecure about himself or herself was worried about being different in some way. A senior girl at Columbine summed it up: "It's a rat race inside the school to see who's going to be more popular. Everybody's thinking: 'Am I going to look cool for the popular kids? Are they going to accept me?'" Another student said, "With all the animosity between the various social groups at Columbine, something like this was bound to happen" (Dube, 1999).

Pervasiveness of Bullying

From firsthand accounts (Dube, 1999; Prendergast, 1999) and from the killers' own videos (Gibbs & Roche, 1999), we know that Harris and Klebold were repeatedly bullied and subjected to verbal put-downs, leading to their plan of violent revenge. Initially, the role of bullying in the Columbine killings was played down. The role of bullying in the Columbine shootings is discussed in more detail later in this chapter.

Bullying is the most common form of violence in our society, and it is what drives the culture of violence. Dominating males and females bully people whom they perceive as weaker and less powerful. Men bully their female partners, women bully their children, older children bully their younger siblings, and younger children bully their pets.

Bruce Perry (1996b) calls this phenomenon the "vortex of violence." He says that violence always travels from the strongest to the weakest or from the most powerful to the least powerful. Known as the *talionic response*, it is part of the adage in the Bible, "an eye for an eye and a tooth for a tooth" (Weinhold, 1991). Men and women who are adult bullies are violent toward less powerful men and women. Men who are adult bullies are violent toward less powerful women. Women who are bullies commit the most violence against children. Older children who bully are the most violent toward younger children. Younger children who have been bullied take it out on their pets. Young children, who are at the bottom of this vortex, often do not have anyone to pass it on to, so they absorb it, accumulate it, and wait until they are old enough, big enough, or strong enough to erupt in some dramatic way that hurts other people.

Bullying in Schools

Although more than 97 percent of U. S. schools report having some sort of violence-prevention program, very few of them are effective, according to the U. S. Department of Education. In a study of the top 84 violence-prevention programs, only 10 were seen as effective (Lederer & Varela, 1998). Less than 10% of the nation's 85,000 public schools have comprehensive school-based mental-health services for kids (Joseph, 1999). Most of the violence-prevention initiatives and studies of the causes of violence, not just those dealing with bullying or school violence, focus on violence of a specific type—family violence, school violence, gang violence, and so on. They do not understand the interrelatedness of the culture of violence, and they usually start too late.

Few programs feature early intervention and primary prevention even though primary prevention programs cost significantly less and are far more effective. Most people are inclined to wait until the problem is acute, and then they try to fix it. In addition, few programs look at the culture of violence for the underlying causes of bullying and school violence. Many homes actually instill in their children dominator values that support bullying and school violence. Instead, we need to instill partnership values in our schools to counter some of the dominator values that kids bring with them to school. Using reactive and shortsighted approaches to try to prevent violence is like trying to avoid hitting an iceberg by rearranging the deck chairs on the Titanic. It has no effect on the outcome.

What is bullying? There is some confusion about what constitutes bullying. Bullying is defined as something that someone repeatedly does or says to gain power over or to dominate another person. The following are some typical examples of bullying:

- Name calling, put-downs, cruel teasing
- Saying or writing nasty things about others
- Deliberately excluding certain people from activities
- Not talking to certain people
- Threatening others with bodily harm
- Taking or damaging others' things
- Hitting or kicking
- Making people do things they don't want to do

Among several kinds of bullies are the following (Marano, 1995):

1. *Proactive bullies* need no provocation and are naturally more aggressive toward others. This group frequently has poor social and relational skills and compensates for this lack of skills by picking on others.

2. *Reactive bullies* often are victimized by other bullies and then retaliate by becoming bullies as well.

3. *Provocative victims* provoke fights or aggressive encounters with others. They are quick to become oppositional or defiant and cry or display exaggerated responses in conflict situations. This group is mostly rejected by their peers and has the fewest friends.

It is often difficult for even peers to identify who are the bullies and who are the victims because the vortex of violence is so prevalent and so many participate in it (Paulk et al., 1999).

Brown's Broken Toy Project

Tom Brown (1999), the founder of the Broken Toy Project and conductor of school workshops on bullying, asked kids to describe bullying. Here is what they told him, in their own words:

- New kids
- Fat kids
- Skinny kids
- Boys that "suck" in sports
- Boys that act like "fags"
- Lesbians
- Kids who are smart
- Kids who are dumb
- Geeks
- Computer-freaks
- Kids who wear geeky out-of-style clothes
- Kids who stink and smell
- Teacher's pets
- Kids with unkempt hair
- Retarded kids
- Kids who talk funny
- Kids who walk funny
- Minority kids
- Kids in wheelchairs
- Kids who get good grades
- Kids who get poor grades
- Girls with blonde hair
- Kids with curly hair
- Kids with freckles
- Kids with funny looking ears or noses
- Kids with diseases

As you can see from this list, just about any kid in school could become a target of a bully. All they have to do is be different in some way that causes them to stand out.

The kids in Tom Brown's study were explicit about *where* kids get bullied. They said:

the bus
the bathroom
the halls
recess
P.E. class

When Tom Brown asked the students why they thought bullies picked on other kids, the students gave the following answers:

They have low self-esteem.
Other kids egg them on.
For attention.
They're mean and don't care about other kids' feelings.
It's cool. You get a lot of friends when you're a bully.

Tom Brown's kids were explicit about why they don't tell grown-ups about bullying incidents:

Fear of a parent or guardian going to school and yelling at the bullies or teachers or principal.
Fear of being told to fight back when they have no desire to fight back.
Shame.
Not wanting to scare or worry their parents.

Tom's kids indicated that they got mixed messages from grown-ups:

Fight back.
Walk away.
Tell your teacher.
Quit being a baby. Start taking up for yourself.

The kids gave their reasons why kids are afraid to confront bullies:

You get instant retaliation.
You get ganged up on by bullies and their friends.
You get in trouble with the school.
You get a reputation of being a bully yourself.
The bully's older brother or sister will get after you.
You might hurt the bully and get sued or in trouble with the police.

When Tom Brown asked kids what three things kids usually do when they see someone being bullied, he got an answer that is at the heart of why bullying persists. The students said:

Run over and watch.
Run over and watch.
Run over and watch.

What keeps bullying going isn't just the bullies and the victims. It is also the bystanders who watch the incidents of bullying and do nothing to stop them. Bystanders provide an audience for the bully and give bullies the peer attention they crave. Any intervention designed to stop bullying must address the role of the bystanders.

What do kids do when they are bullied? Again Tom Brown's kids told it like it is:

Walk or run away.
Get a teacher to help.
Use humor.
Tell the bully to leave you alone.
Yell to attract a lot of attention.

Brown (1999) summarized some of the most ineffective methods that educators use to deal with bullying:

Punish both the bully and the victim.
Look the other way; ignore bullying behavior, passing it off as horseplay or kids being kids.
Bring the bully and the victim together in one room and ask the bully if he or she has been bullying the victim.
Tell the victim to quit being a crybaby and start standing up for himself or herself.
Tell the victim to make better friends.
Tell the victim to quit tattling on other kids.
Punish the bully without any attempt to resolve the situation—for example, setting up a meeting between the bully and a counselor or someone else who can talk to this student without coming off as a threat.
Yell at either or both the victim and the bully in front of other children.
Show an educational film dealing with bullying without processing the contents of the film before or afterward.
Spend money to bring an anti-bullying program into a school without doing follow-up activities.

Brown (1999) summarized his research by saying, "This is what I hear from children everywhere I go to present my program. It doesn't matter what kind of school or if the child is a first or a sixth grader. Kids know exactly what is going on."

Olweus's Research on Bullying

Dan Olweus (Olweus, 1994), from the University of Bergen in Norway, did an extensive study of bullying. Here are his definition and conclusions:

Bullying occurs when one or more persons deliberately and repeatedly try to hurt another person through words or actions. Relevant conclusions follow:

■ Bullying is an act of violence, and it is against the law.

- The bully's ultimate goal is to achieve domination and control over another person.
- Bullies often are not good students and have academic problems in school, such as a learning disability.
- Bullies often lack power in their own lives and compensate for it by dominating others.
- Children who bully become adults who bully unless they receive help.
- Bullying is a cry for help.

Why is bullying important to us?

1. *All school violence begins with bullying.* All serious school violence starts with seemingly innocent bullying or put-downs which eventually can escalate into violence involving guns or knives. The lack of respect for another person's human rights—the most common factor in all criminal behavior—begins with school bullying. Schools that do not deal with bullying when it first appears can become a breeding ground for criminal behavior and pose a serious threat to public safety.

2. *Serious school violence is on the increase.* One of the first cases of school violence to reach the national press occurred in 1994. Fifteen-year-old Brian, from Woodstock, Georgia, cried out in his school classroom, "I can't take this any more," and then, with a single gunshot, ended his life. After his death, his parents and the school officials learned that Brian had been the victim of repeated harassment, humiliation, and bullying at school. Actually, since 1992, there have been 250 violent deaths in schools that involved multiple victims, culminating with the Columbine massacre (Joseph, 1999).

The great majority of these deaths occurred in cities and towns with populations of under 80,000 people, showing us that there is no safe place for our kids. Almost all the killers were white males from relatively affluent families, not gang-members or teens from the inner city. In virtually every school shooting, bullying has been a factor. As in the Columbine shootings, most of the students who committed these violent crimes were "reactive bullies" who finally decided to get revenge against the other bullies who had picked on them.

Some of the other school shootings that involved bullying are as follows.

Feb. 2, 1996:   Two male students in Moses Lake, Washington, were shot to death by a 14-year-old male honor student who had been the target of repeated bullying by those students.

Mar. 24, 1998:   An 11-year-old boy and a 13-year-old boy shot and killed four girls and a female teacher in a Jonesboro, Arkansas, middle school. They had made repeated threats to others in the school about their intent to do violence, but they were ignored. The 13-year-old was described as a bully.

Sept. 1998:   Two school outcasts in Green River, Wyoming, 18-year-old Cody Bradley and 16-year-old David Taylor, who were ostracized and bullied by other students, stabbed and killed a 17-year-old boy who they said stole Bradley's girlfriend, and then they shot themselves a day later in a suicide pact.

Oct. 1998:   A 12-year-old middle-school student from Woodstock, Georgia, was beaten up by a known 15-year-old bully as he got off the bus at school. The victim went into a coma and a few days later was taken off life support.

Nov. 1998:   Five Burlington, Wisconsin, boys were arrested for plotting the deaths of their teachers, administrators, and the other students who they said were picking on them. They told school officials that the other students "treated them like trash."

3. *Bullying was at the root of the Columbine massacre.* We must learn the lessons of the Columbine massacre if we are to prevent it from happening again. The group of Columbine students identified as the "trenchcoat mafia," which included Eric Harris and Dylan Klebold, was harassed, bullied and put down daily for years. This practice was initiated by a clique of student athletes and later joined many other Columbine students.

Every day when Harris and Klebold came to school, they were met at the door by a group of students who harassed them by pouring orange juice on their trenchcoats so they would have to wear the sticky stuff all day. Harris, Klebold, and others in this group who were bullied tried to sneak into school through a side door or back door to avoid this daily ritual. They also were harassed in the hallways and cafeteria and were called names. Frequently the football players would throw a body block on them, knocking them into the lockers or the wall, and call them "dirt bags" or "dirt balls." One 15-year-old Columbine student said, "It must have been hell for them" (Dube, 1999).

Time magazine (Gibbs & Roche, 1999) quoted a 255-pound defensive lineman at Columbine as saying,

> Columbine is a clean, good place except for those rejects. Sure, we teased them. But what do you expect with kids who come to school with weird hairdos and horns on their hats? It's not just the jocks; the whole school's disgusted with them. They're a bunch of homos, grabbing each other's private parts. If you want to get rid of someone, usually you tease 'em. So the whole school would call them homos, and when they did something sick, we'd tell them, "You're sick and that's wrong."

Even though this happened in front of many students and teachers, no one tried to stop it. The killers wore weird clothing to call attention to themselves and even wore armbands that said, "I hate people." As they opened fire on their classmates, Harris and Klebold were heard to say, "This is for all the people who made fun of us all these years" (Dube, 1999).

Notwithstanding their obvious cries for help, no one gave these boys the kind of attention they really needed. They were very bright and very lonely, yet no one seemed to try to redirect their behavior in more positive ways. Further, cliques like those that bullied and harassed Harris and Klebold at Columbine High School exist in every school in this country. In most schools, the athletes are at the top of the heap. They act out the dominator behaviors that many school athletic programs highly value.

Killing is a learned behavior. Children don't naturally kill. They learn it from their experience of violence in their home and, most pervasively, from violence as entertainment on television, in the movies, and by playing interactive video games. Killing requires the availability of weapons and training because there is a built-in aversion to killing one's own kind. Law enforcement and military personnel know this because they have to go through rigorous training before they are able to shoot someone, if necessary. And then they are trained not to kill but, instead, to maim or disarm a dangerous person with a weapon (Grossman, 1998).

Research on the effects of television is clear. In nations or regions where television is introduced for the first time, the murder rate doubles within 15 years. The American Medical Association concluded that long-term childhood exposure to television is a causal factor behind approximately half of the violent crimes committed in the United States, or about 10,000 homicides, 70,000 rapes, and 700,000 injurious assaults (Grossman, 1996).

David Grossman (1998) said:

> The result is a phenomenon that functions much like AIDS, which I call AVIDS— Acquired Violence Immune Deficiency Syndrome. AIDS has never killed anybody. It destroys your immune system, and then other diseases that shouldn't kill you become fatal. Television violence by itself does not kill you. It destroys your violence immune system and conditions you to derive pleasure from violence. And once you are at close range with another human being and its time for you to pull that trigger, Acquired Violence Immune Deficiency Syndrome can destroy your midbrain resistance. (p. 36)

Further, violent video games are teaching our children how to shoot to kill with increasing accuracy. In the Jonesboro, Arkansas, killings, one boy had no experience shooting guns and the other had only some experience in shooting guns. Yet, they fired 27 shots from 100 yards and hit 15 people. That's pretty good shooting. Why were they so good? They both had played violent video games for hours at a time that taught them how to hit targets. Video games train kids to shoot a gun to kill someone (Grossman, 1998).

On a dare from a friend, a 15-year-old boy in South Carolina tried to rob a local convenience store. In the process, he reflexively shot and killed the clerk. From 6 feet away, he pointed a snub-nosed .38-caliber pistol at the back of the clerk's head, and when the clerk turned around to face the boy, the boy shot the clerk right between the eyes. This boy had spent hundreds of hours playing video games, learning to point and shoot, point and shoot. When asked why he did it, the boy replied, "I don't know. It was a mistake. It wasn't supposed to happen" (Grossman, 1998).

Those who have been in the military or law-enforcement know that the correct option is often not to shoot. But when kids put their quarter in a video machine, their intention is to shoot to kill. In a video game, there is always a stimulus that sets them off and instructs them to start shooting.

In the case of the 15-year-old boy in South Carolina—he said he got excited and scared when the convenience clerk turned around; his heart rate went up; the flow of adrenaline closed down his forebrain, he panicked and reflexively he did what he was conditioned to do: He pulled the trigger, shooting just as accurately as he had done hundreds of times before when he was playing video games. Our children are learning to kill and to enjoy it (Grossman, 1998).

Here are some additional statistics:

■ 60 percent of men on TV dramas are depicted in violent scenes; 11% are killers (Grossman, 1998).

■ In the media in general, the majority of victims are women and children (Grossman, 1998).

■ 20 percent of suburban high-school students endorsed the idea of shooting someone "who has stolen something from you" (Grossman, 1996).

Bullying is pervasive in most schools. Some statistics that bear this out are as follows:

■ Half of all violence against teenagers occurs in school buildings, on school property, or on the street in the vicinity of the school. Most begins as bullying or put-downs (NIDR, 1999).

■ The National School Safety Center estimates that more than 525,000 attacks, shakedowns, and robberies occur per month in public secondary schools in the United States (Weinhold & Weinhold, 1998).

■ The National Education Association estimates that 160,000 students miss school every day (totaling 28 million missed days per year), because of fear of attack or intimidation by a bully (Fried & Fried, 1996).

■ Students receive an average of 213 verbal put-downs per week, or 30 per day (Fried, personal communication, 1996).

■ In a survey of 558 students in a Midwestern middle school, the researchers found that 80 percent of the students had engaged in bullying behaviors in the previous 30 days (Espelage et al., 1999).

■ 80 to 90 percent of adolescents report some form of victimization from a bully at school (Espelage et al., 1999).

■ 90 percent of all students thought that bullying caused social, emotional, or academic problems for the students who were bullied (Weinhold & Weinhold, 2000).

■ 69 percent of all students believe that schools respond poorly to bullying and victimization (Weinhold & Weinhold, 2000).

How does bullying differ from grade to grade? (Olweus, 1994)

- Bullying occurs in every grade, but it happens most frequently in grades 4 through 8.
- Bullying usually starts as teasing and put-downs with younger bullies and then becomes more physical and more violent as bullies get older.
- Bullies can be easily identified in each grade by the sixth week of the school year.
- Potential bullies can be easily identified as early as preschool if we recognize the early warning signs.

How does bullying differ between boys and girls? (Saunders, 1997)

- Boys tend to use direct physical and verbal attacks to bully others.
- Girls tend to use more indirect, subtle, and social methods such as exclusion, manipulation, and spreading rumors.
- Boys tend to bully other boys (80 percent) and girls (60 percent).
- Boys are more likely than girls to be both perpetrators and victims of aggressive physical and verbal bullying by peers.
- In middle-school, girls who mature early are often bullied and sexually harassed by boys.
- Girls tend to bully only other girls.
- Boys usually bully alone, and girls bully in groups.

Bullying Outside of School

How pervasive is bullying outside of schools? Considering that bullying is a hidden part of the overall culture of violence that is supported by dominator values, you can see that it occurs almost everywhere—at home, at work, and on the road.

At home, some key points in bullying are as follows:

- Older siblings often bully their younger brothers and sisters.
- Bullies and victims of bullying often grow up to become batterers. Adult perpetrators of domestic violence often have been identified as bullies or victims of bullying while they were in school (Straus & Gelles, 1988).

Bullying occurs in the workplace as well. Bully OnLine (1999) reported the results of a study, as follows:

- Bullies at school who get away with it often become serial bullies at work.
- Children who get bullied at school tend to become targets for bullying at work.
- More than one million U. S. workers are assaulted annually.
- The most common reasons people are bullied on the job are that they are good at their job and they are popular with other employees (the workplace bully is driven by jealousy and envy).

- In the United Kingdom, one in three people leave their job because of bullying.
- The same study showed that 53 percent of UK employees have been bullied during their working life.

Road rage has become recognized in recent years. Nerenberg (1999) reported the following:

- Road rage is another form of bullying.
- In 1996, 28,000 Americans died because of aggressive driving.
- There are 2 billion episodes of road rage per year in the United States.
- Violent incidents of road rage have increased 51 percent over the last five years.

Collective Denial About Effects of Bullying

The most common way that schools deal with bullying is to ignore it. Many teachers don't see anything wrong with bullying. One Columbine student reported, "Teachers would see them push someone into a locker, and they'd just ignore it" (Prendergast, 1999). A junior at Columbine said, "I can't believe the faculty couldn't figure it out. It was so obvious that something was wrong" (Dube, 1999). In another study, teachers were able to identify only 10 percent of the students who reported being a victim of a bully (Paulk et. al., 1999). A prevailing attitude among some teachers is that those who get bullied probably had it coming to them. In families, fewer than one in 10 incidents of bullying involving suspected child abuse or domestic violence ever get reported, and of the incidents that are reported, few are ever investigated and almost none result in any criminal charges (Weinhold, 1991).

How does bullying differ from normal peer conflicts? The collective denial is supported by misconceptions about how bullying situations differ from normal peer conflicts. There is a big difference between these situations (Weinhold, 1999a). A bullying situation has six defining factors:

- *Intent to harm.* The perpetrator finds pleasure in taunting or trying to dominate the victim and continues even when the victim's distress is obvious.
- *Intensity and duration.* The bullying continues over a long period and the extent of bullying is damaging to the self-esteem of the victim.
- *Power of the bully.* The bully has power over the victim because of age, strength, size, or gender.
- *Vulnerability of the victim.* The victim is more sensitive to teasing, cannot adequately defend himself or herself, and has physical or psychological qualities that make him or her more prone to victimization.
- *Lack of support.* The victim feels isolated and exposed. Often, the victim is afraid to report the bullying for fear of retaliation.
- *Consequences.* Damage to the victim's self-esteem is longlasting and leads the victim to markedly withdraw from school or, conversely, to become aggressive.

In a normal peer conflict situation, in contrast, none of these elements is present. Those who are involved in a normal peer conflict

■ do not insist on getting their own way,

■ give reasons why they disagree,

■ apologize or offer win-win suggestions,

■ are free to bargain and negotiate to get their needs met,

■ can change the topic and walk away.

Effects of Bullying

What are the short-term effects of bullying in our schools? Here are some examples of the immediate or short-term effects of bullying in schools:

■ 10 percent of students who drop out of school do so because of repeated bullying (Weinhold & Weinhold, 1998).

■ 20 percent of all high school students surveyed report avoiding the restrooms out of a fear of being bullied (NIDR, 1999).

■ In the United States, about 2 million teenagers carry guns, knives, clubs, and razors (NIDR, 1999).

■ As many as 135,000 take these weapons to school (NIDR, 1999).

■ Nearly one-third of the students have heard a classmate threaten to kill someone (Langer, 1999).

■ 78 percent who knew of the threats to kill someone said they didn't report them to an adult (Langer, 1999).

■ 40 percent of high school students say there are potentially violent cliques at their school (Langer, 1999).

■ One in five of the students say they personally know a classmate who has brought a gun to school (Langer, 1999).

■ Of those who knew a classmate who brought a gun to school, 83 percent say they did not report it to an adult (Langer, 1999).

■ 54 percent of the students say it would be easy for them to get a gun (One student said it was as easy as buying candy at the corner store) (Langer, 1999).

■ 67 percent say it would be easy for them to make a bomb (Langer, 1999).

What are the known long-term effects of bullying? Some of the conclusions of the Olweus (1993, 1994) studies follow.

Studies on Those Who Are Bullied (Olweus, 1993)

■ Being bullied during middle school is predictive of low self-esteem 10 years later.

- By age 23, children who were bullied in middle school were more depressed and had lower self-esteem than their peers who had not been bullied.

- Bullied children feel more isolated than their peers, who often reject them out of fear that they, too, will become a target of bullies if they are seen with targeted students.

- Being bullied can lead to suicide.

- Some victims of bullies resort to eventual violent retaliation against the bully.

Studies on the Bullies Themselves (Olweus, 1994)

- By age 23, about 60 percent of the boys identified as bullies in middle school had at least one conviction of a crime, and 35 percent to 40 percent had three or more convictions.

- 50 percent of all identified school bullies became criminals as adults.

- Bullies at age 8 are three times more likely to be convicted of a crime by age 30.

- Bullies are less likely than nonbullies to finish college or locate a good job.

Why do children bully and put others down? There is a clash between the old and the new thinking on the causes of bullying and school violence. The new thinking is based on the recent research findings cited in this chapter. Table 8.1 presents a comparison.

Causes of Bullying

If we are going to eliminate the causes of bullying, a multitude of risk factors have to be addressed. Consider the following risk factors.

Family factors

- The home is the most violent place in the United States (Straus, 1994).

- Children from violent homes are three to four times more likely to become bullies. Contrary to popular belief, most of the violence directed at young children in the home comes from the mother and older siblings (Straus & Gelles, 1988).

- Three primary predictive family factors are (Weinhold & Weinhold, 2000):
  — a lack of solid bonding/attachment with the young child.
  — poor supervision and neglect of the child's needs.
  — acceptance and modeling of aggressive or bullying behaviors by parents or older siblings.

- Few early identification and intervention programs are available to help young children who show aggressive tendencies.

Table 8.1   Conventional Versus New Thinking

CONVENTIONAL THINKING	NEW THINKING
Bullying is genetic. Bullies are born that way.	Bullying is shaped by early childhood experiences.
Bullies should just be expelled.	Bullying is a cry for help.
Bullying is normal kids' behavior.	Bullying is a symptom of untreated trauma.
Bullying is harmless.	Bullying is traumatic for those being bullied.
Bullies will grow out of it.	Without intervention, bullying leads to further violence.
Bullies are influenced by peer modeling.	Bullies are influenced more by media and family modeling.
Watching violence on TV or movies is harmless.	TV and movie violence traumatizes kids.
Violent video games are harmless fantasy.	Traumatized kids can't separate reality and fantasy.

Personality factors

■ Children with an impulsive temperament are more inclined to develop into bullies (Olweus, 1994).

■ Bullies often have attachment disorders (Weinhold, 1999).

■ Boys who are physically bigger or stronger than peers of the same age are more likely to become bullies (Olweus, 1993).

■ Bullies like to be in charge, dominate, and assert their power. They like to win at any cost (Olweus, 1993).

■ Bullies crave attention, so they show off and act tough to get it from peers (Olweus, 1994).

■ Bullies lack empathy for their victims and have difficulty feeling compassion (Olweus, 1993).

■ Bullies believe that the victim provoked the attack and deserves the consequences (Olweus, 1994).

■ Bullying is a cry for help (Olweus, 1994).

School Factors

■ The amount of adult supervision is directly tied to the frequency and severity of bullying in schools (Saunders, 1997).

- A negative school climate where negative behavior gets most of the attention encourages the formation of cliques and bullying (Espelage et al., 1999).

- Some teachers threaten, tease, shame, or intimidate students to maintain control of their classroom (Olweus, 1994).

- 25 percent of teachers see nothing wrong with bullying and put-downs. Schools often condone this behavior and do nothing to prevent bullying and put-downs (Olweus, 1994).

- The learning environment can be poisoned by bullying and put-downs, raising the fear and anxiety of all students (Johnson & Johnson, 1995).

- Early identification and intervention programs are lacking. Bullies can be identified as early as preschool (Olweus, 1994).

Community Factors (Hawkins, Catalano et al., 1992).

- Schools in poor urban neighborhoods experience more violence in and around schools.

- People feel less safe in neighborhoods that show evidence of crack houses, drug dealing, and related violence. This spills over into the neighborhood schools, where there is more drug-dealing and related violence.

- Schools located in neighborhoods with high turnover mobility and transiency also have more bullying.

- State and local policies about early prevention, identification, and intervention are lacking.

Role of PTSD and Trauma as a Hidden Cause of Violence

A book on conflict resolution, *Conflict Resolution: The Partnership Way* (Weinhold & Weinhold, 2000) presents research indicating that most conflict situations involve stimulus conditions that remind those involved of previously unresolved conflicts and traumas. In a conflict situation, people frequently show symptoms resembling a post-traumatic stress reaction, or when they witness violent conflicts involving others, they may actually regress to an earlier trauma or conflict. They are actually existing in two realities at once, and usually they are unaware of why they are reacting the way they are.

Symptoms of PTSD

Clinical symptoms of post-traumatic stress disorder (PTSD) (APA, 1996) are as follows:

- *Reexperiencing old traumas*—Recurrent and intrusive recollections, distressing dreams, flashbacks, intense reactions to ordinary events.

- *Persistent avoidance of triggering situations and a "numbing" effect on general responsiveness*—Compulsive efforts to avoid people, thoughts, or feelings that arouse memories, depression, or detachment from others; a restricted range of affect.

- *Increased hypervigilence*—Difficulty sleeping, irritability and outbursts of anger, difficulty concentrating; an exaggerated startle response.

Activation of the Adrenal Stress Response

Another effect of repeated exposure to conflict and violence is that people become desensitized to violence. When I give talks on violence, I typically ask members of the audience to raise their hand if they have personally witnessed violence or if they were the victim of violence. Typically, about one-third of the audience members raise a hand. To not have witnessed any violence, they would not have seen a violent television show or a violent movie and would not have seen anyone in the family, workplace, highway, school, or neighborhood being violent. Highly unlikely! Why did they not raise their hand then?

They likely had to dissociate so they could cope with the amount of violence they were exposed to. At the same time, they remain in a constant hypervigilent state to avoid being triggered by memories of past violence. If people are in a persistent hyperaroused state, adrenal horomones are flowing through their bloodstream, and they are likely to fight, flee, or freeze if the current conflict situation contains even the slightest hint of an earlier conflict situation that they did not resolve. These classic adrenal stress reactions are wired into us to help us deal with situations in which we perceive danger. We don't even have to think about it (Weinhold & Weinhold, 2000).

When bullies pick on others, they likely have been triggered into the fight mode of the adrenal stress reaction. They hope they can discharge the accumulated fear, anger, and hurt from an earlier traumatic incident by picking on those they perceive as weaker. Untreated symptoms of PTSD may be a major factor in why people own more than 250 million guns in the United States. They just don't feel safe.

Accompanying the fear of violent encounters is a companion factor that causes people to be attracted to and fascinated by violence. The natural learning style of humans is to repeat a behavior until it is learned or understood or the trauma is healed. Freud called this *repetition compulsion*. Thus, we are drawn to what we fear. That is why so many people like to watch violent events, such as wrestling and seem to enjoy being scared out of their wits by violence on TV and in the movies.

People actually seem to be addicted to violence at the same time they are still trying to understand and heal what happened to them when they were traumatized by it during early childhood. Children see violence on TV and it traumatizes them. They then either compulsively try to stay away from anything that might remind them of this kind of violence and at the same time are drawn to it (Weinhold & Weinhold, 2000).

Parental Neglect and Emotional Abandonment of Our Children

In Ken Magid's and Carol McKelvey's book *High Risk: Children Without a Conscience* (1989), they state that severely abused and neglected children will grow up to become violence-seeking adults unless there is an intervention in their lives before age 16. These authors estimate that up to 20 million adults fall in this category and the numbers are growing more rapidly than the population. They advise that we must do a better job of protecting these children and intervening in the lives of young children who exhibit symptoms of attachment disorder. If we don't, Magid predicts that "soon there will be more of them than us and then we will be in real trouble" (Magid, 1992).

Research by Dr. Bruce Perry of Baylor College of Medicine (1996a, 1996b) has pointed to a particular family environment that will turn a normal child into a killer. He uncovered the effects on the brain of repeated stress caused by abuse, neglect, or terror, which cause physical and maybe permanent changes in young children. He found that the constant flood of adrenaline causes the brain to reset the brain's alarm system on an almost constant hair-trigger alert. Children who are constantly exposed to abuse or who witness the abuse of others, such as a sibling or a parent, can also cause their brains' system of adrenal stress horomones to become unresponsive.

These are the high-risk kids that Magid is talking about. They have antisocial personalities and typically have a low heart rate and impaired emotional sensitivity including a lack of empathy. They often kill or torture animals (Begley, 1999).

A Profile of the Character-Disturbed Child

Cline (1979) was one of the first to profile the characteristics of a high-risk child who has an attachment disorder. He listed the following characteristics:

- Lack of ability to give and receive affection
- Self-destructive behavior
- Cruelty to others
- Phoniness
- Severe problems with stealing, hoarding, and gorging on food
- Marked control problems
- Lack of long-term friends
- Abnormalities in eye contact

The three types of maternal attachments are: secure, avoidant, and anxious/ambivalent. Campos, Barrett, et al. (1983), found that 62 percent of infants are securely attached, 23 percent are avoidant, and 15 percent are insecure/ambivalent. The type of early attachment a child has causes him or her to develop what is called an internal "working model" of the world (Ainsworth, 1989; Bowlby, 1988). There are also three identifiable sub-types of avoidantly attached children: (a) the lying bully who blames others; (b) the shy, dissociated loner who seems emotionally flat, and (c) the obviously disturbed child with repetitive twitches and tics who daydreams and shows little interest in his or her environment. The two ambivalent subtypes are: (a) the fidgety, impulsive child with poor concentration who is tense and easily upset by his or her failures, and (b) the fearful, hypersensitive, clingy child who lacks initiative and gives up easily (Karen, 1998).

The *DSM-IV* (APA, 1996) has updated these characteristics in its diagnosis of a "Conduct Disorder." This diagnosis applies to anyone under 18 years of age, and for those over 18, it usually is called an Antisocial Personality Disorder. The symptoms are as follows:

Aggression toward people and animals:

■ Often bullies, threatens, or intimidates others

■ Often initiates physical fights

■ Has used a weapon that can cause serious physical harm to others

■ Has been physically cruel to people

■ Has been physically cruel to animals

■ Has stolen while confronting a victim

■ Has forced someone into sexual activity

Destruction of property:

■ Has deliberately engaged in fire-setting with the intention of causing serious damage

■ Has deliberately destroyed others' property (other than by fire-setting)

Deceitfulness or theft:

■ Has broken into someone else's house, building, or car

■ Often lies to obtain goods or favors or to avoid obligations

■ Has stolen items of nontrivial value without confronting a victim

Serious violations of rules:

■ Often stays out at night despite parental prohibitions, beginning before 13 years of age

■ Has run away from home overnight at least twice while living in parental or parental surrogate home

■ Is often truant from school, beginning before 13 years of age

To be diagnosed with this disorder, a persistent pattern of three or more of these behaviors must be present over the past 12 months, with the presence of at least one of the behaviors for the past 3 months. Most of these behaviors are similar to the ones that Cline found in his study on the effects of poor bonding and attachment. Clearly, parental neglect, abuse, and emotional abandonment play an important role in creating the internal "working model" of these kinds of young people. If we are going to stop bullying and school violence as well as the rest of the antisocial behaviors of children and adults, we have to help parents achieve a secure bond or attachment with their children.

In addition, Perry's research has indicated that parents who are withdrawn and remote, neglectful and passive or depressed, are at risk of causing their child's brain to stop developing. Perry found that neglect impairs the development of the brain's cortex, where feelings of belonging and attachment occur. According to Perry, these neglected kids desperately need positive adult attention to compensate for the lack of attention or negative attention they received early in life from their parents or family members (Perry, 1996b).

Violato and Russell (1994) conducted a Canadian meta-analysis of 88 published research studies on the effects of nonmaternal care on the development of infants and young children. They found that if the mother is gone for more than 20 hours a week, it can seriously affect the social-emotional, behavioral development and maternal attachment of infants and young children. Lero, Goelman, et al. (1992) found that 70 percent of Canadian mothers with children under 6 years old are working fulltime. In the United States, the figure is estimated to be 75 percent. This form of neglect has serious implications for our national policy of federal and state support for daycare so mothers can work.

Other research has confirmed that once the internal working model of the world is formed in early childhood, it persists into adulthood virtually unchanged (Pearson, Cowen, et al. 1993). Krause and Haverkamp (1996) summarize the research this way:

Existing research does suggest that the bond between parent and child is likely to remain in effect across the life span and plays an important role in later life parent-child relations. (pp. 85–86)

From their meta-analysis cited above, Violato and Russell (1994) concluded that the absence of the mother for more than 20 hours per week during infancy and early childhood increases the prevalence of insecure/ambivalent attachments by approximately 50 percent.

Developmental Trauma

As a part of the author's research on conflict resolution, he has identified the presence of developmental traumas during early childhood as the main cause of a later fear of or fascination with violence. These traumas often are caused more by neglect than abuse and, therefore, are harder to identify because "nothing happened," except that the child's needs were neglected and the significant adults disconnected from them (Weinhold & Weinhold, 2000).

The following are the usual causes of developmental traumas (Weinhold & Weinhold, 2000):

■ Child abuse, neglect, or emotional abandonment during the first 2 years of life
■ Disruptions in the normal sequence of development
■ Prolonged or repeated separations between mother and child during early bonding because of illness
■ Daily small disconnects between mother and child
■ Repeated encroachment of the child's physical, psychological, and emotional boundaries
■ A lack of understanding of the child's needs
■ Lack of support for safe exploratory behavior
■ Using the child to satisfy the parent's needs

This research (Weinhold & Weinhold, 2000) has shown that developmental traumas may be the cause of the following problems:

■ Developmental delays—"late-bloomers"
■ Attachment disorders (ambivalent or anxious/avoidant)
■ Attention deficit/hyperactive disorder
■ Cognitive impairment because of cognitive neglect
■ Primitive problem-solving strategies that involve use of violence
■ Dissociation in females
■ Aggressive, impulsive, reactive, and hyperactive behaviors in males

The author of *Real Boys* (Pollack, 1998), says that when parents or other adults disconnect from young boys, the boys learn to suffer in silence and, rather than crying tears, they eventually "cry bullets." This fits with the description of events in the lives of Eric Harris and Dylan Klebold. Their pent-up abandonment rage, exacerbated by the marginalization at school, discharged through violence. By studying brain scans, Perry found that neglected children had more damage to the cognitive functions of their brain than did abused children. The brain actually atrophies when it isn't stimulated enough. Another of Perry's findings is that children who were traumatized early in life develop more primitive, less mature styles of conflict resolution. They tend to be more impulsive, more easily triggered by stimulus events, and less likely to consider the consequences of their actions. Looked at through this lens, bullying can be seen as adapting to the effects of early traumas and using bullying as a protective mechanism to try to feel safe again (Perry, 1996b).

Conclusions from this research can be summarized as follows (Weinhold & Weinhold, 2000):

■ Many bullies and victims of bullying show classic signs of PTSD and possibly suffer from the effects of the neglect of their basic attachment needs early in life.

■ Bullying incidents usually begin with a triggering event that leads to a traumatic reenactment of previous unresolved developmental traumas or conflicts experienced by the bully or the victim, or both.

■ Bullies and victims need counseling that teaches them trauma-reduction techniques and conflict-resolution skills, and provides them with the positive attention they missed in their early childhood experiences.

The Kindness Campaign: A Primary Prevention Program to Curb Bullying and School Violence

The Kindness Campaign was started in July 1994 under the National Program for the Study and Prevention of Youth and Family Violence at the University of Colorado at Colorado Springs. It was designed as a primary prevention program to address the rising tide of violence among youth, in families, and in schools. Though the National Program receives in-kind support from the university, it depends upon grants and contributions from individuals and corporations. The Kindness Campaign is based on the idea that the best way to eliminate a negative behavior (bullying, put-downs, aggressive behaviors) is by focusing everyone's attention on the opposite of these behaviors: kindness. The program addresses each of the hidden elements of the culture of violence. Below is a summary of how the Kindness Campaign addresses these hidden elements and the results achieved thus far.

Promoting Humanistic Values

The predominant message of the Kindness Campaign is that domination and violence can be stopped if schools and communities use their resources to promote humanistic values such as kindness, respect for the law, peaceful resolution of conflicts, and understanding and tolerance of differences. The campaign's co-sponsor, the local CBS television affiliate, conducted a random sample interview of its viewers in late 1994 and found that 75% of its viewers believed the Campaign was having a positive impact on the community (Weinhold, 1996). Since then, the Kindness Campaign has co-sponsored many community events designed to build common ground and increase understanding and tolerance. These events include an Annual Interfaith Celebration of Kindness and neighborhood ceremonies to recognize the positive activities of residents.

Kindness Campaign programs have been started in more than 105 schools, reaching over 70,000 students in Colorado Springs. Ten other U.S. cities have adopted the Kindness Campaign in their community and schools. As a result of the efforts of the Kindness Campaign's programs, in 1997 the city of Colorado Springs was one of three U.S. cities to be named a "Community of Kindness."

Creating a Positive School and Community Climate

More than 105 area schools have used the Kindness Campaign to improve their school climate. Their results indicate that children who get more recognition for positive behaviors don't have to bully others or wear trench coats to get attention. The Kindness Campaign has produced a curriculum guide, *Spreading Kindness: A Program Guide for Preventing Peer Violence in Schools,* which contains 154 activities for schools to use in designing their own program.

One suggested activity shows how to develop a school Kindness Code that would include the following:

1. "We will say and do kind things to others in this school."
2. "We will recognize the kind things that other people say and do."
3. "We will help those who are having trouble being kind."

In most schools that started the Kindness Campaign, student to student put-downs dropped significantly. One elementary school reduced put-downs by 94 percent after the Kindness Campaign was introduced (Weinhold, 1999a).

Reducing Bullying and Aggressive Behaviors

When bullies see other kids getting recognized for positive behaviors, they begin exhibiting more positive behaviors. In three different middle schools where the Kindness Campaign was introduced, discipline referrals to the office dropped by more than 30 percent. The Kindness Campaign's Creating Kind and Safe Schools program helps schools develop an anti-bullying policy. Faculty and students learn about the negative effects of bullying and then collaborate to create a schoolwide anti-bullying policy. Such a policy might include the following:

1. "Teachers and staff agree to confront all incidents of bullying and put-downs that they see."
2. "Students agree to help those being bullied or put down by speaking out and/or getting adult help."
3. "All students, faculty and staff agree to include everyone in their activities. No one is marginalized."

Dealing With Student Traumas

One of the best ways to deal with untreated trauma is the use of peer mediation programs and schoolwide conflict-resolution classes. Peer mediation involves identifying a group of students, who are selected for their leadership and interpersonal qualities, to become identified as peer mediators. These peer mediators are trained to intervene in peer-conflict situations, where they attempt to get the parties to resolve their conflict peacefully or get adult help, if necessary. This helps prevent peer conflicts from escalating into more aggressive actions. They are trained to approach students engaged in a peer conflict and to offer to help them mediate the conflict.

Usually the agreement is that if the parties can resolve the conflict to everyone's satisfaction, the matter is ended. If not, the peer mediator takes the parties to see a teacher, a counselor, or an administrator, who then will intervene. In combination with a conflict-resolution curriculum, peer mediation helps prevent peer conflicts from escalating and helps prevent bullying. Again, excellent peer-mediation training materials are available on the market. More than 8,500 of the some 85,000 schools in the United States teach conflict resolution to all students (NIDR, 1999).

Research (Johnson & Johnson, 1995) shows that a conflict-resolution curriculum in the schools

- decreases physical violence in the school,
- leads to less disruptive behavior,
- improves academic performance,
- empowers kids to solve their own problems, and
- increases student leadership.

Developing Cooperative Learning Methods to Resolve Conflicts

Many schools have found that, by adding cooperative learning to their curriculum, they are able to reduce bullying and related school violence. In the 1960s, David and Roger Johnson (1995) from the University of Minnesota created a cooperative learning program called Teaching Students to be Peacemakers. This K–12 program has been operating for more than 30 years and teaches all students

- to recognize what is a conflict and what is not a conflict,
- to negotiate win-win solutions to conflicts, and
- to help mediate schoolmates' conflicts.

After conducting numerous research studies to determine the effectiveness of this program, they found that it resulted in a schoolwide discipline program focused on empowering students to regulate and control their own and their classmates' actions. As a result of this program, when a conflict occurred, the students involved would first try to negotiate a resolution. If that failed, they would ask a classmate to help mediate the conflict. If that failed, they would ask a teacher to help mediate the conflict. If that failed, the teacher would be asked to arbitrate the conflict. If that failed, they would ask the principal to help mediate the conflict, and if that failed, they would have the principal arbitrate the conflict (Johnson & Johnson, 1995).

In addition, teachers and counselors need to be trained to identify the symptoms of PTSD and how to intervene effectively in these cases. I have developed training materials and, through the Kindness Campaign, offer inservices and train teachers and counselors in these skills. The whole field of traumatology has had a number of breakthroughs that have led to the development of new trauma reduction techniques that school counselors and teachers can learn to use when they encounter students who are experiencing symptoms of PTSD (Weinhold & Weinhold, 2000).

Addressing Parental Abuse and Neglect

The Kindness Campaign has produced an activity guide for parents, *Raising Kind Kids: An Activity Guide for Fostering Kindness in Families* (Weinhold, 1999b). This guide contains 25 family-kindness activities that parents can use to instill more kindness into their families. Working through the PTAs in schools, the Kindness Campaign offers inservices to parents who want to increase their ability to relate to their children in positive ways. In addition, the Kindness Campaign has produced a guide for preschools, *Kind Beginnings: An Activity Guide for Fostering Kindness in Preschools* (Weinhold, 2000). This activity guide contains 36 field-tested activities that preschool teachers can utilize to teach young children how to be kind and respectful toward each other.

Businesses Adopting a Kind and Safe School

One of the main intervention programs of the Kindness Campaign in schools is the Adopt a Kind and Safe School project. Area businesses that are interested in helping make area schools kinder and safer for the children of their employees have "adopted" schools. The business donates funds for the Kindness Campaign to work intensively with their adopted school to create a positive learning climate and put in place an anti-bullying policy. The business also arranges for its employees to volunteer at the school as aides or tutors in the classroom. The Kindness Campaign conducts inservices with the faculty and students, plans school assemblies, and installs follow-up evaluation procedures. An outline of the process that the Kindness Campaign uses to deliver this program follows.

I. Conduct a needs assessment.
    A. Determine what is needed to make this a kind and safe school.
    B. Meet with faculty and students.
    C. Develop a contract with the school to provide the program it needs.
II. Establish the Kindness Campaign to change the overall school climate.
    A. Conduct inservices with faculty and staff.
    B. Select a Kindness Committee and School Coordinator(s).
    C. Help committee design program to meet school needs (Utilize the Program Guide: *Spreading Kindness*).
    D. Organize kick-off assembly for the students.
    E. Do follow-up consultation with faculty and students.
    F. Start Kind Kids Council(s).
    G. Conduct ongoing evaluation of outcomes.

III. Create an all-school policy on bullying and put-downs.
  A. Conduct student and teacher survey/needs assessment.
  B. Do inservice for faculty and staff.
  C. Design classroom activities for students.
  D. Develop classroom and school rules.
  E. Do follow-up in-service/consultation.
  F. Design and conduct ongoing evaluation (formative and summative).

IV. Help the school establish primary prevention/school safety methods (optional).
  A. Help establish a peer mediation program.
  B. Help establish a conflict-resolution curriculum for all students.
  C. Help create an emergency disaster plan.
  D. Help create an overall school safety plan.

 V. Conduct in-service trainings (optional).
  A. Trauma Reduction Techniques for Counselors and Teachers.
  B. Understanding Gender Differences: Real Boys and Real Girls.
  C. High-Risk Kids: Early Identification and Intervention.
  D. Kids' Rights: The Legal Rights of Children to Protection Against Violence.
  E. Conflict Resolution/Peer Mediation Training.

VI. Provide other services, if needed. Sometimes schools need help with special projects such as designing a better system to deal with students who are disruptive. The Kindness Campaign has designed community and school service programs as an alternative to school suspension.

VII. Help develop long-term cooperative relationships between the school and the business sponsor. The Kindness Campaign staff attempts to encourage the development of a cooperative, long-term relationship between the school and the business. This varies with each school and business. Most businesses arrange to have their employees volunteer at the school they have adopted. Some tutor or read to students who don't get much help at home, and others assist the teacher in the classroom in various ways. Some businesses encourage their adopted schools to provide them with a wish list of equipment or supplies that the school needs and then, if possible, the business provides it.

VIII. Develop programs for the business employees and their families. This is a vital link in the Adopt a Kind and Safe School project. Here, the staff of the Kindness Campaign offers inservice training to the employees of the businesses that have adopted a school. These programs include parenting classes for employees who have families, teaching them how to discipline using kindness and nonthreatening methods. An ambulance company was noticing that its employees were suffering from vicarious trauma and burn-out because of their daily exposure to traumatic and crisis situations. The staff of the Kindness Campaign offered to teach the employees how to recognize their own trauma symptoms and then teach them practical trauma reduction techniques that they could use with each other and with themselves.

Will we wake-up in time? George Kennan, former Secretary of State, likened the American public to a sleeping dinosaur. He said every now and then something would disturb the dinosaur and it would wake up and flail about, trying to find who or what was to blame for waking it up. In the process, it would destroy or damage much of its surroundings. Finding no one to blame, it would go back to sleep.

It seems to me that we are in danger of having a repeat of the Columbine shootings. We may say, "It isn't going to happen here, so we don't have to worry" or, "We can't seem to find who is to blame." So we may go back to sleep until something wakes us up again. I assure you that the next time will be an even more dramatic wake-up call.

The Cost of Failure to Act

Unless we take action to deal with the hidden elements of the culture of violence, the problem will get worse. We will see some of the following:

■ The dropout rate as a result of bullying will continue to rise. (It is currently 10 percent.)

■ The number of high school students who are afraid to go to restrooms at school will increase. (It is now 20 percent of high school students.)

■ The number of kids who report being bullied will increase. (Currently it is 80 to 90 percent among middle school students.)

■ The number of kids who stay home to avoid bullying will increase. (Currently, 162,000 students stay home each day because they are afraid to go to school.)

■ More short-sighted, reactive solutions, such as installing metal detectors, hiring more police to patrol the halls, and putting in more surveillance cameras, will be tried with no tangible results.

■ More school shootings will occur. (64 percent of adults believe it will happen in their own community.)

■ The government will be forced to intervene and pass restrictive legislation holding schools and parents legally accountable. (A description of a first attempt at this is presented below.)

Bullying and Human Rights

Bill and Rita Head, Georgia parents of a 15-year-old who shot himself in front of his classmates after suffering repeated bullying, have proposed new legislation to better protect our children. As a result, a bill was introduced into the Georgia State Legislature that amends the Georgia Criminal Code to give children the same protection under the law that persons 21 years old and older have.

Currently, the Criminal Code in Georgia, as well as some other states, excludes children from protection under the law concerning five types of violent behavior: simple assaults, simple battery, battery, stalking, and using so called "fighting words" or engaging in disorderly conduct. The Heads also want mandatory posting of the rights of children under the law in all schools and mandatory reporting of violations of these laws by the teachers (Brown, 1999).

This is an attempt to classify bullying and put-downs as violations of the rights of children "to be secure and protected from fear, intimidation and physical harm caused by the activities of violent groups and individuals." This represents an intriguing proposal because, using the standard definitions of assaults and battery, stalking, fighting words, bullying, and put-downs are violations of human rights under the laws that cover adults. The same human rights clearly should be extended to children and youth under 21 years of age. This would get the attention of school officials who until now have essentially turned their backs on bullying and put-downs. If such a law had existed in Colorado, the Columbine shootings would not have occurred. The Juvenile Code in Colorado covers these five categories of violent behavior, but it does not call for posting these laws in schools and it does not call for mandatory reporting by teachers. You might check on the Criminal Code in your state.

Summary

Hidden aspects of the culture of violence that keep it going include the dominator value system, an over-focus on negativity, the pervasiveness of bullying, collective denial of the effects of bullying, the presence of PTSD, and an increase of parental abuse and neglect. These hidden factors must be addressed if we are going to change the culture of violence. The Kindness Campaign is an effective primary prevention program that addresses these hidden elements of the culture of violence in schools and communities.

References

Adler, J. & Springen, K. (1999). How to fight back. *Newsweek,* May 3, 1999, p. 37.

Ainsworth, M. (1989). Attachments beyond infancy. *American Psychologist, 44,* 709–716.

American Psychiatric Association (APA). (1996). *The diagnostic and statistical manual (DSM-IV), (4th ed.).* Washington, DC: American Psychiatric Association Press.

Begley, S. (1999). Why the young kill. *Newsweek,* May 3, 1999 p. 32–37.

Bowlby, J. (1988). *A secure base: Parent-child attachment and healthy human development.* London: Routledge.

Brown, T. (1999, January 18). *The bullying reference,* 1(4), Zanesville, OH: The Broken

Toy Project. Retrieved February 6, 1999 from World Wide Web: http:/members. tripod.com/-Ghoul2x/Bully1.html

Brown T. (1999). *The broken toy project.* 846 1/2 McIntire Ave. Zanesville, OH, 43701.

Bully OnLine. (1999). *Web Site of the UK National Workplace Bullying Advice Line.* URL: <www.successunlimited.co.uk/ costs.htm>

Campos, J., Barrett, K., et al. (1983). Socioemotional development. In M. M. Haith & J. J. Campos (Eds.), *Handbook of child psychology: Vol. 2. Infancy and psychobiology.* New York: Wiley, pp. 783–915.

Cline, F. (1979). *Understanding and treating the severely disturbed child.* Evergreen, CO: Evergreen Consultants in Human Behavior.

Dube, J. (1999). High school hell. *ABC NEWS.com,* April 24, 1999, p. 1.

Eisler, R. (1987). *The chalice and the blade.* San Francisco: Harper & Row.

Espelage, D., et al., (1999, Aug.). Interviews with middle school students: Bullying, victimization, and contextual factors. Presentation at American Psychological Association Annual Conference, Boston, Aug. 21.

Fried, S., & Fried, P. (1996). *Bullies and victims: Helping your child survive the schoolyard battlefield.* New York: M. Evans & Co.

Gibbs, N., & Roche, T. (1999). The Columbine tapes. *Time,* 154 (25), 40–51.

Grossman, D. (1996). *On killing: The psychological cost of learning to kill in war and society.* New York: Little, Brown & Co.

Grossman, D. (1998). Trained to kill. *Christianity Today,* Aug. 10, 1998, pp. 31–39.

Hawkins, D., Catalano, R., et al. (1992). *Communities that care: Action for drug abuse prevention.* San Francisco: Jossey-Bass.

Heise, L., Ellsberg, M., & Gottemoeller, M. (1999, Dec.). *Ending violence against women.* (Population Reports, Series L, No. 11). Baltimore: Johns Hopkins University, School of Public Health, Population Information Program.

Johnson, D. W., & Johnson, R. (1995). *Teaching students to be peacemakers.* Edina: MN: Interaction Book Co.

Joseph, J. (1999). Sugar, spice and ready to kill. *ABCNEWS.com,* April 28, 1999, pp. 1–2.

Karen, R. (1998). *Becoming attached.* New York: Oxford University Press.

Krause, A. & Haverkamp, B. (1996). Attachment in adult child-older parent relationships: Research, theory, and practice. *Journal of Counseling & Development, 75,* 83–92.

Langer, G. (1999). Students report violent peers. *ABCNEWS.com,* April 26, 1999, pp. 1–2.

Lederer, L., & Varela, S. (1998). *Safe schools, safe students: A guide to violence prevention strategies.* Washington DC: Substance Abuse & Mental Health Services Administration.

Lero, D., Golman, H., et al. (1992). *Parental work patterns and childcare needs* (Catalogue 89-529E) Ottawa: Canadian National Child Care Study.

Magid, K., & McKelvey, C. (1989). *High risk: Children without a conscience.* New York: Bantam Books.

Marano, H., (1995). Big. bad. bully. *Psychology Today,* 28, 50–68.

National Institute for Dispute Resolution. (1999). *Conflict resolution education facts.* URL: <www.CRFnet.org>

Nerenberg, A. (1999). *Road rage.* Web Site URL: <www.roadragenerenberg.com>

Olweus, D. (1993). Victimization by peers: Antecedents and long-term consequences. In K. H. Rubin & J. B. Asendorf (Eds.), *Social withdrawal, inhibition, and shyness in childhood.* Hillside, NJ: Erlbaum.

Olweus, D. (1994). *Bullying at school: What we know and what we can do.* Oxford, UK: Blackwell Publishers.

Paulk, D. et al. (1999). Teacher, peer and self-nominations of bullies and victims of bullying. Presentation at American Psychological Association Annual Conference, Boston, August 21, 1999.

Pearson, J., Cowen, P., et al. (1993). Adult attachment and adult child-older parent relationships. *American Journal of Orthopsychiatry*, 63, 606–613.

Perry, B. (1996a). Aggression and violence: The neurobiology of experience. *AACAP Developmentor*. Spring.

Perry, B. (1996b). Neurodevelopmental adaptations to violence: How children survive the intergenerational vortex of violence. In *Violence and childhood trauma: Understanding and responding to the effects of violence on young children*. Cleveland, OH: Gund Foundation Publishers, 66–80.

Pollack, W. (1998). *Real boys*. New York: Random House.

Portner, J. (1997). Zero-tolerance laws getting a second look. *Education Week on the Web*, March 26.

Prendergast, A. (1999). Doom rules. *Denver Westword*. August 5–11, 1999, pp. 1–16. URL: <westword.com>.

Saunders, C. (1997). When push comes to shove: Dealing with bullies requires adult supervision. *Our Children*, March/April.

Sebastian, S. J. (1996). Domestic violence. In A. L. Harwood-Nuss (Ed.): *Emergency medicine—A comprehensive study guide* (4th ed.). New York: McGraw Hill.

Straus, M. (1994). *Beating the devil out of them*. New York: Lexington Books.

Straus, M & Gelles, R. (1988). How violent are American families? Estimates from the national family violence resurvey and other studies. In G. Hotaling, et al. (Eds.), *Family abuse and its consequences: New directions in research.*

U. S. Department of Education, National Center for Educational Statistics, *Principal/school disciplinarian survey on school violence* (1997). (Fast Response Survey System, and FRSS 63). Washington, DC: Government Printing Office.

Weinhold, B. (1991). *Breaking free of addictive family relationships*. Walpole, NH: Stillpoint Publishing.

Weinhold, B. (Ed.) (1996*). Spreading kindness: A program guide for reducing youth violence in the schools*. Colorado Springs, CO: Kindness Campaign.

Weinhold, B. (1999a). Bullying and school violence. *Counseling Today*, 42(4), 14.

Weinhold, B. (1999b*). Raising kind kids: An activity guide for fostering kindness in families*. Colorado Springs, CO: Kindness Campaign.

Weinhold, B. (Ed.). (2000). *Kind beginnings: An activity guide for fostering kindness in pre-schools*. Colorado Springs, CO: Kindness Campaign.

Weinhold, B. & Weinhold, J. (1998). Conflict resolution: The partnership way in schools. *Counseling & Human Development, 30* (7), 1–12.

Weinhold, B. & Weinhold, J. (2000). *Conflict resolution: The partnership way*. Denver: Love Publishing.

Teaching Children to Care Rather Than Kill

Radha J. Horton-Parker

*I*t's a typical April morning, and school has begun like always at Columbine *High School. With thoughts of graduation, summer vacation, and the vast tomorrow that seems to stretch out endlessly before them, students laugh and converse as the day proceeds. But soon carefree laughter is transformed into terror and tears as two students, armed with guns and grenades, enter the school and begin the massacre that will end the tomorrows of 15 individuals.*

The tragedy in Littleton, Colorado, which brought immediate reactions of shock and disbelief, has begun to awaken us from the complacency that predominates in our culture. Although violence prevails in movies and video games, popular music is replete with hate-filled lyrics, guns are readily available, and bomb-making recipes abound on the Internet, we never expect our children to commit murder. Yet, when two teenagers from affluent homes with apparently caring parents went on a killing spree in a nice, suburban high school, few of us were spared the realization that major changes are needed in our society.

Although controversy abounds about what should be done, nearly everyone agrees that we must do *something*. Legislation regarding gun control, censorship in the media, greater control of the Internet, fining parents for children's misdeeds, and increased security in the schools all have been proposed as possible solutions. On a more therapeutic note, mental health professionals have advocated diagnostic procedures to identify students who may be at risk of violent behavior, as well as counseling interventions to help alienated students fit in better with their peers.

Even though these ideas have merit, a more efficacious strategy might be to engage in primary prevention in early childhood rather than remediation in adolescence. One untapped resource is the potential of humanistic parenting to engender prosocial behavior in children. *Prosocial behavior,* defined as action intended to benefit others without the expectation of an external reward (Eisenberg, 1988), contrasts

219

with aggression, defined as "behavior aimed at harming another person" (Perry, Perry, & Boldizar, 1990, p. 135). Dave Sanders, the teacher and coach who lost his life while protecting his students during the Columbine massacre, is perhaps the ultimate exemplar of prosocial behavior. In contrast, the student assassins represent extreme cases of aggression.

The key to understanding why some individuals selflessly help their fellow humans while others murder them might be found in early childhood. Much evidence suggests that parents—who serve as children's first models—can be instrumental in assisting children to develop the ability to act thoughtfully and kindly toward others (Eisenberg, 1992). Parental influence is so powerful that one longitudinal study found that 36% of the variance in adult levels of empathy could be explained by the child-rearing practices that the participants had experienced in early childhood (Koestner, Franz, & Weinberger, 1990). This is especially significant in that a meta-analysis of the research revealed that empathy and sympathy were correlated positively with prosocial behavior (Eisenberg & Miller, 1987).

Thus, a firm foundation of prosocial behavior, established when children are young, could be essential to curbing violence in the adolescent years. Perhaps, if parents acquire basic skills in humanistic parenting, today's affectionate toddlers with teddy bears will be deterred from becoming tomorrow's maleficent teens with grenades. The purpose of this chapter is to provide information that counselors can use to assist parents in developing practices that will lead to lifelong prosocial outcomes in young children.

Our Culture of Violence

Striking insights into the psychology of extreme interpersonal violence have emerged with the advent of a new field of study, "killology." The foremost authority in this field is Lt. Col. Dave Grossman (1996), a former professor of psychology at West Point and author of the best-selling book, *On Killing*. Grossman maintains that just as AIDS breaks down the body's immune system and leaves it vulnerable to disease, so does constant exposure to rampant violence in the media and video games break down children's natural aversion to killing, effectively "taking off the safety catch" that keeps fatal aggression psychologically in check.

To support his theories, Grossman recounts the history of the development of techniques by military psychologists to increase the kill rate of soldiers. Definitive evidence collected after the end of World War II showed that only 15% to 20% of combat infantry were willing to fire their weapons. Appalled by these findings, military psychologists began seeking and implementing new training strategies to engender a greater willingness to kill in soldiers. The needed strategies were discovered and successfully applied. The fire rate of infantry in Korea rose to 50%, and to more than 90% in Vietnam.

Military trainers accomplished their magic by using three tools: operant conditioning, classical conditioning, and social learning, focusing on the imitation of role models. Soldiers are classically conditioned by being made to view films depicting people being injured or killed in increasingly violent ways. As a result, they become able to disassociate themselves emotionally from the fear or revulsion that arises in empathy for another person being hurt or abused. Operant strategies include the use of *human-shaped* pop-up targets on firing ranges and other life-like simulated situations. Soldiers trained in this way learn to target and shoot reflexively, bypassing any potential rational inhibitions, as they are reinforced by seeing their bullets make their marks.

Finally, we can credit the well known stereotype of the drill sergeant as a heroic, ultra-capable, invincible role model for the social learning component of the initiatives we are discussing. Boot camp was redesigned to be an ever more efficient initiatory rite of passage through which the neophyte soldier's previous value system is stripped away and replaced with a new ethos in which devastating physical aggression and unconditional obedience become the new foundations of self-worth. These qualities are incarnate in the drill sergeant, who becomes a role model and a surrogate father, brother, and even mother to the troops.

Grossman argues convincingly that the same conditioning techniques used successfully by the military to train soldiers to kill are present in the films, music, television programs, and video games that children regularly watch. Hyper-violent films provide an example of classical conditioning at work. The films themselves vie with each other to portray mutilation and murder in ever more graphic detail. Repeated exposure to incrementally more gruesome imagery inevitably desensitizes children and weakens their natural aversion to seeing others harmed. In a kind of *Clockwork Orange* reverse scenario, the enjoyment that derives from sitting in the comfort of a movie theater munching popcorn and enjoying the company of friends becomes paired with the aggression they are witnessing so that observing violence actually comes to evoke a pleasurable state by association.

Similarly, the principles of operant conditioning are powerfully active in children who immerse themselves in the world of violent video games. As children learn to fire weapons reflexively at pop-up villains, they receive instant reinforcement from seeing characters' heads blown off—or worse. As with films, violent video games tend to incorporate increasingly realistic weapons, wounds, and associated trauma. In some cases, the targets are not bug-eyed monsters but, instead, normal human beings, and the child plays the role of an assassin or a monster.

Through this sort of visual programming, children not only develop "automaticity" and learn to see the world through a gunsight, but they also can actually sharpen their shooting skills. Police officers and FBI agents both utilize the same training procedures to develop combat readiness. So effective is this training that "shoot/no shoot" programming was introduced to constrain collateral violence created by officers who receive such training. Of course, video games enjoin no such restraints.

Finally, as children watch powerful action heros successfully defeat their foes, they learn that violence is a rewarding and effective way of problem-solving.

Because media characters often are shown killing others for minor slights, youth learn that murder is an acceptable response to injustice, imagined or perceived.

Grossman (1996) also offers readers a thoughtful reappraisal of the actual extent of youth violence occurring in our society. Between 1985 and 1991, the homicide rates for males 15 to 19 years of age increased 154%, with homicide the second leading cause of death for all males in this age group and the first leading cause of death in Black males. As shocking as these statistics are, things actually are significantly worse than they appear. Grossman points out that advanced medical capabilities, such as resuscitation technology, save the lives of many persons who certainly would have died in the past. Grossman cites UCLA professor James Q. Wilson's estimate that if trauma care were the same now as in 1957, the homicide rate would be close to three times what statistics reflect now.

Even though the youth violence rate is higher in the United States than in any other industrialized nation, most industrialized nations having a similar level of media violence have witnessed parallel increases in teen violent activity. The one significant exception to this rapid rise in youth aggression is Japan. Although Japanese children partake of the same violent media influences as other youth, a protective "bubble" immunizes them from acting out the aggression they observe. The key to this phenomenon is theorized to be the incredibly strong sense of interdependence between the individual and the family and social structure that is intrinsic to Japanese culture. Japanese children are taught to engage in prosocial behavior from an early age, and that lesson is reinforced at every stage of life. Perhaps by strengthening our families and helping parents learn to influence their children positively, we, too, may turn the tide of violence in our society.

Parenting Styles

Because fads in parenting come and go, parents and counselors often are left wondering what methods actually lead to the most desirable outcomes in children. The answers may lie in Diana Baumrind's ground-breaking research showing that parenting styles significantly impact children's behavior in ways that may be permanent.

In her landmark study, Baumrind (1967) observed children in a nursery school for 14 weeks. Based on their differing patterns of behavior, she categorized the youngsters into three groups: energetic-friendly children, conflicted-irritable children, and impulsive-aggressive children. Baumrind then interviewed the children's parents and observed them interacting with their children in home and laboratory settings.

On the basis of these observations, Baumrind identified three styles of parenting that appeared to be associated with the differing behavioral patterns in children. She labeled these three parenting styles as authoritarian, permissive, and authoritative. In a longitudinal study of the children from early childhood through adolescence,

Baumrind (1991) found that these three parenting styles were associated with specific outcomes, which will be described in the following section.

Using Baumrind's typology of authoritarian, permissive, and authoritative parenting styles as a basis, Maccoby and Martin (1983) added a fourth category—indifferent parenting—and proposed that the four parenting styles could be distinguished by the relative balance of control/ demandingness and warmth/responsiveness present in each.

1. *Control/demandingness* refers to the extent to which parents set high standards and exert firm control to ensure that their children exhibit mature behavior. This continuum represents the extent to which parents insist that their children perform developmentally appropriate tasks that require increasing social and cognitive competence.

2. *Warmth/responsiveness* refers to the extent to which parents convey affection and acceptance in their communication and are responsive to their children's feelings and needs. This continuum relates to the parental warmth and responsiveness so critical to forming attachment bonds in infancy and in maintaining loving, trusting relationships with children as they mature.

The following description of the four parenting styles is based on the models of Baumrind (1967) and of Maccoby and Martin (1983). Figure 9.1 depicts these styles.

Authoritarian Parents

In the Sutter home, the parents like to think that they "run a tight ship." Frank and Miriam Sutter are strict disciplinarians and do not allow any divergence from the expected norms of behavior. When faced with any resistance from their children, the Sutters quickly exert pressure to produce the desired result. "Do it now or else" is often stated in their home, and the children intimately know that the "else" means either a spanking or a sojourn in their rooms for an extended time. When the children occasionally ask their parents why they have to do something, the inevitable reply is "because we said so," and the children then are told to "just stop complaining and do what we say."

Authoritarian parents are high in control/demandingness, but low in the humanistic qualities of warmth/responsiveness. These parents set rigid standards, demand unquestioning compliance, and allow no opportunities for their children to articulate any concerns they have about their parents' expectations. The parents show little warmth or respect in interactions with their children, and parental authority is absolute. Punishment follows quickly when their children disobey orders, and even though the children might have legitimate needs that are not being met, divergent views are not allowed expression.

Baumrind (1967) found the authoritarian parenting style to be correlated with the child behavioral pattern identified as *conflicted-irritable*. In nursery school, the children of authoritarian parents appeared unhappy, withdrawn, mistrustful, and

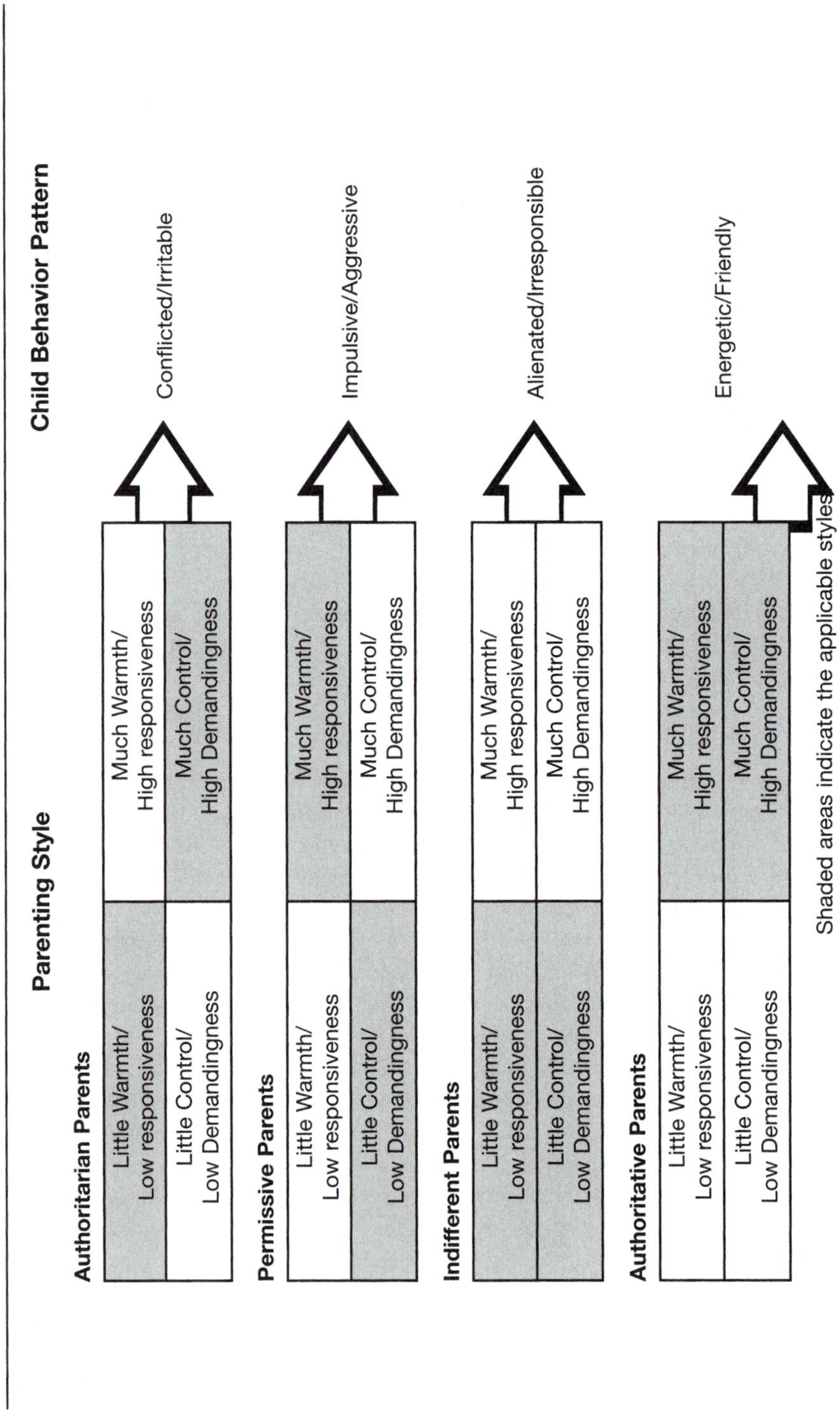

Parenting Style

Child Behavior Pattern

Authoritarian Parents

Little Warmth/ Low responsiveness	Much Warmth/ High responsiveness
Little Control/ Low Demandingness	Much Control/ High Demandingness

Conflicted/Irritable

Permissive Parents

Little Warmth/ Low responsiveness	Much Warmth/ High responsiveness
Little Control/ Low Demandingness	Much Control/ High Demandingness

Impulsive/Aggressive

Indifferent Parents

Little Warmth/ Low responsiveness	Much Warmth/ High responsiveness
Little Control/ Low Demandingness	Much Control/ High Demandingness

Alienated/Irresponsible

Authoritative Parents

Little Warmth/ Low responsiveness	Much Warmth/ High responsiveness
Little Control/ Low Demandingness	Much Control/ High Demandingness

Energetic/Friendly

Shaded areas indicate the applicable styles

Based on the studies of D. Baumrind, and E. E. Maccoby & J. A. Martin, and related research.

Figure 9.1   Parenting Styles Related to Child Behavior Patterns

socially anxious. When frustrated with their playmates, these preschoolers often responded with hostility. The negative impact of authoritarian parenting did not end when the last days of childhood had passed, but instead extended into adolescence. The effects were more pronounced for boys than girls. The adolescent sons of authoritarian parents were socially incompetent, unfriendly, and lacking in initiative and self-confidence (Baumrind, 1991).

Other studies also suggested that authoritarian parenting produced children with low self-esteem who lacked self-confidence and spontaneity (Coopersmith, 1967; Lamborn, Mounts, Steinberg, & Dornbusch, 1991; Lempers, Clark-Lempers, & Simons, 1989). Adolescents from authoritarian homes were obedient but lacking in competence (Steinberg, 1990). When corporal punishment was employed as a central component of authoritarian parenting, the results were especially detrimental. Children developed aggressive behaviors themselves when they were exposed to spanking and other harsh disciplinary practices (Dodge, Bates, & Pettit, 1990; Weiss, Dodge, Bates, & Pettit, 1992).

Permissive Parents

The Jenkins family is at the end of the continuum opposite from the Sutters. Fran and Jake Jenkins allow their children total freedom and shower them with compliments and praise. These parents rarely discipline or set limits for their children and, instead, encourage them to do whatever they wish. The children face no real consequences for failing to fulfill parental requests and often are unaware that their parents have any expectations for them other than to be themselves.

In situations in which one of the Jenkins children is asked to help with a household task, the child typically objects ("I can't. I'm busy playing this video game, and I can't stop."). When the child resists, the parents usually just do the chore themselves so their child can continue to play. Sometimes they even say, "Don't worry about it, honey. You're busy, so we'll take care of it. Go ahead and finish your game."

As this illustration shows, permissive parenting contrasts starkly with authoritarian parenting in that it is low in control/demandingness but high in warmth/responsiveness. Permissive parents offer unconditional love and acceptance but fail to provide adequate guidelines for mature, responsible behavior. Instead, they allow children to have greater freedom than is appropriate for their developmental levels and permit them to make choices that require more maturity than they possess.

Although permissive parents often believe that they are nurturing their children's growth, they could be unintentionally cultivating their children's self-indulgence and fostering a lack of social concern. By showering youngsters with unlimited material possessions and expecting nothing in return, some permissive parents think they are teaching their children to be correspondingly generous and loving. In reality, they likely are teaching their children to think only of themselves. Because this approach affords so little structure or consistency, prosocial behavior in children is not a likely outcome of permissive parenting.

Baumrind (1967) noted that the preschoolers of permissive parents exhibited the behavioral pattern categorized as *impulsive-aggressive.* These children not only had difficulty controlling their impulses but also exhibited highly immature behavior. Lacking confidence in themselves, they were extremely demanding and dependent on adults (Baumrind, 1971). Although some of the children were creative and friendly, others were socially inept. They frequently gave up when they encountered any frustration in their nursery school tasks and became aggressive when other children's needs conflicted with their own. Later research showed that adolescents from permissive homes were likely to be self-confident but to have higher levels of substance abuse and more problems in school (Steinberg, 1990).

Authoritative Parents

Ike and Samantha Freeman clearly state what they want their children to do and how they expect them to behave. The children know that disobedience will have consequences directly related to their misbehavior. Sometimes, however, the children have valid reasons for being excused from doing expected tasks or for asking for special considerations. In these cases, the children voice their concerns, and their parents listen respectfully.

Recently one of the Freeman children asked to be allowed to stay up an hour and a half later than her customary bedtime on a school night to watch a television show about a topic she had studied in her science class. Although Ike and Samantha recognized their daughter's interest as being legitimate, they let her know that they thought it was important for her to get adequate rest. After discussing the issue, the Freemans agreed that everyone's needs would be met if the parents were to tape the show and let the daughter watch it immediately after school the next day. Although this solution meant that Ike had to make an unplanned trip to the store to purchase a blank videotape, everyone was satisfied with the outcome.

Unlike the former two parenting styles, authoritative parenting is high in both control/demandingness and warmth/responsiveness. The Freemans could have flatly denied their daughter's request and said, "You know the rules—go to bed," as the Sutters would have. Or the Freemans could have given in to whatever their daughter wished to do and said, "Sure, sweetie—we wouldn't want you to miss your show," as the Jenkinses would have. The Freemans, however, chose the authoritative approach of maintaining their parental authority while also ensuring that their daughter felt respected and that her concerns were adequately addressed. Authoritative parents set firm limits for children's behavior and also exhibit warmth and flexibility in responding to their children's needs while encouraging them to be involved in problem solving.

The children of authoritative parents exhibited the behavioral pattern that Baumrind (1967) labeled as *energetic-friendly.* Of all the children in the nursery school, this type was found to be the most well adjusted. These preschoolers showed friendliness, confidence, self-control, and high achievement. In addition, they appeared to be happy and were less likely than their peers to engage in disruptive and defiant behaviors. For these reasons, the authoritative approach is associated with the best outcomes for children. As adolescents, the children of authoritative parents continued to exhibit these positive qualities (Baumrind, 1991). Other studies have yielded similar findings, showing that children experience the most positive outcomes when parents practice child-centered patterns of discipline accompanied by clearly communicated demands, careful monitoring, and an atmosphere of acceptance (Maccoby, 1984; Maccoby & Martin, 1983).

Indifferent Parents

The Schmidts pay little attention to their children. Struggling to survive on their meager incomes, they worry more about having enough money to pay for groceries and rent than about what their children are doing. George and Bertha each work two part-time jobs with schedules that change from week to week, so their children often are left at home alone. Sometimes a teenage girl from the neighborhood watches the children, but when she is not available, the Schmidts have their own 10-year-old son attend to his four siblings.

Because their jobs are so demanding and frequently require them to work late-night shifts, George and Bertha are easily irritated when their children attempt to get their attention. The parents often respond angrily if their children make requests, as happened recently when the 5-year-old asked her mother to help her remove a splinter from her finger. Trying to get a few hours rest before going to her second job, Bertha looked at her daughter and said, "Go away. Can't you see I'm trying to sleep?" No one else was around at the time, so the daughter did go away—and began walking to her grandmother's house, 3 miles away. Concerned neighbors saw the little girl walking alone on the road and called Child Protective Services.

Indifferent parenting lies at the opposite end of the continuum from the authoritative style because it is low in both control/demandingness and warmth/responsiveness. Although Baumrind did not study this group, Maccoby and Martin (1983) described indifferent parents as being both lax in discipline and lacking in warmth. These parents show little concern for their children's welfare, are disengaged from parenting, and do not monitor their children's behavior. As a result of this parental neglect, children fail to form attachment bonds and suffer from social incompetence and low self-esteem. Indifferent parental behavior has been linked to children's noncompliance, aggression, delinquency, truancy, precocious sexuality, and alcohol problems in adolescence and adulthood (Lamborn, Mounts, Steinberg, & Dornbusch, 1991; Patterson, 1982; Pulkkinen, 1982). We therefore could describe the child behavior pattern resulting from indifferent parenting as *alienated/irresponsible*. The children of indifferent parents generally have the worst outcomes of all.

The Need for Humanistic Parenting

Because authoritative parenting has been associated with the best and most prosocial outcomes in children, counselors might help to prevent violence indirectly in the teen years by teaching parents how to interact skillfully with their children authoritatively in early childhood. Learning humanistic, authoritative parenting techniques will enable parents to respond to their children's needs respectfully while setting high behavioral standards and maintaining firm control. This balance of control and respect should provide a firm foundation for fostering positive outcomes in children and for building trusting parent-child relationships that will endure throughout the turbulence of adolescence.

Skillful parenting is not guaranteed by virtue of being able to successfully procreate. Although most parents probably have good intentions toward their children, people tend to adopt a child-rearing style similar to that of their own parents—which may or may not be conducive to helping children learn to care about others as well as themselves. More than in the past, effective parenting is critically needed.

In the remainder of this chapter, I will attempt to address the parenting-skills deficit so prevalent in our society today by presenting ideas that counselors can share with parents to promote prosocial behavior in children. The approach, which I call humanistic parenting, consists of strategies drawn from behavioral research and popular parent-training programs that adopt an authoritative child-rearing style (Horton-Parker, 1998). These humanistic parenting techniques, which can be imparted to parents via workshops, counseling sessions, and newsletters, should provide a solid basis for prosocial behavior as children mature. Because I believe that workshops can be especially beneficial for parent training, I also will include some ideas for activities that counselors can use with parents in a large-group setting.

Before introducing the techniques of humanistic parenting, I would like to point out several points. First, although I use the term "parent" throughout this chapter, it is meant to refer to any adult serving in a parental or caregiving role to a child. Because families come in many forms today, "parents" refers to any individuals serving in a parental capacity, regardless of whether they are biologically or legally related to the children they are rearing.

A second note concerns the exclusive emphasis I have placed on parenting in early childhood. Although all of the techniques contained in this chapter can be adapted with older children, my focus is on parenting the very young. Because early childhood is critical to future development, I believe that counselors can have the most impact by helping parents become more effective during children's formative years. Finding that prevention is preferable to remediation, I encourage counselors to work with the parents of preschoolers to help them develop trusting, loving parent-child relationships and exert consistent, firm control while their children are still highly receptive.

Teaching Children to Care: Humanistic Parenting

Components of humanistic parenting include respectful communication, passive listening, using I-messages, setting limits, giving choices, catching children being good, confronting misbehavior, applying logical consequences, using time-out, conducting family meetings, and conveying love.

Respectful Communication

Mental health professionals sometimes suggest that parents speak to their children as though they were their best friends. Conversely, it is interesting to consider how it might be if we spoke to our best friends as though they were our children. The following dialogue is an imaginary conversation with a couple, Mike and Judy, who have come for dinner:

> So you finally arrived! Do you have any idea what time it is? We had about given up on you two. Mike, don't you ever wear your watch? Maybe you think you can just show up any time you please. Well, think again! Now go wash your hands and we'll be ready to eat. Judy, don't drip water on the floor like you did last time. We're tired of cleaning up your mess. Mike, remember to put the toilet seat down after you use it. This isn't a bus station..
>
> Okay, dinner is served! Come to the table and have a seat. Oh, Judy, don't sit there. You and Mike can't sit next to each other tonight because you might get into another fight. We're sitting between you two so you'll stay out of trouble. You know you can't make it through a whole meal without ruining it for everyone with your bickering. Judy, wipe that nasty look off your face and do what you're told. We don't want any complaints about the seating arrangement.
>
> We're so glad you could come, since we haven't seen you for a while. Mike, how do you like your new job? Make sure that you don't oversleep too often and lose this one like you did the last one. It's about time for you to grow up and be responsible! Judy, you had said you were going on a diet. How's that going? You know, you could actually be quite pretty if you weren't so overweight!
>
> Mike, please pass the gravy. Oh, no! You spilled it again. You're such a klutz! Why do you always have to be so clumsy? Judy, what's your problem? Stop glaring at us and try to be pleasant for once in your life.
>
> Who's ready for dessert? None for you, Mike, until you finish the rest of your spinach. Judy, you may have a small piece of pie, but go easy on the ice cream, or you'll never stop looking like a big, fat pig!
>
> Well, you two certainly haven't had much to say this evening. You'd better just go home and go to bed. Come back when you can behave more like ladies and gentlemen!

This humorous example illustrates the less than respectful manner in which parents communicate with their children. While not intending to hurt their children, many parents issue directives in ways that sometimes are demeaning or insensitive to children's feelings. Disrespectful communication does not convey the warmth and responsiveness that are essential ingredients of humanistic parenting.

In contrast, when parents listen empathically and communicate respectfully, children not only feel loved and valued but also have the opportunity to observe empathy in action as their parents demonstrate. Because children imitate much of what they witness in their parents, they likely will acquire the ability to respond empathically and respectfully themselves simply by emulating that behavior. On the other hand, parental responses such as threatening, commanding, lecturing, and name-calling create roadblocks to communication and produce defensiveness in children by conveying a lack of acceptance. The following scenario exemplifies the differences in parental responding to children's expressed feelings:

When Christy Sutter came crying to her mother because her baby brother had bitten her again, Mrs. Sutter responded, "Don't be such a baby yourself. He doesn't know any better, so just ignore him and stop whining."

When a similar situation occurred in the Freeman home, however, it met with a very different response. Mrs. Freeman stopped what she was doing to listen to her daughter and replied, "That must have really hurt when he bit you, and I can tell you're frustrated because this isn't the first time he's done it. Can you tell me more about what happened?"

Passive Listening

To avoid creating roadblocks to communication, Gordon (1970) recommends that parents use passive listening (silence), verbal and nonverbal acknowledgment responses (nodding, "uh-huh"), door openers ("Could you tell me more?" "How do you feel about that?"), and active listening, which demonstrates accurate empathy by reflecting both the content and the affect of the child's message (e.g., "You're disappointed that we can't afford to buy you that game."). Empathic listening validates children's feelings and enables them to assume responsibility for their own emotions.

I-Messages

Learning to use I-messages rather than you-messages is beneficial in communicating with children. Gordon (1970) offers a simple formula for constructing effective I-messages: "When you _____, I feel _____ because _____" The first blank is to be filled in with the child's *behavior*, the second with the *emotion* the parent experiences in conjunction with the given behavior, and the third with the *reason* the parent feels that way. For example, a parent might say, "When you interrupt me while I'm talking, I feel frustrated because I don't get to finish what I'm saying." This message is likely to be far more productive than other remarks that could be said to the child, such as "Shut up when I'm talking," or "Be quiet, blabbermouth!"

Setting Limits

In addition to responding to children warmly and respectfully, authoritative parenting involves setting clear behavioral limits that provide structure and consistency.

Parents should be kind and firm in their interactions with children while clearly communicating behavioral expectations (Nelson, Lott, & Glenn, 1993). Behavioral expectations should be appropriate to children's developmental stages, and it is normal for children to test the limits as they strive for increased autonomy (Brazelton, 1992).

For example, although a 6-year-old would be expected to know that hitting another child is wrong, a 2-year-old might hit playmates as a way of getting their attention or as a means of social interaction. Although limits should be set with both children, parental reaction to the 2-year-old should take into account that the child's behavior might have been exploratory rather than hostile in nature.

When setting limits, parents should state clearly what constitutes unacceptable behavior, as well as what substitute behavior will be accepted (Ginott, 1971). For example, telling the 6-year-old, "Other children are not for hitting, but you may hit this pillow if you are angry," provides clear guidelines for what will and will not be accepted. Similarly, the 2-year-old might be instructed, "Playmates are not for hitting, but you can touch them gently like a butterfly if you want to say hi or get them to look at you."

Giving Choices

To honor and nurture children's growing sense of autonomy, parents should allow children to choose between at least two acceptable alternatives whenever possible (Ginott, 1971; Nelson et al., 1993). With very young children, the choices have to be limited—for example, "You may come and eat dinner when you are called, or you may wait until breakfast tomorrow to eat." Giving children choices enables them to assume responsibility and to learn that choices have consequences.

Catching Them Being Good

Rather than waiting for children to misbehave and reprimanding them, noticing children's appropriate behavior and praising them is more effective. When children receive positive reinforcement, such as parental approval, for appropriate behavior, they are more likely to increase the behavior and to develop high self-esteem. Parents can easily show approval for their children's behavior through words, such as "Good job!" and gestures, such as a gentle touch, loving hug, approving smile, or friendly wink.

If the given behavior is prosocial in nature, parents might articulate to the child *why* his or her actions were desirable. For example, a father might say to his son, "I really liked the way you just helped your little sister pick up her toys, because that let her know that you care about her."

Confronting Misbehavior

A common mistake that parents make is talking too much and taking too many opportunities to remind their children about what they are expected to do. As many mothers have painfully discovered, children quickly learn to ignore nagging parents as though they were noisy gnats. For this reason, it is more effective for parents to follow through on enforcing rules by taking kind, firm action than by engaging in incessant nagging or punishing (Nelson et al., 1993).

For example, if a young child refuses to stop playing outside and come inside when called, the parent could simply state, "Time to come in," and take the child by the hand into the house. If the child resists, the parent could provide a limited choice, such as, "We need to get ready to go to your grandmother's house, so would you rather get dressed first or pack your toys?"

As mentioned previously, I-messages are also helpful for parents to let children know how their behavior is affecting others (Gordon, 1970; Popkin, 1993). For example, a parent might say, "When you don't come when I call you, I feel annoyed because I have to stop what I'm doing to go and get you."

Using Logical Consequences

When children misbehave discipline is required, and parents must decide what to do. Although punishment sometimes brings an end to a given undesirable behavior, it often is accompanied by unwanted side effects. For example, when his mother yells at him for spitting on his older sibling who has called him a nasty name, a little boy might stop ejecting saliva on his big sister but might smash her porcelain horse instead. Corporal punishment, such as spanking, can be detrimental because children could learn to imitate the aggression they have experienced as they interact with others. Even subtle forms of punishment, such as ridicule and humiliation, can damage the parent/child relationship and destroy trust.

A viable method of discipline that avoids the negative effects of punishment is logical consequences. Logical consequences are actions that logically follow from the child's behavior but that are not arbitrarily punitive (Dinkmeyer & McKay, 1973; Popkin, 1993; Nelson, 1987; Nelson et al., 1993).

To be effective, logical consequences must be composed of the "three *R's*": They must be directly *related* to the child's behavior, *respectful* of the child, and *reasonable* to both child and parent (Nelson et al., 1993).

For example, if a child draws a picture on the wall with a crayon after being told that paper is for drawing, a logical consequence would be for the child to help scrub the markings off the wall. This logical consequence is related directly to the child's misbehavior and is respectful and reasonable. On the other hand, sentencing the child to a week without television for this transgression would not be related to the offense, to call the child "a moron who thinks he's Picasso" would not be respectful, and to expect the child to wash all the walls in the entire house would not be reasonable.

Logical consequences can be especially effective if parents enlist children's help in planning them before misbehavior occurs. When children are involved directly in discussing what the consequences should be for not doing what is expected, they will be much less likely to feel that they are being punished unfairly when consequences are applied. For example, a parent might ask a child, "What should be a logical consequence for splashing water on the floor as you play with your toys in the bathtub?"

Using Time-Out

When children are actively engaging in misbehavior, time-out is another disciplinary strategy that parents can employ. Time-out typically consists of removing the child from the situation in which the problematic behavior is occurring, for a short time appropriate to the child's developmental level. The child could be placed in a separate room or simply asked to sit in a chair in the same room in a designated spot away from where he or she was misbehaving.

Time-out also may consist of the parent withdrawing his or her attention from the child for a specific period. Four minutes was found to be an effective length of time for 4- to 6-year-olds, and a longer duration of up to 30 minutes could be used with older children (Howard, 1996; Roberts & Powers, 1990). Parents should explain that the purpose of time-out is to give children a chance to calm down, and that they can return when they have worked through some of their feelings and are more in control of their behavior (Nelson et al., 1993). Time-outs must be brief, and expressions of affection are important when children return. A hug and a caring message will let children know that they are loved but that they must develop the ability to behave appropriately. For example, parents might say, "I love you, but I can't let you do this. Someday you'll learn to stop yourself, and then I won't need to stop you" (Brazelton, 1992, p. 253).

Conducting Family Meetings

Weekly family meetings provide an invaluable means of addressing issues and allowing family members to brainstorm solutions to family problems. Because these meetings should be democratic in nature, leadership rotates from week to week, and all family members are allowed to raise issues. Solutions are reached by consensus rather than by majority vote, and each person in the group is allowed to give input and play an essential role in the decision-making process (Nelson, 1987; Nelson et al., 1993).

Family meetings also can be used to discuss the tasks that have to be accomplished during the week and to delegate responsibilities for attending to household chores (Eyre & Eyre, 1994). The main purpose of family meetings, however, should be to address issues that arise in the family and to resolve conflicts between family members rather than simply assigning chores (Dreikurs, 1968). For example, a family meeting might focus on a younger child's resentment that an older sibling is allowed more freedom or an older child's frustration with a younger sibling always demanding to tag along.

Conveying Love

Finally, parents must let children know that they are deeply loved and valued so they will develop high self-esteem (Brazelton, 1992). Each child should receive some special time alone with each parent every week (Nelson et al., 1993). The quality of the time spent together is more important than its quantity.

Family rituals provide an excellent means for busy parents to maximize limited time with their children and to achieve high-quality interactions with them (Parker, 1999; Parker & Horton, 1996). The rituals may be simple or elaborate, and may be short and occur daily or longer and reserved for special occasions or unique needs. Reading a bedtime story, giving a goodbye kiss, and saying "Good morning—I love you!" are all simple rituals that parents can perform daily to strengthen their bonds with their children. Other rituals, such as attending religious services or having Sunday dinner together, can be conducted at certain times during the week; and seasonal rituals, such as going trick-or-treating or exploding fireworks, might happen just once a year.

In addition to developing rituals to celebrate special events, such as birthdays and holidays, parents can create rituals to address family issues, such as dealing with grief, facing transitions, and healing from emotional wounds. For example, planting a tree to celebrate the birthday of a recently deceased loved one can help to alleviate some of the pain the family is experiencing and allow family members to express their feelings and support one another. Although family rituals might seem insignificant at the time, they often comprise some of our most lasting and important childhood memories and can be a powerful means of conveying love.

Teaching Children to Engage in Prosocial Behavior

In addition to adopting a humanistic parenting style, parents can employ specific strategies to promote prosocial behavior in children. The development of prosocial behavior can be cultivated through a variety of methods, such as modeling, induction, didactic instruction, and assigning responsibility for tasks.

Modeling

One of the best ways by which parents can help children learn to treat others with care and respect is to demonstrate these behaviors themselves. Research has shown that children exposed to models that demonstrated altruistic behavior were more likely to exhibit similar behaviors themselves, especially if the children were given an explanation for *why* the behavior was performed and that the act was done to help another person in distress (Yarrow, Scott, & Waxler, 1973). For example, the caregiver could say to the child, "He's upset because he spilled his drink and doesn't have any more, so I'm going to help him feel better by giving him some of mine."

In addition to observing models who demonstrate altruistic behaviors and giving a verbal rationale for doing them, children need to be allowed to practice these behaviors themselves. One study showed that 12-month-old infants were more likely to share things with their mothers if they had been exposed previously to models who both shared objects with them and asked them to share in return (Hay & Murray, 1982). By asking children to share back with them, parents also teach children about the reciprocal nature of relationships.

When considering the effects of modeling on children's development, another issue that must be addressed is the influence of the media. Some television shows with altruistic models, such as Mr. Rogers, have been found to increase prosocial behavior in children (Huston et al., 1992). Unfortunately, however, children have many more opportunities to observe aggression than altruism in the media, and the influence of viewing violence begins early. Research shows that children as young as 15 months of age copy the aggressive acts of television characters (Centerwall, 1992). Young children are especially vulnerable to the effects of viewing violence because of their limited conceptual understanding of what actually is happening and the consequences of the action. For example, aggressive characters might appear to be attractive and powerful to young children who do not recognize the antisocial ramifications of their behavior. Similarly, the true impact of action figures killing others might have little meaning for preschoolers who do not understand either the finality of death or the fictional nature of the characters.

For these reasons, parents have to carefully monitor the shows children watch and the video games they play. All shows and games that consist primarily of gratuitous violence should be avoided, as they have the potential to teach children to behave aggressively and callously toward others. Even shows that are mostly acceptable sometimes contain momentary displays of aggression. Parents can counteract some of the negative influence of such media violence by watching the shows with their children and discussing with them the impact of the characters' actions on others and their own feelings.

Induction

Just as parents need to provide a verbal explanation while modeling altruistic behaviors, giving a verbal rationale is also helpful as they apply discipline for their children's antisocial actions. Induction refers to the the act of explaining the consequences of actions and suggesting solutions to interpersonal dilemmas. This promotes the development of children's inductive reasoning and expands their capacity to understand how their behavior impacts others and to empathize. For example, a mother might say to her young child, "When you hit me, it hurts and I don't like being with you when you hurt me. I'm going away from you until you can stop hitting me." The mother's explanation allows the child to understand that hitting causes pain to another person, and thus to develop empathy.

Because the ability to empathize with others is a prerequisite to altruism, induction provides a foundation for prosocial behavior. Many studies have confirmed the positive relationship between parental inductions and prosocial behavior in children (Brody & Schaffer, 1982; Dekovic & Janssens, 1992; Karylowski, 1982; Krevans & Gibbs, 1996; Moore & Eisenberg, 1984; Radke-Yarrow, Zahn-Waxler, & Chapman, 1983).

Didactic Instruction

Although lecturing children does not often bring the desired results, parents may find that providing them with moral instruction does foster prosocial behavior. One study showed that children as young as 15 to 20 months of age were more likely to show sympathy toward or attempt to help another child in distress when their mothers frequently explained to them how their behaviors affect other children (Zahn-Waxler, Radke-Yarrow, & King, 1979). Several other studies suggest that moral instruction such as, "You ought to make a get-well card to help your aunt feel better because she's very sick," can be as effective as modeling in eliciting prosocial behavior in children (Grusec, Saas-Korsaak, & Simutis, 1978; Rice & Grusec, 1975).

Didactic instruction is most effective when parents verbalize reasons for acting altruistically that evoke empathy or sympathy in children, and least effective when parents use coercive overtones or threats to pressure children. In the above example, pointing out the aunt's sickness is likely to evoke the child's sympathy and lead to prosocial behavior. In contrast, telling the child, "You'd better make a get-well card for your aunt or no television tonight," is likely to lead to resistance and to elicit little regard for the aunt's welfare.

Assigning Responsibility for Tasks

Another strategy that parents can use to nurture prosocial behavior is to make their children responsible for household tasks at a young age. Cross-cultural research in India, Kenya, Japan, Mexico, and the Philippines indicates that children from societies that make youth responsible for major domestic tasks, such as caring for younger siblings, develop more prosocial behaviors than their peers in cultures that do not promote such active involvement (Whiting & Edwards, 1988). By assisting others, children learn to think of themselves as helpful people and to develop increased prosocial behavior (Eisenberg et al., 1987).

In the process of carrying out family tasks, children discover how others feel, experience reinforcement such as parental approval, develop a sense of personal competence, and acquire a repertoire of prosocial skills they can use in the future (Eisenberg & Murphy, 1995). On the other hand, children who are given few responsibilities are more likely to have an underdeveloped ability to be helpful and to recognize the needs and rights of others.

Parents can foster children's aptitude for altruism and concern for others by establishing routines in which all family members participate in doing chores. Routines can be planned in the weekly family meeting, and visual aids, such as a pictorial chart on the refrigerator, can be used to remind each person of his or her tasks (Nelson, Lott, & Glenn, 1993). For example, the family can set up a house-cleaning routine in which each person is in charge of specific tasks, such as vacuuming, dusting, washing windows, and mopping floors.

Routines can be especially beneficial for children if the whole family performs the tasks together at a designated time during the week. Working together with parents and siblings not only helps to ensure that the tasks are accomplished but also promotes a sense of family unity and esprit de corps. Through this group effort, children can learn the tremendous value of assisting others to achieve the common good.

A common question that parents have concerns the types of tasks young children can be assigned. Children's chores must be age-appropriate, but even preschoolers can participate in family routines and be responsible for a variety of tasks (Nelson et al., 1993). For example:

■ Two- to three-year-olds can do simple chores such as putting away their toys, sweeping the floor, folding socks, putting magazines in a rack, helping put groceries on lower shelves, unloading utensils from the dishwasher, clearing their own place at the table, and dressing themselves.

■ Four-year-olds can put groceries away, dust furniture, feed pets, bring in the mail, prepare cold cereal, and help with tasks such as vacuuming, making the beds, filling the dishwasher, and yardwork.

■ Five-year-olds can accomplish more advanced tasks, such as cleaning their rooms, scrubbing sinks and toilets, cleaning mirrors and windows, taking out garbage, making their own sandwiches, folding clean clothes and putting them away, and helping with meal planning and grocery shopping.

As children grow and mature, the variety of tasks they can be assigned expands, and they can be expected to assume more responsibility in performing family routines.

A Workshop for Parents

Although many avenues can be pursued in providing information to parents—such as written materials, family counseling sessions, and consultation—I particularly like working with parents using a workshop format. The educational nature of workshops reduces much of the stigma associated with asking for help and also provides a means for parents to see that others have similar concerns. Parenting sometimes is a lonely proposition, and parents can easily inflict guilt on themselves by assuming that everyone else knows how to do it right while they continue to struggle.

The length and format of parenting workshops should be determined by the needs of the participants, but conducting more than one session may be desirable.

After attending a parenting workshop, parents can benefit from participating in support groups to reinforce each other as they practice the skills they have acquired.

In beginning the parenting workshop, I like to mention that it seems somewhat ironic that we must pass both written and performance tests to drive a car, yet no prerequisites or requirements prepare us for functioning in perhaps the most important and difficult role there is—being a parent. I emphasize that none of us are born knowing how to be perfect parents and that most of us probably are prepared inadequately for the challenges that seem to arise constantly. I then commend them for seeking help and for wanting to become better at what they do.

To introduce the topic of parenting styles, I ask parents to think about their own parents' child-rearing practices. Questions to be considered might include the following:

How do you feel about the way you were raised?

How strict were your parents?

What means of discipline did they use?

How did you feel about your parents when they disciplined you?

How consistently did they apply discipline?

How did each parent's method of discipline compare and contrast with each other?

What were their expectations regarding your behavior?

How responsive were they to your issues?

To what extent were you able to confide in your parents and feel understood?

Which parent were you more likely to confide in, and why?

What were some of the things you liked about the way you were parented?

If you could have changed anything about the parenting you received, what would it have been? Why would you have changed that?"

Finally, I like to ask, "How much similarity is there between how you were raised and the way that you are trying to parent your children?"

By considering questions like the above, parents begin to gain insight into the impact of parenting practices on children from a personal perspective. Sharing these perceptions with others in small groups provides a valuable means of gaining first-hand information about varying child-rearing styles and to discover that others have had quite different experiences. For partners to realize that some of their difficulties in disciplining their children stem from their own experiences in their families-of-origin can be illuminating.

In processing the information derived from this exercise, I point out that although certain forms of harsh discipline can control misbehavior effectively, these can have lasting adverse emotional consequences for children. Similarly, lack of parental control might seem desirable as a child but could have a less than positive impact on a child's overall development. Some adults who were reared by strict parents veer toward extreme permissiveness with their own children, which results in a lack of balance not unlike that of their parents.

After presenting a description of the parenting approaches and asking parents to consider which style their family-of-origin resembles and which is most like their own, I begin to explore the issue of discipline. Parents are asked to volunteer examples of misbehavior that they have found to be challenging to change in their children. In discussing these problem behaviors, I like to have them give a brief description of a specific incident in which the misbehavior occurred, what the parent did to change the behavior, and how the child responded to the disciplinary action. The behavior, the disciplinary action, and the child's response can be listed on a flipchart. After parents have volunteered a number of examples, they can be asked, "How satisfied were you with the outcome of your disciplinary action?" I then tell parents that we will return to these examples later.

As I present the techniques of humanistic parenting, I give parents opportunities to practice skills such as empathic listening, using I-messages, and giving choices in dyads or small groups. Handouts with scenarios can be provided, and the attendees can be asked to practice responding using the skills they have just learned. Brainstorming logical consequences for various problem behaviors is another excellent exercise that the workshop participants can practice with others in a small group. Their responses have to be processed so that the logical consequences adhere to the 3 Rs and are not punitive in nature.

To introduce the strategies for developing prosocial behavior, I first ask parents how they were taught to consider the needs of others and to act kindly toward them. I then ask them to volunteer any examples of altruistic behavior they have observed in their children. I also inquire if they have any ideas regarding what prompted each instance of altruism and, if so, how the parent responded. At this point, I reemphasize the importance of catching children being good and reinforcing desirable behavior, especially if it is prosocial in nature.

After concluding the discussion regarding engendering prosocial behavior, I return to the examples of misbehavior on the flipchart. Parents can be asked to use the skills they have practiced and the information they have received to brainstorm alternative ideas for dealing with each incident listed on the chart. The possible solutions and their probability for success can be processed with the whole group and fine-tuned to achieve the best possible outcome. Finally, parents can be asked to use what they have learned in the workshop to develop and commit to a simple plan to address at least one parenting issue they have encountered with their children.

Conclusion

Parents—who are children's first models—are key to instilling altruistic attitudes and prosocial behaviors in the generation of tomorrow. When parents provide a nurturing environment that abounds with both limits and love, children not only learn the art of relationship but also have opportunities to accept responsibility for their own behaviors and to develop high self-esteem.

The respectful and caring interactions that parents have with their children offer a blueprint for these youngsters to use as they develop their own modes of relating to others. By helping children understand the impact of their actions on others and develop empathy for others' distress, parents can help to prevent their children from committing travesties such as the one that occurred at Columbine High School. The isolation and alienation that fuel such desperate acts of interpersonal destruction can be displaced by the altruism and self-respect that enable us all to live up to our highest potential.

References

Baumrind, D. (1967). Child care practices anteceding three patterns of preschool behavior. *Genetic Psychology Monographs, 75,* 43–88.

Baumrind, D. (1971). Current patterns of parental authority. *Developmental Psychology Monograph, 4,* 1–103.

Baumrind, D. (1991). The influence of parenting style on adolescent competence and substance use. *Journal of Early Adolescence, 11,* 56–95.

Bombeck, E. (1974). Etiquette lesson. *The Reader's Digest.*

Brazelton, T. B. (1992). *Touchpoints: Your child's emotional and behavioral development.* New York: Addison-Wesley.

Brody, G. H., & Schaffer, D. R. (1982). Contributions of parents and peers to children's moral socialization. *Developmental Review, 2,* 31–75.

Centerwall, B. S. (1992). Children, television, and violence. In Schwartz, D. F. (Ed.), *Children and violence* (Report of the 23rd Ross Roundtable on Critical Approaches to Common Pediatrics Problems. Columbus, OH: Ross Laboratories.

Coopersmith, S. (1967). *The antecedents of self-esteem.* San Francisco: Freeman.

Dekovic, M., & Janssens, J. M. A. M. (1992). Parents' child-rearing style and child's sociometric status. *Developmental Psychology, 28,* 925–932.

Dinkmeyer, D., & McKay, G. (1973). *Raising a responsible child: Practical steps to successful family relationships.* New York: Simon & Schuster.

Dodge, K. A., Bates, J. E., & Pettit, G. D. (1990). Mechanisms in the cycle of violence. *Science, 250,* 1678–1683.

Dreikurs, R. (1968). *The new approach to discipline.* New York: Dutton.

Eisenberg, N. (1988). The development of prosocial and aggressive behavior. In M. E. Lamb & M. H. Bornstein (Eds.), *Developmental psychology: An advanced textbook* (pp. 461-495). Hillsdale, NJ: Lawrence Erlbaum Associates.

Eisenberg, N. (1992). *The caring child.* Cambridge, MA: Harvard University Press.

Eisenberg, N., & Miller, P. A. (1987). The relation of empathy to prosocial and related behavior. *Psychological Bulletin, 101,* 91–119.

Eisenberg, N., & Murphy, B. (1995). Parenting and children's moral development. In M. H. Bornstein (Ed.), *Handbook of parenting* (Vol. 4, pp. 227–257). Mahweh, NJ: Lawrence Erlbaum Associates.

Eisenberg, N., Shell, R., Pasternack, J., Lennon, R., Belber, R., & Mathy, R. M. (1987). Prosocial development in middle childhood: A longitudinal study. *Developmental Psychology, 23,* 712–718.

Eyre, L., & Eyre, R. (1994). *Teaching your children responsibility.* New York: Simon & Schuster.

Ginott, H. G. (1971). *Between parent and child: New solutions to old problems.* New York: Macmillan.

Gordon, T. (1970). *Parent effectiveness training.* New York: Wyden.

Grossman, D. G. (1996). *On killing.* Boston: Back Bay Books.

Grusec, J. E., Saas-Kortsaak, P., & Simutis, Z. M. (1978). The role of example and moral exhortation in the training of altruism. *Child Development, 49,* 920–923.

Hay, D. F. & Murray, P. (1982). Giving and requesting: Social facilitation of infants' offers to adults. *Infant Behavior and Development, 5,* 310–310.

Horton-Parker, R. (1998). Teaching children to care: Engendering prosocial behavior through humanistic parenting. *Journal of Humanistic Education and Development, 37,* 66–77.

Howard, B. (1996). The short- and long-term consequences of corporal punishment. *Pediatrics, 98,* 809–817.

Huston, A. C.. Donnerstein, E., Fairchild, H., Feshbach, N. D., Katz, P. A., Murray, J. P., Rubenstein, E. A., Wilcox, B. L., & Zuckerman, D. (1992). *Big world, small screen: The role of television in American society.* Lincoln, MN: University of Minnesota Press.

Karylowski, J. (1982). Doing good to feel good versus doing good to make others feel good: Some child-rearing antecedents. *School Psychology International, 3,* 149–156.

Koestner, R., Franz, C., & Weinberger, J. (1990). The family origins of empathic concern: A 26-year longitudinal study. *Journal of Personality & Social Psychology, 58,* 709–717.

Krevans, J. & Gibbs, J. C. (1996). Parents' use of inductive discipline: Relations to children's empathy and prosocial behavior. *Child Development, 67,* 3263–3277.

Lamborn, S. D., Mounts, N. S., Steinberg, L., & Dornbusch, S. M. (1991). Patterns of competence and adjustment among adolescents from authoritative, authoritarian, indulgent, and neglectful families. *Child Development, 62,* 1049–1065.

Lempers, J. D., Clark-Lempers, D., & Simons, R. (1989). Economic hardship, parenting, and distress in adolescence. *Child Development, 60,* 25–39.

Maccoby, E. E. (1984). Socialization and developmental change. *Child Development, 55,* 317–328.

Maccoby, E. E., & Martin, J. A. (1983). Socialization in the context of the family: Parent-child interaction. In P. H. Mussen (Series Ed.) & E. M. Hetherington (Vol. Ed.), *Handbook of child psychology: Vol. 4. Socialization, personality, and social development* (4th ed., pp. 1–101). New York: Wiley.

Moore, B., & Eisenberg, N. (1984). The development of altruism. In G. Whitehurst (Ed.), *Annals in Child Development* (Vol. 1, pp. 107–174). New York: JSI Press.

Nelson, J. (1987). *Positive discipline.* New York: Ballantine Books.

Nelson, J., Lott, L., & Glenn, H. S. (1993). *Positive discipline A Z: 1001 solutions to everyday parenting problems.* Rocklin, CA: Prima Publishing.

Parker, R. (1999). The art of blessing: Teaching parents to construct rituals. *Professional School Counseling, 2,* 218–225.

Parker, R., & Horton, H. S. (1996). A typology of ritual: Paradigms for healing and empowerment. *Counseling & Values, 40,* 82–97.

Patterson, G. R. (1982). *Corrective family process.* Eugene, OR: Castalia.

Perry, D. G., Perry, L. C., & Boldizar, J. P. (1990). Learning of aggression. In M. Lewis & S. Miller (Eds.), *Handbook of developmental psychopathology.* New York: Plenum.

Popkin, M. (1993). *Active parenting today.* Marietta, GA: Active Parenting Publishers.

Pulkkinen, L. (1982). Self-control and continuity in childhood delayed adolescence. In P. Baltes & O. Brim (Eds.), *Lifespan development and behavior* (Vol. 4, pp. 64–107). New York: Academic Press.

Radke-Yarrow, M., Zahn-Waxler, C., & Chapman, M. (1983). Prosocial dispositions and behavior. In P. H. Mussen

(Series Ed.) & E. M. Hetherington (Vol. Ed.), *Handbook of child psychology: Vol. 4. Socialization, personality, and social development* (pp. 469–545). New York: Wiley.

Rice, M. E. & Grusec, J. E. (1975). Saying and doing: Effects on observer performance. *Journal of Personality and Social Psychology, 32,* 584–593.

Roberts, M. W., & Powers, S. W. (1990). Adjusting chair timeout enforcement procedures for oppositional children. *Behavior Therapy, 21,* 257–271.

Steinberg, L. D. (1990). Interdependence in the family: Autonomy, conflict, and harmony in the parent-adolescent relationship. In S. S. Feldman & G. R. Elliot (Eds.), *At the threshold: The developing adolescent* (pp. 255–276). Cambridge, MA: Harvard University Press.

Weiss, B., Dodge, K. A., Bates, J. E., & Pettit, G. S. (1992). Some consequences of early harsh discipline: Child aggression and a maladaptive social information processing style. *Child Development, 63,* 1321–1335.

Whiting, B. B., & Edwards, C. P. (1988). *Children of different worlds: The formation of social behavior.* Cambridge, MA: Harvard University Press.

Yarrow, M. R., Scott, P. M., & Waxler, C. Z. (1973). Learning concern for others. *Developmental Psychology, 8,* 240–260.

Zahn-Waxler, C., Radke-Yarrow, M., & King, R. (1979). Child rearing and children's prosocial initiations toward victims of distress. *Child Development, 50,* 319–330.

School-Based Interventions

Jon Carlson and Judith A. Lewis

The junior and senior high schools have a major influence on adolescents. Unfortunately, their impact is not always positive. For most teenagers, school is a "necessary evil" with one primary benefit: It is a prime place for socializing. No other nonfamily setting consumes so much of their time, involves so much attention, or demands so much effort. They often view the actual process of formalized classroom activity as secondary to social aspects. The way in which students feel about their school experience is determined largely by their teachers' opinions. Parents often suggest that adolescents ignore their teachers' shortcomings and concentrate on the subject matter, but this is hard to accept, as everything in a classroom is filtered through the teacher's personality.

What can be done about teenagers who are turned off to school and learning, who are disinterested, who are not working up to their capabilities? The first step is to uncover the reason. In most cases, however, there is not a simple answer. Sometimes parents themselves are at fault. With the best intentions in the world, parents tell their children, "You have to learn to do things you don't like to do," and all too often schoolwork falls into this category. Parents foster this attitude because they want their teenagers to realize that schoolwork must take precedence over hobbies and pleasurable activities, but these words can backfire if their children attend school with the attitude that they are doing so at sacrifice of all pleasure and fun.

In schools, as in other settings, counselors have trouble providing effective services in today's world. The confusion, uncertainty, and alienation that young people experience today derive from problems that past generations did not face. Increases in adolescent depression and suicide, drug and alcohol use, and the growing number of single-parent families present staggering issues for our society. In addition, today's counselors are affected by social conditions that did not, to the same degree, touch professionals of the past, such as the effects of unemployment (and underemployment), the rising rate of adult alcoholism, and the alarming prevalence of child abuse. These social conditions, as well as crime, violence, socioeconomic inequalities, and the public's disillusionment with the quality of education in general, have contributed to a disaffected view of counseling services in the school.

Because of these conditions, today's counselors must be more active; they must be willing to experiment and must realize that traditional counselor roles and strategies will not alleviate these problems. Although counseling techniques for young people have been improving over the years, many strategies that have consistently not worked have not yet been discarded. Of course, discarding ideas and theories that one has learned in training from respected teachers is not easy.

Pamela O. Paisley and Richard L. Hayes discuss in chapter 10 the transformations that school counselor preparation and practice has seen over the years. The focus of school counseling has shifted many times since its inception, favoring at different times career development, social and personal development, and educational development. Educational reform has lately played a large part in the direction school counseling is headed and how preparation programs will respond to new school visions.

Joyce Williams Bergin and James J. Bergin explore the concept of inclusion in chapter 11. Although many school districts have embraced the idea of inclusion, it can be a difficult concept to implement effectively, as communication, coordination, and collaboration are required and schools and teachers can be ill-equipped to proceed. Bergin and Bergin explore the role that school counselors can take in the inclusion movement, as they are fully trained to spearhead the communication efforts and can offer counseling strategies, consultation, group guidance, and group counseling skills.

In chapter 12, Elsie Moore discusses inequalities in education and how counselors can help minority youngsters achieve. According to Moore, teenagers from minority backgrounds have lost performance because of low expectations. Cultural differences are evaluated incorrectly and misunderstood, impacting learning and achievement. Minority children are often relegated (sometimes voluntarily) to inferior positions. IQ scores, achievement tests, and other culturally loaded forms of assessment label minority students as not being as capable as others. Moore provides suggestions for counteracting these problems.

In chapter 13, Peter Leone, Matthew Mayer, Kimber Melmgren, and Sheri Meisel examine issues related to school violence and disruption. They have created practical violence prevention initiatives and guidelines for parents, teachers, and administrators.

In chapter 14, Patricia Gallagher and Linda Satter describe a comprehensive high school that promotes a positive and supportive environment. This is accomplished by involving students, faculty, and the community in a variety of prevention and intervention activities that respond to students' needs. A safer environment is imperative before any other counseling interventions can occur.

Beverly Johns and John Keenan discuss how counselors can help schools handle traumatic events in chapter 15. They provide general guidelines for dealing with traumatic crises in schools and procedures to follow in the event of the death of a student or staff member or the potential death of a student.

In chapter 16, effective crisis management teams are addressed. Alan Basham, Valerie E. Appleton, and Cass Dykeman discuss the need for such teams in schools, as well as how to build crisis teams and how to implement crisis programs and plans. The authors convey the importance of caring for staff in such sensitive situations and include two exercises to allow team members opportunities to process.

Despite all the improvements in modern life, conflicts still persist. The results of the 26th annual Gallup poll (Elan, Rose, & Gallup, 1994) reveal that Americans view fighting, violence, and gangs, along with discipline, as the primary issues facing today's schools. David and Roger Johnson assert that students must be taught to be peacemakers if schools are to be places where quality education occurs. In this chapter they describe how to create a peacemaker program and further enhance the safety of the school.

Marguerite Carroll delves into developmental groups in school counseling in chapter 18, both for elementary schools and high schools. Based on the ideas that people can explore more satisfying ways of behaving, experience growth in a self-actualizing paradigm, and expand their personal development, developmental groups depend heavily on self-disclosure and feedback. Carroll investigates the different types of groups and the logistics, specific considerations, and issues of accountability.

Mary Cook, in chapter 19, brings to light the predicament that many school counselors face today: being unprepared to deal with students who struggle emotionally or behaviorally, students who need services outside of school but are not receiving them. Cook offers interventions and strategies, focusing on social skills training, for counselors to use as building blocks as they develop their own group programs.

References

Elam, S., Rose, L. & Gallup, A. (1974). The 26th annual Gallup poll of the public's attitudes toward the public school. *Phi Delta Kappa, 76,* 41-56.

Transformations in School Counselor Preparation and Practice

Pamela O. Paisley and Richard L. Hayes

School counseling in the United States is an evolving specialty within the profession—one that emerged and continues to change as a result of social, educational, political, and economic trends (Paisley & Borders, 1995). This history of school counseling has been well documented in the literature (Baker, 2000; Gysbers & Henderson, 2001; Herr, 2001; Myrick, 1997; Paisley & McMahon, 2001). The specialty was shaped initially by the social reform movement of the late 19th century and has evolved from an early focus on career and character development to today's comprehensive, developmental, and collaborative programs. During the intervening years, school counseling programs and their specific areas of interest have alternated based on the issues facing schools, communities, families, children, and adolescents.

At times, school counselors have worked more exclusively in educational and career arenas, while at other times much more attention has been paid to children's personal and social development. In the past 10 to 15 years, the most significant transformations in the school counseling specialty have been grounded in the context of educational reform and have influenced both preparation and practice.

American Education as the Context for School Counseling Transformation

American education is undergoing significant change. The public, no longer content to accept "effort" as a substitute for "evidence," demands that educators make observable differences in the lives of every child. In this era of educational reform, more emphasis is being placed upon making school personnel accountable for bringing all students to high levels of academic performance (Eriksen, 1997; Fields & Hines, 2000). Making educators accountable for helping all students meet high levels of academic achievement has necessitated a shift in the very mission of public schooling from "teaching" to "learning." This shift from a teacher-centered to a learner-centered curriculum means that "student outcomes" have replaced "teacher activities" as the accepted measure of educational excellence.

This change in mission comes at a time when globalism, multiculturalism, and rapid changes in technology create the demand for a differently skilled and more knowledgeable workforce and foster the need for a literate citizenry of lifelong learners.

Clearly, meeting the demands of living in a global society and maintaining the status of the United States as a world leader are increasingly dependent on developing and better utilizing all of our human resources (Elam, 1993). Increasing diversity has necessitated a heightened sensitivity to cultural differences through changes in educational programs, policies, and procedures.

Despite three decades of school reform efforts, however, the dropout rate in American schools remains alarmingly high (Hayes, Nelson, Lusky, Pearson, & Worthy, 2002). Significantly, data from states and local school districts show that economically poor and minority students are systematically denied access to an education that prepares them for success in the workplace (Education Trust, 2000). Recognizing the great diversity among today's public school students, this reality points to the importance of getting students into the right curriculum and supporting them to become full participants in the society of the 21st century (Fields & Hines, 2000; House & Martin, 1998; Schneider & Stevenson, 1999). Consequently, ensuring that every student has the supports necessary to remain in school until graduation has become a national priority (American School Counselor Association, 1996).

Under such a mandate, all school personnel and educational policymakers are responsible for establishing responsive policies and initiating new strategies to prevent students from leaving school prior to graduation. Ensuring that every student is successful, of course, is the responsibility of teachers and administrators—and also school counselors, psychologists, social workers, staff, students, parents, business people, and the community at large (House & Hayes, 2002). Clearly, school counselors have a significant role to play in ensuring students' success. Because they have a schoolwide perspective on serving the needs of every student, school counselors are in an ideal position to serve as advocates for all students and as agents for removing systemic barriers to academic success. Recognizing that minority and low-income students actually receive fewer counseling services than their more affluent White peers (Hart & Jacobi, 1992) serves to point out that differences in achievement are systemic issues that play a significant role in perpetuating the observed gaps in academic achievement.

Educational reform has focused on accountability for student performance by setting more rigorous academic standards, devising new assessment strategies, and restructuring preservice and inservice training for teachers and administrators

(Mohrman & Lawler, 1996). Despite the recent emphasis upon a radical transformation of schooling, however, practicing counselors and the educators who prepare them have been largely absent from school reform efforts (Aubrey, 1985; House & Martin, 1998).

Critically, the majority of school counselor education programs have adopted a mental health orientation that reflects little concern for how school counselors address the academic achievement of students (Collison et al., 1998; Education Trust, 1997). Although considerable change in school counseling was already being discussed in schools and universities in 1996, a national assessment of school counselor preparation and practice conducted by The Education Trust found little substantive change under consideration that reflected the dominant reform movement under way in education. Reasons for this were as follows:

1. There was no single or unifying vision for transforming the profession.

2. Curricular changes most often amounted to adding courses.

3. Counselor educators generally lacked experience as school counselors, and they were not in regular contact with practicing school counselors.

4. The core counselor preparation curriculum focused primarily on generic counseling courses better suited to the preparation of mental health specialists.

The picture in the schools was hardly better with "large numbers of practicing school counselors functioning as highly paid clerical staff, quasi administrators and/or inadequately trained therapeutic mental health providers with unmanageable client loads . . . [although] many school counselors believe they have the best jobs in the world" (Martin, 2002, p. 150).

A Legacy of Social Action

Borne along by the social reforms that marked the beginning of the 20th century, "guidance" arose as one of several movements that addressed the turmoil created by the 19th-century Industrial Revolution. Committed to improving the health and safety of an American workforce fueled by unprecedented immigration and the demand for human capital created by mass production technology, early guidance workers believed that sweeping social reform could be achieved through education (Aubrey, 1986).

Over the ensuing century, the guidance movement would adopt, and then be transformed by, the mental health movement that came to characterize the emerging "counseling profession." Ironically, a movement that had sought systems change to improve social welfare through education had been transformed into a mental health profession that promotes individual human welfare by adjusting the person to the system.

Just as guidance arose in response to rectifying the exploitation of workers in the new industrial workplace of 20th-century America, today's counseling profession is faced with preparing a new kind of worker for participating in the global society of the new millennium. Despite its own technological advances, however, the counseling profession struggles to improve the human condition in this "postmodern world." At the dawn of a new century, we are witnesses to a strikingly similar revolution that challenges contemporary counseling professionals to improve the lives of America's citizens through education. Unlike the technological advances that encouraged the exploitation of workers at the turn of the 20th century, however, today's technology threatens to displace or replace them.

At the turn of the last century, America's "great melting pot" promised new immigrants a homogenized society in which anyone willing to work hard enough could be successful. Today, America is recognized as a land of great cultural diversity that is challenged to build a community where everyone can get along with one another. With individuals now freer than perhaps at any time in history to choose the course of their own personal destinies, too many Americans still feel powerless in the face of overwhelming economic and social forces to realize a future of their own making (Hayes, 1994).

The emergence of multicultural counseling at the end of the 19th century increased both the counselor's awareness of the diversity of client concerns and the capacity to be effective across cultures. A culturally more sensitive profession now acknowledges those who have been marginalized by the notion that some are closer to a "central vision." Nonetheless, women, people of color, people with disabilities, gays and lesbians, children raised in poverty, and others find they still must demand to be regarded and treated as individuals. Those living in the new millennium must face their obligation to others and be willing to extend their full support to those who have been marginalized in becoming full citizens and active participants in American society.

A (Re-)Newed Vision for School Counseling

Accepting the challenge to raise the educational attainment of every student to enable full citizenship participation presents a significant role shift for today's school counselor. It means moving from service provider to program and student advocate, from an emphasis on mental health to academic success, from promoting individual adjustment and control to fostering social emancipation and personal empowerment. The vision of today's school counselor is as a school leader who advocates for the academic, career, social, and personal success of every student. In so doing, the new-vision school counselor demonstrates a fundamental belief in the capacity of all students to achieve at high levels on rigorous and challenging academic course content when provided with the necessary encouragement and supports to ensure their success.

Consistent with the new mission of education, the contributions of the new-vision school counselor to the academic success of all students are evaluated against a set of performance standards. Rather than documenting counselor actions in meeting stated program objectives, however, assessment is directed to systems as well as individual change in enhancing student achievement. Rather than focus on *what school counselors do*, the focus has shifted to assessing *how students are different as a result of what counselors have done* (Wong, 2002). Just as the pioneers who gave life to the guidance movement were inspired to translate professed beliefs into deliberate actions, the new-vision school counselor is committed to realizing documented outcomes that affirm a belief in the capacity of every child to become an effective and contributing citizen.

Contrary to some interpretations, this new-vision school counselor does not represent an abandonment of concern for the personal and social development of children and adolescents. Instead, it reflects the requirement that school counselors link interventions to the mission and purposes of schooling while holding themselves accountable for their contributions to student outcomes. New-vision counselors have a fundamental and profound commitment to social justice and recognize that they often are in the best position to assess the school for systemic barriers that hinder success in all domains of student development.

Issues of equity, access, and lack of supporting conditions come to rest on the counselor's desk in the form of data files, referrals, and academic and social reports of whole school and individual student progress. The new-vision school counselor uses this information to serve as an assertive advocate, to remove systemic barriers, to design supportive programs, and to assist all students in their academic, career, and personal/social development. They serve as leaders as well as effective team members working with teachers, administrators, other school personnel, and parents to make sure that each child succeeds. Most significantly, these counselors help students by nurturing their dreams and defining pathways for fulfilling those dreams.

For school counselors to become this type of contributor to educational reform and student success requires transformation of both preparation and practice. Although models for preparing school counselors date back to the early 1920s (Aubrey, 1985). Clearly, we need new preparation and service delivery models that can be responsive to every student within a multicultural, technologically sophisticated, and rapidly changing global society (Hayes, Dagley, & Horne, 1996).

In fact, during the past 10 to 15 years, several initiatives have occurred simultaneously within school counseling that move the specialty in new directions and also position school counselors as critical players in educational reform. These initiatives have some components in common:

1. Each is an effort to acknowledge the unique characteristics of the practice of counseling within an educational setting.

2. These initiatives are all grounded in principles of social justice.

3. The initiatives represent interest in tying school counseling program development to the central premises and purposes of schooling.

Examples of transformative initiatives are apparent in both preparation and practice.

Transformation in School Counselor Preparation

One of the most significant examples of new directions in school counselor preparation is reflected in activities associated with the Transforming School Counseling Initiative funded by DeWitt Wallace—Reader's Digest. In addition, the 2001 revised standards for school counselor preparation by the Council for the Accreditation of Counseling and Related Educational Programs (CACREP) is another excellent example of a shift in paradigm.

The Transforming School Counseling Initiative (TSCI)

The Dewitt Wallace–Reader's Digest Fund's National Initiative for Transforming School Counseling (www.edtrust.org) has been a multi-stage, multi-year initiative to improve school counseling by focusing on the graduate-level preparation of school counselors. The Initiative was based on a series of assumptions related to the potential role that school counselors could play in student outcomes and their previous lack of training and support for doing so. Specifically, school counselors were seen to have an enormous impact on the choices that students make and their post-secondary options. Furthermore, school counselors were seen as being ideally positioned in schools to serve as advocates who create opportunities for all students to define, nurture, and accomplish high academic aspirations.

This initiative required that issues of educational equity, access, and support for student success become central to the school counselor's role. Although these assumptions and goals are in keeping with the current educational reform efforts, it was equally apparent that school counselors, in large part, had been left out of all reform programs. Further, graduate-level preparation programs offered little to prepare preservice students fully to become effective advocates for all students, particularly those who traditionally had been underserved by the educational and social systems.

In 1996, DeWitt Wallace–Reader's Digest, in collaboration with The Education Trust, began phase I of TSCI by identifying what school counselors needed to know and be able to do to help all students succeed academically. In phase II, 10 school counselor preparation programs from institutions of higher education and their K–12 district partners were awarded planning grants to develop new models for school counselor preparation. In phase III, six of the 10 partnerships were selected to implement the designed programs. Grant recipients were required to review admissions processes and policies, their curricula, field experiences, relationships with all stakeholders, and the professional development needs of faculty members. Coordination of the TSCI and technical assistance were provided across the process by consultants from The Education Trust.

Although the designed models had variations, all implemented programs were committed to principles of social justice and to preparing school counselors who are

1. knowledgeable about schools and schooling;

2. equipped to assist students in meeting their educational and personal goals;

3. proactive advocates for system change, working to remove barriers that impede the academic success of poor and minority students.

All programs also used components identified as critical in school counselor development by The Education Trust: educational leadership, advocacy, team-building and collaboration, counseling and coordination, and use of assessment data to improve practice and support student advocacy.

This initiative also sought to disseminate information about the need for change and the directions that change should take, as well as to create fertile ground for discussion and the revision of school counselor preparation. Twenty-eight companion institutions and partnerships have joined in the work. Summer school counseling academies sponsored by The Education Trust and coordinated with the six sites have grown in size from approximately 65 participants in the first summer (2000) to more than 150 in the third (2002).

The 2001 CACREP Standards for School Counselor Preparation

In 2001, the Council for Accreditation of Counseling and Related Educational Programs (CACREP) adopted new standards for the preservice preparation of all counselors. Revisions were particularly apparent in the school counseling specialty standards. Revisions reflected the unique context of school-based practice and the specialized skills required of counselors in that setting. The language of the standards points to skills and content areas similar to those specified in TSCI. In addition to the common core curricular experiences required of all counselors, CACREP required the following curricular experiences and demonstrated knowledge and skills of all students in a school counseling program (www.cacrep.org):

CACREP REQUIREMENTS

A. Foundations of School Counseling

- History, philosophy, and current trends in school counseling and educational systems
- Relationship of the school counseling program to the academic and student services program in the school
- Role, function, and professional identity of the school counselor in relation to the roles of other professional and support personnel in the school
- Strategies of leadership designed to enhance the learning environment of schools
- Knowledge of the school setting, environment, and pre-K curriculum
- Current issues, policies, laws, and legislation
- The role of racial, ethnic, and cultural heritage, nationality, socioeconomic status, family structure, age, gender, sexual orientation, religious and spiritual

beliefs, occupation, physical and mental status, and equity issues in school counseling

■ Knowledge and understanding of community, environmental, and institutional opportunities that enhance, as well as barriers that impede, student academic, career, and personal/social success and overall development

■ Knowledge and application of current and emerging technology in education and school counseling to assist students, families, and educators in using resources that promote informed academic, career, and personal/social choices

■ Ethical and legal considerations related specifically to the practice of school counseling (e.g., the Code of Ethics of the American Counseling Association (ACA) and the Ethical Standards for School Counselors of the American School Counselor Association (ASCA)

B. Contextual Dimensions of School Counseling
Studies that provide an understanding of the coordination of the counseling program components as they relate to the total school community, including all of the following:

■ Advocacy for all students and for effective school counseling programs

■ Coordination, collaboration, referral, and team-building efforts with teachers, parents, support personnel, and community resources to promote program objectives and facilitate successful student development and achievement of all students

■ Integration of the school counseling program into the total school curriculum by systematically providing information and skills training to assist pre-K–12 students in maximizing their academic, career, and personal/social development

■ Promotion of the use of counseling and guidance activities and programs by the total school community to enhance a positive school climate

■ Methods of planning for and presenting school counseling-related educational programs to administrators, teachers, parents, and the community

■ Methods of planning, developing, implementing, monitoring, and evaluating comprehensive developmental counseling programs

■ Knowledge of prevention and crisis intervention strategies

C. Knowledge and Skill Requirements for School Counselors

1. Program Development, Implementation, and Evaluation

■ Use, management, analysis, and presentation of data from school- based information (e.g., standardized testing, grades, enrollment, attendance, retention, placement), surveys, interviews, focus groups, and needs assessments to improve student outcomes

■ Design, implementation, monitoring, and evaluation of comprehensive developmental school counseling programs (e.g., the *ASCA National*

Standards for School Counseling Programs), including an awareness of various systems that affect students, school, and home
■ Implementation and evaluation of specific strategies that meet program goals and objectives
■ Identification of student academic, career, and personal/social competencies and the implementation of processes and activities to assist students in achieving these competencies
■ Preparation of an action plan and school counseling calendar that reflect appropriate time commitments and priorities in a comprehensive developmental school counseling program
■ Strategies for seeking and securing alternative funding for program expansion
■ Use of technology in the design, implementation, monitoring, and evaluation of a comprehensive school counseling program

2. Counseling and Guidance
   ■ Individual and small-group counseling approaches that promote school success, through academic, career, and personal/social development for all
   ■ Individual, group, and classroom guidance approaches systematically designed to assist all students with academic, career and personal/social development
   ■ Approaches to peer facilitation, including peer helper, peer tutor, and peer mediation programs
   ■ Issues that may affect the development and functioning of students (e.g., abuse, violence, eating disorders, attention deficit hyperactivity disorder, childhood depression, and suicide)
   ■ Developmental approaches to assist all students and parents at points of educational transition (e.g., home to elementary school, elementary to middle to high school, high school to postsecondary education and career options)
   ■ Constructive partnerships with parents, guardians, families, and communities in order to promote each student's academic, career, and personal/social success
   ■ Systems theories and relationships among and between community systems, family systems, and school systems, and how they interact to influence the students and affect each system
   ■ Approaches to recognizing and assisting children and adolescents who may use alcohol or other drugs or who may reside in a home where substance abuse occurs

3. Consultation
   ■ Strategies to promote, develop, and enhance effective teamwork within the school and larger community

■ Theories, models, and processes of consultation and change with teachers, administrators, other school personnel, parents, community groups, agencies, and students as appropriate

■ Strategies and methods of working with parents, guardians, families, and communities to empower them to act on behalf of their children

■ Knowledge and skills in conducting programs that are designed to enhance students' academic, social, emotional, career, and other developmental needs

---

As with the other specialty areas for CACREP, school counseling graduate students are required to complete a 600 clock-hour internship in a school setting, under the supervision of a site supervisor. The requirement includes a minimum of 240 direct service hours.

Transformation of School Counselor Practice

As TSCI and CACREP focused on the preparation of school counselors, parallel initiatives were undertaken related to practice. The American School Counselor Association (ASCA) developed standards for school counseling programs and conducted training to familiarize participants with the expectations. ASCA is in the process of developing and disseminating a national model for school counselor practice. Simultaneously, Metropolitan Life Insurance Company funded professional development activities for school counselors based upon the TSCI program components.

American School Counselor Association

In 1994, as part of general educational reform, most academic disciplines developed national standards to influence how teachers teach and how students learn (Dahir, Sheldon, & Valiga, 1998). These standards established expectations for what students would learn and what they would be able to do as a result of a K–12 education.

In 1997, ASCA examined and established similar standards indicating what students should know and be able to do as a result of participating in a school counseling program. The standards and the supporting printed materials (Campbell & Dahir, 1997; Dahir et al., 1998) provided practicing counselors with a common vocabulary and framework for program development as well as a process for involving other stakeholders and building support. The standards incorporated expectations related to academic development, career development, and personal/social development:

ASCA STANDARDS

Academic Development

1. Students will acquire the attitudes, knowledge, and skills that contribute to learning in school and across the life span.
2. Students will complete school with the academic preparation essential to choose from a wide range of substantial postsecondary options, including college.
3. Students will understand the relationship of academics to the world of work, and to life at home and in the community.

Career Development

1. Students will acquire the skills to investigate the world of work in relation to self and to make informed career decisions.
2. Students will employ strategies to achieve future career success and satisfaction.
3. Students will understand the relationship among personal qualities, education and training, and the world of work.

Personal/Social Development

1. Students will acquire the attitudes, knowledge, and interpersonal skills to help them understand and respect self and others.
2. Students will make decisions, set goals, and take necessary action to achieve goals.
3. Students will understand safety and survival skills.

In 2001, ASCA expanded these efforts to develop a National Model for School Counseling Programs (Hatch & Bowers, 2002). This model reflects a comprehensive approach to program foundation, delivery, management, and accountability. The model provides the mechanism by which school counselors and school counseling teams will design, coordinate, implement, manage, and evaluate their programs for students' success. It provides a framework for the program components, the school counselor's role in implementation, and the underlying philosophies of leadership, advocacy, and systemic change.

ASCA advocates implementing a national model in which school counselors switch their emphasis from providing a set of services for selected students to offering a program designed to meet the needs of every student. Such a program would answer the question, "What do school counselors do?" and also would require school counselors to respond to the more significant question, "How are students different as a result of what we do?"

The MetLife Foundation National School Counselor Training Initiative (NSCTI)

As the processes and products of TSCI were disseminated, one of the recurring questions was how practicing school counselors, outside of the partnership districts, could become familiar with the new model. The MetLife Foundation funded the development and dissemination of four modules to be used in a series of workshops for school counselors (Stone & House, 2002). MetLife also funded a training of trainers from across the United States to facilitate dissemination of the modules.

The four modules were designed to teach school counselors that they could connect themselves to school reform and become an integral part in creating an equitable education system. Each of the four modules was designed as a one-day workshop. Thus, school districts that opt to have their counselors participate in this training are required to allow the time for 4 days of professional development over a period of time. In the four modules, participants are expected to acquire and apply skills in leadership, advocacy, teaming and collaboration, and the use of data—all directed toward systemic change designed to provide access and equity for all students. Participants also are required to develop an action plan to be implemented in their building or district. The four modules are as follows:

1. Connecting School Counseling to the Mission of Schools
2. Working as Advocates for Systemic Change
3. Transforming School Counseling Through Teaming and Collaboration
4. Taking Action: Putting It All Together.

Each of the four modules has specific objectives for each day of training. The following overall goals for the workshop series are used to inform school districts of the nature and intent of the workshop series:

1. Establish how counselors can be critical participants in educational reform and effective contributors to the central mission of schools—to educate all students to high levels.
2. Challenge the participants' belief systems.
3. Provide skills that will assist participants to work systemically as well as individually in leadership, advocacy, teaming and collaboration, and use of assessment data to help schools and school systems achieve educational equity and excellence for all students.

The MetLife Foundation NSCTI emphasizes principles of social justice, addresses the inequities in systems, and requires a commitment to diversity, technological competence, and an emphasis on accountability.

The UGA Model: A Partnership for Transformation

Many of these initiatives related to school counseling in recent years have involved partnerships between school counseling preparation programs and local school districts to simultaneously transform both preparation and practice. One example of such a co-reform partnership is available in the collaborative relationship between the School Counseling Program at The University of Georgia (UGA) and the school counselors from the Clarke County School District (CCSD) in Athens, Georgia. This partnership was one of six sites to receive both planning and implementation grants from the DeWitt Wallace–Reader's Digest Fund to engage in the transformation process.

The Preparation Program

The School Counseling Program at The University of Georgia is housed within the Department of Counseling and Human Development Services, College of Education (www.coe.uga.edu/echd). The program is 48 semester-hours, is nationally accredited by CACREP, and meets the standards for certification of the Professional Standards Commission for the State of Georgia.

Currently, the program mission is to prepare and retrain counselors in elementary, middle, and secondary schools who are educational leaders and self-reflective practitioners, who serve as advocates for all students, who understand and apply principles of group work in building school and community partnerships, and who accept responsibility for improving educational practices through an active program of research and evaluation. This model is based on five program components:

1. Counseling and coordination
2. Educational leadership
3. Advocacy
4. Team building and collaboration
5. Research and evaluation

Three related program strands are addressed across these components:

1. Awareness, knowledge, and skills related to multiculturalism
2. The use of technology and data to improve educational practice
3. The application of the ASCA National Standards for School Counseling Programs

Partnership with Local Counselors

The Clarke County Counselors Collaborative (CCCC) was founded in 1991 to provide mutual support and professional development opportunities for school counselors and counselor educators in the county. Since its initial meetings with high school counselors and faculty at the University of Georgia, the CCCC has grown to include school counselors at all levels within the Clarke County School District. The name was changed in 2001 to the Classic City Counselors Collaborative as this group prepared to host the Georgia School Counselors Association (GSCA) Fall Conference in Athens, known as the Classic City.

One Friday morning each month the CCCC meets at UGA to engage in ongoing dialogue and professional development. These meetings have provided a venue for the development of ongoing research projects and grant-related activities. Counselors in the Collaborative regularly serve as supervisors for practica and internships, guest lecturers, adjunct faculty, members, program consultants, members of the admissions committee, and co-authors of presentations and publications disseminating the outcomes of the collaboration. Descriptions of the Collaborative, including sample projects and activities and a listing of relevant presentations and publications, are available through the departmental website (www.coe.uga.edu/echd).

Key Activities

Planning and implementation grants from the DeWitt Wallace–Reader's Digest Fund and technical assistance provided by The Education Trust allowed this partnership to extend the work begun in 1991. Key activities or components in the collaboration have included the following:

1. Monthly meetings between counselors, counselor educators, and graduate students

2. Best Practices Conference—an annual conference for local counselors, graduate students, and alumni that updates participants and provides opportunities for sharing successes from the field

3. Counselor Academy—an annual summer professional development opportunity for partnership counselors, graduate students, and counseling program faculty members on topics related to the new role for school counselors

4. Community Caucus—an annual gathering of counselors, graduate students, program faculty members, other school system and university personnel, and community leaders to consider issues facing children and adolescents

5. Counseling and Performance Assessment Lab—a technology laboratory to support counselor, faculty, and student development related to the use of applications to support the new vision for school counseling and to promote student achievement

Accomplishments

In working together in a partnership between the university and the school district, UGA and CCSD have conducted numerous activities and, over time, have accomplished a great deal. Counselors, counselor educators, and graduate students have published and made presentations to professional audiences together, have received substantial grant funding, and have conducted significant research studies on ways to improve the educational experiences of local students. Together, these groups of professionals

1. have improved the curriculum at the university and have challenged the practice of counseling in the district;

2. have completed a document for the school district superintendent outlining what every child can expect from participating in a K–12 school counseling program;

3. have, most recently, been successful in advocating for the designation and hiring of a lead counselor in the district.

Perhaps most significantly, the collaboration informs and enhances the quality of what graduate students receive in their preparation programs and what K–12 students are provided through comprehensive programming.

Summary

Rapid economic, social, and technological changes on a global scale have necessitated significant reform in school counselor preparation and practice if all students are to meet high academic standards that prepare them to be effective participants in the emerging global society of the 21st century. In meeting this demand, university faculty members and professional school counselors and their colleagues have responded to the demands of professional organizations, with significant financial and organizational support from private foundations, to design, implement, and evaluate programs that provide a new vision for school counseling. This new vision proposes that the school counselor is an educational leader who serves as an advocate for all students. By providing a comprehensive developmental counseling program, the new-vision school counselor is committed to advancing the personal, social, and career development of every student in promoting their academic success.

With a century of significant contributions to the human welfare of school-age children, the profession of school counseling has rediscovered its heritage in social action. In transforming the preparation and practice of today's school counselor, an extensive partnership of committed educators is making a significant contribution to the central task of preparing all of America's children for full participation as global citizens in the new millenium.

References

American School Counselor Association. (1996). *Advocacy, alliances & partnerships: The role of the school counselor.* Alexandria, VA: Author.

Aubrey, R.F. (1985). A counseling perspective on the recent educational reform reports. *School Counselor, 33,* 91–99.

Aubrey, R. F. (1986). The professionalization of counseling. In M. D. Lewis, R. L. Hayes, & J. A. Lewis (Eds.), *An introduction to the counseling profession* (pp. 1–35). Itasca, IL: F. E. Peacock.

Baker, S.B. (2000). *School counseling for the twenty-first century* (3rd ed.). New York: Merrill/Prentice Hall.

Campbell, C.A., & Dahir, C.A. (1997). *Sharing the vision: The national standards for school counseling programs.* Alexandria, VA: American School Counselor Association.

Collison, B., Osborne, J. L., Gray, L. A., House, R. M., Firth, J., & Lou, M. (1998). Preparing counselors for social action. In C. C. Lee & G. R. Walz (Eds.), *Social action: A mandate for* counselors (pp. 263–277). Alexandria, VA: American Counseling Association.

Dahir, C.A., Sheldon, C.B., & Valiga, M.J. (1998). *Vision into action: Implementing the national standards for school counseling programs.* Alexandria, VA: American School Counselor Association.

Education Trust, The (1997, February). *The national guidance and counseling reform program.* Washington, DC: Author.

Education Trust, The (2000). *Achievement in America: 2000* [Computer diskette]. Washington, DC: Author.

Elam. S. (Ed.). (1993). *The state of the nation's public schools.* Bloomington, IN: Phi Delta Kappa.

Eriksen, K. (1997). *Making an impact: A handbook on counselor advocacy.* Washington, DC: Taylor & Francis.

Fields, T. H., & Hines, P. L. (2000). School counselor's role in raising student achievement. In G. Duhon & T. Manson (Eds.), *Preparation, collaboration, and emphasis on the family in school counseling for the new millennium* (pp. 135–162). Lewiston, NY: Edwin Mellen Press.

Gysbers, N.C., & Henderson, P. (2001). Comprehensive guidance and counseling programs: A rich history and a bright future. *Professional School Counseling, 4,* 246–256.

Hart, P., & Jacobi, M. (1992). *From gatekeeper to advocate: Transforming the role of the school counselor.* New York: College Entrance Examination Board.

Hatch, T., & Bowers, J. (2002). The block to build on. *ASCA School Counselor, 39,* 12–17.

Hayes, R. L. (1994). Counseling in the postmodern world: Origins and implications of a constructivist developmental approach. *Counseling and Human Development, 26*(6), pp. 1–12.

Hayes, R. L., Dagley, J., & Horne, A. M. (1996). Restructuring school counselor education: Work in progress. *Journal for Counseling and Development, 74,* 378–384.

Hayes, R. L., Nelson, J., Lusky, M., Pearson, G., & Worthy, G. (2002). Using school-wide data to advocate for student success: Charting the academic trajectory of every student. *Professional School Counseling, 6*(2).

Herr, E.L. (2001). The impact of national policies, economics, and school reform on comprehensive guidance programs. *Professional School Counseling, 4,* 236–245.

House, R. M., & Hayes, R. L. (2002). School counselors: Becoming key players in education reform. *Professional School Counseling, 5,* 249–256.

House, R. M., & Martin, P. J. (1998). Advocating for better futures for all students: A new vision for school counselors. *Education, 119,* 284–291.

Martin, P. J. (2002). Transforming school

counseling: A national perspective. *Theory Into Practice, 41*(3), 148–153.

Mohrman, S. A., & Lawler, E. E. (1996). Motivation for school reform. In S. H. Fuhrman & J. A. O'Day (Eds.), *Rewards and reform: Creating educational incentives that work* (pp. 115–143). San Francisco: Jossey–Bass.

Myrick, R. D. (1997). *Developmental guidance and counseling: A practical approach* (3d ed.). Minneapolis: Educational Media.

Paisley, P.O., & Borders, L.D. (1995). School counseling: An evolving specialty. *Journal of Counseling and Development, 74,* 150–153.

Paisley, P.O., & McMahon, H.G. (2001). School counseling for the 21st century: Challenges and opportunities. *Professional School Counseling, 5,* 106–115.

Schneider, B., & Stevenson, D. (1999). *The ambitious generation: America's teenagers motivated but directionless.* New Haven, CT: Yale University Press.

Stone, C., & House, R. (2002). Train the trainers program transforms school counselors. *ASCA School Counselor, 39,* pp. 20–21.

Wong, K. R. (2002). A new question. *ASCA School Counselor, 39,* p. 2.

Additional References

Collison, B. (1998, January). *Active admissions: You get what you look for.* Paper presented at meeting of The Education Trust, Washington, DC.

Gardner, S. (1992, Fall). Failure by fragmentation. *California Tomorrow,* pp. 18–25.

Gelatt, H. B, & Hayes, R. L. (1993, May). *Rethinking education.* Paper presented at meeting of ACA Think Tank: The Crisis in School Counseling, Alexandria, VA.

Gerstner, L. V., Semerad, R. D., Doyle, D. P., & Johnston, W. B. (1994). *Reinventing education: Entrepreneurship in America's public schools.* New York: Penguin Books.

Goodlad, J. (1990). Studying the education of educators: From conception to findings. *Phi Delta Kappan, 70*(9), 698–701.

Hayes, R. L. (1993). A facilitative role for counselors in restructuring schools. *Journal of Humanistic Education and Development, 31,* 156–162.

House, R. M., & Sears, S. J. K. (2002, Summer). Preparing school counselors to be leaders and advocates: A critical need in the new millennium. *Theory Into Practice, 41*(3).

Lieberman, A. (1992). The meaning of scholarly activity and the building of community. *Educational Researcher, 21*(6), 5–12.

Newmann, F. (1993). Beyond common sense in educational restructuring: The issues of content and linkage. *Educational Researcher, 22*(2), 4–13, 22.

Parry, T. (1993). Without a net: Preparations for postmodern living. In S. Friedman (Ed.), *The new language of change: Constructive collaboration in psychotherapy* (pp. 428–459). New York: Guilford Press.

Schorr, L. B. (1997). *Common purpose: Strengthening families and neighborhoods to rebuild America.* New York: Anchor Books.

CHAPTER 11

Consultation and Counseling Strategies to Facilitate Inclusion

Joyce Williams Bergin and James J. Bergin

he regular education initiative (REI) emerged from the Office of Special Education within the U.S. Department of Education during the later portion of the 1980s, in response to the perception that a dual curriculum existed for public school students with and without disabilities. In addition, there was a concern over the efficacy and the cost effectiveness of teaching disabled and non-disabled students in any mode other than the general classroom setting (Wang, Reynolds & Walburg, 1986). Little research supported the tenets upon which the REI was based, yet the inclusion philosophy grew directly and rapidly out of REI and has had an impact on both general and special education across the nation.

Inclusion requires that all children, regardless of extent of disability, can be served best in the general classroom environment. Public laws—including 94-142 and 101-476—support a continuum of services that reflect the unique educational needs of children with disabilities. Although returning exceptional children to the mainstream has always been a goal of special education, the need for more than one method of service delivery has been viewed as critical to rendering adequate services to students whose disabilities are varied and range from mild to profound.

Many school districts have embraced the inclusion philosophy with the assumption that good, regular education teachers can instruct all students appropriately. Although this assumption sounds flattering to the general education teacher, it overlooks the realities inherent in moving a variety of students with learning and behavior disorders into the typical classroom.

Both the American Federation of Teachers and the National Education Association voiced the concern that scarce resources in many school systems nationwide was propelling full inclusion at the expense of focusing on the instructional needs of the students (CEC , 1993). The reality that most teachers faced involved the arrival of a variety of students having mild to severe disabilities with no advance preparation of the classroom, the teacher, or student peers.

Viewed by many administrators as a cost-cutting measure, inclusion has been implemented with no increase in support personnel, specialized instructional materials, or adaptive technology to help the mainstream teacher meet the instructional needs of the exceptional students who now were part of his or her professional responsibilities. Nor did professionals receive training in how roles were to be delineated to collaborate and coordinate their efforts (CEC, 1993).

The debate over inclusion continues, and schools are left to develop their own models and schemes for implementing full inclusion. Little research is available to offer guidelines, and infusion of funding has not materialized to provide the kinds of support systems needed to address the move from a continuum of services to a one-size-fits-all paradigm.

Although collaboration between general and special educators is believed to be the key to successful inclusion, few models are offered for the kinds of intensive, consistent collaboration required. Of those that do exist, the general education collaboration model (Simpson & Myles, 1996) demonstrates the kind of collaborate effort required for including students with mild to moderate behavioral and learning disabilities in the inclusive classroom.

Simpson and Myles (1996) base their model upon the following assumptions: school personnel and parents desire inclusion: inclusion is the best service option for all students involved in special education; teachers and other support professionals are capable and willing to serve the students: *communication* will serve as the basis for coordination and collaboration. The need for shared decision making is new to teachers who heretofore have been trained and evaluated as fairly autonomous in their classroom roles.

Inclusion assumes communication, coordination, and collaboration. In fact, the general education collaboration model assumes that reducing class size, using trained paraprofessionals, engendering positive attitudes toward inclusion on the part of all school personnel, implementating the consultation-collaboration model with general and special educators, building in sufficient planning time, and making available sufficient numbers of professional support personnel are essential to effective and successful inclusion practices (Simpson & Myles, 1996, pp. 436–446).

Of all the elements that Simpson and Myles suggested, perhaps the most readily implemented and the least understood is the communication that underlies consultation and collaboration. It requires mutual respect, good listening skills, willingness to focus on the needs of all the students in the inclusive classrooms as opposed to viewing only accommodations and adaptations for students with disabilities, commitment to the inclusion philosophy, and willingness to work cooperatively as team members. Few general and special education teachers come to the table trained to meet these requirements. By contrast, school counselors are thoroughly trained in these areas. Therefore, they can engender the necessary communication and collaboration by implementing counseling strategies, as well as by presenting and modeling consultation, group guidance, and group counseling skills.

Consultation

School counselors can provide much assistance through mediating, facilitating, and supporting the kinds of dialogue needed among teachers who are being required to plan and implement inclusion. Counselors can facilitate communication between administrators and teachers about commitment to inclusive practices within their assigned schools.

Rogers (1993) offers 10 questions (see Figure 11.1) that can help school personnel evaluate whether their practices are consistent with the inclusion philosophy. Each question answered negatively can become the basis for discussion and exploration of commitment. Counselors can use questions such as these to help initiate the kinds of discussion that may lead to greater understanding of the assumptions, fears, and issues that must be addressed before change can come about. Counselors can help develop the kind of exploration of issues that is essential to determining whether a school is ready to launch an inclusion plan.

By virtue of training and their role on the professional staff, counselors are in a unique position to lend perspective to faculty consultation and collaboration efforts. They can provide support to teachers who are frustrated in the exploratory sessions or when difficulties arise as a result of inclusive practices. Teachers need this kind of support to feel that they are not alone and that their concerns are heard and respected.

Likewise, counselors can offer valuable support for parents of students with and without disabilities who may be concerned about the faculty's exploration of the inclusion process or implementation of the inclusion process within their children's school. Counselors can facilitate discussion between the faculty and parents to ensure that accurate information is disseminated and parental concerns are expressed in the appropriate forum.

Counseling

Two counseling strategies—group guidance and group counseling—are strong complements to consultation with teachers, parents, and staff in facilitating the inclusion process by providing direct assistance to included students and their peers. Group guidance can be used to teach cooperation and communication skills to large groups of students in the general classroom setting (Mehaffey & Sandberg, 1992; Myrick, 1997, Reeder, Douzenis, & Bergin, 1997; Utay & Lampe, 1995; Vernon, 1989a & 1989b). Counselors and classroom teachers can collaborate on teaching a unit of activities that builds group cohesion and reinforces all students' acceptance of and cooperation with each other.

Activities should require that students cooperate with each other so that they can be successful in completing the activities. Activities should focus the students' attention on competing against time limits instead of competing with their teammates or

1. Do we genuinely start from the premise that each child belongs in the classroom he or she would otherwise attend if not disabled (or do we cluster children with disabilities into special groups, classrooms, or schools)?
2. Do we individualize the instructional program for all children whether or not they are disabled and provide the resources that each child needs to explore individual interests in the school environment (or do we tend to provide the same sorts of services for most children who share the same diagnostic label)?
3. Are we fully committed to maintenance of a caring community that fosters mutual respect and support among staff, parents, and students in which we honestly believe that disabled children can benefit from friendships with nondisabled children (or do our practices tacitly tolerate children teasing or isolating some as outcasts)?
4. Have our general educators and special educators integrated their efforts and their resources so that they work together as integral parts of a unified team (or are they isolated in separate rooms or departments with separate supervisors and budgets)?
5. Does our administration create a work climate in which staff are supported as they provide assistance to each other (or are teachers afraid of being presumed to be incompetent if they seek peer collaboration in working with students)?
6. Do we actively encourage the full participation of children with disabilities in the life of our school including co-curricular and extracurricular activities (or do they participate only in the academic portion of the school day)?
7. Are we prepared to alter support systems for students as their needs change through the school year so that they can achieve, experience successes, and feel that they genuinely belong in their school and classes (or do we sometimes provide such limited services to them that the children are set up to fail)?
8. Do we make parents of children with disabilities fully a part of our school community so they also can experience a sense of belonging (or do we give them a separate PTA and different newsletters)?
9. Do we give children with disabilities just as much of the full school curriculum as they can master and modify it as necessary so that they can share elements of these experiences with their classmates (or do we have a separate curriculum for children with disabilities)?
10. Have we included children with disabilities supportively in as many possible of the same testing and evaluation experiences as their nondisabled classmates (or do we exclude them from these opportunities while assuming that they cannot benefit from the experiences)?

Source: From The Inclusion Revolutions, *Phi Delta Kappan, 11*, 5.

Figure 11.1 Inclusion checklist

members of other teams. Emphasis can be placed upon enhancing participants' attending and responding skills and in communicating using their tactile, auditory, and visual abilities.

Implementing cooperation activities provides some advantages to the inclusion process:

1. By providing direct practice in communication, the teacher is afforded the opportunity to reinforce students for their attending and responding per se without having to refer to any academic context or outcome. Thus the included students can focus on the skills themselves without worrying about grades or being rejected by their peers for academic failure.

2. The requirement that students must collaborate to achieve success in the activities showcases the positive effects of cooperation versus competition. It reinforces the concept that members of a team are necessarily interdependent. They are not to act as independent agents "doing their own work" as is the norm for most school activities, especially academic achievement activities.

3. This latter point leads to a third advantage in that it addresses the "family" environment of the inclusive classroom. It reinforces the principle that all students must work together for the good of the whole class. Through good cooperation and communication with each other and the teacher, the students create and maintain an optimal, supportive learning environment in the classroom so that all students have a fair opportunity to learn and achieve in accordance with their individual abilities and needs.

Group counseling provides a unique opportunity for students to acquire and practice a wide range of skills that promote personal growth and social integration (Americkaner & Summerlin, 1982; Bergin, 1991; Campbell & Myrick, 1990; Huey, 1983; Morganett, 1990, 1994; Omizo & Omizo, 1987, Phillips-Hershey & Kanagy, 1996; Wick, Wick, & Peterson, 1997; Wilde, 1996). The counseling group is a model of teamwork, requiring cooperation, communication, and interdependence among participants in both the establishment and the maintenance of group norms and rules for behavior.

The group also underscores the importance of each individual, emphasizing equality among group members, the rights of each individual to be heard, and the value of each person's ideas and actions as they contribute to the group. The group has a responsibility to the individual as well as the individual to the group. The group is committed to helping the individual improve his or her knowledge and skills, and to reinforce his or her efforts and achievements.

Therefore, group counseling affords the "included" student a special opportunity to build friendships with peers in a structured, supportive environment. The student is allowed to discuss feelings of frustration experienced in the classroom. Moreover, the student can learn socially acceptable methods of handling those frustrations. The group setting also reinforces the student's peers in the group for respecting diversity among the members and for accepting responsibility to help each other achieve personal successes.

These benefits can be extended by selecting all of the group members from the same classroom. This affords greater opportunity for the members to transfer their learning from the group to the classroom, and to receive positive reinforcement of their acquired skills "in vivo" from peers, the teacher, and each other.

Group counseling and group guidance interventions complement individual counseling. They add preventive and developmental components to the remedial aspects of individual counseling by extending the direct-counseling services to the classroom peers of the included student who is referred for counseling. In conjunction with consultation interventions directed to the student's teachers and parents, these counseling strategies can provide strong support for inclusion of the student in the classroom and his or her integration with peers.

Case Study

Randy was an eight-and-a-half-year-old second-grade student. He was repeating second grade and functioning below grade level. Randy had a history of overreacting to frustration, resorting to crying, withdrawing from peers in social situations, and complaining about being distracted by classmates. The results of psychoeducational evaluations, social and medical histories, and systematic classroom observations indicated that Randy had difficulties attaching meaning to symbols. His difficulties were manifested in poor receptive skills (learning new material), expressive skills (organizing and expressing his thoughts), and reproducing written symbols (writing was a slow process for Randy).

Because of these difficulties, Randy was easily frustrated. When he became frustrated, he could not express his feelings adequately, so he withdrew, or cried, or struck out at others. This behavior was disruptive to the learning environment of the classroom and was counterproductive to his teacher's efforts to promote Randy's inclusion in the classroom and, ultimately, to social integration with his peers.

The school-based interdisciplinary pupil services team arranged for Randy to be placed in the learning disabilities resource program. The LD specialist and Randy's classroom teacher collaborated in designing and implementing instructional strategies to improve Randy's receptive and expressive vocabulary, as well as his writing skills. The team recommended that the school counselor and teacher devise and implement activities to teach Randy how to cope with his frustrations in the classroom by actively seeking the assistance of his teacher and by collaborating with his classmates. The counselor, teacher, and LD specialist collaborated on the development of a three-stage counseling intervention plan.

In stage one, the counselor met with Randy for individual counseling sessions twice a week for 4 weeks. The sessions focused on helping Randy monitor his frustration level in the classroom and in the LD resource room. He was instructed to cue his teachers whenever he was unclear about "instructions" or "how to express his ideas" so they could assist him before he became overly frustrated. Emphasis was placed on developing nonverbal cues so as to avoid distracting others and calling negative attention to Randy.

Through role play, the counselor helped Randy rehearse the use of appropriate manners for social interaction and develop clear vocabulary for appropriately expressing his ideas and feelings to adults and agemates. The teachers reinforced

Randy for using the cuing systems in their classes and praised him for taking responsibility for his feelings and behaviors.

Stage two involved Randy, along with five of his classmates, participating in group counseling sessions with the counselor. Developed in consultation with the teachers, the group was composed of six boys, all of whom were performing at or near Randy's level of reading achievement. Two of the boys received services through the LD resource program and three were in Randy's mainstream classroom reading group. All five peers had expressive skills that were average for their ages and grade placements. Two were among the best-liked students in the class, and the teacher identified them as having "very good manners."

The group met twice a week for 6 weeks. The theme for the group was cooperative problem solving. The counselor used *Escape from Pirate Island* (Bergin, 1990), a collaborative decision-making game, to facilitate participants' interactions. Playing the game required the participants to discuss problem situations and to come to unanimous agreement regarding the solutions. Group participation also involved sharing leadership and interaction in cohesion-building activities.

The final stage involved the classroom teacher and counselor collaboratively conducting group guidance activities with Randy's entire mainstream class. The unit of eight activities (Bergin, 1989) focused on teaching the students communication and cooperation skills.

Weekly classroom sessions began when Randy's counseling group had reached its fourth week of work. This allowed the counselor to enlist the groups assistance in conducting the eight designated activities in the mainstream classroom. Randy and his group were able to model teamwork for the class and received their teacher's and classmates' praise.

Results of the 15-week intervention indicated that Randy had made significant progress in several areas. Most significantly, he became well integrated with his classmates, especially his counseling group peers. He was included in recess games, invited to sit with others in the lunchroom, and chosen as a teammate for classroom activities.

His teachers reported fewer instances of peer complaints about Randy's behavior and said he did not complain about others picking on him. Both teachers indicated that the cuing system worked effectively in their classes to reduce Randy's outbursts of frustration. The teachers also believed that Randy's use of cues helped him relate more positively to them, thereby affording them an opportunity to praise him appropriately in front of his peers.

Academically, Randy did not demonstrate significant gains in achievement during this period. The teachers stated, however, that he showed a marked improvement in time spent on task, completion of written assignments, and motivation to achieve. They also concluded that Randy's attempts to articulate his feelings verbally increased his vocabulary and augmented his language development. Finally, his parents reported that Randy's acquired social skills had transferred to his home behavior and he now played with same-age peers in the neighborhood. The parents reported that Randy previously had interacted and played only with much younger children.

Summary

Inclusion is a challenging task for teachers and general education students, as well as for students with disabilities. Cooperation among counselors, teachers, parents, and students themselves is necessary if inclusive programs are to become successful. Through consultation strategies with parents, teachers, and other specialists, counselors can help schools create a climate conducive to inclusion. By providing direct services to students through group and individual counseling and group guidance, counselors can help students acquire the skills necessary to work cooperatively and accept diversity.

References

Americkaner, M., & Summerlin, M. (1982). Group counseling with learning disabled children: Effects of social skills and relaxation training on self-concept and classroom behavior. *Journal of Learning Disabilities, 15*(6), 340–343.

Bergin, J. (1989). Building group cohesiveness through cooperation activities. *Elementary School Guidance and Counseling, 24*(2), 90-95.

Bergin, J. (1991). *Escape from pirate island* [game]. Doyleston, PA: Mar*Co Products.

Campbell, C. & Myrick, R. (1990). Motivational group counseling for low-performing students. *Journal for Specialists in Group Work, 15*(10), 43–50.

Council for Exceptional Children. (1993, fall). CEC takes the lead for appropriate inclusive schools. *Teaching Exceptional Children* , 86.

Huey, W. (1983). Reducing adolescent aggression through group assertiveness training. *School Counselor, 30*, 193–203.

Mehaffey, J., & Sandberg, S. (1992). Conducting social skills training groups with elementary school children. *School Counselor, 40*, 61-67.

Morganett, R. (1990). *Skills for living: Group counseling activities for young adolescents.* Champaign, IL: Research Press.

Morganett, R. (1994). *Skills for living: Group counseling activities* for elementary students. Champaign, IL: Research Press.

Myrick, R. (1997). *Developmental guidance and counseling: A practical approach* (3rd. Ed.). Minneapolis: Educational Media.

Omizo, M., & Omizo, S. (1987). The effects of group counseling on classroom behavior and self-concept among elementary school learning disabled children. *Exceptional Child, 34*(1), 57–64.

Phillips-Hershey, E., & Kanagy, B. (1996). Teaching students to manage personal anger constructively. *Elementary School Guidance and Counseling, 30*, 229–234.

Reeder, J., Douzenis, C., & Bergin, J. (1997). The effects of small group counseling on the racial attitudes second grade students. *Professional School Counseling, 1*(2), 15–18.

Rogers, J. (1993). The inclusion revolution. *Phi Delta Kappan, 11*, 5.

Simpson, R., & Myles, B. (1996). A general education collaboration model: A model for successful mainstreaming. In E. Meyen, G. Vergason, & R. Whelan (Eds.), *Strategies for teaching exceptional children in inclusive settings* (pp. 435–450). Denver: Love Publishing.

Utay, J., & Lampe, R. (1995). Use of a group counseling game to enhance social skills of children with learning disabilities. *Journal for Specialists in Group Work, 20*, 114–120.

Vernon, A. (1989a). *Thinking, feeling, behaving: An emotional education curriculum for children.* Muncie, IN: Research Press.

Vernon, A. (1989b). *Thinking, feeling, behaving: An emotional education curriculum for adolescents.* Muncie, IN: Research Press.

Wang, M., Reynolds, M., & Walberg, H. (1986). Rethinking special education. *Educational Leadership, 44*(1), 26–31.

Wick, D., Wick, J., Peterson, N. (1997). Improving self-esteem with Adlerian adventure therapy. *Professional School Counseling, 1*(1), 53–56.

Wilde, J. (1996). The efficacy of short-term rational emotive education with fourth grade students. *Elementary School Guidance and Counseling, 31*, 131–138.

Enhancing the Educational Attainment of Minority Youth

Elsie G. J. Moore

Inequalities exist in the life opportunities of young Americans from various social classes and ethnic groups. This is obviously not a new observation. The issue became the focus of considerable sociopolitical concern in the early 1960s as larger segments of our society were confronted with the reality that some groups were experiencing unmitigated intergenerational poverty and social and cultural isolation at a time when the majority was benefiting from prosperity and opportunities for upward mobility in an expanding economy.

Although the historical social forces of segregation and exclusion on the bases of race and national origin undoubtedly had contributed to the problems, legally banning these practices was clearly not sufficient to solve them. The fact remained that most individuals in the excluded groups were not developing the skills and credentials required by an increasingly technical society. That poor children and those from isolated ethnic groups consistently showed lower levels of educational attainment and scholastic achievement was recognized as a major contributor to socioeconomic disparities.

Also, public education clearly was not entirely succeeding as the great "equalizer" in providing—regardless of family background—the opportunity to learn, develop, and achieve. Black Americans, Hispanics, Puerto Ricans, and other ethnic minority children were not developing literacy and mathematic skills at a level necessary to compete with their more advantaged agemates in the majority culture.

Although general agreement existed that the socioeconomic immobility of these groups was strongly related to their lack of educational achievement, considerable disagreement emerged over what factors were contributing to their school failure and how these factors might be mediated by social class and ethnic group membership. Many experimental intervention programs were developed with the common goal of reducing or eliminating the school achievement deficiencies of minority status children. The focus and content of these programs varied depending upon the theoretical orientation of program developers to the nature and causal sequence of factors in minority children's educational difficulties.

In addition to numerous isolated experimental programs, Project Head Start was implemented at the national level in 1965 with federal funds allocated for the War on Poverty. The purpose of this national program for poor and minority status children ages 3 to 5 years was to ameliorate handicaps that prevent children from benefiting from public education, and thereby to increase their potential for upward social mobility.

After more than two decades of educational innovations, interventions, and research, considerable disparities remain in the scholastic achievement and educational attainment of minority status youth and their majority culture peers. Why this is the case and what can be done to facilitate school success of minority status young people are the issues addressed in this chapter. Suggestions as to how counselors may play a role in enhancing the educational attainment of minority youths are particularly focused upon in this discussion.

A Closer Look at the Problem

Young people from certain ethnic groups consistently show lower levels of educational attainment (i.e., number of years of schooling completed) than their majority culture peers. Blacks and Hispanics, for example, show significantly lower educational attainment than their Anglo counterparts.

Comparative Studies

Recent estimates indicate that, among American youth between ages 18 and 23 in the summer of 1980, the proportion of Blacks who had not obtained a high school diploma was twice that of the White population (32% vs. 16%) (U.S. Department of Defense, 1982). The proportion of Hispanic youths in this age range who had not completed high school was even higher than that of Blacks—42%. Differences in the proportions of these ethnic groups, ages 18 to 22 years, who had completed at least 1 year of postsecondary education (i.e., some college) were not as great as those seen for high school completion, but they were considerable.

Regardless of ethnicity, individuals with more education obtain higher status jobs and, generally, higher salaries. Therefore, educational variation between groups is an important factor in the persistent inequalities in life opportunities and ultimate occupational and income attainment observed between them (Jencks et al., 1979).

Increasingly, educators and social science researchers are focusing not only upon how much schooling young people from various groups complete but also on the level and types of skills they attain while in the educational system. Technological advances have reduced the demand for unskilled and semiskilled workers while increasing the demand for clerical, technical, and professional workers. What this means is that basic literacy *and* numeracy skills are absolute prerequisites for performance in occupations at even the lowest end of the skilled labor continuum. Individuals with basic science, electronics, and mechanical knowledge, as well as basic academic skills (in reading, writing, and mathematics) can be expected to create a competitive advantage in selection for jobs, higher educational placements, and job-training programs leading to higher status and more lucrative careers in today's labor market.

Studies of academic skill development among American school-age children have consistently shown that, on the average, minority youth are not developing basic academic skills, such as reading, writing, mathematics, and science, at the same rate as their White counterparts. The discrepancy in skill development among minority status youth quite clearly relates to social and educational processes that undermine their opportunities for quality education.

This point was substantiated by Coleman et al. (1966) in reporting the results of their national study of the skill development of American school children at various grade levels. The study demonstrated the unevenness with which public education serves individuals from various life circumstances. It alerted educators, social scientists, and policy makers to the fact that Black and other minority status children were not developing even basic academic skills at the same rate as their White agemates, even when they had the same amount of schooling. Subsequent studies such as the periodic National Assessment of Educational Progress, conducted by the Education Commission of the States, and analyses of results of the yearly administration of the Scholastic Aptitude Test (SAT) (see Jones, 1984, for a review of these studies) generally confirm the persistence of ethnic group differences in specific skill development over time.

Profile of American Youth

In 1980 a unique opportunity to examine the skill level of the contemporary American youth population, to assess their vocational potential (as indexed by aptitude test scores) and to compare the performance of persons of varying ethnic and educational backgrounds, resulted from a study sponsored by the Department of Defense in cooperation with the Department of Labor. This study, called *Profile of American Youth,* involved administration of the current version of the Armed Services Vocational Aptitude Battery (ASVAB) to nearly 12,000 young people ages 15 to 22 at the time of testing. The study sample was developed to yield data that could be projected to represent the entire U. S. population in this age range. Because the young people who were administered the ASVAB were participants in the Department of Labor's large-scale study, National Longitudinal Study (NLS) of Youth Labor Force Behavior, a considerable amount of background data were available for each person tested, including educational information, family background data, ethnicity, and so on.

What makes the results from the *Profile of American Youth* study so unique is that the data come from persons of all segments of our society who were sampled by direct home visits. Consequently, they give a much broader picture of the skill development of American young people than tests administered to school children (e.g., the National Assessment of Educational Progress) or to high school seniors who are college-bound [e.g., Scholastic Aptitude Test (SAT) and American College Testing (ACT) program results reported annually]. In addition, because the ASVAB is a broad-range aptitude test battery that assesses not only school-intensive skills such as reading, word knowledge, general science, and mathematics, but also technical skills such as electronics information, mechanical comprehension, and auto and shop information, the Profile study permits an analysis of vocationally relevant skills that usually are not covered in the routine testing of students.

Results of the Profile study revealed that for all American young people, poor and non-poor, Black, Hispanic, and White, the more schooling they complete, the higher are their skill levels in the school-intensive areas and the technical areas. But Black and Hispanic youth who had completed the same amount of schooling as their White peers, including those who had at least some college, generally scored considerably lower than Whites.

As a matter of fact, a clear pattern of increasing difference in level of skill development with education emerged when the performance of Black and White youths was compared. That is, the smallest difference in their scores was seen among those who had completed 8 or fewer years of education, and the greatest difference was seen among those who had completed at least some college. In the case of the Hispanic young people, the smallest differentiation of their skill level relative to White peers also was seen among those who had completed 8 or fewer years of schooling. Beyond this educational level, a larger, but essentially constant, difference was shown in favor of White youth. (See Bock & Moore, 1986, for a complete analysis and discussion of the Profile study results.)

Other Studies

Although researchers consistently have observed considerable differences in the level of skill development of ethnic minority youth as compared to that of their White peers, positive changes are beginning to appear. For example, Burton and Jones (1982), from their analysis of National Assessment of Educational Progress (NAEP) test results for children ages 9 and 13 years old between 1970 and 1980, reported a significant decline in performance differences between Black and White pupils in writing skills, science, mathematics, social studies, and reading. Similarly, Jones (1984) reported a decline in differences between Black and White students in SAT-Verbal and SAT-Mathematics performance between 1976 and 1983.

Even though considerable differences remain between the average scores of Black and White students, these trends of declining differences are encouraging. Why we now are beginning to see encouraging changes in the relative performance of White youth and their ethnic minority peers is difficult to specify. Most observers, however, conceptualize the declining differences as long awaited returns on societal investments in innovations, interventions, and general efforts to improve the quality of education available to ethnic minority youth.

Some Early False Starts

In the 1960s and early 1970s the development of most experimental intervention programs aimed at facilitating school success of minority status children was predicated upon the belief that the children's academic difficulties were a consequence of cognitive deficiencies that characterized them at the onset of formal schooling (see Horowitz & Paden, 1973, for a review of these programs). That is, many psychologists, educators, and other authorities assumed that ethnic minority children did not develop prerequisite intellectual skills during the preschool years to allow them to optimally benefit from school instruction. Although theorists at the time differed in their ideas about why the children were deficient (whether the deficiencies were primarily the result of environmental factors or of biological factors), they did generally agree that children from certain ethnic minority groups were disproportionately deficient in the skills necessary for successful school performance and learning.

This notion of pervasive cognitive deficiency among ethnic minority children— particularly Black children—was attributable primarily to the consistent finding that the children on the average scored significantly lower on standardized intelligence tests than did their White peers. Indeed, ethnic group differences in IQ performance and performance on other standardized measures designed to assess learning potential were the empirical bases for assuming that cognitive deficits were the sources of the children's school achievement difficulties.

The logic of this assumption stems from the belief that IQ tests can inform us of the quality of cognitive functioning that characterizes all children and that differences in functioning indicated by variations in test scores play a significant causal role in differentiated school performance (Eckberg, 1979). Both facets of this assumption can be challenged on the basis of accumulated research findings on factors affecting minority children's IQ test performance (see Moore, 1986a, for a discussion of this issue).

In the belief that ethnic minority children suffered from cognitive deficiencies, most of the early programs were designed to provide experiences and instruction that were thought to promote cognitive competency in general and the development of prerequisite academic skills in particular. As might be expected, the effectiveness of those programs typically was evaluated by noting changes in children's IQ scores at the completion of the intervention.

Most of these early programs were successful in boosting the children's IQ scores, but follow-up data revealed that by the third grade the children's scholastic achievement was not significantly different from that of their ethnic peers who had not experienced special preparation for public school entry. Had the programs failed? The unqualified answer is *no,* they had not failed, but many of the guiding assumptions of the programs on which long-term projections for the children's school success were based were in error.

As our knowledge of human developmental processes evolves, we must adjust our assumptions and hypotheses. These early programs based their projections of future school success for the participating children on the assumption that experiences in early infancy and childhood have a lasting effect on the individual—an impact on development throughout the course of development.

Clarke and Clarke (1976) and Brim and Kagan (1980) have compiled evidence from a number of sources to indicate that the effects of early experience, both positive and negative, are not permanent over the life course. Human development is a dynamic process, and individuals change as a result of continual interaction between their person and their changing environments. From this perspective, Ramey and Haskins (1981) concluded that the failure of ethnic minority children to achieve in the public school system consistent with projections made on the basis of their IQ scores after program interventions was attributable to public school characteristics. That is, public schools do not generally provide continued support for these children's intellectual development at the level provided by high quality preschool programs.

The lesson to be learned from early attempts to enhance minority children's educational attainment is rather obvious. Attempts to boost the children's scholastic achievement and attainment cannot be a one-time effort in the preschool years. Efforts to facilitate their academic growth have to be reflected in all segments of the curriculum, in the process of classroom instruction, and in the planning and program development of administrators, teachers, and counselors.

Making the Schools Work for Minority Youths

Each school year a disproportionate number of ethnic minority children are relegated to inferior positions in the curriculum on the basis of test results such as IQ scores and reading readiness assessments (Scarr, 1981). These early school decisions later translate into lower track positions in high school (if the student does not drop out of school from boredom before that time) and generally lower skill development at the completion of their public school experience. The reason for this is that children who are placed in special education classes other than gifted classes often are stereotyped by the larger social system of the school as being not as capable as others.

Teachers, counselors, and other school personnel often use the lower standardized test performance of these children to set a similarly low ceiling on the type, amount, and level of exposure to curriculum materials and on acceptable levels of mastery. Instruction is limited to the level of the test score, with only modest attempts to provide intellectual growth experiences (Haskins, Walton, & Ramey,

1983). Consequently, the children get farther behind their peers who achieve higher curriculum placements early in the schooling process. The effects of this under-education are cumulative, resulting in greater disparities in skill development between groups at the higher educational levels than at lower levels.

Many unsophisticated users of test data interpret lower scores on standardized measures of the sort mentioned earlier as indicators of fixed deficits. Thus, they feel justified in setting lower educational standards and expectations for children who are thought to be less capable, especially if "hard" evidence, such as a test score, exists to verify that position. Therefore, test data users in the school setting must be aware of the importance of cultural relativity for determining educational potential. Schools and school personnel all too often have a monocultural view (i.e., that of the White middle-class) of what behaviors, skills, attitudes, and values on the part of a pupil and his or her family are indicative of a "high ability" child. This same view generally is reflected in the standardized test measures used to empirically support placement and classification decisions.

Children from different ethnic groups enter this system with learning experiences, skills, attitudes, and achievement orientations derived from their unique socialization experiences, which are quite often different from those expected or even desired by the school (Gilbert, 1985; Shade, 1982). But this does not mean that they have not developed the prerequisite cognitive skills to be successful learners of skills the schools are charged to provide. Schools must become more attuned to ethnic minority children's needs as learners and avoid relying on test scores to account for their failure to do so.

Certainly the standardized test scores of ethnic minority children can be useful— if used wisely and in conjunction with carefully collected observational data of the child in various contexts, not just the school classroom. These data can be used to identify the child's relative strengths and weaknesses in preparation for curriculum placements appropriate for her or his age. But these data must be used to capitalize on apparent strengths in the instructional process, and to plan and implement appropriate remediation, if necessary, to ensure the child's continual academic growth.

The Cultural Context of Educational Processes

School personnel have to recognize that the school context is not a culturally neutral environment. Gilbert (1985) noted that the culture of the school is one that encourages and expects competitive behavior among pupils, demonstrated competency in standard English in oral exchanges, willingness to follow pre-set rules for involvement in the instructional process (e.g., only one person speaks at a time), and that involvement is limited to cognitive participation, not affective and motorical participation.

Shade (1982) suggested that a particular style of information processing is required by the culture of the school for students to be remarkably successful in the educational process. Characteristics of this accepted style of information processing include the spontaneous tendency to focus on the task itself and to ignore the people in the situation, an attending preference for verbal rather than nonverbal cues, abstraction ability that separates ideas and concepts into parts and reconstitutes them into a unified whole, and an analytic thinking style. According to Shade, the schools expect and require cognitive strategies that are "sequential, analytic, and object-oriented" for school success, which means that children who are, as a result of their particular cultural socialization, "universalistic, intuitive, and . . . person oriented" are likely to experience achievement difficulties (p. 238).

More often than not, ethnic minority children enter the schools demonstrating information processing skills, attitudes, and understandings of involvement in the classroom that conflict with the instructional modes and expectations of the typical classroom teacher. Many believe that this mismatch between the skills and orientations to learning that ethnic minority children bring to the school and what the school system expects and values is a major source of the children's achievement difficulties (see Bock & Moore, 1986, for a review of this literature).

If this is the case, adjusting instructional modes to fit the styles of the children rather than attempting to force the children to be responsive to the preestablished style of the school could function to facilitate minority children's achievement. It also might function to facilitate their remaining in school through high school completion to the extent that the adjustment might encourage children's greater feelings of belonging to the system rather than feelings of "foreign-ness."

High Expectations of Pupils' Achievement

Much literature has accumulated on characteristics of so-called effective schools for poor and ethnic minority children—schools wherein these children show high academic achievement. Characteristics of effective schools generally include a strong leader who is knowledgeable about and involved in the instructional program, programs of instruction in reading and mathematics that are systematically implemented and for which goals of instruction are clearly articulated, and high expectations of children's achievement, particularly in basic verbal and numerical skills, by the teachers and administrative staff (Brookover et al., 1978; Edmonds, 1979).

The latter characteristic has been consistently found to affect the achievement of ethnic minority students. Those who experience school settings wherein high academic standards are set and school personnel, particularly teachers, expect them to be successful in achieving the standards show high achievement. Teachers in these situations tend to provide a considerable amount of encouragement, praise, and support for achievement efforts, and the children respond with continued persistence and efforts toward skill mastery.

Unfortunately, many ethnic minority children find themselves in educational settings wherein academic standards are low, as are expectations of their achievement. Why this is the case is not clear, but in these settings ethnic minority children appear to not only fail to achieve skill development at levels that would allow them to be competitive with peers from the majority culture but also develop lower personal standards of achievement and lower expectations of their own achievement potential.

Early Academic and Vocational Counseling

Ogbu (1978) theorized that the high dropout rate and lower scholastic achievement among Black students, in particular result from their lack of awareness of the relevance of the skills taught in school for future career options. If this is the case, teachers, counselors, and other school officials must make special efforts to continually demonstrate the relationship between the academic skills taught and their application to the larger world of work.

Moore (1986b) verified that Black youth have a significantly lower knowledge of the world of work—what people in various occupations actually do—than their White peers. This is perhaps the result of the rather limited representation of career roles available to ethnic minority young people in their home communities. The literature has consistently shown that Black youth, even those who attend college, show a limited range of vocational interests. They tend to gravitate toward the social sciences, education, and the health fields, while White college students favor biological and physical sciences, at least as freshmen (Astin, 1982).

Underrepresentation of ethnic minorities in scientific and technical careers has been the focus of considerable concern in recent years. This is because lucrative career opportunities in the contemporary economy are expanding in these areas, Ethnic minority youth, however, generally do not express an interest in these careers, nor are they prepared to be competitive for educational placements and job-training programs in these areas. Their lack of preparation is related to their lower average mathematics skills and science knowledge upon completion of their secondary education.

The literature clearly reveals that minority youths do not enroll in academic mathematics and science courses in high school in the same proportions as their White peers (Jones, 1984). Large numbers of ethnic minority students who aspire to careers in engineering or other mathematics-related careers, who are perceived as mathematically capable by their teachers and counselors, do not enroll in advanced level mathematics courses in high school. Obviously, better counseling would facilitate their preparation and achievement of career goals.

What Can Counselors Do?

Counselors' potential to facilitate the educational attainment of minority youth is enormous. Counselors can provide the leadership to develop systematic, comprehensive career exploration programs in elementary, junior high, and high schools that serve large numbers of ethnic minority students and can ensure that these programs are implemented and appropriately evaluated for effectiveness. Counselors can help classroom teachers develop strategies to demonstrate the relationship between skills taught in the classroom and effective, productive functioning in the larger world.

Further, counselors can monitor the use of standardized test results for purposes of classification and placement of ethnic minority students. They also can take the lead in dispelling the myth that any test score is fixed or is a stable index of what the child can achieve. Educating teachers and principals about the appropriate interpretation of standardized test scores would definitely facilitate the achievement efforts of these children.

Counselors can take the lead in developing opportunities for school personnel to explore their own cultural orientations and to consider how their ethnic minority pupils may differ from them on various dimensions. Along this line, teachers also might consider how cultural differences between them and their pupils may negatively impact the learning and achievement of pupils in their charge. Particular attention could be given to the possible mismatch between pupils' typical styles of perceiving and processing information and the style required to achieve under the teacher's preferred mode of instruction.

Finally, counselors can take the lead in educating school personnel on the importance of their expectations for children's achievement striving and attainment. Certainly, teachers and principals need to clarify their performance expectations for ethnic minority students. If they are low, educators should clarify how the expectations were formed and whether they can be verified in fact.

Obviously ethnic minority students' perception of the availability and openness of counselors to meeting with them and discussing their concerns and problems is important. From her study of successful rural Black adolescents, Courtland (1985) reported that many saw school counselors as important providers of academic and personal-social assistance. This component of what the researcher described as "positive school experiences" of these young people is particularly noteworthy in this context.

References

Astin, A. W. (1982). *Minorities in American higher education.* San Francisco: Jossey-Bass.

Bock, R. D., & Moore, E. G. J. (1986). *Advantage and disadvantage: A profile of American youth.* Hillsdale, NJ: Lawrence Erlbaum.

Brim, O. G., & Kagan, J. (1980). *Constancy and change in human development.* Cambridge: Harvard University Press.

Brookover, W. B., Schweitzer, J. H., Schneider, J. M., Beady, C, H., Flood, P. K., & Wisenbaker, J. M. (1978). Elementary school climate and school achievement. *American Educational Research Journal, 15,* 301–318.

Burton, N. W, & Jones, L. V. (1982). Recent trends in achievement levels of Black and White youth. *Educational Researcher, 11*(17), 10–14.

Clarke, A. B., & Clarke, A. D. B. (1976). *Early experience: Myth and evidence.* New York: Free Press.

Coleman, J. S., Campbell, E. Q., Hobson, C. J., McPartland, J., Mood, A. M., Weinfeld, F. D., & York, R. L. (1966). *Equality of educational opportunity.* Washington, DC: U.S. Government Printing Office.

Courtland, C. L. (1985). Successful rural Black adolescents: A psycho-social profile. *Adolescence, 20*(77), 129–142.

Eckberg, D. L. (1979). *Intelligence and race.* New York: Praeger.

Edmonds, R. (1979, March/April). Some schools work and more can. *Social Policy,* pp. 28–32.

Gilbert, S. E. II. (1985, October). Improving the success in school of poor Black children. *Phi Delta Kappan,* pp. 133–137.

Haskins, R., Walden, T., & Ramey, C. T. (1983). Teacher and student behavior in high and low ability groups. *Journal of Educational Psychology, 75,* 799–810.

Horowitz, F. D., & Paden, L. (1973). The effectiveness of environmental intervention programs. In B. Caldwell & H. Riccuiti (Eds.), *Review of Child Development Research* (Vol. 3) (pp. 331–402). Chicago: University of Chicago Press.

Jencks, C., Bartlett, S., Corcoran, M., Crouse, J., Eaglesfield, D., Jackson, G., McClelland, K., Mueser, P., Olneck, M., Schwartz, J., Ward, S., & Williams, J. (1979). *Who gets ahead?* New York: Basic Books.

Jones, L. V. (1984). White-Black achievement differences: The narrowing gap. *American Psychologist, 39*(11), 1207–1213.

Moore, E. G. J. (1986a). Family socialization and the IQ test performance of traditionally and transracially adopted black children. *Developmental Psychology, 22,* 317–326.

Moore, E. G. J. (1986b). *The influence of knowledge of the world of work on ethnic group differences in career aspirations.* Paper presented at the Annual Meeting of the American Educational Research Association, San Francisco, CA.

Ogbu, J. (1978). *Minority education and caste.* New York: Academic Press.

Ramey, C. T., & Haskins, R. (1981). Early education, intellectual development and school performance: A reply to Arthur Jensen and J. McVicker Hunt. *Intelligence, 5,* 41–48.

Scarr, S. (1981). Testing for children: Assessment and the many determinations of intellectual competence. *American Psychologist, 36*(10), 1159–1166.

Shade, B. (1982). Afro-American cognitive style: A variable in school success. *Review of Educational Research, 52,* 219–244.

U.S. Department of Defense. (1982). *Profile of American youth.* Washington, DC: Dept. of Defense, Office of Assistant Secretary of Defense, Manpower, Reserve Affairs, & Logistics.

School Violence and Disruption: Rhetoric, Reality, and Reasonable Balance

Peter E. Leone, Matthew J. Mayer, Kimber Melmgren, and Sheri M. Meisel

During the past few years the specter of school violence has caused many parents, teachers, and administrators to rethink their basic assumptions about the safety of schools. Tragic and senseless shootings of students by students in public schools in the United States have left us stunned and distraught. Images of school shootings and the demand that schools become safe for all children have shaped responses by politicians, parents, and school administrators (Sheley, 2000).

Recent and widely publicized school shootings raise a number of questions: Are public schools less safe than they were 10 years ago? Twenty years ago? Can teachers teach and children learn in an atmosphere where concerns about safety interfere with instruction and management? In addition to these questions, parents and others want to know who has been involved in these school shootings and whether schools have taken steps to ensure that these incidents don't happen in their schools.

Most parents and members of communities believe that schools should be places where children develop intellectually and socially. The idea that school violence, in whatever form, interferes with the orderly operation and safety of schools is anathema to the public. Beyond concerns about physical injury to children, disruption of the school environment interferes with others' learning and can create a climate of fear in which children avoid school or engage in behaviors to protect themselves (Chandler et al., 1998). There is also the concern that minor problems, if ignored, will escalate into major events.

The most current data on school violence and youth victimization in the United States indicate that violence has been declining since 1993. Data reported by the Federal Bureau of Investigation as part of the Uniform Crime Reports (Rand, 1998), as well as students' self-report of victimization that are part of the National Crime Victimization Surveys (Brener et al., 1999), indicate that violence perpetrated by and against youth continues to fall. In spite of this, many segments of the public believe that school violence is increasing (Brooks, Schiraldi, & Ziedenberg, 2000). Some of this misperception may be associated with the widely publicized school shootings at Columbine High School in Colorado and similar incidents in Kentucky, Oregon, and Michigan in the past few years.

Nevertheless, Uniform Crime Reports and data from other sources indicate that schools are the safest places for children to be. Fewer homicides and violent crimes are committed against children at school than in their homes or on the streets (Kaufman et al., 1998; Kaufman et al, 1999; Snyder & Sickmund, 1999). Students are greater than 100 times more likely to be the victim of a homicide away from school than at school (Kaufman et al., 1998).

Another issue that occasionally surfaces when the discussion turns to school violence is the role played by students with mental health problems or other disabling conditions. Some critics believe that special education rules and regulations have tied school principals' hands with regard to discipline and students with disabilities (Hymowitz, 2000). The reauthorization of IDEA (Individuals with Disabilities Education Act) in 1997, however, gave schools a great deal of latitude in responding to disciplinary problems exhibited by students with disabilities. Principals can unilaterally remove special education students involved in weapons or drug offenses and those at risk of harming themselves or others and place them in interim alternative programs (Bear, 1999).

In this chapter we examine issues related to school violence and disruption. We begin by examining the sociocultural context within which school violence occurs, using a nested ecological schema. The first section presents a review of major changes in the status of children and their families, a discussion of availability and consequences of easy access to firearms, and the increase in prevalence of violence in popular media. We also examine media coverage of recent, widely publicized school shootings and the effect that media coverage has on parents' and students' perceptions of school safety. In the second section of the chapter, we examine prevalence and trends in school violence, with particular attention to the use of firearms on school property. This discussion explores some of the difficulty associated with defining and measuring school violence.

We then discuss the challenge of balancing the right to education with the importance of maintaining safe and orderly schools. In particular, we look at available data on the role of students with disabilities in school suspensions and discuss possible interpretations of these data. Finally, we examine how local schools and school districts have addressed violence and disruption in their buildings and communities. We describe violence-prevention initiatives and present guidelines for parents, teachers, and administrators to assist in ensuring that their schools are safe places that promote academic achievement and healthy behavior among all children and adolescents.

The Contexts of School Violence

School violence is a multifaceted phenomenon. Preventing school violence and responding to violent acts that occur within schools require an understanding of the larger community and society. Human behavior is shaped by social-ecological contexts that include individuals with whom we interact daily as well as broad societal contexts that deliver messages about appropriate behavior and relationships among people (Bronfenbrenner, 1979). A widely accepted model (Tolan & Guerra, 1994) of youth and family violence depicts a nested ecological system (see Figure 13.1) of individual factors, close interpersonal relations (e.g., peers and family), proximal social contexts (e.g., school and neighborhood), and societal macrosystems (e.g., media and laws governing gun use). Schools have created prevention activities and

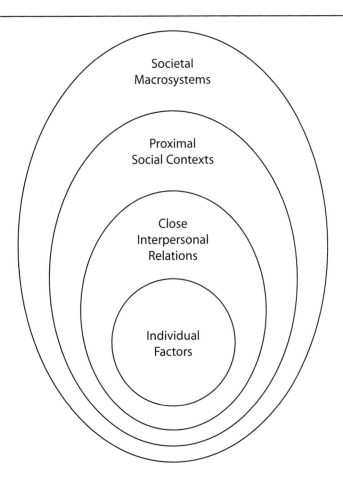

Source: Adapted from "Prevention of Delinquency: Current Status and Issues," (1994), by P. H. Tolan & N. G. Guerra, *Applied & Preventive Psychology, 3,* 254.

Figure 13.1   A Nested Ecological System of Influences on Youth Behavior

developed school-wide management plans that have reduced disciplinary referrals and suspensions, addressing risk factors and needs at multiple levels (Taylor-Green et al., 1997; Sugai, Sprague, Horner, & Walker, 2000). These efforts and similar community-based initiatives have the potential to make schools more safe and orderly places for children. In this chapter, we will address aspects of the outer three levels of this nested system that surround the individual, looking at several school, family, and larger societal level factors.

The problem of school violence is linked to changes within our culture and society. Significant changes in family structure and changes in the status of children contribute to the problems that educators see in schools. Violence in the entertainment and news media has increased dramatically in recent years (Lichter, Lichter, & Amundson, 1999) and contributes to a sense that youth are being negatively influenced by the movies they see, the television they watch, the popular music they hear, and the video games they play.

Many youths have easy access to guns (Ward, 1999). At the same time, print and broadcast news media regularly report on a wide range of violent crime committed not just in our own communities but in any hamlet served by an affiliate or a subsidiary of a large media conglomerate (Goldstein, 1994). It is difficult to establish causal relationships between school violence and changes in family structure, violent themes in popular entertainment, the availability of guns, and the reporting of violence by the news media. In each of these areas, however, there have been significant changes in recent years.

Family Structure and Poverty

Changes in family structure and changes in the relative distribution of income within society in recent decades have affected children. In 1950, fewer than 20% of all children in the United States lived in households that were dual-earner nonfarm families and one-parent families. At present, nearly two thirds of all children live in dual-earner nonfarm and one-parent families (Hernandez, 1995). The effect of this drastic change in living arrangements is that fewer adults are at home and available to support students during the non-school hours. Although some of this change may have been offset by an increase in number of parents who work at home, evidence suggests that less time is available for parents to assist and monitor their children. Survey-based estimates suggest that from 4% to 23% of children regularly care for themselves, and several major surveys found that about 12% of children ages 5–12 were in self-care at least once a week (Kerrebrock & Lewit, 1999; U.S. Department of Education, 1999b).

Another major change since 1980 that affects children has been a shift in the distribution of family income. While the mean income of families in the United States has risen, there has been an increasing gap between children in families living at the lowest income levels and those at the highest levels. From 1968 to 1994, income inequality in the United States increased 22.4% (Weinberg, 1996). While the percentage of children living in luxury approaches 20%, an even larger percentage of children live in relative poverty or near-poor frugality (Hernandez, 1995; U. S. Bureau of the Census, 1998; Weinberg, 1996).

More recent data from the U.S. Bureau of the Census, based on the *Gini Index* and quintile shares of aggregate household income (widely used measures of income inequality), show for the most part, from 1993 to 1998, no significant change in income distribution (A. Jones, personal communication, July 17, 2000). Poverty and the availability of parents to supervise their children do not directly create or cause school violence and or disruption. Nevertheless, poverty is one of a number of factors that place youth at risk for school failure, dropout, and delinquent behavior (Walker & Sprague, 1999), and inadequate monitoring and supervision of children is associated with the development of antisocial behavior and delinquency (Patterson, 1982; Farrington, 1995; Hawkins et al, 2000).

Violence in the Entertainment Industry

A study by the Center for Media and Public Affairs documented the frequency with which violent images are featured in popular entertainment (Lichter et al., 1999). They examined made-for-television movies, television series, music videos, and movies, to determine the prevalence with which violent content was featured. They found that across all forms of entertainment, serious violent images or scenes were featured on the average of 14 times per hour of viewing. When just high violence shows were examined, they found an average of 54 violent acts per hour. Although causal effects between viewing violent images and engaging in violent or disruptive behavior in school are difficult to establish, evidence suggests that exposure to television violence does have an effect on violent behavior (American Psychological Association, 1993; Felson, 1996; Reiss & Roth, 1993).

Media Coverage of School Violence

During the past few years, news media have ratcheted up their coverage of violence in communities and across the country. The evening news and the daily paper chronicle violent acts, both local and across the country, involving juveniles and adults. In the wake of the tragic events and the massive media blitz at Columbine High School in April, 1999, a *USA Today* poll found that 68% of Americans surveyed thought that it was likely or very likely that a school shooting could occur in their town. Other polls of parents' perceptions of school safety taken in the past year revealed similar results (Brooks, Schiraldi, & Ziedenberg, 2000).

Consolidation within the media industry has placed control of radio, television, and newspapers in the hands of fewer and fewer companies (Howard, 1995). As corporate giants compete for audience share or circulation, reporting of violence has become a marketing tool to increase market share (Felson, 1996). Local events in one part of the country become national events as affiliate television and radio stations and newspapers carry reports throughout the country. Although juvenile crime rates fell in the 1990s, the public, informed by media coverage of violence, largely believed that juvenile crime was up and that schools were unsafe (Brooks et al., 2000).

Access to Guns

Handguns and other firearms are more widely available in the United States than in any other industrialized nation in the world, reflecting a permissive policy approach. A 1997 National Institute of Justice report estimated that approximately one third of all households in the United States have guns, with two thirds of gun owners possessing more than one gun (Cook & Ludwig, 1997). At the time of a recent survey 20% of gun owners reported having unlocked, loaded guns in their houses (Cook & Ludwig, 1997). In 1997, more than 4,200 children ages 0–19 were killed by firearms in the United States. More than 2,500 of these killings were homicides and another 1,200 were suicides (Ward, 1999).

Proportionately, young black males are more likely than white youths to be the victims of gun violence. Though federal law restricts sales of guns to minors by licensed gun dealers, in some states children as young as 12 can legally possess semi-automatic weapons and other firearms (Ward, 1999). Yet, unmistakably, the horrific killing of students by students in schools in recent years could not have happened without easy access to firearms by children.

Accountability, Achievement, and Zero Tolerance at the School Level

Our public schools also have changed dramatically during the past decade. Among other things, there has been an increased focus on accountability, information technology, and achievement. At the same time, there has been a decrease in tolerance of deviant behavior. Accountability and an emphasis on literacy for the Information Age have created a greater sense of urgency among educators. Teachers, principals, and superintendents are being asked to measure and demonstrate tangible academic gains in their students' performance. In this climate, disruptive students, particularly those who score poorly on tests that measure the performance of the classroom, school, or school district, are at-risk for being excluded from the education community.

Under the mantle of zero tolerance, schools and school boards have instituted policies that suspend students from school for a wide range of rule infractions that range from threats of violence to possession of weapons to use or possession of drugs on school property. Zero tolerance has created situations in which principals have no latitude or discretion in administering disciplinary sanctions. Thus, students have been suspended for sharing Midol tablets, for bringing a plastic knife to spread peanut butter at lunch, for sharing cough drops, for displaying a manicure kit with a 1-inch knife, and for sharing a prescription inhaler with a student experiencing anaphylactic shock (Tebo, 2000; Skiba & Peterson, 1999).

In sum, changes in the family and the status of children, increases in violent images in popular entertainment, changes in media coverage of violent events, increased availability of guns, and increased accountability at school all set the stage for understanding the current state of school violence and disruption. In the next section, we examine authoritative reports concerning school violence and discuss the difficulty of measuring school violence.

Understanding School Violence

Interest in school violence is a relatively recent phenomenon. How we conceptualize and define school violence shapes how schools think about and respond to the problem (Furlong & Morrison, 2000). Depending upon one's definition of the term, acts of school violence can range from threats of physical violence, to bullying, physical assaults, and homicide.

Data on School Violence

Schools are safer than individual homes and neighborhoods. Children are more likely to encounter serious violent crime away from school than at school. Multiple sources suggest that students are approximately three times safer in school than away from school (Elliott, Hamburg, and Williams, 1998; Kaufman et al., 1999; Snyder & Sickmund, 1999). There is less than a one in a million chance of a student experiencing a school-related violent death. Furthermore, the vast majority of school-related injuries are not violence-related and the majority of school crime is non-violent theft (U.S. Department of Education, 1999a).

The picture of school violence that has emerged over the past decade provides reason for concern, yet optimism for the future. The findings are mixed. In 1997, there were 202,000 serious violent crimes (rape, sexual assault, robbery, and aggravated assault) against students ages 12–18 in school and 2.7 million total school crimes (Kaufman et al., 1999). Centers for Disease Control (CDC) data collected in 1999 from the Youth Risk Behavior Surveillance (YRBS) (Kann et al., 2000) found the following:

■ 6.9% carried weapons at school nationally during 30 days prior to the survey, with males (11.0%) reporting much higher rates of weapon-carrying than females (2.8%).

■ 7.7% of students nationally reported having been threatened or injured with a weapon on school property during the past 12 months.

■ 14.2% of students had been in a physical fight at school during the prior 12 months.

Some longer-term data show that certain measures of violence in schools have remained fairly constant over the past 20 years while other measures of violence have shown a clear pattern of decrease during the 1990s. For example, YRBS data (Centers for Disease Control and Prevention, 2000) show a steady, dramatic decline in students reporting having carried a weapon on school property during the 30 days prior to the survey, from 11.8% in 1993 to 6.9% in 1999 (see Figure 13.2).

The same YRBS data show a similarly impressive decline in students reporting having carried a gun during the 30 days prior to the survey, from 7.9% in 1993 to 4.9% in 1999. Also, from 1993 to 1999, the percentage of students who reported having been in a physical fight at school during the 30 days prior to the survey dropped from 16.2% to 14.2%. The *Annual Report on School Safety* (U.S. Department of Education, 1999a) also reports a decline in several measures of school violence during the 1990s.

Several indicators of school violence have remained fairly constant over the past 20 years. For example, from 1976 to 1997, approximately 5% of high school seniors report having been injured with a weapon at school during the previous 12 months,

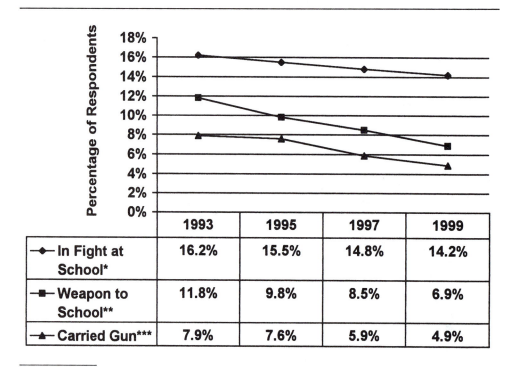

	1993	1995	1997	1999
—◆— In Fight at School*	**16.2%**	**15.5%**	**14.8%**	**14.2%**
—■— Weapon to School**	**11.8%**	**9.8%**	**8.5%**	**6.9%**
—▲— Carried Gun**	**7.9%**	**7.6%**	**5.9%**	**4.9%**

Source: Centers for Disease Control and Prevention. (2000). *Fact Sheet: Youth Risk Behavior Trends*

* Involved in a fight *on school property* at least one time during the 12 months preceding the survey
** Carried a weapon *on school property* at least one time during the 30 days preceding the survey
*** Carried a gun at least one time during the 30 days preceding the survey

Figure 13.2   Self-Report of Risk Related Behaviors: 1993–1999 Trends

according to data from the ongoing *Monitoring the Future* study (University of Michigan). During the same period, approximately 12% of seniors report having been injured without a weapon and about 12% report having been threatened with a weapon at school during the previous 12 months (U.S. Department of Education, 1999b; Institute for Social Research, 1997). Other data sources, such as the so-called Principals' and Disciplinarians' Report (U.S. Department of Education, 1998a), show relatively less crime in the schools. That report was based on incidents in which the school called the police. Understandably, administrators may be reluctant to call police or to submit reports suggesting that their school environment is out of control.

This discussion demonstrates that reported measures of school violence differ somewhat depending on the source. A reasonable question to ask is: Why do we see clear signs of decline in some measures, yet relative stability in other measures? Also, how do we decide whether, and to what extent, school violence and disruption is a serious problem? To begin to answer these questions, we need to consider a number of issues surrounding school violence, as well as community-based violence data collection and reporting.

Making Sense of the Numbers

National data on school violence come from several sources. Some sources focus on criminal acts per se, others focus on injury from a health agency perspective, and some privately commissioned surveys (e.g., Metropolitan Life Survey of the American Teacher) focus on various aspects of school violence. The FBI Uniform Crime Reporting (UCR) Program gathers reports from local law enforcement agencies directly or through respective state agencies (Cook & Laub, 1998). As illustrated by Cook and Laub, the UCR data can seriously underestimate true levels of violent crime and provide no information on age of victim or assailant.

Furthermore, some data on juvenile crime are presented in terms of arrests, whereas other data represent convictions. These two categories are quite different, as arrest figures can include innocent individuals (Loeber, Farrington, & Waschbusch, 1998, p. 21). Arrests records do not offer a viable sample of actual crime perpetrators (Cook & Laub, 1998). In addition, law enforcement agencies vary considerably in their reporting of data to the UCR system, thus making year-to-year and other comparisons risky.

A separate source of national level data on violence comes from the National Crime Victimization Survey (NCVS), using household interviews conducted every 6 months (since 1973), and from the School Crime Supplement (SCS) to the NCVS, which is conducted every 4 or 5 years. The NCVS provides information on victimization of youths age 12 and older. Like other forms of self-report, however, this one is subject to errors from a variety of sources, including sampling frame problems, instrument problems, and respondent errors such as inaccurate recall, comprehension problems, omissions, and telescoping effects (Biemer et al., 1991).

Data gathering methods to assess school violence vary considerably, and perceived violence is consistently reported at higher levels than self-reports of violent incidents (Furlong and Morrison, 1994). Methodologically, studies on school violence usually take a [confirmatory] hypothesis verification approach. That is, school violence is assumed to exist and survey questions elicit responses that confirm its existence. A Congressional Research Service report (U.S. Library of Congress, 1994) found problems in data collection efforts regarding school violence in terms of inconsistent definitions and wording of indicators, varying time frames among studies, and underreporting of criminal acts.

Reiss and Roth (1993) offer a detailed analysis of data collection issues pertaining to violence. They cite differences between UCR, NCVS, and National Center for Health Statistics (NCHS) data in terms of: "(a) domain of events, (b) unit of count, (c) timing of counting, and (d) sources of discretion and error in recording and counting events."

Furthermore, events that are measured are social constructs that depend on society's view of crime—something that changes over time. Reiss and Roth also note that crime incidents can be described differently as a function of the location and circumstance, whether they are defined in terms of the perpetrator (arrest) or victim (injury), and whether multiple offenders or offenses are involved. All of these issues can contribute to varying depictions of violent activity in the community as well as in schools.

Agencies responsible for data collection, analysis, and reporting have attempted to ameliorate the situation throughout the 1980s and 1990s. The CDC has supported many efforts to standardize definitions and reporting of injury-related data (CDC, 1997; Mercy, Ikeda, & Powell, 1998). The National Education Statistics Agenda Committee (U.S. Department of Education, 1996) assessed the current status of data collection and reporting among the states regarding criminal and violent behaviors in schools. The committee issued a report describing the existing state of affairs, providing model definitions for data collection and a description of a model data system that states could choose to implement.

Reconciling the differences between CDC data showing a clear decline in school violence and *Monitoring the Future* data that shows stability over two decades is a challenge. The participants, time frames, and wording of questions differ between these surveys. For example, several of the CDC-YRBS survey questions pertain to frequency of weapon-carrying and involvement in a fight. Several of the questions from the *Monitoring the Future* survey pertain to being threatened or injured with a weapon, and having property damaged or stolen.

Although we may choose to think of these questions as proxy variables for school violence and disruption, just because they fall under a common umbrella concept does not necessarily mean that they measure the same behaviors. They each need to be evaluated within the context of the specific survey effort. Unfortunately, no existing procedure allows clear reconciliation of these data differences. The best one can do is to conclude that some serious problems remain with school violence, but that there are several clear signals of an improving situation and that, generally speaking, schools are safe.

Balancing Educational Rights With an Orderly School Environment

Public schools are charged with providing all children with educational opportunities. School administrators and teachers have a vested interest in creating environments in which their students can best learn. Given the diversity and the numbers of children who walk through the public school doors, this is no small feat. School systems and personnel must constantly balance the need for orderliness and efficiency in schools with the rights and entitlements of individual students. Although the needs and desires of school systems often are aligned with the needs and desires of the students they serve, at times the two are at odds.

In the following sections we will discuss some of the entitlements due students in general, and how these entitlements have affected schools' abilities to provide appropriate educational environments. We also will discuss the impact of those additional entitlements afforded students with disabilities, including some of the pitfalls and misperceptions associated with these entitlements.

Educational Entitlements

Compulsory school-attendance laws give children the right, as well as the responsibility, to attend school. Schools must serve all the children in their communities— even children who prefer not to attend. The public schools cannot pick and choose whom they serve, even if picking and choosing would result in more efficiency, higher achievement scores for the school as a whole, or less disruption.

Over time, compulsory school-attendance laws have created problems for schools in jurisdictions where schools and school districts have not adapted to their changing school clientele. Problems have included truancy, disruptive or disrespectful behavior, drug use, threats of violence, and acts of violence. As problems have cropped up, individual schools, school districts, and governmental agencies have crafted ways for schools to deal with those problems. Responses have included (and continue to include) the use of behavioral modification strategies, timeouts, and corporal punishment. For serious violations of the school code, schools have expelled students and placed them into alternative education settings (Yell, 1990; Yell, Cline, and Bradley, 1995; Yell, 1998, ch. 15). Sometimes these responses have been effective in restoring order to the school environment. Other times these responses have gone too far and threatened the rights of the students to whom they are applied.

The U.S. Supreme Court has examined the issue of school discipline on several occasions. In 1977, the Court examined the constitutionality of corporal punishment (*Ingraham v. Wright,* 1977). Although the Court eventually decided that corporal punishment did not constitute "cruel and unusual punishment" and that students were not entitled to a hearing prior to the administration of corporal punishment (under the due process clause of the 14th Amendment), the justices did reiterate that individual teachers or administrators could be held liable or subject to criminal penalties if the corporal punishment administered was later found to be excessive. Even though the *Ingraham v. Wright* decision did not change the legal status of corporal punishment, the very fact that the Supreme Court heard this case influenced state legislatures to pass additional laws governing the use of corporal punishment (Yell, 1990; Yell, 1998, ch. 15). Corporal punishment remains an option for schools in some states, but its use is limited by requirements such as approval by the principal, presence of an adult witness, and prior parental approval. These limitations protect individual students from capricious and overzealous use of corporal punishment by frustrated school personnel.

Another disciplinary action that has been called into question is suspension from school. In 1975, the U.S. Supreme Court heard *Goss v. Lopez,* in which nine high school students alleged that their constitutional right to due process (under the 14th Amendment) had been violated when they were each suspended for up to 10 days without a formal hearing. In this case, the Court sided with the students, declaring that schools must provide evidence of a student's misconduct at a hearing prior to (or immediately following) the suspension. The Court ruled that students' rights to attend school supersede schools' rights to unilaterally exclude students for misconduct. Although school suspensions for disciplinary purposes are allowable, the process must include oral or written notice of the offense and the right to be heard (Yell, 1998, ch. 15).

In *Honig v. Doe* (1988), the Supreme Court set the stage for revised procedures in dealing with aggressive and violent students. This contributed to a change in attitudes among educators, politicians, and the public with regard to the behavior of students with disabilities. Bill Honig, Superintendent of Instruction for California schools, argued that a dangerousness exclusion to the "stay-put provision" of disability law existed, whereby schools could exclude students who threatened the safety of others. The Court denied his argument and made it clear that the stay-put provision held, and that schools could not unilaterally remove students considered dangerous while their change of placement was being appealed.

The Court's ruling also supported the position that a suspension of more than 10 days is a change of placement. The court affirmed that normal procedures, including temporary suspensions of up to 10 days, timeout, study carrels, and detention could be used with dangerous students (Sorenson, 1993; Tucker, Goldstein, and Sorenson, 1993; Yell, 1998).

In the last 5 to 10 years, particularly in the aftermath of the *Honig* decision, a number of state and local education agencies have revised school disciplinary codes to reflect the tenor of recent Safe and Drug-Free Schools legislation (Skiba & Peterson, 1999, 2000). This legislation was aimed at eliminating weapons and controlled substances on school grounds. This type of disciplinary approach—popularly referred to as zero tolerance—has serious flaws in its implementation. Some administrators have overlooked small infractions by otherwise well-behaved students (e.g., an honor student who forgets to remove a miniature Swiss army knife from his keychain), and others have enforced the letter of the law to such an unyielding extent that they attract national media attention (e.g., the second-grader who brought his grandfather's watch to show and tell; a 1-inch mini-pocketknife was attached; the student was suspended and sent to an alternative school for 1 month).

The real problem with a zero-tolerance posture is that serious punishments, such as suspensions from school, have been handed out in an arbitrary and inconsistent manner (Harvard University Civil Rights Project, 2000; Skiba & Peterson, 1999; Tebo, 2000). Students with disabilities who have behavioral problems and who typically have few advocates in the schools, as well as African-American students, are particularly vulnerable to harsh disciplinary tactics (Harvard University Civil Rights Project, 2000; Townsend, 2000).

Entitlements of Students With Disabilities

Although basic educational entitlements apply to all students, those with disabilities are afforded separate, additional protections under the IDEA, most recently amended and reauthorized in 1997. Provisions of IDEA pertaining to discipline are frequently a source of contention. For example, if a student engages in aggressive or disruptive behavior as a consequence of his or her disability, a school is not at liberty to unilaterally suspend that child from school for that very behavior. This is not to say, however, that schools have no recourse whatsoever when a student with a disability misbehaves.

A wide-range of commonly used discipline tactics are still available to use with students with disabilities. These include behavior management strategies, restrictions on privileges, and in-school suspension. Even suspension from school is still an option as long as that suspension does not last 10 days or become part of a pattern of suspensions that accumulate up to 10 days in length.

The stay-put provision of IDEA (IDEA Regulations, 34 C.F.R. § 300.514) is a common concern for teachers and administrators. When a student with a disability engages in serious acts of misconduct that could result in that student's removal from his or her current placement, school administrators and the student's parents often concur on a plan of action. When parents and school administrators disagree and parents request a due-process hearing, the stay-put provision comes into play. Under the stay-put clause, schools are not allowed to remove a student from his or her current placement while the disciplinary action is under review.

The stay-put provision often is misinterpreted to mean that children with disabilities can engage in dangerous conduct without fear of ever being removed to a more restrictive setting. To the contrary, if a student with a disability brings a weapon or controlled substance to school, that student is subject to the same disciplinary actions that apply to a student without a disability. The student then can be referred to an Interim Alternative Education Placement (IAEP).

Regardless of the disciplinary outcome, the school system must provide special education services to any student with a disability who ends up being suspended from school for more than 10 cumulative days in a school year. In addition, if a child with a disability engages in behavior that school administrators believe is likely to result in injury to self or others in the school community, the child with a disability can be removed to an IAEP for up to 45 days (Bear, 1999). The critical element is that the child with a disability not lose access to his or her educational services. The educational services provided to children with disabilities—including services designed to address their behavioral and social-skill deficits—are critical to their eventual success.

Occasionally schools use homebound instruction as an IAEP. These cases seem to violate both the spirit and intent of IDEA discipline provisions. Homebound instruction typically is limited to about 6 hours per week. In such circumstances, it is virtually impossible to provide appropriate academic instruction, and this level of service precludes meaningful implementation of a student's IEP.

Behaviors of Students With Disabilities

How often are students with disabilities involved in school violence and disruption? Apart from anecdotal accounts, it is difficult to find authoritative analyses, as data sources are limited. Several sources from recent years, however, present a partial picture and enable us to draw some tentative conclusions. We will examine two reports on implementation of the Gun-Free Schools Act, an analysis of suspensions and expulsions in Kansas, an analysis from Kentucky schools, a look at recent data from Maryland, and data regarding suspensions in Delaware and Minnesota. We also examine a national-level study of suspensions and expulsions by the Research Triangle Institute, a survey of state and local practices from state directors of special education services, and findings in the 21st Annual Report to Congress on IDEA.

Gun-Free Schools Reports

Subsequent to passage of the Gun-Free Schools Act of 1994, Congress mandated that annual reports be issued concerning implementation of the Act, including data on involvement of students with disabilities. The Act required each state receiving federal funds under the Elementary and Secondary Education Act (ESEA) to have a state law in effect mandating a minimum 1-year expulsion of students who brought a firearm to school, allowing chief administering officers the right to modify expulsion terms on a case-by-case basis.

During the 1996–97 school year, 6,093 students were expelled from school under the Act. Of the 43 states reporting on shortened expulsions, 39 states reported on the disability status of these students. Of the 699 students reported, 37% had disabilities under IDEA (U.S. Department of Education, 1998b). During the 1997–98 school year, 3,930 students were expelled from school under the Act. Of the 49 states reporting on shortened expulsions, 48 states reported on the disability status of these students. Of the 1,459 students reported, 38% had disabilities under IDEA (U.S. Department of Education, 1999c).

Suspensions and Expulsions in Kansas

Cooley (1995) examined suspension/expulsion data in Kansas, using survey data from 441 secondary school principals. This study found that students with disabilities had more than double the likelihood of suspension/expulsion than students without disabilities. Students with learning disabilities and behavior disorders were disproportionately represented among the students with disabilities who were suspended/expelled, compared to their proportions among students with disabilities in Kansas.

According to the researchers, however, students receiving special education services were no more likely than nondisabled students to engage in injury-causing behaviors. Furthermore, the acts committed by the suspended students with disabilities were found to be no different than those committed by nondisabled students. The report concluded that the students with disabilities were not receiving IEP-related services appropriate to their needs.

Analysis of Records in Kentucky

An analysis of records of 465 students in an Eastern Kentucky school district (Fasko, Grubb, and Osborne, 1995) found that about 20% of the suspended students were disabled, although students with disabilities composed about 14% of students included in the study. Approximately 83% of the suspensions were given to male students, and 17% to females. Males and females made up 53% and 47% of the student population, respectively.

Maryland Data

Data from Maryland (Maryland State Department of Education, 2000) showed that statewide, 64,103 students were suspended during the 1998–99 school year. Of those students, 15,669 (24.4%) were students with disabilities. Students with disabilities made up 13.1% of the statewide enrollment that year. Prior Maryland data for the 1997–98 school year (Maryland State Department of Education, 1999) provided an inconclusive picture of suspensions of students with disabilities because duplicated and unduplicated counts were mixed, using both incident- and person-specific data. This made comparisons to statewide percent of students with disabilities impossible, because, depending on relative rates of multiple offenses among disabled and nondisabled populations, different conclusions could be drawn.

Suspensions in Delaware

Along a similar vein, data from a study of suspensions in Delaware (cited in Sinclair and others, 1996) found that 23% of the incidents resulting in out-of-school suspensions during the 1994–95 school year involved special education students. These data were based on *incident* counts, not *person* counts. Therefore, we cannot conclude that 23% of the suspended students were special education students. Interestingly, the 1997–98 Maryland data (also not conclusive for similar reasons) found that 23.5% of short-term suspension incidents were associated with students with disabilities.

Suspensions in Minnesota

A University of Minnesota policy research brief (Sinclair et al., 1996) reported that in Minnesota, the overwhelming percentage of suspensions of students with disabilities involved students with learning disabilities and behavior disorders. The study found that, based on data from several other state studies, about 25% of suspension incidents were associated with students with disabilities.

Research Triangle Institute Report

Fiore and Reynolds (1996) conducted an exhaustive study gathering data on discipline issues in special education. The researchers found that for aggregated data from responding states and districts, approximately 20% of suspended students were students with disabilities, a percentage much larger than their proportion of the student population. Approximately 80% of the misconduct by students with disabilities was considered less serious, with about 20% of the misconduct falling into more serious categories. Also, the vast majority of students with disabilities who were suspended were males. Students with emotional disabilities were overrepresented among students with disabilities who were suspended.

The authors noted the paucity of available data on suspension/expulsion of students with disabilities. Only six states and 16 districts provided data on suspensions that included information on students with disabilities. The report demonstrated a tremendous variability among the states with regard to data systems on suspensions and on students with disabilities. The authors urged caution in interpreting the results, as many jurisdictions either had no such data-recording system or failed to provide the requested data. In turn, the available data cannot be construed as a nationally representative sample for students with disabilities.

21st Annual Report to Congress

The 21st Annual Report to Congress on IDEA (U.S. Department of Education, 2000) addressed school discipline and students with disabilities and reviewed some of the research cited above. Citing a 1994 Office of Civil Rights (OCR) report that found no overrepresentation of students with disabilities among suspended students, the Department of Education report discussed discrepant findings concerning discipline and students with disabilities.

Survey of State Departments of Education

A survey of state departments of special education (Morgan, Loosli, & Striefel, 1997) found improvements in maintaining and disseminating behavior standards compared to a similar survey done 5 years earlier. Of the 41 state respondents, 14 states reported that they had no such standards on behavioral procedures. The researchers found considerable variability among the states with regard to maintaining an information dissemination, monitoring, and training system for behavioral procedures for students with disabilities.

Conclusions Drawn From Studies

Although the data discussed above do not constitute a nationally representative sample of students with disabilities, we can still draw several tentative conclusions from these studies.

1. Mounting evidence suggests that a disproportionately high percentage (possibly close to 20%) of suspended students are students with disabilities, compared to a national proportion of about 11% of students ages 6–21 receiving services under IDEA. One OCR study (cited in the 21st Annual Report to Congress) contradicts this conclusion. Several studies demonstrate that students with learning disabilities and emotional disturbance are overrepresented among suspended students with disabilities.

2. Several studies have found that the majority of suspension-related behaviors seem to be nonviolent and generally do not result in injuries to others.

3. The nature of the suspension-related behaviors of students with disabilities may not be substantively different than the behaviors of the students' nondisabled peers.

4. Some evidence suggests that procedures to guarantee a system of consistent behavioral procedures for students with disabilities vary tremendously among the states and that students in some states may not be receiving appropriate services. Rather, suspension may be the procedure of choice in lieu of more proactive, supportive approaches.

Research by Mayer and Leone (1999), as well as publications by the Justice Policy Institute and the American Policy Forum (Brooks, Schiraldi, & Zeidenberg, 2000; Mendel, 2000) suggest that punitive, controlling approaches do little to solve continuing problems of school violence and disruption or juvenile crime in the community.

More data regarding specific school experiences with violence, individual school practices, and the role of students with disabilities will be gathered with the new School Survey on Crime and Safety (SSOCS), sponsored by the U.S. Department of Education, National Center for Education Statistics (NCES). NCES plans to conduct the SSOCS every 2 years, and the first SSOCS report is due in December 2000.

Gun-Free Schools Act suspension data revealed 37%– 38% representation by students with disabilities among cases shortened to less than one year for states reporting disability-related data. While it is logical that a relatively high percentage of cases meriting chief administering officer review would involve examination of disability-related factors, these data raise several concerns. *First,* the data (U.S. Department of Education, 1998b, 1999c), is a small and possibly unrepresentative subset of the complete dataset, precluding thorough analysis of the situation. The data must be interpreted with caution.

Second, there is reason to believe that often, students with disabilities get caught more often than nondisabled peers, because of problems with social communication, poor judgment, poor planning skills, and attributional biases that can lead to more confrontation with authority figures. These students may be more easily identified by the system for their infractions. That is not to lessen the egregiousness or unacceptability of such behaviors. Rather, it may simply point to a state of affairs in which students with disabilities are represented disproportionately in such cases, in part, because their nondisabled peers are more adept at eluding detection.

Third, the 37%–38% data could be fairly accurate, in which case schools need to develop new understandings and find more effective interventions to reduce weapon-carrying, particularly by students with disabilities. Additional research may shed more light on the exact nature of this phenomenon.

Schools clearly face many challenges in maintaining a safe and orderly environment. The next section presents several approaches to school- and community-based programming.

How Schools Have Responded to Problems of School Violence

Understanding and Shaping School Environments

School-based violence prevention initiatives are considered a best-practice approach to foster positive youth development (Dwyer & Osher, 2000; Mendel, 2000; Walker & Horner, 1996). Federal and state policy makers increasingly are viewing schools as excellent sites for prevention activities, although federal expenditures for these efforts are relatively modest (Gottfredson, 1997). Schools provide consistent access to youth in the early developmental years, and they employ staff members who are focused on ensuring successful academic and behavioral outcomes for students. Another critical advantage is that many risk factors (see Figure 13.3) associated with youth violence are school-related and therefore may be modified within school settings.

Schools should consider three fundamental principles when planning violence prevention initiatives. *First,* evidence strongly supports the effectiveness of *school-wide violence prevention* initiatives based conceptually on a public health model. This model organizes prevention efforts so that schools can systematically address the needs of all students, including those with severe academic, emotional, or behavioral problems.

Second, approaches that emphasize punishment, control, and containment have been demonstrated to be ineffective in preventing or intervening in disruption and violence; punitive orientations may actually exacerbate school disorder (Mayer & Leone, 1999).

INDIVIDUAL RISK FACTORS	**PEER RISK FACTORS**
• Poor academic skills • Impulsivity • Substance use • Poor social problem-solving skills • Inability to understand the perspective of others • Poor conflict-resolution skills • Difficulties in understanding the moral consequences of actions	• Low social status • Rejection by peers • Gang involvement • Shared deviant peer norms • Association with delinquent peer groups
FAMILY RISK FACTORS	**SCHOOL/COMMUNITY RISK FACTORS**
• Inconsistent discipline • Reliance on coercion • Harsh or abusive discipline • Poor monitoring of activities • Insecure attachments • Defensive communication • Deviant shared values • A high percentage of negative interactions • Low levels of emotional closeness • Inefficient use of family resources	• Lack of student/parent involvement • Low academic achievement • Lack of social organization and social support • Few opportunities for recreation • Unemployment and economic disparities • High levels of community crime • Availability of firearms

Source: *A Program Planning Guide for Youth Violence Prevention* (1996, p. 15), by N. G. Guerra and K. R. Williams (Boulder, CO: Center for the Study and prevention of Violence). Copyright © 1996 by the Institute of Behavioral Science, Regents of the University of Colorado. Reprinted by permission.

Figure 13.3   Risk Factors for Youth Violence

Third, effective school-wide prevention initiatives are comprehensive, have several components, and involve a broad range of services and supports provided over a sufficient period. Because the antecedents of youth violence are highly correlated (Dryfoos, 1990; Hawkins et al., 2000), prevention programs that address a range of interrelated risk and protective factors have greater potential than single-focus programs.

The public health approach underlying school-wide violence prevention initiatives was defined by the Institute of Medicine (1994) as a three-tiered ecological perspective incorporating a continuum of strategies at graduated levels of intensity. This

FOCUS ON SCHOOLS: CALVERTON MIDDLE SCHOOL

Calverton Middle School in Baltimore serves nearly 1,200 students in grades 6 through 8. The school has had a history of low achievement test scores, high rates of student and teacher absenteeism, and discipline problems. Seventy percent of the students at Calverton are eligible for free or reduced-price lunches. During the 1999–2000 school year, 56 of the 85 teachers at the school held provisional or probationary certification. Seven teachers were on long-term leave.

Performance at Calverton was among the lowest for middle schools in the state of Maryland. Daily attendance by students for the 1998–1999 school year averaged 69%, and during the Fall of 1999, more than 300 students were tardy to school each day. The school was chaotic and experienced frequent interruptions resulting from pulled fire alarms, fights, and classroom disruptions.

Scores on the statewide Maryland School Performance Assessment Program (MSPAP) from 1993–99 indicated that fewer than 6% of eighth grade students scored excellent or satisfactory in reading and fewer than 5% of eighth graders scored excellent or satisfactory in mathematics. On the Maryland State Department of Education's Middle School Performance Index (SPI), Calverton scored from 22.57 to 28.24 each year from 1993 to 1999. The SPI is the weighted average of a school's relative distance from the satisfactory standards, where a score of 100 is considered satisfactory. Several years ago, Calverton was placed on a list of schools eligible for reconstitution or takeover by the Maryland State Department of Education.

In February, 2000, a new principal, Karl Perry, assumed administrative responsibility for Calverton. To begin the process of turning Calverton into an effective and caring school, Perry, with the support of staff, instituted a series of measures designed to refocus the attention of staff and students on academic excellence. Following consultation with other administrative staff, the Five Ps—be Present, Punctual, Prepared, Polite, and Positive—were introduced. Perry's primary objectives in assuming the principalship were to gain control of the school and improve the school climate. Principal Perry also introduced the *Drop Everything And Read* (DEAR) program, a regular part of the school day at Calverton. He met with parents, local business owners, and members of the community to develop shared strategies to combat truancy and tardiness.

As a result of using an appropriately tailored combination of universal and selective level interventions, Calverton Middle School has showed early signs of improvement. For example, student attendance has risen from about 69% to over 76%. Tardy arrivals have dropped from about 300 per day during the Fall to about 150 during the Spring semester. Office referrals dropped from more than 2,600 during the Fall semester of 1999 to under 2,200 during the following semester.

model promotes the use of a comprehensive framework of *universal, selective,* and *indicated* prevention strategies (Tolan, Guerra, & Kendall, 1995).

■ Universal strategies are the foundation of school-wide prevention efforts because they apply a primary prevention approach to the entire school population. Consistent use of these strategies provides sufficient support for a majority (80%–90%) of students in each school, thereby avoiding most instances of new problem behavior. Examples of universal prevention strategies include unambiguous behavioral expectations, proactive classroom management strategies, teacher expectations that support positive student outcomes, opportunities for positive attachment to school, consistent use of incentives and consequences, and school-wide literacy programs.

■ Selective strategies provide increased support for a smaller number of students (10%–15%) in each school. Secondary prevention strategies such as small-group instruction, social-skills training, behavioral contracting, and mentoring are designed to avoid the escalation of emerging academic and behavioral problems.

■ Indicated strategies support a relatively small number of students in each school (1%–5%) who demonstrate significant academic or behavioral problems requiring the most intensive level of support. Prevention strategies for these youth are individualized and often involve long-term involvement of education, mental health, social service, and juvenile justice agencies. Wraparound planning (Burns & Goldman, 1999) and school-based mental health services (Weist & Warner, 1997; Woodruff et al., 1999) are widely regarded as important advances in violence prevention for high-risk youth.

The variety of strategies incorporated in school-based violence prevention plans can be organized as individual or as environmental approaches. Prevention plans may focus on individual risk factors including alienation from school, truancy, poor academic performance, low levels of social competency, and antisocial behavior in the early grades. More broadly, prevention plans may focus on risk factors in the school and community, such as availability of drugs and weapons, negative peer experiences, and inadequate academic or behavioral support. Although examples of prevention strategies at the individual and environmental level are presented separately below, the interdependence of risk factors calls for integrated approaches that incorporate more than a single type of support.

Strategies frequently included in school-wide prevention plans that target individual risk factors include the following:

1. Instructional programs (identified as the most common prevention strategy used in schools) (Womer, 1997; Larson, 1994). These curriculum-based approaches focus on a range of social competency and academic skills with the goals of preventing or remediating academic failure, heightening awareness and knowledge of social influences on violent behavior, and teaching appropriate responses to these influences.

FOCUS ON SCHOOLS: RICHARD MONTGOMERY HIGH SCHOOL

Richard Montgomery High School (RMHS) in Rockville, Maryland, serves approximately 1,650 students in grades 9–12 in a suburban Washington, DC, school district. The school serves a diverse student body that is 12% African-American, 15% Asian, 16% Latino, and 55% non-Latino Caucasian students. Nearly 9% of students receive services because of limited English proficiency, 7% of the students receive special education services, and 10% of the students receive free and reduced-price meals. The mobility rate at RMHS is 6%. Students at RMHS perform well academically; approximately 500 students in the school are enrolled in the International Baccalaureate program—a rigorous college preparatory program—and 69% of students attend 2- or 4-year colleges after graduation.

In spite of average daily attendance above 90% and a strong academic program, the school has had an unacceptably high number of serious disciplinary incidents in recent years. In the 1997–98 school year, there were 35 serious disciplinary incidents at the school, including racial incidents, major vandalism, fights, and drug incidents. Mark Kelsch, a new principal appointed at the beginning of the 1998–99 school year, set out to reduce serious disciplinary incidents and improve academic performance of the school through greater participation and involvement of students and teachers in all aspects of the school. Kelsch's approach—a form of universal or primary prevention—combines a strong emphasis on relationships between adults and students and among students with rules that count and are fairly enforced.

The changes Kelsch has brought to RMHS include a daily 10-minute televised program produced by students and broadcast throughout the school. The program includes information from the principal, student groups, teaching staff, and others. Other changes include a focus on student achievement and recognition, reorganization of the school schedule so that all teachers in an academic area have common planning time, and consistent enforcement of attendance and tardy policies. These changes appear promising. During the 1999–2000 school year, 12 serious disciplinary incidents occurred—a reduction of nearly two thirds from just 2 years ago. The number of students losing course credit because of unexcused absences and being tardy to class dropped by 50% from the previous year. This past year Richard Montgomery High School received the Blue Ribbon Award for excellence from the U.S. Department of Education. For more information about the school, visit the web site: http://www.mcps.k12.md.us/schools/rmhs/

2. Behavior-management techniques designed to change antisocial behaviors and promote positive behavioral skills. These strategies will be most effective when based on systematic screening to identify students at risk for antisocial behavior (Sprague & Walker, 2000).

3. Peer strategies including peer coaching, mediation, and counseling.

4. Counseling and mentoring strategies.

Examples of environmental strategies are a strong academic mission, defining norms for appropriate behavior, promoting student attachment to school, and modifying organizational and structural conditions in the school by decreasing class size and providing a consistent climate of emotional support (Leone, 1997). In this context, prevention strategies should become a normative part of the school routine. For example, programs that teach nonviolent problem-solving strategies have a greater chance for success when the school climate regularly supports and models that approach to conflict (Gottfredson, 1997). School-wide prevention plans should be a high priority for the school and school system, a commitment reflected by strong administrative leadership at the school and district level and the provision of sufficient fiscal resources.

Efficacy of These Approaches

Although prevention science strongly supports the efficacy of school-wide approaches that incorporate multiple interventions and link schools and their environmental contexts, research on the impacts of these approaches is lacking (University of Vermont, 1999). As a result, numerous prevention initiatives have been implemented but reliable data of their effectiveness are not widely available. Despite the limited availability of rigorous evaluation studies in the 1990s, efforts to document the effectiveness of youth violence prevention programs are increasing. Schools using prevention plans report positive outcomes including improved academic performance and staff morale (Dwyer and Osher, 2000), as well as reduced behavior problems, reflected by fewer disciplinary referrals and suspensions (Sugai, Sprague, et al., 2000).

In an exhaustive study of school-based crime prevention efforts, Gottfredson (1997) found positive effects for programs that clarify behavioral norms, offer comprehensive instruction in a range of social-competency skills over a long period, provide behavior modification, and restructure schools to create smaller and more supportive units of instruction. Evidence also points to approaches that are *not* effective, including insight-oriented individual counseling and peer counseling (Gottfredson, 1997; Tolan & Guerra, 1998).

Our discussion of the advantages and strategies associated with school-wide prevention approaches is extended in the next section. We also present examples of research-based, school-wide prevention programs that show promise in reducing school disorder and promoting successful academic and social outcomes.

Promising Approaches

Numerous programs across the United States have shown positive results. Although it is beyond the scope of this chapter to review specific programs, we highlight three promising approaches to provide a perspective of the wider prevention and early intervention landscape. The listing of resources and websites (at the end of the chapter) leads to many other excellent program approaches and models.

Positive Behavioral Interventions and Supports: PBIS

Positive behavioral interventions and supports (PBIS) is a systems approach to creating and sustaining school environments that foster academic and behavioral competence for all students. As compared with traditional school-based approaches that target problem behavior demonstrated by individual students, PBIS focuses broadly on identifying policies and practices of the school itself that support or impede successful outcomes.

In this approach, classroom management and instructional practices are viewed as parallel processes; effective teaching of both academic and social skills involve strategies such as direct instruction, positive reinforcement, modeling, and precorrection (Sugai, Kameenui, et al., 2000). The PBIS framework emphasizes data-based assessment of the school climate and individual student progress through measures such as disciplinary referrals, attendance rates, and suspension rates. Functional behavior assessments are used in response to more intense problem behaviors.

Skill-Building: Violence Prevention Curricula

Violence prevention curricula based on social learning theory are used widely in school settings to improve students' problem-solving and anger-management skills, and to increase their knowledge of nonviolent responses to interpersonal conflict (Kenney & Watson, 1999). Conflict resolution and social skills are taught directly as a distinct curriculum or through integration in other coursework.

Numerous models for violence prevention through problem solving are available. For example, an interpersonal cognitive problem-solving approach with demonstrated effectiveness focuses on primary prevention in the elementary grades (Shure, 1999). In this approach, parents and teachers are trained to instruct children directly in using specific thinking and communication skills designed to prevent conflict in school and at home. *Second Step* is a violence prevention curriculum designed for use in preschool through ninth grade (Frey, et al., 2000). The curriculum emphasizes building protective social and emotional competencies and reducing aggressive and antisocial behaviors.

The Violence Prevention Curriculum for Adolescents (Prothrow-Stith, 1987) is designed to teach alternatives to aggressive behavior and to create supportive classroom environments in urban schools. Evidence suggests that the program is effective in reducing aggressive conflicts among students.

Mental Health and Social Services in Schools: Linkages to Learning

Linkages to Learning is a primary prevention model for the delivery of mental health, health, and social services for at-risk children and their families at 11 elementary and middle schools in Montgomery County, Maryland. The program was established in 1992 as a joint effort among public and private nonprofit agencies to respond to the increased needs of low- income children and their families. Parents are viewed as partners in this effort, taking an active role in developing solutions to individual, family, and community challenges. The overall goal of the program is to address social, emotional, and somatic health problems that undermine children's ability to succeed in school.

Participating children and families receive mental health assessment and counseling; assistance in obtaining shelter, food, housing, and employment; medical/dental care; assistance with immigration, translation, and transportation; and educational support including academic tutoring, mentoring, and adult education classes. Researchers at the University of Maryland completed a comprehensive longitudinal impact evaluation of children in a participating school and a control school (Fox et al., 1999). The evaluation found positive outcomes for children and parents, including improved academic achievement and behavioral functioning at home and school, increased consistency in parenting practices and overall family cohesion.

Developing a Plan to Prevent School Violence

In this section we present an overview of the major steps involved in establishing an effective school-wide violence prevention plan.

1. Assessing school needs.

Even though fundamental principles for organizing effective prevention plans can be identified and consistently applied, schools cannot follow "one size fits all" formulas or blueprints. The first step in developing a violence prevention plan that incorporates promising practices and responds to the local school context is to conduct a needs assessment.

A systematic needs assessment enables the staff to understand the structural, economic, cultural, linguistic, and developmental variations that influence the functioning of specific schools. The unique features of schools that would be addressed in needs assessment include differences in size and physical structure; personal and cultural attributes of students, staff, and the community; prior experiences with prevention strategies; and current perceptions of the level of order and disorder. Using information gathered in needs assessment helps to shape a school-wide prevention plan that incorporates specific performance goals tailored to the strengths and priorities of each school and community (Walker & Horner, 1996).

2. Developing parent and community support.

Because schools operate within environmental contexts, prevention initiatives that incorporate strong parent and community partnerships can mediate positive outcomes for youth. Kellam (2000) underscores the promise or perils associated with school/community partnerships when he emphasizes that "how prevention program leaders relate to community concerns will dictate the fate of their efforts (p. 2)."

Effective school-wide prevention plans operate best when they involve individual parents and parent organizations in meaningful ways. Parent/school collaboration enhances opportunities for schools to work successfully with troubled youth, extending prevention initiatives beyond schools and into local communities.

Links between the school and the larger community may take many forms, including collaboration among child-serving agencies, local business, law enforcement, and advocacy organizations. An important consideration in developing community support is to ensure that violence prevention initiatives are culturally competent. This is especially critical given the differential application of school disciplinary practices that result in the disproportionate suspension of African American youth (Townsend, 2000).

3. Developing a leadership team.

School-wide prevention plans that are actively supported by school- and district-level personnel, students, and families will likely produce the most effective and durable results. Team-based decision making can enhance ownership and acceptance of school violence prevention plans. Such a leadership team would be composed of staff members representing the various disciplines and roles within the school (e.g., general and special education teachers, counselors and school psychologists, administrators, paraprofessionals), and may include students, parents, and community members. Given the many risk factors associated with youth violence, the leadership team also could function as the organizational mechanism for systematic collaboration with mental health, social service, law enforcement, and other community agencies.

The leadership team conducts and analyzes the needs assessment, formulates short- and longer-term goals, identifies potential prevention strategies, monitors progress, and evaluates results (Dwyer & Osher, 2000). Teams can be formed specifically to address school-wide prevention efforts, or they can be built from and coordinated with other school-based management teams that exist in many schools.

4. Providing staff development.

As is the case in all school reform efforts, staff training is essential to ensure understanding, support, and consistent use of the school-wide violence prevention plan. Carefully designed and implemented training, available for *all* school staff, operationalizes the concept of a school-wide violence prevention agenda. This training involves teachers, counselors, bus drivers, cafeteria workers, clerical staff, and others working in the school. An important focus of training is skill development that supports achievement of instructional and behavioral competence for all students.

The content of training is also tailored for staff with specialized responsibilities, such as members of the leadership team. Further, given the complex nature of youth violence, staff development should reflect sustained rather than isolated training activities. Inservice training that follows this approach supports the reliable and consistent application of prevention strategies throughout the school.

5. Evaluating the plan.

Evaluation is the systematic collection and analysis of relevant data to inform decision making (Muraskin, 1993). Despite growing evidence supporting the use of school-wide violence prevention plans, specific prevention programs and practices have not typically been evaluated through rigorous research. Without benefit of evaluation, school staff and policy makers may respond to troubling behavior based more on political expediency than empirically validated practice.

Evaluation begins with needs assessment and can extend to process, outcome, and cost-benefit research (Flannery, 1998). When examining school-wide prevention programs one or more of the major types of evaluation may be appropriate to use.

- *Process evaluations* address the qualities that make school-wide prevention programs work or not work.

- *Outcome evaluations* focus on determining the impact of school-wide prevention programs on the school climate and for individual students.

- *Cost-benefit evaluations* identify whether specific programs are cost-effective.

Evaluation design has been constrained by difficulties in identifying and measuring outcomes related to prevention of violence in schools (discussed in previous section). Further, the impact of violence prevention programs has not been measured reliably because most evaluations have focused on immediate results in a limited number of sites rather than on longer-term results and replication in different types of schools and communities.

Challenges Ahead: Next Steps

Many reports have shown that school and community-based adolescent violence has been declining in recent years and that schools are considerably safer than surrounding neighborhoods. At the same time, addressing school violence remains an appropriate concern for educators, parents, political leaders, and other members of the community. We've learned from program evaluations, as well as a vast body of research in the fields of education, mental health, social services, and juvenile justice, that school violence must be addressed on the individual, family, school, neighborhood, and larger societal levels. Multifaceted interventions must target specific risk factors, be developmentally appropriate, and be culturally sensitive. In addition, interventions should involve parents and members of the community, promote interagency collaboration, address multiple levels of the child's life (e.g., school, family, neighborhood), and involve an evaluation component.

Schools will continue to face challenges while working with students with disabilities. State and local school systems must develop, disseminate, and monitor the interventions used in addressing behaviors of students with disabilities, using research-based best practices. Schools need to explore alternatives to school suspension, keeping students engaged in their school responsibilities and promoting their academic success. Responsive and flexible approaches require, and real progress demands, long-term investment and commitment. There are no quick fixes. Schools should examine their climate and programming to ensure that they are addressing their students' needs. Successful school programs require a buy-in by *all* school staff—teachers, support staff, and school administration—not just by a particular program's leadership team.

Data collection and analysis of prevention efforts should be ongoing, using rigorous methodology, as exemplified by the PBIS approach (Sugai, Kameenui, et al., 2000). School- and community-based programs have to maintain ongoing data collection and record keeping and should evaluate student and family needs and progress. At present, the role of students with disabilities in school violence and disruption is not well understood. Meaningful prevention and intervention efforts require thorough understanding of the challenges facing school administrators in serving students with disabilities, particularly those with behavioral problems.

In the face of pressure to offer politically expedient responses to media accounts of school violence and disruption, all members of the community must cultivate a balanced approach to the problem. Parents, educators, administrators, local officials, and other community members should gather accurate information relevant to their community circumstances and needs. A wide range of resources and supports now available from federal agencies, public interest advocacy groups, and private foundations are listed below.

A Final Note

Professionals sometimes are affected by the pressures and circumstances of their daily working environment and may react to problems by seeking the most expedient solution. In addressing the complex needs of students with behavioral difficulties, we must force ourselves to take stock of the situation and proceed thoughtfully, in a reasonable and balanced manner. Teamwork and collaboration among all stakeholders, careful study and thorough planning, and a commitment to reflection and self-evaluation all hold the promise of ultimate success.

Resources

Reports Available Online

Many reports issued under the auspices of the U.S. Department of Education can be obtained (via mail) through the *ED Pubs* online ordering system at http://www.ed.gov/pubs/edpubs.html.

1999 Annual Report on School Safety
   http://www.ed.gov/PDFDocs/InterimAR.pdf
Early Warning, Timely Response: A Guide to Safe Schools
   http://www.ed.gov/offices/OSERS/OSEP/earlywrn.html

Indicators of School Crime and Safety 1999
   http://nces.ed.gov/pubs99/1999057.pdf
Juvenile Offenders and Victims: 1999 National Report
   http://www.ncjrs.org/html/ojjdp/nationalreport99/toc.html
Less Hype, More Help: Reducing Juvenile Crime, What Works—and What Doesn't
   http://www.aypf.org/publications/mendel/index.html
Metropolitan Life Survey of the American Teacher, 1999
   http://www.metlife.com/Applications/Corporate/WPS/CDA/Page
   Generator/0,2117,P2323,00.html
Safeguarding Our Children: An Action Guide
   http://www.ed.gov/admins/lead/safety/actguide/index.html
School House Hype: Two Years Later
   http://www.cjcj.org/pubs/schoolhouse/shh2.html
Violence and Youth, Psychology's Response (American Psychological Association, 1993) is included free as part of a kit: "Creating Safe Schools: A Resource Collection for Planning and Action [Kit]." It can be obtained (via mail) under "School Safety" category at ED PUBS at http://www.ed.gov/pubs/edpubs.html.

Organizations With Websites and Online Resources

Center for Effective Collaboration and Practice (CECP)
   http://cecp.air.org/
Center for the Prevention of School Violence
   http://www.cpsv.org
Center for the Study and Prevention of Violence
   http://www.colorado.edu/cspv/
Center on Juvenile and Criminal Justice (CJCJ)
   http://www.cjcj.org
Kentucky Center for School Safety (KCSS)
   http://www.kysafeschools.org/
National Center on Education, Disability, and Juvenile Justice (EDJJ)
   http://www.edjj.org/
National School Safety Center
   http://www.nssc1.org/
National Youth Gang Center (NYGC)
   http://www.iir.com/nygc/
Office of Juvenile Justice and Delinquency Prevention (U.S. Department of Justice)
   http://ojjdp.ncjrs.org/
Office of Safe and Drug-Free Schools (U.S. Department of Education)
   http://www.ed.gov/offices/OESE/SDFS/
Partnerships Against Violence Network (PAVNET)
   http://www.pavnet.org/
Positive Behavioral Interventions & Supports (PBIS)
   http://www.pbis.org

Books

Elliott, D., Hamburg, B., & Williams, K. (Eds.). (1998) *Violence in American schools.* New York: Cambridge.

Gabarino, J. (1999). *Lost boys.* New York: Simon and Schuster.

Loeber, R., & Farrington, D. P. (Eds.). (1998) *Serious and violent juvenile offenders.* Thousand Oaks, CA: Sage.

Tonry, M., & Moore, M. H. (Eds.). 1998) *Youth violence.* Chicago: University of Chicago Press.

References

American Psychological Association. (1993). *Violence and youth: Psychology's response.* Washington, DC: Author.

Bear, G. G. (1999). *Interim alternative educational settings: Related research and program considerations.* Alexandria, VA: National Association of State Directors of Special Education, Project Forum.

Biemer, P. P., Groves, R. M., Lyberg, L. E., Mathiowetz, N. A., & Sudman, S. (1991). *Measurement Errors in Surveys.* New York: Wiley.

Brener, N. D., Simon, T. R., Krug, E. G., & Lowry, R. (1999). Recent trends in violence-related behaviors among high school students in the United States. *Journal of the American Medical Association, 282*(5), 440–446.

Bronfenbrenner, U. (1979). *The ecology of human development: Experiments by nature and design.* Cambridge, MA: Harvard University Press.

Brooks, K., Schiraldi, V., & Ziedenberg, J. (2000). *School house hype: Two years later.* Washington, DC: Justice Policy Institute.

Burns, B. J., & Goldman, S. K. (Eds.) (1999). Promising practices in wraparound for children with serious emotional disturbance and their families. *Systems of care: Promising practices in children's mental health, 1998 series, Vol. IV.* Washington, DC: Center for Effective Collaboration and Practice, American Institutes for Research.

Centers for Disease Control and Prevention. (1997). *Recommended framework for presenting injury mortality data.* Morbidity & Mortality Weekly Report, 1997; 46 (No. RR-14): 4–5.

Centers for Disease Control and Prevention. (2000). *Fact sheet: Youth risk behavior trends.* [online], http://www.cdc.gov/nccdphp/dash/yrbs/ trend.htm

Chandler, K. A., Chapman, C. D., Rand, M. R., & Taylor, B. M. (1998). *Students' reports of school crime: 1989 and 1995.* Washington, DC: U.S. Departments of Education and Justice. (NCES 98-241/NCJ-169607)

Cook, P. J., & Laub, J. H. (1998). The epidemic in youth violence. In M. Tonry, & M. H. Moore (Eds.), *Youth Violence* (pp. 27–64). Chicago: University of Chicago Press.

Cook, P. J. & Ludwig, J. (1997, May). Guns in America: National survey on private ownership and use of firearms. *Research Brief* (NIJ Rep. No. NCJ-165476). Washington, DC: U.S. Department of Justice, National Institute of Justice.

Cooley, S. (1995). *Suspension/expulsion of regular and special education students in Kansas: A report to the Kansas State Board of Education* (ERIC Document Reproduction Service No. ED 395 403). Topeka: Kansas State Board of Education.

Dryfoos, J. (1990). *Adolescents at risk.* New York: Oxford University Press.

Dwyer, K. & Osher, D. (2000). *Safeguarding our children: An action guide.* Washington, DC: U. S. Departments of Education and Justice, American Institutes for Research.

Elliott, D., Hamburg, B., & Williams, K. (Eds.). (1998). *Violence in American schools.* New York: Cambridge.

Farrington, D. P. (1995). The challenge of teenage antisocial behavior. In M. Rutter (Ed.), *Psychological disturbances in young people: Challenges for prevention* (pp. 83–130). New York: Oxford University Press.

Fasko, D., Grubb, D. J., & Osborne, J. S. (1995, November). *An analysis of disciplinary suspensions.* Paper presented at annual meeting of Mid-South Educational Research Association, Biloxi, MS. (ERIC Document Reproduction Service No. ED 393 169)

Felson, R. B. (1996). Mass media effects on violent behavior. *Annual Review of Sociology, 22,* 103–128.

Fiore, T. A., & Reynolds, K. S. (1996). *Analysis of discipline issues in special education.* Research Triangle Park, NC: Research Triangle Institute. (ERIC Document Reproduction Service No. ED 425 607)

Flannery, D. J. (1998). *Improving school violence prevention programs through meaningful evaluation.* New York: ERIC Clearinghouse on Urban Education. (ERIC Document Reproduction Service No. ED 417 244)

Fox, N., Leone, P., Rubin, K., Oppenheim, J., & Friedman, K. (1999). *Final report on the linkages to learning program and evaluation at broad acres elementary school.* Unpublished manuscript, University of Maryland at College Park.

Frey, K. S., Hirschstein, M. K., & Guzzo, B. A. (2000). Second step: Preventing aggression by promoting social competence. *Journal of Emotional & Behavioral Disorders, 8*(2), 102–112.

Furlong, M. & Morrison, G. (1994). Introduction to miniseries: School violence and safety in perspective. *School Psychology Review, 23*(2), 139–150.

Furlong, M., & Morrison, G. (2000). The *school* in school violence: Definitions and facts. *Journal of Emotional & Behavioral Disorders, 8*(2), 71–82.

Goldstein, S. Z. (1994). Corporate communication: A futurist vision. *Communication World, 11*(1), 26–28.

Goss v. Lopez, 419 U.S. 565 (1975).

Gottfredson, D. C. (1997). School-based crime prevention. In L. W. Sherman, D. C. Gottfredson, D. L. MacKenzie, J. Eck, P. Reuter, & S. D. Bushway. *Preventing crime: What works, what doesn't, what's promising: A report to the United States Congress.* [online] http://www.preventingcrime.com/report/index.htm

Gun-Free Schools Act, 20 U.S.C. § 1415 (e) (3).

Harvard University Civil Rights Project. (2000). *Opportunities suspended: The devastating consequences of zero tolerance and school discipline policies.* [online] http://www.law.harvard.edu/groups/civilrights/conferences/zero/zt_report2.html

Hawkins, J. D., Herrenkohl, T. I., Farrington, D. P., Brewer, D., Catalano, R. F., Harachi, T. W., & Cothern, L. (2000, April). Predictors of youth violence. *Juvenile Justice Bulletin.* Washington, DC: U.S. Department of Justice, Office of Juvenile Justice and Delinquency Prevention.

Hernandez, D. J. (1995). Changing demographics: Past and future demands for early childhood programs. *The Future of Children, 5*(3), 145–160.

Honig v. Doe, 479 U.S. 1084 (1988).

Howard, H. H. (1995). TV station group and cross-media ownership: A 1995 update. *Journalism & Mass Communication Quarterly, 72*(2), 390–401.

Hymowitz, K. S. (2000). Who killed school discipline? *City Journal, 10*(2), 34–43.

Ingraham v. Wright, 430 U.S. 651 (1977).

Institute of Medicine (1994). *Reducing risks for mental disorders.* Washington, DC: National Academy Press.

Institute for Social Research. (1997). *Monitoring the future study.* Ann Arbor: University of Michigan.

Kann, L., Kinchen, S. A., Williams, B. I., Ross, J. G., Lowry, R., Grunbaum, J. A., & Kolbe, L. J. (2000). Youth risk behavior surveillance—United States, 1999. *Morbidity & Mortality Weekly Report, 49* (SS–5).

Kaufman, P., Chen, X., Choy, S. P., Chandler, K. A., Chapman, C. D., Rand, M. R., & Ringel, C. (1998). *Indicators of school crime and safety, 1998.* Washington, DC: U.S. Departments of Education and Justice. (NCES 1998-251/NCJ-172215).

Kaufman, P., Chen, X., Choy, S. P., Ruddy, S. A., Miller, A. K., Chandler, K. A., Chapman, C. D., Rand, M. R., & Klaus, P. (1999). *Indicators of school crime and safety, 1999.* Washington, DC: U.S. Departments of Education and Justice. (NCES 1999-057/NCJ-178906)

Kellam, S. G. (2000). Community and institutional partnerships for school violence prevention. In S. G. Kellam, R. Prinz, & J. F. Sheley, *Preventing school violence: Plenary papers of the 1999 Conference on Criminal Justice Research and Evaluation—Enhancing Policy and Practice Through Research* (Vol. 2, pp. 1–21). Washington, DC: U.S. Department of Justice, National Institute of Justice.

Kenney, D. J., & Watson, S. (1999, July). Crime in the schools: Reducing conflict with student problem solving *Research brief* (NIJ Rep. No. NCJ-177618). Washington, DC: U.S. Department of Justice, National Institute of Justice.

Kerrebrock, N., & Lewit, E. M. (1999). Children in self-care. *The Future of Children, 9*(2), 151–160.

Larson, J. (1994). Violence prevention in the schools: A review of selected programs and procedures. *School Psychology Review, 23,* 151–164.

Leone, P. E. (1997). The school as a caring community: Proactive discipline and exceptional children. In J. Paul, M. Churton, W. Morse, A. Duchnowski, B. Epanchin, P. Osnes, & L. Smith (Eds.), *Special education practice: Applying the knowledge, affirming the values, and creating the future.* (pp. 91–103). Pacific Grove, CA: Brooks-Cole.

Lichter, S. R., Lichter, L. S., & Amundson, D. (1999). *Merchandizing mayhem: Violence in popular culture.* Washington, DC: Center for Media and Public Affairs.

Loeber, R., Farrington, D. P., & Waschbusch, D. A. (1998). Serious and violent juvenile offenders. In R. Loeber & D. P. Farrington (Eds.), *Serious and violent juvenile offenders* (pp. 13–29). Thousand Oaks, CA: Sage.

Maryland State Department of Education (1999, January). *Suspensions from Maryland public schools (1997–98).* Baltimore: MSDE Results Branch.

Maryland State Department of Education (2000, January). *Suspensions from Maryland public schools (1998–99).* Baltimore: MSDE/PRIM-Information Management Branch.

Mayer, M. J., & Leone, P. E. (1999). A structural analysis of school violence and disruption: Implications for creating safer schools. *Education & Treatment of Children, 22,* 333–358.

Mendel, R. (2000). *Less hype, more help.* Washington, DC: American Youth Policy Forum.

Mercy, J. A., Ikeda, R., & Powell, K. E. (1998). Firearm-related injury surveillance: An overview of progress and challenges ahead. *American Journal of Preventive Medicine, 15*(38), 6–16.

Metropolitan Life Insurance Company. (1999). *Metropolitan Life survey of the American teacher, 1999: Violence in America's Public Schools.* New York: Author.

Morgan, R. L., Loosli, T. S., & Striefel, S. (1997). Regulating the use of behavioral procedures in schools: A five year follow-up survey of state department standards. *Journal of Special Education, 30*(4), 456–470.

Muraskin, L. D. (1993). *Understanding evaluation: The way to better prevention programs* [online], http://ed.gov.offices/OUS/eval/primer1. html

Patterson, G. R. (1982). *Coercive family process.* Eugene, OR: Castalia.

Prothrow-Stith, D. (1987). *Violence prevention curricula for adolescents.* Newton, MA: Education Development Center.

Rand, M. (1998). *Criminal victimizations 1997: Changes 1996–97 with trends 1993–97.* Washington, DC: US Department of Justice, Bureau of Justice Statistics.

Reiss, A. J. & Roth, J. A. (Eds.). (1993). *Understanding and preventing violence.* Washington, DC: National Academy Press.

Sheley, J. F. (2000). Controlling violence: What schools are doing. In S. G. Kellam, R. Prinz, & J. F. Sheley, *Preventing school violence: Plenary papers of the 1999 Conference on Criminal Justice Research and Evaluation—Enhancing Policy and Practice Through Research* Vol. 2, pp. 37–57). Washington, DC: US Department of Justice, National Institute of Justice.

Shure, M. B. (1999, April). Preventing violence the problem-solving way. *Juvenile Justice Bulletin.* Washington, DC: U.S. Department of Justice, Office of Juvenile Justice & Delinquency Prevention.

Sinclair, M. F., et al. (1996, December). On a collision course? Standards, discipline, and students with disabilities, *Policy Research Brief, 8*(4). Minneapolis: Institute on Community Integration, University of Minnesota. (ERIC Document Reproduction Service No. ED 404 793)

Skiba, R. J., & Peterson, R. L. (1999). The dark side of zero tolerance: Can punishment lead to safe schools? *Phi Delta Kappan, 80*(5), 372–378.

Skiba, R. J., & Peterson, R. L. (2000). School discipline at a crossroads: From zero tolerance to early response. *Exceptional Children, 66*(3), 335–347.

Snyder, H. N., & Sickmund, M. (1999). *Juvenile offenders and victims: 1999 national report.* Washington, DC: Office of Juvenile Justice and Delinquency Prevention.

Sorenson, G. (1993). Update on legal issues in special education discipline. *Education Law Reporter, 81,* 399–411.

Sprague, J. & Walker, H. (2000). Early identification and intervention for youth with violent behavior. *Exceptional Children, 66*(3), 367–379.

Sugai, G. M., Kameenui, E. J., Horner, R. H., & Simmons, D. C. (2000). *Effective instructional and behavioral support systems: A school-wide approach to discipline and early literacy.* [online], http://ericec.org/ osep/eff-syst.htm

Sugai, G. M., Sprague, J. R., Horner, R., & Walker, H. M. (2000). Preventing school violence: The use of office discipline referrals to assess and monitor school-wide discipline interventions. *Journal of Emotional & Behavioral Disorders, 8*(2), 94–102.

Taylor-Greene, S., Brown, D., Nelson, L., Longton, J., Gassman, T., Cohen, J., Swartz, J., Horner, R. H., Sugai, G., & Hall, S. (1997). School-wide behavioral support: Starting the year off right. *Journal of Behavioral Education, 7,* 99–112.

Tebo, M. G. (2000). Zero tolerance, zero sense. *ABA Journal, 86,* 40–45.

Tolan, P. H. & Guerra, N. G. (1994). Prevention of delinquency: Current status and issues. *Applied & Preventive Psychology, 3,* 251–273.

Tolan, P. H., & Guerra, N. G. (1998). *What works in reducing adolescent violence: An empirical review of the field.* Boulder, CO: Center for the Study and Prevention of Violence, University of Colorado.

Tolan, P. H., Guerra, N. G, & Kendall, P. C. (1995). Introduction to special section: Prediction and prevention of antisocial behavior in children and adolescents. *Journal of Consulting & Clinical Psychology, 63*(4), 515–517.

Townsend, B. L. (2000). The disproportionate discipline of African American learners: Reducing school suspensions and expulsions. *Exceptional Children, 66*(3), 381–391.

Tucker, B. P., Goldstein, B. A., & Sorenson, G. (1993). *The educational rights of children with disabilities: Analysis, decisions and commentary.* Horsham, PA: LRP.

U.S. Bureau of the Census, Current Population Reports (1998). *Measuring 50 years of economic change using the March current population survey* (Rep. No. P60-203). Washington, DC: U.S. Government Printing Office.

U.S. Department of Education, National Center for Education Statistics. *Recommendations of the crime, violence, and discipline reporting task force* (Rep. No. NCES 97-581). 1996. Washington, DC: National Education Statistics Agenda Committee.

U.S. Department of Education, National Center for Education Statistics (1998a). *Violence and discipline problems in U.S. public schools: 1996–1997* (Rep. No. NCES 98-030). Washington, DC: Author, 1998.

U.S. Department of Education, Office of Elementary and Secondary Education and Planning and Evaluation Service. (1998b). *Report on state implementation of the gun-free schools act—School Year 1996–97.* (Contract N0. EA94052001). Prepared by Westat, Rockville, MD.

U.S. Department of Education (1999a). *Annual report on school safety.* Washington, DC: Author.

U.S. Department of Education, (1999b). *The Condition of Education 1999.* Washington, DC: National Center for Education Statistics. (ERIC Document Reproduction Service No. ED 430 324)

U.S. Department of Education, Office of Elementary and Secondary Education and Planning and Evaluation Service. (1999c). *Report on state implementation of the Gun-Free Schools Act—school year 1997–98.* (Contract No. EA94052001). Prepared by Westat, Rockville, MD.

U.S. Department of Education (2000). *Twenty-first annual report to Congress on the implementation of the Individuals with Disabilities Education Act.* Washington, DC: Government Printing Office. Author.

U.S. Library of Congress, Congressional Research Service. *Violence in schools: An overview* (CRS Report for Congress No. 94-141 EPW). Washington, DC: Author.

University of Vermont. (1999). Prevention strategies that work: What administrators can do to promote positive student behavior. Burlington, VT: Department of Education, School Research Office.

Walker, H. M., & Horner, R. H. (1996). Integrated approaches to preventing antisocial behavior patterns among school-age children and youth. *Journal of Emotional or Behavioral Disorders, 4*(4), 194–220.

Walker, H. M. & Sprague, J. R. (1999). The path to school failure, delinquency, and violence: Causal factors and some potential solutions. *Intervention in School and Clinic, 35*(2), 67–73.

Ward, J. M. (1999). *Children and guns.* Washington, DC: Children's Defense Fund.

Weinberg, D. H. (1996). *A brief look at postwar U.S. income inequality* (Rep. No. P60-191). Washington, DC: U.S. Bureau of the Census.

Weist, M. D., & Warner, B. S. (1997). Intervening against violence in the schools. *Annals of Adolescent Psychiatry, 21,* 235–251.

Womer, S. C. (1997). *What kinds of school-based prevention programs are publicized?* Ellicott City, MD: Gottfredson Associates.

Woodruff, D. W., Osher, D., Hoffman, C. C., Gruner, A., King, M. A., Snow, S. T., & McIntire, J. C. (1999). The role of education in a system of care: Effectively serving children with emotional or behavioral disorders. *Systems of care: Promising practices in children's mental health, 1998 Series* (Vol. 3). Washington, DC: Center for Effective Collaboration and Practice, American Institutes for Research.

Yell, M. L. (1990). The use of corporal punishment, suspension, expulsion, and timeout with behaviorally disordered students in public schools: Legal considerations. *Behavior Disorders, 15,* 100–109.

Yell, M. L., Cline, D., & Bradley, R. (1995). Disciplining students with emotional and behavioral disorders: A legal update. *Education & Treatment of Children, 18,* 299–308.

Yell, M. L. (1998). *The law and special education.* Upper Saddle River, NJ: Prentice-Hall.

Promoting a Safe School Environment Through a Schoolwide Wellness Program

Patricia A. Gallagher and Linda S. Satter

When school officials have metal detectors at school entrances for weapon checks, conduct random drug testing of athletes, use breathalyzers to detect alcohol, inspect lockers, forbid pagers and cell telephones, and install video cameras in buses, they are doing so to protect youth from injury and tragedy. "Although some safety measures may need to be in place, this approach cannot be at the forefront of safe school plans" (Lantieri, 1997, p. 157).

A balance can be created between promoting safe school environments through inspection practices and surveillance equipment and presenting a comprehensive wellness program that promotes a positive and supportive environment. School curricula should be taught by competent and caring teachers who provide students with experiences in problem solving and decision making strategies and opportunities to practice responsibility and respect. Teachers need to involve students as active participants and collaborators in program activities and extracurricular experiences to help them undertake commitments that encourage and reinforce kinder and gentler relationships.

IMPACT is such a program. It is a comprehensive high school program that promotes a positive and supportive environment by involving students, faculty, and the community in a variety of prevention, collaboration, and intervention activities in response to students' needs. The long-range goal of the program is to equip students with essential skills to be healthy adults.

Origin of the Total Wellness Program

The program at North Kansas City High School (NKCHS), a small community adjacent to Kansas City, Missouri, grew out of an incentive grant written by the building principal to secure funding for safe-school training. The grant enabled eight of her teachers and some from area high schools to complete 36 hours of professional training through the Baptist Medical Center in Kansas City, Missouri.

The training is referred to as a student assistance program. Student assistance programs became prominent in the middle 1970s as an approach to addressing the growing problems related to adolescents' use and abuse of alcohol and other drugs. Over the years, advocates of student assistance programs realized that substance abuse is the result of, and is accompanied by, many problems. These include parental drinking or substance abuse, family frustrations with rearing children in today's culture, teenage depression and suicide, teen pregnancy, sexually transmitted diseases, divorce, and nicotine addictions.

As a result, the original training expanded to address the many and varied issues affecting adolescents today. It taught the adult learners the roles they can play to improve the school climate, promote students' self-image, and provide a home base where students can go to get help. As such, the program emphasized a comprehensive program designed to meet adolescents' needs. It also encouraged participants to find and network with human and community resources to assist the youth and their families. Essentially, the program teaches the value of enabling.

From its "humble" beginning, which focused on keeping kids in and drugs out of school, IMPACT expanded each year with the addition of innovative programs to meet the needs of safety in the school and community. Currently, IMPACT is a total wellness and awareness program that provides students with a support network of peers, teachers, parents, and school and community programs. It is designed to recognize troubling trends and respond to societal changes that can consume the lives of youth and drive some from the education system. The ultimate outcome is to provide students with the necessary skills to be healthy adults.

When the initial group of North Kansas City High School teachers returned from their student assistance training, they reported their experiences at a faculty meeting. Their enthusiasm for what could be done at the school was contagious and encouraged other colleagues to become part of this new wellness program. Now when new faculty members arrive at the school, they are encouraged to take the training offered at Baptist Medical Center.

Students learn about the program's activities during registration and the freshmen orientation session. Throughout the school year posters and announcements are made inviting students to join.

Block-scheduling arrangements give students and staff members interested in the IMPACT program opportunities for participation. This scheduling allows students to meet their seven classes on Monday and four 85-minute classes from Tuesday through Friday. Two of these classes are designated as seminar times encompassing a variety of activities. For example, students can use seminar time to plan skits, organize events, and present lessons to children in nearby elementary and middle schools. Teachers are assigned to five classes, two planning periods, and three extra-duty assignments. Teachers can fulfill their extra-duty requirements by acting as sponsors for an IMPACT program.

The Current Wellness Program

IMPACT consists of two major components: a "participation" and a "helping" component. The *participation component* is composed of a variety of student activities that include SAVE, peer mediation, Impact Improv, SADD, Hi-Step, PAL, high school heroes, and TRY. The *helping component* includes PATHS, a student's resource officer services, individual counseling, community counseling services, conflict-resolution meetings, support groups, ethical decision-making and problem-solving workshops, teen institute, and referral services to outside agencies. The following descriptions will reveal an interconnection between these two major components of the wellness program.

In addition, there is a complementary relationship between IMPACT and the school discipline policies and procedures. For example, peer mediation may be an alternative to suspension or arrest. If word reaches IMPACT that a potential fight may erupt, the likely violators can be offered a mediation session that potentially can prevent a suspension or arrest. Peer mediation also has been used after an incident that resulted in disciplinary action. In this case, mediation assists the violators to think ahead to acceptable responses if a similar incident, temptation, or problem should arise.

Participation Component

SAVE

Students Against Violence Everywhere is a group of concerned students who work closely with local police departments and community agencies to find ways to decrease violence in the schools and communities. The program was designed to address violence in the high schools and to carry the message that school is a safe environment. At first it was concerned with six topics: gangs, cliques, weapons, students feeling like outcasts, racial problems, and drugs.

SAVE began in 1991 when the Kansas City, Missouri, Police Department decided that a comprehensive program was needed to make the school environment safer. Faculty members at the four high schools within two school districts in the North Patrol Division of Kansas City, Missouri, were asked to provide a group of students that the police could talk to about violence in their schools. The students gave their perceptions of violence in the schools, and recommendations on how to combat it.

Students from each grade level in each high school were brought together to discuss the problem of violence in the area's high schools and to design a program that would address the problem. They suggested that the following three committees be formed to help carry out a series of activities as outlined below:

■ A Student Steering Committee, composed of three students from each of the four high schools

■ An Administration Committee made up of representatives from law enforcement, the school administration, social service agencies; IMPACT coordinators from the four high schools who represented the teachers; and juvenile justice officers

■ An Advisory Committee composed of community leaders

Once the committees had been established, the following 10 activities were recommended as a means to address violence in the schools.

1. *Mediation.* Students were to be trained to serve as mediators to handle disputes between fellow students.

2. *Police.* Uniformed police were to be present in the school to interact with the students and to enforce the laws. The officer would instruct, counsel, and arrest.

3. *Disciplinary procedures.* The police would be called and appropriate action taken when students commit acts of violence in schools. Students would be disciplined by assigning them jobs at the school, such as assisting the custodians in cleaning the school or in the community, such as working at the city's recycling center. Suspension from school was not seen as punitive. Therefore, detention periods were recommended during the offender's free time, such as Friday nights and Saturday mornings.

4. *Family counseling.* Services were to be made available to families needing counseling assistance. This would include problem counseling for the students and assistance for parents who were having difficulty with parenting skills.

5. *Awareness.* As an initial effort to change some destructive attitudes of students and adults, it was recommended that publicity be generated about SAVE and the causes of violence in the schools.

6. *Teen hotline.* A hotline was to be established. Through the hotline, individuals could notify school administrators and the police about illegal activity, such as students carrying weapons and engaging in gang activity.

7. *Legislation.* Legislation was recommended for holding parents accountable for the weapons they have in their homes.

8. *Student body.* A cross-section of the student body was to give suggestions to students with disciplinary problems.

9. *Activity night.* Occasional nights were to be designated for dances at a neutral place for all high school students.

10. *Questionnaire.* A questionnaire was to be developed and distributed to all students to secure their perceptions of violence in their school and to solicit suggestions on how to combat violence. This was to be the basis for further program development.

As an initial step, the Student Steering Committee developed a questionnaire and gave it to each student in the four high schools. More than 4,000 students responded. The questionnaire and responses are shown in Figure 14.1.

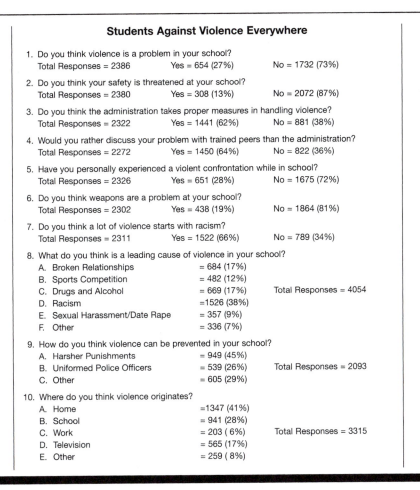

Figure 14.1 Results of Questionnaire

After the responses to the questionnaire were analyzed, the Student Steering Committee, faculty, school administrators, IMPACT coordinators, law enforcement personnel, and social service agencies proceeded to implement their safe school programs. North Kansas City High School implemented the following:

■ A faculty member teaches students to mediate disputes between peers. This peer mediation enables students to negotiate differences before they escalate. The training also covers information on racial and cultural differences.

■ A uniformed police officer is present. The officer is available to teach in the classrooms, assists in counseling sessions with students, and serves as a liaison between the school and outside agencies, such as the county juvenile justice personnel. In addition, the officer takes reports and makes necessary arrests.

■ A disciplinary procedure requires parent involvement and alternative solutions to after-school detention periods. Detentions are on Friday from 2:40 p.m. to 5:00 p.m. Parents or guardians are asked to check their child into the detention period.

■ A process enables students to work out personal problems and directs students and their parents to family counseling. A youth and family service agency provides services including counseling, a place for runaways, and a girl's home. The program offers a 24-hour hotline for personal problems. The telephone number is displayed on a SAVE poster.

■ Displays of SAVE posters and SAVE certificates for participating classrooms endorse the SAVE concept. The poster, designed by a student, contains two telephone numbers: one number for personal problem counseling and the other for reporting illegal activity.

■ A method has been established to report illegal activity. Students call to report illegal activity anonymously. The Kansas City Crime Commission, staffs the telephone number, and contacts the appropriate school administrator to report the information. When necessary, the school administrator works with the police to address the activity.

■ Mandatory reporting of violent activities is required. Missouri Code, Chapter 12.3, requires that certain crimes be reported to the police; therefore, every school has to report violent crimes to the police who would handle each case on its merit. During a meeting, representatives from the juvenile justice system informed the students, police, IMPACT coordinators, and administrators about prosecution for juvenile crimes.

■ A curriculum that addresses violence is in place. The material promotes a decrease of dating/domestic violence and abuse of children and their families. In addition, it advocates prevention in educational videos and during lectures and discussions. The program is designed to promote (a) effective interpersonal communication skills, (b) conflict resolution in a peaceful manner, (c) self-awareness and appropriate identification and expression of feelings, and (d) awareness and understanding of the dynamics of abusive relationships. The program is taught by classroom teachers who have been trained at a facility for abused children and adults.

The SAVE program is reviewed annually. When the first year ended, new Steering Committee members were selected to replace graduated seniors. In addition, a brochure was designed to describe the SAVE programs. Funding was secured from an advertising agency and a printing company to have a brochure printed for every student in the four high schools.

Among the comments of SAVE students is the following from a junior who plays varsity football and plays golf. He said the program had a direct effect upon him by helping curb his tendency to get involved in fights.

> I had a short quick temper. I've learned to control it and realize there is no point giving into violent behavior. I have other solutions and ways out. I will back off.

Another student shared his experiences:

> SAVE has given me the opportunity to voice my opinion of how we should deal with the growing amount of violence. Not only have I told my ideas, but I see them going into effect.

Peer Mediation

Peer mediators are students who, with adult supervision, help resolve disputes between students. Issues that create disputes include rumors, threats, name-calling, fighting, and loss of property. Peer mediators are selected for their abilities of fairness, reliability, and good communication. In addition to training in effective communication techniques, problem solving, and critical thinking skills, they are taught a conflict resolution approach wherein disputants have the chance to sit face-to-face and talk uninterrupted so each side of the dispute is heard.

As the outside persons who lead the discussion, peer mediators do not take sides, and they keep all information confidential. After the disputants relate their versions of the incident the mediators define the problem. Then the mediators and disputants brainstorm options to resolve the conflicts and write them on the Brainstorming Worksheet form (Figure 14.2). They discuss what could have been done differently, what they can do to solve the immediate dispute, and what options they could choose if a similar problem should arise again in the future. When a solution is reached and agreed upon, it is written on the Peer Mediation Agreement Form (Figure 14.3), which the disputants and the mediators sign.

After the conflict resolution session, the peer mediators are responsible for completing a self-evaluation form designed to encourage the student's mastery of the mediation skills (Figure 14.4). Mediators receive feedback and support throughout their work with peers.

A peer mediator, who was the senior class president, wrestler, and down lineman for the football team, said he believes that involvement in athletics is a healthy outlet for potentially aggressive behavior:

> I'm not a fighter. When I see a fight, I think there are other ways out. I like to help people and look for reasonable solutions for problems. There are a lot of things we can do through peer mediation.

Impact IMPROV

Impact IMPROV is a group of students who perform skits with wellness themes to preschool, elementary, middle school, and high school students. IMPROV students receive education in drug and alcohol abuse, family dysfunction, peer pressure, dating issues, eating disorders, and other social ills. Then they and a teacher work together to plan skits on requested topics. After the students give a performance, they ask questions of the audience to initiate dialogue. For example, at a day care center where the students performed *Stranger Danger,* the 4-year-olds were asked to

Brainstorming Worksheet

List all the possible options.

▲ What could be done to resolve this dispute?

▲ What other possibilities can you think of?

▲ In the future, what could you do differently?

1. _____

2. _____

3. _____

4. _____

5. _____

6. _____

7. _____

8. _____

9. _____

10. _____

Figure 14.2 Brainstorming Worksheet

identify the stranger in the performance. They were asked why they should not go with strangers and were asked what they would do if a stranger were to approach them.

IMPROV activities have been effective in that they not only keep everyone's attention but also elicit great conversations. One of the actresses said,

> We enjoy performing for our audiences. It makes us feel that we're helping them solve their problems. In return it makes us feel better.

IMPROV activities are described in a brochure circulated to the elementary schools and in verbal communications with civic groups. Requests for performances

Peer Mediation Agreement

Peer mediator _____ Date _____

Briefly describe the conflict: _____

_____

_____

_____

_____

_____

Type of conflict (check one) ☐ Rumor ☐ Threat ☐ Name-calling ☐ Fighting

☐ Loss of property ☐ Other (specify) _____

The students whose signatures appear below met with a peer mediator and with the assistance of the mediator reached the following agreement.

Disputant_____

Agrees to_____

_____

_____

Disputant_____

Agrees to_____

_____

_____

We have made and signed this agreement because we believe it resolves the issue(s) between us.

_____	_____
Disputant signature	Disputant signature
_____	_____
Peer mediator signature	Length of mediation (minutes)

Figure 14.3 Peer Mediation Form

come from elementary counselors, teachers, day care centers, civic groups such as the Rotary, church groups, and PTAs. During a given year, IMPROV performed at four elementary schools during each of five lunchtimes. In addition, the group does after-school, breakfast, evening, and weekend performances. Requests are now coming in from other cities and school districts.

Thank-you notes have come from preschool children, parents, teachers and community members. The group has become very popular. Demands for after-school performance have become so extensive that IMPROV has been included in the school's Drama II class.

Peer Mediator Self-Evaluation

Peer mediator _____ Date _____

Directions: Place a checkmark (✓) by each step where you did quality work. Place an asterisk (*) by each step where you think the quality could improve.

☐ Step 1: Open the session

☐ Step 2: Gather information

☐ Step 3: Focus on common interests

☐ Step 4: Create options

☐ Step 5: Evaluate options and choose a solution

☐ Step 6: Write the agreement and close

1. What did you do well?

2. If you could do this mediation again, what might you do differently?

3. Were certain steps more difficult for you than others? If so, what could you do to strengthen these steps?

4. Do you have any other concerns or questions?

Staff supervisor_____ Date _____

Comments:

Figure 14.4 Peer Mediation Self-Evaluation

SADD

Students Against Destructive Decisions (formerly known as students against drunk drivers) is a program designed to raise students' awareness of the dangers of drinking and driving. To reinforce its message, the group engages in a number of activities throughout the academic year. For example, in May SADD presents a skit to demonstrate the risks of drinking and driving. During a mock scene, members of SADD wear "fatal vision" goggles that simulate the effects of alcohol by impairing their ability to walk a straight line.

In a docudrama held outdoors, police, medical technicians, squad cars, and ambulances join the SADD group for a DWI mock car accident. The emergency personnel attend to the accident victims, and the police question the witnesses to highlight the consequences of drinking. After the audience has watched the scene, they wear "fatal vision" goggles to learn firsthand how vision, coordination, driving skills, and mental judgment become impaired after drinking. Thus, the potential for fatal consequences becomes very real. The goggles give students the opportunity to understand the dangers of alcohol and drug ingestion without actually experimenting with them.

SADD members also send birthday cards, with a quarter enclosed, to sophomores when they turn 16. Students are encouraged to use the money to call home for a ride if they have been drinking. A week in the fall is designated Red Ribbon Week. This is a time when students are asked to wear red ribbons to remind everybody of the dangers of drinking and driving. During this week SADD also places small white crosses on the school grounds to demonstrate how many teenagers die daily in alcohol-related deaths. During Christmas week the student body is encouraged to stay safe over the holidays.

Hi-Step

High School-Taught Elementary Program is a cross-age teaching program in which high school students teach fourth graders about peer pressure, conflict mediation, drug and alcohol abuse, and relationships. Two faculty members sponsor the program.

Because Hi-Steppers are viewed as role models for the younger students, candidates are carefully screened. They are chosen for having good academic records and an interest in helping fourth grade students grow emotionally and socially.

Hi-Step students receive their training during late winter and early spring. They attend an 8-hour training session to become familiar with the characteristics of fourth graders, learn to investigate topics, plan activities, and learn to write lesson plans. After their training, Hi-Step participants develop six lessons. Students meet with one of the sponsors weekly during seminar time to review their lessons, receive feedback, and practice with the other students in their group.

After the six lessons are ready, the group is assigned to an elementary school. Hi-Steppers are responsible for meeting with the fourth grade teachers and setting up times to meet with their classes. For this purpose, the Hi-Steppers have permission to leave high school during the seminar times. They have time to arrive at their assigned elementary school and teach the hour-long lessons with their accompanying activities, and return before their own academic periods begin.

Although publicity for the program is done in the classrooms through the school's television channel and posted flyers, the most compelling publicity comes from the enthusiastic Hi-Steppers. Telephone calls start coming in October of the year preceding the performance.

Hi-Step experiences are great for the high school students who have a career interest in teaching or social services and for the fourth graders who have met teenage models. Hi-Step students tell how important they feel when they meet the fourth graders at the mall and are introduced to the parents.

The president of the Hi-Steppers summarized the group's intentions:

> If we reach one child, giving them the courage to do what is right, then we've met our goal. We want kids to know that their high school years can be a great time in their lives if they make the right decisions, and we help them to realize what those good decisions are. Most of all, we want them to know that we care.

PAL

Peers Always Listen (PAL) provides a group of students to whom other students can talk. PALS make a commitment to do what they can to encourage a positive and supportive atmosphere at the school. PALS do not give advice but, instead, listen and try to help their peers sort out their feelings. Consequently, all PALs receive training in assertive listening skills. They learn that emotion can be "energy" in motion and that the best way to defuse an emotional moment is to give the excited student an opportunity to "let the air out." They accomplished this by listening attentively. A student who is "highly charged" may talk only in syllables or phrases. A PAL listens until the peer is able to express himself or herself coherently. PALs are committed to the positive action of listening with care.

PALs also take part in other IMPACT programs such as SADD and IMPROVS. They tutor, distribute, and hang red ribbons for Red Ribbon Week and participate in activities that have the potential to improve the school atmosphere. They welcome new students and help them adjust to school.

One of the latest activities to be included in PAL is to spend some seminar time in a special day school for students who have behavior disorders. PALs engage in nonacademic tasks such as playing board games, shooting baskets, and making crafts. They have been well received by the students and teachers alike.

A PALs participant stated:

> The group teaches students how to be more aware of their peers' feelings and about themselves. It introduced me to many new students like myself who are interested in the well-being of their classmates. The training teaches great people skills.

High School Heroes

High School Heroes is a group of students who teach a tobacco prevention program to fourth, fifth and sixth graders, sponsored by the American Lung Association. This organization prepares the students to be peer educators regarding the forces that influence children's decisions to smoke or not to smoke. In preparation for their roles, the High School Heroes learn about the immediate effects of smoking, how to reinforce positive attitudes about being a nonsmoker, how to make specific decisions, and how to use the refusal skills necessary to resist pressures to smoke. They also learn how to lead a discussion about the respiratory system that includes a demonstration of the effects of smoking.

The American Lung Association recommends that the Heroes program be used as part of a health curriculum to enhance the existing substance abuse program. The Association provides a guide with activities for tobacco education. After the Heroes complete their training, they work in groups of five to prepare a 1-hour tobacco education lesson. After completing their lesson work, they contact fourth-, fifth-, and sixth-grade teachers to set up times for delivering their lesson.

The Lung Association suggests that peer education can have a significant influence on students' knowledge and attitudes about smoking. They believe their training can have an impact on high school students' leadership skills and can reinforce positive attitudes about being a nonsmoker.

TRY

Teaching and Reaching Youth (TRY) is composed of parents and community members from business, police, the service agencies, and education. Its main purpose is to engage the community in focusing on developing knowledge, attitudes, and skills concerning tobacco, alcohol and other drug abuse, and related wellness issues. Specific efforts familiarize the community with state laws, school district policy, and local ordinances relating to these topics. The group's mission is to promote physical and mental wellness in young people through community involvement.

TRY recognizes that youth can be at risk when drugs and alcohol are present during social events. It knows that some students will be pressured by peers to participate. Therefore, one of its programs is Safe Homes for Teens, in which information is sent to parents to secure their support in providing safe homes for student parties. Safe Homes provides homes free of drugs and alcohol. Safe Home parents have access to other committed parents who have pledged to support this cause. TRY has also met with hotel and motel managers requesting that they deny room reservations to prom students who seek accommodations for their parties.

TRY has provided some of the financial support for a popular annual youth activity, school lock-in, in which the SAVE group is also involved. A lock-in provides a safe environment, such as a community center, for a night of social activities that include music, dancing, basketball, swimming, gameroom fun, food, and nonalcoholic beverages.

Some of TRY's other activities include sponsorship of Red Ribbon Week with a community kick-off rally. The group purchases ribbons to tie on utility poles and trees, and yard signs caring the message Drug Free and Proud throughout the city. TRY also sponsors community PIE (Parent Informational Evenings) nights. Here, speakers from the community share information about current topics—for example, the issue of methadone laboratories and what to do about their accessibility to the youth. Methadone labs, for some reason, are prevalent in the surrounding area; hence the need to address the situation.

Helping Component

PATHS

Practical and Academic Transitions to High School (PATHS) is a 3-week summer course designed to prepare eighth graders for a smooth transition to high school. During this course incoming students receive an orientation to the school and community and participate in a special curriculum that promotes student bonding and thematic learning.

For the development phase of PATHS, the building principal recruited a group of teachers interested in the PATHS concept. They developed the summer program, an environment in which students making the transition from middle school to high school could feel more secure and successful. The principal presented the idea to the central office and received funding for the 3-week program.

Two faculty members became co-directors of PATHS. They were joined by four teachers, an instructional assistant, and an attendance secretary to develop the summer program's activities. Peer helpers representing a diverse student population were also selected to give special presentations to middle school students, the potential participants for the summer program.

Peer helpers serve as tutors, conflict mediators, teacher assistants, and hall monitors. They operate the school store during the breaks, are group leaders in the homerooms, and run errands.

In the first PATHS program in 1994 four middle schools enrolled 91 students. They received one-half elective credit for attending all the sessions and completing assignments. The five peer helpers received credit also. The 3-week program began with student bonding activities that continued into week two and week three, which focused on thematic learning.

Week 1. The main objective of the first week was to encourage the students to bond as a team and to become oriented to the school and community. The activities were as follows:

■ *The Challenge* consisted of high and low rope courses designed to teach cooperation, communication, peer support, team building, and self-confidence through a series of well supervised physical challenges. Students spent a full day off campus at an adventure site in the woods.

■ *Being Successful* focused on characteristics that successful people have in common. These include being responsible, hard-working, and team players, as well as going the extra mile. Students became acquainted with successful peers and guest speakers who taught the school's expectations for its students. They were asked to reflect and write about someone whom they considered successful. In addition, they were instructed in the components of peer mediation leading to win/win situations.

■ *Community Orientation* involved students in a picture-taking walking tour of North Kansas City. Students learned about aspects of the city including its history, architecture, and culture. The mayor welcomed the students and discussed city government. When the students returned from the day's adventures, they worked together to develop a travel brochure of the city.

■ *School Orientation* familiarized the students with traditions of the high school. The students went on a walking tour of the campus and learned the buildings and locations of departments. Course offerings, transcripts, school rules, and expectations were discussed. Students became acquainted with the school planner, which they are responsible to keep during their freshmen year.

■ *Diversity Training* was presented by Anytown USA, a program sponsored by the Council of Christians and Jews. It begins with participatory situations for students to experience being different, such as having the disability of blindness, deafness, or confinement in a wheelchair. These are followed by decision-making activities that promote an understanding of and appreciation for diversity of people in the community and school. The experiences encourage positive self-image, communication skills, leadership ability, male/female perceptions, police/ youth relations, racial understanding, cultural awareness, and family and peer relationships.

Week 2 and Week 3. A thematic learning experience focused on the music industry and provided continuity throughout the second and third weeks. A music theme was selected because of its appeal to the adolescents. Students attended three classes per day. At the end of each day, students assembled in the auditorium to participate in musical enrichment. A variety of musical groups performed, and students responded to and critiqued the performances. Three specific academic areas were imbedded in the learning: mathematics, communication, and study skills and are described as follows.

■ *The Mathematical Skill Program* invited the students to use their skills to manage a band. They were responsible for scheduling performance events, figuring time cards, using charts and graphs to record number of performances and the time schedules, mapping travel routes, and writing paychecks. Students were scheduled individually to work in the Computer Curriculum Corporation, a programmed learning of computer use for the development of math skills.

■ *The Communication Skills Program* prepared students to read, discuss, and analyze music reviews. Students wrote critiques of the musical performances they heard in the afternoon. They practiced proofreading skills and oral presentation of their work. They engaged in an art activity by making a collage around the theme of music.

■ *The Study Skills Program* familiarized the students with teacher expectations. Students were taught techniques for previewing lessons and learning the value of understanding each section. Techniques for oral and written reviews also were taught and applied to the materials they were using in the thematic unit. Test-taking skills were presented. Instruction included the teaching of skills required to pass verbal, multiple-choice, and essay tests successfully. Students also were exposed to the assessment procedures the faculty used for grading assignments.

PATHS participants get together several times during the academic year. They have plays, speakers, and casual conversation periods to talk about how school life is going. The Peer Helpers have initiated many informal one-on-one meetings with the freshmen.

School Resource Officer

The School Resource Officer is available to assist students with various legal concerns. These concerns have been about abusive parents, abusive boyfriends, DUI arrests, traffic tickets, and probation contingencies.

The School Resource Officer program, begun in Phoenix, Arizona, in the mid-1980s, has been adopted by some police departments throughout the United States. The duties of the School Resource Officer in the IMPACT program are as follows:

1. To be a resource to instructional units to students on issues related to a basic understanding of the law and the role of law enforcement

2. To be a resource for instruction to students on issues related to violence, prevention of violence, and personal safety

3. To facilitate individual and small-group discussions based on material presented in class, or other topics such as date rape, driving while intoxicated, and automobile accidents relevant to student/officer interests. These groups take place during school time or outside of school time.

4. To hold conferences with students to assist them with problems regarding alcohol, other drugs, law enforcement, crime prevention, or personal safety

5. To meet with students and make referrals to community agencies that offer assistance to youth and their families

6. To provide informational services to the staff on issues related to alcohol and other drugs, the law, violence, gangs, safety and security

7. To provide faculty training on skills related to violence prevention, violence diffusion, creation and maintenance of a safe environment

8. To meet and interact with the Student Steering and Administrative Committees to assist them in any of the programs or legislative issues that SAVE is pursuing

The SRO commented at the conclusion of his 4 years in the school:

My job as an SRO has been a very rewarding period of my law enforcement career. I've been able to interact with, educate, and positively influence more kids over time than many officers do throughout a career. Since the inception of my role, the number of fights, gang activity, thefts, and drug-related cases has consistently declined. An SRO should be mandatory for every middle school and high school. The value of a safe school environment and the positive law enforcement presence cannot be overstated. SROs are a necessity in schools today. They not only assist in maintaining a safe school environment but also help in building responsible adults.

Operation Drug Dog

In 1997 the entire community took a proactive position on the drug issue by purchasing Twiko, a black Belgian Malinois dog, born and trained in the Netherlands for police work. His specialty is sniffing for drugs, especially marijuana, cocaine, heroin, and methamphetamines. Twiko became part of the community as a result of a campaign spearheaded by a trio of adults—the School Resource Officer, the IMPACT coordinator, and a mathematics teacher.

Although drug reduction efforts had been established in the school and community, not all drugs are found because they are concealed so easily. Teachers had been concerned about the prevalence of drugs in the community and how it was reflected in the school. Some students were returning "high" from open lunch and some were passing drugs on school grounds. At a faculty meeting the teachers said, "We're sick of losing students to drugs." The School Resource Officer, dedicated to the students' welfare, was adamant about finding ways, in addition to his work, to eliminate drugs from the school. The SRO, the IMPACT coordinator, and a mathematics teacher approached the school administration, police chief, community organizations, and city council regarding a plan, "Operation Drug Dog." They received approval, but not financial support, for the plan.

The School Resource Officer searched for other communities that had raised the $20,000 required to cover the cost of the dog, his training, travel, kennel and cage, the travel lodging and training of the officer (who is not the SRO) assigned to Twiko. After finding a community that issued stock to raise funds, the trio decided to use that approach for fundraising. Stock was sold to individuals, including students and senior citizens, civic organizations, and corporations, for $10, $25, and $100, respectively. Within 4 months the funds had been raised. The dog was purchased and trained with the officer. Then Twiko arrived to live in the community that owns him.

After his arrival each contributor was presented with a stock certificate and a photograph of Twiko with his officer. Their duties include night patrols, searching for drugs at sporting events, and random visits to the high school. There Twiko is treated to plenty of petting and attention. He is successful in sniffing out drugs, even minute amounts.

Counseling Services

Counseling services are available for individuals and groups during school hours and with a variety of community agencies. Students are referred by parents, teachers, friends, and self-referrals to the IMPACT coordinator, who devotes all her time to the role. Reasons for referrals include suspected drug and alcohol abuse, poor or failing grades, eating disorders, pregnancy, abuse, depression, and suicidal tendencies. When a student discusses a problem with the IMPACT coordinator, it is followed by an appraisal relevant to the type of support that will be needed. This may include school support, a community referral, a support group, or professional counseling.

The IMPACT coordinator contacts others, such as the parents, teachers, or community personnel, to gather pertinent information that will be useful in an intervention and treatment plan. If a student receives services outside the school, the coordinator is in contact with the agency to facilitate communications and coordinate everyone's efforts. In addition, if the student spends time in a treatment facility, the coordinator notifies the student's teacher, collects homework, and maintains communication between the agencies.

One student commented:

> Being sent for treatment saved my life because it helped me realize that I did have things to live for and look forward to when I'm older.

A parent noted:

> I really appreciate your efforts, your compassion, and your understanding during all of this with my daughter. We have been down a long, rocky road, and without the support of others like you, I don't think the ending of this story would have turned out nearly so well.

The IMPACT coordinator has seen a change in students' attitudes about getting help with their problems:

> It's no longer "un-cool" to talk about having problems. In fact, I can see where students have become more comfortable about dealing with their issues. I can't think of anything more important than the emotional well-being of our youth. If students aren't ready emotionally, they are never going to get it together academically.

Grief Counseling

Grief counseling became prominent in 1995, when the staff at NKCHS and other high schools throughout the United States recognized changes in the emotional health of students after traumatic events. Fatal and near-fatal injuries from accidents and acts of violence, as well as serious illness, were touching students' lives. When adolescents suffer grief from the loss, injury, or illness of someone they love, the emotional experience affects their behavior and can affect academic performance. They are particularly vulnerable to loss. "Grief is a keen and complex emotional experience that includes fear, anger, relief, despair, peace, guilt, numbness, agitation, and sorrow" (Naierman, 1997, p. 62). As students go through the stages of bereavement, they do not always know that others are having similar experiences. In an effort to reach out to the students, NKCHS established guidelines to help the students heal. A plan was written describing an organized way to respond to a crisis.

During the time when the committee was working on the plan, a tragedy occurred: Four students were killed in an automobile accident. The developing guidelines were immediately put into operation, subsequently reviewed, and changes made. The IMPACT coordinator contacts community agencies for their support and obtains trained teachers to lead support groups. The guidelines delineate duties between the administrative team and the counseling team, and the lines of communication to students, staff, parents, community agencies, and the media. The teams provide crisis counseling and crisis rooms as long as they are needed. All activities are documented on a checklist for the management of a traumatic event.

Data and Results of IMPACT

The success of IMPACT is revealed informally by the participants in their comments cited throughout this article. In addition to these statements, data records for the number of student fights and student conflicts reveal a decline in student to student confrontations. Data on peer mediation illustrate an increase in the number of sessions. Figures 14.5 and 14.6 present these data. It is reasonable to assume that the following variables contributed to the decline of fighting: (a) the SAVE program had been initiated in the 1993-94 school year; (b) the peer mediation program was initiated in 1994-95; (c) a school resource officer was assigned to the school; and (d) a zero-tolerance policy relevant to fighting was implemented in the 1995-96 school year.

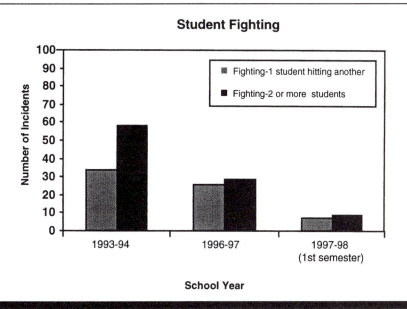

Figure 14.5 Number of Student Fights

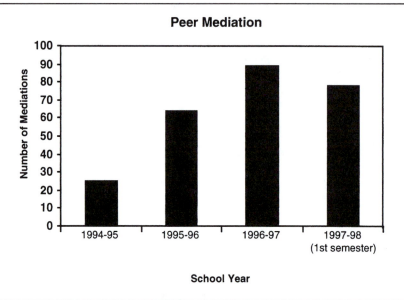

Figure 14.6 Number of Peer Mediation Sessions

Summary

One midwestern high school is taking proactive, constructive steps to protect students and strengthen their relationships with their peers, the faculty, and the community. The IMPACT program focuses on the importance of improving the entire school environment as a significant way to enhance students' wellness and safety. When students, faculty, and community members nourish inviting relationships, caring communities develop. Schools that implement only measures such as metal detectors, student identification badges, and locker inspections have confined themselves to solutions that are problematic. If, on the other hand, schools include practices that promote cooperation, teach conflict resolution, highlight the value of service to others, encourage empathy, and promote belonging and trust, they truly create safe schools.

References

Lantieri, L. (1997). From punishment to prevention: Educating the heart. *Reclaiming Children and Youth.* 6:(3).

Naierman, N. (1997). Reaching out to grieving students. *Educational Leadership. 55* (2).

We thank the many persons who have contributed to the success of IMPACT, the schoolwide wellness program, especially Evelyn Matthys, IMPACT coordinator for North Kansas City School District; Dr. Vicki Baker, Associate Superintendent of North Kansas City School District; Debbie Burns, Special Education Teacher; Rob Russell, School Resource Officer; IMPACT Care Team; IMPACT Student Participants; Bob Kelly and John Admire, Baptist Medical Center, Kansas City, Missouri.

Appendix

Demographics of NKCHS

North Kansas City High School (NKCHS) is one of three high schools serving the North Kansas City School District, which includes 20 elementary schools and four middle schools. The school is located in the small town of North Kansas City; therefore, most of the students are residents of the surrounding areas. The school district is north of the business and financial nucleus of metropolitan Kansas City, Missouri. It is a campus-style facility composed of five separate buildings, the oldest of which was constructed in 1925.

The population represents nearly a complete cross-section of socioeconomic groups. Primary employers of the parents include the major airport, federal and state government agencies, automobile, electronic, paint, and agriculture industries.

The school has 1,400 students. The ethnic make-up of the school is 90% caucasian; the minority populations are represented equally by African American, Asian American, and Latin/Hispanic American cultures.

The school is a Missouri A+ school. A major benefit of this designation is that students who plan to attend a Missouri 2-year community college or vocational school after graduation may be eligible for State-reimbursed fees, books, and tuition. To be eligible, a student must complete the standards for graduation set by the school. In addition, the student must (a) have attended an A+ school for at least 3 years, (b) maintain 95% attendance, (c) have a 2.5 grade-point average on a 4.0 scale, (d) complete 50 hours of unpaid tutoring or mentoring, and (e) maintain good citizenship.

Intervention Procedures for Traumatic Crises in Schools

Beverley H. Johns and John P. Keenan

The school community, like any other close-knit community, is seriously affected by the death of any of its members as well as by other major crises, such as an attempted suicide or a serious accident or illness. As stated by Watson, Poda, Miller, Rice, and West (1990), schools must have in place plans for the management of events that cannot be predicted. We believe that such guidelines must be developed not only for humanistic reasons but also to ensure that a rational, tempered atmosphere will prevail when traumatic crises occur.

In this chapter we provide general guidelines for dealing with traumatic crises in schools and specific guidelines to follow in the event of the death of a student or staff member or the potential death of a student.

Developing and Implementing a Basic Crisis Plan

Throughout this chapter, we have stressed the importance of being prepared for situations that may occur. Unpredictable crises are no exception: A crisis plan is a must. We are not suggesting that schools develop 300-page manuals that cover every possible type of disaster—no one would read them—but we do advocate the development of a basic disaster plan. The following is a step-by-step guideline for developing such a plan.

1. School officials should conduct periodic inventories of the potential for a disaster to occur in their school. For example, do any students or staff have serious illnesses? Is there a feeling of unrest among any group(s) of students?

2. Schools should review what other schools have done when crises have occurred. Educators can learn from both the mistakes and successes of other schools.

3. When developing policies and procedures for dealing with crises, school officials should seek assistance from the local police department. (All of the procedures provided in this paper were developed jointly by the police department and the school.) They should also seek input from all other agencies that would be impacted by the procedures.

4. All crisis policies and procedures should specify the following:

   a. Who will serve as the school's spokesperson if this type of crisis occurs? According to St. John (1986), a single spokesperson should be designated to speak for the school. If more than one spokesperson is designated, there is the possibility that contradictory statements may be made.

      The spokesperson will also be the individual who talks to the press. As Jay (1989) discussed, responding to the media with "No comment" will encourage the media to get the story from other, far less reliable sources. The school spokesperson should stick to the facts and give the media as much information as has been verified. If a specific timeline exists for investigating the situation, he or she should let the media know that timeline.

   b. Who will serve on a crisis intervention team?

   c. What communication system will be used to alert students and staff of the crisis?

   d. What special equipment will be needed for dealing with the crisis?

   e. Who will tell the staff and who will tell the students (individual teachers, social workers, psychologists)?

   f. Who will contact the students' parents?

   g. Who will provide support and counseling to students and staff?

   h. Who will determine whether any changes will need to be made in the school schedule?

   i. Who will subsequently evaluate the process?

5. Once policies and procedures have been developed, they must be disseminated and explained to all personnel who would be impacted. Periodic reviews of the policies and procedures must be made.

6. Schools may wish, as St. John (1986) suggested, to index the crisis plan and place the plan and index in a loose-leaf binder. St. John recommended that the school administrator keep an outline of the crisis plan and all relevant phone numbers on a card in his or her wallet so they are always readily available.

7. Following any traumatic crisis, the school should, within a timely framework, assess the potential impact of the event on all parties involved and arrange appropriate follow-through to provide those parties with closure on the event. Jay (1989) noted the following three actions that the school should take after the immediate crisis is over:

   a. Those who provided extra assistance, were courageous, and were patient throughout the crisis should be thanked.

b. Efforts should be made to help heal any wounds that remain after the crisis, to help allay any fears that may follow an accident, and to acknowledge the sadness that occurs after a loss.

c. The crisis team should consider what they could do better next time.

We cannot stress enough the importance of having a crisis plan in place. Few people will be level-headed enough to create such a plan "on the spot" when a crisis occurs. We are reminded of a sad event that occurred in the school at which one of us works. A dedicated and committed teacher was stricken with cancer. For five years, she continued to teach her class of students with severe behavioral disorders. When her illness became very serious, she was hospitalized and spent the last two weeks of her life in the hospital. Many of the staff and students had watched her brave effort to fight the illness and admired her courage. All of her students, some of whom had been in her class for three years, were devastated by her death, and the staff members were in a state of shock and sadness. All of the staff were grateful that the school had a plan in place for dealing with such sad events. No one was in any condition to create such a plan "on the spot."

In another incident that affected the staff and students in one of our schools this year, a young student was beaten, almost to death, by an older man on a weekend. On Monday, school personnel had to notify the staff and talk with the students. Many of the children were afraid that the same thing might happen to them. Counseling had to be made available to the students.

When dealing with any crisis, school personnel should always do as follows:

1. Stay calm.

2. Tell the truth.

3. Be as precise as possible.

4. Provide facts to the media. (We recommend that school personnel work with the press; remember, they will always have the last word.)

5. Follow the school's policies and procedures.

What to Do in the Event of the Death of a Student or Staff Member

The following outline details a sample action plan that a school may want to use in the event of the death of a student or staff member.

I. Foster Understanding

    A. The school administrator or designee notifies the crisis intervention team.

        1. When? The team should be called together whenever a student or staff member dies. The team should meet immediately, either during the school day or, if the crisis occurs outside of school hours, at 7:00 a.m. the following day, having been contacted at home by the principal. That meeting should be immediately followed by a full staff meeting to update staff, answer concerns, and outline the specific process to be followed.

2. **Who/What?** The members of the team and their roles follow:

   a. School administrator or designee—chairs the team; formalizes or oversees its functioning; ensures that the team carries out its agenda

   b. School administrator or designee—directs staff on actions to be taken, contacts bereaved family for information about assistance needed, and funeral arrangements

   c. School administrator or designee—supervises and coordinates necessary activities that occur in school

   d. Psychologist and social worker—coordinate their roles and responsibilities

   e. School administrator or designee—contacts the press; contacts students' parents (e.g., sending a letter or memo or calling parents)

   f. Teacher and alternate, selected by school administrator—serve as liaison with faculty

   g. Floating member, selected by school administrator—provides information to other team members on individual who has died, including his or her friends, enemies, etc.

B. The school administrator or other appropriate staff member contacts the family of the person who has died (this should be done before team meets, if possible) in order to do the following:

   1. Verify information and facts surrounding the crisis

   2. See how the family defines or understands the crisis (e.g., accident, illness, suicide)

   3. See what the family's wishes are, if any, with regard to sharing information about funeral arrangements, etc., with students and staff

   4. Briefly outline the general process the school plans to follow

C. School administrator or designee on crisis intervention team notifies faculty of the death. This person also does the following:

   1. Identifies faculty who may be the most vulnerable to the crisis and provides support if necessary

   2. Prepares a paragraph to give to faculty members to *read to their classes* providing the true facts and briefly explaining what will happen next

   3. Leads a faculty meeting as soon as possible on the day of the death to explain events and procedures

      a. Two meetings may be needed so that teachers can cover one another's classes.

      b. The faculty meeting may be held after school.

    D. Students are notified.

        1. Individual teachers announce the death to their classes rather than using written notification.

        2. Teachers should offer a support system to students so that they may discuss their concerns.

    E. School administrator or designee on crisis intervention team notifies parents of all students to explain the facts and any special arrangements to be made.

        1. Notice can be hand-carried by each student.

        2. Memo can be mailed to parents, though it will not arrive until the next day.

        3. Parents of students close to the trauma or students having a hard time with it should be called.

        4. If it is deemed necessary for a student to be dismissed from school, parents should be notified. The student should be picked up only by a parent or guardian.

    F. School administrator or designee should be prepared to speak to the press, responding to press inquiries with a factual statement based on the immediate family's definition of the crisis and specifying what is being done in the school.

    G. The crisis intervention team meets at the end of the day to review what has been done and what still needs to be done.

        1. Reviews information dissemination

            a. Was everyone notified, and how was news received?

            b. Is it necessary to update anyone? Parent letters can be written and mailed; an update memo can be provided to staff, who can read it to students the next day; a faculty meeting can be held after school to review progress.

            c. Were school administrator and all team members updated as described earlier?

            d. What was reported to the press, if anything, and how was the press handled?

        2. Reviews adequacy of support services

        3. Reviews likely sequence of activity for those most affected by the crisis

        4. Reviews procedure for moving forward for students and faculty

II. Assist in the Grieving Process

    A. Grieving is appropriate for both students and staff, and everyone should be allowed to show their grief. (Note that it is appropriate to not grieve.)

        1. Grief may come out as sadness, but anger must also be recognized as a part of the grieving process.

2. Close friends and enemies are most vulnerable when someone dies and should be seen in separate groups as determined by the crisis intervention team. (Worst enemies are at risk because of guilt and thinking, "I caused it.")

3. Teachers need to be sensitive to their students' need to grieve and should encourage students to participate in the programs noted in "B," below.

B. Grieving can be done in the following ways:

1. Group sessions in the classroom or elsewhere

   a. Groups may be open to anyone who needs and/or requests such sessions.

   b. Specific groups may be brought together, such as close friends, enemies, and teachers who worked closely with the person who died.

2. Classroom discussions led by the teacher or a support team member, at the teacher's request

3. Individual counseling

   a. By the social worker

   b. By the psychologist

   c. By the guidance counselor

C. The student's belongings and school items, in the event of a student's death must be dealt with.

1. Personal belongings should be returned to the family in an appropriate manner.

2. What to do with school items, such as the student's desk, can be discussed with the class (e.g., remove it, leave it empty, etc.).

III. Explain School Policy for Commemorating the Death

A. Funerals

1. School will not be closed for a student's funeral. However, the school will do the following:

   a. Provide support

   b. Help keep individuals from feeling isolated

   c. Clarify misinformation

2. School may be closed for a faculty member's funeral.

3. Students who go to the funeral of another student or a staff member should be accompanied by an adult.

4. Experiences may be shared the next day, if needed, in class or with support services.

B. Suicides

1. The school approach is to commemorate all lives that are cut short.

2. The school's emphasis should *not* be on glorifying the act but on discussing what can be done to prevent such acts in the future; a suicide should be viewed as a teachable moment.
3. The victim should not be eulogized.
4. The school schedule should be maintained as much as possible.
5. If the suicide occurs at school, the police should be called immediately and students should be kept away from the area of the building.

IV. Help Students and Staff to Move Forward

  A. Students and faculty need to know that it is appropriate to go on with the business at hand even though they are still grieving and to know that laughter and fun are appropriate.

  B. For adolescents, grieving may be a prolonged process, sometimes lasting throughout adolescence.

   1. Students having a particularly hard time can be referred for counseling.
   2. Students who are struggling at times but are able to function may require some understanding from time to time.

  C. The crisis intervention team should meet to evaluate the situation and the effectiveness of the actions taken.

V. Points to Remember

  A. Paradoxically, through a crisis such as death can come a closer, more caring, supportive school community.

   1. Administrators and faculty can be seen in a more caring, supportive, human role.
   2. Community relations can improve as a result of outreach to parents.

  B. Numerous teaching points can be made during this period of time. For example:

   1. How such a crisis may be prevented
   2. How to deal effectively, on a personal level, with a crisis
   3. How to handle crisis situations

  C. All staff, including teachers, administrators, and support team members should make note of students or staff who may require follow-up services and report their names to the school counselor or a member of the crisis intervention team.

What to Do When a Student Makes a Suicide Threat

The July 22, 1996, issue of *Newsweek* featured an article entitled "Suicide's Shadow" (Gleck, 1996), which relayed the story of two young female students from

California who committed suicide just before graduating from ninth grade. Earlier in the school year, another student from the same school committed suicide. The events reminded the community of how dangerous the teenage years have become. The article included recent figures compiled by the Centers for Disease Control that show that teen suicide rates are rising steadily. Between 1980 and 1993, suicide rates rose 120% for 10- to 14-year-olds and 30% for 15- to 19-year-olds.

Some of the increase, as Liotta (1996) contended, is attributable to the fact that more students are depressed today than were in the past. Liotta listed a number of signs that may indicate the presence of depression in teenagers—and should be warning signs for parents and educators. These include lack of interest or pleasure, irritability, behavioral changes, loss of weight, change in eating habits, feelings of guilt, lack of energy, difficulty concentrating, low self-esteem, decline in schoolwork, sense of helplessness, sadness, sense of hopelessness, change in sleep patterns, restlessness, death-related thoughts, and suicidal thoughts.

With today's high rates of childhood depression, and increasing rates of teen suicide, one of the most common questions asked of us is what to do when a student makes a suicide threat at school. In our work with many students with serious emotional and behavioral problems, we have had to respond to such situations many times. We follow the guidelines set forth for educators by Guetzloe (1989), who made the following points about youth suicide and its prevention:

1. Never take a student's suicide threats or gestures casually. Do something, mobilize. A suicidal person may interpret any disregard of his or her suicidal signals as a covert wish that he or she should carry out the threat.

2. Do not be afraid to bring up the subject of suicide. The discussion will not encourage the student to go through with his or her plans; on the contrary, it will help the student to know that someone cares. By talking honestly with the student, you may save his or her life.

3. Question the student closely and carefully about a possible suicide plan. Ask: "Are you planning to hurt yourself?" "Do you have a gun (or pills)?" "When do you plan to do this?"

4. Do not debate the morality of suicide with the student. Do not preach. The suicidal person is not thinking about morality but about an unbearable emotional stress.

5. Through discussion with the student, identify the major stresses or events that precipitated the suicidal behavior. Do not pretend to understand when you are unsure about the student's feelings.

6. Do not respond to what the student says with such statements as, "You have so much to live for," or "Think of all the things you have that others don't." Such statements may make the student believe that his or her thoughts are ridiculous.

7. Encourage the student to make use of other supports, such as parents, friends, a minister, school personnel, neighbors, and the mental health clinic. Let the student know that you will help him or her make contacts with those supports.

8. If the problem was precipitated by the loss of a romantic relationship, do not make such comments as, "There are lots of fish in the sea," and do not pass judgment. The loss of love may feel like the end of the world to a teenager.

9. Never leave a suicidal student alone. Stay with the student.

10. Remove anything from the immediate environment that the student could use as a weapon, and remind the student's parents to do the same.

11. Mention school and community events that will occur later in the day, week, month, and so forth. Try to get a commitment from the student to attend or participate in those events.

12. Be aware of the student's responses to you. If the responses are accepting and the student's mood improves, continue with your present tactic. If, however, the student says, "Leave me alone!" respond with such statements as "I care about you," "I want to help you," and "I'll be here for you."

13. Be sure that the student has the telephone number of a crisis hotline or a counseling service.

14. Do not promise the student that you will keep his or her suicidal behavior secret. It must be reported to parents and a counseling center.

15. Try to get a commitment from the student to not hurt himself or herself and to call for help if he or she feels any kind of suicidal impulse again. You may want to write a contract with the student to get the student's commitment in writing.

16. Involve others in the school who may be able to provide support to the student. Other school personnel may assist in contacting the parents and the counseling service. Other staff may also be able to provide needed information about what is going on in the student's life.

17. Document all actions taken.

Specific Procedures for Suicide Threat Situations in Schools

We strongly recommend that all schools have in place specific procedures for dealing with suicide threats. Sample procedures that educators can adopt, or adapt, follow.

For all staff:

1. Take any suicide threat seriously.

2. Do not leave the student alone.

3. Remove anything from the immediate environment that could be harmful to the student.

4. Immediately inform the school social worker and administrator.

For the school social worker:

1. Talk to the student privately to assess the seriousness of the threat.

2. During all discussions, be supportive and encouraging; use active listening.

3. Do not hesitate to involve other significant staff members in developing an action plan for the student.

4. Keep the student's teacher(s) and the school administrator informed of what steps are being taken.

5. Call the local mental health center for consultation if needed. However, do not mention the student's name at this point.

6. If the student is under age 18, notify his or her parent or guardian and ask the parent to come in and sign a written release so that the local mental health agency can be contacted.

7. If the student is 18 years old or older and is her or his own guardian, discuss all plans with the student and obtain his or her permission to release information to others (by having the student sign a release of information form), including the student's parents and any other relatives with whom the student is living. If the threat of suicide is perceived to be imminent and the student is uncooperative, however, the student's signature is not needed: The parent should then be contacted immediately.

8. If the student's parent or guardian is willing to take the student to the local crisis evaluation site, offer to help in making the arrangements. Emphasize the need for immediate help if that is perceived to be the situation. Coordinate a plan of action with the local mental health center.

9. If the student's parent or guardian is unavailable and the threat of suicide is perceived to be imminent, seek the help of any significant other adult in the student's life, such as a relative, friend, minister, or doctor, and emphasize the need for immediate help. If any of these people are willing to help, offer to assist in making arrangements for transporting the student to the local crisis evaluation site. Coordinate this with the local mental health center.

10. If the student's parent or guardian or other significant adult is unwilling to help and the need for help is judged to be immediate, call the Children and Family Services hotline to report the neglect and to seek assistance. If necessary, call the local police for assistance in transporting the student to the local crisis evaluation site. Coordinate this with the local mental health center.

11. If the action specified in #9 or #10 is taken, a school staff member should accompany the student to the crisis evaluation site or meet the student there. If the student's parent or guardian does not arrive within a reasonable period of time, the staff member should contact the Children and Family Services hotline to report the neglect and to seek assistance.

12. Document the incident on a suicide threat record form.

School Security

In this section we provide practical tips for dealing with the following school security issues: weapons in the schools, bomb threats, visitors, procedures in place for dealing with crises in these areas, for they may occur in any school. To assist educators, we have included in this paper sample procedures that schools can adopt or adapt.

Weapons in Schools

J. Portner (1995) writes that a 1995 report issued by the U.S. Department of Justice stated that the number of teenagers arrested for weapons offenses—carrying or selling guns, explosives, or some types of knives—had more than doubled since 1985. According to the report, the increase in the number of juveniles arrested for gun possession reflected a larger trend of increased youth involvement in violent crimes.

Reports of student involvement in violent crime are all too common. Schools in cities and small towns, in rural and urban areas, have been affected. The following is just one of many such incidents. The Associated Press reported that on October 12, 1995, a suspended student walked through a back door at Blackville-Hilda High School in Blackville, South Carolina, armed with a revolver. He passed by two classrooms and entered a third, where he fired the gun at a math teacher. He then continued down the hall, where he confronted another math teacher, whom he shot to death.

With the increase in juvenile possession of weapons, schools must be prepared for incidents in which students confront school staff or other students with a weapon. Specific procedures must be in place. The following are our suggestions for what a teacher or other member of the school staff should do if he or she observes a student pointing a gun or other dangerous weapon at someone else in school.

1. Concentrate on staying calm. Instruct everyone not directly involved in the incident to leave the area. Another staff member should press an alarm button or immediately call the police from the nearest phone.

2. Stand a short distance from the student. Rather than directly facing the student, stand at an angle to the student's side. Use a nonconfrontational stance.

3. Focus on the student; avoid looking at the weapon.

4. Using a quiet and calm voice, attempt to negotiate with the student. Ask the student questions such as whether you can move back three steps. The more "yes"es you are able to get, the higher the chance that the student will not use the weapon. Further, the questioning will help you buy time until the police arrive. Again, the longer you can talk calmly to the student, the less likely it is that the student will use the weapon.

5. Do not attempt to disarm the student unless you believe that doing so is the *only* way to prevent the student from using the weapon.

6. When the police arrive, follow their directions.

It is illegal for a student to carry a gun, concealed or in the open, at school. If a teacher or other member of the school staff has reasonable cause to suspect that a student has a gun or other weapon in his or her possession at school, we recommend the following procedures.

1. Follow the school's search procedures. The search should be conducted by a team of school staff in an area that is away from other students but offers access to emergency exits, a phone, or both.

2. Should the staff conducting the search feel that the student is dangerous or threatening and in possible possession of a gun, the designated school officials should notify local police immediately.

3. Should a student suspected of having a concealed weapon refuse the search, the search team should explain to the student that, due to the perceived dangerousness of the situation, the police will be called if the student fails to comply with the staff search.

4. In the event that a weapon is confiscated during a search, school officials should notify the police and the student's parents. School officials should also call the police if a search reveals a questionable item (such as bullets) and request direction on how the school should proceed. Whenever a weapon is found, the law enforcement procedures for the illegal action should be invoked.

5. All searches should be documented by the individuals involved in the search. The student's behavior during the search, the reasonable cause for the search, the staff involvement, parent notification, and search results should be included in the documentation. In the case that a crime was committed, the documentation should be sent to the officer in charge of the case, to the local probation office, and to the assistant state's attorney.

6. In the case that a search reveals a student to be in possession of a knife, it is up to the school to determine whether the police should be involved. It is not a crime for a student to carry a pocketknife in school; a switchblade, however, is considered a weapon and its possession in school is illegal. We believe that it should be against school rules to carry *any* type of knife at school or at school events. We recommend that school staff confiscate any knife that is found and render consequences as specified in school policy.

Procedures for Handling Bomb Threats, Bombs Found, and Bomb Explosions in Schools

In any public institution, including schools, the possibility of a bomb threat always exists. In the author's small city (with a population of 20,000), the local police respond to several bomb threats every year. While it is true that the vast majority of bomb threats are false, they never should be ignored. A sound procedure for handling this type of threat is imperative.

In the Event of a Bomb Threat

In the event of a bomb threat at school, the following steps should be taken:

1. The school principal should immediately notify the local police and all necessary staff.

2. The police and the school principal should evaluate the seriousness of the threat based on the following:

   - Is there a sign of illegal entry into the school?
   - Has there been a report of missing chemicals from the Chemistry lab or elsewhere in the school?
   - Have other recent bomb threats proven to be hoaxes?
   - Is it a day that students may not want to be in school, such as the first day of spring?
   - Was there giggling in the background when the bomb threat call was made?
   - Has there been a recent pattern of student, parent, or staff unrest?
   - Which students have been reported absent on the day of the threat?

3. The police and school principal should conduct a search of the building.

In the Event That a Bomb Is Found

In the event that a bomb is found in the school, the following steps should be taken:

1. The area in which the bomb is found should be sealed off while the police remove the suspected device.

2. The school should be evacuated in stages starting with those rooms nearest the device.

3. School officials should instruct students and staff to reenter the building after being so advised by the police.

In the Event of a Bomb Explosion

In the event of a bomb explosion while staff or staff and students are in the school building, the following steps should be taken:

1. One of the alarm buttons to the police department should be pressed immediately, and the fire alarm should be activated.

2. If the phones in the school are still working, the fire department should be notified. If the phones are not working, the police should be asked to notify the fire department.

3. The building should be immediately evacuated and every effort should be taken to keep students calm. School officials should instruct students and staff to reenter the building only after being so advised by the police and the fire department.

4. School officials should develop a list of casualties.

5. School officials should notify the school attorney.

6. An information center, staffed by school officials, should be set up to handle all inquiries about injured persons and the status of the school.

7. If the decision is made to close the school for the rest of the day or longer, transportation should be arranged by school officials to get the students home.

8. School officials should fully document the incident.

Procedures for Handling School Visitors

Visitor control is perhaps one of the areas of school security that is most often overlooked. The authors have noticed that we are almost never challenged when we visit a school. Many schools simply ignore persons who are walking the hallways and have no procedure in place for visitor control. Schools are public-supported institutions and belong to the community. It is difficult to develop a mindset that the community should not necessarily be allowed free access to all school areas. The safety of children and staff must be balanced against the public expectation of free admittance to community schools. Visitor control is a means to accomplish this task.

The format we have used in the following sample is one that is common to many school handbooks.

Purpose: The school believes in maintaining a safe environment for students and staff at all times. To maintain safety and promote the orderly functioning of the educational environment, the school requires that all visitors adhere to the following procedures:

1. All visitors will use the administrative entrance to the building.
   1.1 Signs will be posted to indicate the appropriate entrance.

2. All visitors will check in with a secretary.
   2.1 Visitors will notify a secretary of their business with the school.
   2.2 Visitors will sign in and sign out on a visitor register.
   2.3 Visitors will wait in the designated visitor waiting area while the secretary notifies the staff of their arrival.

3. Visitors will be given a visitor badge for use on the day of their visit.
   3.1 The visitor is to wear the badge at all times while in the school.
   3.2 A visitor who is seen not wearing his or her badge will be asked to wear the badge or leave the school.

3.3 The visitor will return the badge to the secretary at the end of the visit.

4. Visitors will be escorted or directed to their destination by the secretary or school personnel.

5. All visits to the school, a classroom, or staff should be prearranged with school personnel.

   5.1 Visits during school hours should be for legitimate school business purposes.

   5.2 Classroom visits or observations should be prearranged with the classroom teacher, his or her supervisor, or another designated individual.

   5.3 Visitors who wish to monitor a classroom via an observation room must have permission from the teacher or his or her supervisor.

6. Students will be given an explanation of the school's expectations and procedures concerning visitors.

   6.1 At the beginning of the school year, teachers will explain the visitor procedures to their students.

   6.2 Students will be given directions (as specified herein) about what to do if they see a visitor in the school who is not wearing a visitor badge.

      a. Students will, calmly and quietly, immediately report the presence of the visitor to the nearest staff member.

      b. Students will not confront the visitor.

7. Staff will adhere to the following procedures with regard to school visitors.

   7.1 All staff will review the school's visitor procedures with their supervisors at the beginning of the school year.

   7.2 Staff will be aware of visitors and check to be sure that they are wearing their badges.

   7.3 In the event that a visitor is seen not wearing his or her visitor badge, the following procedures will be followed:

      a. Two to three staff members will, together, approach the visitor and ask him or her to walk with them to the visitor entrance, where they are to obtain a visitor badge and sign in.

      b. Should the visitor resist complying with the school procedures, one staff member should quietly leave the area to notify the school administrator and the police, if he or she feels that police involvement is needed. (That staff member will let the others know his or her intent by using a prearranged hand signal.)

      c. In the event that a visitor who resists complying with school rules is unruly or appears to be potentially dangerous, one staff member should immediately notify the police department for assistance. (Again, the staff member will use a prearranged hand signal to alert the other staff of his or her intent.) When talking to the police, the staff member will clearly state that the safety of the students may be at stake.

      d. The staff members who did not leave to notify the authorities should remain in the proximity of the visitor/intruder. The staff member who made the initial contact with the visitor/intruder should continue to talk to the intruder, if possible, to gain his or her compliance with the school procedures. The staff member who left to notify the authorities will, after doing so, alert all classroom teachers through a coded message over the intercom system to have everyone remain in the classrooms. (The code will be determined by staff at the beginning of the school year.) Teachers and staff in the classrooms will close and lock the classroom doors when this code is given.

e. Whenever a situation of visitor noncompliance arises, the staff members who intervened should, immediately after the incident, file a written summary of the incident with the school principal. A copy of the report should be placed in an appropriate file.

Procedures for Dealing With Hostage Situations in Schools

For the purposes of this discussion, we define a hostage situation as a situation in which one individual or a group of individuals prevents, through the use of verbal threats, intimidation, force, threats with weapons, or other means, another individual or group of individuals in a school from moving freely. In the event that an individual or group of individuals places students or staff in a hostage situation at school, we recommend that the following procedures be followed. The purpose of these procedures, as of all other procedures in this chapter, is to maintain the safety of all students and staff.

1. One entrance to the school will be designated as the official entrance into the building. A secretary will be stationed close to that entrance to check in visitors. All visitors shall check in with the secretary, who will explain the school procedures for visitors. All entrances other than the official entrance shall be locked, so that no one may enter through them during the school day.

2. An emergency alarm system shall be established whereby alarm buttons, directly connected to the local police station, will be strategically placed in the school. The alarms are to be used only in the following situations: a hostage situation, a situation in which an individual is brandishing a weapon with the intent to harm, and other situations that present clear and imminent danger to students, staff, or both, that cannot be managed without outside assistance. The alarm buttons shall be pressed only by school-designated officials.

3. A hand signal, which shall be determined by staff at the beginning of the school year, shall be used to indicate the need for someone to press an emergency alarm button. The signal shall also be used to indicate the need for further action, such as clearing the building.

4. In the event of a hostage situation in which a weapon is involved, all students and staff who are not hostages will be evacuated, to the preestablished location

including everyone in the administrative wing. The evacuation procedure will be the same as that established for fire drills with the exception that notification of the evacuation will be made by word of mouth rather than by audible alarm. The use of an alarm could escalate the hostage situation.

Students and staff who are evacuating will reassemble at a preestablished meeting area some distance from the school building. They will be directed to stay away from any window area or area visible to the hostage taker.

Teachers will be in charge of their students and will be responsible for keeping their classes occupied and calm.

Law enforcement officials will assist in transporting students to the preestablished location.

5. The staff member(s) (administrator or designee) directly dealing with the hostage situation should handle it in the following manner:

   a. Remain calm. (Bear in mind that as long as everyone is alive, your efforts are working.) Make every effort to keep everyone involved in the situation calm.

   b. Refrain from making any deals with the hostage taker. Law enforcement officials should be the only individuals to negotiate with a hostage taker.

   c. In the event that both students and staff are taken hostage, suggest that the hostage taker release the students.

   d. Cooperate with the hostage taker.

   e. Avoid trying to negotiate with the hostage taker other than to suggest the release of students.

   f. Avoid questioning any law enforcement tactics or actions while students or staff are being held hostage.

   g. Make every effort to keep the hostages from questioning law enforcement tactics.

   h. Remain patient. Expect that resolving the hostage situation will take time.

   i. Do not be alarmed if power is disconnected, food is not sent, or deadlines are missed. Such occurrences are not unusual in a hostage situation.

   j. Realize that experts are working hard to effect the hostage release. All of their tactics and actions, even those that may appear to be unrelated to the hostage release, do have that purpose.

   k. Know that law enforcement officials will act immediately if a violent act occurs. Should such an act occur, take cover, get away, and cooperate with any police command.

   l. In the aftermath of a hostage situation, avoid discussing the situation until law enforcement officials have completely finished their investigation.

   m. Be aware that bonding and sympathizing syndromes may occur in a hostage situation.

   n. Remember to respect the confidentiality of students and possible items of evidentiary value if you are interviewed by the media.

6. All staff should receive in-service training at the beginning of each school year on the procedures and precautions set forth herein. During that training, the warning hand signal discussed previously shall be established. (We have used the following hand signal: The signaler puts one hand behind his or her back or out to the side and discretely extends one finger if the situation is manageable and no assistance is needed. If the situation is questionable and the signaler feels that he or she may need help, two fingers are extended to request assistance. If the signaler considers the situation dangerous, he or she extends three fingers to signal that another staff member should press the alarm button.)

References

Associated press. (1995, October 13). Teacher, student killed in high school shooting. *Jacksonville (Illinois) Journal-Courier,* p. 7.

Gleck, E. (1996, July 22). Suicide's shadow. *Newsweek,* pp. 40–42.

Guetzloe, E. (1989). *Youth suicide: What the educator should know.* Reston, VA: Council for Exceptional Children.

Jay, B. (1989). Managing a crisis in the school—tips for principals. *National Association of Secondary School Principals Bulletin, 73*(513), 14, 16–18.

Liotta, A. (1996). *When students grieve: A guide to bereavement in the schools.* Horsham, PA: LRP Publications.

Portner, J. (1995, November 22). Juvenile weapons offenses double in decade, report says. *Education Week,* p. 3.

St. John, W. (1986, October). How to develop an effective school communications crisis plan. *National Association of Secondary School Principals: Tips for Principals.* An occasional publication of the National Association of Secondary School Principals, 1904 Association Drive, Reston, Virginia 22091, 1–2.

Watson, R., Poda, J., Miller, C., Rice, E., & West, G. (1990). *Containing crisis: A guide to managing school emergencies.* Bloomington, IN: National Educational Service.

School Crisis Intervention: Building Effective Crisis Management Teams

Alan Basham, Valerie E. Appleton, and Cass Dykeman

$\mathcal{T}$his chapter is intended to show the school counselor, social worker, psychologist, or administrator how to build an effective crisis management team. The chapter begins with a discussion of the dual nature of crisis and the need to evaluate the traumatic impact of crises on students and staff. A model for designing a school-based crisis program is then presented that includes the multilevel assessment of trauma and the components of psychological first aid. Finally, implementation issues and caring for staff are considered. Exercises designed to debrief the crisis team and to increase the crisis team's sensitivity to burnout conclude the chapter.

Defining a Crisis

Every school needs to have a crisis intervention plan in place. Schools that do not develop a written plan that articulates the roles of staff, teachers, and administrators are reactive, and their efforts in the event of a crisis can increase, rather than decrease, the impact of trauma. Furthermore, with the number of crisis events that impact students' lives continuing to grow, even schools that have a written plan in place must find new ways of managing crisis situations (Kline, Schonfeld, & Lichtenstein, 1995).

The experience of crisis is extremely personal. What is a crisis for one person will not be a crisis for another. Indeed, crisis has a dual nature, as indicated by the two Chinese characters that represent the word Weiji, or "crisis," which mean danger and opportunity (Aguilera & Messick, 1986). On the one hand, crises pose terrible threats to continuity, equilibrium, and safety and may result in serious impacts such as suicide, trauma, and post-traumatic stress disorder. On the other hand, crises may also provide an opportunity for change in life, provoking the tension needed to seek new solutions and resources. It is useful to discuss the dual nature of crisis when preparing and debriefing a crisis team. It is also critical to evaluate the traumatic impact of the crisis that has occurred on the students and staff.

Assessing Traumatic Impact

Crises faced in schools range from those that are more personal, such as the death of a loved one, to those that affect the broader community, such as school-based violence.

Terr (1991), who studied the impact of violence on children, including those who were kidnapped and buried in a school bus in the Chowchilla crisis, found it helpful to discriminate between two levels, or types, of trauma. Type I trauma results from an unexpected traumatic event in an otherwise normal life. Such events include violence, death, illness, and natural or man-made disasters. Individuals who experience Type I trauma are generally responsive to counseling and other efforts to contain the impact of the crisis. Personality changes are not expected with this type of trauma, although post-traumatic stress disorder can result if the crisis is severe. Post-traumatic stress disorder symptoms include intrusive thoughts, psychic numbing, hyper-vigilance, exaggerated startle response, fear of separation from parents, regressive behaviors (thumb sucking, enuresis), and night terrors.

Type II traumas result from the anticipated, prolonged, or repeated experience of pain or threat. Events causing Type II trauma include abuse, poverty, war, and other environmental violence. The impact of Type II trauma is severe and includes delayed development and central nervous system impairment, personality dysfunction (antisocial behavior, dissociative disorder), self-abuse, victimization cycles, and provocative behaviors. Stress, including that which comes with a crisis, amplifies these symptoms. Children and adults who have experienced chronic trauma require particular attention and evaluation both during and after a crisis. Further, they require highly specialized and professional interventions for recovery.

Today, most people are in agreement with Terr (1991) that it is important to discriminate the type of trauma the students and staff may be experiencing in the face of a crisis. Having determined the type of trauma, the crisis management team can make appropriate referrals for mental and physical services.

Developing a Crisis Program

When developing a crisis program for a school, it is important to evaluate what resources are already available and what roles are expected of the personnel. The following three questions originally posed by Slaikeu (1990) provide a framework for evaluating the responsiveness of a school to crisis:

> Is the provision of crisis services part of the school policy? For example, are specific crisis management activities written into the job descriptions of teachers, administrators, counselors, and support personnel?

> Are physical resources (space, orientation) available for offering both psychological first aid (the first intervention offered by those closest to the event) and crisis therapy (the second-order intervention offered by trained counselors and therapists) to students when needed?

> Are appropriate school personnel trained in the techniques of psychological first aid and crisis therapy?

Once you have completed your initial evaluation, the next step is to clarify the responsibilities for each member of the crisis team.

Roles and Expectations of Crisis Team Members

Crisis Decision Team

The Crisis Decision Team is the first to meet in response to a crisis event. This team should be composed of a small group of individuals who represent administration (principal and assistant principal), social services (counselors, social workers, and psychologists), and management (office manager, secretaries, and head custodian). The location for Crisis Decision Team meetings should be specified in advance and identified for all members of the team. The assistant principal's office is a good choice, leaving the principal's office free for linking with the outside world. It is important that this team has a listing of telephone numbers for emergency services, the police, the fire department, district security, communications (the media), student services, the School Superintendent's Office, and the local child protective services agency.

The Principal

The role of the principal in the event of a crisis is that of liaison between any outside sources, including the media, parents, emergency services, and other community members, and the school. It is critical that all information and needs are expressed to one consistent figure of authority who can respond for the school and also help to calm the crisis situation. In the event that the principal is not available, a second in command must be designated to take over this function.

Crisis Security Team

The Crisis Security Team is composed of teachers, social workers, psychologists, and counselors who are assigned pre-planned positions in the school and serve (a) to assist anyone not aware of the crisis or failing to respond to the instructions to move to the nearest room or space available (e.g., the auditorium) and (b) to stay in contact with and assist the Crisis Decision Team by providing them with current information regarding the crisis from their vantage point. In this way the Crisis Decision Team can confirm and define the situation and contact the appropriate authorities when necessary.

Support Staff

Non-classified staff such as food preparation and serving staff, bus drivers, and maintenance personnel can, as members of the Crisis Security Team, provide tremendous help during school-based emergencies. They know the grounds and services and are often on friendly terms with the students and teachers. Once the crisis is under control, their participation is also critical to help normalize school life.

The Crisis Response Plan

When developing a school-based crisis response plan, it is helpful to include a measurement guide that can be used to specify different levels of severity. With such a guide in place, all personnel will know how to gauge the seriousness of the situation. One method is to qualify the crisis according to three code levels: Code I, Code II, and Code III. An example of each code level and a corresponding plan for action follow.

Code I

Code I crises are described as life-threatening emergencies that require specific action to maintain the safety of the students and staff. They include situations in which imminent physical danger exists, such as fire, natural disaster, and dangerous persons or weapons. The steps for a Code I crisis are as follows:

1. Signal the crisis. All members of the crisis team move to their preassigned positions (e.g., next to the fire alarm).

2. Implement classroom security (all students are to remain seated and quiet or in the event of fire, they are to evacuate the building in an orderly fashion).

3. For crisis other than fire, secure the building (lock doors, close blinds, put paper on windows).

4. Report need for medical assistance or perceived imminent threat (dangerous person, etc.) by intercom, but use the intercom for these purposes only. Then report your name, location, and a brief description of the problem to the Crisis Decision Team.

5. Await the "all clear" signal (e.g., the bell rung three times followed by an announcement from the principal). A memo is then read to the students and staff clarifying the event and its outcome.

6. Debrief the crisis response staff as soon as the situation is under control. At this time, evaluate the plan for its effectiveness. This important part of the crisis resolution helps the teams to improve their crisis response.

Code II

Code II crises are serious situations that require conflict resolution and specific action to ensure the safety of staff and students. They include traumas students bring to school (e.g., deaths, child abuse), intrusions by dangerous or upset people, threats to the school facility (smoke, chemical spills), and threats of violence made against persons in the school. The principal mobilizes the Crisis Decision Team to implement a plan for action. When warranted, the team designates a member to contact the appropriate emergency or community service agencies. When the safety of students and staff is ensured, disciplinary actions may be implemented, the team is debriefed, and the incident plan is reviewed for effectiveness.

Code III

Code III crises are serious situations of tragedy or loss for the students, staff, and community that occur away from the school. Although they may require action by the school, the crisis itself does not interrupt regularly scheduled teaching activities. These crises include suicide, police-related incidents, and other human-made or natural disasters. The principal obtains the information from the police and prepares a written statement containing the facts about the incident for the school staff and outside community (including media and parents). An early morning meeting serves to brief the entire staff before school starts.

To inform students, an announcement is made at the appropriate time in a school assembly, over the intercom, or by each classroom teacher. Counseling for students should be available in those situations where it is warranted.

Keeping the Story Straight

With any type of crisis, once the response teams are operating within their assigned roles and tasks, an important next step is to control the rumor mill. To keep rumors from flying, the facts that are relayed must be accurate and consistent. Furthermore, only one person in authority should deliver them to the staff, parents, community, and media. As suggested, the principal is typically the appropriate person for this job.

Teachers can help to create a sense of continuity in the school process when crises occur. They can read a statement written by the principal to their students, conduct a period of silence when appropriate, or integrate discussion in their lessons that honors tragedy and/or loss. Another important task of teachers is to inform the students that counselors, social workers, and psychologists are available at specific times and locations (e.g., in the gym all day or in their offices) for students who need support. Not only teachers but the entire school staff should be called on to monitor students' traumatic reactions. Particularly important to monitor are those students and staff who exhibit Type II trauma and have histories of tragedy and loss.

The attitude of the staff should be one of active concern without letting the situation become melodramatic. It is better to discuss the crisis with students in classrooms, small groups, or one-on-one counseling sessions than in a large assembly, where students are more likely to overreact.

Implementation Issues

Training sessions with the whole staff are an important part of preparing for potential crises. A crisis team made up of staff who have been trained in the elementary levels of crisis intervention will be more effective than untrained staff in the face of real events. The training should include simple methods for assessing the impact of the crisis and for providing immediate care.

Assessing Impact

Slaikeu (1990) developed an effective tool called BASIC that crisis teams can use to assess the levels of impact of a crisis situation and determine who is in the most critical need of care. The letters of the acronym stand for symptoms that may be seen following a crisis. These symptoms, and examples of typical characteristics of each, are as follows:

B — Behavioral (poor appetite, sleeplessness, forgetfulness)
A — Affective (anxiety, sadness, anger, depression, numbness)
S — Somatic (sleep problems, headaches, stomachaches, fatigue)
I — Interpersonal (isolation, avoids asking for help, social conflicts)
C — Cognitive (catastrophizing, obsessive ruminations, self-blame).

A quick way to assess the symptoms in a student or staff member is to count their frequency, duration, and severity. Seen on a continuum ranging from 1 to 10, the most frequent, long-lasting, and severe symptoms would rank as 10. The most infrequent, brief, and minimal symptoms would rank as 1.

BASIC can also be used to assess potential lethality in students. In addition to using this model, it is important to consider the individual's traumatic history, lethality of plan, previous attempts to harm, levels of support and coping (particularly isolation), and the nature of the crisis. Threats made by a person to harm herself or another person indicate a high level of lethality. By law, any persons who could be in danger must be informed. Further, support from trained professionals (counselors, social workers, police, emergency room team) is critical.

A team trained in BASIC will have the advantage of everyone using the same language when reporting the impact of crises. Further, the use of an assessment model such as BASIC is a critical part of the initial crisis intervention or "psychological first aid" (Slaikeu, 1990, page 108).

Psychological First Aid

Both professionals and lay persons in the school setting should receive training in psychological first aid. The main goals of psychological first aid are to help maintain a sense of control during a crisis event, assess needs, give support, reduce lethality, and link needy persons to helping resources. Getting the hurt or disorientated persons help is the critical task of this first-level intervention. A simple sequence you can use for psychological first aid could be as follows:

1. Make psychological contact with the person you are assessing by inviting her to talk. Listen with empathy to the feelings and facts relayed, summarize what you have heard, and communicate concern. The goal is to bring calm control to the situation.

2. Explore functioning strengths and weaknesses with the BASIC assessment tool.

3. Examine possible solutions by discussing what has already been done and what else the person can do. Create a menu of options with the person about new behaviors, redefinition of the problem, and resources for outside help.

4. Assist the person in taking action. A facilitative stance is useful when the potential for reactive self-harm is low and the person is capable of acting on his own behalf. A directive stance is essential if the lethality is high and the person is not capable of acting on her own.

5. Follow up on the plan created with the person or refer the person for psychological and social services.

Debriefing the Team

It is critical to debrief the team once the incident is over. After the team has contacted parents of the students involved or injured, it is important for the principal to debrief the staff members and for teachers to debrief their classes. Additionally, the principal should write a memo to all staff and read it to them before the end of the day clarifying the crisis events and outcome. The principal also should prepare a statement for media and parents. Finally, as soon as possible, you should hold an emergency all-personnel meeting at which you evaluate the crisis resolution.

Debriefing the team and others provides chances to review what did and did not work. Team action such as designing new assignments as needed will empower the team and can transform danger into opportunity. Exercise 16.1 provides a structured way to debrief a team after a crisis.

Caring for Staff

A frequently overlooked component of the debriefing process is to take time to care for the crisis team and school staff. While the team members are helping others, they may postpone their own reactions to the crisis. Providing an opportunity for team members to express personal responses will give the team much needed support. Additionally, it will bring to light team members' concerns that they may not be able to carry out their assigned roles and tasks.

Among the highest sources of burnout in service professionals is fear of expressing fatigue, disillusionment, and emotional burdens. Anticipating burnout and openly discussing feelings leading toward it will prevent needless suffering. A caring attitude toward the team includes active support of interpersonal honesty. Such support will increase both trust and longevity among the team members. Conducting a workshop that examines personal values will help to mitigate the stress inherent in crisis work. Exercise 16.2 provides a method for examining burnout within a crisis team.

Conclusion

Schools are increasingly demanding places to work. The level of violence is significant and has the potential for creating a climate of fear in the school. Carefully designed crisis teams and plans will promote a better sense of preparedness throughout the school. Counselors, psychologists, and social workers are essential leaders in the development, implementation, and evaluation of such crisis teams and plans.

References

Auguilera, D. C., & Messick, J. M. (1986). *Crisis intervention: Theory and methodology.* St. Louis, MO: C. V. Mosby.

Kline, M., Schonfeld, D. J., & Lichtenstein, R. (1995). Benefits and challenges of school based crisis response teams. *Journal of School Health, 65,* 245–249.

Slaikeu, K. (1990). *Crisis intervention: A handbook for practice and research* (2nd ed.). Boston: Allyn & Bacon.

Terr, L. C. (1991). Childhood traumas: An outline and overview. *American Journal of Psychiatry, 148,* 10–20.

EXERCISE 16.1
Debriefing a Team—Listening to Stories

Theme: Debriefing the team after a crisis

Materials: Paper and pen for each member
             Masking tape
             Felt-tip pens
             18" × 24" paper, one per person

Steps: (Allow about 2½ hours for this exercise)

1. **Gather the Team** (10 minutes)
   Hold an emergency meeting of the entire team as soon as the crisis is under control. Report the incidents, facts, and outcome of the crisis briefly to ensure that everyone knows the accurate story of what happened. Then move into the story-exchange process (Step 2). Note that a further review of team members' roles and actions can be conducted after everyone has had a chance to express their stories in dyads.

2. **Story Exchanges** (50 minutes)
   a. Break the group up into dyads. Have everyone write down the acronym BASIC on a sheet of 18" 3 24" paper. Define the acronym if necessary.
   b. Have the partners decide who will be the interviewer and interviewee for the first part of the story exchanges. Explain that they will switch roles after 15 minutes.
   c. Instruct the interviewers to listen to their partners' stories of what they experienced during the crisis. State that the attitude of the interviewer should be one of support, empathy, and caring. Have the interviewers use BASIC to guide the interviews, recording relevant information next to each of the five components. It is important that the person telling the story not have to write while talking.
   d. After both partners have been interviewed, have them review the experience of telling the stories. Be prepared for the fact that some of these stories will evoke emotions. It is also important for the interviewers to receive feedback about their active listening skills.

3. **Large-Group Sharing** (20 minutes)
   a. Encourage comments from the whole group about how this crisis intervention process went.
   b. Put two large pieces of paper on the wall. Write "Dangers" at the top of one and "Opportunities" at the top of the other. Record group contributions on the papers according to where they think they belong.

4. **Review of Roles and Actions** (50 minutes)
   (Depending on time and the inclination of the group, this part of the exercise may be passed to a future meeting. If that is the case, proceed to closure.) To review team members' roles and actions, have two or three dyads combine to form groups of 4–6 people. Instruct these groups to develop a list, in two columns, of what did and did not work from their perspectives. Have them make recommendations for changes to the plan.

5. **Closure** (15 minutes)
   a. Acknowledge the efforts of the team members in controlling the situation.
   b. Develop a list of new, or action, items to be reviewed to determine how the situation could be handled next time. These items may also serve as the agenda for a subsequent meeting.

End Goals of This Exercise

1. To provide an opportunity for all team members to debrief the experience of the crisis.
2. To provide an opportunity for team members to practice psychological first aid.
3. To develop an agenda for assessing the crisis response plan.

EXERCISE 16.2
Expressive Arts Collage—Weiji and Burnout

Theme: Examining the danger and opportunity of burnout in the professional crisis.

Materials: (For a team of 20 people)
Pens and sheets of lined 8½" × 11" paper
   (20 of each)
18" × 24" newsprint or white paper (20 sheets)
White glue
Scissors (10–20 pairs)
Collage materials: magazines, tissue and
   origami paper, crafts supplies
   (feathers, ribbons,glitter, small pieces of fabric)
Masking tape

Steps: (Allow about 2 hours for this exercise)

1. **Role and Values Clarification** (10 minutes). Distribute the pens and lined paper. Instruct the team members to divide their paper into two vertical columns. Explain that in one column they should write names they are called for their loving self, and in the other column they should write names they are called for their working self. For example, they might write friend, teacher, mom, "slow-poke," and so forth. Allow everyone to work independently and with no guidance.
2. **Discussion** (20 minutes). Break the team into dyads. Have the partners discuss their lists and their response to having to divide their roles while making the list.
3. **Art Process** (20–25 minutes)
   a. Instruct each team member to create a collage of his or her love and work selves on the larger paper. Encourage an exploration of the materials provided. Promote a feeling of exploration by asking team members to place materials and create symbols in ways that represent the different aspects of their love and work identities.
   b. If members complete their collages early, prompt them to jot down notes in a journal for future reference.
   c. After 20 minutes call stop and have everyone clean up.
4. **Post-Art Discussion** (20–30 minutes)
   a. Prompt the team to share about the collage-making process in their dyads (10 minutes). Then bring the larger group back together for discussion.
   b. Have the larger group share their collages and process. As they do so, write down on a large piece of paper with a felt-tip pen the insights they have gained. Some points for discussion include:
      • The juxtapositions of the love and work selves. How do they overlap or how are they separated on the paper?
      • Do individuals feel these roles contribute to or detract from their levels of stress? How do the team members relax and find renewal?
5. **Closure.** End the discussion by pointing out the concept of Weiji. Examine what roles may be dangerous and what roles provide opportunity for the team members. Develop a list of the methods the team uses for mediating stress and burnout.

End Goals of This Exercise

1. To create an opportunity for team members to examine their personal and collective values around love and work.
2. To increase the sensitivity of the team to burnout.

Peacemakers: Teaching Students to Resolve Their Own and Schoolmates' Conflicts

David W. Johnson and Roger T. Johnson

"Joshua was chasing Octavia. He pushed her down and she kicked him."

"Jane was going to beat up Joan after school. They were spitting in each other's face and calling each other names."

"Tom shoved Cameron up against the lockers and threatened him. Cameron said he's going to bring a knife to school tomorrow to get even."

Schools are filled with conflicts. Considerable instructional, administrative, and learning efforts are lost because students and faculty often manage their conflicts poorly. The frequency and severity of conflicts seem to be increasing, and for the first time, the category "fighting, violence, and gangs" is tied with "lack of discipline" for the number-one problem confronting local public schools (Elam, Rose, & Gallup, 1994). Conflicts will not go away. Students are clearly fascinated by and drawn to conflicts. They like to start them, watch them, hear about them, and discuss them. To make schools orderly and peaceful places in which high quality education can take place, conflicts must be managed constructively without physical or verbal violence. To do so, students must be taught to be peacemakers.

How Conflicts Can Be of Value

A number of points can help clarify the value of conflicts. *First*, conflicts are inevitable. You might as well try to stop the earth from turning on its axis as to try to eliminate conflicts from your life. No matter what you do, conflicts arise. *Second*, conflicts are desirable if they are managed constructively. *Conflicts occur whenever people have goals they care about and are involved in relationships they value.* The absence of conflict often signals a dysfunctional situation wherein neither the goals nor the relationship is valued. Conflict often signals a commitment to the goals and the relationship. This commitment fuels an engagement in conflict that can lead to either constructive or destructive outcomes. On the destructive side, conflicts can (a) create anger, hostility, lasting animosity, and even violence, (b) result in pain and sadness, and (c) end in divorce, lawsuits, and war. There is nothing pretty about a conflict gone wrong. On the positive side, conflicts are constructive when (a) all disputants are satisfied with the outcome (the agreement maximizes joint benefits and allows all participants to achieve their goals and, therefore, everyone goes away satisfied and pleased), (b) the relationship between the disputants is strengthened and improved (disputants are better able to work together and have more respect, trust, and liking for each other), and (c) disputants are able to resolve future conflicts constructively.

Besides these direct outcomes, conflicts have value in a number of other ways. Conflicts do the following:

1. *Focus attention on problems that have to be solved.* Conflicts energize and motivate us to solve our problems.

2. *Clarify who you are and what your values are.* Through conflicts, your identity is developed.

3. *Clarify how you need to change.* Conflicts clarify and highlight patterns of behavior that are dysfunctional.

4. *Help you understand who the other person is and what his or her values are.* Conflicts clarify the identity of your friends and acquaintances.

5. *Strengthen relationships by increasing your confidence that the two of you can resolve your disagreements.* Every time a serious conflict is resolved constructively, the relationship becomes less fragile and more able to withstand crises and problems.

6. *Keep the relationship clear of irritations and resentments so positive feelings can be experienced fully.* A good conflict may do a lot to resolve the small tensions of interacting with others.

7. *Release emotions (such as anger, anxiety, insecurity, and sadness) that, if kept inside, make us mentally sick.* A conflict a day keeps depression away!

8. *Clarify what you care about, are committed to, and value.* You only fight over wants and goals you value. And you fight much more frequently and intensely with people you value and care about. The more committed you are to your goals, and the more committed you are to the other person, the more frequent and intense are the conflicts.

9. *Add fun, enjoyment, excitement, and variety to your life.* Being in a conflict reduces boredom, gives you new goals, motivates you to take action, and stimulates interest. Life would be incredibly boring in the absence of conflict.

Third, what determines whether a conflict is constructive or destructive are the procedures taken to manage the conflict. To manage conflicts with skill, finesse, and grace, you need the following:

1. An understanding of the procedures for managing conflicts constructively. Further, everyone involved must understand and use the same procedures. Different individuals often have quite different ideas about how to manage conflicts. Some rely on physical dominance through threats and violence. Others use verbal attack, the cold shoulder, giving in, or getting even. When two individuals involved in a conflict are using different procedures, chaos results. If conflicts are to be managed constructively, everyone has to use the same procedures to resolve them. Because the procedures for resolving conflicts constructively are *not* learned in most families or from television, movies, or novels, students must learn them at school.

2. The opportunity to practice, practice, practice the procedures to gain real skill and expertise in their use. Resolving conflicts takes great skill and considerable practice. Schools need to emphasize overlearning of the conflict resolution procedures by having students practice the procedures again and again.

3. Norms and values to encourage and support use of the procedures. Just because people know how to manage conflicts constructively does not mean that they will do so. As long as school norms emphasize working alone and valuing "winners," students will "go for the win" in a conflict rather than by trying to solve the problem.

Based on these points (conflicts are inevitable, a sign of commitment, and potentially constructive), schools are advised to welcome and face conflicts rather than to avoid and repress conflicts. To do so, students need to learn how to be peacemakers.

Teaching Students to Be Peacemakers Program

We began the *Teaching Students to Be Peacemakers Program* in the 1960s. It originated from the following:

1. Our research on integrative negotiations (Johnson, 1967), perspective taking in conflict situations (Johnson, 1967, 1971a), conflict resolution in the school (Johnson, 1970, 1971b; Johnson, Johnson, & Johnson, 1976), communication in conflict situations (Johnson, 1974), and constructive conflict (Johnson, 1970; Johnson & Johnson, 1979).

2. Our development of social interdependence theory (Deutsch, 1949; Lewin, 1951; Johnson, 1970; Johnson & Johnson, 1989; Watson & Johnson, 1972).

3. Our training of elementary, junior-high, high-school and college students and adults in how to manage conflicts constructively (Johnson, 1970, 1972/1993, 1978/1991, 1983; Johnson & Johnson, 1975/1994a). Besides regular students,

teachers, and administrators, we taught delinquents, runaways, drug-abusers, and married couples in therapy how to manage their conflicts more constructively.

The Teaching Students to Be Peacemakers Program is a 12-year spiral program in which students learn increasingly sophisticated negotiation and mediation procedures (Johnson & Johnson, 1995b, 1995c). *It focuses on teaching all students in a school to be peacemakers.* We have implemented the peacemaker program in schools throughout North America, Europe, and several countries in Asia, Central and South America, the Middle East, and Africa.

The Teaching Students to Be Peacemakers Program has six steps.

1. *Create a cooperative context.* Considerable evidence and practical experience demonstrate that when individuals are in competition, they will strive for a "win" in conflicts and not try to solve the problem. A problem-solving approach requires the disputants to recognize their long-term interdependence and the need to maintain effective working relationships with each other—conditions that exist only in a cooperative context.

2. *Teach students to recognize when a conflict is and is not occurring.* Many students see conflicts as always involving anger, hostility, and violence and do not recognize conflicts as such when they lead to laughter, insight, learning, and problem solving.

3. *Teach students a concrete and specific procedure for negotiating agreements.* Everyone involved can thus achieve their goals while maintaining or even improving the quality of their relationship. Telling students to "be nice" or "talk it out," or "solve your problem" is not enough.

4. *Teach students to use a concrete and specific mediation procedure.* Give them enough practice in using this procedure to develop some expertise. If students are to mediate their schoolmates' conflicts, they must know how to do so. This initial training of the nature of conflict and how to negotiate and mediate usually consists of approximately 30 half-hour lessons.

5. *Implement the peer mediation program.* Working in pairs, at first, mediators are made available to help schoolmates negotiate more effectively. The mediator's role is rotated so each student is a mediator.

6. *Continue the training in negotiation and mediation procedures weekly throughout first through twelfth grades* to refine and upgrade students' skills. To become competent in resolving conflicts takes years and years. Any thought that a few hours of training is enough to ensure constructive conflict management is terribly misguided.

Each of these steps will be discussed in more detail in the following pages.

Creating a Cooperative Context

In beginning a conflict resolution and peer mediation program, we have to focus on the total school environment and create an awareness of students' interdependence and interaction. A conflict resolution program should seek to do more than change individual behavior. Instead, it should transform the total school environment into a learning community in which students live by a credo of nonviolence and problem solving. In addition, students need to recognize that they manage conflicts in long-term, ongoing relationships in a different way than they do in ad hoc, one-time, temporary relationships. In ongoing, long-term relationships, the future of the relationship has to be taken into account along with the interests of each disputant. Schools involve long-term, ongoing, interdependent relationships and, therefore, conflicts should be managed accordingly.

If conflicts are to be managed constructively, they must occur in a cooperative, not a competitive, context. Attempting to teach students to manage conflicts constructively makes little sense if the school is structured so students are pitted against each other in competition for scarce rewards (such as teacher attention and grades of "A") and students have to defeat each other to get what they want. In competition, rewards are restricted to the few who perform the best (Johnson & Johnson, 1989). Competitors typically have a short-term time orientation and focus all their energies on winning with little or no paid to the long-term interest in maintaining good relationships. Competitors tend to avoid communicating with each other, misperceive each other's position and motivations, be suspicious of each other, deny the legitimacy of others' needs and feelings, and see the situation only from their own perspective.

For conflicts to be resolved constructively, a cooperative context must be established. A cooperative context entails setting mutual goals that all participants are committed to achieving (Deutsch, 1973; Johnson & Johnson, 1989). Cooperators tend to seek outcomes that are beneficial to everyone involved. Cooperators typically have a long-term time orientation and focus their energies both on achieving goals and on maintaining good working relationships with others. Communication is apt to be frequent, complete, and accurate, with each person interested in informing the other as well as being informed. Cooperators are more likely to perceive other participants' positions and motivations accurately. Because they tend to trust and like each other, they usually are willing to respond helpfully to each other's wants, needs, and requests. Cooperators tend to recognize the legitimacy of each other's interests and search for a solution that accommodates the needs of both sides. Conflicts are more likely to be defined as mutual problems to be solved in ways that benefit everyone involved.

A cooperative context is established most easily by structuring the majority of learning situations cooperatively (Johnson & Johnson, 1989; Johnson, Johnson, & Holubec, 1993). Students should spend most of the day working together in cooperative learning groups so their ongoing interdependence and need for future interaction are clear. Hundreds of studies indicate that cooperative learning, compared to competitive and individualistic learning, tends to promote greater effort to achieve (which includes retention, higher-level reasoning, process gain, intrinsic motivation, achievement motivation, transfer), more positive relationships among students (including students who are heterogeneous in terms of ethnicity, gender, culture, and achievement as well as academic and personal social support), and greater psychological adjustment (encompassing psychological health, self-esteem, and social competence) (Johnson & Johnson, 1989). Because cooperative learning has considerable benefits, most teachers should welcome the opportunity to create a cooperative context that will enhance the success of conflict resolution programs.

When conflict resolution and peer mediation programs are implemented in the existing competitive/individualistic context of schools, their effectiveness can be compromised severely (Johnson & Johnson, 1975/1994b, 1995c). When the context and the procedures used to manage the conflict are congruent (an integrative procedure used in a cooperative context or a distributive procedure used in a competitive context), conflicts tend to be managed constructively. When the context and the conflict resolution procedures are incongruent (an integrative procedure used in a competitive context or a distributive procedure used in a cooperative context), destructive outcomes tend to result. To teach students how to seek solutions to problems rather than to strive for a "win," educators must create a cooperative context in the classroom and school.

Once a cooperative context has been established, students may be taught directly to recognize conflicts when they occur. Then they are able to learn the procedures and skills required to manage conflicts constructively.

Teaching Students What Is and Is Not a Conflict

Most of the diverse conflict resolution programs in schools are either cadre or total student body programs. In the *cadre approach*, a few students are trained to serve as peer mediators for the entire school. In the *total student body approach*, every student learns how to manage conflicts constructively by negotiating agreements and mediating schoolmates' conflicts. The responsibility for peer mediation is rotated throughout the entire student body (or class) so every student gains experience as a mediator. The greater number of students trained in how to negotiate and mediate, the greater is the number of conflicts that may be managed constructively in the school.

Whether training a cadre or an entire class or student body, teaching students what is and is not a conflict is an important early step in conflict management training. Students generally have a *negativity bias*, in which they tend to view conflicts as involving anger and violence and, therefore, tend to overestimate the frequency of conflicts involving anger and violence and underestimate the incidents of actual conflicts. The most common types of conflicts in schools are verbal harassments (name-calling, insults), verbal arguments, rumors and gossip, physical fights, and dating/relationship issues. Although physical and verbal aggression may be more frequent in urban than in suburban schools, it almost never involves serious altercations or violations of law. The first part of the Teaching Students to be Peacemakers Program, therefore, is to teach students what is and is not a conflict so they can become aware of (a) how they manage their conflicts and (b) how to manage conflicts constructively. Once students understand what is and is not a conflict, they are taught how to negotiate constructive resolutions to conflicts and how to mediate the conflicts of their peers.

Teaching Students to Negotiate

The best way I know how to defeat an enemy is to make him a friend.

(Abraham Lincoln)

The heart of conflict resolution training is teaching students how to negotiate constructive resolutions to their conflicts. *All* students in all schools need to learn how to negotiate (and mediate). *Negotiation* is a process by which people try to work out a settlement when they (a) have both shared and opposing interests and (b) want to come to an agreement (Johnson & Johnson, 1994). The two types of negotiations are *distributive* or "win-lose" (in which one person benefits only if the opponent agrees to make a concession) and *integrative* or problem solving (in which disputants work together to create an agreement that benefits everyone involved). Only in very limited conflicts involving ad hoc, one-time relationships are win-lose negotiations appropriate. In ongoing relationships that have a future as well as a present, an integrative approach to negotiations is the only constructive alternative. The steps in using problem-solving negotiations are as follows (Johnson & Johnson, 1995b, 1995c):

1. *Describing what you want.* "I want to use the book now." This means using good communication skills and defining the conflict as a small and specific mutual problem.

2. *Describing how you feel.* "I'm frustrated." Disputants must understand how they feel and communicate it openly and clearly.

3. *Describing the reasons for your wants and feelings.* "You have been using the book for the past hour. If I don't get to use the book soon, my report won't be done on time. It's frustrating to have to wait so long." This includes expressing cooperative intentions, listening carefully, separating interests from positions, and differentiating before trying to integrate the two sets of interests.

4. *Taking the other's perspective and summarizing your understanding of what the other person wants, how the other person feels, and the reasons underlying both.* "My understanding of you is . . ." This includes understanding the perspective of the opposing disputant and being able to see the problem from both perspectives simultaneously.

5. *Inventing three optional plans that maximize joint benefits.* "Plan A is . . ., Plan B is . . ., Plan C is . . ." This requires inventing creative options to solve the problem.

6. *Choosing one plan and formalizing the agreement with a hand shake.* "Let's agree on Plan B!" A wise agreement is fair to all disputants and is based on principles. It maximizes joint benefits and strengthens disputants' ability to work together cooperatively and resolve conflicts constructively in the future. It specifies how each disputant should act in the future and how the agreement will be reviewed and renegotiated if it does not work.

Students need to practice this procedure again and again until it becomes an automatic habit. If students have to stop and think what they should do, it may be too late to manage the conflicts constructively. Overlearning the integrative negotiation procedure is needed so it is available for use in conflicts with intense emotions such as fear and anger. Students need to overlearn the negotiation procedure and become skillful in its use in relatively easy situations before they can be expected to use it to resolve emotionally charged conflicts. Mediation, furthermore, is easier and more effective when all students are skilled in integrative negotiating procedures.

Teaching Students to Mediate Schoolmates' Conflicts

A soft answer turneth away wrath. (Bible)

When students cannot negotiate a constructive resolution to their conflicts successfully, peer mediators should be available. *In the Teaching Students to Be Peacemakers Program, all students are taught the procedures and skills they need to mediate their classmates' conflicts of interests* (Johnson & Johnson, 1995c). A *mediator* is a neutral person who helps two or more people resolve their conflict, usually by negotiating an integrative agreement. The mediator has no formal power over either disputant. A mediator does *not* tell disputants what to do or decide who is right and who is wrong. When you mediate, you stand in the middle and help disputants go through each step of problem-solving negotiations so they reach an agreement that is fair, just, and workable.

Mediation usually is contrasted with arbitration. *Arbitration* is the submission of a dispute to a disinterested third party (such as a teacher or a principal) who makes a final and binding judgment as to how the conflict will be resolved. Mediation consists of four steps (Johnson & Johnson, 1995c):

1. *End hostilities*. The mediator ensures that disputants end hostilities and disputants cool off. Usually the disputants ask the mediator for help. In some cases the mediator may see a dispute taking place and ask if he or she can be of service. In rare instances the mediator may have to get a teacher or an administrator to break up a fight. The mediator must be sure that all disputants are emotionally capable of problem solving and conflict resolution. If disputants are too angry to problem solve, they must cool down before mediation begins.

2. *Ensure that disputants are committed to the mediation process*. The mediator introduces the process of mediation and sets the ground rules to ensure that disputants are committed to the mediation process and ready to negotiate in good faith. The mediator first introduces him- or herself. The mediator then asks the disputants if they want to solve the problem and does not proceed until both answer "yes." Then the mediator explains:

   ■ "Mediation is voluntary. My role is to help you find a solution to your conflict that is acceptable to both of you."

   ■ "I'm neutral. I won't take sides or attempt to decide who is right or wrong. I'll help you decide how to solve the conflict."

- "Each person will have the chance to state his or her view of the conflict without interruption."

- "The rules you must agree to are (1) agree to solve the problem, (2) no name calling, (3) do not interrupt, (4) be as honest as you can, (5) if you agree to a solution, you must abide by it (you must do what you have agreed to do), and (6) anything said in mediation is confidential (you, the mediator, will not tell anyone what is said)."

3. *Help disputants negotiate successfully with each other.* The mediator carefully takes the disputants through the negotiation procedure by helping disputants do the following:

  - Define the conflict by having disputants jointly define the conflict by asking each disputant, "What happened, what do you want, how do you feel?" The mediator paraphrases what each disputant says when necessary to demonstrate that the mediator is listening to and understanding what the disputants are saying and when the mediator believes the other disputant does not understand clearly what the other person is saying. The mediator also enlarges the shadow of the future by highlighting the ways the disputants will have to work cooperatively with each other in the future.

  - Exchange reasons for their positions by helping the disputants present their reasons and the rationale for their positions and understand the differences between their positions. The mediator keeps disputants focused on the issue, not on peripheral issues such as their anger toward each other, equalizes power between the disputants, recognizes disputants' constructive behaviors during negotiations, and reframes the issue by helping disputants change their perspectives.

  - Reverse perspectives so that each person is able to present the other's position and feelings to the other's satisfaction. The mediator also may role play the conflict and switch roles at critical points.

  - Invent at least three options that maximize joint outcomes and leave disputants feeling they have benefited. The mediator encourages creative thinking.

4. *Formalize the agreement.* Reach a wise agreement and shake hands to formalize it. The mediator helps disputants weigh the advantages and disadvantages of each alternative and select the one they wish to implement. The disputants sign a Mediation Report Form to formalize their commitment to implement the agreement and abide by its conditions. The mediator becomes the keeper of the contract and checks back with the disputants a day or so later to see if the agreement is working.

Table 17.1 summarizes the steps in mediation and offers possible mediator statements.

If mediation by peers fails, the teacher mediates the conflict. If teacher mediation fails, the teacher arbitrates by deciding who is right and who is wrong. If that fails, the principal mediates the conflict. If that fails, the principal arbitrates.

Table 17.1 Steps to Mediation

STEPS	POSSIBLE STATEMENTS
End hostilities	"Would you like a mediator?"
Ensure commitment to mediation	"You must follow four rules."
Facilitate negotiations	"How do you feel?"
Formalize the agreement	"Are you willing to sign the agreement?"

Teaching all students negotiation and mediation procedures and skills and implementing a peer mediation program results in a schoolwide discipline program that empowers students to regulate and control their own and their classmates' actions. Teachers and administrators are then freed to spend more of their energies on instruction.

Implementing the Peacemaker Program

If civilization is to survive, we must cultivate the science of human relationships— the ability of all peoples, of all kinds, to live together, in the same world, at peace.

(Franklin Delano Roosevelt)

Once students understand how to negotiate and mediate, the teacher implements the Peacemaker program. Each day the teacher selects two class members to serve as official mediators. Any conflicts that students cannot resolve themselves are referred to the mediators. The mediators wear official T-shirts, patrol the playground and lunchroom, and are available to mediate any conflicts that arise in the classroom or school. The role of mediator is rotated so all students in the class or school serve as mediators an equal amount of time. At first students mediate in pairs. This ensures that shy and nonverbal students get the same amount of experience as more extroverted and verbally fluent students. Mediating classmates' conflicts is perhaps the most effective way of teaching students the need for the skillful use of each step in the negotiation procedure.

The processes of negotiation and mediation allow students to practice joint decision making within a structure that emphasizes a solution/settlement acceptable to all parties involved and, therefore, is fair. Students are given the power to decide the outcome (within the constraints of school policy and the law) and solve a joint problem. For a settlement to be reached, they take responsibility for their conflict. Negotiation and mediation are self-empowering. These procedures enable students to make decisions about issues and conflicts that affect their own lives rather than have a decision imposed on them by teachers and administrators.

Continuing Lessons to Refine and Upgrade Students' Skills

Booster sessions are needed throughout the year to maintain the use of the negotiation and mediation procedures. Gaining real expertise in resolving conflicts constructively takes years and years of training and practice. It may even take a whole lifetime. A few hours of training clearly is not sufficient to teach students how to negotiate or mediate skillfully. The initial Peacemaker training is not enough to create highly skilled negotiators and mediators. At least twice a week or so, students should receive further training or practice in negotiating and mediating. The Teaching Students to Be Peacemakers Program is intended to be a 12-year spiral program that is retaught each year at a more sophisticated and complex level.

One of the most natural ways to integrate negotiation and mediation training into the fabric of school life is to integrate it into academic lessons. Literature, history, and science involve conflict. Almost any lesson in these subject areas can be modified to include role-playing situations in which the negotiation or mediation procedures are used. In our recent research, for example, we have integrated the Peacemaker training into English literature units involving a novel. Each of the major conflicts in the novel was used to teach the negotiation or mediation procedures, and all students role played how to use the procedures to resolve the conflicts in the novel constructively. With some training, teachers can integrate the Peacemaker program readily into academic units.

Research on Peacemaker Program

We have conducted more than 10 studies on the effectiveness of the Teaching Students to Be Peacemakers Program (Johnson & Johnson, 1995d; Johnson, Johnson, & Stevahn, 1995). The studies focused on peer mediation programs in elementary, middle school, and high school settings. The programs were evaluated over a period of several months to a year. The schools were in urban and suburban school districts. Students varied from lower to upper middle class socioeconomically and were from diverse ethnic and cultural backgrounds. Mediators were drawn from a wide variety of ethnic backgrounds. The studies were carefully controlled field-experimental studies with high internal and external validity. The research addressed the following series of questions:

■ *How often do conflicts among students occur, and what are the most commonly occurring conflicts?* The findings indicate that students engage in conflicts daily. In the suburban schools studied, most of the conflicts reported centered on the possession and access to resources, preferences about what to do, playground issues, and turn-taking. Some conflicts involved physical and verbal aggression. In the urban elementary school studied, the vast majority of conflicts referred to mediation involved physical and verbal violence.

■ *Before training, what strategies did students use to manage their conflicts?* Before training, students generally managed their conflicts through trying to win by (a) forcing the other to concede (either by overpowering the other disputant or by asking the teacher to force the other to give in) or (b) withdrawing from the conflict and the other person. One of the teachers stated in her log, "Before training, students viewed conflict as fights that always resulted in a winner and a loser. To avoid such an unpleasant situation, they usually placed the responsibility for resolving conflicts on me, the teacher." Students seem to lack all knowledge of how to engage in problem-solving, integrative negotiations.

■ *Was the Peacemaker training successful in teaching students the negotiation and mediation procedures?* After the Peacemaker training, the students knew the negotiation and mediation procedures and retained their knowledge up to 7 months after the training ended.

■ *Could students apply the negotiation and mediation procedures to conflicts?* For all three types of measures used, students were able to apply the negotiation and mediation procedures to a variety of conflicts.

■ *Do students transfer the negotiation and mediation procedures to nonclassroom and nonschool situations?* Our studies demonstrated that students did in fact use the negotiation and mediation procedures in the hallways, lunchroom, and playground. In addition, students used the procedures in family settings.

■ *When given the option, would students engage in "win-lose" or problem-solving negotiations?* Following the Peacemaker training, students were placed in a negotiation situation in which they could either try to win or maximize joint outcomes. Untrained students almost always strive to win. Most trained students, on the other hand, focused on maximizing joint outcomes.

■ *Does the Peacemaker training increase students' academic achievement?* In three of our studies, we integrated the Peacemaker training into English literature units. While studying a novel, students also learned the negotiation and mediation procedures and used them to understand the dynamics among the major characters. The students were given an achievement test following the end of the unit and again several months later. The results indicated that the students who received the integrated training achieved significantly higher on the achievement and retention tests than did students who spent all their time studying the novel without learning the conflict resolution procedures.

■ *Does the Peacemaker training result in fewer discipline problems that have to be managed by the teacher and the administration?* In our studies the number of discipline problems the teacher had to deal with decreased by about 60 percent, and referrals to the principal dropped about 95 percent.

■ *Does the Peacemaker training result in more positive attitudes toward conflict?* Untrained students uniformly had negative attitudes toward conflicts. After training, students had more positive attitudes toward conflict. Teachers and administrators and parents perceived the peacemaker program to be constructive and helpful. Many parents whose children were not part of the project requested that their children receive the training next year, and a number of parents requested that they receive the training themselves so they could use the procedures to improve conflict management within the family.

Overall, these findings provide considerable empirical validation of the effectiveness of the Peacemaker program and of conflict resolution and peer mediation training in general.

School Discipline Program

Classroom and school discipline programs may be classified on a dimension from a basis in giving external rewards and punishments that control and manage student behavior to a basis in teaching students the competencies and skills required to resolve their interpersonal conflicts constructively, cope with stress and adversity, and behave in appropriate and constructive ways. At one end of the continuum, the focus is on the faculty and staff controlling and managing student behavior. At the other end of the continuum, the focus is on students regulating their own and their peers' actions.

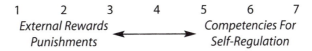

Most discipline programs are clustered at end of the continuum in which adults administer external rewards and punishment. Thus, the faculty has to monitor student behavior, determine whether it is or is not within the bounds of acceptability, and force students to terminate inappropriate actions. When the infractions are minor, the staff often arbitrates ("The pencil belongs to Mary; Jane be quiet and sit down") or cajoles students to end hostilities ("Let's forgive and forget"; "Shake hands and be friends"). If that does not work, students may be sent to the principal's office for a stern but cursory lecture about the value of getting along, a threat that if the conflict continues, more drastic action will ensue, and a final admonition to "Go and fight no more." If that does not work, time-out rooms may be used. Eventually, some students are suspended or expelled from school. Such programs teach students that adults or authority figures are needed to resolve conflicts. These programs cost a great deal in instructional and administrative time and work only as long as students are under surveillance. Students are not empowered. Adults may become more skillful in how to control students, but students do not learn the procedures, skills, and attitudes required to resolve conflicts constructively in their personal lives at home, in school, at work, and in the community.

At the other end of the continuum are programs aimed at teaching students self-responsibility and self-regulation. *Self-regulation* is the ability to act in socially approved ways in the absence of external monitors. It is the ability to initiate and cease activities according to situational demands. Self-regulation is a central and significant hallmark of cognitive and social development. To regulate their behavior, students must monitor their own behavior, assess situations and take other people's perspectives to make judgments as to which behaviors are appropriate, and master the procedures and skills required to engage in the desired behavior. In interaction with other people, students have to monitor, modify, refine, and change how they behave in order to act appropriately and competently.

If students are to learn how to regulate their behavior they must have opportunities to (a) make decisions regarding how to behave, and (b) follow through on the decisions made. Allowing students to be joint architects in matters affecting them promotes feelings of control and autonomy. Then teachers and administrators can concentrate on instruction rather than control.

Structuring Academic Controversies

In addition to implementing the Teaching Students to Be Peacemakers Program, faculty may use intellectual, academic conflicts as an inherent part of the instructional program to increase student achievement, higher-level reasoning, motivation to learn, and conflict skills (Johnson & Johnson, 1995a). *Academic controversy* exists when one student's ideas, information, conclusions, theories, and opinions are incompatible with those of another student, and the two seek to reach an agreement. Over the past 25 years, we (with colleagues such as Dean Tjosvold and Karl Smith) have developed a theory of controversy, tested it by conducting more than 20 experimental and field-experimental studies, developed a series of curriculum units on energy and environmental issues structured for academic controversies, and trained teachers to use academic controversies in schools and colleges throughout the United States, Canada, and a number of other countries (Johnson & Johnson, 1979, 1989, 1995a).

Structuring academic controversy into learning situations results in students learning that conflicts are potentially constructive and even enjoyable. The procedure for structuring academic controversies is to have students follow these steps:

1. Prepare scholarly positions on an academic issue.
2. Advocate these positions.
3. Refute the opposing positions while rebutting criticisms of their position.
4. View the issue from both perspectives.
5. Come to a consensus about their "best reasoned judgment" based on a synthesis of the two positions.

Participating in academic controversies teaches students how to (a) prepare, present, and defend a position, (b) take an opposing perspective, (c) make creative, high-quality decisions that integrate the best information and reasoning from both sides, and (d) engage in a set of social skills such as "criticizing ideas without criticizing people." Similar to cooperative learning, the use of academic controversy may be welcomed by educators because it results in improved student achievement, critical thinking, higher-level reasoning, intrinsic motivation to learn, and a number of other important educational outcomes (Johnson & Johnson, 1979, 1989, 1995a).

Engaging in academic controversies demonstrates the value of conflict and promotes positive attitudes toward engaging in conflict. The skills learned in controversy support and reinforce the skills used in negotiation and mediation. A detailed program to train teachers in how to structure academic controversies to ensure that all students are intellectually challenged within the classroom is presented in Creative Controversy: Intellectual Challenge in the Classroom (Johnson & Johnson, 1995c).

Creating a Conflict-Positive School

Schools do not become orderly and peaceful places in which high-quality education can take place by suppressing the occurrence of conflicts among students. For a variety of reasons, many students want to engage in conflicts. In interviewing inner-city, seventh grade, lower-class, minority students in New York City, Opotow (1991) found that the students perceived fights as being more constructive than destructive.

The students viewed fights as necessary and desirable to maintain valued social norms, deter harmful behavior, provide protection from victimization, provide gains in status, increase self-awareness, clarify personal identity, clarify others' identities, clarify dominance hierarchies, initiate friendships, and provide enjoyable and entertaining experiences. The students reported that in conflicts they found opportunities for (a) modifying the status quo and the behavior of troublesome peers, (b) increasing self-protection, social advancement, personal worth, interpersonal insight, conflict resolution, and excitement, (c) providing heroic drama that generated an oral history of danger, heroism, and good versus evil, and (d) providing moral discourse and clarification of values and codes of behavior. Opotow concluded that these inner-city seventh graders were fascinated clearly by and drawn to conflicts. They liked to start conflicts, watch them, hear about them, and discuss them. Telling students not to fight obviously is not an effective strategy to pursue.

Schools are much better advised to seek an orderly and safe learning environment by encouraging conflicts and their constructive management. A *conflict-positive school* is one where conflicts are encouraged and managed constructively to maximize their potential in enhancing the quality of teaching, learning, and school life in general (Johnson & Johnson, 1995c). Conflicts are not the problem; they are part of the solution and should be a pervasive part of school life. Conflicts not only are inevitable, but also, *when they are managed constructively,* they are healthy and valuable and revitalize and rejuvenate the school. Conflicts can be constructive and valuable.

To summarize:

- Conflicts can increase achievement and long-term retention of academic material.
- Conflicts are the key to using higher-level cognitive and moral reasoning and healthy cognitive, social, and psychological development.
- Conflicts focus attention on problems that have to be solved and energize us to solve them.
- Conflicts clarify who you are, what your values are, what you care about and are committed to, and how you may need to change.
- Conflicts help you understand who the other person is and what his or her values are.
- Conflicts strengthen relationships by increasing your confidence that the two of you can resolve your disagreements and by keeping the relationship clear of irritations and resentments so that positive feelings can be experienced fully.
- Conflicts can release anger, anxiety, insecurity, and sadness that, if kept inside, makes us mentally sick.
- Conflicts can be fun.

What determines whether conflicts result in these positive outcomes is how skillfully students (and faculty) use the integrative negotiation and mediation procedures.

A Lifelong Advantage

A number of recent research studies have found that executives in high-level positions spend much of their time dealing with conflicts. The more skillful they are at doing so, the more successful their careers. Because conflicts occur continually, and because so many people are so unskilled in managing conflicts, teaching students how to resolve conflicts constructively is one of the best investments schools can make.

Once learned, conflict skills go with students to every situation and every relationship. Students do not have to manage every conflict constructively, but the ability to do so should be in their repertoire. Knowing how to resolve conflicts with skill and grace will give students a developmental advantage and increase their future academic and career success, improve the quality of relationships with friends, colleagues, and family, and generally enhance their lifelong happiness.

Summary and Conclusions

The frequency of conflicts is not the problem facing schools. In many cases schools are too conflict-avoidant and need to increase the frequency with which conflicts occur among students and between students and faculty. Conflict has many positive outcomes that cannot occur unless conflict is encouraged. The problem facing schools is how to manage conflicts in constructive and healthy ways. The major barrier to solving this problem is students' lack of effective skills in conflict resolution. Students do use procedures for managing conflicts, but often these procedures are not constructive and not shared by all classmates. The many different methods of managing conflicts within classrooms create some chaos in how conflicts are managed. This is especially true when students are from different cultural, ethnic, social class, and language backgrounds. Life in schools gets easier when *all* students (and staff members) use the same set of negotiation and mediation procedures in managing conflicts.

When students are taught how to negotiate and are given opportunities to mediate their classmates' conflicts, they are given the tools to (a) regulate their behavior through self-monitoring, (b) judge what is appropriate given the situation and the perspective of the other person, and (c) modify how they behave accordingly. Students then have the opportunity to resolve their dispute themselves, in mutually satisfactory ways, without having to engage a teacher's attention. This empowers the students and reduces the demands on teachers and administrators, who then are able to devote less time to establishing and maintaining control over students and spend more time on instruction.

Teaching *all* students negotiation and mediation procedures and skills and implementing a peer mediation program results in a schoolwide discipline program focused on empowering students to regulate and control their own and their classmates' actions. When a conflict occurs, the students involved first try to negotiate a resolution. If that fails, a classmate mediates their conflict. If that fails, the teacher attempts to mediate the conflict. If that fails, the teacher arbitrates by deciding who is right and who is wrong. If that fails, the principal mediates the conflict. If that fails, the principal arbitrates.

Every student needs to learn how to manage conflicts constructively. Without training, many students may never learn how to do so. Teaching every student how to negotiate and mediate will ensure that future generations are prepared to manage conflicts constructively in career, family, community, national, and international settings. The process is neither easy nor quick. Reducing smoking in America took more than 30 years. Reducing drunk driving took more than 20 years. Ensuring that children and adolescents can manage conflicts constructively may take even longer. The more years students spend learning and practicing negotiation and mediation procedures, the more likely they will be to actually use the procedures skillfully both in the classroom and beyond the school door.

References

Deutsch, M. (1949). A theory of cooperation and competition. *Human Relations, 2,* 129–152.

Deutsch, M. (1973). *The resolution of conflict.* New Haven, CT: Yale University Press.

Elam, S., Rose, L., & Gallup, A. (1994, September). The 26th annual Gallup poll of the public's attitudes toward the public schools. *Phi Delta Kappan, 76,* 41–56.

Johnson, D. W. (1967). The use of role reversal in intergroup competition. *Journal of Personality & Social Psychology, 7,* 135–141.

Johnson, D. W. (1970). *Social psychology of education.* Edina, MN: Interaction Book Co.

Johnson, D. W. (1971a). Role reversal: A summary and review of the research. *International Journal of Group Tensions, 1,* 318–334.

Johnson, D. W. (1971b). Students against the school establishment: Crisis intervention in school conflicts and organizational change. *Journal of School Psychology, 9,* 84–92.

Johnson, D. W. (1974). Communication and the inducement of cooperative behavior in conflicts: A critical review. *Speech Monographs, 41,* 64–78.

Johnson, D. W. (1983). *Resolving marital conflicts constructively.* Edina, MN: Interaction Book Co.

Johnson, D. W. (1972/1993). *Reaching out: Interpersonal effectiveness and self-actualization* (5th ed.). Englewood Cliffs, NJ: Prentice-Hall.

Johnson D. W., & Johnson, F. (1975/1994a). *Joining together: Group theory and group skills* (5th ed.). Englewood Cliffs, NJ: Prentice-Hall.

Johnson, D. W., & Johnson, R. (1975/1994b). *Learning together and alone.* Englewood Cliffs, NJ: Prentice Hall.

Johnson, D. W., & Johnson, R. (1979). Conflict in the classroom: Controversy and learning. *Review of Educational Research, 49,* 51–61.

Johnson, D. W., & Johnson, R. (1987). *Creative conflict.* Edina, MN: Interaction Book Co.

Johnson, D. W., & Johnson, R. (1989). *Cooperation and competition: Theory and research.* Edina, MN: Interaction Book Co.

Johnson, D. W., & Johnson, R. (1995a). *Creative controversy: Intellectual challenge in the classroom.* Edina, MN: Interaction Book Co.

Johnson, D. W., & Johnson, R. (1995b). *My mediation notebook* (3d ed.). Edina, MN: Interaction Book Co.

Johnson, D. W., & Johnson, R. (1995c). *Teaching students to be peacemakers.* Edina, MN: Interaction Book Co.

Johnson, D. W., & Johnson, R. (1995d). Teaching students to be peacemakers: Results of five years of research. *Peace and Conflict: Journal of Peace Psychology.*

Johnson, D. W., Johnson, R., & Holubec, E. (1993). Circles of learning. Edina, MN: Interaction Book Co.

Johnson, D. W., Johnson, R., & Johnson, F. (1976). Promoting constructive conflict in the classroom. *Notre Dame Journal of Education, 7,* 163–168.

Johnson, D. W., Johnson, R., & Stevahn, L. (1995). *Three new studies on conflict resolution/peer mediation training.* Paper presented at annual meeting of National Association for Mediation Education (NAME), Seattle.

Lewin, K. (1951). *Field theory in social science.* New York: Harper.

Opotow, S. (1991). Adolescent peer conflicts. *Education and Urban Society, 23*(4), 416–441.

Watson, G., & Johnson, D. W. (1972). *Social psychology: Issues and insights* (2nd ed.). Philadelphia: Lippincott.

Developmental Groups in School Counseling

Marguerite Carroll

he developmental group provides an opportunity for students to explore more satisfying ways of behaving in relation to themselves and in relation to one another. This type of group focuses on the concept that people can experience growth in a self-actualizing paradigm and expand their personal development.

Educational settings may be defined in numerous ways. Elementary schools will include grades K through 4, 5, or 6; middle school grades may vary between grades 5 through 8; and high school includes grades 9 or 10 to 12. Obviously, individual and group characteristics overlap enormously. We have attempted to be sufficiently general to absorb much of the overlap. For that reason, in this chapter we have differentiated between elementary and high school levels only, as it is difficult to define age and grade groups precisely. There has been an attempt to minimize repetition in both levels, as many of the suggestions at the elementary level are adaptable to the high school. Younger-aged groups, however, require considerably more preplanned structure than do older groups.

Some group processes are appropriate in elementary or high school, whereas others are more appropriate in private practice, hospitals, or clinics. For purposes of clarification, group guidance, task-oriented, and small instructional groups are directed toward normal functioning groups, whereas psychotherapy groups are directed toward persons who are less able to cope with daily functioning and possess less personal ego strength.

Groups specific to elementary and high schools are generally conducted within different parameters from groups outside of schools, not only because schools are usually public institutions dealing with minors but also because young children and adolescents do not possess the ego strength to handle the intense level of interaction characteristic of adult groups. After young people in their late teens pass through the typical "identity crisis" of that age, the sense of self strengthens, and psychological resources are likely sufficient to benefit from explorations at a deeper level. Until this occurs, however, group leaders must modify their behavior to create group processes appropriate for the young person still in a developmental stage and not psychologically mature.

The developmental group model applied to children still depends heavily on self-disclosure and feedback, but younger members are more dependent on structured activities and prepared materials for achieving interaction. However, this does not mean that younger children cannot interact spontaneously or that older members cannot profit from structured activities.

Types of Groups

In April 1991, the Association for Specialists in Group Work (ASGW) adopted a new set of standards for training group workers. Conyne, Wilson, Kline, Morran, and Ward (1993), in a discussion of the applications of the "standards" in a counselor education training program, defined group work "as a broad professional practice that refers to the giving of help or the accomplishment of tasks in a group setting . . . by a professional practitioner to assist an interdependent collection of people" (p. 12). They also named the four categories of groups endorsed by ASGW (1992) as follows:

- Task/work groups
- Guidance/psychoeducational groups
- Counseling/interpersonal problem-solving groups
- Psychotherapy/personality reconstruction groups

Using this basic conceptual framework for counselors, Johnson and Johnson (1995) presented a paradigm (see Figure 18.1) that categorizes the various group processes. One category, *content groups,* includes task/work groups and guidance/psychoeducational groups; the other category, *process groups*, includes counseling groups (which are used most frequently in school counseling) and therapy groups. Adaptations of the developmental model may be applied to guidance/psychoeducational groups and counseling groups. Both have the aim of assisting students to learn new material, develop specific skills, or alter attitudes toward something or somebody. Johnson and Johnson (1995) advise that guidance/psychoeducational groups and counseling groups are the most misunderstood by the lay public, and educators and even school counselors may suffer from a lack of knowledge of the distinction between them. In delineating their paradigm of group processes, Johnson and Johnson (1995) believe, "When presented and explained, the model should clarify for the general public, students, parents, teachers, and administrators that all these group processes are designed to reinforce learning" (p. 1).

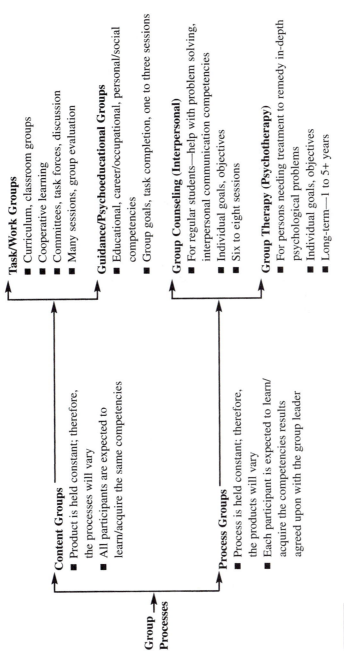

Figure 18.1 Categories of Groups

From "Group Process: A Results Approach," by S.K. Johnson and C.D. Johnson, 1995, *Counseling and Human Development, 27(9)*, p. 3. Reprinted with permission.

Johnson and Johnson (1995) describe task/work groups (content) as related closely to classroom instruction and organizational work forces. Although counselors may be involved in these groups periodically, classroom teachers use them most often to deliver content curriculum. Administrators use them to facilitate adult-related, faculty, parent, and community functions. Most educators understand the function and purpose of these groups.

On the other end of the spectrum are psychotherapy groups whose purpose, as Trotzer (1999) indicates, ". . . is to effect personality change with group effort directed toward reconstructing, reeducating, or rehabilitating individual members relative to personality characteristics that are creating problems in their lives" (p. 39). Johnson and Johnson (1995) affirm that "therapy groups are not appropriate within the public school educational program. Even when private mental health resources are scarce, providing therapy groups goes beyond what is legally sanctioned by local and state boards of education" (p. 2).

All the group processes described in Figure 18.1 contribute to learning, and all, to some degree, involve different skills on the part of the group leader. The use of diverse skills depends on the purposes of the group, the setting in which it is conducted, and the composition of group membership. In a guidance/psychoeducational group, the leaders will have in mind information they wish to transmit to the group as a whole. In other words, participants are expected to learn some content while the dynamics of group interaction are used. There is a group goal whereby students are to acquire similar learning, most of which is primarily in the cognitive domain. In contrast, in a counseling group the leader will emphasize individual goals and focus on individual growth, and leader techniques that emphasize the affective (cognition) domain will be in evidence.

Parameters of Learning

The parameters defining the boundaries within which a group operates are governed to some extent by the setting; thus, group leaders must be able to use facilitative techniques suitable for the type of group they are leading.

To achieve guidance group goals, small group activities and small group discussion as well as teaching skills are applicable. The leader will select approaches that best suit the group goals. Discussion techniques, decision-making analysis, simulations, games, multimedia stimuli such as slides, videotapes, and films, role playing, self-assessment procedures, and vocational exploration are some of the common approaches. Problem-centered groups composed of "school attendance problems," "high-risk chemical dependency," "acting-out students," and "divorce groups" may be the focus of content groups. In addition, Johnson and Johnson (1995) explain that groups may include issues of self-esteem, underachievement, conflict resolution, interpersonal relationships, helping peers, making decisions, and handling authority. All of these types are aimed at helping group members cope with the demands of the culture (whether it be the institution or society at large) so they can become functioning and productive citizens.

Fortunately, there is recognition in our society that the individual is also important; that is, a recognition that each individual is in some way different from anyone else, and that these differences are a valuable resource. Enculturation must be effected to some degree *before* primary forces can be focused on individuation, or a society would be in chaos. If *only* enculturation were achieved, society would be changeless.

The *primary* focus of groups where the developmental model is appropriate is to strengthen individual competencies. Members examine their values, priorities, individual strengths, and lifestyles. The content of developmental groups focuses on how members differ one from another and what each can do because of—not in spite of—such differences.

Mixing the Message

Both the learning and individuation processes interweave and are complementary. Therefore, no precise line of demarcation can be drawn between the two processes. The group whose main focus is on learning specific competencies, such as the values, mores, and conventions of society, is obviously different from the group whose focus is on values and behavior that create a unique lifestyle. However, Johnson and Johnson (1995) caution us that mixing the message can create confusion for group members:

> The intentional or unintentional process of mixing content and process groups creates confusion and mistrust in participants. If a group member signs up for a content group or is mandated to attend such a group with the stated expectation of learning a specific skill or attaining information, the participant has a right to feel violated if the group moves into personal and social areas that the individual is unprepared to address. Likewise, an individual seeking a personal growth experience may feel disillusioned if the group turns out to be a process for teaching specific skills that may not apply to the student's individual goals. For example, a student seeking a group experience as a way of exploring life goals may be impacted negatively if the group turns out to be a group designed to encourage students to attend college and provide strategies for how to get into college. In both instances, when groups are misrepresented or if a group evolves from one type of experience to a different type of group, the long-range impact of the group process may hinder instead of help the individual's progress. (pp. 4-5)

Privacy and Legalities

Issues of privacy and legal implications for counselors and group members (of all age groups) are addressed by Corey & Corey (1997), who suggest that counselors make clear promises to group members in respect to privacy. Ordinarily a school counselor can promise school age children that what is discussed in a group session is confidential, and that no content will be repeated to teachers, parents, or administrators. However, issues related to harm—both to and against others—must be followed up with the proper authorities, as will the suspected abuse of minors. Most state laws require that events related to abuse, discussed in a group setting or otherwise, must be reported to the proper authorities. Corey & Corey (1997) emphasize the need to "Be aware of your legal responsibility to report abuse or suspected abuse of minors" (p. 297).

In addition, it is important for group leaders to obtain informed consent from parent/guardian if this is school policy. This involves providing specific information about the group so that the parent/guardian can make an intelligent decision about whether or not to participate.

Elementary School Group Counseling

The Purpose

The purpose of elementary school counseling has not changed over time. Both Redl (1966) and Morganett (1994) offer reasons for establishing guidance and counseling groups in the elementary school. Redl (1966) identified areas of application: draining off hostilities and daily frustration so they do not accumulate to an intolerable degree; providing emotional support when children are overwhelmed by feelings of panic or guilt; offering a relationship that keeps the child from retreating into his or her own world as a consequence of emotional upheaval; and serving as a setting in which to work out feelings about disputes, fights, and other matters.

Morganett (1994) describes group work as providing a safe and accepting environment to practice new behaviors and receive the support of others; offering role models for positive attitudes, social values, and behaviors; showing how working together is important and providing models for giving and receiving help; providing a place where children can learn tolerance and respect for others' differences; and providing a place to teach children how to trust and how to share ideas, attitudes, and feelings honestly.

Group counseling with elementary school children is, in essence, no different from counseling in groups with participants of any age, but special considerations must be given to groups composed of elementary school–aged children.

In an elementary school–aged counseling group, it is important to preserve the integrity of the home and family, and the leader must be alert to assure that the young student does not discuss issues that would violate this privacy. Elementary school children cannot be expected to have the degree of social sophistication older students will have; thus, the leader must vigorously protect each child's privacy as well as that of their families. This may involve more frequent intervention than is usually necessary when working with an older group.

Composing the Group

Some special considerations must be observed when organizing and conducting counseling groups of elementary school children. The size of the group and the length of each session depend on the ages of the children. For example, in early childhood (ages 5 through 9) the group should contain only three or four members who meet no longer than 20 to 30 minutes at one time. In the event there is apparent cultural diversity among the members, Halverson (2002) believes that gaining an understanding of the complex social and cultural background of each member of the group is difficult but must be encouraged. Regardless of age groups, Halverson (2002) believes "Counselors must be aware of the tensions that surround different cultural and social norms, traditions and beliefs" (p. 379).

There are leaders who prefer to work with groups of young children of the same gender, similar physical prowess, social sophistication, and of the same developmental stage; others do not. Bednar and Kaul (1994) suggest there is no significant research to support either view. Riva and Smith (1997) report that there are many unanswered research questions in respect to group composition, namely member selection and the matching of individuals to special groups. Most practitioners are prone to make their own conclusions about group composition based on experience and intuition.

It is suggested, however, that the method of developing a counseling group (at any grade level) should not be left to chance. The composition of a group may be of great importance to the kind of group experience that will develop and the effects the group will have on its members. Recruiting and screening students for group work is crucial. Children ought not be put into a group where they do not belong because they will seriously disturb the group. Not every child is ready for a group and children should be selected in such a way that overactive or aggressive children are not grouped together. One such child per group is sufficient. Of course, as suggested earlier, there are other examples of a "poor mix." Among elementary school students, the possibilities of contagion (meaning "one bad apple will spoil the barrel") are greater than they are when students are older.

Leaders who work with elementary school groups find that they must do more "teaching" of listening skills, membership skills, and individual behavior than would be necessary or desirable in older age groups. Children need a great deal of help in labeling emotions, as well as in articulating their value systems. Positive emotional development in children is analogous to self-actualization in adults.

Communication Patterns

Group leaders who work from an existentialist framework with the developmental model find that the principles and procedures of enhancing communication as advanced in this book are appropriate when working with groups of all ages. Children of elementary school age, however, have limitations in communication. They are not as practiced at verbalizing feelings as are older students. And even more than older students, they tend to respond with "it" type comments—facts, events, and things away from the group that deal with the there-and-then. Children also tend to make "they" responses. They will focus on people away from the group rather than deal with each other. Thus, young students need help with the skills that stimulate genuine communication. A leader should be alert to these types of responses and may either model more productive interaction or discuss ways of interacting directly.

As an example, young students usually "chain" at first; they respond to one another's comments with replies that indicate no verbalized recognition of the content of the other's remarks. For instance, David, a group member, might state that he had a bad fight with his sister. A chaining response might be, "I just have a new sister in my house. She's really neat!" This type of response chains to the output but gives the previous speaker no indication that his comment held meaning for the receiver. Elementary school children particularly need to be helped to make associative responses as well as to give feedback.

In the associative response, the child will give some recognition that he or she has heard the speaker but centers the response geocentrically. Taking David's comment about the fight with his sister, the child might reply, "Yeah, I know what you mean. I fight with my sister sometimes." This type of response leaves the original speaker with some small degree of satisfaction, but the feedback has been only minimal. He was heard, but does not know whether he was understood.

A group leader's task is to assist the group member to add to the associative response some meaningful feedback that contains some affect. Affective responses require highly developed listening skills; this is one of the functions of the group process—to help members learn to listen to each other. The feedback level of response centers on what the speaker is saying, responds to it, and enriches it. This kind of response is "interactive" in that it enables the dialogue to move back and forth between two people rather than reach a dead end. In responding to the comment about fighting with a sister, a feedback response might be, "I have fought with my sister, and it isn't a nice feeling." All group participants have some difficulty in learning to give this sort of feedback, but elementary school students have a particular struggle in learning how to communicate at a level in which they transmit "hearing" feelings.

So far we have discussed the developmental group model as it pertains to counseling. Elementary school classroom groups (guidance/psychoeducational groups) are more topically oriented than are counseling groups. Factors to be considered in elementary school groups, particularly those at the youngest levels, are that considerably more structure and preplanning of activities are necessary in comparison to groups of older children. Puppets (Dinkmeyer & Dinkmeyer, 1982), "magic circle" (Bessell & Palomares, 1970), classroom meetings (Glasser, 1975), open-ended stories (Morganett, 1990, 1994), art work (Gladding, 1998), and role plays are suggested activities for young children's groups.

Goals for Classroom Group Activities

Typical goals of classroom group activities include the following:

- Achieving a curriculum or instructional goal
- Helping new students get acquainted

■ Problem solving

■ Demonstrating democratic principles

■ Increasing confidence to participate in discussions

■ Clarifying values

When students enter a newly formed class, they wonder, "What's this teacher going to be like?" "What are my classmates going to be like?" "Are they going to be smart? tough? friendly?" Teachers are usually concerned about their students' personal uncertainties and curiosities about their class members. It would take very little time away from instructional objectives for a teacher, using a group approach, to attend to these natural concerns of students.

School children spend a lot of their time in groups of some kind as part of their educational experience. In the classroom setting, group activities tend to be highly structured as compared with other types of group settings. The teacher is usually the primary influence on the content of discussion and controls the directions taken by the group. We believe that classroom group leaders (teachers) can utilize certain elements of the developmental model to be more effective in performing their duties. We hasten to emphasize that we are proposing the developmental model as an *adjunct* to the traditional role of the teacher and certainly not as a replacement of any existing educational model.

Values are formed and protocols of behavior are established that are as distinctive as they are implicit. Such micro-societies are inevitable in any classroom. Good teachers are aware that these micro-societies have an important influence on students' achievement and attitudes. The influence can be positive or negative, and even when teachers are aware of the class social structure, they may be uncertain about what to do to contribute to its healthy development. Group-type activities can serve as a vehicle for influencing the positive development of the classroom's micro-society, and thus improve its educational and emotional climate.

This statement is based on two assumptions: First, we assume that students learn more efficiently when they are personally involved in the learning process. Second, we assume that peers are extremely influential in affecting student attitudes and behaviors. When students can be accepting of themselves, they are more likely to be accepting of others. Only when they function well within their peer group will they be able to attain the utmost of their potentials. We would expect, therefore, greater achievement with comparatively less effort in an educational environment where positive interaction among peers is built into the curriculum, and where students are encouraged to explore and examine their feelings about themselves, their classmates, and their educational experiences.

Resources for Elementary School Classroom Groups

As mentioned previously in this chapter, we are convinced that group work should be considered in a broader context than just counseling—for example, guidance and psychoeducational groups. The distinction between group counseling and classroom group discussion is sometimes obscure. Their purposes differ, and *counseling* usually calls for a departure from the normal classroom routine. But the process of interpersonal contact, speaking spontaneously in the here-and-now, and receiving feedback is just as important to a skilled teacher as it is to a skilled group leader. Both of them are, in reality, group facilitators. Whereas group leaders may focus *entirely* on the interactive process of the group participants, classroom teachers call upon their awareness and group leadership functions at times when they think their students' learning can be positively effected.

The literature directed to group activities for elementary school classroom groups is limited in comparison with the literature focusing on human relations training, older adolescent groups, and adult groups. Morganett (1990, 1994) has developed two excellent books of activities for the use of teachers and counselors. The earlier publication is for those working with young adolescents and includes group activities for what she calls "group agendas," dealing with topics such as "Meeting, Making, and Keeping Friends," and "Better Ways of Getting Mad: Anger Management Skills." Her second volume includes "agendas" for group experiences with children from the second to the fifth grade. A sampling of the agendas are, "I'm Somebody Special: Building Self-Esteem," "Friends: Getting Along with Others," "Kids in Divorce Stress," and "I'm Responsible." How materials such as these are used depends on leader emphasis and the group setting.

High School Group Counseling

The Adolescent Dilemma

Leading a group of young people involves strategies and an organization that differs significantly from those employed for adults and young children. The tumultuous world of the adolescent is fraught with experiences unlike those of adults, which in turn creates an enigmatic haze around their attitudes and behavior. Adolescents are constantly in the process of change—change in body image, change in mood, change in emotions as a result of hormonal development, and change in thinking and patterns of response to events in their lives. As a result of these turbulent changes, adolescents in groups are apt to be more cunning in dealing with their adult leaders and will create interpersonal barriers, often displaying ongoing resistance with a vigor that will test the patience of most leaders.

Adolescence is also a period when young people eagerly experiment with adult behavior and attitudes while gradually relinquishing the securities of childhood. It is an exciting yet, at times, frightening period of growth for many teenagers. Adults who attempt to advise and counsel young people through this transition period are often more impressed with the wisdom of their guidance than are the recipients. The values and experience gap between adults and adolescents can be sizable and, as a result, frustrating to adults who are genuinely trying to be of help. Nevertheless, it is no less frustrating and confusing to teenagers who are seeking a sense of self-identification in which they feel competent, independent, and accepted among peers. This is a common adolescent concern, although the intensity of the concerns and confusion varies considerably. Adolescents are most likely to turn to their peers in search of answers and support. In their bid for independence and self-identification, most teens are particularly conscious of the peer-relevant mores and values that are in vogue.

Acceptance by peers is significantly more important to high school students than are the opinions and advice of adults. Among adolescents, what is acceptable and unacceptable by teen standards is known by all and is constructed and imposed by the students themselves. Simply stated, students decide that some aspects of their existence are "safe" to share. Other interests, thoughts, and aspirations that they might genuinely wish to share are not shared because students suspect they would be ridiculed or rejected by volunteering them. Involvement in almost any variety of sporting activity is preferable to and "safer" than speaking with pride about beekeeping. Sharing the excitement of a weekend party is less risky than describing the excitement of a book read over the weekend.

In many classrooms peer influence can develop an insidious character. For whatever reasons, some students are judged by their peers to be not "with it" by contemporary peer standards. Even if these individuals are not patently ostracized, they are often intentionally "not noticed."

Students spend a good part of their school day in some form of group activity— committees, task-oriented classroom groups, and so on. Most often, though, group interaction takes place in casual gatherings in the classroom, corridors, cafeteria, and after school.

It has already been proposed that group interaction offers the potential for growth and positive change, and because young people are in groups anyway, why doesn't this potential emerge naturally? One of the basic reasons it does not emerge naturally is that teenagers typically are beginning to monitor their behavior, how they dress, what they say, and so forth. The proclivity toward fads and conformity is probably the most obvious verification that teens are concerned, to varying degrees, about how they are perceived by others. In their peer consciousness, teens are beginning to manifest characteristics to protect themselves from possible peer rejection. In high school, students with a weak self-identity or poor self-concept typically are concerned about behaving as they think they ought to rather than as they are. Many high school students have difficulty revealing themselves authentically, and often what looks spontaneous is really a facade. Other students appear bored and sullen because that is the image they wish to convey.

It can be assumed that young people have serious thoughts and concerns that they would like to communicate to others. Unfortunately, many educational settings do not encourage this type of interaction. Adolescents' natural strengths and resources can be channeled and shared for mutual benefit if a sensitive and knowledgeable adult (group leader, teacher, counselor) is available to facilitate interaction. Because peer influence is such a pervasive force among teens, we should capitalize on its power for constructive purposes. The school climate and instructional efficiency would be improved if such opportunities were made available. The abilities of teachers and counselors can be utilized in structuring group situations in which students may share their opinions and perceptions. This may lead to confrontation between students or between students and teachers, but confrontation can be constructive. Frequently, a peer confrontation includes the same information with which an adult might confront the student. The main difference is the identity of the confronter. Our hypothesis is simple: It is more difficult for an adolescent to reject or deny the opinions of a peer than those of an adult. The feelings expressed by peers seem to have more impact.

The following examples indicate the importance of peer interaction. Imagine the following statements being made to adolescents by an adult. Then imagine the same interaction between adolescents.

■ I really think you have a lot to be proud of. You're attractive and intelligent.

■ You don't bore me. I think you have had many interesting experiences.

■ I think you're blowing it. You look strung out all the time.

■ You always act so hard. You don't need to act that way. I don't think you are really that way at all.

These examples are excerpted from student comments made in actual high school group counseling sessions. If teachers were to say the same things to students, however, the statements would probably be rejected as being "your values, not mine." If a student makes the same kind of statement to another student, it stands a better chance of being heard and considered. Consequently, the group leader should try to develop and maintain an environment designed to maximize listening and assimilation of the information and opinions being shared among adolescents.

The developmental group model seems to be an ideal vehicle for focusing on interaction that is honest, spontaneous, and positive. Group leaders do not prohibit feedback that is negative or calculated, but they are careful not to permit continued negative feedback intended to be destructive or vindictive. Leaders can use negative feedback in the group process to influence authentic, positive interaction. Developmental group techniques, however, are not designed or employed for evoking negative confrontations. Our approach to the group process centers on capitalizing on positive feedback.

Learning and personal growth are maximized when we feel good about ourselves and when we have confidence in the support and acknowledgment of our peers. When inviting adolescent members into a group, counselors can acknowledge the potential of a group member. After receiving an invitation, a parent called the counselor to inquire, "What's wrong with my son?" The counselor replied, "We're inviting your son to participate because there is something he can contribute to the group. The reason he was invited to join wasn't because there is something wrong with him!"

Each group member is unique. Each group leader is unique. The extraordinary qualities of individual members and individual leaders make each group unpredictable to some degree. The complexities that comprise the entity called "group" are so intricate that they defy definition and, therefore, anticipation. Experienced and inexperienced leaders alike approach each group as an unknown. Perhaps a major difference between experienced leaders and inexperienced leaders is that the former know they can never be sure what will evolve in a group and the latter still believe that, in time, they might.

Getting Organized

Morganett (1990) recommends the following procedures when organizing a group experience for students:

1. *Conduct a needs assessment.* Find out what group services are needed by the students in a particular setting.
2. *Develop a written proposal.* After need has been established, develop a proposal detailing what you are going to do and how you are going to do it.
3. *Advertise the group.* See "Staff Preparation" and "Presentation to Students."
4. *Obtain informed consent from parent/guardian if this is school policy.* This involves providing specific information about the group so that the parent/guardian can make an intelligent decision about whether or not to allow the student to participate.
5. *Conduct a pregroup interview.* Talk to the student about your expectations, as well as their expectations (what their interests might be) of the group.
6. *Select group members.* Specific guidelines are detailed elsewhere in this article.
7. *Conduct postgroup follow-up and evaluation.* This is essential for accountability for reporting to administrators, teachers, or parents. See "Accountability."

Letter to Parents

Goals and Objectives

Educational goals that can be achieved through the use of group counseling in public schools are a legitimate concern of school counselors. Bates (1968) conducted research to identify which of those goals could be achieved through group processes when working with adolescents in a high school setting. According to her study, group counseling could be used to help students become more receptive to the learning process through the reduction of tension and hostilities. In one group format of her study, students were helped to maintain a grade-point average, improve behavior in the classroom, demonstrate more applied effort, and increase

---

HUBBARDSTON CENTER SCHOOL

Hubbardston, MA 01452

Dear Parents/Guardians,

One of the services offered at Hubbardston Center School is small group counseling. Groups are formed and designed around the needs of the individual students, which can vary from year to year.

Groups are typically made up of four to six students who get together on a weekly basis for approximately six to ten weeks. Depending on the age of the children, each group session meets for about thirty to forty minutes. Developmental issues such as friendships, peer pressure, stress, and transition to middle school are covered, as well as life change issues like death, moving, and divorce.

Referrals for small groups come from teachers, parents, and students. If you are interested in finding out more information, return the form below or give me a call at _____.

I look forward to hearing from you.

Sincerely,

Naida Johnson, School Counselor

I would like more information about small groups being offered at Hubbardston Center School.
Please give me a call at _____.

Signature _____

A Member of the Quabbin Regional School District

---

daily attendance. Students in the groups expanded the occupational choices into which they projected themselves, and these chosen occupations were more realistic when assessed against the student's academic potential.

It is unrefuted that the goals and objectives that can be achieved through group counseling are consonant with the goals and objectives of education. In the developmental model, leaders assist prospective group members in identifying the goals and objectives that each wishes to achieve. A group leader's goals might include the young person's ability to improve interpersonal skills and develop self-management strategies, problem-solving techniques, and active coping skills. The criteria for group membership is directed toward individuals within a "normal" population who, with the help of the group, can attain such goals.

Staff Preparation

The typical high school staff probably misunderstands the purpose of group to a greater extent than does any other institution. Counselors who wish to initiate group counseling will likely find their time in staff preparation well spent. Without the staff's understanding and support, almost any group counseling program will encounter difficulty.

First of all, the administrators' support *must* be obtained — not just permission, but support, preferably enthusiastic support. If an administrator gives only lukewarm agreement, counselors may want to delay the group counseling program until they are able to elicit clearer understanding on the part of administrators of the educational advantages of a group counseling program.

After the support of the administration has been gained, a general presentation concerning the nature of group counseling, its values, and its educational components should be made to the faculty. At this point, it is recommended that the building administrator express support of the group counseling program to the entire faculty.

Defining Membership

The first step in working with young people in a group is to define criteria for membership. As discussed earlier in this chapter, there are those who should be in groups and there are those who should not. The question is, how does the leader know beforehand that a potential member will be a good group member. Some leaders advise an individual interview with each potential member before the sessions begin. This appears to be the most popular method of screening among group leaders, but the literature has not provided consistent opinions and successful practice (Riva, Lippert & Tackett, 2000). Persons often behave differently in an individual interview than they behave in a group session.

The best group member is a self-referred group member; group counseling should be optional for participants. Among adolescents it is advisable to exclude those whose behavior is so bizarre that other group members will be frightened or whose behavior is beyond the mores of acceptance for group members. Other unsuitable candidates include withdrawn or passive individuals and those who are so troubled that they spill their anxieties at an uncontrollable pace.

Corey (2000) recommends candidates for exclusion whose behavior characteristics are detrimental in the group setting, such as those who are withdrawn, have a need to monopolize or dominate, are hostile or aggressive, are extremely self-centered, are in extreme crisis, or are suicidal. They go on to state: "We are concerned that candidates benefit from a group but even more concerned that they might be psychologically hurt by it or might drain the group's energies. Certain members while remaining in the group sap its energy for productive work . . . the potential gains of including certain of these members must be weighed against the probable losses to the group as a whole." (pp. 112-113). Carroll and Wiggins (2001), as well, advise, "Group members should be acceptable to each other. Warring factions and members who have known personal dislikes for one another should not be in the same group. If this cannot be judged accurately in advance, the leader should prune inappropriate members from the group, after the first one or two sessions" (p. 23).

Particular combinations of group members also may cause problems. For instance, a group should not be put together to benefit one person; benefits derived in group work are for the group as a whole. If the group bogs down and members drop out, inadequate choice in membership is most often the cause. Finally, in composing a group, leaders should take into consideration the degree to which each of the participants is verbal; too few or too many highly verbal members may inhibit group interaction.

With respect to grade level and same-sex or mixed-sex groups, there is really no hard and fast rule. No significant body of research suggests that young people function more productively with peers of the same grade level or with the same sex. Yet, as a general practice, it is best to form groups according to grade level when working in a school setting. Not only are developmental issues a consideration, but the social events and behavioral expectations of students also vary as they move from grade to grade.

Group progress may be hampered if students are too divergent in age or development. With older adolescents, however, mixed-sex groups are generally preferred. Young people in grades 6 through 8 usually work better in single-sex groups as preteen boys are unpredictable in their behavior and their loyalty to the opposite sex. Single-sex groups are better able to work on understanding these inconsistencies. The developmental stages of both boys and girls can have a troublesome effect on the group.

Group Size, Number, and Length of Sessions

The usual size for an adolescent group is seven or eight, which allows for dropouts. After a group falls below five members, the dynamics change and the group becomes less productive.

The school-based developmental group model suggests that leaders schedule eight group counseling sessions. Thus, a counseling group can be organized, conducted, and evaluated within the framework of a school quarter. If the group leaders are skilled, eight sessions should be sufficiently productive. The notion of continuing one group for a semester or a year (or two!) in the public school setting is neither necessary nor desirable.

Usually the group meets weekly for one class period. It is suggested that no groups be organized before or after school or during the lunch hour. If counseling is a legitimate part of the educational program, time ought to be available for group counseling as well as classroom instruction.

After the group has been informed of the number of weeks it is scheduled to meet, the group's life should not be extended. If the need arises to extend the duration beyond the contracted period of time, Carroll and Wiggins (2001) suggest leaders might ask themselves, "Have I helped group members recognize that meeting individual goals is not strengthened by endless participation? Or, am I fostering dependency by continuing the group?"

During the time the group meets, no new members should be added. Achieving group cohesiveness within the established number of meetings is important to provide the emotional security needed for members to explore new growth experiences. Because counseling groups have an established, limited number of meetings, allowing changes in membership hinders the formation of group cohesiveness (Johnson & Johnson, 1995).

When considering the length of individual group meetings, groups move more productively when there is a known beginning and a known end. Time limits should be set not only for the number of weeks the group is to meet but also for the length of the individual sessions. Above all, adhering to specific time limits is important for consistency. It cannot be overemphasized that groups move more productively when there is a time frame for each session and a known number of weeks the group will meet. Consistency is imperative for adolescents.

Seating Arrangement

Does the place where group members choose to sit have any significance? The answer is yes and no. Carroll and Wiggins (2001) believe that the leader should avoid making interpretations in regard to who sits where. Of course, certain hypotheses can be drawn, and these can be tested as the group proceeds. More important, though, the leader should watch for neurotic pairings, such as adolescents who pair off by sitting next to each other in every session and whisper, continually nudge each other, and snicker periodically. Leaders can separate such pairs in a way that does not seem negative or uncaring. One possibility is for the leader to attempt to sit between the pairs, as subtly as possible, as the pairs attempt to sit together in the group. Another suggestion is to have each group member sit in a different place each session. It is important to remember that separating problem members can be essential to the life of the group.

Logistics

If possible, a group should meet in other than a classroom setting. Privacy should be maximum, with no interruptions permitted. Chairs should be arranged in a circle, not around a table.

The leader must begin on time, even if only one member is present. The session also must end on time. Beginning group leaders tend to want to extend the time of their sessions, as groups led by beginners characteristically get down to work toward the end of a session. If neophyte leaders allow the time to be extended, they are denying group members the opportunity to learn limits and therefore to gain experience in reality testing.

Issues of Diversity

Diversity issues in groups are a fact of life in today's culture. Corey (2000) broadly defines culture, including race, ethnicity, affectional orientation, class, religion, sex, and race. And Axelson (1993) views culture as "any group of people who identify or associate with one another on the basis of some common purpose, need, or similarity of background (p. 33). The multicultural nature of schools today means that children and adolescents are immersed in issues of racism as well as issues concerning differences of gender, sexual orientation, and disability (Capuzzi and Gross, 2002). Although it is impossible to have an in-depth knowledge of all cultural backgrounds, it is essential to have a grasp of the general principles of diverse populations. Corey (2000) calls attention to ". . . cultural encapsulation, or provincialism, which can afflict both group members and the group leader. As group counselors, we have to confront or own distortions as well as those of the members" (p. 22). In addition, Corey (2000) reminds, "As a group practitioner you cannot, afford to ignore the issue of culture, for culture will influence both the clients' behavior and yours" (p. 15).

The following is an example of how a leader can use his or her observations in an attempt to bring group members to a higher level of understanding of themselves and others in respect to cultural diversity.

> *Leader:*   (*speaking to the group as a whole*) I have noticed that many of you seem to be tentative in the way you respond to Wong. Is there something about Wong that causes you not to draw him into the group?
>
> *Leader:*   (*After Wong has shared that he is aware that he is the only Chinese member of the group*). Although Wong has spoken, it seems no one is responding. I wonder if each of you would share what you are experiencing right now.

Each person responds to Wong, speaking of embarrassment, shyness, discomfort, uneasiness, apprehension, etc.

> *Leader:*   Wong, would you be willing to tell the members of the group how you feel about this, and how you would like them to respond to you?

According to Kline (2003), "The more personal and emotionally connected the confronting of diversity issues are to the here and now of group interaction, the more powerful they are" (p. 272). In the preceding scenario the leader brings issues of diversity to the forefront of the group experience. This allows the group members to deal with what could be hidden emotional agendas that would hinder the group's development. Confronting such issues can be a powerful learning experience for all members.

The simulation game BaFa BaFa has become widely used to teach cultural awareness in group work.

> BaFa BaFa is a mythical land with two distinct cultures: Alpha and Beta. Whereas people from Alpha are warm, friendly, patriarchal, and possess a strong in-group, out-group identity, the people from Beta speak a foreign language, and are highly competitive and task oriented. Upon being formerly trained in the rules of one culture, participants must then visit the other culture and must cope on a trial and error basis with no formal instruction. Upon visiting the foreign culture, participants initially become bewildered and eventually become critical of and hostile toward their hosts—labeling them strange or weird. In the postsimulation discussion, participants learn the cultural rules of the foreign culture with this realization; attitudes reportedly change from hostility to tolerance. Through further discussion, the experience can be generalized to real world cultural groups." (Merta R.J., in Trotzer, J.T., 1999, p. 302.)

Special Considerations

When high school counseling groups begin to acquire the potential for intense interaction of the type that is observed among adult groups, some special concerns may arise. Examining long-term values, assuming personal responsibility, planning for the future, understanding sexuality, clarifying self-identification, and getting along with parents and authority figures are issues that do not normally emerge in groups of younger children but are common in adolescent groups.

Because of the potential for "heavy" issues, the group leader should have a clear picture of why group counseling seems appropriate and desirable for his or her particular group of high school students. Being absolutely clear on this point is a requisite for enlisting the support and understanding of the faculty and administration.

Communication Patterns of Adolescents: What to Look For

The range of and gaps in social and communication skills seem more pronounced among adolescents, particularly those in their early teens, than among any other age group. Interaction with members of the opposite sex is often awkward. Preoccupation with status, age, and grade-level differences can interfere with clear and sincere communication. Even sustaining normal eye contact is a problem for some teens. In short, adolescence is a time of relative uncertainty about oneself, demonstrated sometimes by social clumsiness and difficulty with clear, personal articulation.

Understanding the developmental and transitory personality aspects of adolescence can guide group leaders in their efforts to help members express themselves openly and to learn from their experience with other teens. The awkwardness observed in many adolescents requires, perhaps, more leader vigilance for encouragement and support than is required for other types of groups.

A communication pattern that lingers from pre-teen days is difficulty with conscious self-disclosing in the here-and-now and the tendency not to listen to group mates. This statement is a generalization about teens, and adults are certainly not immune to such group behavior. But the pattern seems to be more noticeable among adolescents, partly because of their self-consciousness and partly because schools rarely encourage the kind of interaction that is encouraged in group.

What a teen may intend to be self-disclosure is frequently an impersonal narrative, as if the teen were describing himself or herself as a character in a movie or TV script, through phrases like, "and I go . . . and she said . . . and then I said . . . and she goes . . ." Personalizing pronouns as a part of speaking directly about oneself is foreign to most adolescents, as well as to most adults. Instead of saying "I" or "my" when referring to themselves, they tend to detract from the intensity of a personal statement by saying, "you," "it," "we," "us." "Ya know" and "OK?" are examples of "filler-phrases" that mean nothing in themselves but may give adolescents the feeling that they have added substance to their statements. These detractions are not used consciously to avoid deeper, more personal interaction; they are speech habits developed over time. Speech patterns are copied, just as music and clothing styles are copied.

Consider the following dialogue taken from a group session with high school freshmen:

> *Paula:*   . . . and my name comes blaring over the intercom, ya know . . ."
> Paula C., please report to the vice principal's office . . ." and I go,
> "Oh, no! (rolling her eyes) Not again!" . . . Okay . . . and then, ya
> know what? The teacher, she goes, "PAULA, did you hear your
> name?" . . . and I go, "If he wants to see me, why doesn't he come
> here?" . . . just kidding, ya know . . . and the class cracks up laughing
> . . . Okay . . . Well, she gets mad, ya know, and starts yelling her lungs
> out . . . ya know.
>
> I mean . . . ya know . . . ya kinda get embarrassed when your name
> comes blaring over the intercom . . . that's a bummer, ya know . . .
> cheez, everybody in school knows you're in trouble . . . ya know . . .
> and then, having this teacher screaming like a banshee . . . ya know
> . . . and it was just a little joke . . . Okay. It's like a prison around here
> . . . Okay . . . and the teachers are like guards . . . ya know.

The leader's task in developmental groups is to help Paula focus on speaking personally and to distinguish between the description of a historic event and the feelings she might be experiencing about it in the present.

Another communication pattern to which all groups are subject, but one that is particularly noticeable among adolescents, is the tendency not to really listen to each other. They may *hear* the words spoken by another, but they do not understand or empathize. For example, in Paula's statement, while she is talking about her experience, nonlisteners are recalling when they got called to the vice principal's office, and if they respond in the group they will likely narrate their experiences. "Storytelling" is a common communication pattern in adolescent groups, and a leader must work to rechannel it to more productive here-and-now interaction. "Story telling" is never a here-and-now expression.

Presentation to Students

If possible, it is suggested that the group leader make presentations in the classroom to introduce students to the program. At this time it is important to avoid using group pressure to stimulate individual interest. The leader does not ask students to indicate an interest in joining a counseling group at this time. Instead, after explaining the purpose of the group, a pamphlet that the counselor has prepared can be given to the students. Another technique that has proven successful is that students make presentations in the classroom or in small groups in the school about their personal experiences in group counseling. In addition, students must be informed as to how they can contact the counselor. This may be in the form of a personal visit to the counselor's office, leaving one's name in a box outside the office, or any other unique way the counselor can suggest.

Counselors should consult with the administration, informing them of procedures, objectives, and potential benefits of the group counseling program; with the support of administration, counselors can then inform faculty and parents.

Checklist for Organizing School Counseling Groups

Finally, when the leader feels that all preparations are complete, a checklist can be useful as a quick reference.

1. Did you clear with administration and faculty?
2. Have you made a general presentation to students in the classroom setting? (optional)
3. Have you selected the potential members?
4. Do you have permission slips (if school policy requires) prepared for parents to sign?
5. Are students of all one grade level?
6. Are students of the same sex (or mixed) depending upon grade level?
7. Did you clearly explain to each student his or her membership responsibility?
8. Is everyone in the school (administration, faculty, and students participating) aware of time limits, location, and number of sessions?
9. Are you assured of uninterrupted privacy in the setting you will use?
10. Do you know how you are going to follow up or evaluate the group sessions?

Accountability

According to Carroll and Wiggins (1990), leaders have to be accountable to themselves as they seek to improve, and to others as they try to demonstrate that time and effort spent in group work is worthwhile. Leaders cannot depend on the research completed by others; that research doesn't address the groups they are leading or their effectiveness as leaders. So each leader is personally responsible for proving that his or her efforts result in measurable benefits to group members. Carroll and Wiggins suggest a five-step model that demonstrates accountability:

1. Setting goals
2. Assessing current status
3. Planning interventions
4. Evaluating outcomes
5. Reporting results (pp. 79-83)

Setting Goals

What does the leader—or the group—want to have happen as a result of the group process? The leader may determine these goals and either share them with group members or simply keep them in mind as a desirable outcome. For example, a leader may have this goal: "My clients should have a higher internal locus of control as a result of going through this group experience." This implies that clients will become more independent and less influenced by group opinion as a result of group interactions. Another possible goal would be to raise measured self-esteem on a pre-group and post-group (pre-post) basis. The possibilities are many and varied.

Assessing Current Status

Prior to starting counseling, the leader may want to determine the current functioning levels of group members. Many locus of control and self-esteem instruments are available for use as needs assessment measures for members. They could be administered to all members at the first session or to each member individually when selecting group members.

Other needs assessment methods of a less formal nature may include pre-post testing of member concerns, completion of adjective checklists describing oneself, very formal assessments using personality inventories administered by third parties, the use of logs or diaries subjected to leader critiques, and many other possible methods.

Planning Interventions

After goals have been set and an assessment of needs completed, the leader has to decide whether a specific type of intervention is needed to help reach the listed goals.

Leaders should also attempt to determine whether their specific types of interventions work. Do group members truly have improved self-esteem, a higher internal locus of control, or receive more favorable ratings by external observers after the group intervention? If so, can these be improved even more? If not, is it because of leader skills, poor selection of members, or other reasons? The purpose of evaluation is to demonstrate success or to help plan for changes that will lead to success.

Evaluating Outcomes

For group leaders who are not concerned with rigorous research, the pre-group and post-group assessment will be sufficient to accomplish their purpose—evaluating an individual member's progress. The perennial problem that has clouded the results of studies of the effectiveness of group work will need to be faced, however. If a group mean statistic is used, the basic stance that a group does not have a group goal but only individual objectives for each individual member is contradicted. A gain for one group member may be a loss for others; therefore, leaders who do research must be prepared to state individual hypotheses for each of their subjects if they are to remain consistent. The fact that this complicates research procedures is recognized. The leader is obligated to become familiar with the abundant literature on groups in which different (desired) directions in movement of individual members canceled out statistical significance.

Reporting Results

Most organizations require results of the evaluations to be submitted to administrators and other decision-makers. Notwithstanding the research problems of the validity of self-report instruments, criterion problems, and statistical significance, some form of evaluation is better than none.

Summary

An important aspect of the developmental group model is that teachers can instigate it, can be involved in the activity themselves, and can control it for educational purposes. Group counseling, however, is to be provided by a trained professional school counselor. Counselors are cautioned that educators may object to using valuable educational time to encourage students to get to know each other and themselves better, particularly if structured activities are used exclusively as part of the developmental group process and are perceived as "games."

Counselors would be prudent to look at their own accountability in group work. Setting goals, assessing the current status of members, planning interventions, evaluating outcomes, and reporting results are methods by which a leader can show responsibility to administrators. It is part of the professional leader's responsibility to show that there has been an attempt to help others change in positive ways. In addition, accountability allows the group leader to build a resource base for the future.

References

Association for Specialists in Group Work: Professional standards for training of group workers (rev.) (1992). *Journal for Specialists in Group Work, 17*(1).

Axelson, J. A. (1993). *Counseling and development in a multicultural society.* (Rev. ed.). Monterey, CA: Brooks/Cole.

Bates, M. (1968). A test of group counseling. *Personnel and Guidance Journal,* April, 749–753.

Bednar, R. L. & Kaul, T. J. (1994). Experiential group research: Can the cannon fire? In S. L. Garfield & A. E. Bergin (Eds.), *Handbook of psychotherapy and behavioral change: An empirical analysis* (4th ed.). New York: Wiley.

Bessell, H., & Polomares, U. (1970). *Methods in human development.* San Diego: Human Development Training Institute.

Capuzzi, D. & Gross, D.R. (2002). *Introduction to group counseling* (3rd ed.). Denver: Love Publishing.

Carroll, M. R., & Wiggins, J. (1990). *Elements of group counseling: Back to the basics.* Denver: Love Publishing.

Carroll, M. R. & Wiggins, J. (2001). *Elements of group counseling; Back to the basics* (3rd ed.). Denver: Love Publishing.

Conyne, R., & Wilson, F. R., Kline, W. B., Morran, D. K., & Ward, D. E. (1993). Training group workers: Implications of the new ASGW training standards for training and practice. *Journal for Specialists in Group Work,* 18(1), 12–19.

Corey, G. (2000). *Theory and practice of group counseling* (5th ed.). Pacific Grove, CA: Brooks/Cole.

Corey, G., & Corey, M. S. (1997). *Group process and practice* (4th ed.). Pacific Grove, CA: Brooks/Cole.

Dinkmeyer, D., & Dinkmeyer, D., Jr. (1982). *Developing understanding of self and others* (D-2). Circle Pines, MN: American Guidance Service.

Gladding, S. T. (1998). *Counseling as an art: The creative arts in counseling* (2nd ed.). Alexandria, VA: American Counseling Association.

Glasser, W, (1975). *Schools without failure.* New York: Harper.

Halverson, S. (2002). Group counseling, children and adolescents. In Capuzzi & Gross, *Introduction to group counseling* (p. 379). Denver: Love Publishing.

Johnson, S. K., & Johnson, C. D. (1995). Group process: A results approach. *Counseling and Human Development,* 27(9), 1–8.

Kline, W.D. (2003). *Interactive group counseling and therapy.* New Jersey: Merrill Prentice Hall.

Morganett, R. S. (1990). *Skills for living: Group counseling activities for young adolescents.* Champaign: Research Press.

Morganett, R. S. (1994). *Skills for living: Group counseling activities for elementary students.* Champaign: Research Press.

Redl, F. (1966). *When we deal with children.* New York: Free Press.

Riva, M. T., Lippert L., & Tackett, M. J. (2000). Selection practices of group leaders: A national survey. *Journal for Specialists in Group Work, 25, 2,* 155–169.

Riva, M. T. and Smith, R.D. (1997). Looking into the future of group research: Where do we go from here? *Journal for Specialists in Group Work, 22 (4),* 266–276.

Trotzer, J. (1999). *The counselor and the group: Integrating training theory, and practice* (3rd Ed.). Philadelphia: Taylor and Francis.

Social Skills Training in Schools

Mary N. Cook, MD

When children experience emotional or behavior problems in school, school counselors are typically the first line of defense. Frequently teachers and parents initially bring their concerns about students to the counselors. The task of screening for emotional problems and assessing for the need for a referral to a pediatric mental health provider often rests with school counselors.

A significant body of research demonstrates that anxiety and depressive disorders in children, especially, are significantly under-recognized and under-treated. In his December 1999 *Report on Children's Mental Health,* the U.S. Surgeon General estimated that one in 10 children and adolescents suffers from a mental illness severe enough to cause some level of impairment. In any given year, however, only one in five of these affected youth receives specialty mental health services. Most children attend school, so it presents a ripe opportunity for early identification, referral, and intervention with children at risk.

I worked full-time in a school-based clinic in an overseas location to provide mental health services to children with emotional and behavioral problems. I aligned myself with a number of school counselors, who frequently were tapped to work with children who were struggling emotionally or behaviorally. Children who go on to qualify for special education on the basis of emotional impairment often require mental health specialty services outside of school, but, nonetheless, school counselors often find themselves continuing to work with these kids and their families in the school setting. The school counselors, I found, typically were devoted to the children and eager to assist, but many expressed that they felt ill-equipped or at a loss at to how to intervene with special-needs children. Some counselors related that they simply didn't know how or where to begin, and some doubted whether they were adequately qualified to intervene with emotionally disturbed children at all.

The interventions in this chapter are geared toward elementary school children, ages 5–12, but could be easily adapted for work with adolescents. The strategies apply to working with kids both individually and in groups and often require the participation and cooperation of parents, peers, teachers, and school administrators. These strategies are intended to serve as beginning building blocks for school counselors, upon which they can develop their own programs based on their own context and experiences. These strategies are not intended as a substitute for pediatric mental health services offered in a medical setting.

The focus here is on social skills training, a service of great value to children with emotional and behavioral problems, who typically are social misfits, subject to much rejection and teasing. The school is clearly among the best venues to provide social skills training, a place where counselors can gather a captive peer group together. Groups work especially well as a medium for social skills training as counselors can strategically employ a few role models of social competence who can mingle and model socially adept behavior for socially impaired students. Groups also provide an opportunity for experiential learning and social-skills practice, in addition to providing an outlet for emotional expression and an avenue for garnering emotional support and acceptance from peers.

The Socially Impaired Child

Most kids seem to acquire social skills naturally, although many social skills probably are taught or modeled by parents, siblings, peers, and others. Most kids seem to sense intuitively how close is too close, how rough is too rough, when is the best time to join in or start a conversation. They can sense how others feel and respond appropriately and sensitively.

If you ask kids whether they like school or what they like best about school, a distinctive pattern emerges. Children who are well liked and have adequate friends generally like school, regardless of their academic standing. Further, they will tell you that their favorite part of school is "chasing the boys" or "playing with my best friend Courtney." Rarely will children answer that what they like best about school is science or learning. If they did answer in that way, most of us would suspect that they're being phony and acting like Eddie Haskell from the old sitcom, "Leave It To Beaver."

Conversely, kids who struggle socially generally dislike school. They often do everything in their power to avoid attending school, such as engaging in tantrums or feigning sickness, or even ditching classes. They tell you that they hate school because no one likes them and they have no friends. Again, you rarely hear mention of academic struggles as the most prominent reason for aversion to school, although many socially impaired children also struggle academically.

Interventions

We all know kids who just don't get it. They play too rough, their sense of humor needs explaining, and they constantly offend and annoy others. What to do? Most of these kids can be taught some basic social skills, either individually or, ideally, in a group setting, to help them get along in the world. The following strategies are offered as a starting point and are best delivered in the setting of a small group of fairly homogeneous kids.

Social Skills Training

Social skills interventions include lessons on how to introduce yourself, make conversation, be a good listener, give compliments, and show empathy.

Introducing Yourself

Kids must learn how to do the right kind of introduction at the right time. Timing is key. They need to be taught to wait for a lull in the conversation. They also need to be taught about personal space. Many socially inept kids are intrusive, crowding others and saying offensive things. They are anxious to be noticed and often use negative ways of garnering attention.

They should be taught to make good and consistent eye contact, to stand an adequate distance away (arm's length), face the other child directly, and, in a formal introduction, shake hands firmly but not crushing the person's hand, briefly and using the whole hand. Children younger than 12 do not customarily shake hands, but it is still a worthwhile concept to introduce. You might suggest they imagine that, when they are older, they are applying for a job, meeting their potential boss, and wanting to make a good impression.

Also, they need to be encouraged to smile. Everyone enjoys being smiled at, and if we are meeting someone who doesn't smile, we might feel rejected or assume they are grouchy or unfriendly. The goal is to convey a sense of warmth, friendliness, and confidence.

Making Conversation

The important points in making conversation are, again, timing, maintaining eye contact, smiling, and behaving in a friendly way. You can point out that everyone likes to talk and appreciates being listened to. Suggest that the best way to maintain a conversation is to ask questions. The right kind of questions are open-ended. For example, saying to someone, "Tell me about your (family, house, hobby, dog, trip….)" leaves a lot of room for an expansive response.

Follow-up questions are helpful, too, asking for more details ("Tell me more…")." Close-ended questions produce one-word answers and are conversation killers. For instance, "What's your favorite color?" will get a one-word response, and the conversation is over. Trying to find the other person's interest or hobby or some common ground is helpful, and showing interest in what the other person says through reflective listening will keep things going.

A fun and easy activity for practicing these skills is to create a talk show. Arm yourself with a video camera, and have the kids come up with a title. There's nothing most kids like more than hamming it up in front of a video camera. You might spend one session videotaping the kids pretending they are talk show hosts, and the next session they could have a party and view the videos while munching pizza or popcorn or other treats.

You might first talk about how talk show hosts make their guests comfortable. The hosts greet their guests warmly with a firm handshake, say nice things about them, and invite them to sit down. They laugh at their guests' jokes, even when they're not funny! Good talk show hosts are friendly, complimentary, and good conversationalists. They ask lots of open-ended questions and follow-up questions and listen well. Before inviting the kids to partner up and take turns pretending to be talk show hosts, you and another group facilitator can demonstrate.

Listening Skills

Kids with social problems are often lousy listeners, and this alienates others. For starters, being a good listener requires maintaining eye contact. It will help kids to learn and use reflective listening, in which they repeat what the other kid says or paraphrase what has been said. This technique is great for keeping conversations going and building relationships with others.

Reflective listening demonstrates that you are interested in what others are saying and are tracking them. Or the child can repeat a line the other child says, but in the form of a question. For example if Susie says, "I want you to draw a pink circle with polka dots," Johnnie could respond, "You want me to draw a pink circle with poke-a-dots?"

The child should respond with a relevant comment or expand on what the other child has said. For example, if Susie says, "I just moved here from Baltimore," Johnnie could say (truthfully, of course), "Oh, my grandmother lives in Baltimore. Tell me about it." Kids also can be coached to use body language that reflects they are listening, such as showing they're interested by leaning in and facing the other child directly.

Some examples of how children can demonstrate they are being good listeners are the following:

1. Make eye contact.
2. Put down anything you're doing or looking at.
3. Don't talk while the other person is talking.
4. Respond to what the other child is saying (e.g., answer a question).
5. Ask a relevant question or make a relevant comment.
6. Repeat part of what the other child is saying.
7. Paraphrase what the other child is saying.

Giving Compliments

Everyone likes compliments. Ask the children how they feel when they are complimented. The key to giving an effective and appreciated compliment is to be specific. Rather than saying, "Oh, you're so wonderful," say something specific like, "I appreciate your honesty." Or, instead of saying, "What a great picture," say, "I love the bright colors in the rainbow, and the dog looks so real!"

It's important not to overdo. If you say, "Wow, that's the best drawing I've ever seen!" you will not appear sincere and your compliment will not mean much. Instead, be real, be specific, and compliment often. Compliments make us feel good, and we like to have friends who compliment us and appreciate us.

Showing Empathy

The capacity for experiencing and expressing empathy may be the most important skill in relationships. Brooks and Goldstein (2001) cite parental modeling and teaching of empathy as a key ingredient in fostering strong parent–child relationships and bolstering *resiliency,* the capacity to rebound from stress. Regular expression of empathy can go a long way toward building and maintaining strong relationships and buffering children from stress. Many adults struggle to master this skill, and most parents do not actively demonstrate empathy to their children. But to be successful socially, kids must regularly employ empathy.

The concept can be introduced by asking the children if feelings are important. They will agree that feelings are important. Then you can ask the kids if they think their own feelings are important and whether they want others to understand their feelings and take them seriously. The kids will agree on this point, too. We all think our feelings are important, and we all want others to understand our feelings and treat them accordingly.

Empathy has two basic components:

1. Understanding another's feelings

2. Telling others that you understand their feelings

You can ask how we can know what others are feeling. The answer? Facial expression, body language, tone of voice, and content of what is said. Sometimes others will tell you what they are feeling, but it's important to point out that many times kids keep their feelings inside and won't spontaneously express them. Some children aren't adept at identifying even their own feelings and might act them out instead. Ask the kids to recall a time when they were upset and whether they found it helpful to talk about their feelings to a friend, parent, or teacher.

Programs for children by Lawrence Shapiro (1994), Phillip Kendall (2000) and others highlight the importance of promoting a "feelings vocabulary" in children, especially in children who demonstrate emotional and behavioral problems. A fun and handy approach is to have small groups of children perform miming exercises using cards, each with a basic feeling word (see Table 19.1)—the more the better,

Table 19.1 Examples of "Feeling Words"

Basic Words	More Sophisticated Words
Sad	Unhappy
Mad	Furious
Glad	Joyful
Happy	Ecstatic
Scared	Terrified
Upset	Frustrated
Hopeful	Disappointed
Dreamy	Thoughtful

using words such as *sad, mad,* and *glad,* as well as more sophisticated words such as *disappointed, frustrated, thoughtful*). You might hand out the cards and ask the kids to act out their feelings while others try to guess what they are, sort of like charades. You could award points, stickers, or tokens for correct guesses.

The group could partner up, and the kids practice making statements of empathy such as, "You seem sad" or "You look frustrated." Those simple statements can be comforting to others and open up conversations in which children can express their feelings and garner support from peers. You can point out that empathy statements convey that you care about that other person, and they also serve as an invitation to talk further about feelings. Moreover, almost all people appreciate a chance to talk about their feelings when they're upset. This is universal stuff.

The following are some responses to be avoided when attempting to empathize with others.

1. *Vague response:* "I understand how you feel." This response is not specific enough and may seem insincere or patronizing. Use a specific feeling word!

2. *Invalidating their feelings:* "That's no reason to be upset." You should emphasize that all feelings are important to the person who is experiencing them. You can ask the kids if the same things that make them sad or angry also make their brother or mother or teacher sad or angry. You can help them recognize that we react differently to the same situation, so what makes another child sad or angry might not affect you the same way.

   The point is that we all have had the same feelings at one time or other. We all know what it is like to feel angry, sad, or disappointed. This is what they can tell a friend who is hurting. Essentially the message is, "I know what it's like to feel _____ " (fill in the blank with a specific word) or, "I can see that you're feeling _____ " (fill in). Also, by conveying that you understand their feelings and inviting them to talk, you are showing that you think their feelings are important. This is a great gift to give a friend—and it's free!

3. *Problem solving:* "It will be easy to fix your bike!" or, "Why don't you just buy another one?"

Many kids (and adults, for that matter) make this mistake when trying to comfort a friend. Problem-solving is a useful skill, but the timing must be right. Initially, what is most helpful to someone who is upset is simply to express empathy, validate their feelings, and invite them to talk about their feelings. Rushing to solve the problem often makes people feel like their feelings are being dismissed or invalidated.

4. *Giving advice:* "Why don't you just go tell the teacher you didn't cheat!"

Again, giving advice right off the bat is not usually helpful or welcomed by a friend who is hurting. Instead, you should wait for the friend to seek your advice. In the meantime, you should express empathy and listen actively. Just be there.

Conflict Resolution

The children should first know the definition of *social conflict*. It is disagreement between two people when they having competing needs or wants. Then, what is a resolution? That's when both parties involved in a conflict arrive at a solution that meets their needs adequately, if not ideally.

Social conflict almost always develops secondary to miscommunication and misunderstanding. It is essential to understand this concept because it follows that most conflict can be resolved fairly simply through discussion and clarification. Also, as one party in a conflict begins to understand the other party's perspective and feelings, the anger, resentment, and frustration usually fade away.

Ask the children to think of examples of conflict from their own lives. Have them give specific examples in which conflict resulted from miscommunication. One example you can give is spreading untrue rumors, leading to hurt feelings and conflict.

It is also helpful to point out that many instances of conflict result from circumstances or accidents. Have the kids give examples and discuss how circumstances out of our control can result in conflict between people. Examples are an accident that causes someone to be late to meet a friend, or one friend but not another making the soccer team.

Ask the kids for their ideas for approaching a conflict. Have them brainstorm as you write their answers on the board. Encourage them to generate a lengthy list, accepting all ideas, even strategies that don't work well. The list might look like this:

> *I could punch his lights out.*
> *I could tell on her.*
> *We could compromise.*
> *I could give in.*
> *I could apologize.*
> *I could make a joke about it.*
> *We could get a mediator.*

Then you will have the kids go through the list and cross off options that don't work well. You can have them offer their opinions regarding which answers are best and which options would cause further problems. The options that generally work best involve compromise, humor, an apology, mediation, or taking turns. Options that usually don't resolve the conflict well and end up with someone getting hurt or teased include aggression and tattling. Tattletales, especially in the school, can be mercilessly teased, and tattlers don't learn the art of resolving conflicts in an ideal way—on their own! It should be noted that, if a child is being bullied excessively, however, adult intervention, even the involvement of school administration or security, may be needed.

Figure 19.1 depicts a sample grid that you could draw for the children. You can ask the kids which box in the grid represents the best outcome—one in which both parties win.

The goal of conflict resolution is to arrive at a compromise in which both kids get something they want, although they also might have to give up something. You can have them generate scenarios (e.g., you and your brother both want to play video games at the same time, or your sister broke your new bike) and role-play efforts at conflict resolution.

Social Problem Solving

When the child is ready to problem-solve around a social conflict, the counselor's role should be to guide and support but *not direct.* The idea is to guide the child to become an independent thinker and problem-solver who makes good choices whether you're in the room or not. The critical importance of teaching durable skills such as independent problem solving is emphasized in the work of Thomas Gordon (2000), who authored the popular *Parent Effectiveness Training,* a book outlining alternative parenting techniques that build character and strong parent-child bonds. Another author, Ross Greene (2001), points to deficits in problem-solving skills, as well as regulating affect, in his book, *The Explosive Child.*

The counselor can introduce the steps of problem solving, easily remembered with the pneumonic DIRT, which stands for the following:

D = DEFINE, as in Define the Problem
I = IDENTIFY, as in Identify Choices
R = REFLECT, as in Reflect on the Choices
T = TRY, as in Try It Out

	Johnnie Wins (+)	Johnnie Loses (−)
Susie Wins (+)	+ +	+ −
Susie Loses (−)	− +	− +

Figure 19.1 Sample Conflict Resolution Grid

The idea is to help children brainstorm as many options as possible for approaching a given problem. The counselor then can encourage the child to work through the options mentally, choose one, and then try it out. The goal, through diligent practice and rehearsal, is to have the problem-solving skills become second nature to the child.

D = Define the Problem

The first step to assist children who are upset is to help them talk out their feelings and cool down. Sometimes it's helpful to assist them in performing relaxation exercises. The goal is to help them arrive at a point at which the intensity of the feelings is no longer overwhelming and they feel back in control. As their arousal is lowered and their brain begins to reason, the counselor helps them define the problem as specifically as possible.

I = Identify the Choices

When the children are ready, encourage them to use their "good brain" to identify options for approaching the problem. During the brainstorming the counselor writes down the children's ideas. This gives validity and weight to their thoughts. Children should be encouraged to develop as comprehensive a list as possible and not reject or withhold any ideas. The counselor may contribute some ideas, too, but should be careful not to be overbearing or critical of any of the child's suggestions.

R =Reflect on the Choices

The next step is to have the children work through the list mentally, visualizing the likely outcome of each approach. Once they have covered the list, they should be encouraged to pick the option they think will result in the best outcome.

T = Try It Out

As the final step, encourage the children to try out their chosen option and report back to you regarding the results.

A sample problem-solving scenario might go like this:

Ben:	"I'm so mad I could just kill Tom. He borrowed my bike and broke it!"
Counselor:	"Boy, you sound really angry. You wish you could get him back the way he hurt you." (use of empathy, defusion emphasized of strong negative affect).
Ben:	"Yeah. I'd really like to break his favorite toy."
Counselor:	"I bet you wish you could smash his new computer game!" (reflective listening, empathy).
Ben:	"Yeah!! I'd like to wreck every one of his games! Then he'd know how I feel!"

Counselor:	"You'd really like him to know how upset you are."
Ben:	"That's right. I want him to pay for what he did."
Counselor:	"Hmmm. I can see that you want something done about this broken bike of yours. Can you think of ways to approach this problem?"

With some encouragement, Ben might generate a list like this:

I could punch Tom's lights out.
I could break one of his things.
I could tell him how I feel. *
I could forget about the whole thing and fix the bike by myself.
I could ask him to help pay for the repairs. *
I could end our friendship and never speak to him again.
I could tell his mom.

During the assessment stage, it is hoped that Ben will conclude that the best outcomes are likely to occur if he chooses the two options with marked with *. The other options will lead to tension or a termination of their friendship. It is not an option to relieve Tom of accountability for his actions because this is a passive response and will cause Ben to feel resentful, bitter, and powerless. Standing up to Tom in the right way, firmly and politely letting him know how Ben feels and asking him to assist with repairs, will likely work best. With problems involving social conflict such as this, it's helpful to have children role-play and trouble-shoot possible pitfalls to any given approach, in advance.

One option for reinforcing these concepts is to have children practice a variety of sample scenarios of common problems they face, such as these:

Your best friend likes the same boy you do.
Your friend borrowed your bike and broke it.
Your mom said you have to clean your room, but your friends are waiting for you outside to play.
You caught your friend cheating on a test.
You have invitations to two birthday parties the same day.
You want to play soccer, but your friend wants to play football.
One of your friends dislikes your other friend.
You failed a test.
You can't agree with your sister on what to watch on TV.
You lost your new jacket.
Your classmate wants to copy your homework.
Your teacher accused you of doing something you didn't do.
Your sister won't stop singing.
Your friend lied to you.
The boy next to you won't stop talking in class.

Assertiveness Training

Kids need to learn how to stand up for themselves (with their words!) and ask for what they want or need in the proper way. Aggression usually goes hand-in-hand with anxiety. Kids often become verbally or physically aggressive when they feel threatened, are hurt, or are afraid they won't get their needs met. Teaching them assertiveness gives them an ideal mechanism for expressing their needs and increases the likelihood that they will get their needs met.

You might begin by introducing the four styles of communication: passive, passive–aggressive, aggressive, and assertive.

1. A *passive* style of communication implies saying and doing nothing when faced with a social conflict or distressing situation.
2. *Passive–aggressive* communication refers to a style in which a person displays hostility or aggression in a covert way. For example, he or she might deliberately lose or forget something or show up late to meet someone with whom they are angry.
3. *Aggressive communication* refers to physical or verbal aggression whereby overt hostility is expressed in a way intended to deliberately hurt others.
4. *Assertive Communication* refers to communication where one person uses written or verbal language to express themselves openly, honestly and directly. Assertive communication does not involve a verbal or physical assault, but simply the open expression of feelings, ideas, opinions and concerns.

You can present some scenarios in which an assertive response is appropriate and offer possible response choices that demonstrate each of the four communication styles, such as the following:

You are in a crowded movie theater and the guys behind you won't stop talking.

1. You ignore them. (Passive)
2. You politely ask them to stop talking so you can enjoy the movie. (Assertive)
3. You start talking loudly, too, to annoy them. (Passive–Aggressive)
4. You throw your popcorn and drinks at them. (Aggressive)

You can have them role-play various scenarios such as the following:

1. The bike repair shop overcharged you $20 and did work you didn't request.
2. The waitress brought you the wrong order.
3. Your sister won't stop teasing you about your freckles.

You can teach kids that asserting yourself is about saying what's on your mind in a firm but polite way. The idea is to put that other person in your shoes and help him or her understand your perspective and feelings, how you are being affected by his or her behavior. Encourage the kids to use "I" statements and express their feelings, but be careful not to attack the other person. Discourage them from name-calling, labeling ("idiot, loser") because those approaches will put the other person on the defensive and probably will not get the person what he or she wants or needs. Instead, suggest that they first say how they feel, point out the person's behavior (remember to be specific!) they don't like, and make a request for a change.

Programs for assertiveness training, such as that by Sheila Helmes (1998), often advocate starting out with a handy formula for assertiveness such as the one that appears below.

I feel_____ ("I" statement—Identify and explain
    your feelings.)

When you _____ (Point out the behavior you don't like,
    without insulting or attacking.)

Because (optional)_____ (Help others understand your viewpoint—
    "Put them in your shoes.")

I would like _____ (Make a request.)

In return / then (optional) _____ (Let them know the positive conse-
    quences for you and them if they comply with your request.)

As kids master this style of communication, they can ad lib more and rely less on such formulas. Still, these are tough skills to master, even for adults, so you might want to have kids practice and commit a similar formula to memory.

An alternative to the above formula is to become a "broken record." For instance, if Johnnie owes Susie $5.00, Susie can say, "I'd like my five dollars back." Then Johnnie may say, "But I don't have enough…" to which Susie responds, "I'd like my five dollars back." And on it goes, with Susie repeating her request the same way, firmly but politely, again and again, in the exact same way, until Johnnie coughs up the $5.00 he owes her.

Joining In

The key to joining a game or other activity, again, is timing. The idea is for kids to learn how to watch for an opportune time to join a group of peers at play. They can start by watching from the sidelines and perhaps wait for a lull in the game or for someone to get called out or call a time-out. Or they can wait for another kid to voluntarily exit the game. Or they can stand by looking interested and hope to be invited to join in. Kids must be cautioned to bear in mind that they are the new guy and to behave in the most polite and cooperative manner. They must be careful not to be too pushy or controlling if they are seeking entry into a group of peers at play.

A good analogy, again, is the concept of interviewing for a job. The children are trying to make a good impression on a group of peers they'd like to join. Sometimes, even when the timing and technique for joining in is right, a child may be consistently excluded. Kids must be prepared for this inevitability. They should be advised to expect to be turned down on occasion, but to keep trying. They can be asked to consider other explanations for why they were turned down, such as the other kids perhaps being locked into a fierce competition. If a child is turned down repeatedly, you can set up exercises to actively role-play his or her attempts to join in and you and peers can troubleshoot for problems with their technique.

Hosting

When setting up play dates, kids and their parents might keep in mind a few things. First, limiting the date to one guest works best. Two guests plus the host make a threesome—a recipe for disaster. Three kids just don't play well together. Another basic rule of "good ol' fashioned southern hospitality" is that the guest is always right. Children should be taught to allow their guest to choose the first activity and to go first. Host kids should be advised to prepare for their guest—to look over their toys and belongings and be sure to stash away in a safe place anything they don't want to share. A brand new toy or newly built Lego tower should be safely stowed in a parent's closet before the guest arrives. That way, everything in view will be up for grabs and the host will be comfortable sharing the possessions that are left out.

Tease Handles

Many kids with social problems are the brunt of much teasing. Kids who don't get along well with peers usually have something about them that makes them stand out in a negative way. They might look different (be overweight, have a facial deformity, or have skin condition), act different, talk funny (have articulation problems), or have learning or behavior problems. These kids need to be taught effective techniques for responding to teasing.

You can begin by explaining why kids tease. Children doing the teasing want to elicit a strong emotional reaction in the victim. They like the thrill of pushing another child's emotional buttons. You can help kids recognize that a strong emotional reaction to teasing (overt anger or tears) is reinforcing to the teaser and is likely to result in more teasing.

Further, you can point out that some kids tease because they feel badly about themselves and think that putting down other kids will help them feel better about themselves. The goal is to teach kids with anger problems some "tricks" for responding to teasing so they are prepared to use their words, not their fists. You can point out to children that grown ups use their words to resolve conflicts and it is more mature and sophisticated to "use your head." Giving children with anger problems some specific concrete solutions to approaching teasing is extremely helpful, so they don't feel compelled resort to violence or verbal altercations.

Some options are as follows:

1. *Ignoring:* the traditional advice that adults give to kids. It's not a bad technique and sometimes results in an end to teasing eventually. But many kids will tell you they can't stand to ignore the teasing or that ignoring doesn't work.

2. *Fogging:* a favored technique, which usually eliminates teasing by leaving the teaser with nowhere to go. A different format of so-called fogging, which is suitable for adults is highlighted by Edmund Bourne (1995) in his work on assertive communication techniques for adults. Essentially this technique involves agreeing with the teaser or even expanding on the tease. The idea is to show that the teasing isn't perturbing you in the least. This reaction is unexpected and boring and usually results in the teaser giving up and moving on.

   A simple example of fogging is to have the child respond to an insult by saying, "So what?!" or "Prove it!" Other examples appear below.

Susie:	"You look scary and weird."
Johnnie's reply:	"Thank you—I've been practicing."
Johnnie:	"You're as fat as an elephant."
Susie's reply:	"That's true, but could you be more specific—an African or an Asian elephant?"

3. *Putting down the tease*: another clever and effective techniques but takes some practice and rehearsal. It is important to distinguish between putting down the tease, which defuses the situation, versus putting down the teaser, which only escalates things. The idea is for victims of teasing to convey to teasers that their teasing is lame, it doesn't phase them, and the teaser might as well give it up.

Susie:	"You're so gay."
Johnnie's reply:	"I've been hearing that since kindergarten!" (implying that the tease is old, unoriginal, and babyish)
Johnnie:	"You're fat."
Susie's reply:	"Duh. I know. It's so obvious!"

   With the techniques of fogging and putting down the tease, you should tell kids they don't really have to agree in their heart with the teasing. You're just giving them a strategy to put an end to the teasing. Fogging and putting down the tease catch the teasers off-guard and usually render them speechless. Also, these reactions are matter of fact, not highly emotional or dramatic, and the teaser will usually find this boring and not pursue it.

4. *Broken record:* a simple but effective technique Lawrence Shapiro (1994) mentions as part of an anger management program for children. You teach kids to respond to teasing with a simple phrase such as, "I don't like your teasing and I'm not going to say anything back." You advise them to try repeating this phrase, exactly the same way, matter of factly, again and again, when they encounter teasing. Eventually most teasers give up and move on, because this reaction, too, is boring.

In most instances of teasing, these techniques will work and the children can learn to handle teasing on their own. At times, however, despite their best efforts to abort the teasing, a child will fall victim to relentless and cruel teasing or bullying and adults have to intervene. Counselors can observe playground and classroom interventions and identify teasers and bullies and intervene with them, involving school administrators and parents when warranted. Teasing can be highly damaging to a child and should be taken seriously.

References

Barkley, R. (1997). *The defiant child: A clinician's manual for assessment and parent training.* New York: Guilford Press.

Barkley, R. (1998). *Your defiant child.* New York: Guilford Press.

Barkley, R (2000). *Taking charge of ADHD.* New York: Guilford Press.

Bourne, E. (1995). *The anxiety and phobia workbook.* Oakland, CA: New Harbinger Publications.

Brooks, R., & Goldstein, S. (2001). *Raising resilient children.* Lincolnwood, IL: Contemporary Books.

Cook, M & Weldon, K (2004). *Counseling children in the schools (in press).* Denver, CO: Love Publishing.Company

Gordon, T. (2000). *Parent effectiveness training.* New York: Three Rivers Press.

Greene, R. (2001) *The explosive child.* New York, NY: HarperCollins Publishers, Inc.

Hermes, S. (1998). *Assertiveness.* Center City, MN: Hazelden.

Kendall, P. (2000). *Cognitive-behavioral therapy for anxious children: therapist manual.* Ardmore, PA: Workbook Publishing.

Shapiro, L. (1994). *The anger control tool kit.* Plainview, NY: Childswork/Childsplay.

U.S. Public Health Service, Report of Surgeon General's Conference on Children's Mental Health: A National Action Agenda. Washington, D.C., Department of Health and Human Services, (2000).

Family-Based Interventions

In our present-day civilization people are not well prepared for cooperation.
Our training has been too much towards individual success, towards consid-
ering what we can get out of life rather than what we can give to it.

—Alfred Adler

The family has been called "the crucible of identity." The sense of personal integration and coherence Erikson (1981) saw as the major achievement
of adolescence depends in large part on the social, intellectual, and emotional
development that is fostered within family relationships.

Family life, which for infants and children is typically marked by gentle
care and appreciation, often becomes a battleground during the teenage years.
Parents who had been almost worshiped become the objects of resentment and
suspicion. Teenagers are in the process of busily carving out a niche and trying to figure out where they belong, how to feel important, and how to belong.
When teenagers carve out niches, parents often dig in their heels. They are
determined to survive this crisis and often feel bitter, angry, and confused—on
the one hand they feel like surrendering, and on the other hand they feel like
creating all-out warfare. The teenage years often translate into a collision
course in the home.

The teen years are a time of rapid physical, psychological, cognitive, and
social changes that affect not only the teens but all family members. Teenagers
begin to look toward their friends more than ever before to formulate their
identities and to try to develop feelings of belonging and worth. Those friends
can become either the allies of parents or the parents' competitors as the parents work to influence their children in appropriate, responsible ways.
Teenagers often feel uncertainty about some important issues, such as identity,

self-importance, self-value, sex roles, belonging, and status. Parenting is a formidable job in the teenage years, and when parenting becomes complicated as a result of divorce, remarriage, or marital problems, the entire situation can become chaotic and filled with conflict.

People often think that the problem with teenagers and their parents is, simply, the generation gap. This belief is an oversimplification and is consistently challenged by research. The real problem in parent-teen relationships—as with all human relationships—is the failure to talk, listen, and try to understand another's point of view. Teenagers often go through the turmoil of adolescence much better than their parents do. They are anxious to make this transition to adulthood, to become independent and self-reliant. But many parents are not willing to let them go.

Surprisingly, more than 8 of 10 teenagers report that they can, at least sometimes, talk with their parents. Even more surprising, research shows that most adolescents want to share more of their lives and feelings with their parents, even though they might not know how (Dinkmeyer, McKay, Dinkmeyer, Dinkmeyer, & Carlson, 1985). Teenagers want to use their parents as sounding boards for new ideas and feelings. They do not want approval or agreement; they simply want their parents to listen. In talking with their parents, teenagers want understanding and involvement. They are in the process of learning how to think for themselves. Although this process can be frustrating for parents, the end product—a mature, self-reliant adult—is surely worth a little agony.

The real key to communicating with young people is a readiness to listen and care about what *they* say, even when one does not agree. For parents, listening is easy when teenagers parrot their beliefs. The hard part is accepting the teens' right to argue, disagree, and speak out against one's tightly held views. If parents want to have open communication with teenagers, they cannot belittle their teens' opinions. Teenagers are testing not only their parents' reactions but also their own, and the response the parents give will determine, to a large extent, the kind of relationship the teens will have with their parents.

Compromise is important, as it gives teenagers credit for knowing something. Rather than lecturing, judging, and criticizing, it is important to show respect. Teenagers will let parents and other adults know if they need more advice or more input. Parents should try to learn to offer advice without demanding that it be followed. Although teenagers tend to prefer talking with their mothers, the power of their contact with fathers should not be underestimated.

In chapter 20, Bonnie Robson discusses the impact of changing family patterns on teenagers. She presents many statistics on divorce and shows how divorce creates both positive and negative aspects for adolescents. For example, following the divorce of their parents, teens have increased responsibility, but they suffer many disadvantages in psychosocial and other areas. She presents several specific methods of intervention and ways of modifying family patterns that children and teens experience. The chapter points out the great need for using preventive methods in these changing times.

Ann Vernon begins her chapter with a vignette that portrays how having accurate information on adolescent development can lead to a counselor's reformulation of adolescent problems and behavior. According to Vernon, it is imperative for counselors to consider developmental factors in problem conceptualization and treatment. In this chapter, she describes developmental characteristics and their implications for counseling and consulting.

In chapter 22, Tom Sayger and Arthur Horne describe the family counseling practice with children and adolescents. The authors make a strong case for the benefits of working with children in the family context. They caution that this modality is not effective in every situation and provide guidelines for when and how to use it effectively.

References

Dinkmeyer, D., McKay, G. D., Dinkmeyer, D., Dinkmeyer, J., & Carlson, J. (1985). *PREP for effective family living*. Circle Pines, MN: American Guidance Services.

Erikson, E. H. (1981). *Youth and challenge*. New York: Norton.

Changing Family Patterns: Development Impacts on Children

Bonnie E. Robson

oday, children are likely to grow up experiencing more than one family pattern. The traditional structure of a family unit or household as a set of parents and children and possibly other blood relatives has been replaced by a multitude of possible family patterns. These include single parents, widowed, separated, divorced, adoptive, or selective families, and blended or remarried families, as well as the adoptive or biological two-parent families with intact first marriages.

Recently the interest of researchers, counselors, and the general public has focused on the effects of various patterns on individuals within the family. This chapter explores the impact of the change from one type of family structure to another on the development of children. It focuses on which developmental styles or coping strategies and which environmental supports potentiate healthy adaptation to a change in family pattern. Using this knowledge, counselors can exert a positive influence on the process of normal development in ameliorating or preventing maladaptive responses.

The Probability of Change in Family Pattern

Most children who have lived in more than one family pattern have experienced parental separation or divorce (Bane, 1979; Norton & Glick, 1979). Since 1972, in the United States, more than one million children under age 18 have been affected each year by their parents' divorce (Carter & Glick, 1976) (although not all marital separations end in legal divorce proceedings). An estimated 40%–50% of children born in the 1980s will spend some time in a single-parent home (Hetherington, 1979; Statistics Canada, 1983).

By the end of the 1980s, almost half of Canadian families and 45% of American families will be of the remarried form (Visher & Visher, 1982). This prediction is not surprising given that 80% of divorced men and 75% of divorced women remarry (widowed persons are much less likely to remarry) (Morrison & Thompson-Guppy, 1985). These statistics suggest that 25% of all children will be part of a remarried family; others will live with parents who are in a blended common-law union. Although the latter is not remarriage, the children will be required to form a relationship with an adult in the stepparent role. Even this readjustment is not the end of the divorce process for some children, as 47% of second marriages eventually dissolve (Morrison & Thompson-Guppy, 1985) and the children of these parents must adapt once more.

Parental Marital Status Effects

That children of divorce are over-represented in psychiatric populations has been known for almost two decades (Kalter, 1977; McDermott, 1970). These children show higher rates of delinquency and antisocial behavior, more neurotic symptoms, depression, conduct disorders, and habit formations such as sleep disturbances than do children in intact homes (McDermott, 1970; Morrison, 1974; Schoettle & Cantwell, 1980). In non-clinic populations the reported maladaptations are numerous. The children are more dependent, disobedient, aggressive, whining, demanding, and unaffectionate (McDermott, 1970). Hetherington, Cox, and Cox (1978) reported that children with divorced parents have generalized feelings of anxiety and helplessness and lower self-esteem. They perform less well on a variety of social and adjustment indices (Guidubaldi & Perry, 1985).

In interviewing 703 children from separated, divorced, and remarried families, Brady, Bray, and Zeeb (1986) found that they differed in both type and degree of problems. Although differences between children with separated parents and children with divorced parents were not significant, the children with separated parents showed more immature behavior, tensions, hyperactivity, and sleep disturbances. Children from remarried families "were found to demonstrate more behavior problems as characterized by conduct problems and hyperactive behavior" (p. 409).

Demographic Variables

In a 6-year follow-up of 60 children of divorcing parents who were compared with 64 children of non-divorcing parents, Hetherington, Cox, and Cox (1985) found that divorce had more adverse long-term effects on boys. Remarriage of the custodial parent was found to be associated with an increase in behavioral problems for girls and a decrease in problems for boys. Further, stability of the problem behaviors was found to be related to the gender of the children. "Early aggressive and antisocial behavior is more predictive of later behavior problems and lack of social competence than is early withdrawal and anxiety. Moreover, early externalizing behavior in girls, perhaps because it is less frequent and viewed as less sex appropriate, is the best predictor of later socially inept behavior" (p. 529). They suggested that these gender differences may be more prominent in younger children.

Brady, Bray, and Zeeb (1986) failed to find any significant interaction among parental marital status and the child's age and sex. Similarly, other studies have not found gender to be correlated significantly with divorce adjustment (Kalter, 1977; Kurdek, Blisk, & Siesky, 1981; Saucier & Ambert, 1986). In a psychiatric population McDermott (1970) found that the proportion of male to female patients was generally equivalent.

Firstborn children, who might feel more responsible for their parents and younger siblings, may experience more stress. The youngest child may have difficulty in later adolescence in identity formation and leaving home to pursue a career if leaving home means abandoning his or her single parent.

Studies of non-clinic populations have suggested that the child's age or specific developmental phase at the time of parental separation is related to the quality as well as the severity of the reaction (Kalter & Rembar, 1981; Wallerstein & Kelly, 1980). Further, the child's age appears to be related to adjustment to the divorce (Kurdek, Blisk, & Siesky, 1981; McDermott, 1970). Generally the younger the child is, the more vulnerable he or she appears to be, because younger children show the most behavioral disturbance (Brady, Bray, & Zeeb, 1986; Hetherington, Cox, & Cox, 1978; Kalter, 1977; Wallerstein & Kelly, 1980).

Developmental Reactions

The child's developmental stage at the time of parental separation appears to be related to the reaction (Hetherington, Cox, & Cox, 1985; Wallerstein & Kelly, 1980; Robson, 1980, 1985). Thus, the following descriptions of the common reactions are divided into age-related (but not age-specific) groupings.

Infants and Preschool Children (0–5)

Following parental separation children under age 5 tend to regress in their development, showing feeding difficulties, toileting problems including soiling, smearing, and enuresis, and frequently disturbed sleeping patterns. Preschool and kindergarten children show, among other symptoms, intense separation anxiety manifested as fear that they will be left alone or abandoned by both parents.

The intensity of this reaction has two possible explanations. These children understand, albeit simplistically, that their parents no longer love each other; they are no longer living together. They reason that if this can happen to their parents, they, too, can be abandoned. An alternate explanation is that having lost one parent, they already have experienced abandonment. Fearing that they will be abandoned by the other parent, they regress to more childish behavior, recalling that when they were babies, they were loved and cared for and in close proximity to both of their parents.

Early responses of anger, fear, depression, and guilt are common in children in this age group. Preschoolers repeatedly state that they miss the non-resident parent. Although these statements may anger the custodial parent, he or she should be helped to realize that this expression of loss does not mean the child loves the resident parent any less—rather, that the child wishes for both parents to be together again.

A child in this age group can develop an attachment to other parental figures and may come to view a resident stepparent as a psychological parent. This result can lead to ongoing discord between the biological parents, with subsequent negative effects on the child.

School-Age Children: Younger (6–8), Older (9–11)

Open denial of the separation or of any difficulties with the separation are frequent findings in early school-aged children. Initially, parents may report that the child is adjusting well, but underlying feelings may not be readily apparent. As one illustration, Virginia, while drawing a picture of her father on the playroom blackboard, announced, "When he's not home, I pretend he's at work and it's okay. When I see him, then I'm sad." Thus, despite the denial, they view the separation as a profound loss. If these children are symptomatic, they appear depressed with anxious mood. They may be extremely hard to control and often have temper tantrums.

To differentiate the vulnerable from the invulnerable in this age group may be difficult for the counselor. The high-risk group appears to express more of a sense of guilt for having caused the separation. Nightmares are common. In addition, refusal to go to school, school failure, and unexplained illnesses are not uncommon.

School refusal may indicate a child who, in the intermediate phase of the divorce process, 6 months to a year after the initial separation, is attempting to get the parents back together. Parents who are concerned about their child's sudden change in behavior sometimes meet to discuss what should be done. This, however, reinforces the behavior and confirms for the child that his or her actions can bring the parents back together. Hence, negative behavior patterns may escalate. Despite the remarriage of one or both parents, children of 7 or 8 remain hopeful that their parents will reunite. For some children these fantasies persist as long as 10 years after the separation (Wallerstein, 1984).

Shock, surprise, denial, incredulity, and disbelief are characteristic of children within the older school-age group. This makes sense when we recall that these children adhere strongly to a sense of fair play. Rules are based on a strong identification with parental guidelines. When parents separate, the image of an all-knowing, all-good, ideal parent is destroyed, and children in this developmental phase can become intensely angry—usually at the non-resident parent. Once their initial anger subsides, they may assume that their parents are still angry with each other. Thus, they are vulnerable to a propaganda game in which they will accept, without question, bitter or false statements by one parent about the other.

Children in this developmental stage experience loyalty conflicts but fail to express them openly. They may attempt to resolve the conflict by becoming excessively dependent on one parent while completely rejecting the other. Susan, who is 9 years old, is unable to go out without her mother. She does not play with friends after school, preferring her mother's company. When the mother and daughter were interviewed, they sat huddled together on a coach. To pry them apart—even to get them to sit in separate chairs—was difficult at first.

These children frequently become enmeshed of their own volition in the custody struggle, and some hang on for years to the image of one parent as all good and the other parent as all bad. Some children engaged in the custody battle are permitted to read court transcripts and even testify on behalf of one parent. They are forced into a position of rejecting not only the other parent's behavior but also all those parts of that parent with which they had previously identified.

Shortly after his parent's separation, Kurt, who previously had shared an interest in soccer with his father, dropped the team despite his obvious enjoyment of the sport. This perceived need to reject all parts of one's life that were associated with the "other" parent can result in a lowered self-image and a concomitant decrease in level of functioning, both socially and academically.

Children in this age group may show anger at the time of a parent's remarriage. Anger that may have been directed at the non-custodial parent may be displaced onto the new marital partner. This can severely disrupt integration of the new family unit (Weiss, 1975).

Adolescents (13–18)

Parental divorce in adolescence can accelerate growth toward maturity, with many adolescents taking on more responsibility than their peers (Robson, 1980). This observation led many people to assert that the adolescent personality was minimally affected by divorce (Reinhard, 1977). If the spurt comes too early, however, it can intensify normal adolescent developmental conflicts and result in a premature attempt at mastery or a pseudo-adolescence (Wallerstein & Kelly, 1980).

Hetherington (1972) has found that adolescent girls, fatherless through separation, tend to change in their interactions with males. They seek attention from men and demonstrate early heterosexual behavior, as compared with the daughters of widows, who tend to be more inhibited around men.

After surveying 1,519 high school students from three different districts, Saucier and Ambert (1986) found that adolescents from divorced families were most disadvantaged on a wide range of psychosocial variables. These included mental health, subjective reporting of their school performance, and perceptions of their life in the future, their parents, and their environment. Those authors also found that boys of widowed parents were more disadvantaged than girls but found no striking difference between boys and girls with divorced parents.

Without conventional support systems and parental guidance, the independent capacity to make judgments and to establish interpersonal relationships is weakened. Lack of parental discipline, which is perceived as emotional withdrawal, is often a crucial factor constituting a further loss and an increased sense of abandonment.

College Students (18–22)

Only recently have young adults been considered when taking a developmental approach to the reactions of offspring to their parents' divorce or remarriage. Cooney, Smyer, Gunhild, Hagestad, and Klock (1986) studied 18 male and 21 female university students whose parents had been divorced 3 years or less. The authors found that in this age group the girls were more likely to experience the divorce as initially stressful.

The students appeared to lack networks, both formal and informal, and only 14% sought formal counseling. This low utilization rate may have been because of a lack of services or a lack of awareness of the availability of services. Entry into a university, with the loss of former peer support systems accompanied by the stress of an unfamiliar environment, is reported to delay adjustment to the parental separation. "The occurrence of multiple transitions was an important issue in the divorce experience in this age group" (Cooney et al., 1986, p. 473). The authors reported that this does not apply to all of the students because some found that living away from home provided protection from enmeshment in the family crisis.

Fifty percent of males and 62% of females reported a change in their relationship with their parents (Cooney et al., 1986). The women seemed more polarized in their post-separation parental relationships and experienced a deteriorating relationship with their fathers.

These are extremely important findings because the quality of relationships cannot be accounted for by custody decisions, as they might be with younger children. Although two-thirds of the college students experienced anger directed at one or both parents, they were equally worried about their parents' future. More students reported being worried about their mothers' ability to cope with independent living situations.

A study of 400 18- and 19-year-old college students revealed that those with divorced or separated parents were anxious about their own future marriages (Robson, 1985). They were less likely to want children. If they planned to marry, they thought they should delay it until they were older—perhaps in their late 20s. More of the students reported that they planned to live with their partners prior to marriage because of their anxiety that their own marriage might end in divorce. Wallerstein and Kelly (1980) reported similar concerns in their interviews with younger adolescents.

Role of the Counselor

From the preceding discussion of the severity and extent of typical reactions of children to their parents' separation, one can readily agree with Hetherington, Cox, and Cox, (1978) that every family breakdown has its victim or victims. The results of Wallerstein's (1980) study are troubling. It revealed that one-third of the children were still distressed and intensely unhappy 5 years after their parents' separation. Of course, two-thirds of the children were coping well and described as emotionally healthy.

Thus, some children cope, and some do not. Viewing divorce as an inevitable disaster may be only one perspective; the divorce process might encourage healthy development for some children. This is not to suggest that these "invulnerable" children have escaped unscathed but, rather, that they may experience the divorce as a growth enhancing process albeit a painful and initially distressing event.

Primary Prevention

Education

Educational programs designed to enhance adjustment fit well with Caplan's (1964) definition of primary prevention as a ". . . community concept. It involves lowering the rate of new cases of mental disorder in a population over a certain period by counteracting harmful circumstances before they have had a chance to produce illness. It seeks to reduce the risk for a whole population" (p. 26). In this instance the population at risk consists of children who are exposed to parental separation and divorce. In discussing children's adjustment, Kurdek, Blisk, and Siesky (1981) stated the following:

> Adjustment involves cultural beliefs, values and attitudes surrounding modem family life (the macro system), both the stability of the post divorce environment and the social supports available to the restructured single parent family (the exo system), the nature of the family interaction in the pre and post separation periods (the micro system), and the child's individual psychological competencies for dealing with stress (the ontogenic system). (p. 569)

The literature contains few reports of community intervention strategies designed to correct cultural misperceptions and attitudes (which might be stated as programming directed at the macro system). Educational programming may be in the forms of *bibliotherapy, programs, public forums, information events, individual parent education groups, group education for children, formal school curriculum, and education for professionals.* Gardner (1979) strongly advocated that educators be involved in all aspects of the divorce process.

Rubin and Price (1979) have recommended education within the school system as a preventive measure that can counteract the perpetuation of divorce in families. This type of intervention is especially important for married teenagers, because we know that this group is at high risk for marriage dissolution. By actively working with this population to further knowledge and problem-solving skills, a higher marital success rate may be ensured.

Warren and Amara (1984) found that parenting groups for custodial parents that begin after legal divorce proceedings are more effective than groups offered immediately after the separation. They further reported that participants in these 6-week groups who benefited most were the parents who had reported the greatest post-divorce stress.

Structured, educationally oriented groups exclusively for children of separated and divorced parents, either within the nursery or primary schools or within community centers and public libraries, have been recommended (Boren, 1983; Fine, 1982; Kurdek, Blisk, & Siesky, 1981; Nevins, 1981; Robson, 1982; Tableman, 1981). These community or non-clinic groups appear to be more effective when they are highly structured and when they adhere to a specific curriculum. Many organizations offer family-oriented parallel group programs similar to the program proposed by Isaacs and Levin (1984).

Freeman (1984) stated that children who participated in an 8-week semi-structured educational group were significantly better adjusted than their wait-listed controls. They showed improved in-classroom behavior, and their parents reported that they were more achievement-oriented. They had developed more specific coping repertoires and responses to stress.

In one unique program Crossman and Adams (1980) used crisis theory and social facilitation programs with preschool children. This intervention was based on the assumption that children of divorce need adult-child interaction in addition to that provided by the mother, to mediate the negative consequences of having only one parent available. In a carefully designed double control study, preschool children with separated parents made marked gains in locus of control and intelligence testing.

Legislation

Most recommendations for legislative changes advocate uniform state laws to avoid child snatching by a non-custodial parent. Others suggest changes to involve children in determining custody and visitation and to promote the concept of no-fault divorce (Atwell, Moore, Nielsen, & Levite, 1984; Payne & Dimock, 1983).

Conciliation counseling may assist families through the legal procedures surrounding a divorce and can help reduce adverse effects (Cleveland & Irvin, 1982; Lebowitz, 1983). Similarly, family mediation can simplify the procedures by proper preparation of the couple for the legalities. A full description of the place of family mediation in the divorce process is described by Haber, Mascari, and Sanders-Mascari (1983).

Much has been written about the best arrangements for custody and visitation of children. In recent years several states have followed the example of California in awarding joint custody as the preferred mode of custody. Joint custody acknowledges the continuation of parenting rights, responsibility, and duties of both parents but does not dictate place of residence or visiting and access practices. Wallerstein and Kelly (1980), Clingempeel and Reppucci (1982), and Steinman (1981) recommend joint custody, while Nehls and Morsenbesser (1980) and Goldstein, Freud, and Solnit (1973) caution against its overuse.

In examining 414 consecutive cases of divorce Ilfeld, Ilfeld, and Alexander (1982) found a significant decrease in relitigation rates when joint custody was awarded. This is not surprising when one considers that a requirement for successful joint custody is the ability to negotiate. In 18 cases the joint custody award was made over the opposition of both parents, and their relitigation rate was the same as when sole custody was awarded.

Is joint custody the best alternative? Certainly some children find a joint custody arrangement that requires frequent changes of residence unsettling and anxiety provoking (Steinman, 1981). In conclusion, joint custody can work, but it is not effective in all cases.

Direct Intervention

Early Identification

To be most effective, programs should be provided first for children and adolescents who are at high risk for maladaptive responses to their parents' separation. The previously described research indicated that the children more at risk are boys (Hetherington, Cox, & Cox, 1985), children with poor academic achievement (Rutter, 1979), first-born children (Despert, 1962), and children whose parents are only recently separated (Wallerstein, 1980).

Several researchers (Chess, Thomas, Korn, Mittleman, & Cohen, 1983; Ellison, 1983; Rutter, 1971) have implicated ongoing parental discord as a high risk factor for maladaptive patterns. Alternatively, children and adolescents who had a supportive peer group and were able to rely on their custodial parent and siblings were less vulnerable (Kalter, 1977; Robson, Homatidis, Johnson, & Orlando, 1986).

The quality and availability of support services, both before and after the separation, appear to differentiate the vulnerable and the invulnerable. Because vulnerable children make less use of their families for support and rely more heavily on fewer friends who also are more likely to have separated parents, peer support groups for these children would seen to be an efficacious preventive program.

School-Based Supportive Group Programs

The education of teachers, administrative personnel, and parents can provide a firm basis for the success of school-based group programs. Supportive groups that are moderately structured and time-limited seem to constitute ideal programming for adolescence and late latency (ages ± 10–12) children for the reasons indicated earlier (Rubin & Price, 1979). During these group sessions, children often project and portray their parents as mean, selfish, abusive, and violent. Ultimately, the parents do emerge as having strengths as well as weaknesses.

Children's divorce groups led by elementary school counselors have been found to be extremely successful (Wilkinson & Bleck, 1976). This type of group, which is based on a developmental model of counseling and includes play activities and crafts, is synopsized by developmental phase in Table 20.1. From personal experience, common themes of these groups are loneliness, fears of separation or abandonment, and feelings of guilt.

While acknowledging that preventive programs based on a crisis intervention model can be effective initially, Kalter, Pickar, and Lesowitz (1984) believe that children go through a reworking of "nodal developmental points." They caution that divorce should be viewed not as a single life event but, rather, as a process. Thus, they recommend that groups within the school setting should assist children "to negotiate more effectively the developmental tasks associated with both divorce and post-divorce experiences" (p. 614). Although they worked with students in grades 5 and 6, they also recommend groups for students at other nodal developmental points and possibly at the point of entry or leaving junior or senior high school and as preparation for college or university entrance.

Themes that emerge for students of about 10–12 years are anxiety over parental fighting, loyalty conflicts, worry about custody decisions, loss of family and loss or partial loss of the father, worry and anger about parents' dating, and concern about stepparents' discipline (Kalter et al., 1984). In adolescent school-based groups, anxiety-charged issues include marital infidelity and family violence. Teens express fear about parents' dating—and about parents who are not socially active. Adolescents feel an increased sense of responsibility and guilt if the parent is not socially active, but when the parent expresses a wish to remarry, the adolescent is concerned about having to revert from the adult position that he or she currently occupies back into a child role.

In addition, anxieties about homosexuality are increased during adolescence. Although this is a normal developmental fear during adolescence, it appears to be increased among students with divorced parents. They express fears about disturbed gender identity formation as a result of living with only one parent—particularly if that parent has preferred an opposite-sex child. Not being of the preferred gender is an issue for both males and females.

Discussion of loyalties is prominent in group sessions when holidays and vacations are imminent—especially summer and Christmas. Girls' groups tend to confirm research demonstrating lower self-concept among girls whose parents are separated (Parish & Taylor, 1979). A persistent theme in girls' groups was that they felt deprived of a normal teenage life and that they felt abnormal and unlike their peers.

An advantage of students participating in school-based groups is the opportunity to observe participants more closely in peer interactions. Close observation can enable the counselor to select students who might benefit from a more individualized approach or who might warrant referral to a clinical setting for treatment.

School-based groups, compared with community-based groups, are less likely to require parallel parent groups. Adolescent groups prefer not to have parents regularly involved, and groups may be more productive when they are free from direct parental interference. To participate actively and openly, adolescents need to be reassured about confidentiality.

Family or Individual Counseling

Reviewing the literature that deals with disruption of the family unit, there are few reports advocating a family approach. Beal (1979) has recommended family counseling as a preventive measure. Multiple family group therapy, as employed by Messinger, Walters, and Freeman (1978), promotes change and realignment with the family.

Parental *support,* not education, is recommended to assist very young children in adapting to separation and divorce of their parents. As Rutter (1971) pointed out, a good relationship with one parent can be highly preventive of later difficulties. Parents who participate in parent support groups report improved self-esteem as they acquire better parental coping skills (Kessler, 1978; Thiessen, Avery, & Joanning, 1980). And if they feel more positive about their own skills, they are likely to have improved relationships with their children.

Parents of preschoolers need support in maintaining appropriate limits in the face of their child's often extreme regression. Parents who already are stressed may become intensely angry and displace their anger at the failure of the marriage onto their preschoolers. If the child is encopretic and smearing or crying and stating repeatedly that he or she wants the absent parent, the resident parent is likely to get even angrier. Preschoolers need to cope with the separation cognitively, but 80% of them are given no explanation for the loss or partial loss of one parent (Wallerstein, 1980).

When parent counseling alone is insufficient to promote security and reassurance, filial therapy, in which the parent is trained to interact in a therapeutic-like play session with the child, is recommended. Filial therapy is especially helpful when a child appears to have an ambivalent attachment to the resident parent and an anxious avoidant attachment to the non-resident parent (Robson, 1982).

Individual secondary prevention or treatment programs should be oriented to the child's developmental phase. Individually oriented programs usually are reserved for secondary prevention or treatment of symptomatic children. One exception is the specific high-risk population of children "kidnapped" by their non-custodial parent. Individual counseling is recommended with these children to avoid post-traumatic stress syndrome, which is specific to this group (Terr, 1983).

Early school-aged children seem to respond extremely well to individual play therapy sessions in which issues of the "neurosis of abandonment," as defined by Anthony (1974), can be represented symbolically. Play therapy assists the child in achieving mastery of the stressful situation by repetition of the feared event in the play situation. Short-term play therapy, supported by frequent visiting with the non-resident father, has been extremely effective in reducing boys' anxiety symptoms such as nightmares or fears of robbers, murderers, or monsters.

Table 20.1 School-Based Groups for Children of Separation or Divorce

DEVELOPMENTAL PHASE	EARLY SCHOOL AGE (6–8)	LATENCY (8–12, 9–11)	EARLY ADOLESCENT (13–15)	MIDDLE AND LATE ADOLESCENT (15–18) (18–22)
Symptoms	Pervasive sadness, crying, suffering, experience loss. Fearful nightmares. Guilt. Reconciliation desired.	Shock and surprise. Intense anger. Blaming and rejecting one parent. Dependency conflicts.	Shock, not surprise. Pain, "loss of family." Anger at loss. Pseudo-maturity. Acting-out, delinquency, promiscuity.	
Group Size	5–6	5–7	5–6	6–8
Sex	Both sexes	Same sex	Same sex	Both sexes
Length of Time	1 hour	1–1½ hours	1 hour	1–1½ hours
Setting	One room. Table, chairs around it. Carpeted floor space.	Two rooms — group room and activity space. Sturdy chairs.	Group room. Video playback and taping. Sturdy chairs.	Group room. Avoid swivel chairs. Lamps, pictures. Regular seating, coffee tables.
Equipment, Supplies, and Materials	Pillows, craft supplies, paper, scissors, glue, crayons, etc. Simple games— Bingo, Twister, ET, Simon Says, Star Wars, Candyland, Plasticine, Polaroid camera, display area. Juice, milk, cookies.	Indoor/outdoor sports— floor hockey, soccer, softballs. Film. Dress-up materials, hats, bells, make-up Polaroid camera, craft supplies, string, paper, cooking supplies. Juice, milk, cookies.	Suggestion box. Paper, pens. Films. Simple dress-up props, collage materials. Soda pop.	Pop, coffee, tea. (15–18) No refreshments. (18–22)
Activities	Individual—crafts or games(2 per session) plus refreshment time (start with snack).	One per session— alternate large motor with quieter. End with refreshment.	Films, guest speakers, videodrama, discussion. Refreshments available at outset.	Discussion. Refreshments available at outset. (15–18)

Counselor Activity	Group preparation. Interpretation of positive transference. Avoid splitting. Modeling. Individual in group. Structure, rules, boundaries. Coaching. Rules—listen when someone is talking, stay in room, keep hands off others and others' work.	Coaching approach. Interpret group process during planning. Define boundaries. Provide security. Stimulate ideas, topics. Promote group cohesion, psychodrama.	Focus on group process. Define boundaries. Assist in maintaining structure and focus. Role play. Participate. Relate group to reality.	Group as whole. Use reasoning. Use events to develop group insights. Use modeling. Allow for verbal confrontation with adult. Relate group to reality.
Parent Involvement	Regular contact (once a week/once a month).	Group meetings irregular, discussed with group. Parents available to transport and wait for children if necessary. Parent groups.	Initially 6–8 weeks.	As indicated; not necessary.
Goals	Have peer support. Reduce anxiety. Reduce unrealistic or catastrophic expectations of adults. Link feelings with language. Help child focus on individual needs. Improve concentration and school motivation through improved self-image.	Have peer support. Reduce guilt. See both sides of parents. Gain insight. Improve behavior. Control, reduce impulsiveness. Improve self-image. Improve interpersonal skills.	See both sides of parents. Tolerate ambivalence. Not use alcohol and drugs for loneliness. Improve self-image. Gain insight.	Share and care. Foster cohesion and confrontation in supportive environment. Develop capacity to resolve conflicts in school and family. Develop hope for future. Improve self-esteem.
Themes	Loneliness. Guilt. Being left out. Abandonment.	Anger. Blame. Rights and fair play, Intolerance of mistakes. Sadness linked with anger.	Hostility. Violence. Rejection. Too much responsibility too soon. Hunger and pain.	Loneliness. Fear of future. Existential anxiety. Loss of adolescence. Sexuality.

Clinical Group Counseling Programs

More symptomatic older children and adolescents in clinic settings similar to those in school-based programs appear to respond well to group therapy. Older school-aged children have a tendency to take sides and become embroiled in parental conflict and intractable custody disputes (Robson, 1982). In this situation, family counseling with the unfavored parent and the child or children is imperative. Separate individual counseling for the favored (usually the custodial) parent is recommended in conjunction with family counseling. The custodial parent must be helped to overcome his or her own anger and resentment at the situation and to support the children in a more reality-oriented approach to visitation.

Adolescents who show more severe reactions, such as acting-out through delinquent behavior or promiscuity or marked withdrawal, can benefit from an intensive psychotherapeutic group experience, which may protect them from developing a personality disorder. The creative drama and videotape playback employed in these groups increases the individual's awareness, facilitates expression of fantasy and feelings, and promotes problem solving (Stirtzinger & Robson, 1985).

The video playback technique is unique in that it allows the adolescent to both invest in the process and maintain a safe distance. In light of these adolescents' loss of alliance with parents and their difficulty in forming a treatment alliance, video playback allows each group member to maintain a sense of control. It allows the adolescent to be an active participant either as part of the audience or as the director of a drama. Thus, the individual is permitted to identify with the group in a role function rather than as a dependent patient.

Creative drama can be viewed as a complex form of play. The adolescent is developmentally intermediate between needing the discharge of play and the ability to bind and delay inherent in talking therapy. Creative drama is intermediate between concrete, symbolic play with toys and personal revelation. It permits displacement on the characters.

In my experience with early adolescent clinic groups, family violence seems to be portrayed with increasing frequency. In client dramatizations fathers set themselves on fire and threaten the family with guns, while mothers take overdoses or suddenly abandon the family. There is much sex stereotyping, often linked with violence and anger (Robson, 1986).

Confusion over the cause of separation and the need to blame is captured in plays about family conflicts. In these plays parents frequently are portrayed as fighting over their adolescent's behavior—such as failing to clean up his or her room or not finishing homework or getting into trouble at school. Portrayal of the parents' continued fighting may represent an ambivalent wish to have the parents reunite. Fathers usually are blamed for the break-up; mothers are viewed as stupid and inadequate. Stepmothers typically are seen in the classic Cinderella sense. Parents who remarry often bear another child, so expression of the theme of being "replaced" by an infant also is common in these groups.

The older adolescent clinic groups, in my experience, tend to be more metaphorical. Through discussion these adolescents rework their understanding of their parents' separation, issues of dating, or the loss of a boyfriend or girlfriend. These themes may reflect a greater sense of parents as individuals with needs of their own. Dramatized solutions to the dilemmas, however, are at times magical and childish, with the main character suddenly becoming a famous rock star, lawyer, or journalist—an individual who goes into the world successfully, needing help from no one.

Families sometimes are portrayed as arguing endlessly with no resolution, but later themes frequently involve asking for and receiving help. A loss of discipline may represent the loss of the family as a unit. The adolescent's strivings for independence and identity can be intensified in an attempt to seek the appropriate discipline. A struggle that extends beyond the family unit into the community suggests that the parent (or both parents) needs support and guidance in providing consistency and structure. Individual counseling for the single custodial parent or separate counseling with the same counselor for both the resident and the non-resident parent may be indicated.

Conclusion

The percentage of students in elementary, secondary, and even postsecondary schools who recently have experienced a change in their family pattern is increasing. This demands the development of more innovative, preventive programming for the students affected. This programming is vital if counselors are to ward off maladaptive responses in later years and help both adults and children cope with changing family patterns.

References

Anthony, E. J. (1974). Children at risk from divorce: A review. In E. J. Anthony & C. Koupernik, *The child in his family* (pp. 461–477). New York: Wiley.

Atwell, A. E., Moore, U. S., Nielsen, E., & Levite, Z. (1984). Effects of joint custody on children. *Bulletin of American Academy of Psychiatric Law, 12,* 149–157.

Bane, M. J. (1979). Marital disruption and the lives of children. In G. Levinger & O. C. Moles (Eds.), *Divorce and Separation* (pp. 276–286). New York: Basic Books.

Beal, E. W (1979). Children of divorce: A family systems perspective. *Journal of Social Issues, 35,* 140–154.

Boren, R. (1983). The therapeutic effects of a school-based intervention program for children of the divorced. *Dissertation Abstracts International, 43* (12-A), 3811–3812.

Brady, C. P., Bray, J. H., & Zeeb, L. (1986). Behavior problems of clinic children: Relation to parental marital status, age and sex of child. *American Journal of Orthopsychiatry, 56,* 399–412.

Caplan, G. (1964). *Principles of preventive psychiatry.* New York: Basic Books.

Carter, H., & Glick, P. E. (1976). *Marriage and divorce: A social and economic study.* Cambridge, MA: Harvard University Press.

Chess, S., Thomas, A., Korn, S., Mittleman, M., & Cohen, J. (1983). Early parental attitudes, divorce and separation and adult outcomes: Findings of a longitudinal study. *Journal of American Academy of Child Psychiatry, 22*(1), 47–51.

Cleveland, M., & Irvin, K. (1982). Custody resolution counselling: An alternative intervention. *Journal of Marital & Family Therapy, 8,* 105–111.

Clingempeel, G. W, & Reppucci, N. D. (1982). Joint custody after divorce: Major issues and goals for research. *Psychology Bulletin, 92,* 102–127.

Cooney, T. M., Smyer, M. A., Hagestad, G. O., & Klock, R. (1986). Parental divorce in young adulthood: Some preliminary findings. *American Journal of Orthopsychiatry, 56,* 470–477.

Crossman, S. M., & Adams, G. R. (1980). Divorce, single parenting and child development, *Journal of Psychology, 106,* 205–217.

Despert, J. (1962). *Children of divorce.* New York: Doubleday.

Ellison, E. S. (1983). Issues concerning parental harmony and children's psychosocial adjustment. *American Journal of Orthopsychiatry, 53*(1), 73–80.

Fine, S. (1982). Children in divorce, custody and access situations: The contribution of the mental health professional. *Journal of Child Psychology & Psychiatry, 21,* 353–361.

Freeman, R. (1984). *Children in families experiencing separation and divorce: An investigation of the effects of brief intervention.* Toronto: Family Service Association of Metropolitan Toronto Press.

Gardner, R. A. (1979). Social, legal and therapeutic changes that should lessen the traumatic effects of divorce on children. *Journal of the American Academy of Psychoanalysis, 6,* 231–247.

Goldstein, J., Freud, A., & Solnit, A. J. (1973). *Beyond the best interest of the child.* New York: Free Press.

Guidubaldi, J., & Perry, J. D. (1985). Divorce and mental health sequelae for children: A two year follow-up of a nationwide sample. *Journal of American Academy of Child Psychiatry, 24,* 531–537.

Haber, C. H., Mascari, J. B., & Sanders-Mascari, A. (1983). Family mediation: An idea whose time has come. *Counseling & Human Development, 16*(3), 1–16.

Hetherington, E. M. (1972). Effects of father absence on the personality development in adolescent daughters. *Developmental Psychology, 7,* 313–326.

Hetherington, E. M. (1979). Divorce: A child's perspective. *American Journal of Psychiatry, 34,* 851–858.

Hetherington, E. M., Cox, M., & Cox, R. (1978). The aftermath of divorce. In J. Stevens & M. Mathews (Eds.), *Mother-child relations.* Washington, DC: National Association for the Education of Young Children.

Hetherington, E. M., Cox, M., & Cox, R. (1985). Long term effects of divorce and remarriage on the adjustment of children. *Journal of American Academy of Child Psychiatry, 24,* 518–530.

Ilfeld, F. W., Jr., Ilfeld, H. Z., & Alexander, J. R. (1982). Does joint custody work? A first look at outcome data of relitigation. *American Journal of Psychiatry, 139,* 62–66.

Isaacs, M. B., & Levin, I. R. (1984). Who's in my family? A longitudinal study of drawings of children of divorce. *Journal of Divorce, 7,* 1–20.

Kalter, N. (1977). Children of divorce in an out-patient psychiatric population. *American Journal of Orthopsychiatry, 47,*40–51.

Kalter, N., Pickar, J., & Lesowitz, M. (1984). School-based developmental facilitation groups for children of divorce: A preventive intervention. *American Journal of Orthopsychiatry, 54,* 613–623.

Kalter, N., & Rembar, J. (1981). The significance of child's age at the time of parental divorce. *American Journal of Orthopsychiatry, 51,* 85–100.

Kessler, S. (1978). Building skills in divorce adjustment groups. *Journal of Divorce, 2,* 209–216.

Kurdek, L. A., Blisk, D., & Siesky, A. (1981). Correlates of children's long-term adjustment to their parents' divorce. *Developmental Psychology, 17,* 565–579.

Lebowitz, M. L. (1983). The organization and utilization of child-focused facility for divorcing, single-parent and remarried families. *Conciliation Courses Review, 21,* 99–104.

McDermott, J. R. (1970). Divorce and its psychiatric sequelae in children. *Archives of General Psychiatry, 23,* 421–427.

Messinger, L., Walters, K. N., & Freeman, S. J. J. (1978). Preparation for remarriage following divorce: The use of group technique. *American Journal of Orthopsychiatry, 48,* 263–272.

Morrison, J. (1974). Parental divorce as a factor in childhood psychiatric illness. *Comprehensive Psychiatry, 15,* 95–102,

Morrison, K., & Thompson-Guppy, A. (1985). *Stepmothers: Exploring the myth.* Ottawa: Canadian Council on Social Development.

Nehls, N., & Morsenbesser, M. (1980). Joint custody: An exploration of the issues. *Family Process, 19,* 117–125.

Nevins, V J. (1981). Evaluation of effectiveness of a group treatment intervention with children of divorce. *Dissertation Abstracts International, 42* (2-B), 781.

Norton, A. M., & Glick, P. S. (1979). Marital instability in America. In G. Levinger & O. C. Moles (Eds.), *Divorce and separation* (pp. 6–19). New York: Basic Books.

Parish, T. S., & Taylor, J. C. (1979). The impact of divorce and subsequent father absence on children's and adolescents' self concepts. *Journal of Youth & Adolescence, 8,* 427–432.

Payne, J. D., & Dimock, J. L. (1983). Legal and psychiatric approaches to marriage breakdown or divorce. *Psychiatric Journal University of Ottawa, 8,* 189–197.

Reinhard, D. (1977). The reaction of adolescent boys and girls to the divorce of their parents. *Journal of Clinical Child Psychology, 6,* 21–23.

Robson, B. (1980). *My parents are divorced, too.* New York: Everest House.

Robson, B. E. (1982). A developmental approach to the treatment of children of divorcing families. In L. Messinger (Ed.), *Therapy with remarriage families* (pp. 59–78). Rockville, MD: Aspen Systems Corp.

Robson, B. (1985). Marriage concepts of older adolescents. *Canadian Journal of Psychiatry, 30,* 169–172.

Robson, B. E. (1986). School-based groups for children and adolescents of divorce. *Canadian Home Economics Journal, 36,* 13–22.

Robson, B., Homatides, G., Johnson, L., & Orlando, F. (1986). *Toronto family study.* Toronto: Toronto Board of Education Publication.

Rubin, L. D., & Price, J. H. (1979). Divorce and its effects on children. *Journal of School Health, 49,* 552–559.

Rutter, M. (1971). Parent-child separation: Psychological effects on the children. *Journal of Child Psychology & Psychology, 12,* 233–260.

Rutter, M. (1979). Invulnerability or why some children are not damaged by stress. In S. J. Shamsie (Ed.), *New directions in children's mental health* (pp. 53–75). New York: Spectrum.

Saucier, J., & Ambert, A. (1986). Adolescents' perception of self and of immediate environment by parental marital status: A controlled study. *Canadian Journal of Psychiatry, 31,* 505–512.

Schoettle, J. C., & Cantwell, D. P. (1980). Children of divorce: Demographic variables, symptoms and diagnoses. *Journal of American Academy of Child Psychiatry, 9,* 453–476.

Statistics Canada. (1983). *Divorce: Law and the family in Canada.* Ottawa: Ministry of Supply & Services.

Steinman, S. (1981). The experience of children in joint custody arrangement: A reprint of a study. *American Journal of Orthopsychiatry, 51,* 403–414.

Stirtzinger, R., & Robson, B. (1985). Videodrama and the observing ego. *Journal of Small Group Behaviour, 16*(4), 539–548.

Tableman, B. (1981). Overview of programs to prevent mental health problems of children. *Public Health Reports, 96,* 38–44.

Terr, L. C. (1983). Childsnatching: A new epidemic of an ancient malady. *Journal of Pediatrics, 103,* 151–156.

Thiessen, J. D., Avery, A. W., & Joanning, H. (1980). Facilitating post divorce adjustment among women: A communication skills training approach. *Journal of Divorce, 4,* 4–22.

Visher, E. B., & Visher, J. S. (1982). Step families in the 1980's. In L. Messinger (Ed)., *Therapy with remarriage families* (pp. 105–119). Rockville, MD: Aspen Systems Corp.

Wallerstein, J. S. (1980). The impact of divorce on children. *Psychiatric Clinics of North America, 3,* 455–468.

Wallerstein, J. S. (1984). Children of divorce: Preliminary report of a ten year follow-up of young children. American *Journal of Orthopsychiatry, 54,* 444–458.

Wallerstein, J. S., & Kelly, J. B. (1980). *Surviving the breakup: How children and parents cope with divorce.* New York: Basic Books.

Warren, N. J., & Amara, I. A. (1984). Educational groups for single parents: The parenting after divorce programs. *Journal of divorce, 8*(2), 79–96.

Weiss, R. S. (1975). *Marital separation.* New York: Basic Books.

Wilkinson, G. S., & Bleck, R. T. (1976). Children's divorce groups. *Elementary School Guidance & Counseling, 11,* 205–213.

Working With Children, Adolescents, and Their Parents: Practical Application of Developmental Theory

Ann Vernon

single-parent father and his 15-year-old son arrived for an appointment with a mental health counselor. The father told the counselor that he and his son Kevin had recently begun to have some major arguments about curfew and chores. They both wanted to address these problems before they escalated. The counselor had previously seen Kevin for school performance and sibling relationship issues and had experienced him as a "good" kid who was concerned about his grades but had to work hard to keep them up. And, although he had trouble controlling his temper when his younger brother did things that annoyed him, he had learned new ways to handle his anger and frustration and their relationship had improved considerably.

As the father and son described their recent conflict, it became apparent to the counselor that the father was seeing his son's refusal to do assigned chores as defiance and was assuming that this defiant behavior would begin to surface in other areas. When the counselor asked Kevin to share his perspective, she began to sense that while this adolescent didn't necessarily like doing chores, the real issue was the arbitrary way in which his dad was instructing him to do them. Kevin also told the counselor that he resented the fact that his curfew was earlier than most of his friends' curfews, but admitted that he hadn't talked to his dad about this because he assumed it wouldn't do any good. Instead, he sometimes stayed out later and then argued with Dad when he was grounded for being late.

Based on what her clients had shared, the counselor felt that many of the problems they were experiencing were a result of the difficulties inherent in the transition from childhood to adolescence. She explained that significant changes occur in parent–child relationships during this period and shared that adolescents are naturally struggling to achieve independence and need the opportunity to make some of their own decisions. Therefore, when parents tell their children what, when, and how to do things, adolescents hear this as a command and feel like they are being treated as children who aren't responsible enough to make any decisions. The counselor assured the father that this didn't mean his son shouldn't assume responsibility, but indicated that there would probably be less defiance if he phrased his request in a way that allowed Kevin to take more control of the task. She also explained that, at this age, many adolescents assume things without checking them out and don't have the cognitive ability to carefully analyze situations and anticipate consequences. Therefore, it was normal for Kevin to assume that his dad wouldn't negotiate on curfew and to take matters into his own hands by just staying out.

With this information about adolescent development, Kevin's father was able to reframe the issue of defiance and recognize that his son was attempting to assert his independence, which is normal at this age. At this point Kevin and his father were able to work out a contract for chores and curfew, with reasonable timelines and consequences if Kevin failed to do what was agreed upon.

As this vignette illustrates, knowledge about developmental characteristics is essential in assessment and intervention with children, adolescents, and their parents. Without this perspective, problems can be easily misconstrued. If parents fail to take into account what is normal at each stage of development, they may assume that the symptom they see is indicative of something more pervasive.

Helping professionals acknowledge the importance of incorporating a developmental perspective into the counseling process with clients of all ages. However, much of the emphasis on applying developmental theory to counseling children has been in comprehensive counseling programs that focus on prevention through classroom and small-group work, rather than assessment and intervention in individual counseling (Vernon, 1993). Although the preventive focus is extremely important, it is also critical to consider developmental factors in problem conceptualization, in designing or selecting age-appropriate assessment instruments, and in developing interventions that take into account the developmental capabilities of the child. In addition, because adult models of assessment and treatment cannot be extrapolated to young clients, knowledge of development is essential in selecting appropriate interventions to engage children in the counseling process.

A further application is to use knowledge about developmental norms and competencies in consultation with parents. If parents have a better understanding about what to expect with their children at various stages of development, they have a better perspective from which to assess symptoms that they may see as problematic.

The purpose of this article is to describe developmental characteristics of children ages 4 to 18, with specific emphasis on applications in individual counseling and consulting.

Developmental Characteristics of Early Childhood

Physical Development

To the 4- and 5-year-old preschooler, the world can be a fascinating place. In their imaginations, anything is possible. Ordinary playrooms transform into museums, and imaginary friends are frequent dinner-table guests. Typical preschoolers are curious, energetic, and eager.

Growth is slower during the preschool years, and gross motor skills such as running, jumping, throwing, and climbing improve dramatically during this period (Berger & Thompson, 1991). Fine motor skills are more difficult to develop. Gradually 4- and 5-year-olds lose their baby fat, so that by age 6 their body proportions are similar to those of an adult. Because growth is slower, it is not uncommon for preschoolers to have smaller appetites.

Cognitive Development

Preoperational thinking characterizes preschoolers' cognitive development (Bee, 1992; Santrock & Yussen, 1992). Although they are beginning to reason more logically, if they are asked to think about familiar things in a familiar context, they still base their problem-solving on what they hear or see rather than logical reasoning. They also have difficulty with abstract concepts such as divorce and death (Garbarino & Stott, 1989).

Also characteristic of their cognitive style is *centration* (Berger & Thompson, 1991). Centration refers to the tendency to center on their perceptions, or on one aspect of the situation, rather than on a broader view. This interferes with their ability to understand cause and effect and makes it difficult for them to see that the same object or situation can have two identities. For example, it is hard for many preschoolers to realize that their teacher could also be a parent.

Animism and *artificialism* are two other aspects of preschoolers' thinking (Vernon & Al-Mabuk, in press). Animism is when children attribute lifelike qualities to inanimate objects (comforting a doll when it falls). Artificialism is the belief that someone causes natural phenomena, such as a 4-year-old thinking that rain occurs because fire fighters are spraying water from the sky. Both of these characteristics contribute to the child's ability to engage in make-believe during play.

Language is another important aspect of intellectual development during this period. By age 5, children can understand almost anything if it is explained to them in context and if the examples are specific (Berger & Thompson, 1991). They have difficulty with abstract nouns and concepts such as time and space, as characterized by the frequent question, "Are we there yet?"

Self-Development

Preschoolers are very egocentric, assuming that everyone thinks and feels as they do. They find it difficult to see things from another's perspective. This egocentrism is also reflected in their excessive use of "my" and "mine." Their self-esteem is quite high, and they tend to overestimate their abilities, thinking that they are competent in everything (Harter, 1983). This is advantageous during this period when there are so many new tasks to master. With each mastery, their sense of competence increases.

Another self-development issue relates to their self-control, which increases during this period. Preschoolers are better at modifying and controlling their own impulses and are not as frustrated and intolerant if their needs are not met immediately (Sarafino & Armstrong, 1986).

Developing initiative is another important self-development task. As they enter preschool, they face more challenges and assume more responsibilities. In turn, they increase their self-initiated behaviors.

Social Development

Play serves an extremely important function for children at this age. Most of the play for 4-year-olds is associative; that is, they interact and share but do not actually seem to be playing the same game. By age 5, they begin to be more cooperative—taking turns, creating games, and elaborating on activities (Charlesworth, 1983).

Selman (1980) noted that children at this age do not understand give and take and are most likely to be quite egocentric and unable to see another child's point of view. They also have difficulty understanding intentionality, so they may respond inappropriately to others' behavior because they misinterpret it.

Gender differences are quite apparent at this age. Boys more readily engage in rough, noisy, aggressive play; girls are more nurturing and cooperative (LeFrancois, 1992).

Emotional Development

Although their vocabularies are expanding, preschoolers still have a rather limited vocabulary for expressing how they feel. As a result, feelings are often expressed behaviorally. According to Harter and Buddin (1987), it is very difficult for children at this age to understand that it is possible to have simultaneous emotions about a situation. However, they can understand the concept of experiencing different emotions at different times.

Toward the end of the preschool period, children develop a better understanding of why someone is upset, and they begin to respond verbally or physically to others' emotions. Their understanding of other peoples' emotions is limited by their perception, and they tend to focus on the most obvious aspects of an emotional situation, such as being mad, happy, or sad (Vernon & Al-Mabuk, in press).

Applications in Counseling and Consulting

Mental health professionals working with 4- and 5-year-olds need to tailor assessment and intervention strategies to the developmental level of their clients. They also need to remain cognizant of the child's physical, intellectual, social, emotional, and self-development characteristics during the assessment and intervention process. Because the attention span of children at this age is limited, practitioners should use a variety of techniques to engage their young clients. They should also use very concrete approaches because the children's ability to remember concepts is enhanced if they can manipulate objects, have a visual representation of the concept, or engage in some form of play to help them resolve issues.

Following is a description of several typical problems characteristic of the preschool child, along with specific examples of developmentally appropriate interventions for a typical problem. Information to share with parents is also included.

Typical Problems Experienced During Early Childhood

The social and emotional development of preschoolers may be manifested in their difficulty engaging in cooperative play; they may also experience problems getting along because of their limited ability to understand give and take or to see situations other than from their own egocentric perspective. In addition, young children take things quite literally. Elkind (1991) shared the example of a young child who refused to go home from preschool because he was going to meet his new "half brother." After discussing his fear, it became apparent that he actually thought he would be seeing half of a brother! This type of thinking is very characteristic and not unlike many of the other fears and uncertainties 4- and 5-year-olds experience because of their preoperational thinking: fear of dark rooms, noises at night, monsters, or bad people (Robinson, Rotter, Fey, & Robinson, 1991). In addition, they may be hesitant to leave the house to play in the yard, visit a friend, or be left at preschool because they are afraid of separation from a parent.

It is important to remember that while these are typical problems that many preschoolers will experience to some degree, there are many other situational problems such as death, divorce, abuse, or other serious events that affect the lives of children. Keep in mind that the way they process these situations is directly related to their developmental capabilities.

A Typical Problem and Possible Interventions

Five-year-old Joshua had recently started refusing to go outdoors to play in the yard. This was confusing to his parents because until the past month, he had shown no hesitation at all in playing in the neighborhood with his friends. They were not aware of any traumatic incident that had occurred when he had been playing outside, nor did they see any other problematic symptoms. They asked the school counselor for help.

The counselor first reassured the parents that this is not an uncommon problem for children at this age because they have vivid imaginations, take things literally, and have limited abilities to process concepts. She explained to them that she would first attempt to determine specifically what Joshua was afraid of and then develop some interventions to help him deal with the problem.

In working with Joshua, the counselor first had him draw a picture of himself playing in the yard. He readily drew himself with several friends playing in the sand pile. The counselor told him that she knew he didn't want to play outside much anymore and asked if he was afraid of something in the yard. At first he denied this by saying that it was too cold outside or that his friends couldn't play, so the counselor read him a book, *Dark Closets and Voices in the Night* (Colman, 1991), to help normalize fears. At this point Joshua did admit that he was a little scared to go outside but couldn't verbalize why, so the counselor asked Joshua to draw a picture to show what he thought might happen. Based on the picture, it appeared that he was afraid that there were "bogeymen" hiding in the trees and that they would come out and hurt him.

The counselor wanted to empower Joshua to handle this fear, as well as others he might experience. She used a combination of self-talk, puppet play, and empowerment strategies to specifically address the imaginative fear, which seemed very real to this 5-year-old.

First, she asked Joshua if he could think of anything that he could put in the yard or on the fence that might scare the bogeymen away. After some brainstorming, he and the counselor decided that he could make scary masks to hang around the yard. The counselor also knew that he had a dog, so she suggested that Joshua put up a sign that said, "This is a bogeyman guard dog." Next, the counselor helped Joshua generate some statements he could say to himself when he was going outside: "My dog will scare them away." "The masks will scare them away." "Even if they aren't scared away, my friends are there with me and we can protect each other." She also suggested that Joshua buy a whistle that he could blow to alert his parents if he felt threatened. Finally, the counselor had Joshua use puppets to act out different ways he could react if he thought he saw a bogeyman in the yard.

In conferring with the parents, the counselor again stressed that this seemed to be a normal problem for a child his age and that they might even see some of this fear transferred to monsters in the room at bedtime. She emphasized that these fears do seem very real and probable to a young child and cautioned them to take the fear seriously and not let siblings tease him about it. They were asked to help Joshua rehearse his self-talk and make his masks. If these interventions were unsuccessful, new approaches could be tried.

As this case illustrates, the problem was conceptualized by taking into account how children at this age experience the world and process experiences. Interventions were concrete and addressed the problem in a variety of ways.

Developmental Characteristics of Middle Childhood

Physical Development

During this period, ages 6 to 11, growth is relatively stable. Children grow taller, their body proportions change, and their muscles grow stronger (Lowrey, 1986). Due to the slow rate of growth, children have a high degree of self-control over their bodies. They can master most motor skills and become adept at running, skipping, jumping, and riding a bike. By the end of this period, there is a major improvement in their fine motor skills as well.

Depending on the rate of maturity, it is not at all uncommon to see some 10- and 11-year-olds entering puberty. Height and weight growth spurts also begin at different times for different children, contributing to self-consciousness and embarrassment.

Cognitive Development

According to Piaget (1967), a transitional period between preoperational and concrete operational thought occurs between the ages of 5 and 7. By age 8, children are definitely concrete operational thinkers. As a result, they are able to understand reversibility, reciprocity, identity, and classification. They begin to apply these principles in a variety of contexts, such as friendships, rules in games, and team play (Vernon, 1993).

During this period of development, their thinking becomes more logical and their problem-solving abilities are enhanced. However, because they are concrete thinkers, they still cannot reason abstractly or consider possibilities, which influences the way they approach situations. For example, if their best friend doesn't sit by them, they logically assume that they did something that made the friend angry, rather than consider a variety of other possibilities.

School-age children learn best by questioning, exploring, and doing (Flavell, 1985). Their language development continues; they can understand more abstract concepts and use vocabulary in more sophisticated ways (Berger & Thompson, 1991).

Self-Development

Children's self-understanding expands during this period. They are able to describe themselves in terms of several competencies at once: "I am short, a good reader, and a fast runner." They are also beginning to develop more of an internal locus of control (Collins, 1984).

As they enter school and begin to compare themselves to others, they become self-critical, feel inferior, and may experience a decrease in self-esteem (Ruble, Boggiano, Feldman, & Loebl, 1980). They may be more inhibited about trying new things and are sensitive to feedback from peers. As they become aware of their specific areas of competence, they may experience self-confidence or self-doubt (Newman & Newman, 1991).

Social Development

Socialization with peers is a major issue during the school-age years. Acceptance in a group and having a "best friend" contribute to children's sense of competence. As they learn to deal with peer pressure, rejection, approval, and conformity, they begin to formulate values, behaviors, and beliefs that facilitate their social development (Berger & Thompson, 1991).

Friendships serve other important functions. Through association with peers, children learn to develop a broader view of the world, to experiment with ideas and roles, and to learn important interaction skills. As they participate in activities, they learn to cooperate and compromise, to make and break rules, to assume roles as leaders and followers, and to understand others' points of view (Vernon & Al-Mabuk, in press).

By age 7, children begin to outgrow their egocentrism and adopt more prosocial behaviors. As they develop the ability to see things from another's perspective, they also become more adept at interpreting social cues and evaluating input (Hartup, 1984). As a result, they become better able to resolve conflicts and solve social problems.

Emotional Development

During the school-age years, children begin to experience more complex emotions such as guilt, shame, or pride. They are also increasingly aware that people are capable of experiencing more than one emotion at once. They are more adept at hiding their emotions when they don't want to hurt someone's feelings (Fischer & Bullock, 1984).

Generally children at this age are more sensitive, more empathic, and better able to recognize and communicate their feelings to others. They realize that feelings can change and that they are not the cause of another person's discomfort (Carroll & Steward, 1984). Because they are experiencing many new situations, anxiety over school performance or peer inclusion is not uncommon (Vernon, 1993).

Applications in Counseling and Consulting

Middle childhood spans a number of years in which there are many "firsts," particularly those associated with school and friends. Although it is a period of relatively stable growth, mental health professionals need to keep in mind that children in the concrete stage of development are limited in their abilities to think logically and to see possibilities. Despite the gradual enhancement of their problem-solving abilities, they continue to need adult guidance in consistently applying their skills to common problems.

Professionals working with this age group should continue to employ concrete interventions to help children resolve problems. Bibliotherapy, art activities, puppets, role-play, and games are very appropriate for this age group.

Typical Problems Experienced During Middle Childhood

Youngs (1985) identified several typical concerns that children this age experience. In particular, she noted issues surrounding peer approval: being chosen last for a team, fear of not being liked, fear of being ridiculed or disapproved of by classmates, or fear of losing a friend. In addition, children worry about school performance, passing to the next grade, or being disciplined by the teacher. As they get older, appearance and emerging sexuality issues become concerns.

Once again, these are typical concerns experienced in varying degrees by most school-age children. Unfortunately, far too many young children today have more serious situational problems, such as growing up in abusive or alcoholic homes, living in poverty, or dealing with difficult adjustments to parental divorce and remarriage. These children must deal with the more serious situational problems in addition to the challenges of dealing with normal growing up. Mental health professionals need to design interventions that are concrete in nature in order to engage the child in the problem-solving process. With school-age children, simply talking about the problem is generally not an effective process (Vernon, 1993).

A Typical Problem and Possible Interventions

Nine-year-old Jennifer asked to see the school counselor because she was afraid to take tests. Although she was a good student, she became so anxious prior to and during a test that she sometimes missed school on the day of the test or felt sick to her stomach at school as the test time approached. Jennifer tended to be very self-critical and was very hard on herself if she didn't get a perfect score.

In order to get a more accurate assessment of the problem, the counselor asked Jennifer to describe

- what she is thinking prior to taking a test,
- what she is feeling physically prior to taking a test,
- what she imagines will happen,
- how she feels emotionally before and during the test.

The counselor also asked her to share what she had tried to do to solve the problem.

Based on what this young client shared, the counselor confirmed her hypothesis that Jennifer was very perfectionistic and looked at the test-taking situation as an "all or nothing, pass/fail" event. In addition, she always imagined the worst, even though she seldom received less than a perfect score. This sort of absolutistic thinking is not uncommon for children at this age, but it is important to help them see the range of possibilities. To help with this, the counselor placed a strip of masking tape on the floor and placed notecard markers from one end of the line to the other in this order:

1. Fail by getting everything wrong.
2. Get a bad grade and miss a lot.

3. Get an average grade and miss quite a few.

4. Get a very high grade but still miss a few.

5. Get the top grade and not miss any.

Next she asked Jennifer to stand on the spot that represented where she stood with her test scores most of the time. Then she asked her to stand on the spot that represented where she was if she didn't get a perfect score. As the counselor had expected, Jennifer stood at the far end of the line (top grade, not miss any) and at the next level down.

The counselor gave Jennifer two pairs of old glasses. She told her that the first pair were the "doom-and-gloom" glasses and that when she put them on she would imagine only terrible things happening when she took a test. She asked Jennifer to verbalize those thoughts while the counselor recorded them. Next, she asked her to put on the "rose-colored" glasses. When she had these glasses on, things would look very good. The counselor asked Jennifer to verbalize her thoughts when she wore the rose-colored glasses. She explained to Jennifer that since she had never failed a test before, nor had she ever gotten an average or below-average grade, that she probably didn't need to wear the "doom-and-gloom glasses." She pointed out that if Jennifer pretended to put on the rose-colored glasses before each test, she could say positive things to herself, such as, "Since I usually do very well, why should I even think that I won't do well this time?" "Even if I got a few wrong, does this mean I'm a stupid kid?" "If I get too nervous, I'll worry too much and make myself sick, but if I just work hard, I'll probably do O.K." After the counselor modeled these rational self-statements to Jennifer, they generated a few more together and put them on note-cards for Jennifer to look at prior to taking a test.

As a final intervention, the counselor taught Jennifer some relaxation exercises that she could use prior to taking a test from *The Second Centering Book* (Hendricks & Roberts, 1977). The counselor also had her interview her sister, her father, and her grandmother. She and Jennifer generated interview questions, which related to a time they had made a mistake, whether they had ever scored less than perfect on an exam, and identifying individual strengths and weaknesses. This activity helped Jennifer see that other people had strong and weak areas, that they also made mistakes, and that they had scored less than perfect on a test and it hadn't been a catastrophe.

To Jennifer's parents, the counselor explained that it was normal for Jennifer to feel more pressure at school because she was more aware of her performance in relation to others. She emphasized the importance of sharing some of their "less than perfect" experiences with Jennifer, of reinforcing her efforts rather than the final grade, and of helping her avoid thinking the absolute worst by looking at her "track record" of performance. She also recommended that they read Jennifer the story "The Less Than Perfect Prince" from *Color Us Rational* (Waters, 1979), a story about a prince who learns that he and the world can't be perfect. She also explained the relaxation exercises so that the parents could help their daughter use them at home the day of her test.

Developmental Characteristics of Early Adolescence

Physical Development

With the exception of infancy, physical changes occur more rapidly during early adolescence (ages 11 to 14) than at any other point in the life span (Dusek, 1991). The increased production of sex hormones and the changes associated with puberty begin at about age 11 for females and at about age 13 for males. At this time, maturation of the reproductive system, the appearance of secondary sex characteristics (breast enlargement, pubic hair, voice change), and a growth spurt occur. This growth spurt can last approximately 3 years and begins about 2 years earlier in girls than in boys (Malina, 1991).

Children in this age group vary tremendously in their rate of maturation, which results in self-consciousness and anxiety. Both males and females will be clumsy and uncoordinated for a period of time because the size of their hands and feet may be disproportionate to other body parts. In addition, their rate of physical change affects how they see themselves. Early adolescents want to be like everyone else and are painfully aware of appearing awkward or different. Because they don't want others to see their bodies, "locker-room phobia" is common during this period of development (Baumrind, 1987).

The physical and hormonal changes characteristic of early adolescence can be very confusing. Sexual thoughts and feelings abound, often accompanied by feelings of shame and guilt. Young adolescents are curious about sex and wonder if others feel the same way they do. Straightforward information about sex is extremely critical prior to and during early adolescence.

Cognitive Development

During early adolescence, the shift from concrete to formal operational thinking begins. Although this change begins at about age 11, it is not attained until the ages of 15 to 20 (Schave & Schave, 1989). As they move into more formal operational thinking, adolescents begin to think more abstractly, develop the ability to hypothesize, and can mentally manipulate more than two categories of variables simultaneously (Newman & Newman, 1991). Although they can also reason more logically and predict consequences of events, they do not always apply these skills to themselves. In other words, they may apply their skill in logic to their work in mathematics, but they may not logically assume that if they stay out past their curfew they might be grounded (Vernon, 1993).

According to Schave and Schave (1989), the shift from concrete to formal operational thinking is "the most drastic and dramatic change in cognition that occurs in anyone's life" (p.7). With these new abilities, young adolescents are able to detect inconsistencies, think about future changes, see possibilities, think of logical rebuttals, and hypothesize about the logical sequence of events (Newman & Newman, 1991). It is important to remember that considerable variability exists in the degree to which formal operational thinking is attained and in the consistency with which it is applied during early adolescence. Because it is easy to assume they are capable of more mature cognitive thought than they actually are, working with members of this population can be confusing.

Self-Development

The tasks of self-definition and integration begin during early adolescence (Dusek, 1991). As adolescents engage in their self-development search, they push for autonomy. Elkind (1984) noted that although they strive for independence, they are still immature and lack life experience. These contrasts, coupled with their cognitive, physical, and pubertal changes, leave them very vulnerable. As a result, they may show increased dependency, which can be very confusing to them and to the adults involved in their lives.

In some ways, young adolescents contradict themselves. They want to be unique, yet they want to look like everyone else. They are very self-conscious, assuming that everyone is looking at them or thinking about them. Elkind (1988) termed this belief that others are as concerned with us as we are the "imaginary audience." As a result of this type of thinking, early adolescents fantasize about how others will react to them, becoming oversensitive about their performance and appearance. Because they feel awkward and ugly, self-esteem usually decreases during this period of development (Baumrind, 1987).

Adolescents can also be very egocentric, seeing themselves as more important than they really are or assuming that no one else experiences things the way they do (Berger & Thompson, 1991). They also assume that because they are unique, they are also invulnerable. Elkind (1984) labeled this the "personal fable"—because adolescents believe they are special, they think bad things can happen to others but not to them. The personal fable accounts for self-deprecating as well as self-aggrandizing behavior, in which the adolescent assumes that he or she will be heroic and world famous.

Social Development

Because young adolescents look to peers as a source of support, they are very sensitive and vulnerable to peer humiliation (Vernon & Al-Mabuk, in press). Peers play an increasingly significant role in their lives and are an important part of the socialization process. The need to belong is very strong, which also means that young adolescents have to learn to contend with peer pressure and decisions about which group to associate with. It is during this period that cliques and distinct groups emerge, with specific "rules" about how to dress and behave.

As adolescents mature, their relationships become more complex. Because it is still difficult for some adolescents to step outside themselves and look at their own behavior objectively, they may behave obnoxiously. This, in turn, influences how others respond to them. They also continue to have difficulty taking others' viewpoints into account because they are still preoccupied with their own needs (Newman, 1985).

Emotional Development

Many early adolescents ride an emotional roller coaster during this developmental stage. Moodiness, accompanied by emotional outbursts, is common. Troublesome emotions such as anxiety, shame, guilt, depression, and anger also occur more frequently (Adelson & Doehrman, 1980).

Because these negative emotions can be overwhelming and cause adolescents to feel very vulnerable, they often mask these feelings of fear and vulnerability with anger, which typically distances people and often results in increased conflict as adults react to the anger and fail to recognize the true feelings behind it.

The increased intensity of emotions permeates all aspects of life. Early adolescents feel anxious about what is happening to them, but because many are unable to think abstractly, they tend to view things from an "either-or" perspective. They don't make good choices about how to deal with the anxiety because they are unable to generate alternatives. This may result in more anxiety, guilt, or shame.

It is particularly important that adults who interact with young adolescents recognize their emotional vulnerability and not exacerbate the problems by reacting insensitively.

Applications in Counseling and Consulting

Working with young adolescents can be challenging because it is often difficult to get at the underlying feelings they mask with their anger, apathy, or acting out. Mental health professionals need to remember that because the attainment of formal operational thinking occurs gradually, many of the problem behaviors occur as a result of incompetencies in thinking and reasoning. This is sometimes easy to overlook because the rapid achievement of physical maturity leads adults to assume that adolescents are more mature than they actually are.

Although many significant changes occur during early adolescence, many researchers contend that what the adolescent experiences is part of a normal, healthy, developmental process (Berger & Thompson, 1991; Newman, 1985; Schave & Schave, 1989). Furthermore, the majority of adolescents do not resort to drug dependence, delinquent acting-out, school failure, sexual promiscuity, or other self-destructive behaviors (Steinberg & Levine, 1987). That is not to say that early adolescents don't have worries and experience problems.

Typical Problems Experienced During Early Adolescence

Young adolescents are easily overwhelmed by their feelings, and many of their problems result from their inability to deal effectively with these feelings. Because they tend to be oversensitive, they overreact to relationship issues with friends and parents. They worry excessively about how they look, how they act, and whether they belong. They also have concerns about dealing with their own sexuality.

Adults often overreact to adolescent behavior and assume that their illogical actions are intentional. This creates additional problems for adolescents, and they may respond with defiance or withdrawal. Mental health professionals working with adolescents need to remember that concrete strategies may still be necessary to help them look at cause and effect, alternative behaviors, and long-range implications.

A Typical Problem and Possible Interventions

Cory's mother referred him to a counselor at a local mental health center because the school had called to inform her that he had skipped school for the last 5 days. Although she had to leave for work before it was time for Cory to go to school, school attendance had never been a problem in the past. His mother indicated that he seemed happy at home and had several friends. He had struggled some with his studies in the seventh grade but generally got average grades. There had been no major changes in his life other than the transition to junior high last year.

When the counselor saw Cory for the first time, he immediately noticed that although Cory was very tall, his feet and hands were still too big for his body, making him appear clumsy and awkward. He had a fair amount of acne and seemed somewhat immature compared with other eighth-graders this counselor had worked with. Cory didn't deny skipping school but wasn't willing to talk about why. In an attempt to elicit more information, the counselor asked Cory to complete the following unfinished sentences:

1. When I go to school, I feel _____.

2. The part of the school day I like best is _____.

3. The part of the school day I like least is _____.

4. The subject I like best is _____.

5. The subject that is easiest for me is _____.

6. The subject I like least is _____.

7. The subject that is hardest for me is _____.

8. If I could change something about school, I would change _____.

9. Other kids in this school _____.

10. Teachers in this school _____.

Cory's responses to these questions appeared to indicate two problem areas: speech class and physical education. The counselor hypothesized that Cory was overly sensitive about his body and didn't want to undress in the locker room after physical education. He also assumed that Cory wanted to skip speech class because he was self-conscious about getting up in front of 25 other students to give a speech.

After some discussion, Cory admitted that he felt self-conscious in these classes. The counselor explained the concept of the "imaginary audience" to him and assured him that these were typical concerns that other classmates were probably experiencing as well. He asked Cory to assess how helpful skipping school had been in dealing with these problems and consequently obtained a commitment from him to work on more productive ways to handle the situation.

The counselor adapted an activity called "Magnify" (Pincus, 1990). In this adaptation several events were listed and Cory was instructed to magnify their importance by turning them into catastrophes. For example:

1. You walk to the front of the room to give a speech. Catastrophic thought: _____.

2. You go into the locker room to change for physical education. Catastrophic thought: _____.

After Cory identified the worst case scenario, the counselor taught him to look at the probable situation by adapting "Getting Straight Our Magnifications" (Pincus, 1990).

You walk to the front of the room to give a speech.

Best case scenario:_____

Worst case scenario:_____

Probable scenario:_____

By identifying best, worst, and probable outcomes and identifying his catastrophic thoughts for several different situations, Cory began to dispute some of his anxieties about his speech and physical education classes. Next, the counselor helped Cory develop self-statements to deal with the anxiety:

■ Even though it seems like everyone is looking at me when I give a speech, probably only a few people are, and that's not the end of the world.

■ If I mess up when I'm giving a speech, I'm not a total jerk.

■ If I'm embarrassed to undress in physical education, other kids probably are too, so it's not worth skipping school over.

Following these activities, Cory and the counselor again looked at the consequences of skipping school and generated alternative ways he could handle the situation if he felt nervous again. The counselor recommended that he read *Changes and Choices: A Junior High Survival Guide* (McCoy, 1989) to help him see that the thoughts and feelings he experienced were normal. Together they drew up a contract for school attendance.

In consulting with Cory's mother, the counselor explained the concept of the imaginary audience and assured her that her son's solution to the problem no doubt seemed very logical to him due to the cognitive incompetencies characteristic at this stage of development. He suggested that the mother might visit with the speech teacher to discuss the possibility of utilizing small groups for some of the speech activities because students wouldn't feel as anxious about performing for fewer classmates. Finally, he praised the mother for being firm about school attendance, yet at the same time trying to understand why Cory had chosen to behave as he had.

Developmental Characteristics of Mid-Adolescence

Physical Development

Depending on when the early adolescent entered puberty, physical development for 15- to 18-year-olds may continue at a rather rapid rate or may gradually slow down. Since males generally lag behind females in the rate of physical development, females often tower over males until this trend is reversed in mid-adolescence (Berger & Thompson, 1991).

Generally, by mid-adolescence, females have achieved full breast growth, have started to menstruate, and have developed pubic hair. Males experience a lowering of their voices at about age 15, and facial hair appears approximately a year later (Newman & Newman, 1991).

Sexual urges are very strong during mid-adolescence. This can evoke anxiety for adolescents and their parents. Sexuality is one way to try out "grown up" behaviors, but many adolescents don't think about the possibly serious consequences, such as sexually transmitted diseases or pregnancy (Vernon & Al-Mabuk, in press). Although most teenagers aren't obsessed by sex and don't have intercourse on a regular basis, good sex education is imperative (Steinberg & Levine, 1990).

Cognitive Development

Formal operational thinking continues to develop during mid-adolescence, allowing 15- to 18-year-olds to think and behave in significantly different ways. For example, as they develop the ability to think more abstractly, they can hypothesize, think about the future, and are less likely to conceptualize everything in either-or terms because their thought processes are more flexible. They are capable of pondering and philosophizing about moral, social, and political issues. They are better able to distinguish the concrete and real from the abstract and possible (Dusek, 1991; Sroufe & Cooper, 1988).

Although their cognitive abilities have improved considerably since early adolescence, mid-adolescents are still likely to be inconsistent in their thinking and behavior. While they might be able to see alternatives, they still may lack the experience or self-understanding to make appropriate choices.

Self-Development

Along with achieving independence, preoccupation with their identities is a primary focus for teens at this stage of development. This process of finding themselves involves establishing a vocational, political, social, sexual, moral, and religious identity (Erikson, 1968). They do this by trying on various roles and responsibilities; engaging in discussions; observing adults and peers; speculating about possibilities; dreaming about the future; and doing a lot of self-questioning, experimenting, and exploring. This may be a period when they spend more time alone, contemplating ideas and trying to clarify their values, beliefs, and direction in life.

Mid-adolescents are generally more self-confident and do not have to look like carbon copies of their peers. In fact, they may do the opposite, dying their hair green if someone else's is red or wearing quirky clothes from secondhand stores to "make a statement." This self-assertion extends to other areas as well. Mid-adolescents are more capable of resisting peer pressure due to increased self-confidence and the ability to look beyond the immediate present and speculate about long-term consequences.

According to Baumrind (1987), much of what happens in terms of self-development at this stage depends on the degree to which the individual has attained formal operational thinking and his or her level of self-esteem.

Social Development

Peer relationships continue to be very important during this stage of development. The increased time spent with peers serves several important functions: to try out various roles, to learn to tolerate individual differences as they come in contact with people with different values and lifestyles, and to prepare themselves for adult interactions as they formulate more intimate relationships (Dusek, 1991).

If they have attained formal operational thinking, adolescents approach relationships with more wisdom and maturity. They are not as dependent on friends for emotional support, and by the end of this period they begin to select friendships based on compatibility and shared experiences as well as on what they can contribute to the relationship (O'Brien & Bierman, 1988).

Intimate friendships increase during mid-adolescence, which helps teens develop more social sensitivity. As they become less egocentric, they are better able to recognize and deal with the shortcomings in relationships. As a result, friendship patterns become more stable and less exclusive (Dusek, 1991). There is also more dating and sexual experimentation during this period (Newman & Newman, 1991).

Emotional Development

As they attain formal operational thinking, adolescents are not as overwhelmed by their emotions and subsequently experience less rapid mood fluctuations. Fifteen- to 18-year-olds tend to be less defensive and are more capable of expressing their emotions rather than acting them out behaviorally (Vernon & Al-Mabuk, in press).

Many adolescents experience loneliness and ambivalence toward the end of this developmental stage. They may be gradually growing away from their friends as their needs and interests change. As high school graduation approaches, they may be apprehensive about the future. Some experience self-doubt and insecurity if they compare themselves to peers or realize that they don't have the skills or ability to qualify for a particular job or postsecondary education.

Adolescents are better able to deal with emotionally charged issues if they have developed formal operational thinking skills. As a result, they are not as impulsive or likely to behave irrationally or erratically in response to emotional upset. Bear in mind that the wide variation in how adolescents manage emotions results from their different levels of cognitive maturation.

Applications in Counseling and Consulting

Counseling the mid-adolescent is easier than working with the 11- to 14-year-old, but a lot depends on the degree to which the adolescent has obtained formal operational thinking. In general, the older adolescent does not feel as vulnerable, is better able to express feelings, and is more willing to be in counseling. That is not to say that all older adolescents are this way; a lot depends on the nature of the problem and the personality of the adolescent.

For the most part they are better able to verbally express themselves, and it is easy to assume that concepts don't need to be reinforced in concrete ways. Because adolescents vary in their rate of maturation and because some are visual rather than auditory learners, it is still very appropriate to use activities to help illustrate points. Use of short homework assignments such as bibliotherapy or journalizing is very helpful for this age group.

Typical Problems Experienced During Mid-Adolescence

Although the emotional turbulence lessens to a large degree during mid-adolescence, a new set of circumstances arises that can create problems for 15- to 18-year-olds. Specifically, adolescents at this age are dealing with more complex relationships that may involve sexual intimacy and with decisions about their future. According to Youngs (1985), teenagers at this age worry about getting enough out of high school to prepare them for life. They also express confusion about career choices and worry about money. Relationships with family may be strained as they push for more autonomy, and yet they may have anxiety about being too independent.

Mid-adolescence serves as a "stepping stone" to the young adult world, in which there are even greater challenges and new opportunities. This can be an exciting time, but it can also create anxiety. Mental health professionals working with adolescents need to be aware of this ambivalence and of the fact that by age 18 most will be making significant transitions involving changes in roles, relationships, routine, and assessment of self.

A Typical Problem and Possible Interventions

Stacie, 17, initiated contact with the school counselor to discuss her relationship with her boyfriend. According to Stacie, the relationship had been very good for the first few months, but lately they had been arguing so much that she was afraid Matt would break up with her. Whenever they went out, she constantly wanted reassurance that he cared about her, which irritated him. When she persisted, he ignored her. If he didn't call when he said he would, she got anxious and was upset if he didn't return her phone calls right away. She was certain he was seeing other girls and assumed that there was something wrong with her. Her response to this situation was to sit home and wait for his phone calls, call his friends to see where he was, and stay awake at night thinking about the situation. She felt depressed and anxious.

In talking with Stacie further, it appeared that the majority of arguments occurred because Stacie wanted to spend all her time with Matt and he insisted on having some space. Stacie expressed concern about what he would do if he wasn't with her, so the counselor had her make a list of all the things that could happen. In the next column, she asked Stacie to put a check next to the things that she could prove had happened. Once this was completed, the counselor explained that there was a difference between probability and possibility and that one way of distinguishing between these was to look at past evidence. For example, it was possible that Matt could take out another girl, but to her knowledge had he ever done this? It was possible that he could get killed in a car accident, but had he ever driven recklessly or while drunk when she had been with him? The counselor instructed Stacie to use this type of questioning to deal with her anxiety about things that could happen but seemed unlikely based on past history and information about Matt.

Next the counselor discussed issues of control in the relationship. She tied some strings to her arms and legs and asked Stacie to pull on them. The harder Stacie pulled, the more the counselor resisted. They discussed the fact that Stacie's attempts to control Matt would probably drive him away, which Stacie acknowledged had happened once already. To help her deal with this, the counselor had Stacie make a list of things she could say to herself when she felt like she wanted to control her boyfriend, such as "Will it do more harm than good to control?" "What's the worst thing that could happen if I don't control him?" "Can I really control another person?"

As Stacie talked about the relationship, it also seemed that there were times when Stacie wasn't being controlling but that Matt was not treating her with respect. The counselor gave Stacie some handouts on personal rights and assertion and explained the concepts to her. They then role-played assertive and nonassertive responses to some issues that Stacie had generated.

When Stacie left the session, she admitted feeling less anxious and indicated she had several things she could work on to help her deal with this relationship issue.

Conclusion

The intent of this article was to provide helping professionals with characteristics of children and adolescents across several dimensions of physical, cognitive, social, emotional, and self-development. This information can be used several ways in assessment and intervention. In assessment, it can serve as a barometer to indicate how a child is progressing relative to normal developmental guidelines. This barometer serves an extremely important function because without it parents and professionals can easily misconstrue or misdiagnose problems. With this information they have a general sense of what's "normal." In addition, knowledge about developmental characteristics is essential in selecting or designing appropriate assessment strategies for the child's developmental stage.

Developmental knowledge is also exceptionally critical in designing effective interventions. Children and adolescents don't respond to the same counseling approaches that work with adults. Because children's attention spans are more limited—at least until adolescence—helping professionals must be more creative and use visual and kinesthetic as well as auditory methods. Games, art activities, play, simulation activities, music, and drama are all examples of interventions that take into consideration the developmental capabilities of the child or adolescent.

Although extensive coverage of consultation could not be provided within the limited scope of this article, the examples with the preschooler, elementary-aged child, and young adolescent demonstrate the significance of sharing information about development with parents. Helping professionals can readily apply the same concept with teachers or other professionals to help them better understand characteristic behaviors and typical problems experienced by a particular age group. In addition, it is very important to share how development affects children's abilities to comprehend concepts, which in turn has an impact on their behavior. Far too often parents and teachers think children (and adolescents in particular) are being obnoxious, when in fact they are acting that way because that is the only way they know to process information in the given situation.

Growing up is challenging. In addition to the normal developmental issues identified in this article, children in today's society have other significant concerns with which to deal. Helping professionals who are well-grounded in developmental theory will be better equipped to understand how young clients process information and how to most effectively work with them to facilitate resolution of typical problems as well as more serious situational problems.

References

Adelson, J., & Doehrman, M. J. (1980). The psychodynamic approach to adolescence. In J. Adelson (Ed.), *Handbook of adolescent psychology* (pp. 99–116). New York: Wiley.

Baumrind, D. (1987). A developmental perspective on adolescent risk-taking in contemporary America. In C. D. Irwin (Ed.), *Adolescent social behavior and health* (pp. 93–125). San Francisco: Jossey-Bass.

Bee, H. (1992). *The developing child.* New York: HarperCollins.

Berger, K., & Thompson, R. (1991). *The developing person through childhood and adolescence.* New York: Worth.

Carroll, J., & Steward, M. (1984). The role of cognitive development in children's understanding of their own feelings. *Child Development, 55,* 1486–1492.

Charlesworth, R. (1983). *Understanding child development.* Albany, NY: Delmar.

Collins, W. A. (Ed.). (1984). *Development during middle childhood: The years from six to twelve.* Washington, DC: National Academy Press.

Colman, P. (1991). *Dark closets and noises in the night.* Mahwah, NJ: Paulist Press.

Dusek, J. B. (1991). *Adolescent development and behavior.* Englewood Cliffs, NJ: Prentice Hall.

Elkind, D. (1984). *All grown up and no place to go: Teenagers in crisis.* Reading, MA: Addison-Wesley.

Elkind, D. (1988). *The hurried child: Growing up too fast too soon.* Reading, MA: Addison-Wesley.

Elkind, D. (1991). Development in early childhood. *Elementary School Guidance and Counseling, 26,* 12–21.

Erikson, E. (1968). *Identity: Youth and crisis.* New York: Norton.

Fischer, K. W., & Bullock, D. (1984). Cognitive development in school-age children: Conclusions and new directions. In W. A. Collins (Ed.), *Development during middle childhood: The years from six to twelve* (pp. 70–146). Washington, DC: National Academy Press.

Flavell, J. H. (1985). *Cognitive development* (2nd ed.). Englewood Cliffs, NJ: Prentice Hall.

Garbarino, J., & Stott, F. (1989). *What children can tell us.* San Francisco: Jossey-Bass.

Harter, S. (1983). Developmental perspectives on the self-system. In P. H. Mussen (Series Ed.) and E. M. Heatherington (Vol. Ed.), *Handbook of child psychology, Vol. 4: Socialization, personality, and social development* (pp. 275–385). New York: Wiley.

Harter, S., & Buddin, B. J. (1987). Children's understanding of the simultaneity of two emotions: A five-stage developmental acquisition sequence. *Developmental Psychology, 23,* 388–399.

Hartup, W. W. (1984). In W. A. Collins (Ed.), *Development during middle childhood: The years from six to twelve* (pp. 240–282). Washington, DC: National Academy Press.

Hendricks, G., & Roberts, T. B. (1977). *The second centering book: More awareness activities for children, parents, and teachers.* Englewood Cliffs, NJ: Prentice Hall.

LeFrancois, G. R. (1992). *Of children: An introduction to child development.* Belmont, CA: Wadsworth.

Lowrey, G. H. (1986). *Growth and development of children* (8th ed.). Chicago: Year Book Medical Publishers.

Malina, R. M. (1991). Growth spurt, adolescent. In R. M. Lerner, A. C. Petersen, & J. Brooks-Gunn (Eds.), *Encyclopedia of adolescence* (pp. 244–289). New York: Garland.

McCoy, K. (1989). *Changes and choices: A junior high survival guide.* New York: Perigee Press.

Newman, B. M., & Newman, P. R. (1991). *Development through life: A psychological approach.* Pacific Grove, CA: Brooks/Cole.

Newman, J. (1985). Adolescents: Why they can be so obnoxious. *Adolescence, 79,* 635–646.

O'Brien, S. F. & Bierman, K. L. (1988). Conceptions and perceived influence of peer groups: Interviews with pre-adolescents and adolescents. *Child Development, 59,* 1360–1365.

Piaget, J. (1967). *Six psychological studies.* New York: Random House.

Pincus, D. (1990). *Feeling good about yourself.* Carthage, IL: The Good Apple.

Robinson, E. H., Rotter, J. C., Fey, M. A., & Robinson, S. L. (1991). Children's fears: Toward a preventive model. *The School Counselor, 38,* 187–192.

Ruble, D., Boggiano, A., Feldman, N., & Loebl, J. (1980). A developmental analysis of the role of social comparison in self-evaluation. *Developmental Psychology, 16*, 105–115.

Santrock, J., & Yussen, S. (1992). *Child development: An introduction.* Dubuque, IA: William C. Brown.

Sarafino, E. P., & Armstrong, J. W. (1986). *Child and adolescent development.* St. Paul, MN: West.

Schave, D., & Schave, B. (1989). *Early adolescence and the search for self: A developmental perspective.* New York: Praeger.

Selman, R. (1980). *The growth of interpersonal understanding: Developmental and clinical analyses.* New York: Academic Press.

Sroufe, L. A., & Cooper, R. G. (1988). *Child development: Its nature and course.* New York: Knopf.

Steinberg, L. D., & Levine, A. (1987). *You and your adolescent.* New York: Harper Perennial.

Steinberg, L. D., & Levine, A. (1990). *You and your adolescent: A parent's guide for ages 10 to 20.* New York: Harper & Row.

Vernon, A. (1993). *Developmental assessment and intervention with children and adolescents.* Alexandria, VA: American Counseling Association.

Vernon, A., & Al-Mabuk, R. (in press). *What growing up is all about: A practical guide to help parents understand children and adolescents.* Champaign, IL: Research Press.

Waters, V. (1979). *Color us rational.* New York: Institute for Rational Living.

Youngs, B. (1985). *Stress in children.* New York: Arbor House.

Family Counseling With Children: Attending to the Children in Our Midst

Thomas V. Sayger and Arthur M. Horne

Conducting family counseling when a child is present can be a humbling experience for even the most skilled professional. Providing family counseling with children requires a "fourth generation" professional, in which skills and knowledge of individual child psychology must be blended equally with skills and knowledge of family dynamics and functioning (Kaslow & Racusin, 1990). Therefore, in the field of child-focused family therapy, we find professionals who retain identities (e.g., counseling psychologist, child clinical psychologist, child psychiatrist) that, at least in part, lie outside the traditional boundaries of family psychology.

Counseling children automatically directs our clinical attention to an ecological perspective in which we explore the interaction of the child with his or her immediate social environment, the family (Garbarino, 1993). Clinicians, however, also must examine the interplay of social systems in the environment that shape the child's experience (e.g., school, society, culture). Children who are identified for counseling, in essence, may be experiencing the traumas of living in an ecological system that is threatening, dysfunctional, and unhealthy. The child's ability to relate stories of his or her experiences with the family therapist is imperative and may provide insights into the child's cognitive abilities and level of self- and social awareness.

Some researchers and clinicians have doubts about the effectiveness of family therapy for addressing clinical issues in general, notwithstanding those related to a child's mental health needs. Most family therapy models have major limitations because they fail to appreciate the importance of key variables that pertain to individual family members and to extrafamilial systems, do not consider important individual developmental issues that should influence the therapist's understanding of the problems and choice of intervention strategies, and rarely utilize proven intervention strategies derived from other treatment models (Henggeler & Borduin, 1990).

According to some professionals, even the terminology of family therapy can elicit negative connotations. Professionals offering family counseling might best perceive their role as consultant rather than treater, therapist, or healer (Johnson, 1993). Subscribing to a position that labels clients as "disturbed," "pathological," or "dysfunctional" can be a disempowering frame of reference that discourages children and families considering their counseling options.

An empowerment position that focuses on clients strengths and resources implies that families and children are people with problems to be addressed, not individuals in need of repair. Empowering families and children entails helping them gain accurate information and access to community resources (e.g., financial assistance, child or respite care, transportation, medical assistance), developing coping skills for managing difficult behaviors or communicating with school personnel, and identifying and establishing a social support network (e.g., prevention programs, extended family/friends networking, parent support groups, individual counseling). Most clinicians agree that family therapy should have therapeutic and healing effects; however, beliefs and language that attribute virtually every emotional or behavior problem of children to parental pathogenesis can become offensive to many parents in the same way that gender-biased or ethnic-biased language can be offensive to women, men, or members of ethnic groups (Johnson, 1993).

Clinical practice with regard to child mental health concerns entails an understanding of the contribution of many different systems (i.e., biological, cultural, economic, political, organizational, legal) to family interactions and the overall quality of family life. Professionals also must be knowledgeable of laws, policies, procedures, and programs that relate to the needs and concerns of families of children with mental and emotional disorders. Parents want family therapists to share what they know about the etiology of emotional and mental disorders of childhood based on current research and the research evidence regarding the effectiveness of different treatment approaches. Professionals must have knowledge about parental views of counseling services, attitudes, and behaviors and be aware of possible connections between counseling ideologies, attitudes, and behaviors that parents view as problematic or contradictory to their beliefs and values. Finally, family therapists must be knowledgeable about the goals and activities of parent support groups and the experiences and needs of siblings of children with emotional and mental disorders (Johnson, 1993).

Clearly, family relationships do not take place in a vacuum. They are affected by biological, cultural, economic, and political dynamics. So, although Bowen (1985) viewed the family as the unit of illness and consequently the unit of treatment, current thinking in child mental health stresses the effects of macrosystems (i.e., dominant culture, governments, mass media) on the quality of family life. When conducting family counseling with children, the family therapist must not forget that any changes effected in treatment will be only as successful as the family's or child's ability to implement those changes in society as a whole.

Why Family Therapy?

Combrinck-Graham (1989) wrote that the family is the child's primary resource system. She envisioned the child's world as a series of concentric circles in which the child is the center, encircled by the nuclear family, which is encircled by the mental health system, and so on. From this perspective it makes sense to assume that children will be most affected, at least during their early developmental stages, by the immediate family, which filters all information from surrounding systems (e.g., the community, culture).

Given that the mental health system in general may have little direct impact (or even contact) with the child, directing specific interventions toward the family system seems plausible and perhaps even desirable. Family therapists often are faced with a dilemma, however, because many families request help for one member whom they view as having individual problems that belong to that person and not to the family as a whole (Nichols & Everett, 1986). When the presenting problem is focused on a child who displays difficulties and disturbances of the kind referred to as symptomatic (e.g., depression, delinquency, school phobia), the family therapist must decide whether that child or other children should be invited to the initial session.

When Garbarino (1993) was asked the question "What do we need to know?" he answered, "It depends on what we want to do" (p. 9). Children referred for clinical services may be traumatized by their life events and have memory problems and distorted information. The family therapist has to be able to help children tell their story and must be sensitive to children's needs to construct a narrative of self and family experiences that meets their emotional needs and is consistent with their cognitive resources.

Families as systems strive to maintain balance or homeostasis. In this way an individual family member (many times the child) may be sacrificed or may sacrifice himself or herself to maintain the system's balance. For example, a child may engage in behaviors that he or she knows will elicit abuse to keep the father from abusing the mother, which may lead to dissolution of the family. The therapist's goal is to facilitate change in which a healthy family balance is maintained by eliminating abuse and developing effective communication patterns (Walker, Bonner & Kaufman, 1988).

Children typically are excluded from family therapy if the therapist deems that the child needs to be protected or if specific information may hurt the child (e.g., parental sexual relations, marital difficulties). Children also may be excluded from family therapy because the therapist has difficulty addressing adult and child modes of interacting at the same time (Chasin & White, 1989). In addition, children may be excluded from therapy if the counselor deems it theoretically inappropriate or determines that the key to the problem and its solution lie in the parental subsystem.

Recalling her experiences as a child playing musical chairs, Hoffman (1993) noted having feelings of exclusion (music is playing, children are having fun, the music stops, someone is kicked out of the game). Are we playing musical chairs with children in the family therapy process if we choose to exclude them from the process because we define them as symptom carriers and assert the belief of accentuating the parental hierarchy as having more importance than the child subsystem? Perhaps clinicians should be adding chairs to our family therapy game of musical chairs as Hoffman suggested, so each family members feels of equal value.

Patterson (1975) suggested that siblings of aggressive children should also be included in any treatment program. Children change their parents, just as parents contribute to changes in their children. In addition, Framo (1992) noted that when a family presents a child as the problem, he works with the whole family, or subgroups of the family, until the symptomatic child has been defocused and the symptoms either have disappeared or have been alleviated. Then, if the parents are motivated, Framo works on the marital relationship, as he views most children's symptoms as a metaphor for the parent's marriage. Framo stated that some of the parents who originally came to therapy out of concern for a child become interested in working out some of their own issues with the family of origin, particularly when the parents recognize that they are repeating with their own children their parents' patterns of parenting.

The primary issues of conducting family therapy with children seem to center on child or family development, psychopathology, and treatment orientation and its history of effectiveness with specific client issues (Combrinck-Graham, 1989). When viewing families, clinicians should reframe their thinking to one in which families are seen as relationship matrices and the primary unit of child development and, therefore, treatment (Chasin & White, 1989).

Issues of Development

The main issue to be addressed in family therapy with children centers on individual adult or child development needs and family development (Zilbach, 1989). Evaluating and understanding a behavior problem in a child as existing apart from the important relationships of his or her life is not possible (Allen, 1990). The child must be understood from the point at which he or she is in his or her own development and how the child is reacting to deal with this experience.

Child Development

To achieve healthy growth and development, we generally believe, children need a warm, loving, and stable home environment (Thompson & Rudolph, 1992). Social crises (e.g., unemployment, poverty, faltering educational systems, latchkey households) and changing value systems (e.g., gender role identities, sexual freedom) have challenged the stability of home environments for children. The high-risk child's better functioning seems to be associated, in part, with maternal warmth, a warm, active, and balanced family interaction, and healthy and benign parental attributions toward the child (Wynne, Jones, & Al-Khayyal, 1982). Morris et al. (1988) found that fathers of aggressive boys reported eight times more negative thoughts about their child and more negative thoughts about their family than fathers of well behaved boys. "Healthy communication" on the part of parents is important in promoting healthy adjustment in children, particularly by providing children a model for developing the cognitive capacities of attending, focusing, remaining on task, and communicating ideas and feelings clearly and directly (Wynne et al., 1982).

In developing clinical interventions for children in the family context, individual techniques and family techniques and modes can be used conjointly. Several treatment goal areas are available to explore when counseling children (Gibson, Mitchell, & Basile, 1993). These goal areas include the following:

1. *Developmental*, assisting children to meet and advance their general human growth and development

2. *Preventive*, helping children avoid some undesired outcome

3. *Enhancement*, helping children to further develop or identify their special skills and abilities

4. *Remedial*, overcoming or treating an undesirable development

5. *Exploratory*, examining options, testing skills, and trying new and different activities

6. *Reinforcement*, helping children recognize that what they are doing, thinking, and feeling is okay

7. *Cognitive*, encouraging children to enjoy the learning process and its intrinsic rewards

8. *Physiological*, helping children acquire the habits of good health

9. *Psychological*, developing effective social interaction skills, learning to understand emotions, and developing a positive self-concept

10. *Protective*, ensuring that children can experience the fun, joy, and happiness of being a child

Young children tend to be trial-and-error learners, are egocentric, and use mental images and imagination, thinking in pictures. Prior to age 7, children also are typically capable of understanding simple rules but often see them as being unchangeable (Thompson & Rudolph, 1992). When counselors are working with preschool or early elementary school children, they should use short sentences in keeping with the length of a child's statements, should use names instead of pronouns, should use the child's terms and words, should ask the child to repeat your message instead of asking "do you understand?", should rephrase, not repeat, questions children do not understand, and should not respond to every answer with another question (Garbarino & Stott, 1989). Because preschoolers and other young children tend to be literal, the counselor should not overinterpret answers a child might give. Encouraging children to expand on their answers might be accomplished by providing short summaries or simply acknowledging the child's responses.

With children ages 5 and younger, the best therapeutic approach is to hold discussions in tandem with play activities, encourage them, tell or read stories that teach, and point out children's strengths to help them develop a sense of self-worth (Gibson, Mitchell, & Basile, 1993). When working with somewhat older children (e.g., ages 7–11 years), a different set of developmental issues arises. Children in this age group are much more active thinkers and are beginning to understand their feelings more fully. These children tend to have high energy levels, be more self-critical, lack self-confidence, and are not comfortable with being singled out for praise. They also are apt to be more social, are moving away from parents as the central focus of their lives to establishing peer group activities, typically are more verbal, and have greater capacities for concentration.

Whereas sessions with very young children should be limited to 20–25 minutes, sessions with pre-adolescent children can be 40–45 minutes long. As children get older, play activities in the counseling sessions become less useful and the traditional verbal approaches can be used more extensively. Pre-adolescent children should experience the feeling of being "understood," and activities such as values clarification, modeling, bibliotherapy, and focusing on more cognitively and affectively complex tasks are more appropriate.

With all children, the school environment becomes a primary system within which they interact. Therefore, the counselor should expect to hear complaints about teachers, principals, or other children. Pre-adolescent children in particular may be unintentionally rude, fidgety, talk quickly and in an animated fashion, and have a roaming memory. To deal with these issues in session, the family counselor should interject direct leads that focus upon the specific problem.

In sum, the task is to determine if the child is having experiences or behaving in ways that are consistent with their developmental stage. As a cautionary note, the family counselor should guard against the tendency to treat children as "little adults." Children typically have different interests, behaviors, and cognitive abilities than adults and should be treated as unique individuals with challenges specific to their development both in and outside the family system.

Family Development

The family life cycle at the time young children are present requires accepting the new generation of members into the system (McGoldrick & Carter, 1982). Second-order changes require adjusting the marital relationship to make space for children, taking on parenting roles, and realigning relationships with extended family to include parenting and grandparenting roles. This stage requires that adults now move up a generation and become caregivers to the younger generation.

When parents cannot make this shift, they may struggle with each other about taking responsibility or refuse to behave as parents to their children. Often parents are unable to set limits and exert the required authority, or they lack the patience to allow their children to express themselves as they develop. Family therapy might reframe the situation to help parents view themselves as part of a new generational level with specific responsibilities and tasks in relation to the next level of the family life cycle.

Changing family systems present the family therapist with a major challenge in addressing family development issues. An increase in teenage pregnancy and subsequent multigenerational family households, increasing divorce rates and consequent single-parent households, dual-career families and latchkey children, and the rising rate of children living in poverty all present the family therapist (and society) with difficult challenges and add to our confusion in attempting to understand the family life cycle.

Multigenerational families organize themselves in different ways (Chase-Lansdale, 1993). Young mothers may be the primary parents of their children, with grandmothers as supportive, background figures. On the other hand, grandmothers may be in charge of the family, with young mothers and grandchildren treated as siblings. Or co-parenting may occur, wherein mothers and grandmothers share child-drearing and child care and coordinate parenting tasks.

Two-parent, two-earner families face two major challenges: marital discord and child care. The stress of maintaining the household and providing child care can place a strain on even the most highly functioning parent. Because of these multiple stressors, marital arguments, lack of time together, and faltering communication, the marital dyad is at high risk for dysfunction. These families need to find ways to divide tasks, set aside time for family meetings, develop times for shared activities as a couple, parent-child, and family, and maintain open lines of communication.

The growing divorce rate has presented the family system with a variety of problems, including poverty and unemployment, custodial versus noncustodial parenting, stepfamilies and stepparenting, and systems that place the child in a tug-of-war between the two parents. Some children living in poverty-related risk conditions do manage to develop in a healthy pattern (Chase-Lansdale, 1993). This resiliency seems to be embedded in the child's internal resources, such as an easy temperament, average or above-average intelligence, and sociability; a good relationship with at least one member of the family; and adequate social support outside the family. Chase-Lansdale argued that these children are not given enough credit for their abilities to make sense of their complex social world or how they derive strength from certain experiences and overcome multiple life stressors.

Noncustodial (usually father) parent research suggests that loss of access to the father has been associated with greater problems in children's adjustment to divorce, and loss of access to their children has been associated with more dissatisfaction and problems for fathers (Goldsmith, 1982). Active, continuing involvement between fathers and children has been linked to successful adaptation to other subsystems, such as the co-parental subsystem and the one-parent household. Involvement and engagement of the father are likely to be crucial when dealing with a two-parent family, whether that be a bioparent family or stepparent family, and in divorced families with noncustodial or joint-custodial fathers. The family therapist should always monitor the relationships between the various subsystems, their boundaries and relative power, and the manner in which the presenting problem is embedded within them (Goldsmith, 1982; Sager et al., 1983).

Cultural Relevancy

Using and developing culturally relevant interventions are important because most of the minority cultures in the United States share a primary emphasis on the importance of the family (Isaacs & Benjamin, 1991). In Native American, African-American, Hispanic-American, and Asian-American families the role of extended family members and support individuals (e.g., grandparents, friends, shamans, religious leaders) may be accentuated. These individuals within the social support or kinship network may have been delegated specific parenting functions within the family. In addition, strong family orientations typically override loyalty to other institutions and, consistent with the ecological perspective, the family and its cultural identity may play the primary role in determining objects of loyalty.

In the dominant American culture the family generally is conceptualized as the parents having ultimate authority over the child. In ethnic minority cultures families tend to be built around eldership, so even when parents are present, the ultimate authority may reside with a grandmother, an elder uncle, a tribal leader, or others the family recognizes as having the greatest wisdom and respect. A thorough understanding of the roles various family members play, as well as an articulation of the family values, especially as they relate to childrearing practices, are critical to the assessment process in determining family development issues and the direction of family therapy interventions.

With respect to their cultural styles, families can be classified on a traditionalism-modernism dimension (Ramirez, 1991). Modern lifestyles and belief systems encourage separation from family and community early in life. Modern orientations to socialization emphasize individual competition, and science is accorded great importance in explaining the mysteries of life. Traditional lifestyles, on the other hand, emphasize close ties to family and community throughout life. Traditional orientations stress cooperation and give spiritualism more importance in explaining life events. Clearly, cultural identity plays a significant role in determining family boundaries, values, beliefs, attitudes, and behaviors and, as such, should be assessed and incorporated directly into the family counseling process.

Psychopathology

Many children experience psychological distress and may receive a clinical diagnosis (Rapoport & Ismond, 1990). Perhaps the most common diagnostic category is that of disruptive behavior disorder (attention deficit hyperactivity, conduct, or oppositional defiance) (Horne & Sayger, 1990). Other diagnostic categories include anxiety disorders, depression, body function disorders such as enuresis and enco-presis, tic disorders, and personality disorders, to name a few. We do not attempt to discuss all of these disorders in this article but, rather, to simply touch on the role of family in the development of childhood psychopathology.

Combrinck-Graham (1989) has come to the conclusion that dysfunction in children may be understood more usefully as a part of patterns of family interaction and, in some cases, family interactions with larger systems. For Bowen (1985) pathology takes a multigenerational twist in which psychopathology results from each generation's unsuccessful attempt to achieve differentiation. He discusses the conceptualization of schizophrenia as a three-generation development characterized by high levels of immaturity and intense early attachments to the mother.

If a child has a serious psychological problem, the parent becomes overinvested in the child, fails to achieve differentiation for self, and blocks the child's attempts at achieving differentiation (Sayger, 1992b). The Bowen systems family therapist focuses on an available family strength to achieve a more stable family structure and works toward helping the parent maintain a more definitive position in relating to the child.

The bottom line for family therapists who determine that the child referred for treatment has a pathology is to select the treatment regimen that has shown the most success in dealing with that issue. Often the family therapist works with children who are taking medication for a disorder by stressing adherence to the medical regimen, developing appropriate social or behavioral skills, and addressing the family's concern regarding the disorder or any one of a number of concerns with which the family and child are being confronted.

Treatment Orientation

Multiproblem families tend not to benefit from traditional mental health treatment, have multiple problems with several symptomatic members, and utilize foster placement and institutionalization at a higher rate than other families (Zarski & Fluharty, 1992). Therapists working with families at risk for child placement can help these families by positively reframing stressful events related to the child at risk and encouraging any efforts by the parents to learn alternative coping styles. Social class, poverty, and associated problems may contribute significantly to the presenting problems of families in treatment. Therapists should explore alternative models for the most effective matching of family to treatment. Matching is needed to ensure that the unique characteristics of children and families are taken into consideration prior to intervention (Zarski & Fluharty, 1992).

Weltner (1985) asserted that therapeutic style also has to be matched to the family need and identified four levels of family functioning:

Level I Families dealing with life and death issues and ineffective parenting. By mobilizing support for the ineffective parenting system, the family is better able to deal with the life stresses at hand.

Level II   Families facing issues of establishing authority and setting limits. The parental system is unable to maintain sufficient control over family members, and this threatens the stability of the entire family. The family intervention should focus upon surveying family strengths and resources and developing a system coalition that is strong enough to offer sufficient authority.

Level III Families with a structure and style that seems to be working and a mixture of coping mechanisms to which they are committed and attempt to pass on to their children. Working with these families involves changing ingrained patterns and dealing with the expected resistance to these changes.

Level IV Families concerned with the fine art of living. Thoughts, feelings, and memories usually become the focus of clinical work. Interventions tend to have insight-oriented goals with more sensitive awareness of the world of relations and understanding of legacies and heritage. Psychoanalytic techniques, along with family sculptures or imaging, work best with these families.

Chasin and White (1989) offered the following criteria for conducting effective family therapy with children:

1. Use constructive family activities in therapy.

2. Assume that parents are in charge of the family, and encourage, not undermine, this role.

3. Stress clear structure for sessions, clear rules and expectations for addressing discipline and safety, and personal rights of individual participants.

Chasin and White also noted that children are more frequently excluded than included in family therapy even though including children makes them available to the therapist for direct intervention, and full understanding of the family cannot be achieved if some members are known only by hearsay.

Strategic Family Therapy

Strategic family therapies seem best suited to families that want symptom relief. This approach has had considerable success with families that have had negative experiences in counseling in the past and resist therapy because the focus is placed immediately on communication strategies and interactions. Because most strategic family therapies are brief, this form of counseling also has been accepted widely by the professional mental health community.

Strategic family therapists believe that families present symptoms that metaphorically represent some other problem. A mother's abuse of her son, for example, may be representative in part of the emotional and psychological neglect she experiences when her husband is drinking (Walker et al., 1988). Watzlawick, Weakland, and Fisch (1974) saw problems occurring from wrong attempts at changing ordinary difficulties. Segal (1982) described these "wrong" attempts as following one of four patterns:

1. Family members attempt to solve their problem by being "spontaneous deliberately." A scenario for "curing" insomnia might be to lie in bed until you fall asleep. This places the individual in a paradoxical trap by attempting to force a specific behavior. Substance abusers force themselves not to drink, and overeaters force themselves not to eat.

2. Family members attempt to find a "no-risk" solution when some risk is inevitable. In responding to a fear of failure or rejection, the child or parent tries too hard or gets "stuck" when trying to resolve the issue.

3. Family members attempt to achieve agreement through arguing. In attempting to discuss and share their feelings, children and their parents become overly sensitive and create problems where none exist.

4. A child or parent attempts to attract attention by attempting to be left alone. A parent, for example, might withdraw from a situation when he or she feels personally attacked or not respected.

When utilizing a strategic family therapy approach with families in which the child is the identified client, the therapist first attempts to determine who the child is protecting and in what way (Madanes, 1981). The therapy is planned in stages, and the therapist decides on an intervention that will change the family organization to one with a single hierarchy in which the parents have the superior position. Specific interventions usually are either straightforward or paradoxical directives to family members to do something in and out of the session with the goal of changing the interaction patterns of family members. The strategic family therapist makes no direct attempt to make family members aware of how communication takes place. If the problem can be resolved without the family's knowing how or why, that is satisfactory. As the client's problem increases in severity, however, knowledge of the rationale for change could be helpful in improving success and client satisfaction (Szykula, Sayger, Morris, & Sudweeks, 1987).

Madanes (1984) presented four paradoxical directives that seem most amenable to family therapy with children. Paradoxical interventions, or prescribing the symptom, encourages a person to perform the symptom, thus emphasizing that the symptomatic behavior is under the person's control.

In the first directive the counselor prescribes *pretending of the symptom*. In this scenario parents request their child to pretend to have the presenting problem. The parents then criticize the performance and make sure the pretending is accurate. Then, when the child presents the real problem, the parents are to behave as they usually do. For example, a child may be asked to pretend to have a temper tantrum while the parents evaluate the performance. Parents must be careful to evaluate in a caring and affectionate manner and avoid hostility. In most cases the therapist does not expect the performance to occur, and the family or child will realize that he or she does have control over the problem.

The second directive prescribes *a reversal in the family hierarchy*. Most problems are seen as stemming from incongruent hierarchies, usually the marital hierarchy, in which either the husband or the wife has more power with regard to intimacy, affection, or decision making. Two common extensions of imbalances in power are as follows: (a) a child's behavior protecting the weaker parent by distracting the stronger parent from direct attacks; (b) the child's problem representing an arena for parental fighting that is less threatening than the parent's real dispute (e.g., fighting about a child's misbehavior rather than a parental lack of sexual intimacy).

Strategic interventions frequently involve rebalancing the marital hierarchy. For example, the parent with lesser power is placed in charge of implementing the directives and the parent with more power serves as expert consultant. Prescribing a reversal of the family hierarchy is a directive that puts the children in charge of the parents. This approach is appropriate when the parents present themselves as incompetent, helpless, and unable to take charge of their children, and at the same time complain that the children are out of control. This directive also can be used with children who are shy and withdrawn or rebellious. For example, children might be instructed to discuss what they would have their parents do if they were in charge of their parents' happiness. This technique is meant to tap in to the child's sense of humor and the natural caring between children and parents.

The third directive involves *asking parents to prescribe the presenting problem or the symbolic representation of the presenting problem*. Parents are asked to request that the child purposefully display the presenting problem. During the child's performance the parents supervise the child and see that he or she does it correctly. For a child with a fire-setting problem, the prescription is that the child is to set fires under the parents' supervision. Later, this behavior is to be replaced by the parents' and child's performing more constructive activities. Hypothetically, this paradoxical intervention addresses the part of the parent-child interaction in which the child helplessly persists in the disturbing behavior while the parents helplessly insist that it should end but are unable to stop it.

The fourth directive entails *prescribing who will have the presenting problem*. In essence, this directive consists of prescribing the symptom but changing who will have it. Strategic family therapists might employ this intervention with more severe problems, such as delinquency, depression, drug or alcohol use, antisocial behavior, or bizarre communication. The underlying hypothesis for this technique is that the presenting problem is distracting the family from conflict with a family member in a way that is benevolent and prevents resolution of the original conflict. For example, an acting-out child might be the family problem for a depressed father in that the antisocial behavior takes the family's focus away from the father's problem. Consequently, by asking another family member to be the "family problem," family members are expected to rebel against this task and progress to a discussion of the "real" family problem.

Sayger (1992b) reviewed two other techniques associated with strategic family therapy:

■ *Benevolent sabotage.* In this technique the counselor tells the child or parent to "go slow" or warns of impending danger if improvement occurs, thus emphasizing the consequences of behavior. Examples of benevolent sabotage are parents' apologizing for the consequences that occur "accidentally" to the child (e.g., not being able to find a favorite shirt after the parent cleans the child's room, being locked out after curfew).

■ *Reframing.* To attempt to change the conceptual or emotional tone of a situation, the counselor suggests a different frame of reference. For example, a child who is demanding of his or her parent's attention may be seen as an irritating, bothersome brat. A strategic reframe might suggest that the child values the parent's attention so highly that he or she is willing to go to extreme lengths to obtain it. Consequently, the parent's frame of reference changes from one of irritation and disgust to one of expression of respect and love.

In presenting a case of a child experiencing night terrors, Madanes (1981) reported that the initial session was directed at obtaining information on the specific scenario of night terrors (e.g., family history, sleep patterns, antecedent events). During session the child was instructed to demonstrate the night terror and the mother was asked to think of causes of the behavior. In this instance the child's night terrors centered on a burglar who was harming the mother. The strategic therapist envisioned the purpose of the night terrors as the child's attempt to protect the mother from the burglar because the mother, hearing her child's cries, would awaken and go to the child's room. In the rest of the treatment scenario, family members were to pretend the symptom every evening, the mother would wake up the child and all other family members, and a sibling kept notes on each family member's performance. Finally, the therapist attempted to strengthen the relationship between the child and the mother's live-in partner and conducted an individual session with the child to change the "night terror burglar" to a more positive vision. The treatment ended when the child began to be involved more actively with other children and the night terrors ceased.

Structural Family Therapy

Rather than focusing on power, structural family therapists emphasize structural aspects of the family (Minuchin, 1974). They interest themselves with intergenerational boundaries and with the formation of alliances and coalitions. Structural therapists believe that difficulties are most likely to arise during critical points in the life cycle. Structural family therapy seems most suited to families that are disorganized, authoritarian, and unmotivated (Sayger, 1992b).

Structural therapy has its roots in crisis intervention and treatment of chronically dysfunctional, inner-city, delinquent, and psychotic families. During critical stages of development, parents who have established nurturing patterns must modify those patterns and develop appropriate methods of maintaining control while encouraging growth during this cycle of family life (Minuchin & Fishman, 1981). New patterns must be explored and stabilized in all family subsystems (e.g., parent-child, sibling, couple, individual), and when children go off to school, for example, the family must learn to relate to a new, well organized, highly significant system. As children grow and learn that their friends' families operate by different, and usually more fair (at least according to the child), rules, the family has to negotiate adjustments, changing some rules and developing new boundaries between parents and children.

Dysfunctional patterns arise most often when generational boundaries are unclear or absent. The classic dysfunctional family structure is *enmeshed* (over-involved) at one end of the spectrum and *disengaged* (uninvolved) at the other. Dysfunction or underfunction, exists when families experiencing stress increase the rigidity of their interactional patterns and boundaries and resist exploring alternative actions. The unit of intervention for the structural family therapist is the family subsystem. Therapy begins with construction of a family map that describes the family structure in terms of its subsystems, the family hierarchy or organization, family relationships and their boundaries, and the family's transactional processes (e.g., coalitions, detouring). The goal of therapy is to unbalance the family members so a new, more adaptive family organization can be achieved. Healthy family functioning is attained when the family demonstrates an ability to adapt to both internal and external stressors.

In the case of physical abuse (Walker et al., 1988), a structural explanation for its occurrence in a family might highlight disengagement of the father and enmeshment of the mother and child. Furthermore, it might be suggested that the mother covertly precipitates the child's acting out, which necessitates the father's presence at home to discipline the child, thereby increasing the father's involvement in the family but also angering the father and increasing the probability of abuse. Structural family therapists attempt to elicit, during a session, a behavior as close as possible to the problem behavior. In this way the therapist has a first-hand opportunity to observe the process of family interaction around this issue. An attempt then should be made to facilitate change in the family's structure. The therapist might either reframe a crucial element of the process or direct family members to respond in a different way. For example, reframing the child's behavior as helpful in keeping the father involved in the family may pave the way to asking the father to suggest more appropriate ways that the child can continue to involve him.

Behavioral/Cognitive/Social Learning Family Therapy

Behavioral/cognitive therapists believe that family dysfunction can be related to some combination of an individual's behaviors, thoughts, and feelings and the environment's response. Behavioral family therapists assume that family dysfunction develops through erosion of positive reinforcement control and is maintained by reciprocal aversive control. Families are viewed as systems of interbehaving people, and a child's behavior is reinforced and maintained by environmental factors.

According to Horne (1991), behavioral family therapy is a systematic method of assessing family interactions, developing intervention strategies, and evaluating change. Behavioral family therapy emphasizes the functional analysis of behavior and, as such, develops highly specific and empirically based treatment methods (Sayger, Horne, & Glaser, 1993). This analysis includes observing behavior, obtaining a baseline assessment of rate and frequency of behaviors, identifying consequences, and altering consequences to change the behavior. According to behavioral family therapists, humans attempt to maximize the pleasurable consequences of their behavior while minimizing the aversive consequences (Horne & Sayger, 1990). As the ratio of costs to benefits increases in a relationship, the more likely is the occurrence of dysfunction.

Family dysfunction is seen as an interpersonal phenomenon resulting from coercive or reciprocal relationships. When family relationships are maintained and controlled through aversive, negatively reinforcing reactions, the relationship is deemed coercive. In situations in which family members maintain their relationships through equitable and mutual positive reinforcement, the relationship is deemed reciprocal (Patterson, 1982). Deviant behavior, therefore, is seen not as crazy, illogical, or dysfunctional but, rather, as an appropriate response to the contingencies in that system. Conceptualization and treatment are focused in the here-and-now as the problem is redefined in interactional-systemic terms, complete with an understanding of the antecedents and consequences of behavior as well as the circularity of the antecedents and consequences for maintaining the dysfunctional system (Horne & Sayger, 1990).

Believing that all family members are doing the best they can, given their circumstances and previous learning experiences, the behavioral family therapist attempts to construct a therapeutic environment in which family members feel safe and comfortable in discussing their concerns (Fleischman, Horne, & Arthur, 1983). Based upon the premise that interpersonal problems often arise from faulty or inadequate learning, the behavioral family therapist accentuates skills training procedures to prevent and solve family problems. Skills taught in therapy include communication, problem solving, negotiation, parenting and child management, self-control, and relationship enrichment.

Sayger (1992a, pp. 16, 36) suggested the following component for treating families with conduct problem children:

A. Prepare the family for a successful outcome.

   1. Set specific, realistic, and achievable goals.

   2. Communicate your belief that the family can change and successfully resolve its problems.

   3. Assess and implement strategies to alter environmental barriers to the client's success.

4. Focus on and accentuate the family's strengths and positive qualities.

5. Elicit cooperation of school personnel and/or social service agency workers.

B. Help family members gain control of their life situation by instituting and teaching strategies to help parents and children repudiate self-defeating thoughts.

C. Identify primary behavioral problems and instruct parents in remedial strategies of discipline (e.g. time-out, loss of privileges, Premack principle).

D. Instruct family members in effective strategies of communication to establish and maintain effective family interactions.

1. Check for the family's level of mastery over new skills.

2. Generalize newly learned skills to other problem areas/settings.

3. Schedule booster sessions to review and assess the family's continued use of effective problem-solving strategies.

A behavioral conceptualization of physical abuse might include identification of skill deficits (e.g., child management skills or communication skills between the couple), unrealistic developmental expectations, feelings (e.g., anxiety), and difficulties in response to environmental stressors (e.g., child-care demands, financial stress). The process of therapy includes modifying behavior or cognition, or both, to facilitate change, prompting further behavioral change to enhance social interaction and facilitating cognitive integration of the true meaning of these changes to ensure that the changes are maintained (Walker et al., 1988).

Behavioral approaches have been demonstrated to be effective in treating a broad range of problems including sexual dysfunction, somaticism, phobias, depression, marital conflict, and child conduct (Sayger, 1992b). Behavioral family therapy's strong adherence to scientific methods and evaluation makes it the most researched approach to family therapy. Because it emphasizes a systematic, structured, assessment-based approach to treatment, it lends itself to both outcome and process research. Behavioral family therapy is the treatment of choice for child conduct problems (Olson, Russell, & Sprenkle, 1980). A combination of family therapy and cognitive therapy may be the most effective approach for working with eating disorders (Weltner, 1985).

Object Relations Family Therapy

Object relations theorists believe that humans have a fundamental drive to be in a relationship. Conducting family therapy from this perspective emphasizes the assessment of developmental levels, defense and anxiety, and transference and countertransference. Common therapeutic strategies include sequencing individual and couples therapies with family therapy and incorporating play with childrearing families. At birth, the child seeks to form an attachment with the mother and becomes vulnerable to her responses. The child's attitudes toward family members and eventually others is determined largely by the gratification or frustration of these needs.

Unhappiness and dysfunction are seen as rooted primarily in the past, existing unconsciously, and operative in both the client's intrapersonal and interpersonal world.

Therapy begins by developing a caring environment in which family members can feel safe and make themselves "known" to the therapist (Luepnitz, 1988). Therapy attempts to help family members understand each other better and open up choices to the family that allow them to be less disconnected from their family context. The process of "remembering" aims to enable family members to review and reexperience what is troublesome, to bring repressed material into consciousness, explore feelings and attitudes, and break up dysfunctional patterns of intrapsychic reacting and interpersonal interacting (Luepnitz, 1988; Scharff & Scharff, 1987). Change, therefore, is achieved via analysis and a process of confrontation, clarification, interpretation, and working through.

People with interpersonal problems are holding onto expectations consistent with childhood (Skynner, 1976). The immediate goal of object relations family therapy is not to resolve the problem but, rather, to progress through the current developmental phase of the family with an improved ability to work together, self-differentiate, and meet the individual needs of its members. As growth occurs, the goals of family therapy from this perspective change. The goal of treatment for individual family members is individuation and ego integration. From the interpersonal perspective the aim is to enable family members to interact as whole persons on the basis of current realities. Once each family member achieves a heightened level of individuation, individuals will be better equipped to make important choices (e.g., mate selection, vocation) based on reality, consciousness, and needs versus unmet, unconscious childhood deficiency needs.

In practice, infants, toddlers, and play-age children are included in treatment so that their contribution to the family system can be observed. Excluding children from the therapeutic process can lead to invalid perceptions of family dynamics, and difficulties in children cannot be detected early if all family members are not seen. Including children in treatment completes the whole picture of the family that is essential to analysis (Scharff & Scharff, 1987). Typically, children between ages 3 and 10 do not seem to understand family defenses and frequently blurt out family "secrets." Similarly, the impact of parental arguments regarding the child is readily visible by watching the child's response. In addition, object relations family therapists frequently utilize play interventions to access the child's internal world, in which play is seen as a normal, age-appropriate way for children to deal with anxiety. In clinical situations play also can serve as a way for the child to feel more comfortable.

Scharff and Scharff (1987) presented a case of a predelinquent, 11-year-old, adopted boy and his family. The child was characterized as argumentative, stated that he hated his family, and was particularly upset with his father and the family's religious orientation. During sessions the child drew violent pictures, many of which depicted deaths and murders of family members, and he played "smuggling" games. The therapist noted that the family members were discussing angry feelings while the child was making his drawings. Using the child's drawings as an intervention strategy, the therapist discussed how the family drawings represented how family members felt they were being treated by each other. This intervention resulted in the family's gaining insight into its family system and becoming gentler and kinder in interactions with one another. The child, likewise, gave up his aggressive tendencies and came to feel a part of a more caring and nurturing family system.

Because object relations family therapy focuses on personal and spiritual growth (Weltner, 1985), it is well suited to families who can tolerate its slower pace, higher cost, and lack of powerful shaping interventions on the therapist's part. This therapeutic approach is geared much more toward creating a deep and warm experience of human contact than toward removing symptoms. Therefore, object relations therapy may best be matched with families at Level IV (Weltner, 1985).

Integrated Family Therapy

Assessment in integrated family therapy should attempt to understand the individual child, other family members, and their reciprocal interactions (Kaslow & Racusin, 1990). The focus is on the psychological symptomatology and functioning of each family member across cognitive, affective, interpersonal, adaptive behavior, and family domains. Incorporating a developmental perspective, integrationist family therapists strive to understand family functioning in the context of normative expectations for the individual's and the family's stage of development.

Depressive symptomatology in the child may be understood as a reflection of family dysfunction. In some families with a depressed child, the child experiencing sadness, helplessness, and low self-esteem attempts to elicit nurturant caregiving and relief from other family members, who, because of their own depression and low self-esteem and the negative moods the child's depression induces in them, often can provide only a form of caregiving characterized by alternating overprotection and rejection. Because it fails to address the child's needs, this form of caregiving reinforces the child's depression, which further engenders a sense of inadequacy in the other family members, who in turn may become more critical, hostile, or withdrawn and thus sustain the cycle of depression in the family.

In other families with depressed children, parents exhibit ambivalence over a child's achievement born out of their own narcissistic needs to keep the child dependent. The parents in these families express mixed expectations for success and failure but actually may provide concrete reinforcement only for the child's failure to achieve. Interventions address the needs of all family members by helping them to identify these problematic patterns and their origins and by facilitating the development of alternative interactional patterns leading out of the depressive cycle. Kaslow and Racusin (1990) see the field of family psychology as consolidating its movement toward an integrationist perspective, drawing more fully upon contributions from object relations theory, family systems theory, cognitive-behavioral psychology, developmental psychopathology, and biological psychiatry.

Play Therapy

Incorporating play therapy into family therapy approaches has been done with varying levels of success. In part, professionals providing family therapy services may have no formal training in child development, child therapy, or specific play therapy concepts. Our training programs seem to have placed a much greater emphasis on adult development and the marital/parental system than on understanding children. In this chapter we have attempted to provide some of this developmental information as it relates to conducting family therapy with children. In addition, many professionals simply do not have the space or funds to develop and furnish a play room.

Chasin and White (1989) identified three categories of play activities that they suggest incorporating into family therapy with young children. Play interventions can be defined on three continua: (a) involved–distanced, (b) directed–nondirected, and (c) imaginative–factual.

1. *Involved play* incorporates child role plays or puppets and requires other family members to become actively engaged in the play activity. Typically this mode of play therapy results in a high level of energy and works well with families because adults and children alike can communicate through actions instead of talk.

2. *Distanced play* involves the child playing with objects (e.g., drawing materials, dolls, clay) in the presence or absence of family members, but not actively involving their participation.

3. *Directed play* requires the child to draw a picture of some specific person or thing or to enact a given scene or play a given role. For example, you have just broken one of your mother's favorite lamps and are sitting at the dinner table. You play yourself and your brother is Mom. What would happen?

4. *Nondirected play* is characterized by giving the child drawing materials or a box of play materials and instructing him or her to draw whatever he or she pleases.

5. *Factual play* involves the documentation of actions and feelings of real people as they are now or realistically could be in the future ("Sally, you be your daughter, and John, you be the doctor. Show us what will happen at her check-up next week").

6. *Imaginative play* is exemplified by free drawing while the adults converse. Through these drawings children might express their concerns about the family that otherwise might not be expressed.

Clearly, involved, directed, and factual play provide access to more specific events and processes that the child and other family members experience. In contrast, distanced, nondirected, and imaginative play allow children to create their own structure and call for interpretation of intrapsychic phenomena. Depending upon the clinician's orientation, each form of play therapy can provide useful and insightful information about families and the children in them.

Parting Comments

Depending upon the needs of the family and the child, the therapist must decide whether to include or exclude the child. If the child is to be included, decisions have to be made as to what has to be done. When asked what we do with children in family therapy, we quote Garbarino (1993): "It depends." It depends upon whether the child is the identified patient. It depends on one's theoretical orientation. It depends on the appropriate training and knowledge to work with children. It depends on space and funds to furnish a play room. It depends on the treatment of choice for the client concern. It depends on professional commitment to provide the most effective treatment possible for encouraging client growth and happiness.

References

Allen, F. H. (1990). Participation in therapy. In C. Schaefer (Ed.), *The therapeutic use of child's play* (pp. 535–542). Northvale, NJ: Jason Aronson.

Bowen, M. (1985). *Family therapy in clinical practice*. Northvale, NJ: Jason Aronson.

Chase-Lansdale, P. L. (1993). The impact of poverty on family processes. *Child, Youth & Family Services Quarterly, 16*, 5–8.

Chasin, R., & White, T. B. (1989). The child in family therapy: Guidelines for active engagement across the age span. In L. Combrinck-Graham (Ed.), *Children in family contexts: Perspectives on treatment* (pp. 5–25). New York: Guilford Press.

Combrinck-Graham, L. (Ed.). (1989). *Children in family contexts: Perspectives on treatment*. New York: Guilford Press.

Fleischman, M. J., Horne, A. M., & Arthur, J. L. (1983). *Troubled families: A treatment approach*. Champaign, IL: Research Press.

Framo, J. L. (1992). *Family-of origin therapy: An intergenerational approach*. New York: Brunner/Mazel.

Garbarino, J. (1993). Childhood: What do we need to know? *Childhood: A Global Journal of Child Research, 1*, 1–10.

Garbarino, J., & Stott, R. (1989). *What children can tell us*. San Francisco: Jossey-Bass.

Gibson, R. L., Mitchell, M. H., & Basile, S. K. (1993). *Counseling children in the elementary school: A comprehensive approach*. Boston: Allyn & Bacon.

Goldsmith, J. (1982). The postdivorce family system. In F. Walsh (Ed.), *Normal family processes* (pp. 297–330). New York: Guilford Press.

Henggeler, S. W., & Borduin, C. M. (1990). *Family therapy and beyond: A multisystemic approach to treating the behavior problems of children and adolescents*. Pacific Grove, CA: Brooks/Cole.

Hoffman, J. (1993). Musical chairs. *Simi Valley Church of Religious Science Newsletter,* September/October, p. 4.

Horne, A. M. (1991). Social learning family therapy. In A. M. Horne & J. L. Passmore (Eds.), *Family counseling and therapy* (2nd ed., pp. 463–496). Itasca, IL: F. E. Peacock.

Horne, A. M., & Sayger, T. V. (1990). *Treating conduct and oppositional defiant disorders in children*. New York: Pergamon Press.

Isaacs, M. R., & Benjamin, M. P. (1991). *Towards a culturally competent system of care: Volume 2. Programs which utilize culturally competent principles.* Washington, DC: CASSP Technical Assistance Center, Georgetown University Child Development Center.

Johnson, H. C. (1993). Family issues and interventions. In H. C. Johnson (Ed.), *Child mental health in the 1990s: Curricula for graduate and undergraduate professional education.* Washington, DC: U. S. Department of Health and Human Services, Center for Mental Health Services.

Kaslow, N. J., & Racusin, G. R. (1990). Depressed children and their families: An integrationist approach. In F. W. Kaslow (Ed.), *Voices in family psychology* (Vol. 2., pp. 194–216). Newbury Park, CA: Sage.

Luepnitz, D. A. (1988). *The family interpreted: Feminist theory in clinical practice.* New York: Basic Books.

Madanes, C. (1981). *Strategic family therapy.* San Francisco: Jossey-Bass.

Madanes, C. (1984). *Behind the one-way mirror: Advances in the practice of strategic therapy.* San Francisco: Jossey-Bass.

McGoldrick, M., & Carter, E. A. (1982). The family life cycle. In F. Walsh (Ed.), *Normal family processes* (pp. 167–195). New York: Guilford Press.

Minuchin, S. (1974). *Families and family therapy.* Cambridge, MA: Harvard University Press.

Minuchin, S., & Fishman, H. C. (1981). *Family therapy techniques.* Cambridge, MA: Harvard University Press.

Morris, P. W., Horne, A. M., Jessell, J. C., Passmore, J. L., Walker, J. M., & Sayger, T. V. (1988). Behavioral and cognitive characteristics of fathers of aggressive and well-behaved boys. *Journal of Cognitive Psychotherapy: An International Quarterly, 2,* 251–265.

Nichols, W. C., & Everett, C. A. (1986). *Systemic family therapy: An integrative approach.* New York: Guilford Press.

Olson, D. H., Russell, C. S., & Sprenkle, D. H. (1980). Marital and family therapy: A decade review. *Journal of Marriage & the Family, 42,* 973–993.

Patterson, G. R. (1975). *Families: Applications of social learning to family life.* Champaign, IL: Research Press.

Patterson, G. R. (1982). *Coercive family process.* Eugene, OR: Castalia.

Ramirez, M., III. (1991). *Psychotherapy and counseling with minorities: A cognitive approach to individual and cultural differences.* New York: Pergamon Press.

Rapoport, J. L., & Ismond, D. R. (1990). *DSM–III–R training guide for diagnosis of childhood disorders.* New York: Brunner/Mazel.

Sager, C. J., Brown, H. S., Crohn, H., Engel, T., Rodstein, E., & Walker, L. (1983). *Treating the remarried family.* New York: Brunner/Mazel.

Sayger, T. V. (1992a). Children with conduct disorders and their families: Discovering the sources for change. *Family Psychologist, 8,* 16, 36.

Sayger, T. V. (1992b). Family psychology and therapy. In C. E. Walker & M. C. Roberts (Eds.), *Handbook of clinical child psychology* (2nd ed., pp. 783–807). New York: John Wiley & Sons.

Sayger, T. V., Horne, A. M., & Glaser, B. A. (1993). Marital satisfaction and social learning family therapy for child conduct problems: Generalization of treatment effects. *Journal of Marital & Family Therapy, 19,* 393–402.

Scharff, D. E., & Scharff, J. S. (1987). *Object relations family therapy.* Northvale, NJ: Jason Aronson.

Segal, L. (1982). Brief family therapy. In A. M. Horne & M. M. Ohlsen (Eds.), *Family counseling and therapy* (pp. 276–301). Itasca, IL: F. E. Peacock.

Skynner, A. C. R. (1976). *Systems of family and marital psychotherapy.* New York: Brunner/Mazel.

Szykula, S. A. (1989). Child-focused paradoxical psychotherapy: Reframing the behavioral picture for therapeutic change. In L. M. Ascher (Ed.), *Therapeutic paradox* (pp. 340–377). New York: Guilford Press.

Szykula, S. A., Sayger, T. V., Morris, S. B., & Sudweeks, C. (1987). Child-focused behavior and strategic therapies: Outcome comparisons. *Psychotherapy, 24S,* 546–551.

Thompson, C. L, & Rudolph, L. B. (1992). *Counseling children.* Pacific Grove, CA: Brooks/Cole.

Walker, C. E., Bonner, B. L., & Kaufman, K. L. (1988). *The physically and sexually abused child: Evaluation and treatment.* New York: Pergamon Press.

Watzlawick, P., Weakland, J., & Fisch, R. (1974). *Change: Principles of problem formation and problem resolution.* New York: Norton.

Weltner, J. (1985). Matchmaking: Choosing the appropriate therapy for families at various levels of pathology. In M. P. Mirkin & S. L. Koman (Eds.), *Handbook of adolescents and family therapy* (pp. 39–53). New York: Gardner Press.

Wynne, L. C., Jones, J. E., & Al-Khayyal, M. (1982). Healthy family communication patterns: Observations in families "at risk" for psychopathology. In F. Walsh (Ed.), *Normal family processes* (pp. 142–164). New York: Guilford Press.

Zarski, J. J., & Fluharty, L. B. (1992). Treating emotionally disturbed youth: A comparison of home-based and outpatient interventions. *Contemporary Family Therapy: An International Journal, 14,* 335–350.

Zilbach, J. J. (1989). The family life cycle: A framework for understanding children in family therapy. In L. Combrinck-Graham (Ed.), *Children in family contexts: Perspectives on treatment* (pp. 46–66). New York: Guilford Press.

Name Index

A

Abrahams, M. J., 143
Abramson, L. Y., 150
Achilles, C. M., 113
Adams, G. R., 82, 97, 440
Adelman, H. S., 25, 40, 41, 43, 44, 54
Adelsheim, S., 1, 44, 45
Adelson, J., 463
Adler, J., 186
Adler, L., 43
Aguilera, D. C., 361
Ainsworth, M., 205
Akiyama, K., 158
Albrecht, T. L., 127
Alexander, J. R., 441
Al-Khayyal, M., 477
Allen, F. H., 476
Allen, M., 120
Allensworth, D., 40, 43
Al-Mabuk, R., 453, 454, 458, 462, 466, 467
Amara, I. A., 440
Ambert, A., 435, 437
Ambrosini, P. J., 140
American Academy of Pediatrics, 73, 74
American Association for Marriage and Family Therapy (AAMFT), 22
American Association of Colleges, 88
American College Health Association, 85
American Psychiatric Association, 140, 203, 206
American Psychological Association (APA), 21, 30, 66, 291

American School Counselor Association, 22, 248
Americkaner, M., 269
Amundson, D., 290, 291
Anderson, J. C., 144, 153–154
Anderson, J. E., 84
Anderson, S., 20
Anderson-Johnson, C., 95
Andraski, F., 157
Angold, A., 144
Annie E. Casey Foundation, 41
Annon, J., 88–89
Annunziata, J., 24, 26
Anthony, E. J., 443
Appleton, V. E., 245
Arday, S., 84
Armstrong, J. W., 454
Arnold, M. S., 6, 13–14
Arthur, G., 23
Arthur, J. L., 487
Askins, R. V., 90
Association for Specialists in Group Work, 390
Astin, A. W., 283
Atkinson, D. R., 14
Attneave, C., 117, 124
Atwell, A. E., 440
Aubrey, R. F., 249, 251
Avery, A. W., 443
Axelson, J. A., 406
Axline, V., 19

B

Bachman, J. G., 73
Baer, P. E., 74
Baker, L., 139
Baker, S., 40
Baker, S. B., 247
Baldwin, W., 79

Balow, I. H., 91
Bane, M. J., 433
Barbero, G. J., 140
Barnea, Z., 96
Barr, R. D., 108
Barrett, K., 205
Bartlett, S., 276
Basham, A., 245
Basile, S. K., 477, 478
Bates, J. E., 225
Bates, M., 401
Battjes, R. J., 96
Baumrind, D., 222–223, 225, 226–227, 461, 462, 467
Beady, C. H., 282
Beal, E. W., 443
Bear, G. G., 288, 300
Beck, A. T., 70, 139, 140, 150
Beck, V., 117
Bednar, R. L., 395
Bee, H., 453
Begley, S., 205
Behrens, J. T., 64, 144, 145, 149, 153
Belber, R., 236
Bell, C. S., 96
Bemak, F., 116
Benjamin, M. P., 480
Bentler, P. M., 73, 74, 96
Bentovim, M., 20
Berger, K., 453, 457, 458, 462, 463, 466
Berger, M., 128, 130
Bergin, J., 244, 267, 269, 271
Berkan, W. A., 72, 95
Berlin, B. M., 84
Bernard, J. L., 29
Bernstein, G. A., 153–154
Bessell, H., 396

Subject Index